A guide to the programming models, numerical methods, and distributed computing tools used in the application chapters (Part II) of this book.

Distributed (

Single proce
optimizatic

Parallel I/O

Load balanci

Performance
on various
architectur

Use of parall
discussed

Networking,

Processing,

Scheduling,
interactive

Graphics an
dering

Parallel soft
libraries

Dynamic
programming

P.1

TABLE

Industrial Strength Parallel Computing

Related Titles from Morgan Kaufmann Publishers

The Grid: Blueprint for a New Computing Infrastructure
   Edited by Ian Foster and Carl Kesselman
Parallel Computer Architecture: A Hardware/Software Approach
   David E. Culler and Jaswinder Pal Singh with Anoop Gupta
Parallel Programming with MPI
   Peter S. Pacheco
Distributed Algorithms
   Nancy A. Lynch
Scalable Shared-Memory Multiprocessing
   Daniel E. Lenoski and Wolf-Dietrich Weber
Parallel Computing Works!
   Geoffrey C. Fox, Roy D. Williams, and Paul C. Messina
Parallel Processing from Applications to Systems
   Dan I. Moldovan
Synthesis of Parallel Algorithms
   Edited by John H. Reif
Introduction to Parallel Algorithms and Architectures: Arrays, Trees, &
   Hypercubes
   F. Thomson Leighton
VLSI and Parallel Computation
   Edited by Robert Suaya and Graham Birtwhistle

Forthcoming

Implicit Parallel Programming in pH
   Arvind and Rishiyur Nikhil
Parallel I/O for High Performance Computing
   John May
Parallel Programming with Open MP
   Rohit Chandra, Leo Dagum, Dave Kohr, Dror Maydan, Jeff Maydan,
   Jeff McDonald, and Ramesh Menon

Industrial Strength

Parallel Computing

Edited by

Alice E. Koniges

Morgan Kaufmann Publishers
San Francisco, California

Senior Editor   Denise E. M. Penrose
Director of Production and Manufacturing   Yonie Overton
Production Editor   Edward Wade
Editorial Coordinator   Meghan Keeffe
Cover Design   Ross Carron Design
Text Design   Windfall Software
Composition, Color Insert Preparation, and
Technical Illustration   Technologies 'N Typography
Copyeditor   Donna King, Progressive Publishing Alternatives
Proofreader   Ken DellaPenta
Indexer   Steve Rath
Printer   Courier Corporation

Designations used by companies to distinguish their products are often claimed as trademarks or registered trademarks. In all instances where Morgan Kaufmann Publishers is aware of a claim, the product names appear in initial capital or all capital letters. Readers, however, should contact the appropriate companies for more complete information regarding trademarks and registration.

Morgan Kaufmann Publishers
Editorial and Sales Office
340 Pine Street, Sixth Floor
San Francisco, CA 94104–3205
USA
Telephone   415–392–2665
Facsimile   415–982–2665
Email   mkp@mkp.com
WWW   http://www.mkp.com
Order toll free   800–745–7323

04 03 02 01 00   5 4 3 2 1

Library of Congress Cataloging-in-Publication Data
Industrial strength parallel computing / edited by Alice Koniges.
      p.   cm.
   Includes bibliographical references and index.
   ISBN 1-55860-540-1
   1. Parallel processing (Electronic computers) 2. High performance
computers. I. Koniges, Alice Evelyn.
QA76.58.I483   2000
004'.35—dc21
                                                      99-30273
                                                        CIP

To Emily, Corwin, and Brigitte

Contents

3   Programming Models and Methods   27

Margaret Cahir, Robert Moench, Alice E. Koniges

4   Parallel Programming Tools   55

Margaret Cahir, Robert Moench, Alice E. Koniges

5   Optimizing for Single-Processor Performance   67

Jeff Brooks, Sara Graffunder, Alice E. Koniges

6   Scheduling Issues   81

Morris A. Jette

9   Petroleum Reservoir Management   129

Michael DeLong, Allyson Gajraj, Wayne Joubert, Olaf Lubeck, James Sanderson, Robert E. Stephenson, Gautam S. Shiralkar, Bart van Bloemen Waanders

10   An Architecture-Independent Navier-Stokes Code   147

Johnson C. T. Wang, Stephen Taylor

13   Simulation of Plasma Reactors   227

Stephen Taylor, Marc Rieffel, Jerrell Watts, Sadasivan Shankar

14   Electron-Molecule Collisions for Plasma Modeling   247

Carl Winstead, Chuo-Han Lee, Vincent McKoy

18 Nuclear Magnetic Resonance Simulations 339

*Alan J. Benesi, Kenneth M. Merz, Jr., James J. Vincent,
Ravi Subramanya*

19 Molecular Dynamics Simulations Using Particle-Mesh Ewald Methods 355

*Michael F. Crowley, David W. Deerfield II, Tom A. Darden, Thomas E.
Cheatham III*

20   Radar Scattering and Antenna Modeling   389

Tom Cwik, Cinzia Zuffada, Daniel S. Katz, Jay Parker

21   Functional Magnetic Resonance Imaging Dataset Analysis   431

*Nigel H. Goddard, Greg Hood, Jonathan D. Cohen, Leigh E. Nystrom,
William F. Eddy, Christopher R. Genovese, Douglas C. Noll*

22   Selective and Sensitive Comparison of Genetic Sequence Data   453

Alexander J. Ropelewski, Hugh B. Nicholas, Jr., David W. Deerfield II

Preface

Parallel computing has become a practical approach to industrial modeling. It brings formerly insoluble problems into solution range and makes formerly difficult-to-solve problems routine. The software challenges for the development of industrial-quality codes for parallel computers, however, are great. In this book, we provide in-depth case studies of 17 applications that were either redesigned or designed from scratch to solve industrial strength problems on parallel computers. We document both the solution process and the resulting performance of the application software. Additionally, we provide an overview of the terminology, basic hardware, performance issues, programming models, software tools, and other details that are necessary for researchers and students to become able parallel programmers. Finally, we show how, in order for industry to continue to participate in the parallel-computing arena, the applications must be portable and tailored to accommodate a rapidly changing hardware environment.

Parallel computing became a significant subfield of computer science by the late 1960s, but only by the late 1980s had hardware and software technology improved sufficiently for parallel computing to affect the day-to-day lives of applications programmers. As such, it spurred the development of a whole new way of thinking about programming for applications. Rather than deal with the old textbook picture of a flow-charted program going from one step to the next in a sequential fashion, the availability of parallel computers has forced us to rethink our algorithms at every step to determine which tasks can be performed independently and simultaneously with others. In the early days of parallel computing, this transition to parallel algorithms and the associated tools and programming languages remained primarily in the research and university setting. As massively parallel computers based on workstation or commodity chips were introduced, however, these machines that are capable of gigaflop performance and terabyte data storage enticed industry into the growing field of parallel computing. Parallel computing is no longer confined to the research arena. The term massively parallel architecture even entered (with definitions provided) into popular magazines such as *Time* and *Parade* when a parallel computer designed by IBM was finally able to defeat the world chess champion Gary Kasparov in 1997. This parallel machine's calculating speed, which was doubled that year, can analyze 200 million possible moves per second—50 billion board positions in the three minutes given for each move.

In industry, parallel computers provide application-specific solutions to concurrent problems in today's marketplace. For the industrial participant, the challenge is to retool computational modeling to harness the cost effectiveness of parallel high-performance computer systems in a way that is not possible with general-purpose computers. This book presents a set of real experiences in porting useful applications to parallel computers. A majority of the applications discussed here were the result of a set of 15 collaborative projects involving two U.S. Department of Energy (DOE) labs—Los Alamos National Laboratory and Lawrence Livermore National Laboratory—Cray Research, and major industrial firms. The program, called the Parallel Applications Technology Project (PATP), was cofunded by DOE and Cray Research. The goal was to take software previously developed in DOE labs and enhance it for industry use, so that it achieved commercial quality and robustness.

This book focuses on tools and techniques for parallelizing scientific and technical applications in a lessons-learned fashion based on the experiences of researchers active in the field of applied parallel computing.

Part I, The Parallel Computing Environment, examines the following critical elements of the programming environment:

+ parallel computing terminology and architectures

+ performance issues—in particular, examing how hardware affects application performance

+ common parallel programming models and languages

+ parallel programming tools for performance analysis and debugging

+ optimization on parallel machines

+ scheduling issues in a production environment

Part II, The Applications, contains detailed case studies of 17 applications, including problem background, approach to parallel solution, and performance results.

In the process of parallelizing a major applications code, it is often the case that one must call upon a variety of numerical methods and techniques. This is because for a complex "real" application code, there are many processes working simultaneously, often on different time scales. Thus, in grouping the applications chapters in the book, we have not attempted to partition them based on numerical schemes and parallel computing techniques. Rather, they are categorized based on the essential length scale of the physical phenomena modeled. On the largest scale, we have meso- to macroscale environmental modeling. Next down from this in primary physical scale length, we have a category that broadly covers fluid dynamics. Although plasmas can be classified as fluids and can also have length scales greater than a typical Navier-Stokes fluid, they often involve processes on shorter time scales that allow for the interaction of the electrons and ions in the plasma. Thus we use this classification next in our rough breakdown and have a section for applied plasma dynamics. Continuing to get smaller in physical phenomena, we categorized certain of the chapters as materials design and modeling. Here, the applications codes tend to deal with primarily particle and/or molecular interactions in contrast to the more global behavior of the plasma category. Finally, an additional set of applications dealt primarily with data analysis rather than a problem characterized by physical length scales, so we have grouped these applications accordingly.

In Part III we summarize results and lessons learned from the applications, give advice on designing industrial applications, and discuss our view of the future of industrial parallel computing. A glossary is included for defining terms in the book including those in the application chapters.

To assist the reader with finding information pertinent to the creation of a new parallel applications code, we have identified the programming models, numerical methods, and performance tools and techniques applied in each chapter in Table P.1.

Web Supplement

The contributors have made available programs, animations, graphs, charts, and various visualizations in support of their work on a homepage at Morgan Kaufmann's Web site, which is dedicated to this book. The URL is *www.mkp.com/ispc.*

	7	8	9	10	11	12	13	14	15	16	17	18	19	20	21	22	23
Programming Models																	
MPI	✦	✦	✦	✦			✦	✦		✦	✦	✦	✦			✦	
PVM			✦	✦	✦										✦	✦	
SHMEM	✦	✦	✦				✦	✦		✦	✦	✦	✦				✦
HPF/CRAFT			✦				✦							✦			
Other models and preprocessors		✦	✦			✦									✦		
Task farming															✦	✦	

	7	8	9	10	11	12	13	14	15	16	17	18	19	20	21	22	23
Numerical Methods																	
Iterative matrix methods and sparse matrices	✦	✦	✦			✦				✦		✦		✦			
Eigenvalues and eigenvectors												✦					
Discrete and Fourier transforms		✦								✦	✦	✦	✦		✦		✦
Finite difference methods	✦	✦				✦			✦	✦							
Finite element methods					✦	✦								✦			
Finite volume methods					✦	✦											
Mesh generation and refinement							✦						✦				
Domain decomposition including multigrid		✦	✦			✦	✦			✦							✦
Particle in cell and particle tracking					✦		✦		✦								
Integral equations and integrals					✦		✦			✦		✦		✦			
Optimization, local						✦									✦	✦	
Parallel random field generation																	

Distributed Computing Tools and Techniques

	7	8	9	10	11	12	13	14	15	16	17	18	19	20	21	22	23
Single processor optimization	♦		♦		♦		♦			♦	♦	♦	♦	♦	♦		
Parallel I/O							♦			♦	♦	♦		♦	♦		
Load balancing					♦		♦	♦	♦	♦	♦	♦	♦	♦	♦	♦	
Performance comparison on various architectures		♦				♦	♦		♦		♦	♦			♦	♦	
Use of parallel tools discussed	♦	♦		♦			♦								♦		
Networking, realtime															♦		
Processing, realtime															♦		♦
Scheduling, interactive															♦		
Graphics and volume rendering	♦						♦			♦					♦		
Parallel software libraries	♦		♦				♦				♦				♦		
Dynamic programming																♦	

TABLE P.1   A guide to the programming models, numerical methods, and distributed computing tools and techniques used in the application chapters (Part II) of this book.

About the Cover

The I Ching is an ancient divination tool and one of civilization's oldest and most enigmatic texts. Featured on the cover are six of the sixty-four hexagrams from the I Ching, selected for their resonance with the concepts we hope are inherent in *Industrial Strength Parallel Computing*. The simple patterns shown here—parallel and almost binary in structure—symbolize fruition, elegance, power, endurance, completion, and development. The parallel we draw is based on the structure of the hexagrams and the powerful means of communication they represent.

Acknowledgments

The creation of *Industrial Strength Parallel Computing* would not have been possible without the support of the PATP program institutional sponsors, managers, and directors. Special recognition among these is given to Dr. Michel McCoy of LLNL, who liked the idea of a book as a means to record successes associated with these special partnerships between industry and national laboratories and provided the personal encouragement to make the book a reality. At each of the additional PATP sites there was a team who provided similar encouragement for their authors. We would like to recognize these PATP program managers and associates, including Drs. Charles Slocomb and Andrew White (LANL), Drs. Larry Eversole and Carl Kukkonen (JPL), Drs. Ralph Roskies and Michael Levine, and Mr. James Kasdorf (PSC), Dr. Michel Reymond (EPFL), and Dr. Alex Larzelere (DOE). We also wish to thank the technical managers at the numerous industrial partner sites. Of particular help and encouragement were Ms. Sara Graffunder, Mr. David Caliga, and Dr. William Camp.

We extend a sincere thank you to the Max-Planck Institute for Plasma Physics/Computer Center in Garching, Germany for providing research support for Alice Koniges while she was also engaged in completion of this book. We thank Dr. Ralf Schneider, Dr. David Coster, Dr. Hermann Lederer, Prof. Dr. Karl Lackner, and Prof. Dr. Friedrich Hertweck for providing both encouragement and technical expertise.

We bring additional attention to the authors of the book's applications chapters. Each of these research team members took the time to isolate the computer science aspects of their technical work and to contribute to a book with an intended audience that is much broader than their usual group of colleagues.

The NERSC Center at LBL provided a Web site for managing the book's elements and contributions. We thank Jeanette Jenness for her talented job of Web programming.

The book benefited enormously from comments and suggestions of the technical reviewers of the manuscript. These included Dr. Tarek Abdelrahman, University of Toronto; Dr. Catherine Schulbach, NASA Ames Research Center; and Dr. George Adams, Purdue University.

We also wish to thank the talented staff at Morgan Kaufmann Publishers who believed in this book from the beginning and worked with all of the authors throughout the process to maintain the highest of standards. In particular, we acknowledge the senior editor, Denise Penrose, editorial coordinator Meghan Keeffe, and production editor Edward Wade. They provided a professional, efficient, and most of all enjoyable environment for the publication of a book.

Financial support for the programs that spawned the applications chapters includes the U.S. Department of Energy, NASA, the U.S. National Science Foundation, the Swiss National Science Foundation, the U.S. National Institute of Health, SGI/Cray Research, Boeing Company, IBM Research Center, Institute for Defense Analysis, Intel Corp., Equator Technologies, and Amoco.

PART I
THE PARALLEL COMPUTING ENVIRONMENT

These six chapters provide information on the terminology, basic hardware, performance issues, programming models, software tools, optimization possibilities, and scheduling issues that are necessary to have a basic understanding of parallel computing and to allow the reader to take full advantage of the information provided in Part II. Sufficient introductory material is presented in Part I to allow someone with little or no background in parallel computing to gain the information needed to understand many of the lessons learned in the application chapters presented in Part II. There is sufficient detail in these six chapters to take someone with some background in parallel computing up to the next level of software development expertise. For someone with significant background in parallel computing, the chapters in this part can be a compact reference for the essential aspects of parallel computing needed to do real-world applications.

An overview of parallel architectures, including a section on historical issues, is presented in Chapter 1. The methods that can be used to measure the performance of parallel computers are present in Chapter 2. Chapter 3 is a very important chapter that describes the programming models and methods necessary to use parallel computers to solve real problems. Two important tools are presented in Chapter 4 that allow a programmer to locate problem areas and to debug a parallel code. An essential aspect of obtaining high performance on parallel computers is to optimize for single-processor performance, which is discussed in Chapter 5. Finally, the majority of parallel computer users must share the resources with other users, and the important issues of scheduling are presented in Chapter 6.

1 Parallel Computing Architectures

Alice E. Koniges
David C. Eder   Lawrence Livermore National Laboratory

Margaret Cahir   SGI/Cray Research

Industrial strength applications have been driving supercomputer architectures for many years. Each year a new machine design appears on the horizon, and with the availability of that new machine the door is open to the applications scientist. The following questions must be asked, Can my application benefit from this new architecture? What speedup is possible? What effort is necessary to port or design a code for this new computer? Fortunately, there is somewhat of a convergence in architectures for the very reason that ultimately, once the decision is made to split a problem up into parallel tasks, there are only a few basic principles that must be understood. In the next sections, we give the reader the appropriate terminology to understand all of the current parallel platforms; presumably these same concepts will be essential in future designs. This material is at the introductory level and provides the necessary foundation for understanding the terminology and techniques used in the applications chapters. For more complete coverage see [1.3] and [1.6].

1.1   HISTORICAL PARALLEL COMPUTING ARCHITECTURES

One of the hardest problems to overcome when getting started in a new field, and this is particularly true of computing fields, is the acronym terminology that prevails. Even at the outset, parallel computing used a wide variety of acronyms. Additionally, due to the rapid pace at which computer architecture is developing, newer architectures do not always fit well into categories that were invented before the architecture was. Historically, the most common classification scheme for parallel computers (devised by Flynn) is based on a four-letter mnemonic where the first two letters pertain to instructions that act on the data and the second two letters refer to the data stream type [1.5]. These are

+ SISD: Single Instruction—Single Data. This is the traditional von Neumann model of computation where one set of instructions is executed sequentially on a stream of data.

+ SIMD: Single Instruction—Multiple Data. This classification includes some of the very early parallel computers such as the Connection Machine, which was manufactured by a company called Thinking Machines. In the SIMD model, multiple individual processors or a single vector processor execute the same instruction set on different datasets.

+ MISD: Multiple Instruction—Single Data. This is not currently a commercially viable system for computing.

+ MIMD: Multiple Instruction—Multiple Data. This is the model of parallel computing that has dominated for most industrial applications. In this model, multiple processors can be executing different instructions on their own data and communicating as needed. There are two subclasses of MIMD machines, Shared Memory (SM) or Distributed Memory (DM).

A diagram showing the basic difference between the MIMD-SM and MIMD-DM is given in Figure 1.1. Another possible programming model is based on the parallel SIMD approach, in which all processors are controlled to execute in a lock-step fashion. This parallel SIMD approach is too restrictive for the applications considered in this book. In the figure, CPU stands for Central Processing Unit. Note that the SIMD computers do not have CPUs; they have Processing Elements (PEs). The difference is that a CPU fetches its own instructions and has its own program counter that points to the instruction to be fetched at a given instant. A processing element is fed instructions by its control unit, which has the only program counter.

Adding to the terminology confusion, we have SPMD, which stands for Single Program Multiple Data and is basically a restriction of the MIMD model. In SPMD, each processor executes exactly the same program on a different subset of the program data. Every data item in the program is allocated to one processor, and often every processor is allocated approximately equal numbers of data items. In practice, however, even with the SPMD model, the programmer can designate a master processor by judicious use of conditional statements. Although some of this terminology is being replaced by a smaller set of acronyms described in the next section (e.g., MIMD-DM becomes simply MPP), it is still found and referred to both in this book and throughout the literature.

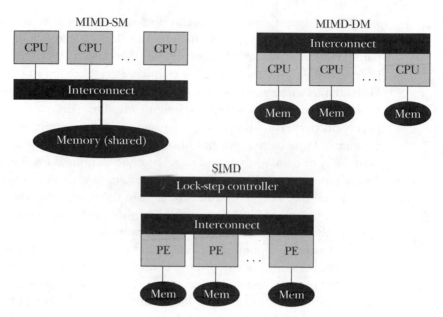

The basic differences between the MIMD-SM, MIMD-DM, and (parallel) SIMD. For simplicity, we class MIMD-DM as Massively Parallel Processing (MPP). DMP, for Distributed Memory Parallel, is also used for MIMD-DM.

Since Flynn introduced the taxonomy (his paper was written in 1969–70 and published in 1972), computers have been advancing at an enormous rate. Despite efforts by computer scientists to revise the terminology, it persists and is referred to in many of the applications chapters. One problem with the historical terminology is where to classify the first (single-processor) vector architectures such as the Cray-1 (introduced in 1976) and the NEC SX-1. There is some disagreement as to whether these machines should be classified as SIMD or SISD. The arguments for using the SIMD classification are that a single instruction operates on many datums and that the programming considerations for performance (i.e., data independence, concurrency) are the same for vectorization as they are for machines like the CM2. The arguments for the SISD classification are that the execution of the operations happens in a pipelined fashion and that modern microprocessors (like those appearing on the desktop and classified as SISD) are starting to incorporate vector instructions. Because this point is somewhat controversial, wherever possible we avoid using the Flynn taxonomy except for historical references. Finally, vector machines with shared memory and multiple processors such as the Cray XMP and the Cray C90 are referred to as PVP for Parallel Vector Platform.

The programs described in this book are written primarily for the MIMD-DM class of computers, which includes the Cray T3D and T3E and the IBM SP parallel systems. We use the term MPP for this class of computers. When the projects described in the applications chapters were initiated in the mid-1990s, the MPP architecture was one of the most difficult of the current high-performance supercomputing architectures to design codes for. This was due not only to the purely distributed memory, which caused the programmer to totally rethink a problem's implementation, but also to the initial lag in the development and availability of parallel tools and programming standards for the MPP machines. Thus, it took a while before the MPP paradigm made its way into general industrial computing. The application chapters of the book detail the case histories of several large scientific and industrial applications that successfully made the jump to the MPP platform. However, because they are large industrial applications, it was not economically prudent to write them to perform on one type of architecture alone. They had to be written to withstand the continual upgrade and redesign of computer architectures. There is still a contention in the field of supercomputing as to which of the architectures will ultimately win the price/performance race. In fact, as this book is being written, architectures are once again undergoing a transformation. Some of the current "hottest architectures" being built now exploit a hybrid of the shared memory and distributed memory models, thus requiring even more complex programming models [1.9].

1.2   CONTEMPORARY PARALLEL COMPUTING ARCHITECTURES

The high-performance computers available today generally fall into one of three major classes, the SMP, the MPP, and the nonuniform memory access (NUMA) generalization of the SMP. The term SMP originally referred exclusively to symmetric multiprocessors, referring to the uniform way in which the processors are often connected to the shared memory. But as Culler points out, the widely used term SMP now causes some confusion [1.3]. The major design issue in a symmetric multiprocessor is that all processors have equal access to the shared resources, namely, shared memory and I/O functionality. The time required for a processor to access the memory should be the same for all processors. As Culler states, even if the location is cached, the access will still be symmetric with respect to the processors. (Part of the confusion here is the occasional use of SMP to mean "shared memory parallel." Following this same line of thinking, the MPP architecture may simply be referred to as a member of the DMP or "distributed memory parallel" class.) The MPP systems originated as a straightforward gener-

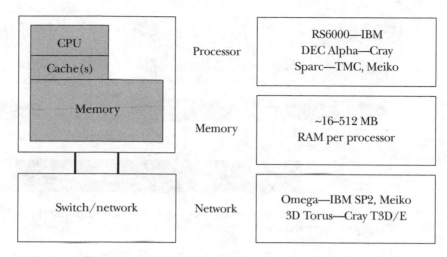

CPU	Processor	RS6000—IBM
Cache(s)		DEC Alpha—Cray
Memory		Sparc—TMC, Meiko
	Memory	~16–512 MB RAM per processor
Switch/network	Network	Omega—IBM SP2, Meiko 3D Torus—Cray T3D/E

1.2
FIGURE

Typical specifications of MIMD-DM or MPP computers in 1998.

alization in which fast workstations or personal computers, which themselves are based on Reduced Instruction Set Computer (RISC) microprocessors, are connected. To simplify the description of an MPP computer, we can partition it into processors, memory with various access levels including cache(s), interconnect network or switch, and support hardware. (See Figure 1.2.) Some details of these various components of an MPP computer are discussed in the following subsections.

The most powerful systems in use by industry today are the SMP and the MPP. In the classic MPP, the memory is truly distinct (and thus the performance is also very scalable). In the SMP, the processors share a global area of RAM (memory). The purpose of such architecture is to avoid some of the problems associated with interprocessor communication. However, the shared RAM design of the SMP can lead to bottlenecks as more and more processors are added (i.e., a bus or switch used to access the memory may become overloaded). Thus, the SMP systems do not share the same potential for scalability as their MPP cousins. One way to avoid the scalability problems on the SMP is the reintroduction of NUMA, into the system. NUMA adds other levels of memory, shared among a subset of processors, that can be accessed without using the bus-based network. This further generalization of the SMP architecture is an attempt to regain some of the scalability lost by offering shared memory. Vendors have come to coin these architectures as ccNUMA, using cc to stress that cache coherency is retained as multiple SMP nodes are linked by a cache-coherent interconnect.

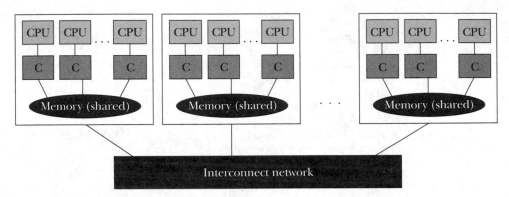

1.3

FIGURE
Example of a cluster of SMPs or symmetric multiprocessors such as the DEC Alpha. Here the single letter *C* denotes cache.

Caches are becoming more important because processor speeds are increasing much faster than memory access speeds. A read or write to cache generally requires less than 10 processor clock periods as compared to 100 clock periods or more to access normal memory. However, the basic problem with using caches is that multiple copies of data can exist. Significant effort at the hardware and software levels is required to ensure that all processors use the latest data. This requirement is referred to as *cache coherency*. The use of caches is discussed in more detail in Section 1.2.2.

One of the latest developments in high-performance computing is the coupling of SMP machines into clusters using very high-speed interconnects. These clusters can have a total number of processors that are comparable to large MPP machines. A typical cluster configuration is shown in Figure 1.3. They give the application developer the benefit of relatively large shared memory within a given SMP and total memory comparable to MPP machines. The clustering concept is not restricted to joining SMPs; many architectures are suitable for nodes of a cluster, and the nodes need not necessarily be all of the same type. This is often referred to as a *convergence of architectures* in the development of high-end computing [1.3].

To use entire clusters effectively, the developer must divide the problem into levels of parallelism and often needs to use a combination of the programming models discussed in Chapter 3. One advantage of clusters is that they are designed to allow computer centers to add additional nodes as needed given the economic driving force. Typical SMPs available now as a cluster can be RISC-based or vector-based. The NEC SX-4 system is a recent example of a vector-based SMP that can be configured into a cluster [1.12]. A single SX-4 SMP or node can have 4 to 32 processors and the cluster can have 2 to 16 nodes. The nodes are connected with a fiber-optic nonblocking crossbar having an 8 GB/s bidirectional bandwidth. For such vector machines, there are now three levels of parallelism: distributed memory parallelism across the nodes; shared-memory parallelism within the nodes; and, finally, vector parallelism associated with the vector units. For each level of parallelism a different programming model (see Chapter 3) may be the appropriate choice, leading to additional complexity and challenges for programming. In order to distinguish these new clusters from clusters of workstations, the latter are generally referred to as Networks of Workstations (NOWs) [1.2]. Although the processor count for NOWs can be large, the first implementations of this architecture had a slow communication speed that limited them to problems that required a very small amount of communication compared to processor usage. As technology advanced, it improved communication speed and the ease with which these systems could be created [1.7], [1.8], [1.11].

Ultimately all systems contain some level of similarity in the minds of the applications programmers because, for example, even memory that is logically shared is still physically distributed on today's parallel machines. Breaking the problem into appropriate tasks is fundamental to all parallel architectures, and doing so in an architecture-independent manner helps to promote the longevity of a particular application code.

1.2.1   MPP Processors

The reason that parallel computers have become a viable means of performing large industrial-scale calculations is the same reason that every business and home has easy access to personal computing—the RISC-processor technology for fast and efficient chips combined with manufacturing improvements to shrink the geometry has made commodity processors very inexpensive. Parallel machines today consist of either off-the-shelf chips or, in certain cases, chips that have been modified from the off-the-shelf version to include additional caches and other support structure to make them ideally suited to being combined into a large parallel computer. For example, in the case of the Cray T3D and T3E line of architectures, the chip is formed using low-cost CMOS technology (based on a metal oxide semiconductor) [1.10]. The result is an extremely fast RISC-based microprocessor (manufactured by Digital Equipment Corporation) called the Alpha EV4 (150 or 200 MHz) in the Cray T3D and the EV5 in the Cray T3E. Initial shipments of the EV5 chip had a peak performance of 600 million floating-point operations per second (megaflops or Mflops) in IEEE standard 32-bit and 64-bit mode running at a speed of 300 MHz. Continual upgrades of the chip increased the speed to 450 and, finally, 600 MHz by 1997. In some instances, the chips implemented in the MPPs run about one year behind their implementation in workstations because the MPP support must be compatible with the new chip.

Another dominant player in the MPP arena is the IBM RS/6000 SP [1.1]. The SP series is available in configurations that we informally term "standard" or "hybrid"; the standard configuration has one processor per node, and the hybrid versions have an SMP on each node. The earlier SP machines were based on the 66 MHz POWER2 processors arranged in a standard configuration. By 1995, according to IDC (International Data Corporation), the IBM RS/6000 SP was the best-selling MPP system in Europe. In 1996, the P2SC technology was introduced, which integrated eight POWER2 chips into a single POWER2 Super Chip, which at 120 MHz was capable of 480 Mflops peak performance. This has been followed by P2SC processors running at 160 MHz and rated at 640 Mflops peak performance. The carefully balanced architecture of these P2SC processors allows them to obtain high levels of performance on a wide variety of scientific and technical applications. In the class of hybrid configurations, a recent SP version has a four-way SMP on each node with each PowerPC 604e processor in the node running at 332 MHz, leading to a peak performance rating of 2.656 Gflops per node (each processor can perform two floating-point operations per cycle). Two of these machines have been placed at the Lawrence Livermore National Laboratories as part of the U.S. government's Advanced Strategic Computing Initiative (ASCI). Each of these machines has 168 nodes with four 332-MHz PowerPC 604e processors sharing memory on each node; one of them has additional POWER2 nodes. A larger machine with 1464 nodes and four processors per node is currently in the installation process. In Figure 1.4, we show a greatly simplified schematic diagram of a generic hybrid architecture that demonstrates distributed memory across nodes and shared memory within a single node. The optimal programming model for such hybrid architectures is often a combination of message passing across the nodes and some form of threads within a node to take full advantage of shared memory. This type of programming will be discussed in some detail in Chapter 3.

1.2.2   MPP Memory

Crucial to the performance of an MPP application is memory hierarchy. Even in computers that are classified as uniform memory access, there are levels of memory associated with the architecture. Consider, for example, an isosceles trapezoid of memory. (See Figure 1.5.)

At the top of the price/performance hierarchy are registers on the chip for actually manipulating the data. Next down, we have cache memory. Here the

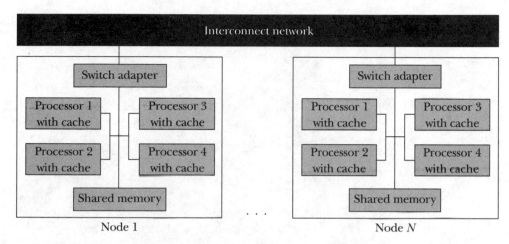

1.4

FIGURE

Generic hybrid architecture, based on the ASCI machine at LLNL.

data is cached for access to the registers. In the first chips used in the Cray T3D, there was one level of cache, and performance of an application was greatly affected by whether or not the problem was conveniently sized for cache access (see Chapter 5 for more details). In the next generation T3E machine, the EV5 contained a seconday cache, which helped improve performance. Additionally, the T3E automatically maintained cache coherency, whereas users of the T3D sometimes had to turn off caching when using certain programming models for remote referencing. By introducing cache coherency, all processors see the same value for any memory location, regardless of which cache the actual data is in or which processor most recently changed the data. Next down in the memory hierarchy is local memory. This is followed by remote memory and, finally, secondary memory such as disk.

Figure 1.6 shows the data flow from local memory (DRAM) to the microprocessor on the EV5 chip used in the Cray T3E. It is useful in understanding the following description of the process of moving data between memory and the microprocessor [1.4].

This EV5 RISC microprocessor is manufactured by Digital Equipment Corporation. The description uses the following abbreviations: E0, E1 (integer functional units); FA, FM (floating-point functional units); WB (write buffer); ICACHE (instruction cache); DCACHE (data cache); SCACHE (secondary data cache); SB (stream buffer); and DRAM (local memory). Only the four key hardware elements are mentioned: the microprocessor, data cache, secondary cache, and local memory. The example assumes the following Fortran loop:

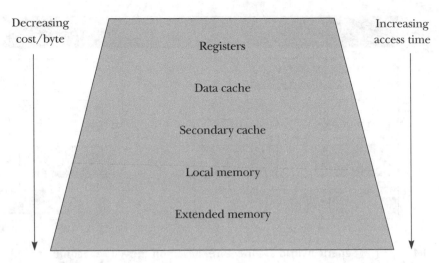

Decreasing cost/byte

Increasing access time

Registers

Data cache

Secondary cache

Local memory

Extended memory

1.5

FIGURE

The price/performance hierarchy for computer memory.

```
DO I = 1,N

A(I) = B(I) * N

ENDDO
```

1. The microprocessor requests the value of B(1) from data cache. Data cache does not have B(1), so it requests B(1) from secondary cache.

2. Secondary cache does not have B(1). This is called a *secondary cache miss*. It retrieves a line (eight words for secondary cache) from local memory. This includes elements B(1–8).

3. Data cache receives a line (four words for data cache) from secondary cache. This is elements B(1–4).

4. The microprocessor receives B(1) from data cache. When the microprocessor needs B(2) through B(4), it need only go to data cache.

5. When the microprocessor needs B(5), data cache does not have it. Data cache requests B(5) through B(8) from secondary cache, which has them and passes them on.

6. Data cache passes B(5) through B(8) on to the microprocessor as it gets requests for them. When the microprocessor finishes with them, it requests B(9) from data cache.

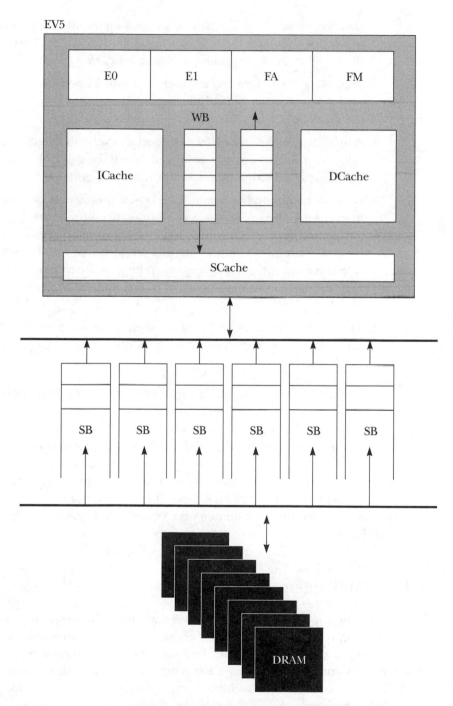

Flow of data on a Cray T3E node. (Figure used by permission from the *Cray T3E Fortran Optimization Guide, SG-2518.*)

7. Data cache requests a new line of data elements from secondary cache, which does not have them. This is the second secondary cache miss, and it is the signal to the system to begin streaming data.

8. Secondary cache requests another eight-word line from local memory and puts it into another of its three-line compartments. It may end up in any of the three lines, since the selection process is random.

9. A four-word line is passed from secondary cache to data cache, and a single value is moved to the microprocessor. When the value of B(9) gets to the microprocessor, the situation is as illustrated in Figure 1.7.

10. Because streaming has begun, data is now prefetched. Secondary cache anticipates the microprocessor's continuing need for consecutive data and begins retrieving B(17) through B(24) from memory before it is requested. Data cache requests data elements from secondary cache before it receives requests from the microprocessor. As long as the microprocessor continues to request consecutive elements of B, the data will be ready with a minimum of delay.

11. The process of streaming data between local memory and the functional units in the microprocessor continues until the DO-loop is completed for the N values.

In general, one can obtain a larger amount of total memory on an MPP machine as compared to an SMP machine, and the cost per megabyte is usually much cheaper. For example, the Cray T3D has 64 MB per node, giving a total of 33 GB for a system with 512 nodes. At the time it was released, its memory was larger than the memory available on shared-memory machines. Currently, the Cray T3E has up to 2 GB per node, and for the maximum number of nodes (2048), a total memory of 4 TB is possible. As discussed in a number of applications, the need for large memory is frequently a major reason for moving to an MPP machine.

1.2.3   MPP Interconnect Network

Another important part of the supercomputer is the system by which the processors share data or the interconnect network. Interconnection networks can be classified as static or dynamic. In a static network, processors are connected directly to other processors via a specific topology. In a dynamic network, processors are connected dynamically using switches, and other links can establish paths between processors and banks of memory.

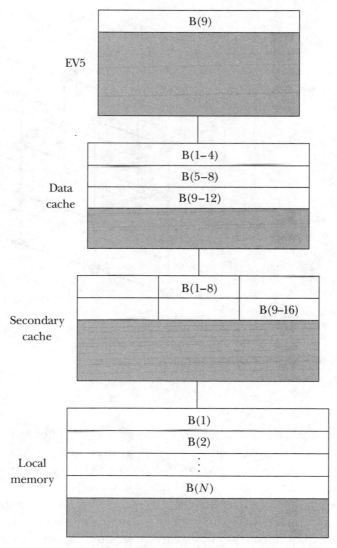

1.7
FIGURE

Ninth value reaches the microprocessor. (Figure used by permission from the *Cray T3E Fortran Optimization Guide, SG-2518*.)

In the case of static interconnects, the data transfer characteristics depend on the explicit topology. Some popular configurations for the interconnect include 2D meshes, linear arrays, rings, hypercubes, and so on. For some of these configurations, part of the job of the parallel programmer was to design the data layout to fit the machine. This was because the nonuniform nature of the

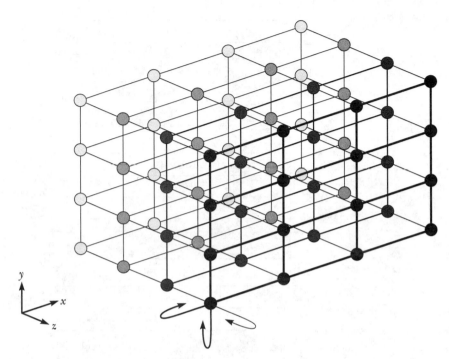

A diagram of the torus interconnect.

interprocessor communication made an enormous difference in the performance of a given application. As technology improved in certain parallel computer designs, these communication latencies were masked from the user or significantly reduced with improved interconnects. The Cray T3D and T3E lines of parallel computers to a great extent overcame this obstacle to performance by arranging the processors in a 3D torus. A diagram of the torus is given in Figure 1.8. In the toroidal configuration, each processing element is connected with a bidirectional interconnect to neighboring processors and, as well, additional connections are made to connect the ends of the array in the perpendicular directions (thus the name 3D torus).

On the IBM RS/6000 SP, a low-latency, high-bandwidth switching network, termed the High-Performance Switch (HPS), connects the nodes. The HPS offers the highly attractive feature of the available bandwidth between any two nodes in a system remaining near constant regardless of the location of the nodes or the size of the overall system (up to the maximum size of the switch available on current SP configurations). This is achieved by a multistage interconnect network that adds switching stages to increase aggregate bandwidth with an increasing number of nodes. Switches use various techniques for directing the data from one port of the switch (connected to a node) to another. These techniques include temporal division, spatial division, and frequency domain division. In general, the bandwidth available to a node is proportional to LN/H, where L is the link bandwidth, N is the number of links in the switch per node, and H is the average number of hops through the switch required for a communication operation. In a multistage network such as the HPS, additional links are added with increasing nodes. The number of hops, H, increases logarithmically with the number of nodes. But this is compensated by the logarithmic increase in the number of links, N, and thus the bandwidth between any two nodes remains constant.

A common and realistic indicator of aggregate network capacity is the bisection bandwidth, which is the maximum possible bandwidth across a minimum network bisection, where the bisection cuts the network into two equal parts. On an IBM RS/6000 SP with an HPS, the bisection bandwidth scales linearly with the size of the system. For large systems, this provides an important advantage over direct connect networks such as rings and meshes, where the bisection bandwidth increases much more slowly. The constant bandwidth between any two nodes on an SP system also eliminates concerns based on "near" and "far" nodes; as far as an application programmer is concerned, all nodes on an SP are "equidistant" from each other.

References

[1.1]   Agerwala, T., J. L. Martin, J. H. Mirza, D. C. Sadler, D. M. Dias, and M. Snir. 1995. SP2 System Architecture. *IBM Systems Journal*, **34,** 2 Reprint Order No. G321–5563.

[1.2]   Anderson, T. 1995. A Case for NOW (Networks of Workstations). IEEE Micro 15, **1;**54–64.

[1.3]   Culler, David E., Jaswinder Pal Singh, with Anoop Gupta. 1999. *Parallel Computer Architecture, A Hardware/Software Approach.* San Francisco: Morgan Kaufmann.

[1.4]   Cray T3E Fortran Optimization Guide, SG-2518. *www.cray.com/swpubs/*

[1.5]   Flynn, M. J. 1972. Some Computer Organizations and Their Effectiveness. *IEEE Transactions on Computing,* **21,** 948–960.

[1.6]   Hennessy, J. L., and D. A. Patterson. 1996. *Computer Architecture: A Quantitative Approach* (second edition). San Francisco: Morgan Kaufmann.

[1.7]   Hill, Jim, Michael Warren, and Patrick Goda. 1998. I'm Not Going to Pay a Lot for This Super Computer. *Linux Journal,* **45,** 56–60.

[1.8]   Katz, D. S., T. Cwik, and T. Sterling. 1998. An Examination of the Performance of Two Electromagnetic Simulations on a Beowulf-Class Computer. *12th Annual International Symposium on High-Performance Computer Systems and Applications (HPCS'98),* May.

[1.9]   May, John M., and Bronis R. de Supinski. 1999. Experience with Mixed MPI/Threaded Programming Models. *International Conference on Parallel and Distributed Processing Techniques and Applications,* June–July.

[1.10] Scott, S. 1996. Synchronization and Communication in the T3E Multiprocessor. Proceedings of the Seventh International Conference on Architectural Support for Programming Languages and Operating Systems. 26–36, October.

[1.11]   Sterling, Thomas. 1997. How to Build a Beowulf: Assembling, Programming, and Using a
          Clustered PC Do-It-Yourself Supercomputer. In *Proceedings of the SC97*.

[1.12]   SXWorld. *www.hpc.comp.nec.co.jp/sx-e/sx-world*.

2 | Parallel Application Performance

CHAPTER

Alice E. Koniges Lawrence Livermore National Laboratory

Performance of a real-world industrial application on a parallel computer is a difficult quantity to measure. Most of the applications described in Part II model a complex interplay of phenomena. These may involve different time scales and coupling of physics and chemistry packages in a dynamic framework. Additionally, efficiency of the parallel application on the industrial computing platform may be an issue, particularly when the platform is shared among users. In this chapter, we provide the minimal set of definitions and concepts needed to understand the basics of parallel application performance and measurement. These are then quantified in the applications chapters and used again in Part III when we discuss the future of industrial parallel computing.

2.1   DEFINING PERFORMANCE

The first level of understanding performance issues requires a few definitions. We have the basic measure of computer performance, *peak performance,* namely, the maximum performance rate possible for a given operation (usually prefixed by mega (10^6)) per second. Thus we have, Mips, Mops, and Mflops for instructions per second, operations per second, and floating-point operations per second. As machines get faster and faster, we introduce Gflops for giga (10^9) and Tflops for tera (10^{12}), and we await the introduction of peta (10^{15}). The performance in operations per second (ops) is based on the *clock rate* of the processor and the number of operations per clock (cycle). At the chip level, there are various ways to increase the number of operations per clock cycle and thus the overall chip ops capability.

Machine	r* (Gflops)	Clock cycle (ns)	Processor count for r*
Cray T3D (150 MHz)	77	6.7	512
Cray Y-MP C90	16	4.1	16
Avalon A12	7	3.3	12
Cray T3E (300 MHz)	307	3.3	512
IBM9076 SP2 (66 MHz)	136	15	512
SGI Power Challenge XL	5.4	13.3	18
Cray T90	58	2.2	32
Intel Paragon	38	20	512

2.1

TABLE

Theoretical peak performance for some machines used in the applications chapters. (Some machines are available with more processors and faster clocks than given here. This would result in larger values for r*.)

When processors are combined into an MPP architecture, we can define the *theoretical peak performance* r* of the system [2.1] as

$$r* = \frac{Number\ of\ arithmetic\ function\ units\ /\ CPU}{Clock\ cycle} P$$

where P is the number of processors, and the number of arithmetic function units per CPU gives a measure of the possible number of floating-point operations in a clock cycle. This measure of supercomputing performance is often jokingly referred to as the "speed that the vendor is guaranteed never to exceed" [2.1]. Table 2.1 gives r* for some machine configurations used in the applications [2.3]. Of course, r* is dependent on the number of processors, and not all applications had access to all processors or even a machine configured with the maximum number of processors allowed by the vendor specifications.

Chip performance and thus r* is only the first of the building blocks in determining the utility of a parallel machine. Perhaps the next most important hardware factor affecting performance is the communication speed on the chip, speed between local memory and the chip, and speed between nodes. Communication speed plays an important role in determining the scalability performance of a parallel application. Communication speed has itself two major components:

+ *Bandwidth:* The rate of data transferred, measured in MB per second
+ *Latency:* How long it takes to get that first bit of information to a processor (i.e., a message of size zero); usually measured in nanoseconds or clock periods (CP).

	Cray T3D latency	Cray T3D bandwidth	Cray T3E latency	Cray T3E bandwidth
Data cache load	20 ns (3 CP per load)	1200 MB (1 word per CP)	6.67 ns (2 CP per load)	4800 MB (2 words per CP)
Secondary cache load	N/A	N/A	26.67 ns (8 CP per load)	4800 MB (2 words per CP)
Data or secondary cache store	N/A	N/A	N/A	2400 MB (1 word per CP)

2.2

TABLE

Memory latencies and bandwidths for Cray T3E with the 300-MHz chip compared to the Cray T3D with a 150-MHz chip.

Together, these two additional factors influence the actual useful performance of a parallel computer's hardware. This performance may depend greatly on both the problem requirements and the parallel implementation. Table 2.2 shows the time required for a Cray T3D (150 MHz) processing element (PE) and a Cray T3E (300 MHz) PE to load data from and store data to data cache. As already discussed, as one goes down the memory hierarchy the amount of memory increases but with increasing latency to access this data. For example, on the Cray T3E the latency to access local memory is 125 CP as compared to 2 CP for data cache and 8 CP for secondary cache. The bandwidth to local memory on the Cray T3E is approximately 600 MB/s. To help users evaluate chip performance, there is a series of benchmarks that reflect not only the clock and peak performance rate but also give the performance on a series of special benchmarks. A vendor consortium known as the Standard Performance Evaluation Corporation designed one often-quoted benchmark series [2.4]. The SPECint95 and the SPECfp95 benchmarks are obtained by computing the geometric mean of performance on a set of eight normalized performance ratios.

2.2   MEASURING PERFORMANCE

The underlying issue for most applications is the period of time required to solve a given problem. Raw Mflops rate is not really the main issue nor is raw CPU time. For the former, it has been shown [2.1] that by judicious choice of the algorithm, a faster time to solution may be obtained by using an algorithm that has an inherently lower flops rate. For the latter, one must realize that raw CPU time does not take into consideration any of the communication overhead. Furthermore, optimization of throughput may result in performing some operations multiple times to avoid the overhead of broadcasting the results computed once to many processors. In other cases, it is desirable to perform multiple sets of instructions on one set of data and retain only one set of result data, depending upon computations conducted by other threads. Both cases inflate the overhead of computing a result, but do so in the fastest overall manner.

2.2.1   MPP Application Speedup

One of the interesting questions asked when dealing with an MPP application is what *speedup* is possible as the number of processors increases. For instance, if an application takes N seconds to run on a single-processor machine, how long does it take to run on a machine with P CPUs? One might hope that the time would be N/P seconds. However, this is not the typical case. One key reason is that at most a fraction, f, of the program may be parallelizable. According to Amdahl's law, for an application to obtain a speedup of 200 on 256 processors, it must be 99.9 percent parallel. Therefore, there is little point to encountering the overhead in requesting and releasing processes because the processors are needed almost the whole time.

$$Speedup = \frac{1}{(1-f) + f/p}$$

This is the famous Amdahl's law. If f is 100 percent, then speedup is P. To make good use of an MPP with a large number of processors, it is necessary to have f fairly close to 100 percent. For example, if f is 75 percent, the speedup cannot be more than 4 even when you employ an infinite number of CPUs (P very large).

The speedup that an application achieves on one processor compared to P processors, on a problem of a given size, is referred to as the *parallel speedup*. Ideally, the speedup should be measured with respect to the best serial algorithm, not just the parallel algorithm on a serial computer. Examples of parallel speedup are given in a number of the applications chapters. In some cases, the speedup scales linearly with processor number up to the maximum number displayed. However, this is not always the case. In Chapter 21 (Figure 21.2), the speedup scales linearly with processor number up to a given number of processors. After that, there is less of a benefit in adding more processors. Such a turnover in speedup curves can be due to Amdahl's law, increased communication costs associated with the larger number of processors solving the same problem, or other issues associated with the algorithms used in the code. A measurement that carries similar information to parallel speedup is *wall clock speedup*. If the reason to add more processors is to get a result faster, and not to run a larger problem associated with larger memory, this is an appropriate measure of performance. Examples of wall clock speedup can be found in Chapters 11 (Figure 11.4), 20 (Figure 20.11), and 22 (Figure 22.5). Another way that speedup results are presented is in terms of floating-point operations per second. With this measure, one can compare to the theoretical peak performance or the speed of the computer on some relevant benchmark code. Such a measure can be useful in determining ways to optimize the code. Results presented in this form are given in Chapters 9 (Figure 9.3), 16 (Figure 16.6), and 17 (Figure 17.9).

One real utility of parallel computers is their ability to solve larger problems by distributing the memory requirements over the processors. Thus, it is perhaps more useful to measure speedup by defining the *scaled speedup*. Here, we compare the application's performance for a problem of size A on P processors to a problem of size $n*A$ on $n*P$ processors, where n is an integer. As the problem size increases, the sequential part typically takes a lower fraction of the total. This reduces the effect of Amdahl's law on the speedup that is possible. For large industrial applications, it is often the case that very large memory problems must be solved. It is efficient to put the largest problem possible on a given machine configuration, and thus the scaled speedup is a useful measure of the effectiveness of the parallel implementation. (In Chapter 6, we show how gang scheduling can be used to allocate various processor sets to a variety of users.) Some examples of scaled speedup are in Chapters 7 (Figure 7.2) and 12 (Figures 12.3, 12.6, 12.7).

One way to standardize performance results, particularly for the evaluation of machine architecture, is the suite of benchmarks particularly designed for parallel machines, the NAS Parallel Benchmarks [2.2]. These consist of a wide variety of relevant scientific and industrial computations, and various levels of optimization are permitted. For instance, NPB 1 is a "pencil and paper" set of the benchmarks. For this set, one is allowed to tailor the specific algorithm and programming to the architecture. Other benchmark suites require the use of a particular algorithm or programming model. Parallel computing vendors work very hard to achieve good performance on the benchmark problems, and thus a typical nonbenchmark application code may have trouble reaching the same absolute performance levels.

References

[2.1]   Dongarra, Jack J., Subhash Saini, Erich Strohmaier, and Patrick H. Worley. 1997. Performance Evaluation of Parallel Applications: Measurement, Modeling, and Analysis. In *Proceedings of the SC97*.

[2.2]   The NAS Parallel Benchmarks home pages: *www.nas.nasa.gov*.

[2.3]   van der Steen, Aad J., and Jack J. Dongarra. 1996. Overview of Recent Supercomputers (sixth edition). Feb 10. *www.crpc.rice.edu/NHSEreview*.

[2.4]   SPEC (Standard Performance Evaluation Corporation). *www.specbench.org/*.

3 Programming Models and Methods

Margaret Cahir
Robert Moench   SGI/Cray Research

Alice E. Koniges   Lawrence Livermore National Laboratory

The standard specifications for the most popular languages used in scientific programming, Fortran and C/C++, do not address programming for multiple processors. Vendors and committees representing a wide range of industries and academia have produced various solutions to the issue, resulting in a broad range of parallel programming methods. This can be confusing to the newcomer, so in the sections below, we describe a few of the current most popular parallel programming models in use on machines with high processor counts. We also describe some active areas of research that are influencing work on programming methods for highly parallel machines.

Parallel programming models are typically designed with a specific hardware architecture in mind. As a result, the variety of parallel programming model architectures is a reflection of the variety of hardware architecture offerings. Although today's machines have converged on a MIMD-style architecture, they still differ significantly in how they handle their collective memory. Some machines have a single-address space, where a memory address is all that is needed to locate the data in the memory. Examples of these include the SGI/Cray parallel-vector machines such as the J90 and some of the newer ccNUMA machines such as the SGI/Cray Origin and HP/Convex Exemplar. MPPs such as the Cray T3D and T3E have globally addressable memory spaces, where memory throughout the machine may be referenced but memory references require a translation to the appropriate node. Machines may also be composed of multiple address spaces, where a special mechanism such as a networking protocol may be required to transfer data between the spaces. Examples of this type of machine include the IBM SP2 [3.1], networks of workstations, and clusters of one of the other types of machines.

Examples of models that were designed for a single-address and globally addressable spaces include work-sharing models and data-parallel models. In work-sharing models, a single process executes until it hits a parallel construct, such as a parallel DO-loop, where work is to be divided among a group of threads and then returns to a single thread of control once all the work in the parallel construct has been completed. Data-parallel models are similar to work-sharing models, but here the parallel constructs are implicit in the array syntax used for specially designated data objects. In both cases, the location of the data may determine where the execution of the instruction referencing that data item will occur.

Models designed for use across multiple address spaces are based on the message-passing and data-passing paradigms. In these models, tasks operate in relative independence and explicitly communicate through function calls to the communication library. Examples of message-passing models include the de facto standard libraries Message-Passing Interface (MPI) and Parallel Virtual Machine (PVM), and examples of data passing include the SGI/Cray Shared Memory (SHMEM) library [3.19] and University of Oxford Bulk Synchronous Parallel Model (BSP) library [3.12].

This taxonomy is complicated by the fact that these models can be applied to hardware types other than that for which they were originally targeted. For example, message-passing models have been implemented quite successfully on shared-memory, single-address machines by using memory copies in place of network-based communication mechanisms. Likewise, some shared-memory models have been implemented on machines with multiple address spaces by replacing memory operations with messages.

Another aspect of parallel programming models is how and when the execution of tasks or processes starts and ends. Models that are targeted for machines with large processor counts, like MPPs, generally have all tasks starting and finishing simultaneously. According to Amdahl's law, an application that must scale well to 512 processors must be close to 99 percent parallel. Therefore, there is little point to encountering the overhead in requesting and releasing processes because the processors are needed almost the whole time. Models that evolved on machines with small numbers of processors tend to have execution models where threads come and go during the application's lifetime.

A comprehensive discussion of all the parallel programming models that have been developed and used in recent years would constitute a book in itself. In Section 3.1, we discuss just a few of the most well-known programming models in use on highly parallel systems today, including PVM, MPI, and SHMEM approaches. In Section 3.2, we discuss data-parallel approaches, including High-Performance Fortran. In Section 3.3, we discuss a few other approaches to parallel programming that may prove to be of interest in future programming developments. The 17 applications in this book use a variety of the programming discussed. Table P.1 in the Preface guides you in finding an application that uses a particular programming model. This same table is shown on the inside front cover and its facing page.

The most commonly used programming model on today's highly parallel systems is message passing. Here we discuss the two most popular message-passing library implementations, PVM and MPI. We also describe the SGI/Cray SHMEM data-passing library, as it is highly utilized on the Cray T3D and T3E platforms and is used in many of the applications described in this book. It has also been influential in the evolution of other programming models. In addition to message passing, there are also significant numbers of codes that utilize the data-parallel method. In Section 3.2.1, we describe the most well-known implementation of this model, High-Performance Fortran or, as it is commonly referred to, HPF.

For each of the model types, it is important to understand the execution model and the memory model that the model is based on. The execution model describes how tasks are created, synchronized, stopped, and otherwise controlled. There are two aspects to the memory model. One describes how memory is viewed by the different tasks, that is, whether data is private to each task or if it is shared among all tasks. The other aspect concerns how the data is physically laid out in memory. We will explain the execution and memory models used in each of the programming types in the following sections.

3.1   MESSAGE-PASSING MODELS

Message-passing models have a number of characteristics in common. The execution model allows for each task to operate separately, manage its own instruction stream, and control its private area of memory. Tasks are generally created at program startup or very shortly thereafter. Communication and synchronization between the tasks is accomplished through calls to library routines. The lower-level mechanism by which the message is sent is transparent to the application programmer. Message passing is largely the model of choice on MIMD computers with physically distributed memory because the close relationship between the model and the hardware architecture allows the programmer to write code in an optimal manner for the hardware. In addition, message-passing libraries are available on virtually all parallel systems, making this paradigm appealing to those who desire portability across a variety of machines. Message passing is currently the only practical choice for use across clusters of machines.

There are a number of functions that message-passing libraries usually perform. These include operations to perform point-to-point communication, collective operations such as broadcasts, global reductions, and gathering data from groups of tasks. Many of the collective functions could be written by the user using the basic point-to-point operations, but they are generally supplied by the library for ease-of-use and for performance. As is the case with libraries for common mathematical functions, optimal versions of communication functions depend on the underlying hardware architecture and can often benefit from nontrivial algorithms. Thus, it is generally advantageous for the application programmer to use routines supplied by the library implementation.

It is worth noting that since message-passing models share the same basic structure, codes may be written so that the same source code is used with different message-passing libraries. Many of the applications described here do just that. Most often this is accomplished by limiting the communication portions of a code to a relatively small set of routines. Versions of this small set of routines are written for each message-passing model desired. Another method is to utilize preprocessors to modify the source code to use the desired message-passing system.

3.1.1   PVM

PVM grew out of a research project at Oak Ridge National Laboratory to harness a group of heterogeneous computers into a single "virtual" machine. In 1991, an implementation of the PVM design, designated PVM 2.0, was made available to the public and included source code for users to build a set of commands and a library that programmers can integrate with their applications. Usage of PVM grew rapidly due to its general availability and its ability to run on a wide variety of machines from large MPPs to PCs. In addition to the publicly available source, many computer vendors supply versions of PVM with optimizations specific to their particular machines.

PVM 3.0 was released in 1993. This version had many changes and enabled PVM applications to run across a virtual machine composed of multiple large multiprocessors. Version 3.3 is the most common version in use today and the one used in many of the applications described in this book. PVM continues to evolve, and Version 3.4 has been released recently.

Under PVM, programs or tasks are initiated under the control of a daemon that spawns the program on the requested computer(s). The user may require multiple instances of a particular application, and the application itself may request tasks to be spawned. Each task is assigned a unique identifier by which it is referred to in communication requests. Task creation and deletion is completely dynamic; that is, it may occur any time during the application's lifetime. The tasks composing the PVM application may be executing different programs. PVM provides fault tolerance by allowing tasks to register for notification if one of the other tasks in the application terminates for some unexpected reason. This allows the notified task to take precautions such that it does not hang and can potentially generate new tasks if desired. This is particularly important to applications running across heterogeneous networks where the likelihood of a "node failure" may be high. PVM supplies mechanisms for resource control by allowing the user to add and delete systems from the virtual machine and to query the status of the systems.

PVM provides functions for point-to-point communications and for synchronization. It provides collective functions for global reductions, broadcasts, and multicasts and allows for the designation of groups that can be used in the collective functions and barriers. (Multicasts are similar to broadcasts with the exception that it is not necessary for all targets to attempt to receive the message.) PVM's strengths lie in its ability to run over heterogeneous networks. Because this includes the possibility that messages will be sent between machines with incompatible numeric formats, PVM performs translations of the data when messages are sent and received. Additionally, PVM provides for bypassing this translation when the application will only be running on a homogeneous system. Messages are queued, meaning that multiple messages may be sent from a task without blocking. Messages can be deleted from the queue. The current version of PVM, 3.4, introduces several new capabilities, including message context and a name service. Context allows PVM to distinguish between PVM messages sent by different components that make up the application, such as PVM-based libraries that may be utilized along with the main body of the application. A name service provides capability for multiple independent programs to query for information about each other. A message handler service to assist in event-driven codes is also part of the new version.

Example 3.1 shows a PVM implementation of a common technique used in numerical codes with regular grids. Each task works on a portion of a rectangular array or grid. It performs computations that require data owned by other processors, so before it can perform its computations, it requests copies of the data that it needs from the other processors. The local grid array is padded with boundary cells, which are also known as "ghost cells" or "halo cells." The data that is needed from the edges of the nearest neighbors' arrays will be stored in these extra cells. In this example, we have a 3D array named 'data', which is distributed along the second dimension, or y-axis.

```
program halo_update
implicit none
include 'fpvm3.h'
integer,parameter  :: nx=128
integer,parameter  :: ny=128
integer,parameter  :: nz=150
real(kind=8),dimension(1:nx,0:ny+1,1:nz) :: data
real(kind=8)       :: result, global_result
integer            :: mytid, ppid, nstart, ier, buf
integer            :: mytid_left, mytid_right
integer            :: mype
integer            :: mtag
integer,parameter  :: ntasks = 2
integer            :: tids(0:ntasks-1)
integer            :: ier
integer            :: nspawn, inst_world
integer            :: myleft, myright, iz, i
call pvmfmytid (mytid)
call pvmfparent (ppid)
if (ppid .eq. pvmnoparent) then
print*,'Calling spawn . . . '
nspawn  = ntasks -1
tids(0) = mytid
call pvmfspawn ('/usr/people/joe/halo_pvm',
*         PVMTaskHost,'.',nspawn,tids(1),nstart)
  if(nstart.ne.nspawn) then
  print*,'Error in starting tasks, only',nstart, 'were spawned'
 else
  print*,'List of Task IDs =',tids
 endif
endif
call pvmfjoingroup ('world', inst_world)
call pvmfbarrier ('world', ntasks, ier)
mtag = 1
if (ppid .eq. pvmnoparent) then
  call pvmfinitsend (PVMDATARAW, ier)
  call pvmfpack (INTEGER4, tids, ntasks, 1, ier)
  do i=1,ntasks-1
```

3.1 Halo (Ghost) Cell Update in PVM.

EXAMPLE

```
              call pvmfsend (tids(i), mtag, ier)
       enddo
     else
        call pvmfrecv (ppid, mtag, buf)
        call pvmfunpack (INTEGER4, tids, ntasks, 1, ier)
     endif
     do i = 0,ntasks-1
        if(tids(i).eq.mytid) mype = i
     enddo
     myleft  = mod(mype+1,ntasks)          ! left neighbor-periodic
     myright = mod(mype-1+ntasks,ntasks) ! right neighbor-periodic
     mytid_left  = tids(myleft)
     mytid_right = tids(myright)
     ! each domain will compute new values for data
     call compute_data (data,nx,ny,nz)
     mtag = 2
     ! update left-right (Y-direction)
     ! pass to the right
     ! use dataraw mode since this application lives on 1 machine
     call pvmfinitsend (PVMDATARAW, ier)
     do iz = 1,nz
        call pvmfpack  (REAL8, data(1,ny,iz), nx, 1, ier)
     enddo
     call pvmfsend      (mytid_right, mtag, ier)
     call pvmfrecv      (mytid_left, mtag, buf )
     do iz = 1,nz
        call pvmfunpack(REAL8, data(1,0,iz), nx, 1, ier)
     enddo
     ! pass to the left
     call pvmfinitsend (PVMDATARAW, ier)
     do iz = 1,nz
        call pvmfpack  (REAL8, data(1,0,iz), nx, 1, ier)
     enddo
     call pvmfsend      (mytid_left, mtag, ier)
     call pvmfrecv      (mytid_right, mtag, buf)
     do iz = 1,nz
        call pvmfunpack (REAL8, data(1,ny,iz), nx, 1, ier)
     enddo
```

3.1   (continued)

EXAMPLE

```
call use_data (data,nx,ny,nz)
! each domain will compute new values for data
call compute_data (data,nx,ny,nz)
! compute an error norm that is some function of the data
call compute_error_norm (data, nx, ny, nz, result)
! perform a global sum reduction on the result
mtag = 3
call pvmfreduce (PvmSum, result, 1, REAL8, mtag, 'world', 0, ier)
if (inst_world.eq.0) print*, 'The Error Norm: ', result
! wait for everyone to be done
call pvmfbarrier ('world', ntasks, ier)
! now we can safely exit from PVM
call pvmfexit (ier)
end
```

3.1   (continued)

EXAMPLE

The first step that must be accomplished is to start up all the tasks that will be part of this program. This is accomplished by the pvm_spawn function, which will only be done by the first process initiated. Each process queries the runtime system to find out its task ID. All tasks join a group, which we call "world." The first or parent task received a list of the spawned tasks' IDs when it returned from the spawn request. It needs to send the list of task IDs to all the tasks so that they may communicate with each other as well as with the parent task. We want to assign each task a portion of the array to work on, so we find their order in the task list. Then each task computes its left and right neighbor using a periodic function and determines the task ID of the nearest neighbors. Each task will compute values for the data array independently. The edge values are updated by first passing edge data to the right. For each message, a send buffer is allocated with the pvmfinitsend call. A vector's worth of data is packed into the message buffer for each x-y plane of data. Finally, the message is sent with a send call. After sending data, each location waits to receive data from its neighbor. When the task has returned from the receive call, the data has arrived and the unpacking can begin. This process is then repeated to update data to the left. In a typical application, the data would now be used, likely for several times. Frequently, some function of the data—for example, an error norm—is to be computed. Each task calculates this value on its portion of the data. To add up each task's contribution, we perform a global reduction by calling the pvmfreduce function with the PvmSum option. Finally, all tasks complete and PVM is exited.

PVM is sometimes criticized for providing less performance than other message-passing systems. This is certainly true on some machines. PVM was targeted to work over networks of computers, with portability and interoperability being the prime design considerations. For situations where performance is of utmost importance, some of the other message-passing systems should be considered. But where there is a need for running across a heterogeneous group of processors, and capabilities such as fault tolerance and resource control are important, PVM may still be an appropriate choice.

3.1.2   MPI

By 1992, when the MPI Forum first started meeting, message passing was a proven concept and experience had been gained with other message-passing systems. The forum was composed of members of academia, government laboratories, and computer vendor representatives. The goal of the forum was to take what had been learned in the earlier efforts and create a standard for a high-performance system that would be portable across many different machines. MPI encompasses a set of library functions that the applications developers integrate into their code. Unlike PVM, MPI does not specify commands to the operating system for the creation of daemons. Soon after the MPI-1 specification was approved by this group in 1994, it became a recognized standard and the message-passing system of choice for most developers of new code [3.15]. This is as much due to its demonstrated performance as to its extensive collection of routines for support of commonly occurring communication patterns [3.10]. The MPI standard is available on the Web and as a book [3.20].

An MPI application may be initiated by a runtime command that includes an option to indicate how many tasks should be created. The tasks will be activated when the MPI_INIT call is encountered, if they were not already created at program initialization. All tasks continue executing until the MPI_Finalize call is encountered unless a task has encountered an error situation, which may cause the MPI application to abort.

The MPI-1 standard does not require that different executables be able to communicate with each other, although most vendor implementations do provide this feature. MPI-1 implementations do not generally provide the capability for different types of machines to talk to each other. For point-to-point communication, a wide variety of message-passing modes exists. The most commonly used modes are the standard send invoked by the MPI_send function and the asynchronous mode invoked with the MPI_isend function. For the standard mode, the message may or may not be buffered, depending on the implementation and the size of the message. For cases where the message is not buffered, the sending task will not return from the call until the message has been sent and received. When the message is buffered or if the MPI_isend function is used, the sender may return from the call before the message is sent out. This mode is usually used where performance is important. The MPI-1 standard is not specific about how the actual message is transferred in order to allow vendors leeway in implementing MPI in the most efficient way for their machines.

MPI allows a form of task groups called *communicators*. A special communicator that includes all the tasks in an application, MPI_COMM_WORLD, is set up at program initiation. Other communicators may be defined by the user to include any arbitrary set of processors. A task has a rank within each communicator, and this rank together with the communicator uniquely identifies a task within the application. Communicators are a convenient device for the user to limit operations to a subset of tasks and are required input for most of the MPI functions.

Within MPI messages, it is possible to send scalar values or arrays of contiguous values for the MPI-defined data types. MPI also provides a method for the user to define noncontiguous patterns of data that may be passed to the MPI functions. These patterns are called *derived types* and may be built by a series of function calls to form virtually arbitrary patterns of data and combinations of data types.

MPI provides a comprehensive set of communication routines that are convenient for high-performance scalable programming. The communicator is passed to the collective functions to indicate which group of tasks is included in the operation. Collective functions are provided to perform global reductions, broadcasts, task synchronization, and a wide variety of gather-and-scatter operations. Additionally, MPI provides functions for defining a virtual Cartesian grid of processors that make it easier to program algorithms that are based on regular grid structures.

The specification for MPI-2 was approved in April 1997 [3.9]. This version adds many new capabilities to the base standard, most notably dynamic process control, shared I/O, and one-sided communications. The dynamic process control capabilities allows an MPI application to spawn another set of tasks and communicate with them. The new I/O features of MPI-2, commonly referred to as MPI-IO, allow tasks to intermix I/O requests to the same file. This provides important new capability for hardware platforms that do not have shared file systems. The one-sided communication method allows a task to put or get data from another task without the other task being directly involved.

Example 3.2 illustrates how we could write our regular grid update code in MPI. First, we call the MPI_init function to indicate that this is an MPI program. We use the MPI functions to determine how many tasks are running and

```
program halo_update
implicit none
include "mpif.h"
integer,parameter :: nx=128
integer,parameter :: ny=128
integer,parameter :: nz=150
real(kind=8),dimension(1:nx,0:ny+1,1:nz) :: data
real(kind=8)       :: result, global_result
integer            :: mype, npes, ier
integer            :: status (mpi_status_size)
integer            :: stag, rtag
integer            :: myleft, myright, iz, i
integer            :: face_y, stride
call MPI_init (ier)
call MPI_comm_rank (MPI_COMM_WORLD,mype,ier)
call MPI_comm_size (MPI_COMM_WORLD,npes,ier)
myleft  = mod(mype+1,npes)       ! my left neighbor (periodic)
myright = mod(mype-1+npes,npes) ! my right neighbor (periodic)
! each domain will compute new values for data
call compute_data (data,nx,ny,nz)
stag = 0
rtag = 0
! update left-right (Y-direction) edges using sendrecv
do iz = 1,nz
  stag = stag + 1
  rtag = rtag + 1
  call MPI_sendrecv(data(1,ny,iz),nx, MPI_REAL8, myright, stag,
*                   data(1,0,iz), nx, MPI_REAL8, myleft, rtag,
*                   MPI_COMM_WORLD, status, ier)
  stag = stag + 1
  rtag = rtag + 1
  call MPI_sendrecv(data(1,0,iz), nx, MPI_REAL8, myleft, stag,
*                   data(1,ny,iz),nx, MPI_REAL8, myright, rtag,
*                   MPI_COMM_WORLD, status, ier)
enddo
! use the new data in computations
call use_data (data,nx,ny,nz)
```

3.2   MPI.

EXAMPLE

```
! each domain will compute new values for data
call compute_data (data,nx,ny,nz)
! this time we will use derived types to send data in 1 message
! this type is composed of columns of the data, each nx long,
! separated by one X-Y plane with is nx*(ny+2) in size
stride = nx * (ny+2)
call MPI_type_vector (nz, nx, stride, MPI_REAL8, FACE_Y, ier)
! MPI requires the type to be committed before being used
call MPI_type_commit (FACE_Y, ier)
stag = 1
rtag = 1
call MPI_sendrecv(data(1,ny,1), 1, FACE_Y, myright, stag,
*                 data(1,0,1), 1, FACE_Y, myleft, rtag,
*                 MPI_COMM_WORLD, status, ier)
 stag = stag + 1
 rtag = rtag + 1
 call MPI_sendrecv(data(1,0,1), 1, FACE_Y, myleft, stag,
*                 data(1,ny,1),1, FACE_Y, myright, rtag,
*                 MPI_COMM_WORLD, status, ier)
 ! use the new data again in computations
 call use_data (data,nx,ny,nz)
 ! compute an error norm that is some function of the data
 call compute_error_norm (data, nx, ny, nz, result)
 ! perform a global sum reduction on the result
 call mpi_allreduce (result, global_result, 1, MPI_REAL8,
   *              MPI_SUM, MPI_COMM_WORLD, ier)
 if(mype.eq.0) print*,' The Error Norm: ',global_result
 call mpi_barrier (MPI_COMM_WORLD,ier)
 call mpi_finalize (ier)
 stop
```

3.2   (continued)

EXAMPLE

what the ranks of the individual tasks are. Each task will compute values for the array 'data'. This happens completely independently within the routine compute_data. To update the edges of the 'data' array the first time, we use the MPI library routine, which combines a send and a receive in one call. The first call updates the left edges, and the second call updates the right edges. Typically, this data would be used and the halo cells referenced several times. We show a second method that utilizes MPI-derived types. This enables us to perform the send and receive for the edge updates in one call for the entire face of the cube. Lastly, an error norm that is some function of the data array is computed in a function call. An MPI global reduction routine is called to sum this value for each task and return the value to all tasks. This example could be extended for a 3D distribution, which would be more representative of real applications but would involve extra complexity. The essential steps and technique would remain the same.

3.1.3   SHMEM

The SHMEM parallel programming model originated with Cray T3D users who desired to have a group of closely related tasks operate separately with minimal synchronization while retaining the ability to access remote memory with the lowest latency possible. Although classified as a message-passing library, the model originated on machines with globally addressable memory, such as the Cray T3D. As is the case for MPI and PVM, SHMEM allows for each task to have its own instruction stream. All tasks start at the beginning of program execution and terminate at the end of program execution. The model allows for tasks to read and write directly to another task's memory.

The primary and overriding design goal of the SHMEM model is high performance. In contrast to the "two-sided" message-passing technique utilized by MPI and PVM, where one task issues a send request and another task issues a receive request, SHMEM performs "one-sided" messaging, sometimes referred to as "gets" and "puts" because a remote-memory load (get) or remote-memory store (put) accomplishes the messaging.

The SHMEM library supplies functions to perform basic communication-intensive operations such as global reductions, broadcasts, global gathers and scatters, and global collections or concatenated lists of data. Functions for global synchronization, subgroup synchronization, and point-to-point synchronization between tasks are also part of the library. SHMEM also provides the unique capability of giving the user access to a remote data object by supplying a pointer to the remote data. That pointer can be associated with an object name, which can then be used to transfer data with direct assignments instead of calling a library function. This is particularly useful when data access in irregular patterns is desired.

In Example 3.3, we revise the previous examples to illustrate what a SHMEM code looks like. All tasks will start at program initiation. In this example, the

```
program halo_update
implicit none
include "mpp/shmem.fh"
integer          :: shmem_my_pe, shmem_n_pes
integer          :: pSync(SHMEM_REDUCE_SYNC_SIZE)
real(kind=8)     :: pWrk(SHMEM_REDUCE_MIN_WRKDATA_SIZE)
save pSync, pWrk
real(kind=8)     :: result
integer,parameter :: nx=128
integer,parameter :: ny=128
integer,parameter :: nz=150
real(kind=8),dimension(1:nx,0:ny+1,1:nz) :: data
save data
real(kind=8)     :: result, global_result
save result, global_result
real(kind=8),dimension(1:nx,0:ny+1,1:*) :: data_left
real(kind=8),dimension(1:nx,0:ny+1,1:*) :: data_right
pointer (ptr_left, data_left)
pointer (ptr_right, data_right)
integer :: npes, mype, myleft, myright, iz, ipe , i, j
call start_pes(0)
npes = shmem_n_pes()  ! return total number of PEs
mype = shmem_my_pe()  ! return my PE number in range 0:npes-1
myleft = mod(mype+1,npes)        ! my left neighbor (periodic)
myright = mod(mype-1+npes,npes) ! my right neighbor (periodic)
pSync = SHMEM_SYNC_VALUE
! each domain will compute new values for data
call compute_data (data,nx,ny,nz)
! synchronize to make sure everyone is done
call shmem_barrier_all()
! update left-right (Y-direction) edges using gets
do iz = 1,nz
   call shmem_get8 (data(1,0,iz) ,data(1,ny,iz),nx,myleft)
   call shmem_get8 (data(1,ny+1,iz),data(1,1,iz) ,nx,myright)
enddo
! use the new data in computations
call use_data (data,nx,ny,nz)
! synchronize to make sure everyone is done
```

3.3   **Halo Cell Update in SHMEM.**

EXAMPLE

```
      call shmem_barrier_all()
      ! each domain will compute new values for data
      call compute_data (data,nx,ny,nz)
      ! second method of updating halo cells
      ! update left-right using pointer function
      ptr_left  = shmem_ptr(data, myleft)
      ptr_right = shmem_ptr(data, myright)
      data(1:nx,ny+1,1:nz) = data_right (1:nx,1,1:nz)
      data(1:nx,0 ,1:nz)   = data_left (1:nx,ny,1:nz)
      ! use the new data in computations
      call use_data (data,nx,ny,nz)
      ! compute an error norm that is some function of the data
      call compute_error_norm (data, nx, ny, nz, result)
      ! perform a global sum reduction on the result
      call shmem_real8_sum_to_all (global_result,result,1,0,0,npes,
     *                             pWrk, pSync)
      if(mype.eq.0) print*,' The Error Norm: ',global_result
      stop
      end
```

3.3   (continued)

EXAMPLE

number of tasks used is determined at runtime by an environment variable. The rank of the task is returned from the shmem_my_pe function. The total number of tasks is returned from the shmem_n_pes function. The data transfer will occur between the 'data' array. The model requires that this be in symmetric storage, meaning that it is at the same relative memory address in each task's memory image. Here we have accomplished that by declaring it in a 'save' statement. As an alternative, we could have used the 'shalloc' function if we did not know the size of the data until runtime.

Each task queries the library to find the number of tasks that exist and its rank within the group. As in the earlier examples, the data array is distributed along the y-axis, so the y face is where the halo cells are. The data array is initialized in the 'compute_data' function. Before updating the halo cells, we perform a barrier to make sure that all tasks have finished computing their data. The halo cells are then updated by the shmem_get calls. The program continues to work on the data. A typical application would reference the data, including the halo cells, several times before an update to the data array is necessary. The next update is performed differently to illustrate use of the shmem_ptr function. Here we have requested a pointer to the location of the 'data' array on the right and left neighbors. These pointers are associated with the arrays data_left and data_right. We can then reference them directly—that is, without library calls. Finally, we illustrate the use of a library routine for performing a global reduction, as is frequently done on an error norm. Here we only allow the master task to print out the result.

3.2   DATA-PARALLEL MODELS

Data-parallel describes models where the execution of instructions in parallel is implicitly driven by the layout of the data structures in memory. The data structures are generally large arrays, and the operations on the elements are performed on the processor that owns the memory where a particular element resides. There is one thread of control, and parallelism is achieved when parallel constructs, such as DO-loops with independent iterations, are encountered. The programmer specifies the storage layout of data objects with compiler directives. Data-parallel languages usually include several types of parallel constructs to allow the user mechanisms in addition to DO-loops for controlling parallelism. In addition, they typically supply intrinsic functions and library routines to perform common parallel operations.

The first data-parallel languages were extensions to compilers, but currently available products may be implemented either as compiler extensions or as source-to-source translators that analyze the code and substitute message-passing requests for the remote references. In the latter case, the resultant source is passed to the native compiler of the computer used.

Data-parallel models have their roots as far back as the early 1970s. The programming model used for the ILLIAC IV, a SIMD machine, was data parallel [3.14]. Thinking Machines, a computer manufacturer that used to produce SIMD machines, used the data-parallel approach for its C* and CM Fortran compilers. Other examples of data-parallel compilers are Vienna Fortran [3.4] and Fortran D [3.8].

3.2.1   High-Performance Fortran

High-Performance Fortran (HPF) has become the most prevalent tool for data-parallel programming today. HPF is the result of a consortium effort to create a standard for data parallelism in Fortran. A group composed of representatives from academia, industry, and government laboratories began this effort in 1992 [3.13]. The participants included some of those involved in the earlier data-parallel languages, and HPF can be viewed as the convergence of those efforts. HPF 1.0 standards were first published in 1992, and an update, HPF-2, became available in January 1997 [3.11].

HPF provides a rich set of directives for specifying the distribution of data across processors. These 'DISTRIBUTE' directives, as they are referred to, can be used for assigning blocks of data to processors or for assigning elements of an array one or more at a time in a round-robin, or cyclic, fashion. Arrays may be distributed along any or all of their dimensions. It is permissible to distribute automatic and allocatable arrays. An 'ALIGN' directive is supplied that allows an array to be aligned relative to another array whose distribution was already specified.

Other directives serve to indicate areas of parallelism. The INDEPENDENT directive specifies that the iterations of the following DO-loop may be executed independently and in any order. HPF also imported the FORALL construct from CM Fortran, which is similar to a parallel DO-loop but requires that the right-hand side of all the enclosing equations be evaluated before the assignments to the left-hand side variable are made. This construct is illustrated in the following example. The FORALL statement is now part of the F95 standard.

HPF provides a comprehensive set of library routines to perform functions necessary for high-performance programming. These include array prefix and suffix functions, sorting functions, and reduction routines. Functions are also supplied for basic inquiries, such as the number of processors and the shape of the processor grid.

Example 3.4 shows an excerpt from an HPF code. Here we show a stencil operation on the array U. Note that in this example, some operations will require values from remote memory locations. The compiler will automatically take care of accessing the remote data. We do not need to worry about overwriting the data because the language stipulates that the right-hand values will be evaluated using the values of U before any updates are affected by this construct. This will likely be accomplished by creating a temporary copy of the U array, which will then be used in the computation. Needless to say, creating this temporary array adds overhead. If we require a global reduction on the U data, this is easily accomplished with the F90 SUM function [3.16]. Again, any data movement required will be performed by the compiler.

Data-parallel modes are particularly useful when there is abundant parallelism appearing in a very regular fashion. Although this is often the case in scientific and some industrial applications, it is just as common to encounter

```
              ! distribute the data array in block along the Y and Z axes
      !$HPF DISTRIBUTE data (*, block, block)
              real(kind=8),dimension(1:nx,1:ny,1:nz) :: U
      !$HPF ALIGN Temp with U
              real(kind=8),dimension(1:nx,1:ny,1:nz) :: Temp
      !HPF$ FORALL (i=2:nx-1, j=2:ny-1, k=1:nz)
              u(i,j,k) = c0 * u(i,j,k) + c1*u(i+1,j,k) + c2*u(i+2,j,k) +
      *               c3 * u(i-1,j,k) + c4 * u(i-2,j,k) +
      *               c3 * u(i,j+1,k) + c4 * u(i,j+2,k) +
      *               c3 * u(i,j-1,k) + c4 * u(i,j-2,k)
       END FORALL
       Temp = some_function ( U )
       Result = SUM (Temp)
```

3.4   **Stencil Operation in HPF.**

EXAMPLE

problems with irregular data structures. Using this type of programming model can be awkward for the latter type of problems. HPF-2 attempts to address some of these problems with the introduction of new features. These new features include formats for irregular distributions of data that allow nonequal-sized blocks of data to be mapped and the ability to map elements of an array individually. Other new capabilities include support for dynamic remapping of data and the ability to map computation directly onto processors. A new directive, TASK_RE-GION, can be used to identify a set of blocks or regions of code that may be executed independently of each other.

To increase the flexibility of programming in HPF, routines written in other languages and styles may be used in an HPF program. These routines are specified with the EXTRINSICS label, and F90 interface blocks must be provided for them to enable the HPF compiler to pass the correct calling arguments. Extrinsic routines may be written in C or written to use a message-passing library. In the latter case, the extrinsic would be of type HPF_LOCAL, meaning that each node involved in the program would call the routine independently and messages could be sent between the tasks.

HPF provides a means to avoid the complexity of explicitly passing messages and takes the same form for the user whether the target parallel architecture is based on a distributed memory machine with pure message-passing communication or an SMP with thread-level parallelism. An explicit message-passing code can generally outperform an HPF implementation, as the programmer has complete control over the amount of communication generated. However, since the portable methods of message passing today involve the use of complicated libraries, HPF still provides a great advantage in terms of ease of use.

3.3 PARALLEL PROGRAMMING METHODS

Approaches to the problem of programming highly parallel machines continue to evolve. Work continues in developing and evaluating new models, while at the same time older models are reevaluated for today's machines. In this section, we provide an overview of some of the topics related to this research: nested- and mixed-model parallelism, POSIX Pthreads, compiler extensions for explicit styles of parallelism, and work sharing.

3.3.1 Nested- and Mixed-Model Methods

Once a group of tasks has been created, it may be desirable to have one or more of these tasks spawn subtasks. This occurs in situations where it is not known until sometime during the execution of an application that one task has more work than others do. Assigning more processors to assist that task could benefit the performance of the entire application. Almost any combination of models is possible, but the most natural approach uses a distributed-memory, coarse-grain model as the top layer and a shared-memory, finer-grain method for the lower layer. Examples of such pairings that have been used successfully include MPI with HPF for Fortran codes [3.7] and MPI with POSIX Pthreads for C codes.

3.3.2 POSIX Threads and Mixed Models

One approach to programming hybrid machines (i.e., MPP machines where each node is an SMP) is simply to view the processors within a node as being additional processors in the distributed-memory framework and program as though they did not share memory. This is a reasonable approach because it allows the use of message-passing code on such a machine without modification. It is also an efficient approach provided that the message-passing libraries are coded to take advantage of the shared memory on each node.

In some instances, however, there may be benefits to coding in a style that explicitly takes advantage of the shared memory on each node. The kind of parallelism employed within a node may be of a different kind from that used across nodes—this may allow finer-grained parallelism within a node than that used between nodes. An example is the use of self-scheduling within a node while using a static decomposition of the problem across nodes. An obvious way to implement such an approach is to use message passing across nodes and use threads within a single node. This only requires that the message-passing library be thread safe. Given such a library, it is possible to get optimal performance using programming models that are most natural to each portion of the machine. In the MPI-2 standard, there are requirements for thread-compliant MPI implementations, and corresponding functions for initializing the thread environment are defined; however, it is not required by the standard that all MPI implementations be thread compliant.

Since the interaction of threads and MPI is a relatively new area of parallel computing that is not yet documented extensively in the literature, we present in an appendix an indication of how this type of parallel programming is evolving. Although it was not necessary to implement this type of programming model in the applications described in this book, it is certainly becoming necessary to implement such concepts on the next generation of computers.

3.3.3   Compiler Extensions for Explicit Parallelism with Distributed Objects

Another approach to the problem of providing both ease of use and high performance to the parallel programmer is to build extensions for explicit parallelism into the compiler. These efforts seek to match the ease of use of parallel compilers such as HPF with the high performance of message-passing methods. Here we briefly describe several approaches for the C language and an approach for the F90 language.

David Culler and Katerine Yelick at the University of California, Berkeley, developed the Split-C language on Thinking Machines' CM5 in the early 1990s [3.6]. Split-C follows a single-program, multiple-data (SPMD) model with processors initiating execution together. Barriers are provided for controlling synchronization. Each task has a global view of the application's entire address space, while at the same time controlling a private region for stack and static storage. Global pointers can reference the entire address space, and standard pointers reference only the memory portion controlled by the local processor. The array syntax is extended to support spread arrays, which are arrays with additional notation to indicate that they are distributed or spread across all processors. For example, an array declared as 'array [len]::' results in the data being distributed in a cyclic fashion across processors. If the length value is larger than the number of processors, the mapping continues in a round-robin pattern. Blocks of data are distributed by adding an extra dimension after the spreader syntax, as in 'array [len] :: [block_size]'. Split-C provides constructs for control of parallel execution. These include a split-phase assignment operator ':=', which indicates that computation and communication may be overlapped. In the case of an operation such as ' a := b', where b may be a global reference, the data transfer and store occur asynchronously while program execution continues. A 'SYNC' function is provided to wait for completion of the operation.

The AC compiler was developed by Bill Carlson and Jesse Draper of the Supercomputing Research Center for the Cray T3D [3.3]. An AC program generates a process for each processor in a system. The processes all execute for the duration of the program. Synchronization is provided by barriers and by sequence points. While barriers operate over groups of processors, sequence points ensure that all operations for a single processor have completed before execution continues past the sequence point. Each processor owns its local data and contains a portion of global data. Data is local and private by default, and global shared arrays and pointers are explicitly declared with the 'dist' qualifier. For example:

```
dist int *pd;          /* pd is a pointer; it points to an int
                          in distributed space */
int *dist dp;          /* dp is a pointer that is distributed; it
                          points at an int that is local */
dist int *dist dpd;    /* dpd is a pointer that is distributed; it
                          points at an int that is in dist space */
```

These same constructs may be applied to arrays as well:

```
int *ap[10];           /* an array of 10 pointers to int */
dist int *apd[10];     /* an array of 10 pointers, each pointing
                          at an int that is in dist space */
int *dist apd[10];     /* a distributed array of 10 pointers,
                          each pointing at a local int */
dist int *dist adpd[10];/* a distributed array of 10 pointers,
                          each pointing at an int in dist space */
```

Pointer arithmetic is defined modulo the number of processors; that is, successive increments of a distributed pointer increment the processor number until the number of processors is reached and then wraps to the starting processor with an additional local offset. A shortcoming of most distribution methods is that the shared object must be the same size on all processors. The use of distributed pointers to local objects allows the creation of remotely accessible objects that may be of different sizes among tasks. Using these declarations provides an extreme level of flexibility of data distribution and the ability to reference these in a manner consistent with the spirit of the C language. AC has been demonstrated to have performance comparable to the SHMEM library on the Cray T3D.

A third effort at Lawrence Livermore National Laboratory by Eugene Brooks and Karen Warren extends earlier work on the PCP language, which is in itself an extension to the C language [3.2]. A specific goal of this work is to provide a single method of programming that provides performance comparable to the best methods on both shared- and distributed-memory architectures. PCP uses distributed pointers and arrays in a manner similar to the AC compiler but uses the keyword 'shared' to designate global pointers and data. PCP provides many of the same parallel constructs that shared-memory programming styles do. Regions designated by 'master' are only executed by the master task. 'FORALL' is used to create loops that will execute concurrently. Unlike shared-memory models, these constructs do not have implicit barriers associated with them in order not to hinder parallel performance. Lock functions are provided to limit access to critical regions of code. The execution model is that all tasks begin execution at the start of the program and continue until the end. In order to address the desire for dynamic distribution of workload, PCP introduces the notion of team splitting. Team splitting allows the group of tasks to be subdivided into subteams and used to execute different portions of a FORALL construct or a structure of blocks of code, similar to task regions or sections in some shared-memory models. Promising initial results with this model on a variety of platforms have been reported [3.2]. The authors of these three efforts are currently engaged in merging the approaches into a single model for parallel C, currently named UPC.

The Co-Array Fortran (also known as F−−) effort within Silicon Graphics/ Cray Research extends the F90 compiler to allow programming in a distributed-memory style. As in the other models just described, the execution model is that all tasks begin execution at the start of the program and finish together at the end [3.17, 3.18]. This model distinguishes between memory images and processes or threads of execution. A memory image is a unit of replication that maps to the number of physically distributed memories of the system used. The number of memory images may or may not be the same as the number of execution threads. The basic language extension is the addition of bracket notation to indicate the replication of a data object on all memory images. Replicated data objects may be referenced remotely by supplying the target memory image within the brackets. For example, if the array A has been declared with the bracket notation, the following statement takes the value of array A from processor P and copies it to the local array B:

```
real, dimension (0:length-1) :: A [n_images]  ! A is replicated on
                                               ! all memory images
real, dimension (0:length-1) :: B, C
B(:) = A(:) [p]            ! the array A is copied from processor P
C(:) = A(:)               ! the local A array is copied to C
```

This model minimizes the number of changes required for an existing code by making optional the inclusion of the bracket notation for local memory references of replicated data. The number of local references should far outweigh the number of remote references for distributed objects in a program that scales well to large numbers of processors. Scalars, F90 pointers, arrays, and F90 derived types may all be replicated with the bracket notation. As in the methods discussed earlier that allow shared pointers to local data, this enables the programmer to create objects of varying sizes on different memory images that are remotely accessible. Dynamic memory management is enabled by use of pointers as well as allocatable arrays.

This approach has advantages for the implementors and for the application programmer. The simple syntax extension makes it easy to implement. The bracket notation makes it possible for the compiler to distinguish between local and remote memory accesses and schedule them accordingly. Remotely accessible storage objects may be created dynamically and be of varying size (including zero length) for different memory images. Additionally, a synchronization function that works over all images or an arbitrary subset is provided. These last two items make the task of creating multidisciplinary applications feasible. Separating the notion of memory image from a process enables this model to function as a top layer for parallelism with a shared-memory model, with dynamic work distribution as the lower layer. This model has been implemented on the Cray T3E, and it should be straightforward to implement it on almost any architecture.

Although each of the approaches described is unique, they have a number of elements in common. The most important common element is how they address data layout. Data is considered to be private to a task unless it is specified to be shared. This is more convenient for highly scalable applications because performance considerations dictate that the majority of data objects should be private. Observations from working with models such as CRAFT and HPF have shown that the arbitrary distribution patterns allowed by these models break the canonical layout of arrays and make the compiler's job difficult. They add complexity in the compiler for handling the many arbitrary patterns of distribution and add overhead during execution because the compiler must perform extra indexing computations or use look-up tables for determining the location of data objects that have been distributed in this way. Some implementations attempt to minimize this effect by putting restrictions on the blocking factors of distributed objects to make the address computations easier. Experience with early MPPs has shown that these restrictions are very unpopular with users. By separating the node location from the array dimensions, it is possible to retain flexibility in sizing and distributing arrays while also making it easy for the compiler to compute the memory address of the data.

The second common aspect of these approaches is that the parallelism and data communication are explicit; that is, the programmer controls the flow of tasks and synchronization and knows when remote data is being accessed. Implicit methods that hide data communication and synchronization from the programmer tend to make it difficult for users to control performance because they may not be conscious of the remote-data communication and synchronization that is being generated by the compiler. On shared-memory machines, issues of false sharing may need to be dealt with. Explicit methods also have the advantage of allowing the programmer to separate single-processor performance from multiprocessor performance because the communication overhead is decoupled from issues of single-processor performance.

The combination of explicit communication and a simpler data layout makes it easier for implementers to use source-to-source translators to substitute remote references with message-passing constructs if desired. This makes these methods promising for use across clusters as well as within a shared-memory node.

3.3.4   Work-Sharing Models

Work-sharing models are characterized by the fact that they divide up the work of an application according to specifications supplied by the user. This is accomplished through compiler directives or through library calls. A class of model originally developed for hardware architectures with uniform shared memory, one of the earliest implementations was the macrotasking model developed for the Cray XMP in 1984 [3.5]. This was designed for coarse-grained parallelism and provided users with functions for starting and stopping tasks, for synchronization, and for locking. The memory model provides for both private and shared portions. The tasks can read and write into the shared memory areas but not into the private areas. The interface and design are similar to Pthreads. Although macrotasking enjoyed some success, particularly in weather-modeling codes, it required users to restructure codes, which was difficult to justify as access to parallel systems was not generally available at the time.

This limitation led to observations that the extra cycles available on the parallel systems at the time could be put to good use if the tasks were lightweight and if users had an easier way to introduce parallelism into existing codes. This led to the development of loop-level parallelism, which allowed users to designate loops to run separate iterations in parallel. By 1987, Cray Research introduced an implementation known as auto-tasking, which allowed the compiler to detect loops where parallelism could be. About this same time, other vendors, such as Convex and Alliant, were also producing shared-memory parallel machines. A standardization effort, ANSI X3H5, otherwise known as PCF, was started. Although ultimately unsuccessful, the proposal did heavily influence the design of vendors' parallel models. The models available today—such as those from Sun, Convex, and SGI/Cray—share much similarity, and indeed, applications exist that can run on all these machines by passing the source code through a preprocessor. All these implementations are based on compiler directives, which are statements inserted into the source code to indicate areas of the code to be executed in parallel. Most also provide a construct for defining segments of code that may execute in parallel, for sections where only one processor may execute at a time, and features for controlling locks.

The Cray T3D and T3E MPP machines support a work-sharing model called CRAFT. This model is similar to the other work-sharing models but also provides directives for explicit data distribution, which are similar to the data distribution directives defined by HPF. In the CRAFT model, all tasks start up at program initiation. CRAFT includes query functions and environment variables to aid the user in controlling parallel execution.

Although the work-sharing models available on shared-memory parallel machines are very similar, application programmers had to use until recently a different set of directives for each computer vendor's machine. A new standardization effort led by a group of computer manufacturers has produced a specification for a set of compiler directives called OpenMP that eliminates that requirement. To date, a specification for Fortran has been done, and work is proceeding on a specification for the C language.

In OpenMP, the user identifies a portion or portions of an application to run in parallel, referred to as a *parallel region,* by the insertion of compiler directives at the beginning and end of the desired region. A team of threads is initiated when a parallel region is encountered, and this team of threads executes all the statements within the region concurrently. Several constructs are provided to break up the work among the tasks. The parallel DO-loop construct directs the compiler to divide up the iterations of a DO-loop among the threads. A section construct allows the user to designate sections of code that are executed concurrently by different threads. The single contruct causes a particular section of code to be executed by only one thread. The directives include options to enable the user to specify whether data should be private or shared among threads. The OpenMP specification also includes a set of inquiry functions and companion environment variables that allow the user to set and query the parallel environment. Open MP does not provide a mechanism for explicit data distribution, but it is expected that implementations for distributed-memory machines will supply extensions for distribution. OpenMP does include a specification for nested parallelism but does not make it a requirement for compliant implementations.

References

[3.1] Agerwala, T., J. L. Martin, J. H. Mirza, D. C. Sadler, D. M. Dias, and M. Snir. 1995. SP2 System Architecture. *IBM Systems Journal,* Reprint Order No. G321–5563.

[3.2] Brooks III, Eugene D., and Karen Warren. 1997. A Study of Performance on SMP and Distributed Memory Architectures Using a Shared Memory Programming Model. In *Proceedings of the SC97.* Nov. 15–21.

[3.3] Carson, William, and Jess Draper. 1995. AC for the T3D. Technical Report SRC-TR-95–141, Feb. Supercomputing Research Center Institute for Defense Analyses.

[3.4] Chapman, B., P. Mehrotra, and H. Zima. 1992. Vienna Fortran—A Fortran Language Extension for Distributed Memory Multiprocessors. *Languages, Compilers, and Run-Time Environments for Distributed Memory Machines.* J. Schultz and P. Mehrutra (eds.), 39–62. Elsevier, Amsterdam.

[3.5] Cray Research, Inc. 1989. *Cray Y-MP, Cray X-MP EA, and Cray X-MP Multitasking Programmer's Manual.* Cray Research Publication SR-0222F.

[3.6] Culler, David C., Andrea Dusseau, Seth Copen Goldstein, Arvind Krishnamurthy, Steven Lumetta, Thorsten von Eicken, and Katherine Yelick. 1993. Parallel Programming in Split-C. In *Proceedings of the Supercomputing '93.* Portland. Nov. 15–19.

[3.7] Foster, Ian, David R. Kohr, Jr., Rakesh Krishnaiyer, and Alok Choudhary. 1996. Double Standards: Bringing Task Parallelism to HPF Via the Message Passing Interface. In *Proceedings of the Supercomputing '96.* Pittsburgh, PA. Nov. 17–22.

[3.8] Fox, G., S. Hiranandani, K. Kennedy, C. Keolbel, U. Kremer, C. Tseng, and M. Wu. 1991. *Fortran D Language Specification.* COMPTR90079, March. Department of Computer Science, Rice University.

[3.9] Gropp, William, Steven Huss-Lederman, Andrew Lumsdaine, Ewing Lusk, Bill Nitzberg, William Saphir, and Marc Snir. 1998. *MPI—The Complete Reference Volume 2, The MPI Extensions.* Cambridge MA: MIT Press.

[3.10]   Gropp, William, Ewing Lusk, and Anthony Skjellum. 1996. *Using MPI, Portable Parallel Programming with the Message-Passing Interface.* Cambridge, MA: MIT Press.

[3.11]   High-Performance Fortran Forum. 1997. *High Performance Fortran Language Specification, Version 2.0.* Jan.

[3.12]   Hill, Jonathan M. D., Bill McColl, Dan C. Stefanescu, Mark W. Goudreau, Kevin Lang, Satish B. Rao, Torsten Suel, Thanasis Tsantilas, and Rob Bisseling. 1997. *BSPlib: The BSP Programming Library.* Technical Report PRG-TR-29–9. Oxford University Computing Laboratory, May.

[3.13]   Koelbel, C., D. Loveman, R. Schreiber, G. Steele, and M. Zosel. 1993. *The High Performance Fortran Handbook.* Cambridge, MA: MIT Press

[3.14]   Mehrotra, P., J. Van Rosendal, and H. Zima. 1997. *High Performance Fortran: History, Status and Future,* TR 97–8 Sept. 1997, University of Vienna, Institute for Software Technology and Parallel Systems.

[3.15]   Message-Passing Interface Forum. 1994. *A Message-Passing Interface Standard,* May. University of Tennessee, Knoxville, Tennessee.

[3.16]   Metcalf, Michael, and John Reid. 1996. *Fortran 90/95 Explained.* Oxford, England: Oxford University Press.

[3.17]   Numrich, R., and J. Steidel. 1997. Simple Parallel Extensions to Fortran 90. *Proceedings of the Eighth SIAM Conference on Parallel Processing for Scientific Computing, 1997.* SIAM Activity Group on Supercomputing.

[3.18]   Reid, J., and R. Numrich. 1998. Formal and Informal Definitions of fmm. Rutherford Appleton Laboratory. In preparation.

[3.19]   *SHMEM, Application Programmer's Library Reference Manual.* Cray Research Inc. Publication SR-2165.

[3.20]   Snir, Marc, Steve W. Otto, Steven Huss-Lederman, David W. Walker, and Jack Dongarra. 1996. *MPI, The Complete Reference.* Cambridge, MA: MIT Press.

4 Parallel Programming Tools

Margaret Cahir
Robert Moench   SGI/Cray Research

Alice E. Koniges   Lawrence Livermore National Laboratory

Designing and writing a parallel program is only part of the effort in developing a parallel application. Typically, a program would not be on a high-level parallel computer if it were not intended to address large problems or if performance were not an issue. Thus, the assessment of performance and the ability to debug large data sets are basic requirements in highly parallel environments.

Unfortunately for the analyst, it is at this stage of the development process that standards fade away and the dependencies on the system hardware and software assert themselves. The underlying issues here are much more complex than merely gaining agreement from different parties on a standard. A good performance tool for a high-end system must have intimate knowledge of the hardware. To be truly useful, it must also have intimate knowledge of the programming environment to be able to interpret the performance analysis data in such a way as to direct the programmer in how to improve the code. Likewise, debuggers benefit from integration with the parallel environment. A particular requirement for debugging parallel codes is to provide the user with some method of controlling the running and synchronization of different tasks, as bugs in parallel code may be due to race conditions. With that in mind, we describe here the performance analysis tools and debugger used on the Cray T3D and T3E to illustrate general issues.

4.1   THE APPRENTICE PERFORMANCE ANALYSIS TOOL

Parallel programmers face all the same issues in assessing program performance that programmers of serial codes face but have the additional problems of assessing the overhead and performance of the communication between tasks, of determining the cost and location of load imbalance, and of quantifying locality of reference. For MPP systems, this information must be assembled and presented for a large number of long-running tasks.

The Apprentice performance analysis tool was designed specifically to address these issues for the Cray T3D and T3E. Apprentice works on two levels: It provides a method of instrumenting the code, which causes data to be collected during the execution run, and it provides a visual interface for the programmer to analyze the data. Apprentice has the capability of recognizing certain libraries as part of the parallel programming support. It provides the user information on the usage of routines from SHMEM, MPI, PVM, HPF, and CRAFT.

The authors of the application chapters made extensive use of a performance analysis tool such as Apprentice. In Chapter 7, the authors used Apprentice to first identify two types of routines to optimize (ones using a large percentage of time and ones running at a slow flops rate) and then to verify improvements. Another good example of using Apprentice is found in Chapter 18. Here, bottlenecks such as poor functional unit pipelining, divides within loops, and cache conflicts giving cache thrashing were identified. Solutions were found for all these problems, yielding dramatic code improvement.

Performance analysis tools tend to fall into one of two categories: those that instrument codes and those that generate traces. The decision to use an instrumented approach for Apprentice was made because instrumented codes generate an amount of data that is proportional to the size of the code, whereas trace-based tools generate data proportional to the number of tasks running and the length of the runtime. Apprentice allows the user to choose to accumulate counters for each processor or on an aggregate basis. This avoids the potential problem of trace-based methods of generating such large amounts of data that disk space becomes an issue or that the I/O demands impact the execution of the job.

Codes are instrumented by compiling them with a special option that causes the compiler to insert the instrumentation at appropriate places in the code. This has the disadvantage of requiring the user to recompile the code but provides two strong advantages. First, the instrumentation is inserted with the knowledge of the compiler to avoid perturbing the performance of the code. Second, this allows Apprentice to correlate the performance information with the source code even when high levels of compiler optimization are used. In addition, it allows information to be gathered over a finer granularity and allows the user to control which routines are to be instrumented.

Apprentice provides an X-window-based interface for the programmer to view the data. Apprentice can also be used on a command line basis to generate reports. This capability is useful for users who may be working over remote

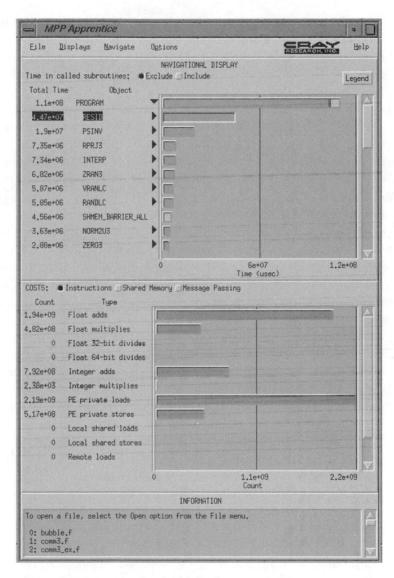

4.1

FIGURE

Apprentice startup navigational display.

network connections or who wish to keep a record of the history of their optimization efforts. An example of the window that Apprentice initially displays to the user is shown in Figure 4.1. Apprentice initially displays the time spent in each routine. This time is broken down into time spent in parallel work, I/O time, overhead time, and called-routine time. It also indicates time spent in uninstrumented sections for routine calls and I/O. Overhead time includes operations such as waiting on barriers. Apprentice also provides a breakdown of the costs for the routines. There are displays for three types of costs: basic instructions, shared-memory constructs, and message passing. The basic instructions include floating-point and integer-arithmetic operations as well as local and remote memory accesses. For the CRAFT/HPF programming model, Apprentice has the capability of reporting whether the memory accesses were to private or shared memory locations. The shared-memory construct costs show where time is spent in barriers and indicate the presence of critical regions. The message-passing costs indicate the time spent in calls to message-passing libraries. The libraries that Apprentice recognizes include SHMEM, PVM, and MPI. Additionally, the Apprentice window provides a spot where messages from the tool to the user are displayed, which include items like explanations of errors. Apprentice is integrated with a language-sensitive source code browser that allows the user to easily find data structures and language constructs in the source to assist in analyzing the Apprentice information. The user can drill down on any routine to see the same times and costs reported for sections of the routine. Because Apprentice inserts the instrumentation with some intelligence, the sections are tied to constructs such as DO-loops or statements with line numbers corresponding to the source code. These statements and numbers are accurate even when high levels of compiler optimization are used (see Figure 4.2).

The interface allows the user to customize the displays from the Preferences menu. Examples of the items the user can control are the units used to display the various quantities reported, the method by which the routines are sorted, and whether context-sensitive help is used. These preferences may be captured for reuse when Apprentice is used the next time. The user has a great deal of control over the displays and can utilize peel-off windows to save various items of interest while continuing to pursue other options with the tool (see Figure 4.3).

The Observations display of Apprentice provides a report for the whole program or for an individual routine that indicates the rates at which various instructions, such as floating-point operations, are executing. The observations also include a detailed description as to where problem spots may be in the code. Examples of this include how much time is lost due to single-instruction issue and instruction and data cache misses. It can also indicate if significant amounts of time are spent in critical regions, which can result in excessive serialization.

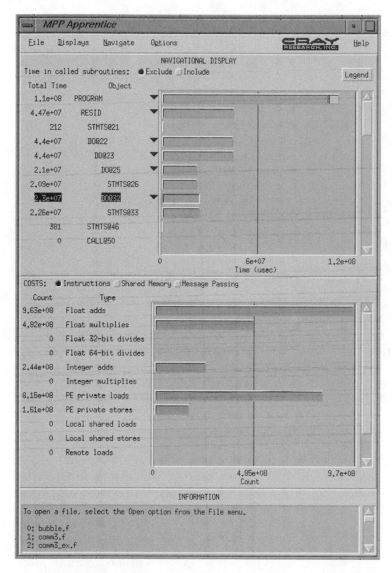

Apprentice display showing performance breakdown within a routine.

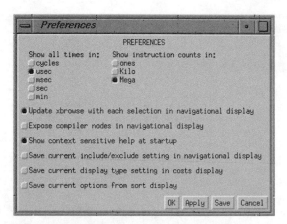

PREFERENCES

4.3   Apprentice Preferences window.

FIGURE

Additionally, it indicates the statements in a given routine where most time is spent and can do this even at high levels of compiler optimization (see Figure 4.4).

4.2   DEBUGGERS

Users of debuggers on single-processor machines and on highly parallel machines want debuggers that are reliable and that do not introduce any changes to the behavior of the code. In addition, they must be easy to use. Ease of use becomes more difficult to provide as the number of processes involved increases. The information for a large number of processes must be presented in a way that can be displayed on a typical workstation screen. Users need an easy way to direct the debugger to insert breakpoints at subgroups of processes and to specify whether all processors should stop whenever one meets a breakpoint. The debugger needs to present the current status of the entire program in a concise manner so that the user can easily determine what the program is doing. From this summary, the user can navigate to a specific processor or set of processors to obtain more detailed information.

The most popular parallel debugger used in the applications chapters is called TotalView. TotalView is a source-level, multiprocess debugger, capable of debugging running programs or performing a post-mortem debug from a core

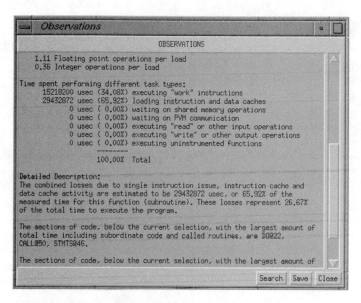

Apprentice Observations window.

file. It has both an X-windows and a line-mode user interface. It supports symbolic debugging of the Fortran 90, High-Performance Fortran (HPF), C++, and C languages. As with most debuggers, TotalView has control functions to run, attach to, step, breakpoint, interrupt, and restart a process. It facilitates the examination and modification of variables, registers, areas of memory, and machine-level instructions. Rather then dwelling on these standard debugger capabilities, however, the focus of the following discussion will address the TotalView features that are beneficial to the specific needs of MPP machines.

4.2.1   Process Control

Perhaps the most crucial MPP capability that TotalView has is its ability to control thousands of processes coherently. The first place this is seen is in the TotalView main window (Figure 4.5). This window displays a summary of the processes being controlled by TotalView. It organizes the processes into process sets, where all processes that are in the same state (breakpointed, stopped, running, etc.) and on the same instruction are grouped and described with a single entry. This technique greatly reduces the amount of data that needs to be displayed to, and ab-

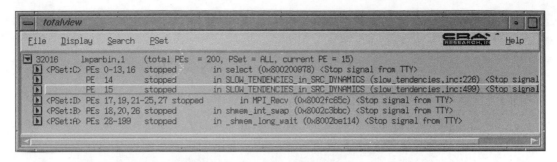

TotalView main window.

sorbed by, the user. The user can "dive" (right mouse-button click) on an entry to bring up a process set window detailing the contents of the set. A process set entry can also be expanded (or collapsed) to view the top of its call sequence.

While the TotalView main window provides a high-level view of the processes being debugged, the TotalView Process window (Figure 4.6) provides details specific to an individual process. There is initially a single process window with sliders that can scroll through each of the processes or jump directly to a desired process. Separate process windows can be created as desired. Near the top of the Process window is a status bar, which displays the current process identifier (PID) and processor element (PE) as well as the PE's state. There is also a process set mode of either ALL or SINGLE. Whenever control commands are given to TotalView (for instance, Continue, Step) the command applies either to all of the processes in the set (ALL) or only to the specific process that the Process window is displaying (SINGLE).

TotalView's breakpoints are configurable with respect to MPP processes. When setting a breakpoint in a Process window, diving on the breakpoint (Figure 4.7) provides an opportunity to define the breakpoint to apply to a single process or to all processes. Additionally, once the breakpoint is hit, all processes can be stopped or only the breakpointed process.

4.2.2   Data Viewing

TotalView has a number of features related to viewing data in an MPP environment. Both the Cray T3D and T3E are distributed-memory machines. As such, each process has its own memory space that is not directly available to the others. To even display the value of any variables, TotalView must access the memory

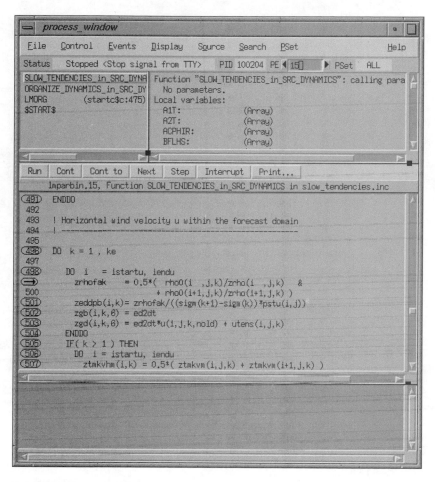

4.6   TotalView Process window.

FIGURE

specific to the process currently being displayed in the Process window. When the window is scrolled to a different process, new values must be fetched from the new memory space.

A common technique when programming MPP applications is to divvy up the processing of a large array among several processes. By default, an array is private; that is, each process will have a separate copy of the array that the other processes cannot access directly. When TotalView displays a private array, the Data Object window (Figure 4.8) used to display the array has a slider to select the process from which the array is coming. Of course, many of the array ele-

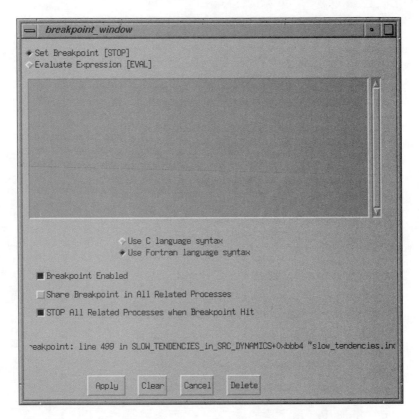

4.7   TotalView Breakpoint window.

FIGURE

ments may be invalid since the selected process is not maintaining them. The elements that the selected process is responsible for are dependent on the design of the application. With the aid of programming models such as CRAFT F77 and HPF, it is possible to use shared arrays instead of private arrays. These models provide TotalView with more complete information regarding which processes are using which array elements. When TotalView displays a shared array, the data object window will not have a slider to select the process. Instead, the array elements are labeled with the process that they are local to, and all of the elements will be valid.

One of the difficulties in developing applications dealing with large amounts of data is being able to "look" at and make sense of so much information. With MPP machines, this is all the more true. Although using TotalView to look at individual array elements is useful and essential, it may be too close a view of the

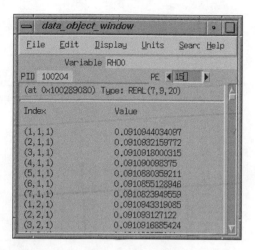

4.8   TotalView Data Object window.

FIGURE

data. TotalView can instead present a two-dimensional slice of the data as a color "picture." The user supplies a minimum and maximum value and a number of colors and TotalView divides that range by the number of colors. In this way, each value falls into a range and is mapped to the range's color. Each element of the array is then "painted" in its color to the rectangular picture. Values outside of the range are given a special color, as are floating-point NAN values on IEEE units. This provides a coarse, high-level picture of the data that can visually highlight data anomalies. TotalView can also provide statistical summaries of the data. It will display the minimum, maximum, and sum of an array. Once again, this can be useful in locating data anomalies.

5

CHAPTER

Optimizing for Single-Processor Performance

Jeff Brooks
Sara Graffunder   SGI/Cray Research

Alice E. Koniges   Lawrence Livermore National Laboratory

Achieving peak performance on MPP systems depends on both how well an application scales across processors and how close the performance of a portion executed on a single processor can come to the peak performance of that processor. Previous chapters in Part I addressed scaling; in addition, the application chapters discuss how different applications are written to take advantage of many processors. The majority (10 of 17) of the applications discussed in this book were concerned with single-processor optimization. (See Table P.1 in the Preface.) In this chapter, common techniques for getting the best performance for one processor are discussed. Single-processor optimization will vary depending on the exact characteristics of the processor, but the principles in this chapter, which apply explicitly to the Cray T3E system, will provide a good background. This chapter is purely introductory; for detailed assistance, the programmer should find the appropriate benchmarker's or programmer's guide to optimizing for a particular MPP computer system.

On the Cray T3E computer system, with its very strong network for interprocessor communication, the key to performance of a whole, well-parallelized application is typically optimizing for good performance on a single node. Substantial single-processor speedup is available from within high-level programming languages and from libraries. Additional performance can be obtained by hand optimization and assembly programming. In all cases, the goals of optimization are to use the processor's functional units at maximum capacity, to align data to take best advantage of the on-chip cache, and to understand and use any techniques available to mask the effects of having to load and store needed data that is not in cache. The goal, overall, is to hide the real time it takes to get data from memory to the processor's functional units and back again—the memory latency. Without attention to single-processor optimization, a programmer may obtain less than a tenth of the theoretical peak speed of the microprocessor. With considerable care, some optimized kernels can obtain up to two-thirds of peak.

5.1 USING THE FUNCTIONAL UNITS EFFECTIVELY

Modern Fortran and, to a degree, C language compilers do quite a good job of keeping any processor's functional units as busy as possible, assuming the programmer exposes sufficient parallelism to the compiler. How to write good code for the compilers and how to take advantage of their capabilities is the subject of other texts and of compiler documentation. In short, a programmer must explicitly place sufficient work inside of loops to allow the functional units to amortize their startup time for an operation, must explicitly "unroll" inner loops with too little work or allow the compiler or libraries to do so, and must understand what operations and library calls inside loops prevent effective pipelining into the functional units and avoid, reposition, or modify them.

Using the Fortran 90 compiler on the Cray T3E system, a programmer can obtain considerable functional unit optimization by selecting the compiler options for general optimization (-O3 will do general optimization and allow calling vectorized versions of intrinsic functions like SIN and COS), for unrolling loops (-Ounroll2 causes the compiler to unroll loops, and -Ounroll1 directs the compiler to unroll loops if indicated via a compiler directive in the program), and for software pipelining (-Opipeline1 or -Opipeline2 will safely expose some additional independent operations to the functional units). In addition, the programmer may use compiler directives inside the program to indicate loop unrolling (!dir$ unroll n) or to tell the compiler that a loop is vectorizable (!dir$ ivdep). On many processors, including the Cray T3E processor, the floating-point divide is so very slow in loops that it is best replaced with multiplication by the reciprocal. Finally, highly optimized, but not always completely standards-compliant, library routines may be available to improve performance. On the Cray T3E system, for example, libmfastv and the unsupported benchlib may both be used, but programmers should take care to understand any possible side effects. The effects on performance of using the functional units effectively can be considerable, as stated above. Factors of three to eight speedup for certain loops can easily be obtained.

Compiler documentation and programmer's guides for particular systems will give the best detail on functional unit optimization for both the novice and experienced parallel programmers. The following example from the Cray T3E system shows how unrolling is done by hand, not unlike what a compiler would do. In addition, it demonstrates clearly that a compiler, with some minimal guidance, can attain better results than a programmer can with substantial effort.

Arrays A, B, and C are each of size 256 and are stored consecutively so that all three arrays can reside in the Dcache at the same time. The loop is repeated many times to get a cache-resident performance figure:

```
DO I = 1, 256
        A(I) = B(I) + 2.5 * C(I)
ENDDO
```

When compiled with f90 -O3, without any unrolling, the loop's performance rate is about 53 Mflops. When compiled with f90 -O3,unroll2, which unrolls by 4, the performance improves to 155 Mflops. Manually unrolling the loop to help the compiler manage the functional unit dependencies, as follows, attains 177 Mflops:

```
TEMP1 = 2.5*C(1)
TEMP2 = 2.5*C(2)
TEMP3 = 2.5*C(3)
TEMP4 = 2.5*C(4)
DO I = 1, 252, 4
        A(I) = B(I) + TEMP1
        TEMP1 = 2.5*C(I+4)
        A(I+1) = B(I+1) + TEMP2
        TEMP2 = 2.5*C(I+5)
        A(I+2) = B(I+2) + TEMP3
        TEMP3 = 2.5*C(I+6)
        A(I+3) = B(I+3) + TEMP4
        TEMP4 = 2.5*C(I+7)
END DO
A(I) = B(I) + TEMP1
A(I+1) = B(I+1) + TEMP2
A(I+2) = B(I+2) + TEMP3
A(I+3) = B(I+3) + TEMP4
```

However, the easiest way to increase the functional unit parallelism is simply to unroll more deeply and let the compiler do the work. Adding the following directive before the original loop:

```
!DIR$ UNROLL 8
```

and recompiling with f90 -O3,unroll1, obtains the best performance of 181 Mflops.

The benefits of using optimization such as loop unrolling are discussed by a number of authors in the applications. In Chapter 7 (Table 7.1), the speedup obtained using different optimization procedures is shown. In Chapter 18, a dramatic speedup is cited for unrolling inner loops.

5.2 HIDING LATENCY WITH THE CACHE

Data caches on the processor provide a first level to hide latency. Data in the caches can be moved to and from the processor in a few clock periods, whereas data in memory may take one or two orders of magnitude longer. On the Cray T3E processor, there is an 8-KB primary data cache (Dcache), an 8-KB instruction cache, and a 96-KB secondary cache (Scache) for both instructions and data. Within the cache, data is loaded and stored in "lines," of 32 bytes for Dcache and 64 bytes for Scache. Characteristics of the Scache help prevent cache thrashing, but the small sizes of the caches may require special attention from the Cray T3E programmer. On the Cray T3E-900 system, the Dcache latency is 2 clock periods, the Scache latency is 8–10 clock periods, and the memory latency is approximately 125 clock periods. Thus, processing data not in the caches takes a great toll because the processors are capable of performing two floating-point operations per clock period.

As with functional unit optimization, compiler directives provide some cache optimization with little reprogramming. For example, both Fortran and C directives force data structures to be aligned on cache-line boundaries for the Cray T3E system and permit padding within common blocks to avoid some conflicts. Cache alignment ensures that successive loads and stores from a data structure will not cause the cache to be flushed unnecessarily. From Fortran, the CACHE_ALIGN directive may be used as follows:

```
      REAL A(M,K), B(K,N), C(M,N)
      COMMON /ACOM/ C
CDIR$ CACHE_ALIGN A,B
CDIR$ CACHE_ALIGN /ACOM/
```

Similarly, in C, alignment is specified with a #Parma:

```
#Parma _CRI cache_align flags
int flags[4096];
```

Even with directives, the programmer may need to exercise some care in programming. In particular, it is important to understand what portions of arrays are used together in program sequences and then to ensure that the array segments and any other data used simultaneously resides in the cache to be accessed without flushing the cache. Finally, when the leading dimension of a cache-aligned array is a multiple of the cache-line size, columns are pulled into the cache on line boundaries. To ensure such alignment, it may be necessary to increase the leading dimensions of the arrays to a multiple of the cache-line size. However, the interplay of cache and buffering schemes in a particular MPP system may mean that choosing a good leading dimension depends on how the data is used.

The following example is adapted from a benchmarker's optimization [5.1] of a finite difference kernel that has a small enough working data set (513) to benefit from optimization for the cache:

```
REAL, DIMENSION(513,513) :: AA, DD, X, Y, RX, RY
DO J = 2,N-1
        DO I = 2,N-1
                XX = X(I+1,J)-X(I-1,J)
                YX = Y(I+1,J)-Y(I-1,J)
                XY = X(I,J+1)-X(I,J-1)
                YY = Y(I,J+1)-Y(I,J-1)
                A = 0.25 * (XY*XY+YY*YY)
                B = 0.25* (XX*XX+YX*YX)
                C = 0.125 * (XX*XY+YX*YY)
                AA(I,J) = -B
                DD(I,J) = B+B+A*REL
                PXX = X(I+1,J)-2.*X(I,J)+X(I-1,J)
                QXX = Y(I+1,J)-2.*Y(I,J)+Y(I-1,J)
                PYY = X(I,J+1)-2.*X(I,J)+X(I,J-1)
                QYY = Y(I,J+1)-2.*Y(I,J)+Y(I,J-1)
                PXY = X(I+1,J+1)-X(I+1,J-1)-X(I-1,J+1)+X(I-1,J-1)
                QXY = Y(I+1,J+1)-Y(I+1,J-1)-Y(I-1,J+1)+Y(I-1,J-1)
                RX(I,J) = A*PXX+B*PYY-C*PXY
                RY(I,J) = A*QXX+B*QYY-C*QXY
        END DO
    END DO
```

The inner loop of this kernel has 47 floating-point operations, 18 array reads, and 4 array writes. The reads are of two 9-point stencils centered at X(I,J) and

Y(I,J), and the writes consist of unit-stride stores to the independent arrays AA, DD, RX, and RY. The two 9-point stencil array references should exhibit good temporal locality provided the three contiguous columns of X and Y fit simultaneously in the Scache. In addition, the writes to AA, DD, RX, and RY may not interfere with X and Y in the Scache. Since all six arrays are the same size and are accessed at the same rate, they will not interfere with each other if they do not conflict initially.

In the benchmarking example [5.1], to prevent a conflict, the arrays are placed in a cache-line aligned common block and padding arrays inserted between them to achieve the desired offsets modulo 4096. The leading dimension of the arrays is changed from 513 to 520 in order to make it a multiple of eight words, the Scache line size. The modified Fortran is as follows:

```
      REAL, DIMENSION(520,513) :: AA, DD, X, Y, RX, RY
      PARAMETER (IPAD=3576)
      COMMON /ARRAYS/ X, P1(IPAD+520*3), Y, P2(IPAD+520*3), &
&        AA, P3(IPAD+128), DD, P4(IPAD+128), RX, P5(IPAD+128), RY
!DIR$ CACHE_ALIGN /ARRAYS/
      DO J = 2,N-1
            DO I = 2,N-1
            {Loop body omitted . . . }
      END DO
  END DO
```

These changes improved the performance of the kernel roughly by a factor of 2 when compiled with f90 -O3,unroll2,pipeline2 on a Cray T3E-900 system. Such benefits have since been adopted into the compiler, making changes to the code more portable. For instance, using the compiler option "-a pad" and the cache-align directive statement in the code without precomputing the optimum array and pad sizes yields almost the same improvement:

```
      REAL, DIMENSION(513,513) :: AA, DD, X, Y, RX, RY
      COMMON /ARRAYS/ X, Y, AA, DD, RX, RY
!DIR$ CACHE_ALIGN /ARRAYS/
      DO J = 2,N-1
            DO I = 2,N-1
                  {Loop body omitted . . . }
            END DO
      END DO
```

To see the further potential benefits of cache-line alignment, consider the case of copying an 8-by-*N* array to another 8-by-*N* array [5.2], in which both arrays have been deliberately misaligned so that each 8-element column spans two Scache lines instead of one:

```
      INTEGER LDX, N
      PARAMETER (LDX=64, N=1000)
      REAL MBYTES, SECS, T1, T2
      REAL A(LDX,N), B(LDX,N)
      COMMON /AB/ BAD(4), A, B
!DIR$ CACHE_ALIGN /AB/
      DATA A / 64000*1.0 /
      CLKSPD = CLOCKTICK()
      T1 = RTC()
      CALL COPYAB( 8, N, A, LDX, B, LDX )
      T2 = RTC()
      MBYTES = 8.0*REAL( 16*N ) / 1.E+6
      SECS = (T2-T1)*CLKSPD
      WRITE(*,*) '8-BY-N BLOCK COPY = ', MBYTES/SECS,' MB/SEC'
      END
      SUBROUTINE COPYAB( M, N, A, LDA, B, LDB )
      INTEGER N, LDA, LDB
      REAL A(LDA,N), B(LDB,N)
      DO J = 1, N
            DO I = 1, M
                  B(I,J) = A(I,J)
            END DO
      END DO
      RETURN
      END
```

In all of these computations, using a routine like CLOCKTICK, which returns the speed in seconds of one clock period in the microprocessor, is useful for comparing results on processors of different speeds:

```
#include unistd.h
float CLOCKTICK(void) {
      long sysconf(int request);
      float p;
```

```
        p = (float) sysconf(_SC_Cray_CPCYCLE); /* CPU cycle time
                                                    in picoseconds */
        p = p * 1.0e-12;              /* cycle time in seconds */
        return (p);
}
```

When compiled with f90 -O3,unroll2, the 8-by-*N* block matrix copy runs at 104 MB/s, counting each byte copied once on the read and once on the write.

Now the arrays A and B are aligned on an 8-word Scache-line boundary by removing the array BAD in the common block declaration:

```
COMMON /AB/ A(LDX,N), B(LDX,N)
```

The performance improves by nearly a factor of 2, to 195 MB/s. However, using cacheable loads and stores leads to inefficient use of the caches in this example because only a small portion of the arrays A and B remain in cache on completion. E-register usage, described briefly in Section 5.4, would improve the performance.

5.3   STREAM BUFFER OPTIMIZATIONS

Stream buffers on the Cray T3E node permit unit-stride or small-stride accesses to local memory to be streamed when an operation causes Scache misses for two consecutive 64-byte blocks of memory. There are six stream buffers on each node, and the hardware keeps track of eight cache misses, so noncontiguous misses may still cause streaming, and stream references may be interleaved. Optimizing for the stream buffers focuses on creating long patterns of unit-stride or small-stride access to memory to keep streaming active and to group operations to limit memory references so that six or fewer streams can satisfy them.

Optimization guides for the Cray T3E system explain a number of techniques for using the stream buffers effectively, including

+ Splitting loops to limit the number of streams
+ Arranging array dimensions to maximize inner loop trip count
+ Rearranging array dimensions to minimize the number of streams
+ Grouping statements that use the same streams
+ Combining streams with temporary vectors
+ Prefetching streams into cache

A couple of examples from those guides will give a flavor of how using the stream buffers well can improve performance:

```
      SUBROUTINE FDTD(CAEX,CBEX,CAEY,CBEY,CAEZ,CBEZ,EX,EY,EZ,
 &  HX,HY,HZ)
      REAL CAEX, CBEX, CAEY, CBEY, CAEZ, CBEZ
      REAL EX(129,129,128), EY(129,129,128), EZ(129,129,128)
      REAL HX(129,129,128), HY(129,129,128), HZ(129,129,128)
      DO J = 2, 127
            DO I = 2, 127
                  DO K = 2, 127
                        EX(K,I,J) =     CAEX*(EX(K,I,J) +
 &                            CBEX*(HZ(K,I,J) - HZ(K,I,J-1) +
 &                            HY(K,I,J) - HY(K-1,I,J)))
                        EY(K,I,J) =     CAEY*(EY(K,I,J) +
 &                            CBEY*(HX(K-1,I,J) - HX(K,I,J) +
 &                            HZ(K,I-1,J) - HZ(K,I,J)))
                        EZ(K,I,J) =     CAEZ*(EZ(K,I,J) +
 &                            CBEZ*(HX(K,I,J-1) - HX(K,I,J) +
 &                            HY(K,I,J) - HY(K,I-1,J)))
                  END DO
            END DO
      END DO
      RETURN
      END
```

At first glance, the six arrays seem an ideal fit for the six stream buffers. But because the loop accesses the well-separated columns j and j − 1 of the arrays HX and HZ, there are at least eight input streams, three of which are also output streams. This loop is a good candidate for splitting because the trip counts are high, there are long sequences of unit-stride references, and the arrays are large enough that they cannot already reside in the Scache. Just directing the compiler to split (-O3,split2) the innermost loop nets a 40 percent improvement. Splitting the loop manually may give different results.

An alternative strategy that works nearly as well is to condense several streams into a temporary vector, as rewriting the previous example shows:

```
      SUBROUTINE FDTD(CAEX,CBEX,CAEY,CBEY,CAEZ,CBEZ,EX,EY,EZ,
 & HX,HY,HZ)
      REAL EX(129,129,128), EY(129,129,128), EZ(129,129,128)
```

```
            REAL HX(129,129,128), HY(129,129,128), HZ(129,129,128)
            REAL TMP(3,128)
            DO J = 2, 127
                 DO I = 2, 127
                       DO K = 2, 126, 2
                             TMP(1,K) = HZ(K,I,J) - HZ(K,I,J-1)
                             TMP(2,K) = HX(K-1,I,J) - HX(K,I,J) +
     &            HZ(K,I-1,J) - HZ(K,I,J)
                             TMP(3,K) = HX(K,I,J-1) - HX(K,I,J)
                             TMP(1,K+1) = HZ(K+1,I,J) - HZ(K+1,I,J-1)
                             TMP(2,K+1) = HX(K,I,J) - HX(K+1,I,J) +
     &            HZ(K+1,I-1,J) - HZ(K+1,I,J)
                             TMP(3,K+1) = HX(K+1,I,J-1) - HX(K+1,I,J)
                       END DO
                       DO K = 2, 127
                             EX(K,I,J) = CAEX*(EX(K,I,J) +
     &            CBEX*(TMP(1,K) + HY(K,I,J) - HY(K-1,I,J)))
                             EY(K,I,J) = CAEY*(EY(K,I,J) +
     &            CBEY*(TMP(2,K)))
                             EZ(K,I,J) = CAEZ*(EZ(K,I,J) +
     &            CBEZ*(TMP(3,K) + HY(K,I,J) - HY(K,I-1,J)))
                       END DO
                 END DO
            END DO
            RETURN
            END
```

The first loop over k contains five streams, consisting of the array tmp and two columns each of HZ and HX. The second k loop also contains five streams: three for the arrays EX, EY, and EZ; one for HY; and one for TMP (which may still be in the cache). This version returns 57.6 Mflops. This is a lot more work than just splitting the loop, but it may be the only option if the inner loop variables all depend on each other.

5.4   E-REGISTER OPERATIONS

Operations directly between the memory of any two PEs on the Cray T3E make use of special hardware components called *E-registers*. These memory-mapped registers reside in noncached memory and provide a means for bypassing the

5.5   How Much Performance Can Be Obtained on a Single Processor?

77

cache when the data structure is such that use of the cache would be a hindrance. The E-registers, which are generally reserved for internal system use such as synchronization and communication with remote memory, can also play a critical role in helping applications scale well on many processors. They have a secondary use for local optimization because they can also assist in providing large-stride and gather/scatter operations very efficiently with respect to local memory. One can use the E-registers to obtain large blocks of data and for loads that would cause large amounts of data to be discarded if loaded into a cache-line. The E-registers can be used directly in a loop by specifying the CACHE_BY-PASS directive. Their use may also be invoked by use of SHMEM library and other special library routines. It is beyond the scope of this section to give the detail necessary for using the E-registers, but one example of a random gather will show the benefit to be gained:

```
!DIR$    CACHE_BYPASS A,X
         DO I = 1, NGATH
                X(I) = A(INDEX(I))
         END DO
```

Bypassing the cache and using the E-registers causes the data transfer rate on a Cray T3E-900 system to improve from 59 MB/s to 339 MB/s. Further improvement is possible by using special benchmarking library routines. The E-registers are used by the compiler, external communications routines, and other libraries, and so the programmer needs to understand how to synchronize direct use of the registers with the other uses.

5.5   HOW MUCH PERFORMANCE CAN BE OBTAINED ON A SINGLE PROCESSOR?

This chapter has given an idea of the techniques available to the applications programmer for automatic, semiautomatic, and manual optimization for the single processor of an MPP system. As demonstrated in some of the examples, giving attention to single-processor performance can be well worth the effort. On the Cray T3E system, an experiment was performed using some of the NAS kernel benchmarks, which demonstrate characteristics of a NASA workload.

When the kernels were run unmodified and various options were chosen on the compiler command line, the overall performance of the set improved by a factor of 4. Intrinsic function vectorization, common block padding, unrolling, software pipelining, and linking with fast math intrinsic functions all contributed to the overall improvement, though some routines benefited more than others. One kernel improved by over a factor of 6. From the experiment, the benchmarkers concluded that the compiler options -O3, unroll 2, pipeline2, and -apad and loading the fast, but not completely IEEE-compliant, libfastmv should be selected for best automatic optimization.

Next, the benchmarkers examined each kernel in detail, modifying them as required. Many of the changes simply involved calling optimized library routines to perform the operations of the kernels. Sometimes, through pattern matching, the compiler was able to do this automatically, but not always. Compiler directives to align data in cache, use of the E-registers and cache-bypass, and rearranging array dimensions and splitting loops for better stream usage are some of the other techniques they used. In the end, they obtained, on average, another factor of 3 for the kernels, giving over a 6X average performance improvement in all. One kernel, which did not benefit much from the compiler-line options, gained a factor of over 6 from hand tuning. The best overall combined improvement was a factor of 21. And one kernel, a matrix multiplication, obtained over two-thirds the peak performance of the processor. These are impressive results, worth some effort, even keeping in mind that the performance of a kernel is often far superior to the average performance of a whole application.

References

[5.1]   Anderson, E., J. Brooks, C. Grassl, and S. Scott. 1997. Performance of the Cray T3E Multiprocessor. In *Proceedings of the SC97*.

[5.2]   Anderson, E., J. Brooks, and T. Hewitt. 1997. *The Benchmarker's Guide to Single-Processor Optimization for Cray T3E Systems*. Cray Research, a Silicon Graphics Company Publication.

6 Scheduling Issues

Morris A. Jette   Lawrence Livermore National Laboratory

In the industrial and scientific parallel computing environment, it is usually the case that a high-end supercomputer has many users at all times. As an applications programmer, it is important to understand some of the issues associated with the scheduling of jobs on a parallel computer. These issues can help the user to both obtain maximum performance for a particular application and also understand the reasons why performance on a particular application may be significantly less than expected in a multiuser environment.

For example, we consider in some detail the generations of schedulers, known as gang scheduling, developed for use on the multiuser and multi-program parallel environments at the Lawrence Livermore National Laboratory (LLNL). Gang scheduling incorporates three principles: concurrent scheduling of each thread of a parallel program, space sharing, and time sharing. Space sharing refers to the ability to concurrently execute different programs on the different processors. Most parallel computers provide only two of these components, resulting in significant loss of capability. Three generations of LLNL-developed gang schedulers have achieved excellent system utilization, good responsiveness, and effective parallel job execution on a variety of computer architectures. Gang scheduling provides parallel computers with capabilities ranging from general-purpose through grand-challenge computing.

Parallel computers are valuable resources from which one should expect a high level of system utilization. A high level of responsiveness is also required for the sake of program developers who execute many small programs. Interactive programs account for 67 percent of all jobs executed on LLNL's Cray T3D while consuming only 13 percent of all CPU cycles delivered. Peak interactive workloads reach 320 processors, a 25 percent oversubscription rate, necessitating a time-sharing mechanism to provide good responsiveness. The remainder of resources are delivered to the larger and longer-running batch jobs.

Most MPP systems provide concurrent scheduling of a parallel program's threads and space sharing of resources. A time-sharing capability is normally lacking, and processors allocated to a program are retained until that program's termination. This paradigm makes high system utilization and good responsiveness mutually incompatible. Given the high value of MPP systems, most are operated to provide high system utilization and limited responsiveness. Interactive work may be limited to a small subset of the processors and short execution times. Alternatively, high-priority batch queues may be constructed for programs having short execution times. Interactive and other high-priority programs cannot be initiated in a timely fashion during periods of high system utilization, precluding general-purpose computing. Programs with high resource requirements must accumulate processors in a piecemeal fashion as other programs terminate, wasting those resources in the interim and reducing system utilization. Long-running programs can prevent the execution of high-priority or high-resource-requirement programs for extended periods. The lasting effect of scheduling a grand-challenge-class problem limits the system's ability to process them.

The addition of a time-sharing capability addresses these issues, with some relatively minor costs. Program preemption does incur some additional overhead, but higher overall system utilization may compensate for this. All running or preempted programs must have their storage requirements simultaneously satisfied. Preempted programs must also vacate memory for other programs. As with nonparallel computers, the increased system capability and effective capacity provided by time sharing should warrant the expense of additional storage. It should be noted that grand-challenge-class problems typically utilize most of the available real memory. The true cost of performing a context switch in this environment may be tens of seconds and result in terabytes of data moving between real memory and disk (virtual memory). This I/O normally prevents the instantaneous responsiveness desired for small problem sizes.

Most symmetric multiprocessor (SMP) systems do provide both time sharing and space sharing, but lack a mechanism for concurrent scheduling of a parallel program's threads of execution. Concurrent scheduling of a program's threads has been shown to improve the efficiency of both the individual parallel programs and the system [6.1, 6.7]. Concurrent scheduling is essential not only within a single SMP but across a cluster in order to harness the computer power available and to address grand-challenge-class problems.

6.1   GANG SCHEDULER IMPLEMENTATION

The objective of gang scheduling is to achieve a high level of system utilization and responsiveness on parallel computing platforms in multiprogrammed environments. The concurrent execution of a parallel program's threads can be viewed as essential for any scheduler implementation. Sustained system utilization rates over 90 percent are practical for SMP architectures and can be extended into the MPP domain. Although maximizing the responsiveness for all programs might be attractive, our design objective was somewhat more refined: to provide high responsiveness only for programs in which the expected benefit outweighs the high context switch times described earlier. The responsiveness requirement for interactive programs is far more critical than that of batch programs. The LLNL gang scheduler was therefore designed to maximize responsiveness for interactive and other high-priority work. Responsiveness for batch and lower-priority work was not a significant concern.

The LLNL gang scheduler was initially developed for the BBN TC2000 system in 1991 [6.3]. It underwent substantial modification for use on the Cray T3D in 1996 [6.2, 6.6]. Its third generation was developed for clusters of Digital Alpha computers in 1997 [6.4, 6.5]. Although the LLNL gang scheduler has evolved during this period and significant system-specific differences exist, many original design features remain.

One significant design feature is the existence of several job classes, each with different scheduling characteristics. These classes permit the scheduler to provide high responsiveness only to programs for which the additional overhead will provide real benefit, primarily in cases where a user is waiting at a terminal for the response. The classes also provide for a variety of throughput rates depending upon programmatic considerations. The following job classes are supported: *express* jobs have been deemed by management to be mission critical and are given rapid response and optimal throughput, *interactive* jobs require rapid response time and very good throughput during working hours, *debug* jobs require rapid response time during working hours but cannot be preempted on the Cray T3D due to the debugger's design, *production* jobs do not require rapid response but should receive good throughput at night and on weekends, *benchmark* jobs do not require rapid response but cannot be preempted once execution begins, *standby* jobs have low priority and are suitable for absorbing otherwise idle computer resources.

Each parallel program has a job class associated with it. The default classes are production for batch jobs, debug for TotalView debugger-initiated jobs, and interactive for other jobs directly initiated from a user terminal. Jobs can be placed in the express class only by the system administrator. Benchmark and standby classes can be specified by the user at program initiation time. Each job class has a variety of associated parameters, the most significant being the class's relative priority. All LLNL gang-scheduling parameters can be altered in realtime to provide different scheduling characteristics at different times. For example, LLNL systems are configured to provide high responsiveness and interactivity during working hours. Throughput is emphasized at night and on weekends. Resource management is provided by other systems that can alter a program's nice value in response to a user's or group's resource consumption rate diverging from the target consumption rate. Nice value changes can result in a program being reclassified to or from the standby job class.

The parallel program to be scheduled must register its resource and scheduling requirements with the appropriate gang-scheduler daemon at initiation time. No user applications modifications were necessary on either the BBN and Cray systems because it was possible to add LLNL-developed software to the vendors' parallel-program initiation software. Initiating parallel programs on Digital computers can be as simple as executing a fork system call, which is impossible to capture outside of the operating system. Therefore, Digital parallel programs must be modified to register their resource requirements, and each process must explicitly register as a component of the program. This typically requires the addition of one function call in the user application and makes use of an LLNL-developed library to issue remote procedure calls to the gang-scheduler daemon. From the point a parallel program has been registered, the gang-scheduler daemons decide which resources are to be allocated to it and when. While executing, each program has the perception of dedicated resources. A program's throughput is primarily dependent upon overall system load and relative priority of the program's job class.

The cost of performing a context switch for typical LLNL parallel programs is quite substantial. On architectures supporting virtual memory, paging essentially removes the entire memory image of one program in order to load that of another program. The time to perform this paging raises effective context switch time into the tens of seconds range (for large programs, into the range of minutes). In order to amortize this substantial context switch time, they should occur at infrequent intervals. The key to providing good responsiveness with infrequent context switching is the prioritized job classes. Rather than providing time sharing of resources among all executable programs, resources are specifically targeted to the highest-priority work through what may be better described as a preemption scheme. For example, an interactive-class job may preempt a production-class job. The preempted production-class job will not resume execution until no higher-priority work can be allocated those resources. If multiple programs at the same job-class priority contend for the same resources, those programs may time-share the resources. The net effect is a high-utilization and low-overhead system with good responsiveness.

The first-generation LLNL gang scheduler was developed in 1991 for the BBN TC2000 "butterfly" [6.3], a 126-processor computer shared-memory architecture. The TC2000 originally supported only space sharing of resources. The gang scheduler reserved all resources at system startup and controlled all resource scheduling from that time. User programs required no modification to take advantage of the gang scheduler, but did need to load with a modified parallel job initiation library. Rather than securing resources directly from the operating system, this modified library was allocated resources by the gang-scheduler daemon. Each time slice lasted 10 seconds, with decisions made as to resource allocation at each time-slice boundary. Context switches were initiated through concurrent transmission of signals to all threads of a parallel program.

The second-generation LLNL gang scheduler required major modification for the Cray T3D system in 1996 [6.4, 6.6]. The LLNL Cray T3D system had 256 processors, each with 64 MB DRAM. Only space sharing of resources was originally permitted on the Cray T3D. In 1996, Cray Research added a capability to save a parallel program's context to disk and later restore it to memory. The implementation also permitted the restoration of a program to different processors, which permitted workload rebalancing and significant improvement in performance. Parallel programs on the Cray T3D are initiated through a vendor-supplied program. LLNL developed a "wrapper" for this program to register its resource requirements with the gang-scheduler daemon at initiation time and receive a specific resource allocation. The gang-scheduler daemon performs context switches by issuing system calls. Scheduling decisions are made whenever a program is initiated or terminated, upon completion of writing a program's state to disk, and on a periodic basis. This event-driven scheduler provides for better responsiveness than would be possible with fixed-period time slices.

The third- and latest-generation LLNL gang scheduler supports Digital SMP systems with the Digital Unix operating system [6.4, 6.5]. Even though Digital Unix does provide for space sharing and time sharing, it fails to coordinate scheduling of a parallel program's threads. This is addressed through program and thread registration with the gang-scheduler daemon and Digital's class scheduler. Rather than providing a mechanism to assign specific processors to specific processes, the class scheduler resembles a very fine-grained fair-share scheduler. Realtime changes to the class-scheduler parameters control which programs are running or preempted. The operating system seeks to take advantage of an active cache, tending to keep a given thread on a specific processor. The net effect is very similar to true gang scheduling. To coordinate scheduling across multiple SMP computers, it was necessary to revert to fixed time-slice periods (currently configured at 30 seconds). If appropriate, newly initiated programs may begin execution prior to a time-slice boundary. Programs with particularly large memory requirements may be scheduled to run in multiple consecutive time slices to limit paging. Each computer has its own gang-scheduler daemon that is capable of operating independently for greater fault tolerance. Programs spanning multiple computers require coordinated scheduling by multiple gang-scheduler daemons. Remote procedure calls are used to establish time-slice allocations across multiple computers. Tickets representing these resources are associated with programs through their lifetime.

Although the LLNL gang scheduler's basic design called for resource allocation to the highest-priority programs, high context switch times necessitated some additional consideration. One additional parameter associated with each job class on the Cray T3D implementation is a do-not-disturb factor. Once a program is allocated resources, it is guaranteed those resources for some period before preemption occurs. This time period is computed by multiplying the number of processors the program is allocated by the do-not-disturb factor. This parameter limits the impact context switches may have upon overall system throughput. Multiple programs with identical job-class priorities will context switch periodically, but memory thrashing will be avoided.

Another parameter associated with each job class is a maximum wait time. A program waiting longer than the maximum wait time for its resource allocation will have those resources reserved for it. Multiple programs of equal or lower priority will be preempted after satisfying their do-not-disturb requirement. This ensures that programs with high resource requirements can be allocated those resources in a timely fashion. To ensure that high responsiveness is provided to nonparallel programs on Digital SMP systems, a parameter specifies a minimum number of processors to be reserved for them. These processors will be available to execute system daemons and nonparallel user programs in a timely fashion. One other parameter will be noted, a maximum workload. Once the system's workload reaches this level, newly initiated programs will be queued for execution but not scheduled. Programs that have already begun execution will continue. The purpose of this parameter is to prevent oversubscription of storage space, especially swap space. The maximum workload is specified in terms of processor count.

6.2   GANG SCHEDULER PERFORMANCE

The introduction of the LLNL gang scheduler on the Cray T3D permitted substantial reconfiguration of the machine. Rather than reserving a substantial number of processors for interactive use during working hours, the batch system was permitted to completely allocate all processors at all times. Interactive work is allocated resources on an as-needed basis. Although the median time required to begin execution of interactive programs has increased slightly, the worst case has been dramatically reduced by time-sharing resources during periods of extreme load. Substantially longer-running programs were permitted to execute and freed from the constraint of only executing during weekend hours.

The overall Cray T3D system utilization improved substantially after deployment of a gang scheduler. This improvement in utilization can be largely attributed to the reconfiguration described here. Weekly Cray T3D processor utilization frequently exceeded 96 percent. About 2 percent of CPU time is lost to incomplete resource allocation due to a workload incapable of utilizing every processor. Context switch time also reduces CPU utilization by about 2 percent because the CPU is idle during the entire time a program's state is moved between memory and rotating storage. In benchmarks run against an early version of the LLNL gang scheduler for the Cray T3D, throughput of interactive work increased by 21 percent without reduction in overall system throughput.

Responsiveness may be quantified by slowdown or the amount by which a program's actual execution time exceeds its execution time in a dedicated environment. Because the LLNL design only ventures to provide a high level of responsiveness to interactive programs, responsiveness for batch jobs will not be considered. The aggregate interactive workload slowdown on the Cray T3D during a 20-day period of high utilization was 18 percent, which is viewed quite favorably. Further investigation shows a great deal of variation in slowdown. Most longer-running interactive jobs enjoy slowdowns of only a few percentage points. Interactive jobs executed during the daytime typically begin execution within 30 seconds and continue without preemption until termination. Interactive jobs executed during late night and early morning hours experienced slowdowns as high as 1371 (a one-second job delayed for about 23 minutes). However, the computer is configured for high utilization and batch-job execution during these hours, so high slowdowns are not unexpected.

Gang scheduling on the Digital systems demonstrates significant improvement in performance for tightly coupled parallel programs, especially at high levels of parallelism and heavy loads. One factor in performance improvement is a fast reduction in spin-wait time at synchronization points. Spin-waiting keeps a processor polling for an event rather than relinquishing the processors. Although this technique maximizes program throughput, it can result in substantial waste of computer resources. Another important factor is a reduction in the cache refresh overhead, which is provided by the long slice times (configured at 30 seconds). While executing with gang scheduling, the program effectively has dedicated memory and processor resources. Figure 6.1 shows the effect of gang scheduling on the performance of a Gaussian elimination benchmark. The computer used for the benchmark was being used concurrently by about 14 other

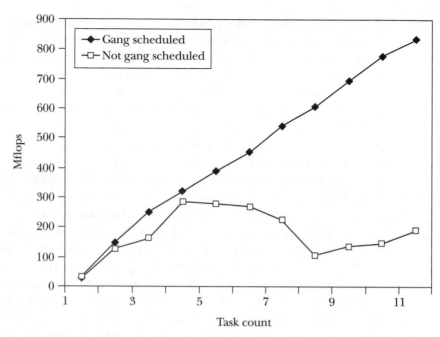

6.1

FIGURE

Gaussian elimination benchmark performance on Digital computer.

runnable threads, the normal state of affairs for our interactive-oriented computers during normal work hours.

No degradation in overall system responsiveness or utilization has been
noted. This is in part due to the Digital class scheduler's ability to reallocate otherwise idle resources should the parallel program wait for some external event. A
wide range of parallel programs demonstrate 5 to 100 percent speedup in response to concurrent scheduling of threads. Figure 6.2 shows the performance
of a parallel program and the computer system executing it. The left window
shows overall system performance. The window on the right show performance
of the parallel application. CPU and memory use information is plotted at each
time-slice boundary to aid in tuning both the computer system and application
program.

The addition of a time-sharing capability to MPP computers can substantially
improve both the system's capability and effective capacity. Good responsiveness provides the user with an effective program-development environment and
the means to rapidly execute short programs. The ability to initiate resource-
intensive problems upon demand, without the piecemeal accumulation of re-

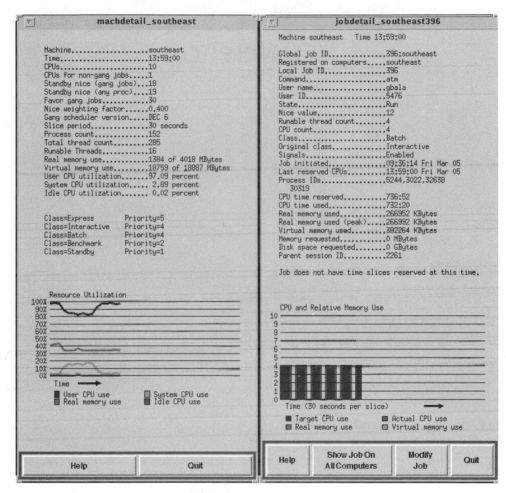

6.2

FIGURE

Display of gang scheduling two parallel programs on Digital computer.

sources, increases overall system utilization. Long-running programs can also be initiated as desired without preventing the reallocation of those resources at a later time for high-priority or resource-intensive problems. SMP systems benefit by the concurrent scheduling of a parallel program's threads, particularly across multiple computers. This extends the range of SMP capabilities beyond general-purpose computing to that of grand-challenge-class problems.

References

[6.1]   Dusseau, A. C., R. H. Arpaci, and D. E. Culler. 1996. Effective Distributed Scheduling of Parallel Workloads. *ACM SIGMETRICS '96 Conference on the Measurement and Modeling of Computer Systems.*

[6.2]   Feitelson, D. G., and M. A. Jette. 1997. Improved Utilization and Responsiveness with Gang Scheduling. *IPPS '97 Workshop on Job Scheduling Strategies for Parallel Processing,* April. *www-lc.llnl.gov/global_access/dctg/gang/gang.sspp.ps.*

[6.3]   Gorda, B., and R. Wolski. 1995. Timesharing Massively Parallel Machines. *International Conference on Parallel Processing,* Vol. II (Aug.), 214–217.

[6.4]   Jette, M. 1997. Performance Characteristics of Gang Scheduling in Multiprogrammed Environments. In *Proceedings of the SC97,* Nov.

[6.5]   Jette, M. 1998. Expanding Symmetric Multiprocessor Capability Through Gang Scheduling. *IPPS '98 Workshop on Job Scheduling Strategies for Parallel Processing,* April, 199–216.

[6.6]   Jette, M., D. Storch, and E. Yim. 1996. Gang Scheduler—Timesharing the Cray T3D. *Cray User Group,* March, 247–252. *www-lc.llnl.gov/global_access/dctg/gang/gang.sched.html.*

[6.7]   Sobalvarro, P. G., and W. E. Weihl. 1995. Demand-based Coscheduling of Parallel Jobs on Multiprogrammed Multiprocessors. *IPPS '95 Parallel Job Scheduling Workshop,* April, 106–126.

II | THE APPLICATIONS

PART

Meso- to Macroscale Environmental Modeling

Applied Fluid Dynamics

Applied Plasma Dynamics

These 17 chapters document the recent experiences of software developers in porting and designing industrial strength applications to run on massively parallel computers. The contributors in these chapters discuss the strategies, techniques, and tools that were used as well as the lessons learned. The applications were created under both distributed- and shared-memory programming models and provide a wide cross section of numerical algorithms and techniques. Please see Table P.1 in the Preface and on inside front cover of this book for cross references to these techniques and methods.

The chapters are grouped by the length scale of the physical phenomena treated by the application. Chapters 7 and 8 involve environmental modeling on the meso- to macro-scale and are very well suited to MPP architectures. Chapters 9 through 12 can be broadly classed as fluid dynamic applications with length scales roughly in the centimeter to kilometer range. For these applications, communication plays a more important role than for the two applications at larger length scales. Chapters 13 through 15 can be classified as applied plasma dynamic applications with length scales roughly in the micron to centimeter range. Chapters 16 through 20 have a wide range of relevant length scales from atomic to laboratory dimensions. For the last three applications there is not a well-defined length scale and we class these chapters as ones dealing with data analysis.

7 Ocean Modeling and Visualization

Yi Chao
P. Peggy Li
Ping Wang
Daniel S. Katz
Benny N. Cheng   Jet Propulsion Laboratory, California Institute of Technology

Scott Whitman   Equator Technologies, Inc.

7.1   INTRODUCTION

Observations suggest that the ocean plays an important role in the Earth's climate system. One of the principal roles of the ocean in the global heat balance is to store and release heat, which moderates seasonal extremes and leads to the contrast between ocean and continent temperatures. The ocean is the major driving force in modulating natural climate variability, such as the El Niño phenomenon. In today's global warming environment, the ocean plays an important role in controlling the onset of atmospheric warming (due to the increase of greenhouse gases induced by the burning of fossil fuels) through absorbing the excess heat trapped in the atmosphere. It is therefore necessary to develop a comprehensive understanding of world ocean circulation and its role in climate change.

Because of the enormous resources required to make ocean observations, it is virtually impossible to continuously monitor the ocean from a basin to global scale. In situ (e.g., ship-based) observations provide only sparse measurements over the global ocean. Despite its global coverage, satellite remote-sensed observations provide information only on the ocean surface. Information below the ocean surface has to be obtained from 3D numerical ocean models constrained by in situ and satellite observations. Therefore, ocean modeling is an indispensable tool for monitoring current climatic conditions and for predicting future climate change.

However, numerical ocean models need to be thoroughly tested against the available observations to establish their validity for describing the real world. This often involves conducting a large number of numerical experiments with different model configurations and parameters and seeking the "best fit" between the model and observations. One of the biggest deficiencies in the existing ocean models is their inability to resolve mesoscale eddies in the ocean (equivalent to synoptic storms in the atmosphere), with spatial scale on the order of 1 degree (or 100 km). One of the major challenges in ocean modeling is to determine the minimum resolution of the model beyond which a further increase of resolution has little qualitative impact on the model simulation.

The last decade has seen tremendous progress in exploring the role of horizontal resolution up to 1/3 [7.4] and 1/4 [7.16] degrees using parallel-vector computing technology. Eddy-resolving calculations beyond 1/4 degree are extremely costly and have only been feasible in recent years using MPP technology. A group at Los Alamos National Laboratory (LANL) has performed a 10-year integration of a 1/5-degree ocean model on the Connection Machine 5 (CM5) [7.19]. Using the Cray T3D, the Jet Propulsion Laboratory (JPL) has conducted a 40-year integration of a 1/6-degree ocean model [7.5]. It is apparent that more eddy-resolving calculations with resolutions higher than 1/6 degree are needed. A one-year integration of the 1/6-degree ocean model takes about 100 hours on a 256-processor Cray T3D. Given the limited computing resources available to the ocean-modeling community and the requirement to conduct multidecade integrations at even higher resolutions, it is therefore necessary to optimize the existing ocean code and reduce the total computation time needed to complete these eddy-resolving calculations.

High-resolution models generate large volumes of data. A snapshot (the data at a single time step) of the 1/6-degree North Atlantic model contains about 600 MB of data. If the ocean model output is saved every 3 simulation days (the typical scale to resolve the synoptic events in the ocean), a 5-year time series of this model corresponds to about 350 GB of data. With existing commercial visualization software on high-end graphic workstations (e.g., the Power Onyx from Silicon Graphics, Inc.), only a very small fraction of a dataset of this size can be analyzed, ignoring the time delay for data transfer between the MPP machine and the local workstation. It is therefore advantageous to develop compatible visualization software on the MPP machines where the ocean modeling is being conducted.

In this chapter, we report our recent experiences in running the ocean model and developing a visualization tool on the Cray T3D. After a brief description of our numerical ocean model, we present a few examples demonstrating how we improved its computational performance. The development of a volume renderer on the Cray T3D will then be described, and its computational performance will be assessed. Finally, the scientific results using the optimized ocean model and the newly developed visualization tool will be presented. Given the short life cycle of MPP machines, the portability of the optimized ocean model and the volume-rendering software will be discussed.

7.2   MODEL DESCRIPTION

We have selected the most widely used ocean model as our base code. This ocean model is derived from the Parallel Ocean Program (POP) developed at LANL [7.19], which evolved from the Bryan-Cox 3D primitive equations ocean model [7.3, 7.6], developed at NOAA Geophysical Fluid Dynamics Laboratory (GFDL) and later known as the Semtner and Chervin model [7.16] or the Modular Ocean Model (MOM) [7.14].

The ocean model used in the present study solves the 3D primitive equations using the finite difference method. The equations are separated into barotropic (the vertical mean) and baroclinic (departures from the vertical mean) components. The baroclinic component is 3D and is solved using explicit leapfrog time stepping. It can be parallelized very well on massively parallel computers. The barotropic component is 2D and is solved implicitly. It differs from the original Bryan-Cox formulation in that it removes the rigid-lid approximation and treats the sea surface height as a prognostic variable (i.e., free-surface). The free-surface model is superior to the rigid-lid model because it provides a more accurate solution of the governing equations. More importantly, the free-surface model tremendously reduces the global communication otherwise required by the rigid-lid model.

7.3   COMPUTATIONAL CONSIDERATIONS

The original ocean code was developed in Fortran 77 on a LANL CM5 [7.19]. This code was then ported to the Cray T3D using Shared Memory Access (SHMEM) routines [7.17]. Because the code on the Cray T3D was still time-consuming when large problems were encountered, improving the code performance was essential. In order to significantly reduce wall clock time, the code was optimized using single-processor optimization techniques [7.2] and other strategies. The remainder of this section discusses these strategies, the corresponding improvement in performance of the ocean code on the Cray T3D, and issues of portability.

7.3.1 Parallel Software Tools

When optimizing any code, the first need is for a tool that accurately measures the performance (the runtime as well as the number of floating-point operations per second) of the overall code and all of its subroutines. On the Cray T3D, we have used the MPP Apprentice tool for this purpose, first to identify two types of routines to optimize (those that took a large percentage of overall time and those that ran at a slow floating-point operations per second rate) and then to verify that applied optimizations caused an improvement in performance. The Apprentice tool is not a hardware monitor; rather, it is a pure software tool. Its use requires recompiling the code with Apprentice options enabled in the compiler and rerunning the code to produce a runtime information file. This file is then viewed by the Apprentice tool, which has many types of outputs to help the user understand exactly what happened while the code was running.

7.3.2 Compiler Options

The optimization techniques we used can be separated into two groups: those that did not require manual code editing, and those that did. The techniques that did not require code editing were implemented by compiler and loading options, such as "-o aggress", "-o noieeedivide", "-o unroll", and "-D rdahead= on", as discussed in Chapter 6. These options had some effect, but we quickly discovered that for the ocean code, we needed to make changes to the code itself to take full advantage of both these and other optimization techniques. The rest of this section provides a detailed discussion of these changes.

7.3.3 Memory Optimization and Arithmetic Pipelines

On the Cray T3D, good performance can be achieved through effective use of cache and pipelined arithmetic. The ocean code uses many 2D arrays, which can be inefficient when frequent stride-one addressing is encountered. One improvement is to change to explicit 1D addressing. For example, the 2D array KMU(IMT,JMT) can be replaced by KMU(IMT*JMT). This type of change can increase performance, both by simplifying index calculations and by making the code easier for the compiler to optimize.

Another useful strategy is to manually unroll loop statements. For the Cray T3D, the loop unrolling achieved using compiler options is not always sufficient. Thus, in order to get the best performance from Fortran code, the user may have to manually unroll some of the loops. Also on the Cray T3D, the divide operation is not a pipelined function. Therefore, the number of divide operations has been minimized by using real variables to store the values resulting from divide operations and moving the divide operation out of loop statements when it is independent of the loop index. The code

```
IF (MIX.EQ.0) THEN
BETA = ALPHA
ELSE
BETA = THETA
ENDIF
```

where MIX equals either 0 or 1, is replaced by

```
BETA=ALPHA*(1-MIX)+THETA*MIX
```

which improves the effective use of pipelined arithmetic.

7.3.4 Optimized Libraries

There are several optimized libraries available on the Cray T3D and other MPP machines, such as the Basic Linear Algebra Subproblems (BLAS) libraries [7.10]. These libraries have been optimized to give the best possible performance when the user applies them properly. There are many matrix and vector computations in the ocean code, which consume a fair portion of the total computation time. We have replaced them by calling BLAS routines. For example, the Hadamard product of two vectors

```
DO I=1,IMAX
X(I)=ALPHA*(Y(I)*Z(I))+BETA*X(I)
ENDDO
```

can be replaced with a call to the extended BLAS routine SHAD:

```
CALL SHAD(IMAX,ALPHA,Y,1,Z,1,BETA,X,1)
```

Furthermore, SHAD also recognizes a special case when BETA = 0.0; thus

```
DO I=1,IMAX
```

```
X(I)=ALPHA*(Y(I)*Z(I))
ENDDO
```

can be replaced with a call to SHAD:

```
CALL SHAD(IMAX,ALPHA,Y,1,Z,1,0.0,X,1)
```

For large values of IMAX, such modification can improve the performance of this particular loop by a factor of 5. It should be pointed out that the use of optimized libraries does not necessarily improve the overall code performance. Thus, one needs to use the MPP Apprentice tool to evaluate each library being added.

7.3.5 REPLACEMENT OF IF/WHERE STATEMENTS BY USING MASK ARRAYS

In the original ocean code, many logical IF and WHERE statements were used to distinguish ocean points from land points. These statements consumed substantial computation time and reduced pipelining of operations inside loops. The compiler often was not able to optimize these loops efficiently (especially using automatic loop unrolling) because some of the computations within the IF and WHERE statements were quite complex. These IF and WHERE statements were replaced by defining land/ocean masking arrays, which store the values 1 for ocean points and 0 for land points, and then using these arrays as multiplying factors. For example, the statements

```
WHERE (KMU.NE.0)
VUF = SUF
ELSE
VUF = 0.0
ENDIF
```

were replaced by

```
CALL SHAD(IMT*JMT,1.0,UMASK,1,SUF,1,0.0,VUF,1)
```

where UMASK, VUF, SUF, and KMU are all of size (IMT,JMT), and UMASK was defined after the geometry initialization by

```
DO I=1,IMT*JMT
IF (KMU(I,1).NE.0) THEN
UMASK(I,1) = 1.0
```

Floating point operations ($\times 10^9$)	Time (s)	Rate (Gflops)	Optimization procedures
1904	6779.26	0.281	Original
2305	6046.90	0.381	Mask
2305	4517.81	0.510	Mask + BLAS
2305	3337.32	0.690	Mask + BLAS + compiler options
2305	2858.56	0.807	Full optimization

7.1

TABLE

A 10-day integration with local grid size of 64 × 32 × 20 on 64 processors.

```
        ELSE
          UMASK(I,1) = 0.0
        ENDIF
      ENDDO
```

where KMU is a function of input geometry, corresponding to 0 over land and 1 over ocean.

7.3.6   Computational Performance

Each of the optimization techniques just described results in an incremental improvement, as shown in Table 7.1. When all the changes were applied, a substantial improvement in the computational performance of the ocean code was seen. The addition of the mask arrays increased the number of floating-point operations and also decreased the total runtime. In addition, using the mask arrays introduced code that can be replaced by BLAS calls, for an additional decrease in runtime. The key in using the mask arrays is that we are substituting floating-point operations for conditional instructions in order to increase performance.

A test problem was chosen with a local grid size of 37 × 34 × 60 cells. Timings were run for machine sizes from 1 to 256 processors, corresponding to a global grid of up to 592 × 544 × 60. The ocean code decomposes the grid in blocks in both x and y, and all z data for a given (x,y) is local to one processor. All results shown in this section refer to scaled size problems, where the problem size per processor is fixed and the number of processors is varied.

Figure 7.1 shows the wall clock time per processor per time step as a function of the number of processors, for both the original code and the optimized code. The optimized code running one processor is faster than the original code by a

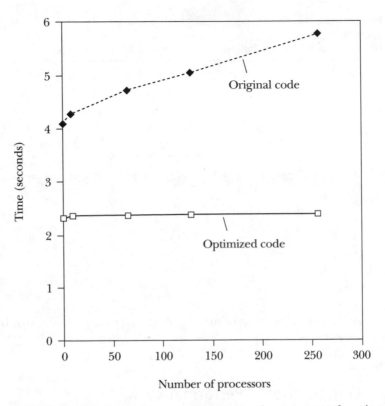

Wall clock time (seconds) per processor per time step as a function of the number of processors for scaled problems.

factor of 1.8. The improvement is more evident when more processors are used, reaching a factor of 2.5 when 256 processors are used.

It is clear from Figure 7.1 that the code's scaling has also been improved. This improvement is depicted explicitly in Figure 7.2, showing the speedup achieved versus the number of processors used in the calculation. For the ideal parallel code, this would correspond to a line with a slope of 1. The optimized code is performing quite well, running 250 times faster than the single-processor code on 256 processors. The original code, however, clearly has scaling problems, as it runs only 182 times faster when 256 processors are used.

Figure 7.3 shows the actual performance achieved in terms of computation rate. The optimized code runs at 3.55 Gflops. It should be pointed out that for many reasons the optimized code performs at only 10 percent of the peak machine speed. One reason is that the ratio of computation to communication is small in these examples. If a larger local grid size was used, this ratio would in-

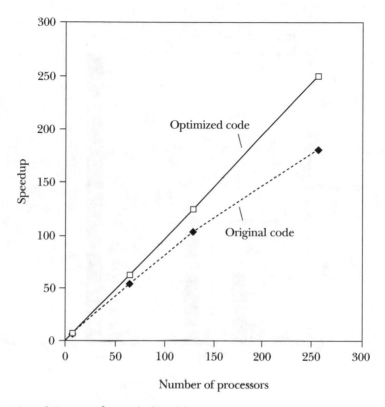

Speedup curve for scaled problems.

crease and the overall performance would also increase. Another reason is poor cache reuse, due to the formulation of the code. It is written in terms of vector-vector routines (replaced by BLAS1-type [7.10] routines), rather than matrix-vector or matrix-matrix routines (which could be replaced by BLAS2-type [7.7] or BLAS3-type [7.8] routines). The overall code formulation doesn't make enough use of the data (each time it is loaded from memory) to achieve very high performance.

7.4   VISUALIZATION ON MPP MACHINES

In this section, we present a new parallel volume-rendering system, ParVox, which is used for visualization of 3D ocean datasets. The ocean model gener-

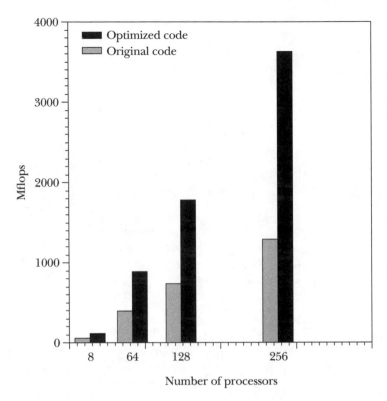

7.3 The ocean code performance rate (Mflops) for scaled problems.

FIGURE

ates very large 3D datasets. For example, a 1/6-degree North Atlantic Ocean model has a dimension of 640 × 624 × 37. Also, there are five model variables: temperature, salinity, and three velocity components. The dataset at one time step is 600 MB. If the model output is saved every three days, a five-year simulation has about 350 GB of data. It becomes impractical and even impossible to visualize such a large volume of data on existing high-end workstations. It is therefore necessary to use parallel computers to visualize and explore such a dataset.

ParVox is designed to serve as either an interactive visualization tool for post-processing or a rendering Application Programming Interface (API) to be linked with application programs. As a distributed visualization system, ParVox provides an X-window-based GUI program for display and viewing control, a parallel input library for reading 4D volume data sets in NetCDF format, a network interface program that interfaces with the GUI running on the remote workstation, and a parallel wavelet image compression library capable of supporting both lossless and lossy compression. ParVox can visualize 3D volume data as a translucent volume with adjustable opacity for each different physical value or as multiple isosurfaces at different thresholds and different opacities. It can also slice through the 3D volume and view only a set of slices in either of the three major orthogonal axes. Moreover, it is capable of animating multiple time-step 3D datasets at any selected viewpoint.

Volume rendering is a very computationally intensive procedure. Forward projection methods, such as splatting [7.12], are best suited for parallel implementation because the voxel splatting can be done in parallel without intervention from other voxels. However, the locally rendered subimages have to be composited globally in the depth order to form the final image. This compositing procedure requires a data redistribution from the object space to the image space, and the main challenge of designing the ParVox parallel splatting algorithm is how to reduce the data redistribution overhead—that is, communication overhead.

The detailed description of the ParVox system and its parallel implementation can be found in [7.20, 7.21]. In this section, a brief summary of the parallel splatting algorithm and a description of how the one-sided communication functions in Cray's SHMEM library are used to optimize the efficiency of the parallel program are provided. ParVox uses a combination of object-space decomposition and image-space decomposition. The input volumes are partitioned into small interleaving blocks distributed into each local processor's memory. Each processor first renders its volume blocks locally by splatting and compositing each voxel to the local accumulation buffer. This results in a correct image for this portion of the volume. This subimage is then composited with other subimages from other processors. The global image compositing is done in parallel by partitioning the image space into small interleaving regions and assigning multiple regions to each of the processors. Communication is required for the compositing processor to obtain the subimage data from the appropriate splatting processors. The rendered subimages will overlap each other in depth as well as in the x and y directions. Final compositing of the subimages then occurs, and the distributed image (among all the processors) is reconstructed to a single image for final display.

The final compositing has to be performed in either front-to-back or back-to-front order; therefore, it cannot begin until all the processors have finished their local splatting and all the subimages have been delivered to the compositing processors. However, the work required at the splatting stage varies over each processor because the time needed to render a piece of an image depends on the exact contents of that piece. We can thus hide some of the communication overhead by overlapping the splatting process with the redistribution of the subimages.

As soon as a processor is finished rendering a block, it sends the individual final compositing regions off to the appropriate preassigned "compositing" processor, and then it proceeds to render the next block. In order to save memory and reduce communication, only the valid pixels in an image region are sent by putting a bounding box around the relevant data. The one-sided communication is accomplished using the Cray SHMEM library with the shmem_put call. However, with this approach, there is a complication if more than one processor tries to send data simultaneously to a given compositing processor. This is remedied by a semaphore mechanism. Each processor maintains a pointer to the memory buffer where the image region data will be put onto the remote compositing processor. The pointer is updated to point to the next available location by a remote processor using an atomic operation. The Cray shmem_swap routine is used to implement this atomic operation. Once the pointer has been updated, the image region can be put to the remote processor's memory because no intrusion is possible by any other processor. This one-sided communication (shmem_put) is very fast on the Cray T3D (up to 120 MB/s). Because it involves no overhead on the other processor, communication can be easily overlapped with computation.

Figure 7.4 shows the speedup curve vs. number of processors for the parallel splatting algorithm on the Cray T3D. The input data is the $640 \times 624 \times 37$ ocean temperature dataset. In this benchmark, four blocks of input volume are assigned to each processor regardless of the total number of processors. The image size is 512×512, and the final image is divided into square regions with five regions per processor. The rendering algorithm scales well from 1 processor to 256 processors. More significant load imbalance is observed in the ocean dataset with a small number of processors due to the fact that the land voxels are grouped together in the dataset, and it is very likely that an entire block may contain no valid data.

7.5   SCIENTIFIC RESULTS

Using the optimized ocean model, we have performed a 40-year integration with 1/6-degree resolution on the 256-processor Cray T3D. Figure 7.5 shows a typical snapshot of the sea surface temperature overlaid by the sea surface height. The ocean surface temperature is represented in color (see color plate 7.5), and

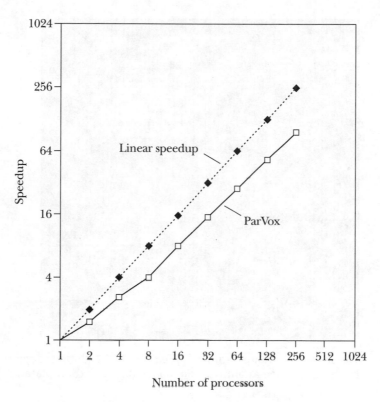

The speedup curve for the parallel rendering algorithm.

shaded relief is used to depict the sea surface height [7.11]. In comparison to the previous eddy-resolving ocean model simulations [7.13, 7.15], this model shows improved Gulf Stream separation off the coast of Cape Hatteras [7.5]. As the horizontal resolution increases, increasingly fine-scale features and intensification of the currents are found with many of the larger-scale features unchanged. These results are quite promising and offer hope that the physical processes responsible for both water mass and eddy formation can be reasonably simulated in models of this class.

In a regional application, we have documented the temporal and spatial evolution of mesoscale eddies in the Caribbean Sea (Figure 7.6). These Caribbean Sea eddies are quite regular, appearing about every 100 days. The eddies progress westward at a speed of near 15 cm/s, growing in amplitude. The 1/6-degree North Atlantic ocean model described earlier is able to reproduce major fea-

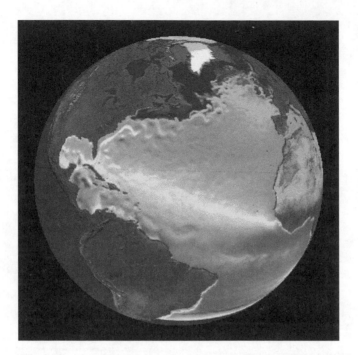

7.5

FIGURE

The sea surface temperature with sea surface height in shaded relief simulated by the 1/6-degree Atlantic Ocean model. (See also color plate 7.5.)

tures of these Caribbean Sea eddies, including their amplitudes, spatial and time scales, and propagation speed, compared with satellite observations. Accurate description and understanding of these eddies are crucial for both coastal monitoring and forecasting, which are of great benefit to regional fishery and oil industries.

7.6   SUMMARY AND FUTURE CHALLENGES

We have developed and used a number of optimization techniques on the Cray T3D to improve the computational performance of the most widely used ocean model. The first step was to use the MPP Apprentice tool available on the Cray T3D to identify performance anomalies and inefficient coding structures. In addition to using compiler options, we have implemented a number of optimization techniques, including manual loop unrolling, rewriting code to equiva-

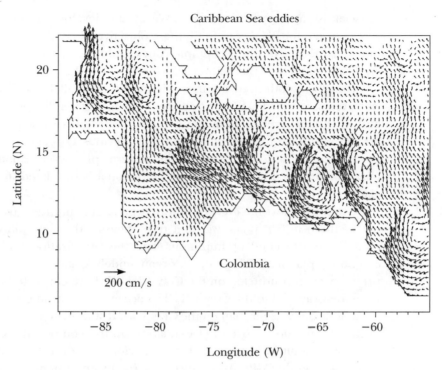

Caribbean Sea eddies

7.6

FIGURE

The surface current vector over the Caribbean Sea simulated by the 1/6-degree
Atlantic Ocean model.

lence multidimensional arrays to 1D arrays, simplifying algebra, reducing the
number of divide operations, using mask arrays to trade slow comparisons
and branches for fast floating-point operations, explicitly rewriting statements in
array notation as loops, and using optimized libraries. It should be pointed out
that not all code changes result in code speedup in all cases. Therefore, it
is very important to use the MPP Apprentice tool to evaluate the performance
impact of each of these optimization procedures. Each optimization procedure provides an incremental improvement. When all of these techniques are
applied, the optimized ocean code is about 2.5 times faster than the original
code.

A parallel volume-rendering system, ParVox, was also developed on the MPP
system for interactive visualization of large time-varying 3D datasets generated
by high-resolution 3D models. The ultimate goal is for ParVox to work in concert
with simulation models as a visualization, data exploration, and debugging tool

for scientists and model developers. We are still developing a number of key features needed for ParVox to fulfill these objectives, including vector and streamline visualization, multiple clipping planes, and function pipelining between the application and the visualization software.

Using the optimized ocean model and the parallel visualization software, we have constructed a 1/6-degree ocean model on the 256-processor Cray T3D and integrated over 40 simulation years. The results show that the solutions are significantly improved compared with previous 1/3- and 1/4-degree model simulations [7.13, 7.15]. Many of the physical processes responsible for both water mass and eddy formation can be reasonably simulated in models of this class.

Given the short life cycle of massively parallel computers, usually on the order of three to five years, we want to emphasize the portability of the ocean model, the associated optimizations, and the visualization tool across several computing platforms. Thus far, our ocean modeling and visualization effort have primarily been conducted on the Cray T3D. We have converted the ocean code from the Cray T3D to the Cray T3E. The ocean code running on the Cray T3E is about four times faster than on the Cray T3D. It should be pointed out that some of the optimization procedures that speed up the code on the Cray T3D don't necessarily result in faster overall code performance on the Cray T3E. On any new machine, the MPP Apprentice tool (or its equivalent) should be used to evaluate the effect of each optimization. Recently, we have also ported the ocean code to the HP SPP-2000 using the MPI communication library. It is expected that the performance on the Cray T3E and HP SPP-2000 can be further improved after implementing some of the optimization techniques described. The current version of ParVox takes advantage of the asynchronous one-sided communication capability in the SHMEM library to overlap communication and computation. Because the newly released version of MPI supports a new set of one-sided communication routines, ParVox can be readily ported to those MPP machines that support this version of MPI.

Despite the recent progress in running high-resolution ocean models, it is still unknown what the minimal resolution is beyond which a further increase of resolution will produce little qualitative improvement on the large-scale circulation. A group at LANL has just accomplished a 10-year integration of a 1/10-degree Atlantic Ocean model on the CM5, and their preliminary results show a further improvement over our 1/6-degree calculation [7.18]. A six-year integration of a 1/12-degree Atlantic Ocean model has been attempted on the Cray T3E [7.1]. Using the new HP SPP-2000, it is possible to construct an even higher-resolution ocean model. It is anticipated that these high-resolution ocean models will collectively reach some convergence on the minimal resolution required for climatic applications [7.9].

ACKNOWLEDGMENTS

The research described in this chapter was performed at the Jet Propulsion Laboratory, California Institute of Technology, under contract to the National Aeronautics and Space Administration (NASA). The Cray T3D used to produce the results in this chapter was provided by the JPL Supercomputing Project. Funding from the JPL Director's Research and Development Fund (DRDF), NASA Office of Mission to Planet Earth's Physical Oceanography program, and NASA High-Performance Computing and Communication (HPCC) program's Earth and Space Science Project (ESS) are acknowledged. The authors wish to thank Rick Smith, Phil Jones, and Bob Malone from LANL for providing the original ocean code; David Shirley from Cray Research, Inc. for doing much of the work on the initial porting of this code to the Cray T3D; Alan Stagg from the U.S. Army CEWES for doing initial timing studies; Chris Ding from NERSC for doing initial optimization work; Tom Clune from Cray Research, Inc. and Martin Lewitt from Hewlett-Packard Company for helping to port the ocean code to the Cray T3E and HP SPP-2000, respectively; Edith Huang of the JPL Supercomputing Project for helping to implement I/O on the Cray T3D; James Tsiao of JPL for the development of the ParVox Graphic User Interface; and Moustafa Chahine, Terry Cole, Dave Curkendall, Robert Ferraro, Lee-Lueng Fu, and Carl Kukkonen of JPL for their institutional support.

References

[7.1]   Bleck, R., S. Dean, M. O'Keefe, and A. Sawdey. 1995. A Comparison of Data-Parallel and Message-Passing Versions of the Miami Isopycnic Coordinate Ocean Model (MICOM). *Parallel Computing*, **21**, 1695–1720.

[7.2]   Brooks, J. P. 1995. *Single PE Optimization Techniques for the CRAY T3D System.* Benchmarking Group, Cray Research, Inc.

[7.3]   Bryan, K. 1969. Numerical Method for the Study of the World Ocean Circulation. *J. Comp. Phy.*, **4**, 1687–1712.

[7.4]   Bryan, F., and W. Holland. 1989. A High Resolution Simulation of the Wind- and Thermohaline-Driven Circulation in the North Atlantic Ocean. In P. Müller and D. Henderson (eds.), *Proceedings of Parameterization of Small-Scale Processes.* Hawaii Institute of Geophysics Special Publication, 99–115.

[7.5]   Chao, Y., A. Gangopadhyay, F. O. Bryan, and W. R. Holland. 1996. Modeling the Gulf Stream System: How Far from Reality? *Geophys. Res. Letts.*, **23**, 3155–3158.

[7.6]   Cox, M. D. *Primitive Equation, 3-Dimensional Model of the Ocean.* 1984. Group Tech. Report 1. GFDL/NOAA, Princeton, NJ.

[7.7]   Dongarra, J. J., J. Du Croz, S. Hammarling, and R. J. Hanson. 1988. Extended Set of FORTRAN Basic Linear Algebra Subprograms. *ACM Trans. Math. Soft.*, **14**, 1–17.

[7.8]   Dongarra, J. J., J. Du Croz, I. S. Duff, and S. Hammarling. 1990. A Set of Level 3 Basic Linear Algebra Subprograms. *ACM Trans. Math. Soft.*, **16**, 1–17.

[7.9]   Drummond, L. A., J. D. Farrara, C. R. Mechoso, J. A. Spahr, Y. Chao, D. S. Katz, J. Z. Lou, and P. Wang. 1997. Parallel Optimization of an Earth System Model (100 GIGAFLOPS and Beyond?). *1997 Society for Computer Simulation (SCS) International Conference*, Atlanta, Georgia, April.

[7.10]   Lawson, C. L., R. J. Hanson, D. Kincaid, and F. T. Krogh. 1979. Basic Linear Algebra Subprograms for FORTRAN Usage. *ACM Trans. Math. Soft.,* **5,** 308–322.

[7.11]   Li, P., W. Duquette, and D. Curkendall. 1996. RIVA—A Versatile Parallel Rendering System for Interactive Scientific Visualization. *IEEE Transactions on Visualization and Computer Graphics,* **2** (3), 186–201.

[7.12]   Li, P., et al. 1997. ParVox—A Parallel Splatting Volume Rendering System for Distributed Visualization. *Proceedings of the 1997 IEEE Parallel Rendering Symposium,* Oct.

[7.13]   McWilliams, J. C. 1996. Modeling the Ocean General Circulation. *Annual Review of Fluid Mechanics,* **28,** 215–248.

[7.14]   Pacanowski, R., R. K. Dixon, and A. Rosati. 1992. *Modular Ocean Model User's Guide.* GFDL Ocean Group Tech. Report 2. GFDL/NOAA, Princeton, NJ.

[7.15]   Semtner, A. J. 1995. Modeling the Ocean General Circulation. *Science,* **269,** 1379–1383.

[7.16]   Semtner, A. J., and R. M. Chervin. 1992. Ocean-General Circulation from a Global Eddy-Resolving Model. *J. Geophys. Research Oceans,* **97,** 5493–5550.

[7.17]   SHMEM. *Application Programmer's Library Reference Manual.* Cray Research, Inc. Publication SR-2165.

[7.18]   Smith, R. 1998. Los Alamos National Laboratory, personal communication.

[7.19]   Smith, R. D., J. K. Dukowicz, and R. C. Malone. 1992. Parallel Ocean General Circulation Modeling. *Physica D,* **60,** 38–61.

[7.20]   Westover, L. 1990. Footprint Evaluation for Volume Rendering. *Computer Graphics* (SIGGRAPH Proceedings), **24** (4), 367–376.

[7.21]   Whitman, S., P. Li, and J. Tsiao. 1996. Volume Rendering of Scientific Data on the T3D. *Proceedings of the CUG 1996 Spring Conference,* March.

8 | Impact of Aircraft on Global Atmospheric Chemistry

Douglas A. Rotman
John R. Tannahill   Lawrence Livermore National Laboratory

Steven L. Baughcum   The Boeing Company

8.1   INTRODUCTION

Atmospheric chemistry and constituent transport are important aspects in the understanding of climate and climate change. Chemical processes influence the distributions of many of the greenhouse gases and the aerosols that determine the radiative forcing on the climate. Many of the greenhouse gases undergo atmospheric chemical and photochemical transformations that alter the natural balance of other important atmospheric constituents. For example, the resulting effects on ozone in both the troposphere and stratosphere are of serious concern [8.11, 8.12, 8.13]. The strong relationship between methane, carbon monoxide, and the hydroxyl radical is also of concern because of the importance of the hydroxyl radical in determining the oxidizing capacity of the atmosphere. Such chemical interactions also influence the time-dependent predictability of global climate change on scales extending from regional to global.

Key elements in atmospheric chemistry models are the boundary conditions and emissions. Carbon dioxide, methane, carbon monoxide, nitrous oxide, chlorofluorocarbons, bromine compounds, sulfur dioxides, and a host of other compounds and aerosols are emitted by human activities such as power generation, chemical production, fire extinguishing, and mining as well as activities such as biomass burning. All these chemical compounds have potential impacts on the environment and climate.

Of these activities, the emission of oxides of nitrogen into the stratosphere by a fleet of supersonic aircraft relates directly to our work. Some of the questions that need to be addressed by chemical-transport modeling include

✦ What are the important chemical processes and reaction channels in the gas, aerosol, and aqueous phases that can influence the distribution of important chemical species? What is their dependence on atmospheric conditions?

✦ What is the potential impact of changing ozone concentrations on climate, and vice versa? What is the effect of changing climatic (or chemical) conditions on the aerosol-initiated stratospheric ozone depletion in the Arctic and Antarctic?

✦ What impact does the close coupling between tropospheric CH_4, CO, OH, NO_x, and O_3 have on projections of climate change, and how might the distributions of these species change? What is the role of anthropogenic emissions on such effects?

✦ How might the exchange of water vapor and other gases between the troposphere and stratosphere change in a changing climate? What effect do changes in stratospheric water vapor have on stratospheric cloud occurrences?

Of key importance is the possibility of the depletion of stratospheric ozone caused by possible fleets of supersonic aircraft. The ozone abundance in the stratosphere is important for three primary reasons. First, ozone is one of the most important species in the atmosphere regulating the amount of ultraviolet radiation reaching the Earth's surface. As stratospheric ozone is depleted, more and more radiation reaches the surface, and it is believed this increases the possibility of additional cases of skin cancer in humans. Second, too much ultraviolet radiation reaching the Earth's oceans can have negative impacts on the production of oceanic plankton, which plays a key role in the marine food chains. And third, ozone is one of many greenhouse gases that play a role in the overall radiative balance of the atmosphere. Human alterations in the radiative balance may affect climate.

8.2   INDUSTRIAL CONSIDERATIONS

Supersonic aircraft would dramatically shorten the flight times of intercontinental air traffic if they could be shown to be economically and environmentally feasible. For example, flight times for long over-water flights could be reduced by a factor of 2 to 3. Supersonic aircraft would fly in the stratosphere (e.g., flight altitudes of 18 to 20 km for a Mach 2.4 aircraft). These flight altitudes are near the maximum of stratospheric ozone concentrations and concerns have been raised that emissions of oxides of nitrogen and water vapor from supersonic aircraft could destroy ozone.

Since a ground rule for the development of a supersonic commercial transport is that it must not have any significant ozone impact, it is important to be able to accurately assess the effect of projected future fleets. These assessments could then help define the technical requirements for such aircraft (e.g., the required NO_x emission levels and thus combustor requirements). Experiments to analyze this impact are difficult to envision because the aircraft have not even been designed. Thus, numerical atmospheric chemistry models will play a key role in this analysis. However, these numerical models are extremely large and require huge amounts of computer time to complete meaningful simulations.

8.3 PROJECT OBJECTIVES AND APPLICATION CODE

The objective of this project is to improve the understanding of the atmospheric chemical and climatic impacts, particularly on ozone in the troposphere and stratosphere, that may occur from future projected fleets of supersonic aircraft. This effort involves a close collaboration between the Lawrence Livermore National Laboratory (LLNL) and The Boeing Company. The primary tool used in these atmospheric chemistry-transport studies will be the LLNL 3D Integrated Massively Parallel Atmospheric Chemical-Transport (IMPACT) model of the troposphere and stratosphere. A significant fraction of this project will be aimed at further development, testing, and validation of this model on the Cray T3D parallel computer to meet the needs of aircraft assessment plus using the model to evaluate aircraft effects on ozone and climate.

The LLNL 3D chemical-transport model, IMPACT, was designed and implemented based largely on the scientific need for coupled atmospheric chemistry/ global climate simulations [8.8]. When coupled, IMPACT will obtain its meteorological data directly from the concurrently running Global Climate Model (GCM). However, IMPACT is also capable of offline (uncoupled) calculations using data-assimilated meteorological fields (winds, temperature, etc.) such as those from the Data Assimilation Program at NASA-Goddard. Using assimilated data provides the advantage of allowing us to treat event-specific chemical phenomena as a technique for validating the processes treated in the model. IMPACT is based on an operator-splitting method in which each of the primary operators (advection, diffusion, convection, photolysis, and chemistry) is dealt with in an independent fashion. Advection in all three dimensions is currently done using a variable-order multidimensional flux form of the semi-Lagrangian method, an upstream-biased monotonic grid point scheme [8.6]. The upstream nature of this method reduces phase errors to a minimum, and the monotonicity control eliminates the need for a filling algorithm and the severe problems that would arise with negative values of chemical species concentrations. This scheme also avoids the strict Courant stability problem at the poles, thus allowing large time steps to be used, resulting in a highly efficient advection operation. Diffusion is currently included using a constant coefficient multiplied by the spatial second derivative of the chemical species distribution. Species transport resulting from convective motion is implemented using the scheme of Lin (private communication), which for infinitely thin layers is essentially the apparent momentum transport of clouds [8.10].

Photolysis implementation allows simulations using either complete diurnal calculations or calculating diurnally averaged coefficients. The photolytic loss rate constants are calculated by integrating the product of absorption coefficient, quantum yield, and solar flux over wavelength, using temperature and pressure dependence where appropriate and available. A two-stream multiple-layer UV-visible model uses 126 wavelength bins to capture the spectral detail needed for photodissociation calculations. The scattering of energy from the direct solar beam is treated using the delta-Eddington algorithm [8.5], while the scattering of diffuse radiation is modeled using the Sagan-Pollack algorithm [8.9]. Both algorithms allow inclusion of the bulk optical properties of clouds and aerosols.

Chemistry in IMPACT is solved with a sparse-matrix, vectorized Gear code, SMVGEAR II [8.3]. The original SMVGEAR code [8.2, 8.4] was derived from Gear's predictor/corrector, backward-differentiation code [8.1]. Gear's original code was extremely accurate but inefficient because it required decomposition and backsubstitution over a full matrix of partial derivatives many times. SMVGEAR gave exactly the same results as Gear's original code but was about 120 times faster when both codes were run on a Cray C-90. The speedup in SMVGEAR was obtained from the implementation of sparse-matrix and vectorization techniques. The major sparse-matrix technique was to reorder the matrix of partial derivatives and then to eliminate, in advance, all multiplies by zero that occurred during subsequent matrix decomposition and backsubstitution.

The sparse-matrix techniques accounted for about half the speedup; the other half resulted from vectorization. To vectorize, the grid domain was divided into blocks of grid cells, and the grid-cell loop was made the inner loop throughout the code. In retrospect, this method was found to be useful for scalar and parallel machines as well as for vector machines. For scalar machines, the vectorized version of the code was useful since it minimized the number of outer-loop array references. The vectorized version was also useful for parallel computing because several blocks of 500 grid cells could be placed directly on each individual scalar node, causing array references to be minimized.

However, a disadvantage of the original SMVGEAR code was that it required the same number of iterations for each grid cell in a block; thus, iterations had to continue until the cell with the stiffest equations converged. To mitigate this problem, a method was developed to reorder grid cells each time interval by stiffness so that the stiffest cells could be solved together in the same blocks. The modified SMVGEAR code is known as SMVGEAR II.

How does the above application address the problem? The atmospheric impacts of supersonic aircraft have been under investigation for many years. In the past, much of this work has been accomplished through the use of a 2D (latitude and altitude) model (zonal-averaged). Although adequate for initial studies, the amount and level of uncertainties related to the zonal-averaged fields required complete global 3D models to be used for analysis and assessments. For example, the impact of aircraft is most clearly seen in the ozone depletion caused by the emission of oxides of nitrogen—that is, NO_x emissions. These emissions of nitrogen obviously occur only where the aircraft fly, and these so-called flight corridors are very much 3D profiles; that is, the emissions are not zonally averaged. Furthermore, the exchange of mass between the troposphere and stratosphere is highly unknown, nonzonal, and important to the analysis of emission deposition and chemical effects because the aircraft fly close to this dividing area, called the "tropopause."

Our general approach is to make use of the computing power of the Cray T3D by implementing our parallelized 3D chemical-transport model and adding the needed physics to further our understanding and analysis of the impacts of supersonic aircraft on the atmosphere.

8.4   COMPUTATIONAL CONSIDERATIONS

This section addresses the need for MPP simulations and the relevant programming and algorithmic issues.

8.4.1   Why Use an MPP?

The very formidable nature and complexity of atmospheric chemistry/transport issues require that model development carefully consider the treatment of chemical and physical processes and the numerical solution techniques used within the model. For example, the mathematical stiffness inherent in atmospheric chemical processes requires integration of the important chemistry equations across time scales ranging from seconds to years. This forces either implementing a complete stiff chemistry solver or applying the family approach (which assumes chemical equilibrium between some chemical species to reduce the computational requirements while conserving mass) to eliminate the stiffness. To maintain maximum accuracy, we have chosen to implement a complete stiff solver. While accurate, these techniques require many calculations and thus large amounts of computer time. The solution of the photolysis package requires the integration of cross sections of chemical species and the flux of solar radiation. Species interact with solar radiation in specific and sometimes small increments of the solar spectrum; thus, for complete and accurate photolysis coefficients, fine resolution in the solar frequency spectrum should be used. Increasing this resolution greatly increases the computational intensity of the simulation. The numerical treatment of constituent transport also requires careful consideration because of the strong gradients inherent in atmospheric dynamics, requiring relatively fine geographic resolution of the meteorological fields. Even though, as we shall see, transport does not require large amounts of computational time, this geographic resolution has implications for the memory usage of the model.

Resolutions for our simulations have been approximately 2 degrees in the latitude coordinate and 2.5 degrees in the longitude coordinate (or 4 degrees by 5 degrees), with 25 to 46 levels in the vertical (approximately from ground to 60 km). This yields approximately 600,000 grid boxes. Our stratospheric mechanism includes approximately 50 chemical species, which, in total, requires about 600-800 Mwords of memory. This typically stresses most supercomputer memory limits. In addition, to provide accurate meteorological data, these data are updated throughout the simulation. Our simulations update the data every 6 hours, which means for a year-long run (or multiyear runs where we simply recycle the year's worth of meteorological data), we must input extremely large amounts of data. In our simulations, the input data is typically between 5 and 50 GB.

Perhaps the strongest reason for MPP applications is the runtime of the simulations. Because the transport lifetimes of species in the stratosphere are fairly long, simulations typically must be run for about 10 years of modeled time. Given that on even the largest vector supercomputers, the computational time is on the order of 250 hours per simulated year, a single 10-year run takes nearly 3 months to complete. Multiply that by at least 5 if using a fast workstation. In addition, full parametric analyses of the aircraft impact will require multiple 10-year runs, suggesting that use of even large vector supercomputers would be quite difficult at best.

8.4.2   Programming Considerations

We have developed a parallelized Climate System Modeling Framework (CSMF) for high-performance computing systems. The CSMF is designed to schedule and couple multiple physics packages in a flexible and portable manner [8.7]. Some of the major packages under the control of our framework and currently running on parallel platforms include

+ LLNL/UCLA atmospheric general circulation model
+ LLNL version of the GFDL Modular Ocean Model
+ LLNL version of the Oberhuber dynamic/thermodynamic sea-ice model
+ LLNL atmospheric chemistry transport model
+ LLNL soil-plant-atmosphere model
+ LLNL ocean biogeochemistry model

IMPACT represents the LLNL atmospheric chemisty model in this package and is integrally coupled with all aspects of the CSMF.

Task decomposition is supported in the CSMF, which has the ability to process major physics packages either concurrently or sequentially on various groups of processors within the MPP platform. Each package is further decomposed using domain decomposition, in which the various subdomain solutions for that package are processed concurrently. Processors are assigned to packages and subdomains in a deterministic manner, and variables local to a given package/subdomain are stored in the memory of the assigned processor. Data, including border zone information, are transmitted between computational processes in the form of messages. Packages are scheduled according to user-specified coupling intervals. Once the processors having responsibility for that package possess the data necessary for advancement, that package is advanced from its present time to the time at which new information is required from one of the other packages.

Within each package, a 2D latitude/longitude domain decomposition is implemented, whereby each subdomain consists of a number of contiguous columns having full vertical extent (relative to that package). The number of meshpoints per subdomain may be nonuniform, under the constraint that the decomposition be logically rectangular. The choice to decompose in only two dimensions is based on the fact that column processes (e.g., radiation transport and convection) strongly couple the elements within the column and do not naturally parallelize along the column. Each package may have its own domain decomposition.

Because of the wide spectrum of computer architectures, which typically have a lifetime of just a few years, it is of paramount importance to maintain a portable source code. For this reason, we have developed this model with close adherence to standard Fortran 77. We have encountered two major issues that affect portability: message passing and dynamic memory management. To address these issues, LLNL has written and incorporated into the CSMF the Macro Interface for Communication and Allocation (MICA), which is a set of macros that make use of the M4 and CPP preprocessors. MICA was recently enhanced to support the shared memory communications library (SHMEM) on the Cray-T3D. Through the use of MICA, our climate and chemistry models run on virtually all leading-edge massively parallel computers, including the Cray T3D, IBM SP2, Intel Paragon, Meiko CS2, and TMC CM5. The models also run on clusters of workstations (IBM, SUN, DEC, SGI) under PVM, MPI, and P4, as well as on the Cray-C90. Although portability is quite important, it is equally important to exploit each architecture as much as possible. Toward that end, we utilize conditional compilation to allow inclusion of optimization constructs particular to given architectures.

8.4.3   Algorithm Considerations

As discussed previously, the model is based on 2D domain decomposition. This decomposition was especially advantageous for atmospheric chemistry simulations because the majority of the computational time is used in the chemistry and photolysis packages. In the case of the chemistry, the calculation is basically a local calculation using local parameters. For photolysis, it is strictly a column-style calculation, and because with a 2D domain decomposition all vertical zones are within a processor, this also required no extra communications. Hence, for these operators, overall performance depends primarily on the per-node performance. Especially given our choice of a SMVGEAR II–based stiff chemistry solution and a highly resolved solar spectrum for photolysis, performance on parallel machines greatly depends on maximizing per-node computational speeds.

Transport relies on per-node performance when using few processors, but as the number of processors increases, the overall performance depends much more on communications and the effiency of message passing. The overriding calculation within the stratospheric transport section is the advection operator.

IMPACT uses a second-order method, which requires two zones on each side of the zone in question to establish information needed to transport species into and out of a grid zone. The algorithm used has a unique attribute near the poles. In the polar region, due to the spherical nature of the Earth, the grids get smaller and smaller, causing tighter and tighter Courant conditions. Hence, near the equator one could accurately advect with a certain time step, but the polar regions force a reduction in time step by as much as a factor of 5. There are various ways to fix this. In past algorithms, we simply subcycled at a smaller time step near the polar regions. However, this is difficult to efficiently implement under the 2D domain decomposition paradigm. The current algorithm automatically switches to a flux form of the semi-Lagrangian method wherever the Courant number goes beyond 1. This flux-form algorithm permits computation at the maximum time step allowed throughout the domain. The penalty for this added capability is the possibility of needing more than two zones of information on each side of the grid zone in question. Near the poles, the Courant number can be as high as 4 and requires information from four zones surrounding the zone in question. All of this adds up to more and more communications. In most cases, the ability to compute at the larger time step more than outweighs the price of added communications, but this may depend on the speed of communications compared to the CPU performance of the computer.

8.5 COMPUTATIONAL RESULTS

This section addresses the code performance on various machines. Numerical techniques with other applications are also discussed.

8.5.1 Performance

Figure 8.1 shows the performance of IMPACT on a Cray T3D and T3E, an IBM SP2, and a Cray C90 (on a single node), using a 4-degree (latitude) by 5-degree (longitude) grid with 25 vertical levels and 50 chemical species. The horizontal line represents the performance using a single processor of the Cray-C90. As the curves suggest, as the number of processors increases, the scalability degrades, although only slightly. Many models suffer from this because of increased overhead in sending messages. In our model, we see relatively little degradation because the model's CPU time is focused in submodels that are local or column in nature. For this resolution, about 80 percent of the CPU time is spent in column

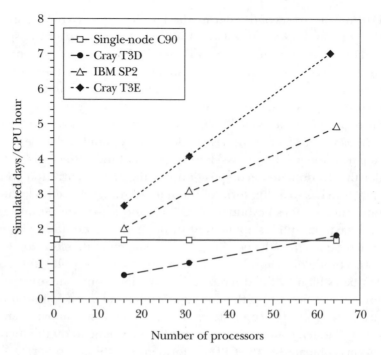

8.1

FIGURE
Speedup curve for the impact chemistry model on four different computing platforms showing increasing simulation capability with increasing processor use.

or local photochemistry-related submodels, while 20 percent is taken in the communication-dependent transport submodels. As mentioned, our model allows larger time steps by moving to a flux-form semi-Lagrangian algorithm near the poles. Information required for the advection scheme from neighboring domains is defined in border zones within the processor. Given that the scheme is second order, only two zones on each domain edge are required. However, near the poles, the Courant condition can become larger than 1, and, at that point, more than two zones are required on the upstream side. Our model does not have the capability of having variable numbers of border zones, so we allow the maximum number of zones everywhere. So far, we have found that four zones are sufficient. Unfortunately, when running at a resolution of 4 degrees by 5 degrees, there can be more border zones than computational zones. While the CPU needs at each point are large, as you increase the number of processors, there comes a point where the communications required for border zone updates increase and can degrade scalability. One solution is to increase the load on each processor. This may—when the resolution, complexity of the chemistry, and amount of physics are increased (which will increase the computational load on a processor)—both increase the quality of the simulation and make more efficient use of the computational platform.

In our development, we have stressed portability more than optimal performance. This is because we have found that our throughput increases more by being able to jump to the newest machine versus optimizing on a certain machine and staying with it for a longer time. Based on one short optimization effort, we estimate that we could get possibly 25 percent faster calculations with more intense optimization. We gladly accept this penalty for the increased portability. Even then, our current model performs quite well. On a single node of a C90, we require approximately 220 hours per simulated year and average approximately 350–400 Mflops. The same run on 64 nodes on an T3D requires 205 hours, on an IBM SP2 about 75 hours, and on a Cray T3E about 58 hours. This provides a very nice speed improvement over the single-node C90 and allows multiyear simulations (i.e., the wall clock time is drastically reduced). However, at 1.5 Gflops with 64 nodes of the T3E, we are averaging only 25 Mflops per node. This clearly leaves room for improvement.

8.5.2   Subsidiary Technology

Although IMPACT is focused on atmospheric chemistry problems, various aspects of IMPACT are useful in a more general way. Of particular note is the SMVGEAR II chemistry package. Developed by Jacobson for atmospheric chemistry, it is in fact a general, coupled stiff ODE solution technique. The technique is not dependent on the source of the chemical mechanism or how the coefficients are obtained. It simply takes in the Ordinary Differential Equations (ODEs) and integrates forward in time based on the methods of Gear. This technique can be used in a host of problems where stiff ODEs must be integrated.

8.6   INDUSTRIAL RESULTS

Complete chemistry assessments are currently ongoing. However, in an effort to provide a sensitivity study of emission scenarios, we have carried out a series of tracer studies using soot emissions as a proxy for emission impacts. These tracer runs were done to identify how supersonic aircraft emissions would be dispersed in the atmosphere as a function of latitude, longitude, and altitude, using projections of where and how such fleets of aircraft might operate.

A near-term effort is evaluating the current chemistry model against observed data to establish its capabilities for producing meaningful distributions of species. This is essential for determining whether simulations are of high-enough quality for industry to use to make decisions regarding future aircraft efforts. A long-term vision would be the coupling of this chemistry model to a climate model to understand whether aircraft can impact the radiative balance of the atmosphere to a point where climate may be altered or, conversely, to evaluate the impact of aircraft on ozone in an altered climate.

8.7   SUMMARY

Until now, the computational power did not exist to attempt full 3D chemistry simulations and aircraft analysis. Advancing hardware capabilities, highlighted by massively parallel computers, now provide that possibility. 3D chemistry models are well suited for parallel computers because of the models' large CPU and memory requirements compared to communication needs. Overall performance of our chemistry model will partly depend on continued increases in communications bandwidths but more so on increasing the per-node performance of computer platforms.

References

[8.1] Gear, C. W. 1971. *Numerical Initial Value Problems in Ordinary Differential Equations.* Englewood Cliffs, NJ: Prentice-Hall.

[8.2] Jacobson, M. Z. 1994. *Developing, Coupling, and Applying a Gas, Aerosol, Transport, and Radiation Model to Study Urban and Regional Air Pollution.* Ph.D. Thesis, University of California, Los Angeles, Department of Atmospheric Sciences.

[8.3] Jacobson, M. Z. 1995. Computation of Global Photochemistry with SMVGEAR II. *Atmos. Environ., 29A,* 2541–2546.

[8.4] Jacobson, M. Z., and R. P. Turco. 1994. SMVGEAR: A Sparse-Matrix, Vectorized Gear Code for Atmospheric Models. *Atmos. Environ., 28A,* 273–284.

[8.5] Joseph, J. H., W. J. Wiscombe, and J. A. Weinman. 1976. The Delta-Eddington Approximation for Radiative Flux Transfer. *J. Atmos. Sci., 33,* 2452–2459.

[8.6] Lin, S. J., and R. B. Rood. 1996. A Fast Flux Form Semi-Lagrangian Transport Scheme on the Sphere. *Mon. Wea. Rev., 124,* 2046–2070.

[8.7] Mirin, A. A, J. J. Ambrosiano, J. H. Bolstad, A. J. Bourgeois, J. C. Brown, B. Chan, W. P. Dannevik, P. B. Duffy, P. G. Eltgroth, C. Matarazzo, and M. F. Wehner. 1994. Climate System Modeling using a Domain and Task Decomposition Message-Passing Approach. *Comput. Phys. Commun., 84,* 278.

[8.8] Rotman, D. A., D. J. Wuebbles, and J. E. Penner. 1993. Atmospheric Chemistry Using Massively Parallel Computers. *1994 AMS Fifth Annual Symposium on Global Change Studies.* Jan.

[8.9] Sagan, C., and J. B. Pollack. 1967. An Isotropic Nonconservative Scattering and the Clouds of Venus. *J. Geophys. Res., 72,* 469–477.

[8.10] Schneider, E. K., and R. S. Lindzen. 1976. A Discussion of the Parameterization of Momentum Exchange by Cumulus Convection. *J. Geophys. Res., 81,* 3158–3161.

[8.11]   World Meteorological Organization. 1989. *Scientific Assessment of Stratospheric Ozone, 1989.* Global Ozone Research and Monitoring Project Report 20, Geneva.

[8.12]   World Meteorological Organization. 1991. *Scientific Assessment of Ozone Depletion, 1991.* Global Ozone Research and Monitoring Project Report 25, Geneva.

[8.13]   World Meteorological Organization. 1994. *Scientific Assessment of Ozone Depletion, 1994.* Global Ozone Research and Monitoring Project Report 37, Geneva.

9

CHAPTER

Petroleum Reservoir Management

Michael DeLong
Allyson Gajraj
Wayne Joubert
Olaf Lubeck
James Sanderson   Los Alamos National Laboratory

Robert E. Stephenson
Gautam S. Shiralkar   Amoco

Bart van Bloemen Waanders   SGI/Cray Research

9.1   INTRODUCTION

In 1994 the Parallel Architectures Team of Los Alamos National Laboratory
(LANL) entered into a cooperative research and development agreement
(CRADA) with Amoco Production Company and Cray Research Inc. to develop a
commercial-quality parallel oil reservoir simulation code. The project was motivated by the oil industry's need to perform field simulations of problems consisting of tens of millions of grid cells and thousands of wells, simulations larger
than any ever performed before. The resulting parallel reservoir simulation software, known as Falcon, is the first-ever commercial-quality parallel oil reservoir
simulation code [9.16]. This code is being made available to the oil industry
through a third-party independent software vendor. The Falcon project has been
a collaborative effort combining the reservoir modeling and simulation expertise of Amoco, the parallel programming and linear solver experience of LANL,
and the high-performance computing abilities and resources of SGI/Cray.

The purpose of this chapter is to present some of the technical challenges
involved with developing the Falcon code. We discuss basic features of the code,
parallel programming and software management issues, the parallel linear solv-

ers used, and performance results, including results of a major field study performed by Amoco using Falcon.

9.2   THE NEED FOR PARALLEL SIMULATIONS

Simulations that predict the flow of oil and gas in underground reservoirs are used by all major oil and gas companies to determine the best recovery strategies. Reservoir simulation is relied upon heavily by these companies for such purposes as assessing potential yield from oil and gas fields, optimizing pumping schedules, making leasing decisions for properties, and planning facilities at production sites. The accuracy of these oil production estimates can be economically substantial—an inaccuracy of a few percentages in a yield prediction can mean tens or hundreds of millions of dollars in lost oil and gas revenue.

World oil production is a $500-billion-per-year business. Over half of the world's oil is produced by large oil fields that cannot be accurately modeled in their entirety by conventional simulation technologies. Typical reservoir simulations run on single-processor computers and use grids of up to 100,000 to 200,000 grid cells. However, to model large fields by such methods, it is necessary either to model a portion of the field at a time or to model the field with a grid that is too coarse to provide accurate predictions. Either of these techniques results in a loss of accuracy in the modeling process.

Accurate modeling of very large fields requires the use of millions or tens of millions of grid cells and, in some cases, hundreds or thousands of wells. Conventional reservoir simulation codes cannot handle problems of this scope because such codes are designed for single-processor computers or shared-memory platforms with small numbers of processors, whereas the huge memory requirements for very large problems can be addressed efficiently only by large distributed-memory computers, which provide much larger memories and much higher aggregate memory bandwidth. Furthermore, even if such large problems could be run on workstation-class computers, the turnaround time for a simulation would be prohibitive. For example, a workstation that could run a 100,000 grid-cell calculation in two hours would require over a week to perform a single 10 million grid-cell calculation of a similar type, even if enough memory were available. Careful reservoir studies typically require many such runs; thus, such runtimes are unacceptable for effective studies.

High-end computing technologies are also desirable to obtain estimates of uncertainties in reservoir predictions. Rock properties such as porosity and permeability of a field are typically known only for a small number of locations in the field—for example, well locations. To obtain rock properties on a fine grid for use in an oil flow simulation, geostatistical techniques such as kriging and sequential Gaussian simulation are used to generate multiple statistically varying but equiprobable estimates of these unknown values. Multiple simulation runs using these different realizations give an estimate of the "error bars" or uncertainties in yield predictions, resulting in the opportunity for better economic decision-making for the field. To perform large numbers of runs on large fields, the speed of each simulation must be reduced substantially. This can only be done by making use of today's high-end parallel computers.

9.3   BASIC FEATURES OF THE FALCON SIMULATOR

The Falcon simulator is able to address these large-scale simulation needs by harnessing the power of modern, massively parallel computers. Falcon is based on the Young/Stephenson compositional reservoir simulation model as embodied in Amoco's earlier GCOMP simulator, a proprietary reservoir simulation code developed by Amoco in the 1980s for serial and vector processors [9.1, 9.22].

The basic approach of Falcon is to solve the partial differential equations governing the underground flow of hydrocarbon fluids and water within porous rock. The fundamental laws that underlie this process are the conservation of mass for each component species used to characterize the fluids and the momentum equations, generally expressed as a generalization of Darcy's law to multiphase flow. Darcy's law states that the volumetric flux of a fluid in a porous medium is proportional to the pressure gradient within the fluid and to the rock permeability and inversely proportional to the fluid viscosity. For multiple phases flowing in a porous medium, the permeability is multiplied by a factor, called the relative permeability, which reflects the fact that the fluids interfere with each other as they flow. For a given pair of fluids, the relative permeability of each fluid is a function of fluid saturations, which are the local volume fractions they occupy. Additional equations are needed to characterize the phase behavior and properties (such as density and viscosity) of the fluids. In the compositional option, the phase behavior is characterized by means of a thermodynamic equation of state and can depend strongly on fluid compositions, whereas in the black-oil option, phase behavior and properties are largely dependent on pressure. The resulting system of coupled equations is highly nonlinear in general and of mixed parabolic-hyperbolic type, and needs to be solved numerically.

Some of the chief features of the Falcon code are as follows:

✦ It currently simulates fields using black-oil, dry gas, and gas-water models; furthermore, fully compositional capabilities are also available. The code performs both implicit pressure, explicit saturation (IMPES) and fully implicit simulations. The code employs a time-stepping algorithm for which a Newton process is used at each time step to solve the nonlinear porous media flow equations, which in turn requires a sparse linear solve at each Newton step.

✦ The current version supports topologically rectangular 1D to 3D grids with 7-point finite differencing. A future version will support alternative stencils, improved gridding at faults, and general unstructured gridding capabilities.

✦ The code has capabilities for multiple rock types and rock compressibilities, vertical and deviated wells, well rate constraints, and restart capabilities.

✦ The code can be run either under High-Performance Fortran (HPF) data-parallel [9.12] or distributed Fortran 90 Single Procedure Multiple Data (SPMD) message-passing [9.5] language environments due to a dual-model programming paradigm used to develop the code.

✦ The code is fully scalable and has been run thus far on up to 512 processors. It runs on Cray Research's T3D and T3E, SGI's Power Challenge and Origin 2000, Thinking Machines' CM5, and IBM's SP2. It also runs on single-processor computers such as PCs and IBM's RS6000. The software architecture of Falcon allows the code to be ported to other platforms as well.

✦ It has run simulations on fields of up to 16.5 million grid blocks. Falcon was also used to perform a major field study, the largest geostatistical reservoir study ever conducted within Amoco, using 50 realizations, each with 2.3 million grid cells and 1039 wells.

9.4   PARALLEL PROGRAMMING MODEL AND IMPLEMENTATION

The development of a commercial production-quality parallel code presents a variety of challenges that are not always present in the development of more research-oriented codes. In addition to having efficient parallel performance, including single-node performance as well as multinode scalability, the code must be well designed and maintainable into the future. The code is expected to have a life span measured in years and will be developed and maintained by a variety of personnel who must be able to grasp the design of the code quickly and easily. The code must also be based on language and software library standards that are likely to persist for the foreseeable future. Achieving all these goals is difficult, especially in the area of production-quality parallel codes, for which industry experience thus far is relatively immature.

The Falcon code was initially developed in Connection Machine (CM) Fortran as a full rewrite of the earlier serial/vector proprietary Amoco simulator code GCOMP. The base language of the Falcon code is Fortran 90, with CM Fortran and HPF layout directives stored in to include files to facilitate executing the code in those environments. The source code for Falcon is maintained with C preprocessor directives, which make it possible to generate either single-processor Fortran 90 code, HPF code, or node Fortran 90 with message passing. Using this approach, most of the code is kept free of machine-dependent constructs. The message-passing layer of the code containing point-to-point messaging, global operations, and so on is kept isolated in a single source file that can be easily changed to port to other environments—for example, PVM, MPI, and so on [9.4, 9.5].

For the purposes of initial code development, maintenance, and rapid prototyping, the relative simplicity of HPF is key. However, message passing allows greater user control of the hardware and the implementation of more intricate algorithms—complex linear solver strategies for example. To balance between these two extremes and to address the full range of target architectures, the development process for new code features begins with an HPF development that is then "MIMD-ized" to run also in message-passing environments. That is, into the HPF code are inserted message-passing calls and other modifications in order to convert the code to a MIMD message-passing code.

For certain compute-intensive parts of the code, such as the linear solver and the matrix coefficient generation, the programming model is locally violated by the inclusion of highly optimized machine-specific code kept alongside the generic code. This permits flexibility in optimizing code "hot spots" while maintaining a more-generic simple version of the code intact.

A number of specific issues had to be addressed to parallelize the code:

✦ The 3D rectangular grid was decomposed in a standard fashion across processors. In both the HPF and message-passing versions, the vertical z-axis was kept on-processor. This choice facilitated the efficient treatment of vertical wells and allowed efficient implementation of z-line relaxation and other techniques for the linear solver, while making little difference compared to full 3D decompositions in terms of surface/volume ratios for interprocessor communication for computer architectures of interest.

✦ For message-passing versions, wells and well perforations were stored on the processor that owns the subgrid where the well or perforation in question was physically located. Perforations for horizontal and deviated wells were stored on multiple processors accordingly. For HPF versions of the code, well and perforation arrays have no imposed locality with respect to the grid. Although technically such layouts might result in load imbalances or excessive communication, our experience has been that the impact of the wells on the total runtime of the code has been minimal, even for very large numbers of wells, and thus these techniques are fully adequate.

✦ Inputs and outputs were all channeled through processor zero for message-passing versions. Data input and initialization typically take up only a very small fraction of the runtime, even when large input datasets are required. This is aided in part by an option for inputting data in the form of binary files, which significantly improves performance compared to ASCII input. Output also requires a small fraction of the runtime, although we expect that the extraction of large amounts of data frequently from the simulation would increase the burden on the output routines.

9.5   IMPES LINEAR SOLVER

Typically, the most expensive part of reservoir simulations is the solution of linear systems, comprising up to 50 to 70 percent or more of the total runtime. Because of this, the efficiency of the linear solver merits careful consideration.

The matrices arising from IMPES simulations corresponding to the pressure equations are typically well behaved, exhibiting favorable near-symmetry and diagonal-dominance properties. In this case, robustness is not usually an issue, and efficient parallelism is the chief concern for the linear solver. Our primary technique for solving such systems is a z-line red/black line successive overrelaxation method (SOR) strategy [9.8]. The main kernels for this algorithm are a 5-point sparse matrix-vector product, implementable by elementwise vector multiplication updates and grid face communications, multiple on-processor tridiagonal solves, global dot products, and simple vector updates such as vector-scalar multiplies and vector adds. This algorithm is not only adequately robust for IMPES problems but also straightforwardly amenable to parallelization.

The chief development platform for the message-passing version of Falcon was the Cray T3D. Parallelization and optimization of code for this platform addressed issues of relevance to most other massively parallel platforms, such as efficient cache utilization and optimization of the communications. The Falcon code has options to use three different implementations of red/black line SOR. The first version is a simple modification of the original HPF version requiring the insertion of small amounts of code to perform subgrid face communications and global sums. This version of the code, however, runs at only about 1–3

Subgrid size	Processor grid	Mflop rate/PE
8 × 8 × 64	1 × 2 × 1	12.194
8 × 8 × 64	2 × 2 × 1	10.781
8 × 8 × 64	2 × 4 × 1	9.716
8 × 8 × 64	4 × 4 × 1	8.747
8 × 8 × 64	4 × 8 × 1	8.694
8 × 8 × 64	8 × 8 × 1	8.674
16 × 16 × 64	1 × 2 × 1	15.314
16 × 16 × 64	2 × 2 × 1	14.064
16 × 16 × 64	2 × 4 × 1	13.138
16 × 16 × 64	4 × 4 × 1	12.211
16 × 16 × 64	4 × 8 × 1	12.145
16 × 16 × 64	8 × 8 × 1	12.113
32 × 32 × 64	1 × 2 × 1	17.265
32 × 32 × 64	2 × 2 × 1	16.466
32 × 32 × 64	2 × 4 × 1	15.837
32 × 32 × 64	4 × 4 × 1	15.138
32 × 32 × 64	4 × 8 × 1	15.042
32 × 32 × 64	8 × 8 × 1	15.016
65 × 65 × 64	1 × 2 × 1	16.268
65 × 65 × 64	2 × 2 × 1	15.965
65 × 65 × 64	2 × 4 × 1	15.689
65 × 65 × 64	4 × 4 × 1	15.378
65 × 65 × 64	4 × 8 × 1	15.322
65 × 65 × 64	8 × 8 × 1	15.271

9.1   Mflop rates per processor for optimized red/black line SOR solver.

TABLE

Mflops/processor on the T3D. A more efficient version of the code was obtained by separating the red and black arrays, which enabled improved cache use due to stride-1 arithmetic.

A third version of the code was obtained by replacing PVM calls with calls to Cray's proprietary SHMEM put/get library to perform faster interprocessor communications and by using assembly-coded library routines (e.g., BLAS—basic linear algebra subprograms [9.13]) to obtain high on-processor performance and careful alignment of vectors to minimize cache interference in these arithmetic library routines. These modifications made possible execution speeds in excess of 17 Mflops/processor on the T3D.

Numerical results for this solver are given in Table 9.1. In general, the results show a comparatively small performance drop from adding more processors and, thus, good scalability behavior. Larger subgrids generally give better single-processor performance because the BLAS routines are more heavily optimized for long vectors. However, performance irregularities do exist because it is hard to predict cache performance precisely, particularly for a direct-mapped cache such as the T3D's.

9.6   FULLY IMPLICIT LINEAR SOLVER

The development of an effective linear solver for fully implicit simulations poses substantially greater technical challenges than the IMPES case. Complex phase-change behavior in the field typically requires fully implicit simulations for accurate modeling, and these fully implicit simulations in turn cause difficulties for linear solvers. The matrices arising from such simulations typically are neither near-symmetric nor diagonally dominant. Robustness as well as efficient parallelization are both critical for such simulations.

The Falcon fully implicit linear solver is based in part on certain conventional iterative techniques, such as the Orthomin [9.18] and GMRES (generalized minimal residual algorithm) [9.15], Krylov iterative solvers, the constrained pressure residual method (CPR) method [9.20] to accelerate convergence via approximate solution of the pressure equations, and line correction [9.21]. However, the preconditioning component of the linear solve is both the most crucial in terms of robustness and also historically the most difficult to parallelize. In particular, conventional preconditioners such as the incomplete and modified incomplete LU factorization methods (ILU, MILU), INV, and nested factorization have a long history of success on conventional computer architectures in effectively solving reservoir simulation problems due to their robustness, which comes in part from their strong coupling properties [9.2, 9.3, 9.17]. However, these effective serial preconditioners have proven to be difficult to parallelize because of the sequential nature of their computations.

The Falcon linear solver uses a new implementation of the ILU preconditioner that scales well on large numbers of processors. The limitations of standard ILU and MILU implementations is illustrated in Figure 9.1 [9.11]. In Figure 9.1 a 3D rectangular finite difference grid is discretized with 7-point finite differences. The computational pattern for the ILU(0) preconditioner applied to this problem with natural ordering is illustrated by a series of planar "wavefronts" that sweep through the grid from one corner to the opposite corner. The result on each wavefront must be computed before the next wavefront's result can be computed. Thus, when a standard 3D domain decomposition is applied to the grid for parallelization, as denoted in Figure 9.1, most processors remain

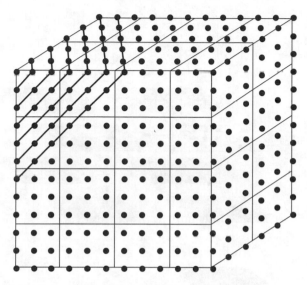

9.1   Wavefront update pattern for ILU(0) sweep.

FIGURE

idle most of the time, waiting for other processors to finish before they can commence their computations.

The new ILU/MILU preconditioning technique implemented for Falcon is based on an alternative domain decomposition and a rearrangement of the order of computations, as illustrated in Figure 9.2. Along the vertical z dimension, data is kept on-processor; that is, a degenerate 2D decomposition is imposed on the grid for distribution across the processors, rather than a full 3D decomposition into subgrids. Furthermore, rather than using the diagonal sweep wavefront pattern to update the grid values as shown in Figure 9.1, the computation order is rearranged so that the points "across the top" are updated first, so all the processors can begin computation immediately.

To illustrate in terms of the example in Figure 9.2, on the first parallel step processor 1 computes the ILU forward sweep result for the first plane of its subgrid. Processor 1 then sends face information to processors 2 and 3, which can then compute the result on their first plane while processor 1 in turn computes the result on its second plane. On the third parallel step, processor 4 receives face data to initiate computation of the result on its first plane. Following this small startup period, all processors have information to begin their computations, and the update sweeps rapidly to the bottom of the grid in parallel.

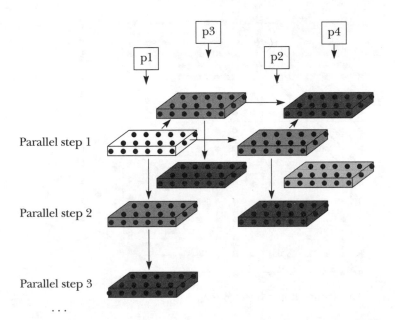

p3

p1

p2

p4

Parallel step 1

Parallel step 2

Parallel step 3

. . .

9.2

FIGURE

Update sequence for parallel ILU scheme on a four-processor computer.

Note that this new scheme computes exactly the same numerical result as standard global ILU with natural ordering. Thus, all the strong convergence properties that have historically been demonstrated by the ILU preconditioner on difficult reservoir simulation problems are preserved. This is in contrast to other standard parallelization techniques such as subdomain decouplings or grid-point reorderings that typically degrade the convergence or robustness of the iteration process.

To illustrate the performance of this technique, several numerical examples are given in Table 9.2. First, a fully implicit problem (four unknowns per grid block) is solved. The problem is run for 1000 days, with 500 days of primary production followed by 500 days of waterflooding. The number of unknowns is $32 \times 32 \times 16$, and the problem has two wells. For this study, the base simulation is performed using the Amoco implicit GCOMP simulator with a GMRES(20)/ILU(0) linear solver on a Cray M98 processor. To obtain estimates of the corresponding linear solver performance on highly parallel architectures, problems of the same size and structure (four unknowns per block and two wells) were solved on the Cray T3D architecture, and the corresponding linear solve times for the simula-

Number of processors	Estimated linear solve time, seconds
2	2684
4	1486
8	783
16	427
32	266
64	166

9.2

TABLE

Estimated parallel linear solve times, 31 × 31 × 16 fully implicit problem.

tion on that architecture were calculated. The resulting timings show that the solver has good scalability properties on many processors.

The strength of the solver, however, is demonstrated on very large problems that can only be solved on highly parallel architectures. Figure 9.3 shows the computation speed for the ILU(0) solve calculation. The largest problem solved contained over 67 million grid cells and was executed on a 512-processor Cray T3D. The results indicate that the algorithm scales well on large numbers of processors, attaining in excess of 3 Gflops on the full machine, demonstrating that the solver gives good performance for large problems on large numbers of processors.

Finally, we give performance results for the GMRES/ILU solver applied to several IMPES problems. Several grid sizes of up to 16.5 million grid cells were used. The simulation length was 2800 days, including 1000 days of primary production followed by 1800 days of waterflooding. Table 9.3 shows timings for these runs on a 512-node Cray T3D.

The results show that for large problems of interest, the new implementation of ILU preconditioning solves difficult, fully implicit reservoir simulation

Grid dimensions	Number of grid cells	Number of wells	Total runtime, seconds	Linear solve time, seconds
255 × 255 × 32	2,080,800	13	671	214
511 × 511 × 32	8,355,872	41	2385	698
719 × 719 × 32	16,542,752	85	3983	1278

9.3

TABLE

Falcon GMRES/ILU linear solver performance on several IMPES problems.

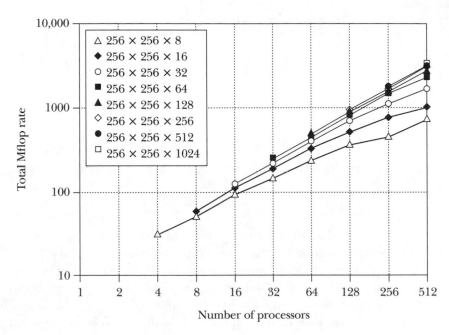

9.3

FIGURE

Scalability of parallel ILU/MILU solve.

problems efficiently and robustly on computer architectures with large numbers of processors.

9.7   FALCON PERFORMANCE RESULTS

The real benefit of Falcon to the reservoir engineer is measured in terms of such factors as the ability to simulate large fields that cannot be simulated in their entirety by conventional software and the ability to perform reservoir studies faster and more thoroughly due to the advanced speed capabilities of Falcon. To illustrate these benefits, we now present some performance data for runs of Falcon on parallel computers.

The basic dataset used for testing Falcon performance corresponds to a $64 \times 64 \times 32 = 131{,}072$ grid-cell simulation, with two wells. The simulation period is 2800 days, composed of 1000 days of primary oil production followed by 1800 days of waterflooding. The scaling behavior of this simulation on a Cray T3D is shown in Figure 9.4. Runtime for each run, as illustrated by the bars of the

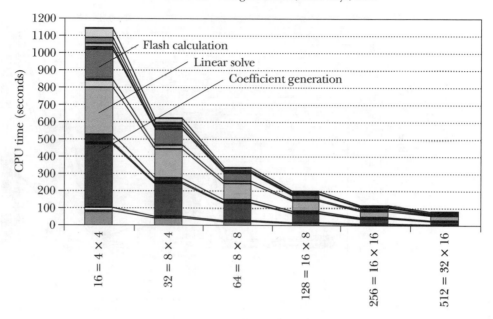

64 × 64 × 32 grid blocks, 2800 days, T3D

9.4   Scalability of a 131,072 grid-cell simulation.

FIGURE

graph, is decomposed into timings for different parts of the code, denoted by differently shaded sections of each bar. The timings indicate that most of the time is spent in the linear solve (in this case, the fast T3D-specific IMPES solver), the matrix coefficient generation routine (COEF), and the flash calculation that is used to determine the phase fractions of the different species of oil, gas, and water. These results show that, even for a comparatively small problem, the Falcon code scales extremely well.

Performance data for a set of much larger runs is given in Figure 9.5. Runtimes for a 64 × 64 × 32 grid on 128, 256, and 512 processors; a 255 × 255 × 32 grid on 128, 256, and 512 processors; a 512 × 512 × 32 grid on 512 processors; a 720 × 720 × 32 grid on 512 processors; and a 768 × 768 × 24 grid on 512 processors of a Cray T3D are shown. The last run uses the heavily optimized red/black line SOR solver; the others use an ILU(0)/GMRES(20) linear solver. These runs show Falcon's ability to solve large problems with comparatively small turnaround times.

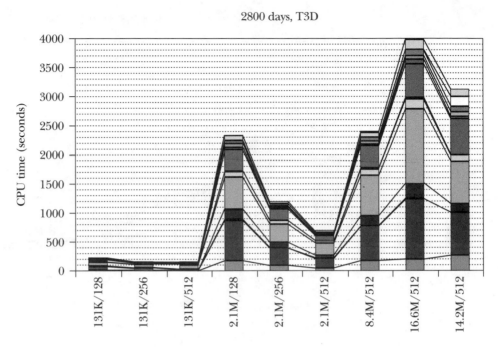

2800 days, T3D

9.5   Timings for very large simulations.

FIGURE

9.8   AMOCO FIELD STUDY

Falcon was used to conduct the largest geostatistical reservoir study ever conducted within Amoco. This study involved the simulation of 50 geostatistically
derived realizations of a large, black-oil waterflood system. The realizations each
contained 2.3 million cells and 1039 wells, and the production history was modeled for a period of 25 years. Each simulation was executed in approximately 4
hours, enabling the simulation study to finish in less than a month. Figure 9.6
shows a snapshot oil saturation profile from the study; the red areas (see color
plate 9.6) show high oil saturation and blue denoting low oil saturation.

✦ The speed of Falcon over conventional simulators enables the modeling of
uncertainties using multiple realizations.

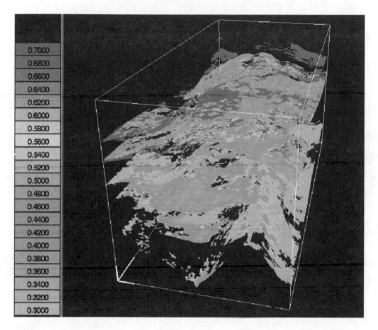

9.6

FIGURE

Oil saturation profile for a 2.25-million grid cell simulation. (See also color plate 9.6.)

✦ Because Falcon can use fine grids for modeling the field, the step of upscaling the geologic data can be eliminated, thus reducing uncertainties and the time required for the study.

Figure 9.7 demonstrates the importance of performing simulations using multiple realizations for a field. This graph shows the oil production rate over time for the 50 separate runs. The range of differences in the predicted oil rates demonstrates the uncertainty inherent in the predictions of the oil field's production. Awareness of this uncertainty can be used to make better economic decisions regarding the field.

9.9   SUMMARY

Falcon's ability to exploit parallel computing technology effectively makes possible the redefinition of the nature of reservoir simulations. Falcon provides large speed and problem-size increases due to the use of parallel computers. Falcon

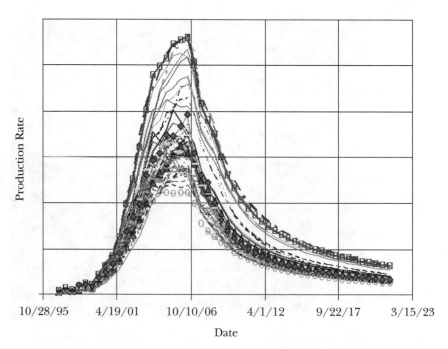

9.7

FIGURE

Production rate versus time for 50 Falcon simulations.

can simulate large economically important fields in their entirety, thus providing the opportunity for significant cost savings in oil extraction and production.

The Falcon project has been awarded a 1997 R&D 100 Award for technological innovation. To obtain further information on the Falcon project, see the project Web site located at *www.c3.lanl.gov/~wdj/amoco.html.*

ACKNOWLEDGMENTS

This work was supported in part by the Department of Energy through grant W-7405-ENG-36 with Los Alamos National Laboratory. This research was performed in part using the resources located at the Advanced Computing Laboratory of Los Alamos National Laboratory, Los Alamos, NM 87545.

References

[9.1]   Amoco. 1992. *Computer User Instructions for the Mass Variable Formulation of GCOMP.* Amoco Proprietary Document.

[9.2]   Behie, A. 1985. *Comparison of Nested Factorization, Constrained Pressure Residual, and Incomplete Factorization Preconditionings.* Paper SPE 13531 presented at the SPE 1985 Middle East Oil Technical Conference and Exhibition, Bahrain, March 11–14.

[9.3]   Eisenstat, Stanley C., Howard C. Elman, and Martin H. Schultz. 1988. Block-Preconditioned Conjugate Gradient-Like Methods for Numerical Reservoir Simulation, *SPERE,* Feb. 307–312.

[9.4]   Geist, Al, Adam Beguelin, and Jack Dongarra (eds.). 1994. *PVM: Parallel Virtual Machine: A Users' Guide and Tutorial for Networked Parallel Computing.* Cambridge: MIT Press.

[9.5]   Gropp, William, Ewing Lusk, and Anthony Skjellum. 1994. *Using MPI: Portable Parallel Programming with the Message-Passing Interface.* Cambridge: MIT Press.

[9.6]   Gustafsson, I. 1978. A Class of First Order Factorization Methods. *BIT,* **18,** 142–156.

[9.7]   Gustafsson, I. 1983. Modified Incomplete Cholesky (MIC) Method. In Evans, D. J. (ed.), *Preconditioning Methods: Theory and Applications.* New York: Gordon and Breach, 265–293.

[9.8]   Hageman, Louis A., and David M. Young. 1981. *Applied Iterative Methods.* New York: Academic Press.

[9.9]   Joubert, Wayne. 1994. *Node Performance of the BLAS-1 Routines on the Cray T3D.* CIC-19 Performance Brief. Los Alamos National Laboratory, Sept.

[9.10]   Joubert, Wayne. 1994. *Port of Amoco Linear Solver Code to the Cray T3D.* CIC-19 Performance Brief. Los Alamos National Laboratory.

[9.11]   Joubert, W., T. Oppe, R. Janardhan, and W. Dearholt. 1997. Fully Parallel Global M/ILU Preconditioning for 3-D Structured Problems. In preparation.

[9.12]   Koelbel, Charles H. *The High Performance Fortran Handbook.* 1994. Cambridge: MIT Press.

[9.13]   Lawson, C. L., R. J. Hanson, D. R. Kincaid, and F. T. Krogh. 1979. Basic Linear Algebra Subprograms for FORTRAN Usage. *ACM Trans. Math. Soft.,* **5,** 308–323.

[9.14]   Meijerink, J. A., and H. A. van der Vorst. 1977. An Iterative Solution Method for Linear Systems of Which the Coefficient Matrix is a Symmetric M-Matrix. *Mathematics of Computation,* **31,** (137), 148–162.

[9.15]   Saad, Youcef, and Martin H. Schultz. 1986. GMRES: A Generalized Minimal Residual Algorithm for Solving Nonsymmetric Linear Systems. *SIAM J. Sci. Stat. Comp.,* **7** (3), 856–869.

[9.16]   Shiralkar, Gautam S., R. E. Stephenson, Wayne Joubert, Olaf Lubeck, and Bart van Bloemen Waanders. 1997. *Falcon: A Production Quality Distributed Memory Reservoir Simulator.* SPE Paper 37975 presented at the 1997 SPE Reservoir Simulation Symposium, Dallas, TX, June 8–11.

[9.17]   Simon, Horst D. 1988. Incomplete LU Preconditioners for Conjugate Gradient-Type Iterative Methods. *SPERE,* Feb.

[9.18]   Vinsome, P. K. W. 1976. *ORTHOMIN, an Iterative Method for Solving Sparse Sets of Simultaneous Linear Equations.* SPE paper 5739 in Fourth Symposium of Numerical Simulation of Reservoir Performance of the Society of Petroleum Engineers of the AIME. Los Angeles.

[9.19]   Volz, Richard, Manny Vale, Bob Stephenson, Kirk Hird, and Gautam Shiralkar. 1995. *Showcase Reservoir Study Using FALCON (Redefining Reservoir Simulation).* Amoco Internal Document, Dec.

[9.20]   Wallis, J. R., R. P. Kendall, and T. E. Little. 1985. *Constrained Residual Acceleration of Conjugate Gradient Methods.* SPE Paper 13536 presented at the 1985 SPE Reservoir Simulation Symposium, Dallas, TX, Feb. 10–13, 1985.

[9.21]   Watts, J. W. An Iterative Matrix Solution Method Suitable for Anisotropic Problems. 1971. *SPE Journal,* **11** (March), 47–51.

[9.22]   Young, L. C., and R. E. Stephenson. 1983. A Generalized Compositional Approach for Reservoir Simulation. *SPE Journal,* Oct. 727–742.

10 | An Architecture-Independent Navier-Stokes Code

Johnson C. T. Wang   Department of Computer Science, California Institute of Technology

Stephen Taylor   Scalable Concurrent Programming Laboratory, Syracuse University

10.1   INTRODUCTION

In the late 1960s and early 1970s, almost every campus in the United States had established computing centers equipped with high-speed computers, such as the CDC 7600 and the IBM 360. Research activities in the field of numerical solutions for either Euler's equations or Navier-Stokes equations started to ferment. It was the dawn of the computation fluid dynamics (CFD) age. During that time, the fundamental concept for code development was "instructing the computer to carry out the computation as if it were to be done by yourself using hand, pencil, and paper." Fluid dynamists were carrying out code development equipped with only some basic knowledge of Fortran. The situation quickly changed, however, in the late seventies and early eighties, when vector supercomputers became available. The vector nature of the computer architecture demanded changes in the concept of code development. For example, the old concept of "storing the computed numbers for later use" was not always advisable. As another example, by inverting the inner and outer DO-loop for a block tridiagonal solver based on the concept of "as if it were to be done by yourself," the computation could be speeded up by an order of magnitude. The CFD code developers started to depend on help from the computer system engineers. To achieve effective vectorization and optimization, a certain degree of knowledge about the computer architecture was needed.

Another huge change occurred at the end of eighties and the beginning of the nineties, when parallel computers entered the CFD arena. As we saw in many conferences—for example, the Computational Aero Sciences Workshop '93 held at NASA Ames Research Center—the arrival of parallel computers was greeted with both welcome and skepticism. They were welcome because we all recognized the power of multitude. We were skeptical because we, as fluid dynamists, didn't know how parallel computers work, and we wondered how we could "take a code that was working on a sequential machine such as a CDC or Cray YMP, install it in a parallel computer system, and expect it to work." As a matter of fact, it will not work; let alone work with efficiency and optimization.

The objective of this chapter is to share with readers how we can make a computer code that works on any computer platform. We will present our efforts and results in developing a Navier-Stokes code that can be operated in sequential computers as well as parallel computers of distributed memory, shared memory, and workstation cluster systems. In other words, the code works independently of the computer architecture. The code has been applied to a variety of launch vehicle systems using the sequential machine C90 and the parallel computers Intel Delta and Paragon and Cray T3D and T3E.

We have experienced the power of multitude. The flow field simulation for the complete Delta II launch vehicle (one core plus nine solid rocket boosters), discussed in Section 10.5.3, took 5 million grid points. The total memory required was 500 million words (double precision). It was estimated that, in the low supersonic region (free-stream Mach number 1.2), a Cray YMP would take about 4 million seconds (46 days) to do this simulation. This is an example of a problem that cannot be solved using sequential machines.

We will first introduce the basic equations and the numerics and then present an implementation method for parallel computers.

10.2   BASIC EQUATIONS

The fundamental equations considered in this chapter are the Reynold-averaged compressible Navier-Stokes equations. This set of equations represents the fundamental laws of conservation of mass, momentum, and energy, and so it is natural that the equations are written in conservation law form and solved by using conservative schemes. In a Cartesian physical space, this set of equations in the conservation law form can be written as

$$\frac{\partial U}{\partial t} + \nabla \cdot \vec{F} = 0 \qquad (10.1)$$

where U is the vector of the conserved variables,

$$U = [\rho \quad \rho u \quad \rho v \quad \rho w \quad \rho e]\,T \tag{10.2}$$

and $\bar{F} = E\hat{e}_x + F\hat{e}_y + G\hat{e}_z$ is the vector form of the fluxes for the conserved variables,

$$E = \begin{bmatrix} \rho u \\ \rho u^2 + p + \tau_{xx} \\ \rho uv + \tau_{xy} \\ \rho uw + \tau_{xz} \\ (\rho e + p + \tau_{xx})u + \tau_{xy}\,v + \tau_{xz}\,w + q_x \end{bmatrix} \tag{10.3}$$

$$F = \begin{bmatrix} \rho v \\ \rho uv + \tau_{xy} \\ \rho v^2 + p + \tau_{yy} \\ \rho vw + \tau_{yz} \\ \tau_{zx}\,u + (\rho e + p + \tau_{yy})v + \tau_{yz}\,w + q_y \end{bmatrix} \tag{10.4}$$

$$G = \begin{bmatrix} \rho w \\ \rho uv + \tau_{zx} \\ \rho vw + \tau_{zy} \\ \rho w^2 + p + \tau_{zz} \\ \tau_{zx}\,u + \tau_{zy}\,v + (\rho e + p + \tau_{zz})w + q_z \end{bmatrix} \tag{10.5}$$

$$\tau_{xx} = -2\mu\frac{\partial u}{\partial x} - \lambda\nabla\cdot\bar{V}$$

$$\tau_{yy} = -2\mu\frac{\partial y}{\partial y} - \lambda\nabla\cdot\bar{V}$$

$$\tau_{zz} = -2\mu\frac{\partial vv}{\partial z} - \lambda\nabla\cdot\bar{V}$$

$$\tau_{xz} = \tau_{zx} = -\mu\left(\frac{\partial u}{\partial z} - \frac{\partial w}{\partial x}\right) \tag{10.6}$$

$$\tau_{yx} = \tau_{xy} = -\mu\left(\frac{\partial u}{\partial y} - \frac{\partial v}{\partial x}\right)$$

$$\tau_{yz} = \tau_{xy} = -\mu\left(\frac{\partial v}{\partial z} - \frac{\partial w}{\partial y}\right)$$

$$\bar{q} = q_x\hat{e}_x + q_y\hat{e}_y + q_z\hat{e}_z = -k\nabla T$$

In Equations (10.1) through (10.6), ρ is the density; p is the pressure; and u, v, and w are the components of velocity vector $\vec{V}$ in the x, y, and z directions, respectively, with corresponding unit vectors $\hat{e}_x$, $\hat{e}_y$, and $\hat{e}_z$. The total energy per unit mass is denoted by e; $\bar{q}$ is the heat transfer vector; T is the temperature; λ is the bulk viscosity; μ is the viscosity; and k is the thermal conductivity. With gas being assumed polytropic, the total energy is related to pressure, p, by the equation of state: $p = (\gamma - 1)\rho[e - (u^2 + v^2 + w^2)/2]$. The viscosity and the thermal conductivity are comprised of molecular and turbulent components as $\mu = \mu^M + \mu^T$ and $k = k^M + k^T$, respectively. Here, μ^T is evaluated using a Baldwin-Lomax turbulence model [10.1].

The equations usually are nondimensionalized using a reference length, a reference density, and a reference velocity. By using these three reference quantities, the reference pressure and the reference time are fixed.

In general, flow solvers are developed using a body-conforming orthogonal curvilinear coordinate system with the following transformation:

$$\xi = \xi(x, y, z); \eta = \eta(x, y, z); \varsigma = \varsigma(x, y, z) \tag{10.7}$$

Using this transformation, Equation (10.1) can be written as

$$\frac{\partial \overline{U}}{\partial t} + \frac{\partial \overline{E}}{\partial \xi} + \frac{\partial \overline{F}}{\partial \eta} + \frac{\partial \overline{G}}{\partial \varsigma} = 0 \tag{10.8}$$

where

$$\overline{U} = U/J, \overline{E}J = E\xi_x + F\xi_y + G\xi_z, \overline{F}J = E\eta_x + F\eta_y + G\eta_z, \overline{G}J = E\varsigma_x + F\varsigma_y + G\varsigma_z$$

and J is the Jacobian of the transformation,

$$J = \frac{\partial(\xi, \eta, \varsigma)}{\partial(x, y, z)} = \begin{vmatrix} \xi_x & \xi_y & \xi_z \\ \eta_x & \eta_y & \eta_z \\ \varsigma_x & \varsigma_y & \varsigma_z \end{vmatrix} \tag{10.9}$$

10.2.1   Nomenclature

Here we describe the nomenclature for equations illustrated in this chapter.

E, F, G = flux vectors in physical space

$\overline{E}, \overline{F}, \overline{G}$ = transformed flux vectors
e = total energy per unit mass
$\hat{e}_x, \hat{e}_y, \hat{e}_z$ = unit vectors in the x, y, and z directions, respectively
J = Jacobian of the transformation
k = thermal conductivity
p = pressure
$\bar{q}$ = heat transfer vector
T = temperature
t = time
U = vector of conserved variables
$\overline{U}$ = transformed vector of conserved variables
u, v, w = Cartesian velocity components
$\bar{V}$ = Cartesian velocity vector
x, y, z = Cartesian coordinates
γ = ratio of specific heats
ρ = density
λ = bulk viscosity
μ = viscosity
τ = viscous stress tensor
ξ, η, ζ = transformed coordinates

Subscripts

x, y, z = partial derivative with respect to x, y, and z

Superscripts

T = transport of a matrix or vector

10.3   A NAVIER-STOKES SOLVER

The parallelized flow solver to be presented in Section 10.4 is based on the ALSINS code [10.11]. The ALSINS code is a fully vectorized Navier-Stokes solver. It is a primary tool used by The Aerospace Corporation for a broad range of practical flow simulations. The code has been applied to a variety of nozzle flows and the flows over multibody launch vehicle configurations, such as the Titan IV. Figure 10.1(a) shows parts of the vehicle and the computational grids used in a CFD flowfield simulation. Further references that explain the vehicle and geometry are given in Section 10.5.2. Notice that the computational grid system is irregular in topology and contains multiple solid objects. In this instance, there

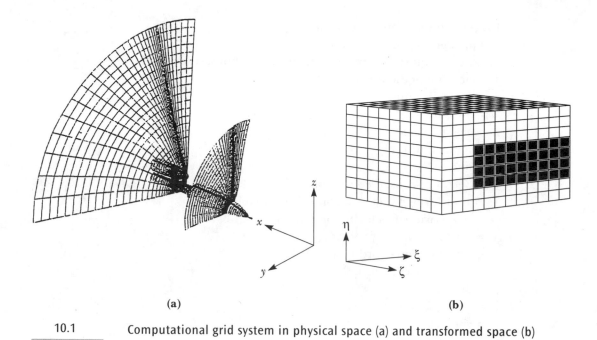

(a)   (b)

10.1

FIGURE

Computational grid system in physical space (a) and transformed space (b)

is a core vehicle and a booster. In the transformed computational domain, the grid system becomes topologically regular, as shown in Figure 10.1(b).

The ALSINS code uses a finite volume approach. By volume integration of Equation (10.1) over a computational cell, the Navier-Stokes equations are discretized into a set of finite difference equations that equate the change of states at the cell center to the net sum of the fluxes across the cell surfaces. This approach allows the 3D operator of the Navier-Stokes equations to be reduced to the sum of three 1D operators. By this approach, the global conservations are preserved.

For the explicit option, the discretized equations of Equation (10.8) become

$$
\begin{aligned}
\mathrm{U}_{i,j,k}^{n+1} = \mathrm{U}_{i,j,k}^{n} &- \Delta t \frac{\mathrm{J}_{i,j,k}}{\Delta\xi\Delta\eta\Delta\zeta}\left(\overline{\mathrm{E}}_{i+1/2,j,k} - \overline{\mathrm{E}}_{i-1/2,j,k}\right)\Delta\eta\Delta\zeta \\
&+ \left(\overline{\mathrm{F}}_{i,j+1/2,k} - \overline{\mathrm{F}}_{i,j-1/2,k}\right)\Delta\xi\Delta\zeta + \left(\overline{\mathrm{G}}_{i,j,k+1/2} - \overline{\mathrm{G}}_{i,j,k-1/2}\right)\Delta\xi\Delta\eta
\end{aligned}
\tag{10.10}
$$

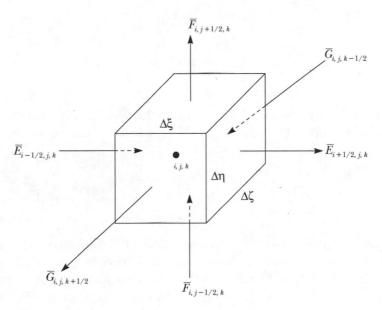

10.2   Flux terms for finite volume calculation.

FIGURE

where Δt is the time interval; the subscripts i, j, and k indicate the spatial location of the cell; and superscript n indicates the time step. The terms inside the brackets, representing the fluxes across the cell surfaces, are depicted in Figure 10.2.

In Equation (10.10), there are two parts, inviscid and viscous, in each surface flux term. We will use superscript inv to indicate the inviscid part and vis the viscous part. For example,

$$\overline{E}_{i+1/2,j,k} = \overline{E}_{i+1/2,j,k}^{inv} + \overline{E}_{i+1/2,j,k}^{vis} \tag{10.11}$$

Details for computing the surface fluxes are given in [10.10, 10.11]. For the purpose of this chapter, it is sufficient to point out that the computation of the inviscid part of $\overline{E}$ requires information concerning $\overline{U}^{n}$ at positions i, $i \pm 1$, and $i \pm 2$ for second order spatial accuracy, that is,

$$\overline{E}_{i+1/2,j,k}^{inv} = \overline{E}^{inv}\left(\overline{U}_{i-1,j,k}^{n}, \overline{U}_{i,j,k}^{n}, \overline{U}_{i+1,j,k}^{n}, \overline{U}_{i+2,j,k}^{n}\right) \tag{10.12}$$

and

$$\overline{E}_{i-1/2,j,k}^{\,\mathrm{inv}} = \overline{E}^{\,\mathrm{inv}}\!\left(\overline{U}_{i-2,j,k}^{\,n}, \overline{U}_{i-1,j,k}^{\,n}, \overline{U}_{i,j,k}^{\,n}, \overline{U}_{i+1,j,k}^{\,n}\right) \tag{10.13}$$

It should be noted that in Equations (10.12) and (10.13), the values of j and k are kept the same. The central difference scheme is used to compute the viscous terms; therefore,

$$\overline{E}_{i+1/2,j,k}^{\,\mathrm{vis}} = \overline{E}^{\,\mathrm{vis}}\!\left(\overline{U}_{i+1,j\pm1,k}^{\,n}, \overline{U}_{i+1,j,k\pm1}^{\,n}, \overline{U}_{i,j\pm1,k}^{\,n}, \overline{U}_{i,j,k\pm1}^{\,n}\right) \tag{10.14}$$

Unlike Equation (10.12), for a given j and k, $\overline{E}^{\,\mathrm{vis}}$ depends on $\overline{U}^{\,n}$ at $j\pm1$ and $k\pm 1$. This is due to the cross derivatives of the viscous terms; for example, see the definition of τ_{xz} in Equation (10.6). The inviscid (convective) fluxes are evaluated using an extension of the total-variation-diminishing (TVD) algorithm of Harten [10.3]. The viscous fluxes are computed using a standard central difference scheme. The numerical solutions are second order accurate in space and first order in time. This option can be applied for steady and unsteady flow simulations, but it is not efficient for steady flow simulations because the stability consideration requires a Courant-Friedricks-Levy (CFL) number less than 1, which renders a very small Δt. Consequently, a large number of iterations is required to reach a steady-state solution.

For the steady flow problems, the iteration is carried out using an implicit algorithm that allows CFL numbers in the order of hundreds. To further accelerate the rate of convergence, a numerical technique was presented [10.11] using a line relaxation procedure. Using this implicit algorithm, the governing equations are cast into a block tridiagonal system of equations with the change of states as dependent variables and the net sum of fluxes as nonhomogeneous parts. The full set of equations is given in [10.11]. In this chapter, we extract only those parts of the equations that are necessary to explain the method of parallel computing.

The discretized equation in the ith direction is a block tridiagonal system:

$$\tilde{A}^-\Delta U_{i-1,j,k}^{\,n} + \tilde{D}\Delta U_{i,j,k}^{\,n} + \tilde{A}^+\Delta U_{i+1,j,k}^{\,n} = \mathrm{RHS} \tag{10.15}$$

where $\tilde{A}^-$, $\tilde{D}$, and $\tilde{A}^+$ are preconditioned 5×5 matrices. The unknowns ΔU^n are defined as

$$\Delta U^{\,n}_{\,i,j,k} = U^{\,n+1}_{\,i,j,k} - U^{\,n}_{\,i,j,k} \tag{10.16}$$

In Equation (10.15), the RHS is the second term on the right-hand side in Equation (10.10). For a steady-state solution, $\Delta U^n = 0$ by definition. When this condition is reached, it implies that RHS = 0, which represents a solution to the steady-state Navier-Stokes equations.

10.4   PARALLELIZATION OF A NAVIER-STOKES SOLVER

An often-quoted concept of parallel computing is "many hands make easy farming." However, there are different ways of practicing this concept. One is to let each hand do different work on the same land—task decomposition strategy. Another is to let each hand do the same task on different parts of the land—domain decomposition strategy. Each strategy has its own merit. For our development of an architecture-independent Navier-Stokes code, a domain decomposition strategy is adapted.

10.4.1   Domain Decomposition

The basic numerical scheme outlined in previous sections is implemented for parallel machines using the technique of domain decomposition. This technique involves dividing the data structures of the problem into parts and operating on each part independently.

To cope with complex geometries, it is necessary to decompose the irregular grid system into blocks of varying sizes. However, a completely arbitrary decomposition is not needed. For a wide variety of practical applications, it is sufficient to decompose the domain along the axes. Figure 10.3 shows an example of this type of decomposition. An irregular grid system, such as that shown in Figure 10.1(a), is first transformed into a regular computational grid system, as shown in Figure 10.1(b), through the transformation described in Section 10.2. The computational grid system is then decomposed into blocks of varying sizes along each axis. For example, in Figure 10.3, decomposition along the ξ axis yields blocks containing 3, 5, and 4 cells; decomposition of the η and ζ axes yields blocks containing 2, 4, and 3 cells.

In generating the decomposition, it is necessary to specify the boundary conditions for each block independently. In addition to the standard solid wall

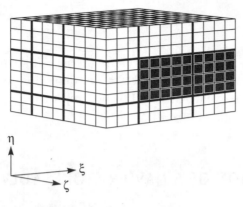

10.3   Irregular domain decomposition.

FIGURE

and free-stream boundary conditions, an extra condition that specifies a face resulting from a cut through the domain is required.

   This decomposition is capable of modeling a variety of single-body geometries but is not sufficiently flexible to model multibody configurations like that illustrated in Figure 10.1(a). To generalize the basic decomposition strategy, we
consider some blocks in the decomposition as holes. These holes are surrounded by solid boundaries and thus represent multibody configurations. Figure 10.3 uses shaded areas to signify the location of holes, representing multiple
bodies, in the decomposition.

10.4.2   Parallel Algorithm

Inviscid Fluxes

The inviscid fluxes across a cell surface are computed using Equations (10.12)
and (10.13). The second order accurate TVD scheme requires information from
two cells on each side of the surface. Thus, to compute an entire block in the decomposition, it is necessary to receive information from two layers of cells from
adjacent blocks.

Viscous Fluxes

Unfortunately, this communication of information alone is not sufficient to calculate the viscous fluxes, as indicated in Equation (10.14), due to the cross derivative terms of the viscous shear. Thus, each block of the decomposition needs to

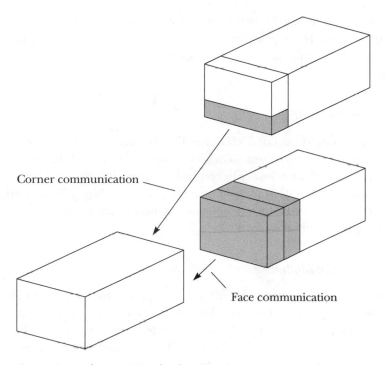

Corner communication

Face communication

10.4

FIGURE

Message-passing communication structure.

have the 12 neighboring corners available from the adjacent blocks. The shaded regions in Figure 10.4 illustrate the types of communication structure necessary to compute all cells in a single block at time t based on values at time $t - \Delta t$.

Implicit solutions

Although this basic communication structure is sufficient for the explicit simulations, it requires some changes to the numerical scheme to handle implicit calculations. Recall, from Section 10.3, that a line-by-line relaxation scheme is used. This scheme is a sequential algorithm that iterates through the entire domain of computation. It cannot, therefore, be executed concurrently within each block. However, in the steady state, the change in dependent variables from one time step to another will be zero:

$$\Delta U_{i,j,k}^{n} = U_{i,j,k}^{n+1} - U_{i,j,k}^{n} = 0$$

We take advantage of this fact by setting the required ΔU^n from an adjacent block to be zero. From previous experience in using the sequential code, we have learned that this approach does not cause instability and even speeds up convergence.

Model for Time

In the construction of TVD fluxes [10.10, 10.11], a Δt bounded by the CFL condition in the entire domain of computation is required. In order to find the next Δt at step t, it is necessary to combine information from all blocks in the decomposition. This is done by finding a local Δt for all blocks independently and then combining these values to provide the minimum value over the entire domain using the utility broadcast.

Turbulence Modeling

To complete the basic algorithm, we require a method for utilizing turbulence models on parallel machines. For simplicity, we achieve this by assuming that turbulent effects are localized within a single block adjacent to a boundary. This assumption is, in general, valid. This allows all turbulent effects to be calculated without communication or adding sequential operations to the parallel algorithm.

Single-Body Algorithm

We represent each block in the domain as a parallel processor and associate with it communication channels to 18 neighbors. These channels connect a block to the 6 neighbors required for face exchanges and 12 neighbors used for corner exchanges. End-around connections are used at the boundaries to ensure that every block has a full complement of neighbors. The basic algorithm may be expressed as

```
block(. . .)
{ load geometry data into block
calculate local Δt and send to minimum calculation
while (time not exhausted) {

receive global Δt
extract 6 faces and 12 corners from block and send to neighbors
compute dependent variables at t + Δt using faces, corners, and Δt
calculate new local Δt and send to minimum calculation
```

```
    }

    }
    minimum(. . .)
    { receive a local Δt from each block
    calculate the minimum and broadcast minimum to all blocks
    }
```

Program 1: Basic Iterative Algorithm

A block can be executed at any computer in the machine. Each block concurrently loads the appropriate geometry information from a unique file. In this manner, a block is informed of its boundary conditions. Notice that the algorithm is self-synchronizing by virtue of the explicit number of the face and corner exchanges required.

Multibody Algorithm

The scheme is adapted to deal with multibody simulations by allowing any block to represent a hole in the domain. A block is informed that it represents a hole when the geometry information is loaded. If a block represents a hole, the compute function does nothing, the extract function returns a vector of length 1, and the calculate function returns infinity.

Load Balancing

Notice that the computation will be reasonably well balanced if the blocks are similar in size. For the most part, our blocks are sufficiently large that a simple mapping technique is sufficient. Each block is numbered to uniquely identify itself, and mapping is achieved by assigning the ith block to the ith computer, thus, for the most part, placing continuous blocks close together. This technique has been sufficient for many practical simulations.

10.5   COMPUTATIONAL RESULTS

In this section we present three of our simulations using the parallelized Navier-Stokes solver. The first one offers a good test case that you can use for developing and debugging a parallel CFD code. The second one is a typical aerospace industry application and the third a demonstration of the power of parallel computing.

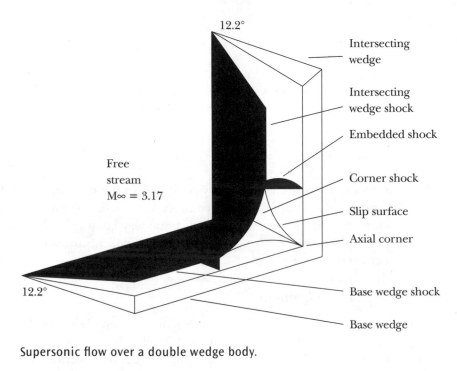

10.5

FIGURE

Supersonic flow over a double wedge body.

10.5.1   Supersonic Flow over Two Wedges

This problem is geometrically simple, but it involves complex shock interactions
and flow physics. The main features of the flow are depicted in Figure 10.5. We
found that this problem is particularly attractive for the development of a parallel CFD code using domain decomposition. The exact inviscid solution is known.
Both inviscid and viscous solutions are symmetrical with respect to the diagonal
line. Therefore, we can detect the implementation error in just a few iterations by
comparing the numerical results at a few symmetry locations. Results of the numerical solution using an Intel Delta machine are presented in [10.6], which
also discusses detailed comparisons on the speedup and concludes that, using 145
nodes of the Intel Delta machine running at approximately 70 percent efficiency,
the performance obtained was 0.028 ms/cell/iteration. It was benchmarked
[10.11] that the performance of ALSINS on a Cray YMP was 0.078 ms/cell/itera-
tion and 2.26 ms/cell/iteration for running in vector mode and scalar mode, respectively. This disparity in running time is due to the fact that the ALSINS code
is fully vectorized. Because the Intel Delta machine is a scalar machine, it is
reasonable to say that the present implementation has reached a speedup of 81 times.

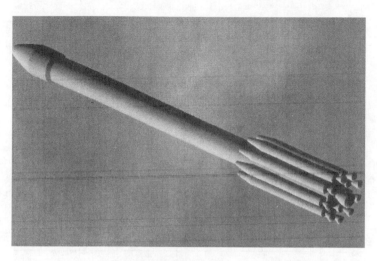

10.6

FIGURE

Delta II 7925 multibody launch vehicle, one center core plus nine boosters.

10.5.2   Titan IV Launch Vehicle

An industrial strength application, this problem involves a flowfield over the forebody of a Titan IV launch vehicle, which includes a hammerhead core vehicle and two solid rocket boosters. Simulated earlier using Cray YMP [10.9], the computational procedures were tedious due to the complexity of geometry. Using the present parallelized code, no extra efforts are required to handle the complexity of the multibody configuration. Results of this simulation and discussions of the efficacy of parallel computing are presented in [10.4].

10.5.3   Delta II 7925 Vehicle

This simulation involves a transonic flowfield over a complete Delta II 7925 vehicle, which includes one hammerhead core vehicle and nine solid rocket boosters. To address the aerodynamic issues, as will be discussed shortly, we needed to perform the simulations with the liquid rocket engine and six of the nine solid boosters firing. The angle of attack was 5 degrees. This kind of large-scale (in terms of computer memory) and complex (in terms of flow field) simulation was at the time one of the most complex simulations to have been performed.

A Delta II launch vehicle, made by Boeing (previously, McDonnell Douglas), is depicted in Figure 10.6. In the first two launches, while passing through the

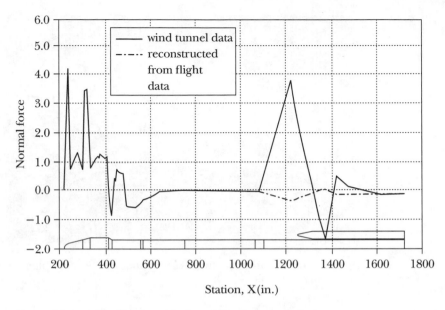

Normal force distribution, Mach = 1.2, alpha = 5 degrees.

transonic regime, the vehicles experienced unexpected aerodynamic characteristics that differed significantly from the wind tunnel data [10.2]. Figure 10.7
shows the wind-tunnel-measured normal force acting on the vehicle in comparison to the normal force reconstructed from the flight data. The free-stream
Mach number was 1.2 and the angle of attack was 5 degrees. The reconstructed
normal force implies that, in flight, the vehicle experienced a forward (upstream) shifting of the center of pressure (cp-shift). Although there is a possibility that the wind tunnel data may not be accurate in the transonic regime, the be-
lief was that the difference between the wind tunnel data and the flight data was
due to the effects of the rocket plumes in flight. The hypothesis was that this cp-
shift phenomenon was caused by the plume-induced boundary-layer separation,
as depicted in Figure 10.8 [10.2]. It was recognized at that time that the proof of
this concept might only be resolved using CFD, because the plume-on situation
cannot be simulated in the wind tunnel. But, in the early 1990s, we concluded
that it is impossible (in terms of computer memory and running time) to carry
out such a simulation using a sequential machine.

Recently, we have completed several simulations for this launch vehicle using the present parallelized Navier-Stokes solver to support some of the launch
activities and to resolve this cp-shift issue. The code has been run on the Intel
Delta machine and on the Cray T3D. The results of simulations, using 502 nodes

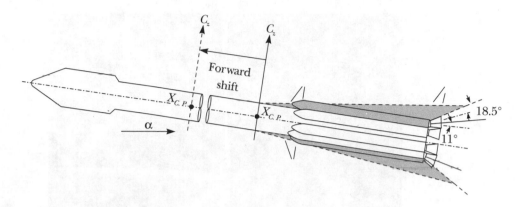

Plume-induced separation and cp-shift.

of the T3D machine at the Pittsburgh Supercomputing Center, addressing this transonic cp-shift issue have been presented in the 20th Congress of the International Council of the Aeronautical Sciences (ICAS) [10.8]. Figures 10.9 and 10.10 show, respectively, the computational grid system and the computed pressure field with six of the nine solid rockets firing. (See also color plate 10.10.) Figure 10.11 shows the flow separation induced by the plumes, a result that confirms the concept of the cp-shift due to plume-induced flow separation. Detailed comparisons of the flowfield with rocket plumes on and with plumes off are given in [10.8].

10.6   SUMMARY

We have demonstrated in this chapter a procedure for developing a parallel Navier-Stokes solver. We have also developed a parallel Navier-Stokes code based on the ALSINS code by using a domain decomposition technique. The code is independent of the computer architecture. It has been used on the Intel Delta and Paragon, Cray T3D and T3E, and is now being tested on a workstation cluster. The same code has also been run on the Cray C90 in a sequential mode with vector optimization. The primary modification to the sequential code required for parallelization is the implementation of an additional boundary condition used to include message passing. Because the information to be passed and the target computers that receive the information are well defined inside the code, the message passing can be accomplished using MPI or any system library. As it turns out, parallel computing using domain decomposition not only simplifies

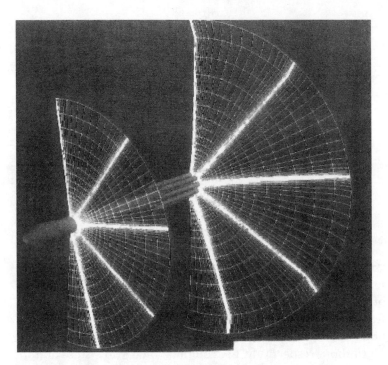

10.9   Computational grid system for Delta II 7925 CFD simulation.

FIGURE

the boundary condition specification but also makes the grid generation easier. Grid generation can be simplified further if one uses a mismatched grid system. However, the use of a mismatched grid system complicates some message-passing issues. Progress in using mismatched grid systems has been made and is discussed in [10.5] and [10.7].

ACKNOWLEDGMENTS

The simulation of the Delta II flowfield was suggested by James R. Taylor, Director of Medium Launch Vehicle Systems Engineering, The Aerospace Corporation. The organization also provided partial support for this study. Additional support came from the Advanced Research Projects Agency, ARPA Order 8176, monitored by the U.S. Office of Naval Research under Contract N00014-91-J-1986. The Delta II simulations were conducted using generous T3D computing allocations from the Pittsburgh Supercomputing Center. Mike Levin and his staff provided timely and efficient aid for this work. We are most grateful for their help.

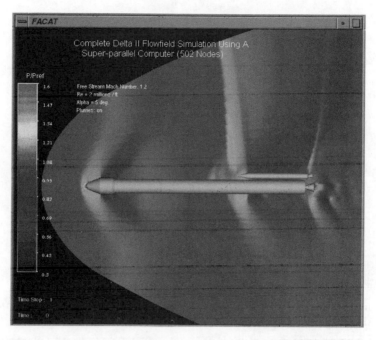

10.10

FIGURE

Pressure contours on the pitch plane of symmetry, plume on. (See also color plate 10.10—only one of the nine SRBs is shown.)

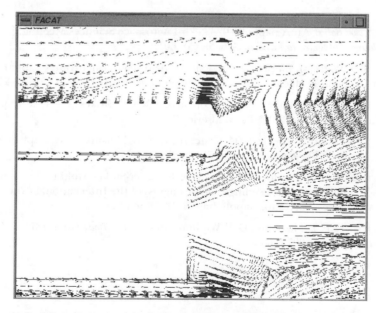

10.11

FIGURE

Velocity vectors on the plane of symmetry, plume on.

References

[10.1]   Baldwin, B. S., and H. Lomax. 1978. *Thin Layer Approximation and Algebraic Model for Separated Flow.* AIAA Paper 78-257.

[10.2]   Cantwell, M. N. 1990. *Delta II Transonic Aerodynamic TIM.* Memo A3-L230-M-90-049. McDonnell Douglas Company, March 12.

[10.3]   Harten, A. 1983. High Resolution Schemes for Hyperbolic Conservation Laws. *Journal of Computational Physics,* **49,** 357.

[10.4]   Taylor, S., and J. C. T. Wang. 1995, 1996. *Launch Vehicle Simulations Using a Concurrent, Implicit Navier-Stokes Solver.* AIAA paper 95-0233, 33rd Aerospace Sciences Meeting, Jan. 1995, and *AIAA Journal of Spacecraft and Rockets,* **33** (5), 601.

[10.5]   Taylor, S., J. Watts, M. Rieffel, and M. Palmer. 1996. The Concurrent Graph: Basic Technology for Irregular Problems. *IEEE Parallel and Distributed Technology,* **4** (2), 15–25.

[10.6]   Wang, J. C. T., and S. Taylor. 1993. A Concurrent Navier-Stokes Solver for Implicit Multibody Calculations. *Parallel CFD 93,* Paris: Elsevier Press.

[10.7]   Wang, J. C. T., and S. Taylor. 1994. Concurrent, Nodal Mismatched, Implicit Navier-Stokes Solver. *Parallel CFD 94,* Kyoto, Japan: Elsevier Press.

[10.8]   Wang, J. C. T., and S. Taylor. 1996. Large Scale Navier-Stokes Multi-Body Launch Vehicle Flowfield Simulations; Proceedings, 20th Congress of the International Council of the Aeronautical Sciences, Sorrento, Napoli, Italy, 8–13 September.

[10.9]   Wang, J. C. T., P. T. Than, and G. F. Widhopf. 1991. *Multi-Body Launch Vehicle Flowfield Similation.* AIAA-91-0072, Jan.

[10.10]   Wang, J. C. T., and G. F. Widhopf. 1989. A High Resolution TVD Finite Volume Scheme for Euler Equations in Conservation Form. *Journal of Computational Physics,* **84** (1), 145.

[10.11]   Wang, J. C. T., and G. F. Widhopf. 1990. An Efficient Finite Volume TVD Scheme for Steady State Solutions of the 3-D Compressible Euler/Navier-Stokes Equations. AIAA Paper 90-1523, June.

11 | Gaining Insights into the Flow in a Static Mixer

Olivier Byrde
Mark L. Sawley   Fluid Mechanics Laboratory, Ecole Polytechnique Fédérale de Lausanne (EPFL), Switzerland

11.1   INTRODUCTION

An understanding of the physical and chemical phenomena that occur in various mixing processes can be greatly enhanced by numerical modeling. Due to the complexity of these processes, numerical simulations generally require large computational resources to provide sufficient detail and accuracy. This chapter presents a study of the use of high-performance parallel computing to analyze the flow in a static mixer. Numerical simulation is shown to provide not only basic knowledge of the flow behavior, but also a means for optimization of the mixer.

11.1.1   Overview

Mixing operations can be found in a number of different process industries, including the chemical, pharmaceutical, petroleum, and plastics industries, as well as in food processing and water and waste treatment. The wide range of chemical mixers commercially available reflects the enormous variety of different mixing processes [11.12, 11.19]. There are two different categories of mixers. Stirred tanks perform the mixing by a motor-driven agitator. This type of mixer is generally employed when the mixing tasks are undertaken in successive batches. The energy required for mixing is supplied by the agitator. Static mixers are in-line devices, generally consisting of mixing elements inserted into a length of pipe. Mixers of this type are used in continuous operation, with the energy for mixing being derived from the pressure loss incurred as the process fluids flow through the elements.

The appropriate choice of mixer and the optimization of the mixing process are central to industrial applications: Insufficient mixing results in poor-quality products, while excessive mixing leads to unwarranted energy consumption. Indeed, insufficient understanding of mixing operations costs the process industries, in the United States alone, an estimated \$1–10 billion per annum [11.12]. Determining which device is the most suitable for a given application is not always obvious, nor is the optimization of the mixing process. The optimization of chemical mixers is traditionally performed by trial and error, with much depending on previous experience and wide safety margins. Some of the difficulties inherent in this approach can be overcome by numerical flow simulation. The ability to simulate numerically the flow in a mixer can contribute significantly to the understanding of the mixing process and provide for better, faster, and cheaper design optimization.

Despite the increasing interest in the numerical simulation of mixing processes, a number of difficulties restrict its widespread use by the process industries. These include

+ inadequate knowledge of the appropriate physical and chemical modeling (e.g., for turbulent swirling flows of reacting mixtures)

+ insufficient computational resources to perform large-scale numerical simulations necessary to obtain accurate flow solutions for multicomponent mixtures

+ the reluctance of the process industry to embrace new technologies until they have been sufficiently tested and validated

11.1.2   Description of the Application

The present study is concerned exclusively with the analysis of the flow and mixing in a static mixer. The geometry considered in the present study corresponds to the Kenics KM static mixer [11.1, 11.4, 11.14]. This mixer design has been employed in the process industry since the mid-1960s, mainly for the in-line blending of liquids under laminar flow conditions. The Kenics mixer is composed of a series of mixing elements aligned at 90 degrees, each element consisting of a short helix of 1.5 pipe diameters in length. Each helix has a twist of 180 degrees with right-hand and left-hand elements being arranged alternately in the pipe. For the present study, a Kenics mixer with six elements is considered, as illus-

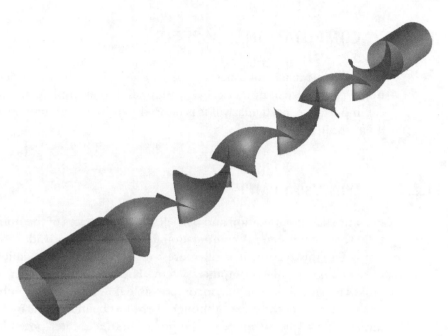

11.1   Perspective cutaway view of the six-element Kenics static mixer.

FIGURE

trated in Figure 11.1. The empty inlet and outlet pipes each have the same length as a mixing element. A uniform axial velocity is assumed at the inlet of the mixer pipe, while at the outlet a constant pressure is imposed.

In this chapter, an efficient and accurate numerical method is presented for the simulation of the laminar, incompressible, isothermal flow in the Kenics static mixer. Previous studies have generally considered an Eulerian approach by resolving the governing Navier-Stokes equations coupled with the species continuity equations [11.17, 11.21]. In this study, the physical problem has been simplified in order to concentrate attention on the basic mixing process. It is assumed that the constituent species have similar physical properties (e.g., density, viscosity) and thus the species distributions do not influence the flow behavior. A fluid composed of only a single species is therefore considered for the flow computation. The simulation is thus composed of two decoupled phases: the computation of the flow fields and the determination of the mixing efficiency. The flow in the Kenics mixer is computed using a conventional Eulerian approach. However, in order to avoid excessive numerical diffusion associated with the resolution of the species continuity equations [11.21], a Lagrangian approach is adopted for the investigation of the mixing by means of the analysis of particle trajectories through the mixer.

11.2   COMPUTATIONAL ASPECTS

There are a number of aspects to be considered for the numerical flow simulations. The choice of numerical algorithms and their implementation are of critical importance, particularly if it is desired that the computations be performed on a parallel computer.

11.2.1   Why Use an MPP?

Both the flow-computation and particle-tracking phases of the numerical simulation require substantial computational resources to provide accurate predictions. For this reason, it is of interest to perform the simulations on a high-performance parallel computer system. The parallel resolution of the Navier-Stokes equations for laminar, incompressible flow has been the subject of numerous studies in recent years. Although there has been a major interest in modest levels of parallelism (up to, say, 16 processors), a greater potential gain should be realizable from massively parallel computations (from tens to hundreds of processors). Because the communication and synchronization overheads can increase substantially with the number of processors, it is important that appropriate techniques be used to minimize the communication and/or synchronization. The techniques required to optimize the computation of the Eulerian and Lagrangian phases are different in this respect.

To obtain accurate solutions from the flow-computation phase, the computational mesh must be sufficiently refined. Previous studies have shown that insufficient resolution of the flow resulting from an overly coarse computational mesh may result in a loss of accuracy of both the flow fields and the mixing efficiency [11.5]. The determination of the mixing efficiency from the particle-tracking phase is based on a statistical analysis of the particle trajectories. To obtain the required accuracy, a large number of trajectories must therefore be calculated and analyzed.

11.2.2   Flow Computation

Programming Considerations

The parallel flow solver used in this study is based on a multiblock code developed for the numerical simulation of 3D steady/unsteady, laminar/turbulent, incompressible flows [11.15]. This code uses a conventional Eulerian approach to solve the Reynolds-averaged Navier-Stokes equations on block-structured computational meshes.

The numerical method is based on a cell-centered finite volume discretization with an artificial compressibility method to couple the pressure and velocity fields [11.9]. For steady, laminar flow, as considered in the present study, the Navier-Stokes equations can be written as

$$\frac{\partial}{\partial t}\int_V \mathbf{IQ}dV + \int_{\partial V} \mathbf{F}\bar{n}dS = \int_{\partial V} \mathbf{G}\bar{n}dS$$

where $\mathbf{I} = \mathrm{diag}(1/c^2,1,1,1)$, $\mathbf{Q} = (p/\rho,\ u,\ v,\ w)^T$ is the vector of the primitive variables, and $\mathbf{F}$ and $\mathbf{G}$ are the flux matrices of the convection and diffusion terms. The artificial compressibility coefficient c^2 is set equal to 3 max$\{u^2 + v^2 + w^2\}$, which has been observed to provide optimal convergence rates [11.16].

A spatial discretization following the Monotone Upstream-Centered Scheme for Conservation Laws (MUSCL) approach [11.25] is employed, using a second order upwind κ scheme and the approximate Riemann solver of Roe [11.20] for the convection terms, while the diffusion terms are discretized using a central approximation. A "diagonal" form of the Alternate Direction Implicit (ADI) method [11.8] is used to solve the set of discretized equations. This choice of spatial discretization is commonly employed for the resolution of the Navier-Stokes equations. The combined convection and diffusion terms are computed by means of a 25-point stencil requiring, for the determination of the fluxes in each cell, information that is at a distance of at most two cells. To facilitate the flow in complex geometries, a multiblock approach is adopted. This involves dividing the computational domain into a number of subdomains (blocks), with the previously mentioned numerical scheme being applied to compute the flow in each of the individual subdomains.

It should be noted that, because the parallelization of the flow computation is achieved at the level of the multiblock implementation (as described later), the choice of the underlying numerical method employed to resolve the Navier-Stokes equations within each subdomain is of secondary importance for parallelization issues. Indeed, a number of different numerical methods have been implemented with success in parallel flow solvers based on the multiblock approach (see, e.g., [11.3, 11.23]). Nevertheless, to obtain good computational performance on a parallel computer system, the underlying numerical method must be efficient and attain a high level of single-processor performance. This is particularly true for a cache-based system, such as the Cray T3D used in the present study, for which inefficient transfer of data from memory to the registers via the cache can lead to significant performance degradation. A number of techniques have been employed in the code (written in Fortran 77) to optimize its single-processor performance. These include

✦ the reordering of DO-loops

✦ loop unrolling

✦ elimination or reduction of expensive operations (e.g., division)

✦ use of optimized libraries for intrinsic functions (e.g., sqrt, exp, log)

✦ use of cache prefetching

The symmetry of the Kenics mixer described earlier allows for the computation of the flow in only one-half of the pipe because tests have shown that the flow is also symmetric for the parameter range considered. The meshes used in the present study, which consist of an H-type mesh in the core of the pipe and an O-type mesh near the pipe wall, alleviate potential problems associated with a singularity at the pipe axis (see [11.5] for more details). Multiblock decomposition is very natural for this mesh; the partitioning used here involved the subdivision of the mesh into a total of 64 blocks.

Parallel Algorithm Employed

Parallelism is achieved by solving the flow equations concurrently on the block-structured mesh by assigning the computation for one block to each processor. Communication between processors is necessary to exchange data at the interface of neighboring blocks. The communication overhead is minimized by data localization using two layers of halo cells surrounding each block (see Figure 11.2 and color plate 11.2). Data are exchanged between blocks using message passing via the PVM library, which provides a good combination of performance and portability [11.22]. Load balancing is achieved by ensuring that each block has an equal, or approximately equal, number of mesh cells.

In the parallel algorithm, the values of the flow variables in the halo cells are updated at the end of each iteration. Thus, for a given iteration, the boundary values of each subdomain correspond to those of the previous iteration. Such an explicit method of imposing the boundary conditions has the advantage of separating the computation and communication phases and is thus relatively straightforward to implement. However, this modification reduces the implicit nature of the numerical algorithm and may therefore lead to convergence degradation. A number of studies [11.2, 11.13, 11.24] have addressed the convergence degradation of such parallel block-implicit methods, the conclusions de-

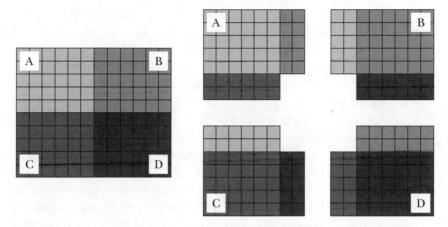

Schematic diagram illustrating the use of two layers of halo cells to increase data localization for parallel computation using a block-structured mesh. (See also color plate 11.2.)

pending on the nature of the implicit algorithm employed and the frequency with which the halo cell values are updated. In addition, it has been shown for external supersonic flows that the convergence is also strongly dependent on the block partitioning, with a partitioning that results in blocks that are approximately cubic in computational space being optimal [11.13]. Indeed, for a parallel block-implicit algorithm, ensuring adequate convergence properties is just as important as the communication-minimization and load-balancing (synchronization) criteria.

11.2.3 Particle Tracking

Programming Considerations

To determine the efficiency of a chemical mixer, it is necessary to establish means by which the fluid mixing can be gauged both qualitatively and quantitatively. For the computation of the flow of a multiple-species fluid in a static mixer, it is possible to determine the extent to which an inhomogeneous species concentration at the inlet becomes more uniform with the passage of the fluid through the mixer. Numerically, this approach has been found to be inappropriate due to the domination of numerical diffusion in the resolution of the species continuity equations compared to the physical diffusion [11.21].

A more accurate determination of the mixing phenomena can be obtained by calculating the trajectories of fluid particles in the flow field of the mixer.

Such an approach, which can be applied to a single-species fluid, has been adopted for the present study. To obtain an accurate global evaluation of the mixing, it is necessary to study the trajectories of a large number of particles, leading to the use of a massively parallel computer system.

For steady flow, as considered in the present study, particle trajectories correspond to streamlines. Some care must be taken in integrating the equation for the streamlines in order to retain a sufficient degree of accuracy. Preliminary tests have indicated that even though lower-order schemes appear to provide acceptable results, they accentuate the problem of "lost" particles—that is, particle trajectories that are trapped near a solid wall (where the local velocity is zero) or leave the computational domain. For the results presented in this chapter, therefore, a four-stage Runge-Kutta scheme was employed. In addition, to avoid problems near stagnation points, the numerical integration of the streamline equation was performed using a fixed spatial increment rather than a fixed time step. For the chosen value of the spatial increment, more than 12,000 integration steps were required to calculate each particle trajectory through the mixer. With these considerations, the number of lost particles was reduced to 1 to 5 percent, depending on the Reynolds number of the flow. No attempt was made to recuperate lost particles by reinjection into the flow field because this may unduly perturb the statistical analysis.

At the inlet of the mixer pipe, the particles were distributed uniformly in the half disc delineated by the line traversing the mixer pipe diametrically at an angle of 90° to the front edge of the first mixing element. This can be viewed as a simplified model for the diametrical feeding of the mixer with two component fluids. Particle trajectories corresponding to only one of the fluids were calculated (and plotted in this chapter); the trajectories corresponding to the second fluid can be determined by symmetry.

Parallel Algorithm Employed

The particles considered for the analysis of the mixing process are non-interacting, and therefore different trajectories can be calculated independently. There is no need for communication between independent calculations, and so such a situation represents an "embarrassingly" parallel application, which lends itself naturally to massively parallel computation. Nevertheless, since the velocity field solution is distributed among the different processors (as described in Section 11.2.2), three different approaches to parallelization of the particle tracking have been investigated.

In the first approach, the same data distribution as was used for the flow computation is retained; that is, the velocity field for different subdomains is

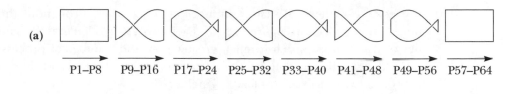

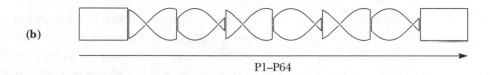

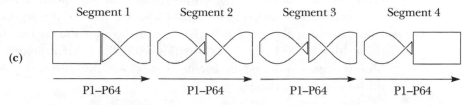

11.3

FIGURE

Schematic diagram illustrating the three approaches to parallel implementation of particle tracking on 64 processors: using the same data distribution as for the flow computation (a), replicating the entire velocity field in each processor's memory (b), and partially replicating the velocity field (c). The inlet and outlet pipes are represented by rectangles and each of the six mixing elements by curved sections (flow is from left to right).

contained in the memory associated with different processors. Each processor then undertakes the calculation of particle trajectories traversing its own subdomain, as illustrated in Figure 11.3(a). The advantage of this approach is the unique data structure and close integration of the flow-computation and particle-tracking phases. Unfortunately, such an approach was found to be inefficient because the computational load of different processors can be significantly different and changes as the particles traverse the mixer. Indeed, if a total of 64 processors are used as illustrated in Figure 11.3, at any given time during the calculation generally at most 8 processors are nonidle. This leads to a strong load imbalance that results in a correspondingly poor parallel performance.

For the second approach, the parallelism is based on the particles rather than the flow field. This involves a reorganization of the underlying data structure, with the entire velocity field stored in the memory of each processor. Each processor can then calculate a number of trajectories throughout the entire mixer, as illustrated in Figure 11.3(b). Each processor calculates the same number of trajectories, which is much greater than the number of processors. Because the calculation time for each processor is therefore almost the same, this approach exhibits excellent load balancing.

For a sufficiently fine mesh there is inadequate memory associated with each processor to contain the entire velocity field. The mixer is therefore divided into segments along the axial direction, as shown in Figure 11.3(c), with the particle trajectories in consecutive segments calculated in a sequential manner. Load balancing is again achieved by each processor calculating the same number of trajectories. This approach, however, involves additional synchronization and redistribution of data between the treatment of each segment.

Due to their high level of parallel efficiency, the second and third approaches are well suited to massively parallel computation. The second approach has been used for the particle-tracking calculation for the coarse and medium meshes with a limited number of particles, while the third approach, due to the greater storage requirements, has been employed for the fine mesh and for larger numbers of particles.

11.3   PERFORMANCE RESULTS

To provide a quantitative evaluation of the suitability of the chosen numerical methods and their parallelization, detailed measurements of code performance have been made for both the flow-computation and particle-tracking phases.

11.3.1   Flow Computation

To analyze the performance of the parallel code with respect to the preceding considerations, a number of test simulations have been performed. Figure 11.4 shows the results obtained for a 3D test problem involving the inviscid incompressible flow in a turbine cascade [11.11] using computational meshes with a total of $120 \times 52 \times 64$ mesh cells. A series of simulations was performed on a Cray T3D system, using different numbers of processors, until the convergence criterion (L2 residual less than 10^{-5}) was attained. For each simulation, the original single-block mesh was subdivided into the appropriate number of equal-sized blocks such that each block was approximately cubic in computational space. By

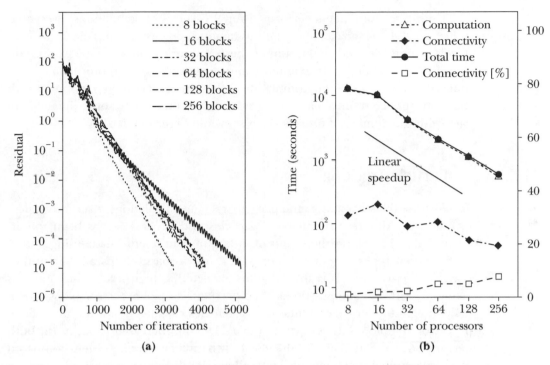

Plots of convergence histories (a) and timings measured on the Cray T3D for a
3D test problem using different numbers of processors (b).

inserting appropriate timing calls into the code, the wall clock times required to
perform the computation and the connectivity (which involves both communication between blocks and synchronization overhead) were measured for each simulation. The small I/O overhead is neglected in these timings.

From Figure 11.4(a) it can be remarked that although a convergence degradation is measured, it is modest. Indeed, increasing the number of processors (and also, therefore, the number of blocks) from 8 to 256 requires only a 24
percent increase in the number of iterations needed for convergence. Surprisingly, it can be observed from Figure 11.4(a) that the convergence degradation
is not monotonic with the number of processors employed, the greatest number
of iterations being required for a 16-block simulation. The origin of this behavior has not been elucidated, although it indicates that the convergence rates for
the present incompressible flow simulations are determined not only by the
number and shape of the blocks but also by the transient solutions within each
block.

Timing measurements performed for this series of simulations, presented in Figure 11.4(b), show that for the full range of processors employed, the connectivity time (defined as the sum of the communication and synchronization times) is very small. The maximum connectivity time for 256 processors is less than 10 percent of the total simulation time. This observation, combined with the convergence results, leads to a performance that scales approximately linearly with the number of processors, as shown in Figure 11.4(b).

11.3.2 Particle Tracking

To illustrate the scalability of the particle-tracking calculations, a series of calculations using different numbers of particles and processors has been undertaken. Table 11.1 shows the results of timing measurements made using both a conventional supercomputer (Cray Y-MP) and a massively parallel computer (Cray T3D). These results show that, as expected, a high level of scalability is achieved, with the computational time per particle per processor being essentially independent of the number of trajectories calculated and the number of processors employed. As shown in Table 11.1, the increased capacity (in both performance and memory) of the massively parallel computer system compared to a conventional supercomputer thus allows significantly more particle trajectories to be calculated.

11.4 INDUSTRIAL RESULTS

A wide range of industrial flow applications can benefit from analysis using the computational approach that has been presented and analyzed in the previous sections. Detailed numerical simulations have been undertaken for the Kenics static mixer, both to gain a knowledge of the basic flow behavior and as a means for optimization of the mixer geometry.

11.4.1 Numerical Solutions

Using the numerical methods described, the flow in a six-element Kenics static mixer has been analyzed for a number of different flow conditions. While previous studies have generally concentrated on creeping flows [11.1, 11.14], the present study considered a range of Reynolds number (Re being based on the

Number of particles	Cray Y-MP time	Cray T3D time
4,160	68 min	17 min (16 proc.)
16,512	270 min	34 min (32 proc.)
65,792		68 min (64 proc.)
262,656		135 min (128 proc.)
1,049,600		540 min (128 proc.)

11.1

TABLE

Computational times required to calculate particle trajectories using two different computer systems.

pipe radius). Only the salient features of the flow fields and mixing analysis are presented here; more details for the range of conditions considered can be found in [11.6, 11.7, 11.21]. The results presented here were obtained using a computational mesh having a total of 1,505,280 cells (for the computation domain of half the mixer). Since the mesh had 64 blocks, the flow in the mixer was computed using 64 processors. All blocks had exactly the same number of cells to ensure optimal load balancing between processors.

The flow in the Kenics mixer is best represented by the crosswise velocity in a helical coordinate system that accounts for the local twist of the mixing elements [11.7]. Figure 11.5 shows plots of the crosswise velocity computed for flow with $Re = 100$ at different axial locations along the mixer. From these plots, it can be seen that the rotation of the fluid in the opposite sense to the helical twist of the mixing element leads to the creation of a vortical structure. For this particular Reynolds number, contrary to observations for creeping flow [11.7, 11.21], a secondary vortex is also seen to develop on the suction side of each element. An axially periodic flow, having the same periodicity as the mixer geometry, is observed to be rapidly established.

Using these computed velocity fields, the trajectories of 262,656 particles injected into the mixer have been calculated. (To simplify the graphical representation, only one of the two component species is considered here, as discussed in Section 11.2.3.) The plots of the particle positions at different axial locations, shown in Figure 11.6, illustrate the redistribution of the particles by means of the combined effect of flow division and reversal, resulting in stretching and folding of the observed structures. Each mixing element is seen to divide by 2 the size of these structures, with the vortices contributing to the elongation of the structures and hence to the mixing process. Such behavior is characteristic of fluid mixing via chaotic advection [11.18].

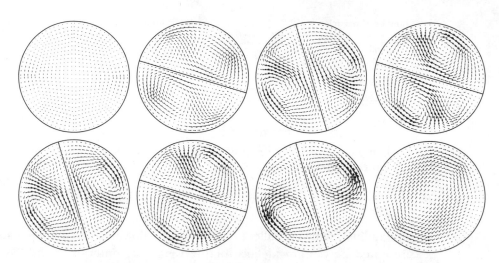

Crosswise velocity vectors in the helical coordinate system computed for flow with Re = 100 at different axial locations along the mixer using the fine mesh. (From top left to bottom right: near end of inlet pipe, near end of each of the six mixing elements, and at the outlet.)

The calculated structures in the particle positions at different axial locations are observed to vary with the Reynolds number of the flow. This is illustrated by Figure 11.7, which shows the particle positions at the mixer outlet for two different values of Reynolds number. In particular, for Re = 25, large structures corresponding to regions of poor mixing persist until the exit of the mixer (see [11.6, 11.7] for more details).

11.4.2　　Optimization Results

In its standard design (as considered previously), the Kenics mixer consists of helical elements of 1.5 pipe diameters in length with a twist angle of 180 degrees. Based on qualitative arguments, this choice of twist angle is often considered optimal for creeping flow, although numerical simulations using simplified models suggest that a smaller angle may provide better results [11.1, 11.10]. Due to the increased complexity of the flow and associated mixing process at higher Reynolds number, it is not obvious that the standard twist angle of 180 degrees is appropriate under all flow conditions.

To evaluate the influence of the twist angle on the mixing efficiency, a series of numerical simulations have been performed for 13 different twist an-

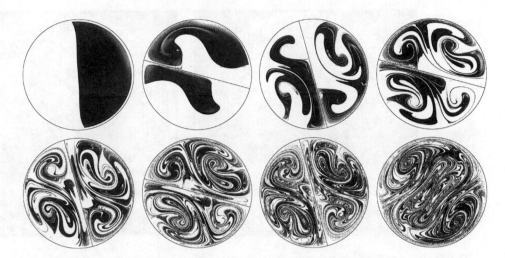

Plots of the positions of 262,656 particles computed for flow with Re = 100 at different axial locations along the mixer. (From top left to bottom right: near end of inlet pipe, near end of each of the six mixing elements, and at the outlet.)

gles between 0 and 360 degrees. Due to the sizable computational resources required (approximately 4800 processor-hours for the flow computation and 3840 processor-hours for the particle tracking), this study has been undertaken only for Re = 100.

A practical measure of the quality of the mixing can be obtained by defining the 2D structure radius at a given axial location, normalized to the pipe radius, to correspond to the radius of the largest circle that can be drawn around a particle of one of the component species that does not contain any particles of the second species. The mixing efficiency can then be defined as

$$E = (-\Delta p\, r_s)^{-1}$$

where $-\Delta p$ is the total pressure drop along the mixer, and r_s is the structure radius at the end of the last (sixth) mixing element.

Figure 11.8(a) and (b) shows the computed dependence of the pressure drop and the structure radius on the twist angle. As expected, with increasing twist angle, the pressure drop along the mixer increases while the structure radius decreases. As a result, Figure 11.8(c) shows that a maximum of the mixing

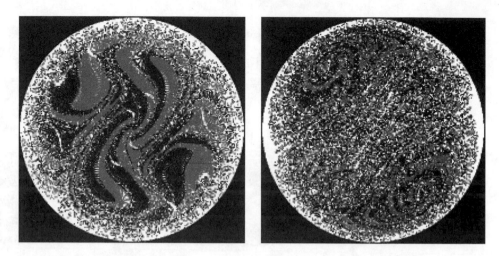

Positions of 65,792 particle trajectories at the mixer outlet for each of the two species for Re = 25 (left) and Re = 100 (right).

efficiency is computed for a twist angle of 180 degrees. Thus, although the qualitative arguments proposed for creeping flow are not valid for flow with Re = 100, nevertheless a twist angle of 180 degrees appears to be optimal.

11.4.3   Future Work

Because the flow in the Kenics mixer is characteristic of chaotic advection, more insight into the nature of the mixing process can be obtained by applying chaotic analysis to the trajectories (e.g., Poincaré sections) and analyzing chaotic quantitative measures (e.g., Lyapanov exponents). Such an extension is presented in [11.6, 11.7]. In addition, the present mixing analysis has neglected any diffusion between the different component species of the mixture. Species diffusion can be incorporated into the particle-tracking technique by superimposing a Brownian motion on the particle trajectories. More details regarding the implementation and results of such an extension can be found in [11.7, 11.21].

In addition, a number of extensions to the present work of direct interest to the process industry can be proposed. These include a more complete determination of the optimal parameters of the Kenics mixer (e.g., element length, pipe diameter) and their dependence on Reynolds number, the study of the mixing of species having different physical properties, and the application to mixers of different types (both static mixers and stirred tanks).

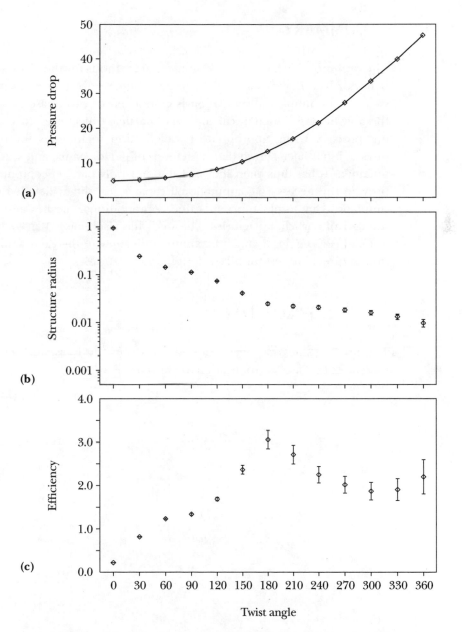

11.8 FIGURE

Dependence on the twist angle of pressure drop along the mixer (a), structure radius (b), and resulting mixing efficiency for flow with Re = 100 (c).

11.5   SUMMARY

The present study has described numerical methods for the investigation of flow behavior in a Kenics static mixer using a high-performance parallel computer system. The numerical simulation is comprised of two phases, computation of the flow fields followed by calculation of particle trajectories, to analyze the mixing process. Using appropriate parallelization techniques for both of these phases, it has been shown that high levels of performance and scalability can be obtained. It has thus been shown that a massively parallel computer system can provide the necessary computational capacity to obtain detailed and accurate simulations by using sufficiently fine computational meshes and an adequate number of particle trajectories. The study has also enabled an evaluation of the optimal twist angle to obtain maximum efficiency in the Kenics mixer, information of direct interest for mixer design optimization.

ACKNOWLEDGMENTS

The present study has been undertaken within the framework of the Cray Research–EPFL Parallel Application Technology Program.

References

[11.1] Arimond, J., and L., Erwin. 1985. A Simulation of a Motionless Mixer. *Chemical Engineering Communications,* **37,** 105–126.

[11.2] Badcock, K. J., W. McMillan, M. A. Woodgate, B. Gribben, S. Porter, and B. E. Richards. 1997. Integration of an Implicit Multiblock Code into a Workstation Environment. In P. Schiano et al. (eds.), *Parallel Computational Fluid Dynamics: Algorithms and Results Using Advanced Computers.* Amsterdam: North-Holland, 408–415.

[11.3] Bailey, D. H., P. E. Bjørstad, J. R. Gilbert, M. V. Mascagni, R. S. Schreiber, H. D. Simon, V. J. Torczon, and L. T. Watson (eds.). 1995. *Proceedings of the Seventh SIAM Conference on Parallel Processing for Scientific Computing,* San Francisco, Feb.

[11.4] Bakker, A., and E. M. Marshall. 1992. *Laminar Mixing with Kenics In-line Mixers.* Fluent Inc. Users' Group Meeting, Burlington, VT, Oct. 1992.

[11.5] Byrde, O., and M. L. Sawley. 1999. Parallel Computation and Analysis of the Flow in a Static Mixer. *Computers and Fluids,* **28,** 1–18.

[11.6] Byrde, O., and M. L. Sawley. 1997. *Analysis of Chaotic Flow in a Realistic Static Mixer under Laminar Non-creeping Conditions.* Technical Report T-97–12. Fluid Mechanics Laboratory, EPF-Lausanne.

[11.7] Byrde, O. 1997. *Massively Parallel Flow Computation with Application to Fluid Mixing.* Ph.D. Thesis No. 1736, EPF-Lausanne.

[11.8] Chaussee, D. S., and T. H. Pulliam. 1980. *A Diagonal Form of an Implicit Approximate Factorization Algorithm with Application to a Two Dimensional Inlet.* IAAA Paper 80-0067.

[11.9] Chorin, A. J. 1967. A Numerical Method for Solving Incompressible Viscous Flow Problems. *Journal of Computational Physics,* **2,** 12–26.

[11.10] Dackson, K., and E. B. Nauman. 1987. Fully Developed Flow in Twisted Tapes: A Model for Motionless Mixers. *Chemical Engineering Communications,* **54,** 381–395.

[11.11]   Gregory-Smith, D. G. 1994. *Test Case 3: Durham Low Speed Turbine Cascade.* ERCOFTAC Seminar and Workshop on 3D Turbomachinery Flow Prediction II. Val d'Isère, Jan. 1994, Part III, 96–109.

[11.12]   Harnby, N., M. F. Edwards, and A. W. Nienow. 1992. *Mixing in the Process Industries,* 2nd ed. Oxford: Butterworth-Heinemann.

[11.13]   Jenssen, C. B. 1994. Implicit Multiblock Euler and Navier-Stokes Calculations. *AIAA Journal,* **32,** 1808–1814.

[11.14]   Ling, F. H., and X. Zang. 1995. A Numerical Study on Mixing in the Kenics Static Mixer. *Chemical Engineering Communications,* **136,** 119–141.

[11.15]   Marx, Y. 1991. *A Numerical Method for the Solution of the Incompressible Navier-Stokes Equations.* Technical Report T-91–3. Fluid Mechanics Laboratory, EPF-Lausanne.

[11.16]   Marx, Y. 1992. *On the Artificial Compressibility Coefficient for the Solution of the Incompressible Navier-Stokes Equations.* Technical Report T-92–2, Fluid Mechanics Laboratory, EPF-Lausanne.

[11.17]   Myers, K. J., A. Bakker, and D. Ryan. 1997. Avoid Agitation by Selecting Static Mixers. *Chemical Engineering Progress,* **93,** 28–38.

[11.18]   Ottino, J. 1989. *The Kinematics of Mixing: Stretching, Chaos, and Transport.* Cambridge: Cambridge University Press.

[11.19]   Pahl, M. H., and E. Muschelknautz. 1982. Static Mixers and Their Applications. *International Chemical Engineering,* **22,** 197–205.

[11.20]   Roe, P. L. 1981. Approximate Riemann Solvers, Parameter Vectors, and Difference Schemes. *Journal of Computational Physics,* **43,** 357–372.

[11.21]   Sawley, M. L., and O. Byrde. 1997. *A Study of Numerical Methods for the Simulation of Mixing of Diffusive Fluids.* Technical Report T-97–11. Fluid Mechanics Laboratory, EPF-Lausanne.

[11.22]   Sawley, M. L., and J. K. Tegnér. 1995. A Comparison of Parallel Programming Models for Multiblock Flow Computations. *Journal of Computational Physics,* **122,** 280–290.

[11.23]   Schiano, P., A. Ecer, J. Périaux, and N. Satofuka (eds.). 1997. *Parallel Computational Fluid Dynamics: Algorithms and Results Using Advanced Computers.* Amsterdam: North-Holland.

[11.24]   Schreck, E., and M. Peric. 1993. Computation of Fluid Flow with a Parallel Multigrid Solver. *International Journal for Numerical Methods in Fluids,* **16,** 303–327.

[11.25]   Van Leer, B. 1977. Towards the Ultimate Conservative Difference Scheme IV. A New Approach to Numerical Convection. *Journal of Computational Physics,* **23,** 276–298.

12 | Modeling Groundwater Flow and Contaminant Transport

William J. Bosl
Steven F. Ashby
Chuck Baldwin
Robert D. Falgout
Steven G. Smith
Andrew F. B. Tompson   Lawrence Livermore National Laboratory

Groundwater contamination is a major problem throughout the world. In the United States, for instance, numerous governmental and industrial sites require remediation. The Department of Energy (DOE) is currently cleaning up several of its contaminated sites, including Lawrence Livermore National Laboratory (LLNL). In an attempt to understand the efficacy of a given remediation approach, as well as to determine the most economical implementation for a specific technique, engineers frequently employ mathematical models to aid in the design and analysis of various strategies. The computing power needed for these simulations can be quite staggering and necessitates the use of massively parallel computers. The ParFlow project is an effort to develop new, efficient algorithms to solve the equations that arise in groundwater and contaminant-transport simulation. The focus is on the underlying numerical algorithms, which are designed for optimal performance in a multiprocessor, distributed-memory environment. Performance results and scalability issues will be discussed.

12.1   INTRODUCTION

The numerical simulation of subsurface fluid flow and chemical migration plays an increasingly important role in several environmental applications, including groundwater remediation studies and groundwater resource management. Although sophisticated simulations have been used for decades in the petroleum industry with considerable success, they have been less widely used in environmental applications; they are gaining in popularity as sites become larger and more complex. Computational environmental remediation is particularly attractive for the design, evaluation, and management of engineered remediation procedures [12.23], especially for large industrial and government sites. Simulations can be used, for instance, to choose the best cleanup strategy for a given site and then, once a scheme is chosen, to manage it in the most cost-effective fashion. They also can be used to perform more realistic risk assessment in support of key decision-making and as an aid in demonstrating regulatory compliance.

Contaminant distributions are usually found in distinct, 3D patterns. This is caused by the complex flow patterns in the medium, including flow in more conductive lenses and strata, diffusion into less-permeable zones, sorption onto variably reactive minerals, and a sporadic history of introduction into the subsurface. Although the dispersive nature of flow in porous media can be described mathematically by a dispersion tensor, this is not a measureable quantity. The heterogeneous nature of porous materials is the primary cause of flow anisotropy and nonuniformity and the dispersion of contaminants carried by the flow field [12.8]. The composition of formations and the associated hydraulic and chemical properties can be measured in the field on some scale. Thus, it is desirable to simulate flow and transport on a scale at which the aquifer properties can be measured in order to study the effect of property heterogeneities on contaminant transport.

Unfortunately, the data required to describe the structure and material characteristics of a subsurface flow formation, as well as the contaminant distribution within it, are usually small because of the high cost of data acquisition and the impossibility of making measurements at all possible locations of interest. In addition, because of the nonuniform nature of the system, the quantitative distribution of properties such as the hydraulic conductivity or reactive mineral abundance can be quite large. The sparsity and variation of the data can introduce a large element of uncertainty into modeling analyses.

Although this uncertainty is usually recognized, little is done to address its subsequent implications in predicting flow and contaminant migration, estimating downgradient health risks, and designing and implementing in situ remediation procedures. Hydraulic heterogeneity may reduce the efficiency of pump-and-treat schemes in removing (diffused) contaminants from low permeability zones or may enhance other remedial approaches that rely on the in situ mixing of injected reagents and contaminants or on natural attenuation processes. Similarly, chemical (or mineralogic) heterogeneity can alter the overall speciation and mobility of reactive contaminant and remedial reagent mixtures and should be considered an important factor in the design and applicability of many in situ remediation technologies. Large-scale computing can be used to estimate the uncertainty in the system by simulating transport using many equiprobable realizations of the site parameters. In this way, engineers can gain some understanding of the range of possible outcomes and their likelihood, even though definitive predictions are impossible without complete knowledge of the system.

The size of the site to be modeled (typically, several square kilometers) and the desire to resolve these heterogeneities adequately lead to very large computational domains. The use of adaptive gridding and local refinement can considerably reduce the total number of zones needed, but huge problems that quickly overwhelm all but the largest of conventional supercomputers remain. Moreover, we need to run hundreds of such simulations as we conduct time-dependent studies, examine different remediation or production strategies, or run the code in a Monte Carlo fashion or within an optimization code. In light of these considerations, it is necessary to employ MPP power; toward this end, we are building a parallel flow simulator called ParFlow. It is designed to be portable and scalable across a variety of distributed-memory MIMD machines with message passing, ranging from workstation clusters to large MPPs.

Massively parallel processing may be necessary for detailed simulations, but it is not sufficient. High-performance algorithms—that is, accurate and fast numerical techniques that can be implemented efficiently on these machines—also need to be employed. As we will see, simply changing the linear-equation solver can result in a reduction in CPU time of two orders of magnitude. This is especially important in time-dependent simulations, where the right numerical method can mean the difference between a 30-hour run and a 30-minute run on an MPP.

12.2   NUMERICAL SIMULATION OF GROUNDWATER FLOW

Flow in porous media and contaminant transport are described mathematically by Darcy's law and the advection-diffusion equation, respectively. The particular form of these equations used in ParFlow is presented here. The discretization scheme used to transform these continuous equations into a discrete algorithm is then reviewed.

12.2.1   Flow and Transport Model

We intend to simulate steady groundwater flow, contaminant migration, and contaminant extraction from a pump-and-treat process inside of this domain. Ultimately, we intend to use the model to study the performance of more advanced remediation methods that are more sensitive to mass transport and chemical reaction issues in heterogeneous media.

Steady, saturated flow in this system is described by

$$\varepsilon v = -K\nabla h \tag{12.1}$$

where $v(\mathbf{x})$ is the average groundwater seepage velocity (L/T), $h(\mathbf{x})$ is the hydraulic head (L), $K(\mathbf{x})$ is the medium hydraulic conductivity (L/T), and ε is the medium porosity. In saturated, nondeforming media with only wells to represent external sources or sinks of mass, h satisfies

$$\nabla \cdot (K\nabla h) = \sum_w Q_w \delta(\mathbf{x} - \mathbf{x}_w) \tag{12.2}$$

where $Q_\omega > 0$ (L^3/T) represents a loss of fluid due to extraction pumping at location x_ω

The migration of a dissolved, neutrally buoyant chemical constituent in the groundwater is described by

$$\frac{\partial(\mathcal{R}\varepsilon c)}{\partial t} + \nabla \cdot (\varepsilon c v) - \nabla \cdot (\varepsilon \mathbf{D} \cdot \nabla c) = -c \sum_w Q_w \delta(\mathbf{x} - \mathbf{x}_w) \tag{12.3}$$

where $c(x, t)$ is the average aqueous concentration (M/L^3) at a point in the medium [12.8]. The quantity

$$\mathbf{D}(\mathbf{x}) \approx (\alpha_T |+ \mathcal{D})\mathbf{I} + (\alpha_L - \alpha_T) \frac{vv}{|v|} \tag{12.4}$$

is the velocity-dependent hydrodynamic dispersion tensor (L^2/T), α_L and α_T are the local longitudinal and transverse dispersivities (L), and $\mathcal{D}$ is the aqueous molecular diffusivity (L^2/T). In (12.3) we have assumed that sorption onto the mineral phase may occur reversibly and in an equilibrium fashion such that the total (aqueous plus sorbed) concentration may be related to the aqueous concentration by $\rho(x, t) = \varepsilon c + (1 - \varepsilon) s = \varepsilon c \mathcal{R}$, where $s(x, t)$ is the sorbed concentration (M/L^3) on the soil matrix and $\mathcal{R}$ is the local partitioning or retardation capacity of the soil, which may generally be concentration dependent.

12.2.2   Discrete Solution Approach

We employ a standard 7-point finite volume spatial discretization on a uniform mesh. After discretization, we obtain a large system of linear equations, $Ah = f$. The coefficient matrix A is symmetric positive definite and has the usual 7-stripe pattern. The matrix has order $N = n_x \times n_y \times n_z$, where the n_i are the number of grid points in the x, y, and z directions, respectively. For problems of interest, N is in the millions; the large number is dictated by the size of the physical site and the desire to resolve heterogeneities on a relatively small scale (tens to a few hundreds of meters). Once the pressure head is computed, the velocity field can be calculated easily using a simple differencing scheme. This field is then passed to a transport code to simulate contaminant migration.

The solution of the large linear system is computationally intensive and must be done efficiently and accurately. Because we are interested in detailed simulations (i.e., high resolution), we must use an iterative scheme. Within the hydrology community, the most commonly used methods are the Strongly Implicit Method (SIP) and Symmetric Successive Overrelaxation (SSOR). Recently, however, the more powerful Conjugate-Gradient Method of Hestenes and Stiefel (CGHS) [12.15] and its preconditioned version (PCG) [12.7] have been used with great success. For example, polynomial preconditioned conjugate gradient method was shown [12.17] to be an order of magnitude faster than SIP and SSOR on groundwater problems.

Multigrid algorithms also are attractive for these types of problems. These techniques are among the fastest currently available for the solution of linear systems arising from the discretization of elliptic partial differential equations. Unlike most other iterative methods, a good multigrid solver's rate of convergence is independent of problem size, meaning that the number of iterations remains fairly constant. Hence, both the multigrid algorithm and its parallel implementation are highly scalable (see Section 12.3.5). On the other hand, multigrid algorithms tend to be problem specific and less robust than Krylov iterative methods such as conjugate gradients. Fortunately, it is easy to combine the best features of multigrid and conjugate gradients into one algorithm: multigrid preconditioned conjugate gradients. The resulting algorithm is robust, efficient, and scalable.

Another advantage of this approach is that one can quickly implement a simple multigrid algorithm that is extremely effective as a preconditioner but perhaps less effective as a stand-alone solver. This is especially valuable when the underlying partial differential equation (PDE) has a nearly discontinuous coefficient function, as in our case.

12.3   PARALLEL IMPLEMENTATION

The problem data is distributed across a virtual 3D process grid consisting of $P = p \times q \times r$ processes. The grid points within a process are arranged as a 3D subgrid, and the code uses a nested loop to access these points. This loop is our key computational kernel, and its efficient implementation is crucial, as we will see in the next section. The computations are organized so as to avoid explicit data redistribution, thereby improving the code's efficiency. (This is one of the benefits of writing the code from scratch.) Although each process has a piece of the problem domain, we are *not* doing domain decomposition in the algorithmic sense. We are solving the *full* problem rather than independent subproblems. When possible, we have overlapped communication with computations, thereby enhancing scalability on machines that support overlapped communication.

We are using message passing to realize portability across a variety of distributed-memory MIMD computing platforms. At present, we are using Another Message Passing System (AMPS), a message-passing layer derived from Zipcode [12.20] with additional I/O capabilities (e.g., parallel file read/write) and persistent communication objects. The layer was designed to map efficiently onto the Message Processing Interface (MPI). We have successfully run ParFlow on the following platforms: an Intel PC running Windows 95 and NT, a single Sparcstation, a cluster of Sparcstations, a multiprocessor SGI Onyx, an nCUBE/2, an IBM SP-1 and SP-2, and the Cray T3D.

12.3.1   Parallel Random Field Generation

The hydraulic conductivity realization is central to the problem definition and is represented by the K function in Equation (12.2). The hydraulic conductivity function can be represented mathematically as a random field (RF). This is a generalization of a random function, well known in probability theory. Conceptually, a random field consists of values at spatial points that are drawn from a prescribed statistical distribution, commonly a Gaussian distribution. The specific values drawn at a given spatial location at a given time are *correlated* to nearby values. That is, high values are more likely to have high values nearby than low values. This kind of spatial correlation is observed in nature.

Of course, we never have enough data to characterize a given site completely. Equiprobable realizations of random fields, such as the K-field, are generated using geostatistical algorithms [12.22]. Flow simulations using many equiprobable realizations allow the use of Monte Carlo and optimization techniques to quantify inherent uncertainty and enable site managers to perform more realistic risk assessments. Although these realizations cannot give the precise value of the hydraulic conductivity at an (x, y, z) coordinate, they do reproduce the statistical patterns of heterogeneity observed in real systems and can be used to evaluate the effectiveness of various remediation strategies.

The generation of the hydraulic conductivity realization is central to the problem definition. The spatial correlation of random fields poses a difficult computational problem for parallel applications. We use domain decomposition to divide the computational domain into subdomains, which are distributed to the computer's processors. Thus, we have had to modify traditional geostatistical algorithms to run efficiently on parallel computers. We have developed two such algorithms.

The first is a modification of the turning bands algorithm [12.22], which is a technique for computing a spectral random field with given statistical properties (mean μ, variance σ^2, and correlation lengths λ_x, λ_y, and λ_z). The algorithm has two phases: the generation of one-dimensional Gaussian distributions along spatially oriented lines, and the projection of grid points onto those lines. In the first phase, a number of rays through the origin (typically, 50–100) are created, and one-dimensional random variables are generated along these. This requires cosines, which are more expensive than multiplications on RISC machines. (On the Cray T3D, the cosine function is about 10 times slower.) The degree of parallelism here depends on the process grid topology: If the topology is too skewed, then each process may compute nearly an entire line, which degrades parallelism. Ideally, the process grid topology should match the topology of the discretized domain. In the second phase, these 1D fields are combined to produce a 3D random field. Specifically, each point is projected onto the lines, and these values are combined to determine the value of the 3D field at the given point. This projection phase is fully parallelizable, meaning that the computations are distributed equally across all processes with no redundancy. In contrast, some of the line-generation computations may be replicated across one or more processes depending on the problem and the virtual process grid topology. See

[12.22] for a description of the turning bands algorithm, and see [12.4] for a discussion of its parallel implementation.

Another algorithm that is commonly used for random field generation is the sequential Gaussian simulation (SGS) algorithm [12.12]. As its name implies, this algorithm is inherently sequential. In all implementations of this method, a limited search radius is employed to survey the neighborhood around a spatial point at which a random field value is to be simulated. This limited search radius is exploited in our parallel random field simulation (prfs) algorithm. The details of this algorithm will be described in [12.6].

12.3.2   Preconditioned Conjugate Gradient Solver

We have implemented several preconditioned conjugate gradient algorithms for solving the large linear systems that result from the discretization of Equation (12.2). The algorithm is well known [12.7] and will not be repeated here; its key components are one matrix-vector multiplication, one preconditioning step, three vector updates, and two inner products. In this chapter, we present results for diagonal, two-step Jacobi, and multigrid preconditionings; the algorithms are denoted DSCG, J2CG, and MGCG, respectively. The multigrid preconditioner consists of a single V-cycle with semicoarsening [12.3].

The coefficient matrix A is viewed as a stencil distributed across the processes analogous to the data distribution. To compute the matvec result at a given grid point (i,j,k), we "apply" the stencil to the grid: For each neighboring grid point specified by the stencil, we multiply the vector value at that point by the corresponding stencil coefficient and then sum these products. That is, component $y_{i,j,k}$ of the matrix-vector product is given by

$$y_{i,j,k} = w_{i,j,k}\, x_{i-1,j,k} + e_{i,j,k}\, x_{i+1,j,k} + s_{i,j,k}\, x_{i,j-1,k} + n_{i,j,k}\, x_{i,j+1,k}$$
$$+ l_{i,j,k}\, x_{i,j,k-1} + u_{i,j,k}\, x_{i,j,k+1} + c_{i,j,k}\, x_{i,j,k}$$

which is equivalent to multiplying a row of the matrix by the vector x. By viewing the matrix-vector multiplication in this way, it is readily apparent which data need to be communicated—namely, process boundary data. We therefore exchange interprocess boundary data at the start of a matvec. To facilitate this, there is a single layer of ghost points for storing the interprocess data; a single layer suffices because we have a 7-point stencil. Once each process has the data it needs, intraprocess matvecs are carried out in parallel. Of course, it is possible to overlap some of the communication with computation. Specifically, the intraprocess matvec can work on the process's internal mesh points first, then update the boundary mesh points after the communication step is complete. For large problems on machines that allow overlapping of communication and computations, this communication will be concluded before the internal mesh points have been updated.

12.3.3   Gridding and Data Distribution

A *grid* in ParFlow is a collection of Cartesian *subgrids*. These subgrids are defined in terms of integer quantities to simplify coding and increase performance (integer arithmetic is faster than real arithmetic, and it is not subject to roundoff error). Specifically, subgrids are defined in terms of the integer index triples, (i,j,k), of an *index-space* I_1. An index-space has a *resolution level, l,* which determines how an integer triple maps to the real-space grid coordinate, $(x_{i,l}, y_{j,l}, z_{k,l})$. This mapping is given specifically as

$$x_{i,l} = x_0 + i \left(\frac{\Delta x}{2^r_{x,l}} \right)$$

$$y_{j,l} = y_0 + j \left(\frac{\Delta y}{2^r_{y,l}} \right)$$

$$z_{k,l} = z_0 + k \left(\frac{\Delta z}{2^r_{z,l}} \right) \tag{12.5}$$

where the reference point (x_o, y_o, z_o) and spacings Δx, Δy, and Δz, together are called the *background* and where $r_{x,l}, r_{y,l}$ and $r_{z,l}$ represent the resolutions of I_l. Note that these resolutions may be positive (finer subgrids), negative (coarser subgrids), or zero. The resolution level, l, allows us to define coarse grids for multigrid algorithms and may also be used to define composite grids in adaptive mesh-refinement algorithms.

A *subregion* is a collection of indices in I_l separated by integer strides in each of the spatial directions. For example, a subregion may consist of every other point in x or every third point in both x and y. Finally, a *region* is just a collection of subregions. We usually use regions to describe pieces of subgrids. As we will see, we can use them to describe grid data that need to be communicated with other processes, or we can use them to describe computation patterns. For example, we can describe red subgrid points and black subgrid points for the red/ black Gauss-Seidel algorithm via two regions, each consisting of four subregions with stride 2 in each direction.

The algorithms in ParFlow all employ a straightforward data-decomposition approach to parallelism. Specifically, problem data is distributed across a logical 3D process grid topology consisting of $P = p \times q \times r$ processes. The data within each process are associated with a subgrid, as defined by the discretization of Equation (12.2). In particular, vector data owned by a process is called a *subvector,* and each element of a subvector is associated with a grid point in the process's subgrid. Similarly, matrix data owned by a process forms a *submatrix.* The rows of this submatrix are viewed as stencils, and each stencil is associated with a grid point in the process's subgrid. Note that although we distribute the problem data by decomposing the problem domain, we are *not* doing domain decomposition in the algorithmic sense. We are solving the *full* problem rather than independent subproblems.

12.3.4   Parallel Computations in ParFlow

Computations in ParFlow proceed in an *owner computes* fashion. That is, processes only do computations associated with their local subgrid, taking care to exchange data with neighboring processes when needed. For example, consider matrix-vector multiplication, $y = Ax$, a key operation in the conjugate gradients (CG) solver. To compute the matvec result at a given grid point (i,j,k), we "apply" the stencil to the grid: For each neighboring grid point specified by the stencil, we multiply the vector value at that point by the corresponding stencil coefficient, then sum these products. (This is equivalent to multiplying a row of the matrix A by the vector x.) However, at subgrid boundary points, some stencil coefficients may reach outside of the process's subgrid. At these points, we must first communicate data from neighboring processes. In general, these communications patterns can be quite complicated. Take, for example, pointwise red/ black Gauss-Seidel. Before a process can do a red sweep, it must exchange black boundary data with neighboring processes. Likewise, red boundary data must be exchanged before a black sweep can be completed. In order to simplify coding and speed application development, subvectors and submatrices have an additional layer of space set aside for storing this communicated boundary data. The grid points associated with this layer are called *ghost points*.

Because the computations in ParFlow are structured, we represent them as *stencils* operating on *grids*. From this stencil/grid description of computations, it is easy to determine the communications required to complete the computations in parallel. Furthermore, we can easily structure the communications and computations so as to overlap them (assuming that the parallel machine has the appropriate hardware support). To do this, we first decompose process subgrids into four regions: an *independent computations region,* which describes those stencil computations that do not require data from neighboring processes; a *dependent computations region,* which describes those stencil computations that do depend on data from neighboring processes; a *send region,* which indicates which data must be sent to neighboring processes to complete the computations; and a *receive region,* which indicates which data must be received from neighboring processes to complete the computations. The parallel computations then proceed as follows:

Initiate communications   (12.6a)

Do stencil computations on independent computations region (12.6b)

Finish communications   (12.6c)

Do stencil computations on dependent computations region   (12.6d)

With the appropriate hardware support, the communications in step (12.6a) and the computations in step (12.6b) can be carried out simultaneously. For large-enough problem sizes, the communications may finish before the computations, effectively masking communications. Note that on most machines with this support, there is a startup communications cost that cannot be overlapped with computations. For large-enough problem sizes, this overhead is negligible.

As an example, consider the Godunov method, where for simplicity we consider only a 2D method. In Figure 12.1, we illustrate the 33-point stencil for this method. The figure also illustrates an example 9×7 subgrid, with neighboring subgrids only partially shown as open unshaded boxes. We will refer to the neighboring subgrids by their compass positions (north pointing upward) relative to the shaded 9×7 subgrid, and we will assume that each of the subgrids lives on a different process. In Figure 12.2, we illustrate a subvector (data represented by ●) with three ghost layers surrounding it (data represented by ○): The left-hand figure shows the send regions (shaded boxes) and receive regions (clear boxes) for the Godunov method. The right-hand figure shows the dependent computations region (shaded boxes) and independent computations region (clear boxes) for the Godunov method.

12.1

FIGURE

Stencil for the Godunov method (left) and a 9 × 7 subgrid (shaded box) with neighboring subgrids (partial boxes) (right).

If we place the Godunov stencil over each grid point in the 9 × 7 subgrid and note the grid points the stencil touches, it is easy to determine that the data needed *from* neighboring processes to complete the stencil computations is given by the receive regions depicted in Figure 12.2. If we apply this same technique to each of the neighboring subgrids, it is also easy to determine that the data needed *by* neighboring processes to complete their stencil computations is given by the send regions depicted in the figure. We see that data must be sent to and received from eight neighboring processes. Note also that the regions sent to and received from corner processes (e.g., the northeast process) are made up of 3 × 1 and 1 × 2 subgrid pairs. Even though each of these corner regions consists of multiple subgrids, each region is either sent or received in just *one* communication. To determine the dependent computations region in this example, we again place the Godunov stencil over each grid point in the 9 × 7 subgrid and note those grid points at which the stencil reaches outside of the subgrid (see Figure 12.2). The independent computations region consists of every grid point in the 9 × 7 subgrid that is not in the dependent computations region. Note that the 3 × 1 independent computations region depicted in Figure 12.2 is much larger for typical problem sizes; it is small in this example to save space.

Subgrids along domain boundaries need to communicate with fewer than eight neighbors. In the preceding example, corner subgrids would need to swap data with only three neighbors. Also, if the subgrids in Figure 12.1 had fewer than three points in any of the directions, communications would involve more than eight neighbors. Note that this can easily be extended to situations with

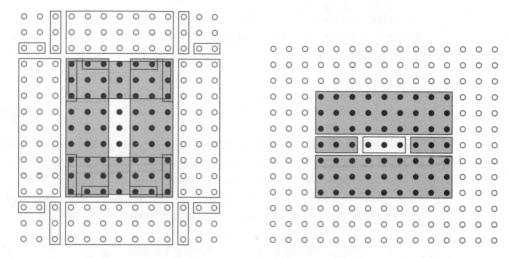

Send (shaded boxes) and receive (clear boxes) regions for Godunov method (left) and dependent (shaded boxes) and independent (clear boxes) regions for Godunov method (right).

overlapping subgrids or subgrids that are not uniformly distributed throughout the domain. Note that in three dimensions, the analogous Godunov stencil has 135 points, and the communications usually involve 26 neighboring processes.

We remark that ParFlow was designed to be parallel from its inception. In particular, computations are organized so as to avoid explicit data redistribution, thereby improving the code's efficiency and parallel performance. The choice of process grid topology P can have a significant impact on performance, largely due to cache issues [12.4]. Thus, in choosing the topology P, the competing needs of various portions of the code must be weighed and the best overall topology determined. We believe different topologies should *not* be chosen for different stages of the calculations and data redistributed within the simulation.

12.3.5   Scalability

There are two types of scalability that we will address in this chapter: (1) the scalability of an *algorithm;* and (2) the scalability of an algorithm's *parallel implementation.* For example, a well-defined multigrid algorithm is a scalable algorithm because the number of iterations required for convergence remains roughly constant as the grid is refined. On the other hand, an algorithm such as

CGHS is not scalable because the number of iterations required for convergence usually depends on the size of the problem (i.e., grid resolution). Scalability of the parallel implementation of an algorithm is a completely different measure.

12.4   THE MGCG ALGORITHM

In this section, we define our Multigrid Preconditioned Conjugate Gradient algorithm (MGCG) [12.2]. We first describe our Multigrid Preconditioner (MG), the key components of which are discussed in each of the following sections. These include the coarsening strategy; the prolongation and restriction operators, P and R; the coarse grid operator, A^c; the smoother, S; and the coarsest grid solver.

The two-level MG algorithm is defined as follows:

for i = 0,1, . . . until convergence:

$$h^- = S(hi, A, f, m) \tag{12.7a}$$

$$r^c = R(f - Ah^-) \tag{12.7b}$$

$$e^c = (A^c)^{-1}r^c \tag{12.7c}$$

$$h^+ = h^- + Pe^c \tag{12.7d}$$

$$h_{i+1} = S(h^+, A, f, m) \tag{12.7e}$$

end for

In (12.7a) we perform m smoothing steps on the fine system of equations (we choose $m = 1$ in this chapter). We then restrict the residual to this coarse grid (12.7b). In step (12.7c) we solve the coarse system of equations, yielding a coarse grid approximation to the fine grid error. This coarse grid error is then prolonged (i.e., interpolated) to the fine grid and added to the current fine grid solution approximation in step (12.7d). Finally, in (12.7e), we carry out m more smoothing steps on the fine system of equations. Steps (12.7b)–(12.7d) together are called the *correction step*, and the algorithm describes a 2-level multigrid *V*-cycle. The full multilevel algorithm is defined by recursively applying the 2-level method to the system of equations in (12.7c). In other words, instead of solving (12.7c) exactly, we obtain an approximate solution by applying one V-cycle of the 2-level algorithm. This yields a new, coarser system of equations, which we may also solve approximately by applying the 2-level algorithm. This process is continued until we reach some coarsest system of equations, which is then solved to complete the V-cycle.

Before we continue, we need to introduce some notation. The fine grid matrix A has the following *stencil structure*:

$$A = \begin{bmatrix} -a_{i,j,k}^{L} \end{bmatrix} \begin{bmatrix} & -a_{i,j,k}^{N} & \\ -a_{i,j,k}^{W} & a_{i,j,k}^{C} & -a_{i,j,k}^{E} \\ & -a_{i,j,k}^{S} & \end{bmatrix} \begin{bmatrix} -a_{i,j,k}^{U} \end{bmatrix} \qquad (12.8)$$

where W, E, S, N, L, U, and C are used mnemonically to stand for west, east, south, north, lower, upper, and center, respectively. Now, split A such that

$$A = T + B \qquad (12.9)$$

where

$$T = \begin{bmatrix} 0 \end{bmatrix} \begin{bmatrix} & 0 & \\ -a_{i,j,k}^{W} & t_{i,j,k} & -a_{i,j,k}^{E} \\ & 0 & \end{bmatrix} \begin{bmatrix} 0 \end{bmatrix} \qquad (12.10)$$

$$B = \begin{bmatrix} -a_{i,j,k}^{L} \end{bmatrix} \begin{bmatrix} & -a_{i,j,k}^{N} & \\ 0 & b_{i,j,k} & 0 \\ & -a_{i,j,k}^{S} & \end{bmatrix} \begin{bmatrix} -a_{i,j,k}^{U} \end{bmatrix} \qquad (12.11)$$

and where

$$t_{i,j,k} = a^C_{i,j,k} - b_{i,j,k}$$
$$b_{i,j,k} = a^S_{i,j,k} + a^N_{i,j,k} + a^L_{i,j,k} + a^U_{i,j,k}$$

Note that A is split in the x direction: T contains the off-diagonal coefficients of A corresponding to the x direction, and B describes the coupling in the y and z directions. We similarly split A in the y and z directions, but for clarity, we will use only the x splitting above in the discourse that follows. Note that since A is diagonally dominant, we have that

$$t_{i,j,k} \geq a^W_{i,j,k} + a^E_{i,j,k} \qquad (12.12)$$

with strict equality holding away from Dirichlet boundaries.

12.4.1   Heuristic Semicoarsening Strategy

Because the ground subsurface is generally stratified in nature, our computational grids typically have skewed cell-aspect ratios. This produces anisotropy in the problem, which causes "standard" multigrid algorithms to converge slowly. To ameliorate this problem, we employ a *semicoarsening* strategy in which the grid is coarsened in one spatial direction at a time. Semicoarsening in the x direction is illustrated in Figure 12.3; the coarse grid is defined by taking every other yz plane.

To determine the direction of semicoarsening, we use a heuristic based on the grid spacing. The algorithm chooses a direction with smallest spacing (i.e., strongest coupling). If this minimum spacing occurs in one or more directions, the algorithm attempts to coarsen first in x, then in y, and finally in z. One important issue in this scheme is determining how and when to terminate the coarsening algorithm. As we will see in Section 12.5, this issue can have a dramatic impact on the performance of multigrid. The results presented there indicate that, in our MG algorithm, semicoarsening down to a $1 \times 1 \times 1$ grid is optimal for typical groundwater problems.

In our numerical experiments, we show that this semicoarsening strategy effectively ameliorates anisotropies due to large grid cell-aspect ratios. However, it does not take into account anisotropies in the rock matrix (i.e., the permeability

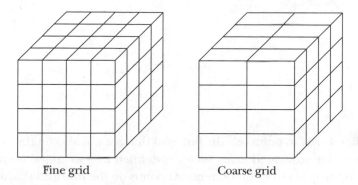

Fine grid   Coarse grid

12.3

FIGURE

Semicoarsening in the x direction.

tensor). We are currently investigating this issue, especially the relevant work discussed in [12.12, 12.15, 12.19, and 12.20].

12.4.2   Operator-Induced Prolongation and Restriction

One of the keys to a successful multigrid algorithm is the definition of the prolongation operator, P, which defines how vectors on a coarse grid are mapped onto the next finer grid. In the case of constant coefficient elliptic PDEs, P is usually defined via a simple interpolation scheme. However, when the coefficient function varies greatly, as in our problem, this is inadequate. Instead, one should use *operator-induced* prolongation, meaning that P is defined in terms of the coefficients of the fine grid matrix. Our prolongation operator is similar to those described in [12.1, 12.9, and 12.13].

To elucidate, consider the prolongation of an error vector e^c from the coarse grid G^c to the fine grid G. For the sake of discussion, let us assume that G^c is obtained by coarsening G in the x direction, as in Figure 12.3. (To be precise, we actually have prolongation operators P_x, P_y, and P_z, corresponding to each of the directions of semicoarsening, but we will drop the subscripts for clarity below.) Prolongation is then defined by

$$Pe^c = p^W_{i,j,k} e^c_{i-1,j,k} + p^E_{i,j,k} e^c_{i+1,j,k}, x_{i,j,k} \in G \backslash G^c$$
$$e^c_{i,j,k} \qquad\qquad x_{i,j,k} \in G^c$$

$$(12.13)$$

where

$$p^W_{i,j,k} = a^W_{i,j,k} / t_{i,j,k}$$
$$p^E_{i,j,k} = a^E_{i,j,k} / t_{i,j,k}$$

In other words, at points on the fine grid that are not also on the coarse grid, the value of the prolonged error vector is defined as a weighted average of x-adjacent coarse grid error components. At points on the fine grid that are also on the coarse grid, the value of the prolonged error vector is the same as the corresponding coarse grid error component. Prolongation in y and z is defined analogously.

The restriction operator, R, is used to project from a fine grid to a coarse grid. As is commonly done, we define $R = P^T$.

12.4.3   Definition of Coarse Grid Operator

Another important issue in multigrid is the definition of the coarse grid operator, A^c. In the literature, this matrix is often taken to be the *Galerkin matrix, $P^T A P$*. This choice for A^c is optimal in the sense that the quantity $\left\| e + P e^c \right\|_A$, the norm of the error after a multigrid correction step, is minimized over all coarse grid vectors e^c. In particular, if the error before correction is in the range of prolongation, then the correction step yields the exact solution. The drawback of this coarse grid operator is that it has a 27-point stencil, which requires additional storage and does not allow us to define the multilevel algorithm by recursively applying the 2-level algorithm.

Another way to define A^c is to rediscretize the differential equation on the coarse grid. This has the benefit of yielding a 7-point stencil structure, which requires less storage than the 27-point stencil and allows recursive definition of a multilevel algorithm. On the other hand, this operator lacks the minimization property of the Galerkin operator.

In our algorithm, we attempt to combine the best of both approaches by algebraically defining A^c as (again assuming semicoarsening in the x direction)

$$A^c = T^c + B^c \tag{12.14}$$

where

$$T^c = P^T T P = \begin{bmatrix} 0 \end{bmatrix} \begin{bmatrix} & 0 & \\ -a_{i,j,k}^{c,W} & t_{i,j,k}^{c} & -a_{i,j,k}^{c,E} \\ & 0 & \end{bmatrix} \begin{bmatrix} 0 \end{bmatrix} \qquad (12.15)$$

$$a_{i,j,k}^{c,W} = a_{i,j,k}^{W} \, p_{i-1,j,k}^{W}$$

$$a_{i,j,k}^{c,E} = a_{i,j,k}^{E} \, p_{i+1,j,k}^{E}$$

$$t_{i,j,k}^{c} = t_{i,j,k} - a_{i,j,k}^{W} \, p_{i-1,j,k}^{E} - a_{i,j,k}^{E} \, p_{i+1,j,k}^{W}$$

and

$$B^c = \begin{bmatrix} -a_{i,j,k}^{c,L} \end{bmatrix} \begin{bmatrix} & -a_{i,j,k}^{c,N} & \\ 0 & b_{i,j,k}^{c} & 0 \\ & -a_{i,j,k}^{c,S} & \end{bmatrix} \begin{bmatrix} -a_{i,j,k}^{c,U} \end{bmatrix} \qquad (12.16)$$

$$a_{i,j,k}^{c,S} = a_{i,j,k}^{S} + \frac{1}{2} a_{i-1,j,k}^{S} + \frac{1}{2} a_{i+1,j,k}^{S}$$

$$a_{i,j,k}^{c,N} = a_{i,j,k}^{N} + \frac{1}{2} a_{i-1,j,k}^{N} + \frac{1}{2} a_{i+1,j,k}^{N}$$

$$a_{i,j,k}^{c,L} = a_{i,j,k}^{L} + \frac{1}{2} a_{i-1,j,k}^{L} + \frac{1}{2} a_{i+1,j,k}^{L}$$

$$a_{i,j,k}^{c,U} = a_{i,j,k}^{U} + \frac{1}{2} a_{i-1,j,k}^{U} + \frac{1}{2} a_{i+1,j,k}^{U}$$

$$b_{i,j,k}^{c} = a_{i,j,k}^{c,S} + a_{i,j,k}^{c,N} + a_{i,j,k}^{c,L} + a_{i,j,k}^{c,U}$$

In other words, A^c is a Galerkin operator in x (the direction of semicoarsening) plus a weighted sum of y and z stencil coefficients. The coefficients in (12.16) describe the connections in y and z of the coarse grid variables, and our reason for

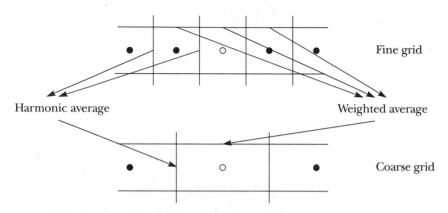

12.4

FIGURE

Definition of the coarse grid operator (2D illustration with x semicoarsening).

choosing these particular weights is illustrated subsequently. Note that A^c is diagonally dominant, and an inequality analogous to (12.12) holds.

Away from the domain boundaries, the algebraic definition of A^c in (12.14)–(12.16) also may be interpreted geometrically as the result of a finite volume discretization of (12.2) on the coarse grid G^c. Consider the grid point marked ○ in Figure 12.4 (where we illustrate only two dimensions for simplicity). The finite volume discretization requires hydraulic conductivity values on the cell faces about this grid point. To generate the matrix coefficients, these values are first multiplied by the area of the cell face, then divided by the grid spacing in the perpendicular direction. So, if grid point ○ in Figure 12.4 has index (i,j,k), then on the fine grid we have

$$a^W_{i,j,k} = \frac{\Delta y \Delta z}{\Delta x} K_{i-\frac{1}{2},j,k}$$

$$a^E_{i,j,k} = \frac{\Delta y \Delta z}{\Delta x} K_{i+\frac{1}{2},j,k}$$

$$a^S_{i,j,k} = \frac{\Delta x \Delta z}{\Delta y} K_{i,j-\frac{1}{2},k} \qquad (12.17)$$

$$a^N_{i,j,k} = \frac{\Delta x \Delta z}{\Delta y} K_{i,j+\frac{1}{2},k}$$

Now, consider the finite volume discretization on the coarse grid. We first compute hydraulic conductivity values on coarse grid cell faces, as in Figure 12.4; for vertical faces, we take a harmonic average of values on adjacent fine grid cell faces; and for horizontal cell faces, we taken an arithmetic average of values on corresponding fine grid cell faces. Because the x grid spacing on G^c is twice that on G, we have that

$$a_{i,j,k}^{c,W} = \frac{\Delta y \Delta z}{2\Delta x} \left(\frac{2K_{i-\frac{1}{2},j,k}\,K_{i-\frac{1}{2},j,k}}{K_{i-\frac{1}{2},j,k} + K_{i-\frac{1}{2},j,k}} \right) \tag{12.18}$$

$$a_{i,j,k}^{c,E} = \frac{\Delta y \Delta z}{2\Delta x} \left(\frac{2K_{i+\frac{1}{2},j,k}\,K_{i+\frac{1}{2},j,k}}{K_{i+\frac{1}{2},j,k} + K_{i+\frac{1}{2},j,k}} \right)$$

$$a_{i,j,k}^{c,S} = \frac{2\Delta x \Delta z}{\Delta y} \left(\frac{1}{2}K_{i,j-\frac{1}{2},k} + \frac{1}{2}K_{i-1,j-\frac{1}{2},k} + \frac{1}{2}K_{i+1,j-\frac{1}{2},k} \right)$$

$$a_{i,j,k}^{c,N} = \frac{2\Delta x \Delta z}{\Delta y} \left(\frac{1}{2}K_{i,j+\frac{1}{2},k} + \frac{1}{2}K_{i-1,j+\frac{1}{2},k} + \frac{1}{2}K_{i+1,j+\frac{1}{2},k} \right)$$

Using (12.17) in (12.18) and noting that equality holds in (12.12) in the interior of the domain, it is easy to see that the coefficients produced by this finite volume discretization on the coarse grid are the same as those given in (12.14)–(12.16).

12.4.4   Smoothers

The smoother is another important part of a multigrid algorithm. A "good" smoother complements the correction step by damping modes that the correction step does not. However, as is often the case with numerical algorithms, the smoother that does the best job of damping these errors is typically the most computationally expensive. For example, line and plane methods are generally better than pointwise methods are at damping high-frequency error components, but they are computationally more expensive and less parallelizable.

We use simple pointwise damped Jacobi (with weighting factor 2/3) and red/black Gauss-Seidel (GS) smoothers in our MG algorithm. Although these smoothers are easy to implement scalably in parallel, the resulting MG algorithm lacks robustness. However, as we will see (Section 12.4.6), we regain robustness by using MG as a preconditioner within a conjugate gradient algorithm—without the additional coding complexity (and possibly greater overhead) of a line or plane smoothing.

12.4.5   Coarsest Grid Solvers

To complete the multigrid algorithm, we must decide when to stop the coarsening procedure and how to solve the coarsest system of equations. For example, should we solve the coarsest system of equations exactly or just do a few smoothing steps to obtain an approximate solution? In Section 12.5.1, we run several experiments in this regard, and we conclude that coarsening down to a $1 \times 1 \times 1$ grid is optimal for our algorithm and for this application. The $1 \times 1 \times 1$ "system" is solved exactly via one sweep of red/black GS. (We employ CGHS and red/black GS as our coarse grid solvers. We could also consider a direct solution of the coarsest grid system via Gaussian elimination, but the iterative solvers are adequate for our purposes.)

12.4.6   Stand-Alone Multigrid versus Multigrid as a Preconditioner

Although multigrid algorithms are extremely fast, they tend to be problem specific and less robust than Krylov iterative methods such as conjugate gradients. Fortunately, it is easy to combine the best features of multigrid and conjugate gradients into a multigrid preconditioned conjugate gradient algorithm that is robust, efficient, and scalable. The main advantage of this approach is that a simple multigrid algorithm can be quickly implemented that is extremely effective as a preconditioner, but perhaps less effective as a stand-alone solver.

The well-known PCG method (Orthomin implementation) [12.5, 12.7] is given by

$$p_0 = s^0 = Cr_0 \tag{12.19a}$$

for $i = 0,1, \ldots$ until convergence:

$$a_i = \frac{\langle r_i, s_i \rangle}{\langle Ap_i, p_i \rangle} \tag{12.19b}$$

$$x_{i+1} = x_i + \alpha_i p_i \tag{12.19c}$$

$$r_{i+1} = r_i - \alpha_i A p_i \qquad (12.19\text{d})$$

$$s_{i+1} = C r_{i+1} \qquad (12.19\text{e})$$

$$\beta_i = \frac{\langle r_{i+1}, s_{i+1} \rangle}{\langle r_i, s_i \rangle} \qquad (12.19\text{f})$$

$$p_{i+1} = s_{i+1} + \beta_i p_i \qquad (12.19\text{g})$$

end for

In the MGCG algorithm, the preconditioning operator, C, is never explicitly formed. Instead, (12.19e) is effected by applying the MG algorithm (12.7) to the residual system of equations, $Ae = r$, using an initial guess of $e_o = \vec{0}$. The resulting approximate solution is s_{i+1}.

When designing a preconditioner for PCG, the preconditioning matrix must be symmetric, and preferably positive definite. For multigrid preconditioning, this condition is satisfied by doing an equal number of symmetric smoothing steps both before and after each coarse grid correction. (The smoothing step is symmetric if the iteration matrix of the associated method is symmetric.) However, this is not necessarily required (see, e.g., [12.21]). Multigrid algorithms also can be applied to nonsymmetric problems (e.g., [12.10]) and to problems with irregular meshes (e.g., [12.16]).

Our current implementation of MGCG is simple but effective. The MG preconditioning step consists of a single V-cycle (as defined) with a choice of weighted Jacobi or symmetric red/black GS smoothing. We use an equal number, m, of smoothing steps before and after correction. (In this chapter, $m = 1$).

12.5   NUMERICAL RESULTS

In this section, we will investigate the performance of our multigrid algorithm in several contexts. In particular, we will study the effect of the following on the rate of convergence: choice of boundary conditions, coarsest grid size, and coarsest grid solver; increasing the resolution (fixed domain size); enlarging the domain size (fixed grid spacing); and increasing the degree of subsurface heterogeneity. We also will describe the algorithm's parallel performance on the Cray T3D massively parallel computer.

All of the experiments in this section are of the following form: The domain, $\Omega = L_x \times L_y \times L_z$, is a parallelepiped, where L_x, L_y, and L_z represent the domain lengths (in meters) in the x, y, and z directions, respectively. The grid is Cartesian with $N = n_x \times n_y \times n_z$ points and $\Delta = \Delta_x \times \Delta_y \times \Delta_z$ spacing. The subsurface is assumed to be a single, heterogeneous hydrostatigraphic unit with variable hydraulic conductivity K. To generate K, we use a turning bands algorithm [12.22] with geostatistical parameters μ, σ, λ_x, λ_y, and λ_z. Here $\ln \mu$ and σ represent the mean and standard deviation of the $\ln K$ field (μ also may be thought of as the geometric mean of K), and λ_x, λ_y, and λ_z represent the correlation lengths in the x, y, and z directions, respectively. Unless otherwise stated, we impose Dirichlet boundary conditions (hydraulic head, $H = h + z = 1$) on the four vertical sides of the domain and no flow conditions on the top and bottom.

We consider three multigrid algorithms for solving the symmetric positive definite system of linear equations that results from the discretization of the elliptic pressure equation. Specifically, we compare the following: MG with symmetric pointwise red/black GS smoothing; MGCG with symmetric pointwise red/black GS smoothing; and MGCG with damped Jacobi smoothing (MJCG). The preconditioning step in both MGCG and MJCG consists of a single MG V-cycle. As discussed in the previous section, the smoothing operation should be implemented in a symmetric fashion when multigrid is used as a preconditioner for PCG. For comparison, we also consider PCG with 2-step Jacobi preconditioning (J2CG). Each of the algorithms was halted once the 2-norm of the relative residual was less than 10^{-9}. Unless otherwise noted, we used $P = 2 \times 4 \times 4$ processors of the Cray T3D. (Some of the larger problems required a larger number of processors because of their memory needs.) All times are wall clock times, and they are given in seconds. Although the test problems are contrived, they serve to illustrate the performance of the MGCG algorithm.

12.5.1   The Effect of Coarsest Grid Solver Strategy

In this section, we study the effect on convergence rate of the choice of coarsest grid solver strategy with respect to the type of boundary conditions. The experiment details are as follows:

$$\Omega = 1024 \times 1024 \times 25.6$$

$$N = 65 \times 65 \times 33, \quad \Delta = 16 \times 16 \times 0.8$$

$$\mu = 4, \quad \sigma = 1.5, \quad \lambda_x = 32, \quad \lambda_y = 32, \quad \lambda_z = 1.6$$

Variant	Coarse grid solver	MG		MGCG	
		iterations	time	iterations	time
1	1 step of RB on $3 \times 3 \times 3$	111	18.6	21	3.8
2	CGHS on $3 \times 3 \times 3$	58	10.9	19	3.9
3	CGHS on $5 \times 5 \times 3$	22	4.9	14	3.5
4	1 step of RB on $1 \times 1 \times 1$	19	3.5	10	2.1

12.1

TABLE

Coarse grid solution strategy: no-flow boundary conditions on the top and bottom; Dirichlet ($H = 1$) conditions on the four vertical faces.

The results are shown in Tables 12.1 and 12.2 for four variants of the basic MG and MGCG algorithms. In variant 1, we coarsen to a $3 \times 3 \times 3$ coarsest grid then do one step of red/black GS. In variant 2, we again coarsen to a $3 \times 3 \times 3$ coarsest grid but solve the coarsest system "exactly" via CGHS. In variant 3, we coarsen as in variant 2, except that we stop at a $5 \times 5 \times 3$ coarsest grid. In variant 4, we coarsen to one equation in one unknown and solve it exactly via one step of red/black GS. To simplify the discussion below, we will refer to these variants of MG as MG1, MG2, MG3, and MG4. The MGCG variants will be named similarly.

Let us consider first the results in Table 12.1. In these experiments, we employ our "standard" boundary conditions: no flow on the top and bottom faces and constant head ($H = 1$) on the remaining vertical faces. Let us also focus first on the issues related to multigrid. From the table, we see that convergence of MG2 is considerably better than that of MG1. The reason for this is that the system of equations on the $3 \times 3 \times 3$ coarsest grid is "almost singular" because of the strong coupling in the direction of a flux boundary condition (i.e., the z direction). Consequently, errors with "smooth" z components are not damped well by one step of GS smoothing. Note that the CGHS coarsest grid solver of MG2 converged to machine tolerance in three iterations. We see further significant improvement in convergence with algorithm MG3. To explain this, consider coarsening the $5 \times 5 \times 3$ grid, first in x, then in y, to a $3 \times 3 \times 3$ grid (as in algorithm MG2). In each of these coarsening steps, we are coarsening in a direction orthogonal to the direction with strongest coupling (i.e., the z direction). These nonoptimal coarsening steps actually slow convergence. Note that here the CGHS coarsest grid solver took 34–36 iterations to solve the coarsest grid problems to the specified tolerance (relative residual less than 10^{-9}). Algorithm MG4 is the best method for this problem. Here, the heuristic semicoarsening strategy coarsens in z in the "optimal" way until the z direction is eliminated altogether (thereby eliminating anisotropy in the z direction). This results in a

		MG		MGCG	
Variant	Coarse grid solver	iterations	time	iterations	time
1	1 step of RB on $3 \times 3 \times 3$	12	2.0	8	1.6
2	CGHS on $3 \times 3 \times 3$	12	2.2	8	1.7
3	CGHS on $5 \times 5 \times 3$	12	2.1	8	1.7
4	1 step of RB on $1 \times 1 \times 1$	15	2.8	10	2.1

12.2

TABLE

Coarse grid solution strategy: Dirichlet ($H = 1$) boundary conditions on all faces.

coarse grid operator that looks like a 2D Laplacian. The remainder of the *V*-cycle (which involves coarsening only in the *x* and *y* directions) gives a good approximation to the solution of this system. Hence, this multigrid algorithm performs quite well.

The MGCG algorithms perform similarly, except that they are much faster. Note that there is only a slight difference in iteration count between MGCG1 and MGCG2 compared to the corresponding MG algorithms. This is an indication that algorithm MG1 is having trouble with just a few of the modes, which the conjugate gradient part of MGCG1 easily eliminates.

Now consider the results in Table 12.2. Here, we repeat the experiments with constant head ($H = 1$) on all six faces. The results are entirely different. First, we observe much faster convergence in this set of all-Dirichlet experiments. This is largely due to the near singularity of the coarse grid matrices in the previous table, as discussed earlier. For the all-Dirichlet problems, it can be shown that both red/black GS and CGHS will solve the $3 \times 3 \times 3$ coarse grid problem in just one iteration. Since red/black GS is cheaper than CGHS, it is faster, as observed in the table. It also can be shown that CGHS will solve the $5 \times 5 \times 3$ coarse grid problems in just nine iterations. Although algorithm MG3 takes a bit longer to solve the coarsest grid problems, there is less semicoarsening than in MG1 and MG2, and the overall algorithm is competitive. Second, we notice that the variant 4 algorithms produce the worst results in Table 12.2 and the best results in Table 12.1. Because our finite volume discretization is vertex centered, the boundary condition equations are not coupled to the other matrix equations. This, combined with our algebraic definition of the prolongation operator, results in prolongation coefficients that are zero at grid points near Dirichlet boundaries. Hence, the $n_x \times n_y \times 3$ coarse grid obtains no effective correction from the coarser $n_x \times n_y \times 2$ grid, which slows convergence of the variant 4 algorithms.

Problem size			J2CG		MJCG		MGCG		MG	
n_x	n_y	n_z	iterations	time	iterations	time	iterations	time	iterations	time
17	17	9	456	1.1	12	0.3	9	0.4	12	0.4
33	33	17	963	5.7	13	0.5	10	0.7	17	1.1
65	65	33	1895	57.1	15	1.9	10	2.1	18	3.4
129	129	65	3706	772.1	16	10.8	11	12.6	21	20.6
257	257	129	7391	*1549.5	N/A	N/A	11	*12.9	23	*23.9

*These times are for 256 processors ($P = 4 \times 8 \times 8$).

12.3

TABLE

Increasing the spatial resolution: the domain size is fixed while the number of grid points is increased.

We remark that the mixed boundary conditions used in the experiments of Table 12.1 are more likely to arise in practice, and so we prefer the coarsening strategy of the variant 4 algorithms.

12.5.2   Increasing the Spatial Resolution

In this section we study the effect on convergence rate of increasing the spatial resolution. Specifically, we increase the number of grid points used to resolve each correlation length but keep the problem domain fixed. (We start with two grid points per correlation length and increase to 32 grid points per correlation length.) The experiment details are as follows:

$$\Omega = 1024 \times 1024 \times 25.6$$
$$\Delta = 1024.0/(n_x-1) \times 1024.0/(n_y-1) \times 25.6/(n_z-1)$$
$$\mu = 4, \ \sigma = 1.5, \ \lambda_x = 128, \ \lambda_y = 128, \ \lambda_z = 6.4$$

The results are shown in Table 12.3.

We see that increasing the spatial resolution has a significant effect on the convergence rate of J2CG (as expected), but has little effect on the MG-based algorithms. Specifically, the J2CG iteration count doubles when the resolution doubles (i.e., problem size increases by 2^3), but MGCG converges in about 10 iterations independent of resolution. As the resolution increases, J2CG becomes increasingly impractical, and a multigrid approach must be used. For example, in the $257 \times 257 \times 129$ case, J2CG takes about 120 times longer to converge than MGCG, and this multiplier would grow if we increased the problem size further. Note also, that although MJCG takes more iterations to converge than MGCG, it converges a little faster. This is due to two things: Jacobi has less communication overhead and, in general, runs at a higher Mflop rate than red/black GS; and in MJCG we do two smoothings per grid level, but in MGCG, we do three smoothings because of an extra half sweep that is done to ensure symmetry. Note that the stand-alone MG algorithm is not as effective as MGCG because of problems with a few extraneous modes (as explained earlier).

We remark that if we did not semicoarsen to a grid with only one grid point in the z direction, the iteration counts in the first few rows of the table would be higher. This is because the first semicoarsening in an x or y direction would occur not because the coupling in these directions was strongest ("optimal" coarsening strategy), but as a result of having too few z points. As discussed in Section 12.5.1, this would have an adverse effect on convergence, which would be more pronounced for the smaller problem sizes. See [12.4] for related experiments.

Remark: The overall slow convergence of J2CG results partly from anisotropy in the problem due to the skewed grid cell-aspect ratio. This is a consequence of how the eigenvalues of A are distributed. When the grid cell-aspect ratio is near 1:1:1, the eigenvalues are more tightly clustered in the middle of the spectrum, and the effective condition number is less than the true condition number. (Recall that the rate of convergence for conjugate gradient methods is governed by the effective condition number, not the true condition number, because conjugate gradients are able to damp outlying eigenvalues quickly.) When the grid cells are skewed, the eigenvalues cluster near the endpoints of the spectrum, and the effective and true condition numbers are nearly identical. Moreover, the flux boundary conditions on the z faces result in a larger effective condition number than would Dirichlet conditions, reducing further the effectiveness of J2CG on this problem.

12.5.3   Enlarging the Size of the Domain

In this section, we study the effect on convergence rate of growing the domain size. In some remediation studies, enlarging the initial site to encompass neighboring property might be necessary if, for instance, a contaminant were discovered to have migrated offsite. In such a scenario, the engineer might wish to use the same geostatistics and grid spacing but enlarge the domain by increasing the number of spatial zones. In our experiments, we maintain a constant two grid points per correlation length. The experiment details are as follows:

Problem size			J2CG		MJCG		MGCG		MG	
n_x	n_y	n_z	iterations	time	iterations	time	iterations	time	iterations	time
17	17	9	453	1.1	11	0.3	9	0.4	12	0.4
33	33	17	957	5.7	13	0.5	10	0.7	14	0.9
65	65	33	1860	56.0	16	2.0	10	2.1	19	3.6
129	129	65	3665	763.4	18	12.1	11	12.6	21	20.6
257	257	129	6696	*1403.8	N/A	N/A	13	*15.1	22	*22.8

*These times are for 256 processors ($P = 4 \times 8 \times 8$).

12.4

TABLE

Enlarging the domain size: the grid spacing is fixed while the number of grid points is increased.

$$\Omega = (n_x - 1)\Delta_x \times (n_y - 1)\Delta_y \times (n_z - 1)\Delta_z$$
$$\Delta = 4 \times 4 \times 0.2$$
$$\mu = 4, \ \sigma = 1.5, \ \lambda_x = 8, \ \lambda_y = 8, \ \lambda_z = 0.4$$

The results are shown in Table 12.4.

The results here are qualitatively and quantitatively similar to the results in Table 12.3. The minor differences in the two tables are due to the differing subsurface realizations (produced by turning bands) in the two experiments.

12.5.4   Increasing the Degree of Heterogeneity

In this section, we study the effect on convergence rate of increasing the degree of heterogeneity. This heterogeneity is represented by the parameter σ described earlier. The experiment details are as follows:

$$\Omega = 1024 \times 1024 \times 25.6$$
$$N = 129 \times 129 \times 65, \ \Delta = 8 \times 8 \times 0.4$$
$$\mu = 4, \ \lambda_x = 16, \ \lambda_y = 16, \ \lambda_z = 0.8$$

The results are shown in Table 12.5.

When $\sigma = 0.0$, the subsurface medium is homogeneous, in which case the coefficient function K is constant, and so the matrix A is Laplacian-like. As σ in-

Heterogeneity		J2CG		MGCG		MG	
σ	σ_K^2	iterations	time	iterations	time	iterations	time
0.0	0×10^0	1701	354.4	9	10.4	13	12.8
0.5	6×10^0	3121	650.3	9	10.4	13	12.8
1.0	7×10^1	3388	705.7	9	10.4	12	11.8
1.5	1×10^3	3670	764.6	11	12.5	22	21.6
2.0	4×10^4	4273	889.5	17	18.8	diverged	
2.5	4×10^5	5259	1094.4	26	28.2	diverged	

12.5

TABLE

Varying the degree of heterogeneity.

creases, so does the degree of heterogeneity. Specifically, the variance, σ_K^2, of the log normally distributed conductivity field K increases exponentially. This variability in K causes the coefficient matrix A to become increasingly ill conditioned. The effect on MG of this increasing heterogeneity is significant, and we see that for two of the runs, it actually diverges. However, when MG is used as a preconditioner for PCG (MGCG), convergence is obtained in each case. Note that the iterations for MGCG grow like the order of the variance. The convergence of J2CG is poor, as expected.

Convergence plots for J2CG and MGCG are given in Figure 12.5 for each of the values of σ in Table 12.5. Notice that the MGCG convergence curves are nearly linear and quite steep in comparison to J2CG, indicating that MGCG is making rapid and steady progress toward the solution. (The log of the 2-norm of the relative residual is plotted against the number of iterations required for convergence.)

12.5.5　Parallel Performance on the Cray T3D

In earlier experiments [12.4], we examined the parallel performance of the ParFlow simulator and its component routines. In this section, we reprise those experiments with respect to the multigrid algorithm. Specifically, we will examine the scalability of the MGCG algorithm on the Cray T3D massively parallel computer system. The results given here differ from those in [12.4] for several reasons, including compiler upgrades, algorithm enhancements, and coding improvements.

In Figures 12.6 and 12.7, we present scaled speedups for the matvec, MG preconditioning, and MGCG routines on the Cray T3D. Our machine has 256 modes, each consisting of a 150-MHz DEC Alpha processor and 64 MB of mem-

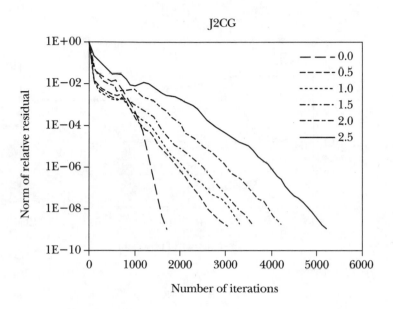

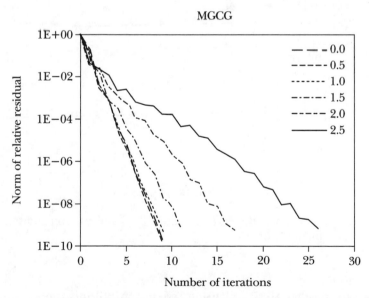

12.5

FIGURE

Convergence plots for J2CG and MGCG for several values of σ (as in Table 12.5). As σ increases, the subsurface realization becomes more heterogeneous, and the underlying matrix problem becomes more difficult.

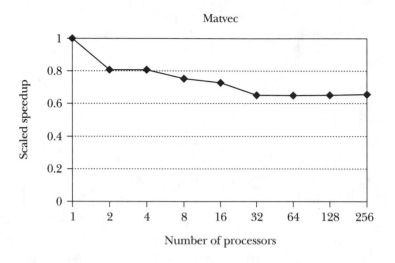

Matvec

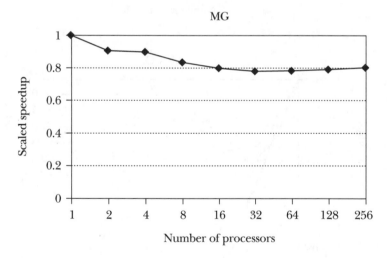

MG

Scaled speedup of the ParFlow matvec (top) and MG preconditioning routines (bottom) on the Cray T3D.

ory; our Another Message Passing System (AMPS) message-passing library developed at LLNL is layered on top of Cray's SHMEM library. In our experiments, each processor is given a $64 \times 64 \times 32$ subgrid, so that the total problem size on $P = p \times q \times r$ processors is $N_P = 64p \times 64q \times 32r$. In other words, we allow the total problem size to grow with P. Moreover, the shape of the problem domain is determined by the process grid topology $p \times q \times r$. The point of this study is to

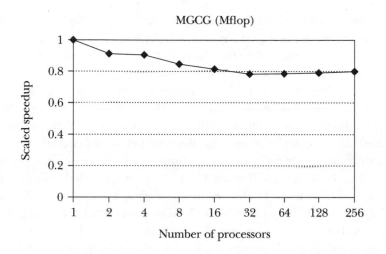

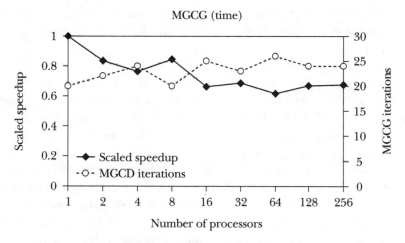

12.7

FIGURE

Scaled speedup of the ParFlow MGCG routine on the Cray T3D. The figure on the top shows the scalability of the MGCG implementation (via Mflop rates); the figure on the bottom shows the scalability of the MGCG implementation and algorithm (via timings that include the effects of differing iteration counts).

see how well the routines make use of additional processors. Our goal is to obtain nearly flat curves (good scalability) that are near 1 (good scaled efficiency).

The first three graphs in Figures 12.6 and 12.7 illustrate the scalability of our implementations of the matvec, MG, and MGCG routines in terms of Mflops. Specifically, we define scaled speedup to be $M_p/(PM_1)$, where M_P is the Mflops achieved by the operation in question on P processes. The scaled speedup graphs are all fairly flat, indicating good scalability. The MG and MGCG routines have nearly identical performance (about 80 percent scaled efficiency) because MGCG spends most of its time in the MG preconditioning routine. The matvec routine has lower scaled efficiency (about 65 percent) because it has a much-higher Mflop rate than the other routines, and so communication costs are relatively higher. (The matvec, MG, and MGCG routines averaged 2.12, 1.25, and 1.37 Gflops, respectively, on 256 processors.) Thus, all three routines are scalable, meaning, for example, that the time per MGCG iteration remains constant as we increase the problem size and number of processes in tandem.

In the last graph (Figure 12.7), we present scaled speedup for MGCG in terms of CPU time. That is, we define scaled speedup to be T_1/T_P, where T_P is the time required to execute the MGCG algorithm (to convergence) on P processes. Because the number of iterations required for convergence fluctuates with P, this graph illustrates the combined scalability of the algorithm itself and our implementation of it. We also plot MGCG iteration count, which varies between 20 and 26 iterations (using the C-norm stopping criterion). Notice the inverted relationship between scaled speedup and iteration count (as one would expect).

Remark: The number of MGCG iterations might be expected to increase monotonically with the size of the problem (which grows with the number of processors), but this is not the case. Recall that in our definition of scaled speedup, the computational domain is growing with P—and changing shape as we move from one process grid topology to the next. This means that the eigenstructures of the underlying matrices change from one run to the next, which accounts for the up-and-down iteration counts. We could largely eliminate this effect by keeping the domain fixed and increasing the resolution as we grow the problem size, but this would require varying the topology of the subgrid assigned to each processor. As discussed in [12.4], this can have a dramatic impact on node performance, causing another set of problems. (In our experiments, we used the following process grid topologies: $1 \times 1 \times 1, 1 \times 1 \times 2, 1 \times 2 \times 2, 1 \times 2 \times 4, 1 \times 4 \times 4, 1 \times 4 \times 8, 1 \times 8 \times 8, 1 \times 8 \times 16, 2 \times 8 \times 16$.)

12.6   SUMMARY

This chapter focuses on the numerical simulation of groundwater flow through heterogeneous porous media. The key computational challenge is the solution of a large, sparse system of linear equations for the pressure head. The size of the sites to be modeled (on the order of kilometers) and the need to resolve subsurface heterogeneities (to within a few meters) necessitate the use of efficient numerical methods and the power of massively parallel processing. In this chapter, we introduce a parallel multigrid preconditioned conjugate gradient algorithm for solving these linear systems.

After defining the various components of the multigrid algorithm and discussing its parallel implementation, we investigated its performance in a variety of numerical experiments. We considered the effects of boundary conditions, coarse grid solver strategy, increasing the grid resolution, enlarging the domain, and varying the geostatistical parameters used to define the subsurface realization. Our multigrid preconditioned conjugate gradient solver performed extremely well. For example, we were able to solve a problem with more than 8 M spatial zones in under 13 seconds on a 256-processor Cray T3D. We also demonstrated the scalability of both the algorithm and its implementation. This solver has been incorporated in the ParFlow simulator and is being used to enable detailed modeling of large sites.

ACKNOWLEDGMENTS

The Cray T3D experiments described in this chapter were run on the 256-processor machine located at Lawrence Livermore National Laboratory as part of the H4P Industrial Computing Initiative funded by DOE Defense Programs. This work was supported by Laboratory Directed Research and Development and by the Mathematical, Information, and Computational Sciences Division of the Office of Energy Research, Department of Energy, by Lawrence Livermore National Laboratory under contract W-7405-ENG-48.

References

[12.1]   Alcouffe, R. E., A. Brandt, J. E. Dendy, and J. W. Painter. 1981. The Multi-grid Method for the Diffusion Equation with Strongly Discontinuous Coefficients. *SIAM J. Sci. Stat. Comput.*, **2**, 430–454.

[12.2]   Ashby, S. F., and R. D. Falgout. 1996. A Parallel Multigrid Preconditioned Conjugate Gradient Algorithm for Groundwater Flow Simulations. *Nuc. Sci. and Eng.*, **124**, 145–159.

[12.3]   Ashby, S. F., R. D. Falgout, S. G. Smith, and T. W. Fogwell. 1995. Multigrid Preconditioned Conjugate Gradients for the Numerical Simulation of Groundwater Flow on the Cray T3D. In *Proc. ANS International Conference on Mathematics and Computations, Reactor Physics and Environmental Analyses, 1995.* Held in Portland, OR, April 30–May 4.

[12.4]   Ashby, S. F., R. D. Falgout, S. G. Smith, and A. F. B. Tompson. 1995. The Parallel Performance of a Groundwater Flow Code on the Cray T3D. In *Proc. Seventh SIAM Conference on Parallel Processing for Scientific Computing, Society for Industrial and Applied Mathematics, 1995*, 131–136. Held in San Francisco, February 15–17. Also available as LLNL Technical Report UCRL-JC-118604.

[12.5]   Ashby, S. F., T. A. Manteuffel, and P. E. Saylor. 1990. A Taxonomy for Conjugate Gradient Methods. *SIAM J. Numer. Anal.* **27**, 1542–1568.

[12.6]   Bosl, W. J. A Parallel Random Field Generation Algorithm. 1998. Unpublished manuscript.

[12.7]   Concus, P., G. H. Golub, and D. P. O'Leary. 1976. A Generalized Conjugate Gradient Method for the Numerical Solution of Elliptic Partial Differential Equations. In J. R. Bunch and D. J. Rose (eds.), *Sparse Matrix Computations.* New York: Academic Press, 309–332.

[12.8]   Dagan, G. 1989. *Flow and Transport in Porous Formations.* New York: Springer-Verlag.

[12.9]   Dendy, J. E. 1982. Black Box Multigrid. *J. Comput. Phys.*, **48**, 366–386.

[12.10] Dendy, J. E. 1983. Black Box Multigrid for Nonsymmetric Problems. *Appl. Math. Comput.*, **13**, 261–284.

[12.11]   Dendy, J. E., and C. C. Tazartes. 1995. Grandchild of the Frequency Decomposition Multigrid Method. *SIAM J. Sci. Comput.*, **16**, 307–319.

[12.12]   Deutsch, C., and A. Journel. 1992. *GSLIB: Geostatistical Software Library and User's Guide.* New York: Oxford University Press.

[12.13]   Fogwell, T. W., and F. Brankhagen. 1989. Multigrid Method for the Solution of Porous Media Multiphase Flow Equations. In *Nonlinear Hyperbolic Equations—Theory, Computation Methods, and Applications.* Vol. 24 of *Notes of Numer. Fluid Mech.*, Vieweg, Braunschweig, Germany, 139–148.

[12.14]   Hackbusch, W. 1987. The Frequency Decomposition Multigrid Method, Part I: Application to Anisotropic Equations. *Numer. Math.*, **56**, 229–245.

[12.15]   Hestenes, M. R., and E. Stiefel. 1952. Methods of conjugate gradients for solving linear systems. *J. Res. Nat. Bur. Standards,* **49**, 409–435.

[12.16]   Mavriplis, D. J., and A. Jameson. 1988. Multigrid Solution of the Euler Equations on Unstructured and Adaptive Meshes. In S. F. McCormick (ed.), *Multigrid Methods: Theory, Applications and Supercomputing,* Vol. 110 of *Lecture Notes in Pure and Applied Mathematics.* New York: Marcel Dekker, 413–429.

[12.17]   Meyer, P. D., A. J. Valocchi, S. F. Ashby, and P. E. Saylor. 1989. A Numerical Investigation of the Conjugate Gradient Method as Applied to Three-dimensional Groundwater Flow Problems in Randomly Heterogeneous Porous Media. *Water Resources Res.*, **25**, 1440–1446.

[12.18]   Naik, N. H., and J. R. Rosendale. 1993. The Improved Robustness of Multigrid Elliptic Solvers Based on Multiple Semicoarsened Grids. *SIAM J. Numer. Anal.*, **30**, 215–229.

[12.19]   Schaffer, S. A. Semi-coarsening Multigrid Method for Elliptic Partial Differential Equations with Highly Discontinuous and Anisotropic Coefficients. To appear in *Siam J. Sci. Comput.*

[12.20]   Skjellum, A., S. G. Smith, N. E. Doss, A. P. Leung, and M. Morari. 1994. The Design and Evolution of Zipcode. *Parallel Computing,* **20**, 565–596.

[12.21]   Tatebe, O. 1993. The Multigrid Preconditioned Conjugate Gradient Method. In N. D. Melson, T. A. Manteuffel, and S. F. McCormick (eds.), *Sixth Copper Mountain Conference on Multigrid Methods,* Vol. CP 3224, 621–634. Hampton, VA.: NASA.

[12.22]   Tompson, A. F. B., R. Ababou, and L. W. Gelhar. 1989. Implementation of the Three-dimensional Turning Bands Random Field Generation. *Water Resource Res.*, **25**, 2227–2243.

[12.23]   Tompson, A. F. B., S. F. Ashby, R. D. Falgout, S. G. Smith, T. W. Fogwell, and G. A. Loosmore. 1994. Use of High Performance Computing to Examine the Effectiveness of Aquifer Remediation. In *Proc. X International Conference on Computational Methods in Water Resources,* A. Peters, G. Wittum, B. Herrling, U. Meissner, C. Brebbia, W. Gray, and G. Pinder (eds.), Vol. 2. Dordrecht: Kluwer Academic Publishers. Held in Heidelberg, Germany, July 19–22, 1994. Also available as LLNL Technical Report UCRL-JC-115374.

13 | Simulation of Plasma Reactors

Stephen Taylor
Marc Rieffel
Jerrell Watts   Scalable Concurrent Programming Laboratory, Syracuse University

Sadasivan Shankar   Technology CAD Department, Intel Corporation

13.1   INTRODUCTION

Plasma processing equipment accounts for approximately 20 percent of the setup cost for a new semiconductor manufacturing plant. The cost of these production facilities is escalating, as are the research and development costs of introducing each new generation of processing technology. One of the key pieces of equipment in microelectronics manufacturing is the *plasma reactor,* used in 30 to 40 percent of processing steps. It is widely recognized that the development of computational tools for modeling plasma reactors is essential to reduce the costs both of validating new reactor designs and of improving manufacturing processes.

Process engineers seek simulation methods that are increasingly realistic, pushing toward 3D models of complex geometries and reacting chemistry. Acceptable simulation results require not only appropriate chemical and physical models but also substantial investments in geometric modeling, grid generation, postprocessing, and analysis techniques. These steps in the design cycle are interrelated, and the process of obtaining a meaningful result is frequently a time-consuming, iterative process. Simulation techniques will continue to have limited engineering applicability until each of these steps is addressed in a comprehensive simulation methodology.

This chapter summarizes a novel concurrent simulation technique intended to address the overall design cycle of a simulation. It is described in the context of the simulation of low-pressure (less than 200 Pa/1.5 Torr) neutral flow in the Gaseous Electronics Conference (GEC) reference cell reactor shown in Figure

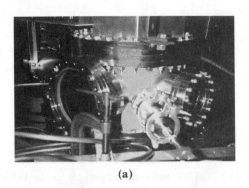
(a)

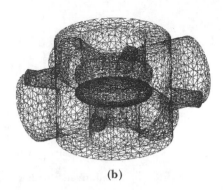
(b)

13.1

FIGURE

The Gaseous Electronics Conference (GEC) reference cell reactor (a) and tetrahedral grid that represents it (b). (See also color plate 13.1.)

13.1(a). (See also color plate 13.1.) The technique integrates a variety of ideas taken from computational fluid dynamics and finite-element methods. A central aim is to exploit existing industrial tools already in use by process engineers to shorten the design cycle to acceptable engineering time scales.

The reactors of interest involve weakly ionized plasmas (with degree of ionization $\approx 10^{-4}$) with electron-impact gas-phase reactions and ion-enhanced surface reactions. Neutral flow is of importance in studying these systems because it determines the reactor pressure, the center-of-mass motion, and the production of chemically active species. In addition, the lateral location and possible agglomeration of particulates are determined by the characteristics of neutral flow. Because pressure drops are higher in low-pressure reactors, the study of neutral flow is critical to optimal design. The flow can be supersonic close to a shower head or inlet nozzle, and good design is necessary to avoid large pressure drops and highly asymmetric flows.

Neutral flow in low-pressure reactors is in the *transition regime*. The mean free path of particles is on the order of the characteristic length of the reactor; this is too large for continuum methods, but too small for free-molecular simulations. The Direct Simulation Monte Carlo (DSMC) method [13.1] is an alternative technique for modeling rarefied gas dynamics. Neutral flow calculations require only simple chemical models yet are extremely useful from an engineering perspective. Moreover, these calculations are a natural precursor to more complex studies of ion and electron transport.

13.2 COMPUTATIONAL CONSIDERATIONS

The concurrent simulation technique involves four primary stages:

1. **Automatic grid generation.** A 3D geometry definition is taken directly from CAD/CAM descriptions already available to process engineers. An unstructured tetrahedral grid is then constructed automatically, using industry-standard tools, as shown in Figure 13.1(b).

2. **Static partitioning.** The grid is subsequently partitioned for execution on any of a wide variety of concurrent architectures.

3. **Concurrent DSMC.** Scalable concurrent algorithms are then used to reduce the numerical simulation time. These algorithms model 3D neutral flow using the DSMC technique. Adaptive gridding automatically maintains the accuracy of the simulation, and dynamic load balancing maximizes processor utilization.

4. **Postprocessing.** Finally, simulation results for each computer are reassembled and analyzed using commercial unstructured visualization tools.

13.2.1 Grid Generation and Partitioning Techniques

Reactors are typically designed using CAD/CAM packages, where engineers specify the curves and surfaces that define the reactor geometry. The concurrent simulation technique uses a boundary-fitted computational grid extracted from this CAD/CAM definition.

Axially aligned grids are unable to represent the curved geometry of a realistic reactor, and structured hexahedral grids are difficult to generate automatically for complex geometries. In contrast, mature techniques exist for automatic generation and smoothing of unstructured tetrahedral grids. These grids are able to efficiently represent complex geometries, and standard algorithms are available for their adaptive refinement.

Realistic computational grids can often be too large to fit in the memory of any single processor. The concurrent simulation technique is therefore based on the concept of *overpartitioning:* The grid is decomposed into a number of partitions, and several partitions are mapped onto each processor. Each of these partitions represents a portion of the grid that can be simulated concurrently by communicating information to neighboring partitions. This allows the memory requirements for each processor to be inversely proportional to the number of processors.

The initial partitioning is based on a volume decomposition that preserves *locality*. Cells are sorted in each dimension and grouped according to their sorted positions. Adjacent cells are therefore likely to be mapped to the same partition. This procedure attempts to minimize the surface area of the partitions and hence the total amount of communication required during a simulation. It also attempts to minimize the number of neighbors for each partition and therefore the number of separate communications required.

This simple partitioning strategy is sometimes inadequate if a large number of partitions is required. It allows the number of cells in a partition to vary widely, and it allows a partition to have an undesirably large surface area. These problems can result in imbalances in processor load and memory usage and in excessive communication. In these cases, static balancing is necessary. This is achieved using a concurrent algorithm that computes the solution to the heat equation, $\frac{\partial u}{\partial t} = \alpha \nabla^2 u$, where u is an estimate of the memory and computational cost of a partition and $\nabla^2 u$ is a measure of local imbalance. The parameter α represents the desired accuracy of load balance specified when setting up the simulation; for example, $\alpha = 0.1$ balances each processor to within 10 percent. The variable μ is computed as the sum over all cells in a partition, $\mu = \Sigma_{cells} A + BV_{cell}$, where A is an estimate of the fixed cost per cell and B is an estimate of the cell cost proportional to the cell volume V_i. Each cell is treated as a discrete quantity of heat that can be transferred between adjacent partitions in order to evenly distribute the cost. Cells are selected for transfer in such a way as to preserve locality and to minimize the area of surfaces shared between partitions. This process terminates when all partitions have roughly the same memory and computational costs.

Figure 13.2 (and color plate 13.2) shows the result of initial partitioning for 24 computers, where it is clear that the partitions are imbalanced as well as the same grid after static volume balancing ($A = 0$, $B = 1$). Note that the volume of the middle partitions has grown to be close to that of the outer partitions. In this case, the ratio of maximum to average partition volume was improved from 1.4 to 1.01.

Partitions are mapped to computers in such a way as to place neighboring partitions in the same or adjacent computers, again maximizing locality. Information is exchanged between partitions on neighboring computers using message passing, while information is directly exchanged between partitions on the same computer (or computers sharing memory). The mapping of multiple partitions to each computer allows the overlap of communication and computation: If one partition is blocked, awaiting communication, another partition on the same computer may still proceed.

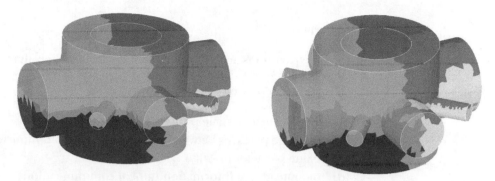

13.2

FIGURE
The grid for the GEC reference cell after initial partitioning (left) and static partition balancing (right). (See also color plate 13.2.)

Overpartitioning allows partitions of differing sizes to be mapped to the same computer in order to balance load and memory. Specifying the number of computers, and therefore the total number of cells per computer, provides control over the *granularity* of the computation—that is, the ratio of computation to communication. Generally speaking, this corresponds to the ratio of the volume (n^3 for a characteristic dimension n) to the surface area of all partitions in a computer (n^2). Adjusting the granularity allows the simulation to be matched to a wide variety of concurrent architectures. On platforms with high communication costs, such as networks of workstations, a small number of large partitions may be used. By contrast, a larger number of smaller partitions may be used on distributed-memory multiprocessors that employ fast communication technology.

13.2.2   Concurrent DSMC Algorithm

The DSMC method solves the Boltzmann equation by simulating individual particles. It is impossible to simulate the actual number of particles in a realistic system so a smaller number of simulation particles is used, each representing a large number of real particles. Statistical techniques are employed to obtain the correct macroscopic behavior. Computational grid cells are initially filled with simulation particles according to density, temperature, and velocity specifications. The simulation takes discrete steps in time, during which a *transport model* is used to move particles, a *collision model* is used for particle-particle interactions, and a *boundary model* is used for interactions between particles and surfaces. Macroscopic properties, such as density and temperature, are computed by appropriate averaging of particle masses, positions, and velocities.

For each partition:

1. Initialize partitions according to initial conditions (locally).

2. While more steps are necessary,

    (a) calculate new particle positions (locally)
    (b) exchange particles between partitions (local communication)
    (c) collide particles (locally)
    (d) compute global information (global communication)
    (e) adapt grid
    (f) balance load

3. Conclude computation.

13.3

FIGURE

Parallel algorithm.

Figure 13.3 outlines the concurrent algorithm executed by each partition of the computational grid. For the most part, particle transport is local within a partition (2a); however, a particle may move across a cell face on the boundary between two partitions. In this case, it is communicated to the appropriate neighboring partition (2b). In a single time step, a particle may cross several partition boundaries and thus require several rounds of communication. In order to improve communication efficiency, all particles exchanged between a single pair of partitions are combined into a single message. Once all of the particles have been placed in their new cell locations, the collision and boundary models are employed independently within each cell (2c). At the end of a time step, global information, such as the total number of particles in the domain, is computed (2d), and a check is made to determine if grid adaption (2e) or load balancing (2f) would be advantageous.

Transport Model

The transport model is concerned with moving particles through the computational grid for a specified period of time. It uses ray-tracing techniques to determine the final location of a particle at the end of a time step. In an unstructured grid, this is achieved by computing a particle's path in each cell that it traverses.

To determine whether a particle will move into another cell, it is necessary to calculate which cell face the particle's trajectory will first intersect. In the presence of a uniform acceleration, such as a gravitational field, particles follow *parabolic trajectories*. The intersection time between the particle's curved trajectory and each cell face is calculated, and the closest face along the trajectory is determined. The intersection time for that face is compared to the time step length, Δt. If the intersection time is greater than Δt, the particle will not hit any faces in the current time step and can therefore be moved directly to its new position. If, however, the intersection time is less than the time step, the particle will hit the closest face. Most cell faces are internal to partitions, and particles move through them to adjacent cells. If the cell face is on the boundary between partitions, the particle is sent to the adjacent partition. If the cell face corresponds to a physical surface, the boundary model is employed to determine the interaction between the particle and the surface.

Because the transport model is primarily local to a partition, only information about the cell containing the particle is used. This contrasts sharply with DSMC implementations that require global grid information in order to move particles. In that case, the entire grid must be replicated at each computer, limiting scalability.

Collision Model

The collision model characterizes particle-particle interactions. Simplistic collision models can lead to erroneous results, and unnecessarily complex models can dramatically increase simulation time. Binary collisions are fundamentally an N-squared interaction for N particles. For simulations involving millions of particles, it is impractical to consider all possible interactions. If the mean free path is larger than the cell size, there can be no statistically significant spatial gradients due to collisions. The DSMC method, therefore, only needs to consider collisions between particles in the same cell. Collisions are thus performed independently within each cell and concurrently in each partition. Statistical techniques are used to determine the correct number of collisions in time proportional to the number of particles in the cell [13.1].

The collision model uses an acceptance-rejection method based on collision tests. The frequency of collision tests in a cell is computed. The collision model makes a series of tests at the appropriate frequency and probabilistically chooses particles to collide, updating their postcollision velocities appropriately. A variety of collision models have been developed; however, for the argon simulation presented here, the Variable Soft Sphere (VSS) model [13.4] is sufficient.

Boundary Model

During grid generation, cell faces on the same surface are grouped together. When configuring a simulation, a surface type is specified for each group. The surface type of a face determines particle-surface interactions on that face. The three surface types used in the GEC simulation are *inflow, outflow,* and *accommodating.* Standard DSMC techniques are used to model inflow and thermally accommodating surfaces. The outflow model allows surfaces of the reactor to be partly reflective. The reflectivity, r, specifies the probability that a particle hitting a surface will be specularly reflected back into the reactor. Particles that are not reflected exit the reactor, as though through an exhaust pump. The reflectivity is adaptively modified during the simulation so as to maintain the pressure at a chosen reference point within the reactor.

During grid partitioning, an additional surface type, *partition,* is created to represent shared boundaries between partitions. Recall that a partition surface is introduced at each cell face located on the boundary between partitions. A particle arriving at a partition surface is sent to the appropriate neighboring partition. The time it takes for the particle to reach the surface is subtracted from the current time step to obtain the remaining time during which the particle must be moved upon arrival at the neighboring partition.

13.2.3   Grid Adaptation Technique

In the DSMC method, error is related to the local Knudsen number, the ratio of the mean free path to the cell size. If the cell size is too large, erroneous results are obtained. If the cell size is too small, computational resources are wasted, and statistical scatter is increased. The mean free path is an average parameter computed during a simulation. Thus, it is not possible to generate an optimal grid before simulations have been conducted.

To resolve this issue, an iterative manual approach can be used. A rough initial grid is used to obtain estimates of the mean free path throughout the grid. Based on visual inspection of these estimates, a new grid is generated with increased or decreased resolution where necessary. This process is repeated until an acceptable solution is found. This approach requires time-consuming manual intervention for nontrivial geometries and increases the overall simulation time. An alternative is to adapt the grid automatically during the simulation to ensure accuracy without wasting cells.

In the present simulations, a coarse initial grid is generated that serves to accurately define the reactor geometry. Periodically during the simulation, the lo-

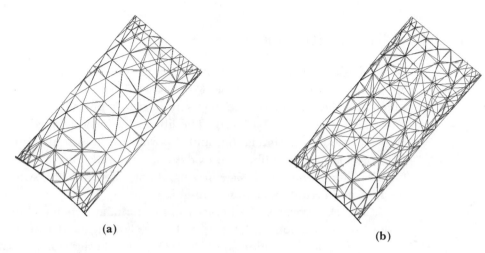

(a)   (b)

13.4   Grid for the inflow port of the GEC grid before (a) and after (b) grid adaptation.

FIGURE

cal Knudsen number is computed in each cell. Cells with insufficient Knudsen numbers are marked for adaptation so long as they contain a sufficient number of particles. The adaptation technique leverages standard methods [13.3] drawn from finite-element analysis. When a cell is marked for adaptation, an edge in that cell is selected. A new point is introduced along this edge, each cell that shares the edge is split into two new cells, and each face that shares the edge is split into two new faces. Careful selection of edges ensures that repeated adaptation does not cause the grid quality to deteriorate.

Figure 13.4(a) shows the grid for a small port in the GEC reactor. This port is configured with an inflow surface at its end (top right). The particle density in these cells is relatively high; therefore, the local mean free path is shorter than the typical cell size, and adaptation is necessary. Figure 13.4(b) shows the same port after several iterations of the adaptation process. Notice a decrease in the average cell size, and therefore an increase in the number of cells, after adaptation has taken place.

Because grid refinement is a local process, it can usually be conducted within a single partition. In cases where an adapting edge lies on a partition boundary, only the partitions sharing that boundary need to be aware of the adaptation. Thus, the communication and synchronization costs of grid adaptation are minimal. Furthermore, grid adaptation can be performed infrequently during a calculation without substantial loss of accuracy.

13.2.4   Library Technology

Communication, load balancing, and other features are implemented using the application-independent Scalable Concurrent Programming Library (SCPlib), which provides basic programming technology to support irregular applications on scalable concurrent hardware. The library has been applied to a variety of large-scale industrial simulations and is portable to a wide range of platforms. On each platform, the library provides an optimized, portable set of low-level functionality, including message passing, thread management, synchronization, file I/O, and performance monitoring.

SCPlib also provides a higher level of functionality, which includes heterogeneous communication and file I/O, load balancing, and dynamic granularity control. Communication and file I/O occur through objects called *ports*. These ports are similar to Unix descriptors in that the same routines can be used to write to a channel port or to a file port. This allows considerable reuse of application code because the same routines used to read and write a data structure can be used for both communication and file I/O. Furthermore, communication through ports is typed; when a port is created, the system inputs a header describing the writer's data type sizes, byte ordering, and so on. The reader can then automatically apply the appropriate transformations, if necessary. This allows communication between tasks running on heterogeneous architectures, as well as the ability to read checkpoints written on different platforms.

An SCPlib application is constructed as a concurrent graph of communicating tasks, called *nodes*. Each node is comprised of a thread of execution, state information, and a set of channel ports for communication with other nodes. The mapping of nodes to computers is transparent to the user because the channels effectively hide the locations of a node's neighbors in the communication graph. The library can thus move a node dynamically, so long as the user provides routines for communicating a node's state. The user can reuse checkpointing routines for this purpose; node movement is essentially checkpointing a node through the network rather than to a file. Furthermore, the library provides functionality to dynamically divide or merge nodes, if the user has provided the necessary support routines. Node movement and dynamic granularity control are used in conjunction to provide portable load balancing.

The load-balancing mechanism is based on the concept of heat diffusion, which provides a scalable, correct mechanism for determining how much work should be migrated between computers, including computers with different processing capabilities or external workloads. Heat diffusion gives only the ideal work transfer, however; to meet that ideal, neighboring computers must exchange nodes. The selection of which nodes to exchange may be guided by both the sizes of the nodes involved as well as the effect a node's movement would have on its communication with other nodes. If there are too few or too many nodes in the system, granularity management routines are used to increase or decrease the number of nodes. The end result is a five-step methodology for load balancing a computation [13.6, 13.7]:

1. Load measurement. The load of each computer is determined either by having the programmer provide an estimate of resource needs of the nodes or by actually measuring their resource usage.

2. Load imbalance detection and profitability calculation. Based on the total load measured at each computer, the efficiency of the computation is calculated. Load balancing is undertaken if its estimated cost is exceeded by the estimated reduction in runtime that would result from load balancing.

3. Ideal load transfer calculation. Using the load quantities measured in the first step, computers calculate the ideal degree to which they should transfer load to or from their neighbors.

4. Node selection. Using the load-transfer quantities calculated previously, nodes are selected for transfer or exchange between neighboring computers. This phase may be repeated several times until the transfer quantities have been adequately met, and it may be guided by cost functions that encourage communications locality or discourage the movement of nodes with large data structures.

5. Node migration. Once the nodes have migrated to their final locations, any data structures associated with those nodes are transferred from their old locations to their new locations, and the computation resumes.

Through the use of such application-independent library technology, it is possible to support a high level of irregularity with minimal cost to the application developer. With the addition of a small set of communication, adaption, and interface routines, the concurrent DSMC algorithm has been extended to support heterogeneous computing, dynamic load balancing, and dynamic granularity control. These features are crucial for ensuring efficient use of a wide variety of platforms.

13.3   SIMULATION RESULTS

A thorough validation of the neutral flow model has been completed. Results for several 1D heat transfer problems have been compared with analytical results [13.5, 13.8]. Results for 2D hypersonic flow past a cylinder, with multiple gas species, each with rotational and vibrational energy modes, have been compared to numerical results from [13.2]. Suitable experimental data is not yet available for neutral flow in the GEC reference cell.

The simulation shown here uses the geometry and grid shown in Figure 13.1. Argon gas was injected at 300 K, with a density of 5×10^{21} m^{-3} and a speed of 37.6 m/s. The reactor walls and wafer were assumed to be accommodating at 300 K. The outflow surface adapts to maintain a pressure of 2.66 (20 mTorr) at a point just above the center of the wafer. A time step of 8×10^{-7} s was used.

Gas was injected through the small port at the bottom left of the plane and again removed through the large port on the left, separated by 135 degrees. The effects of the inflow and exhaust ports make this simulation completely asymmetric. There would thus be no way to capture the true flow field with a 2D axisymmetric calculation.

Figure 13.5 shows results in two 2D slices through the reactor, one above and parallel to the wafer and the other perpendicular to the wafer in the vertical plane. Projections of CAD surfaces onto the cut plane appear as solid lines. In the horizontal cut, the largest complete circle in the center of the reactor indicates the edge of the wafer. In the vertical slice, the wafer appears as a thin, horizontal element in the middle.

The plots are colored by pressure, with a scale from 0 to 5 Pa, and 20 contour lines are shown for this interval. The orientation and spacing of the contour lines provides an indication of the uniformity of the flow above the wafer. Closely spaced parallel contour lines indicate a steep gradient in pressure, while scattered and separated lines suggest reasonable uniformity. The prominent features in these plots are the high pressure in the inflow region and a slightly lower pressure in the exhaust region.

Figure 13.6 (right) shows the measured gas pressure at the pressure probe point, above the center of the wafer. The measured pressure can be seen to converge to within 5 percent of the target pressure, 2.66 Pa (20 mTorr), as the pressure-regulation mechanism adaptively adjusts the exhaust rate. Because the pressure-regulation mechanism is the slowest process in the simulation, the convergence shown in this figure demonstrates convergence of the entire system. The flow results shown in Figure 13.5 were sampled after pressure convergence had been reached.

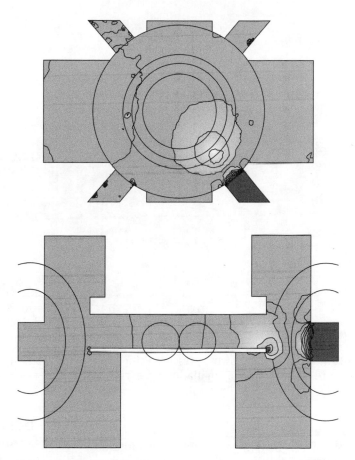

13.5   Pressure in the horizontal (top) and vertical (bottom) planes.

FIGURE

13.4   PERFORMANCE RESULTS

The following figures show performance and scalability on a variety of platforms for simulations of the GEC reference cell. The platforms considered in this study include the Cray T3D, the Avalon A12, a network of Dell multiprocessor workstations, and a Silicon Graphics Power Challenge. For each architecture, a message-passing programming model was used. No changes to the high-level algorithm were required. On shared-memory systems, such as the SGI Power Challenge, shared-memory optimizations enable fast message passing through the

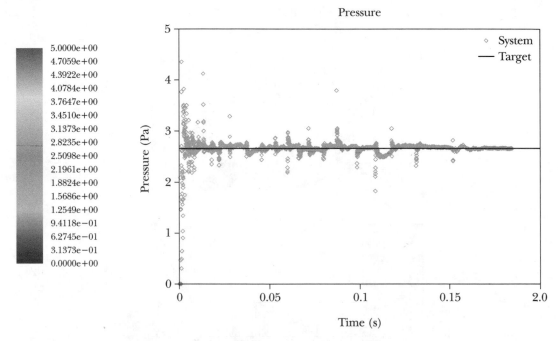

FIGURE

Plots in Figure 13.5, showing pressure values from 0 to 5 Pa (left), and probe pressure as a function of simulation time (right).

use of pointer-copying. Message passing on the network of Dell workstations is achieved with TCP/IP socket communications between processors in separate workstations and by using pointer-copying between processors in the same workstation. The combination of a unified high-level model and low-level architecture-specific optimizations makes efficient computation possible on a wide variety of computer architectures and connection topologies.

For each platform, the number of particles used in the simulation is proportional to the memory available to those processors. In other words, as the number of processors is increased, the number of particles is increased so as to maintain a constant fraction of memory usage. Performance is measured as the rate at which particles can be processed for each time step and will ideally increase linearly as a function of the number of processors.

Figure 13.7(a) shows performance on the Cray T3D, which is composed of 256 200-MHz 21064 DEC Alpha processors with 64 MB RAM each but without secondary or tertiary caches. Due to the small memory size, it is impossible to run this problem on fewer than 16 T3D processors, as the GEC grid alone requires approximately 16 MB. The ideal T3D performance was therefore estimated by benchmarking against the Avalon A12. On 256 processors, load balanc-

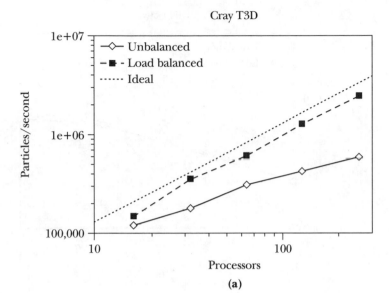

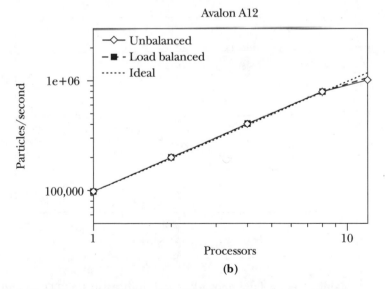

13.7

FIGURE

Scalability results for the Cray T3D (a) and the Avalon A12 (b).

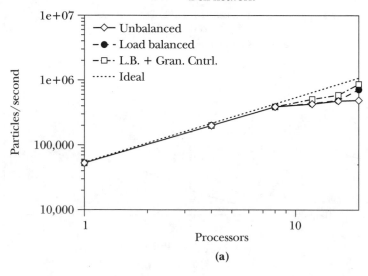

(a)

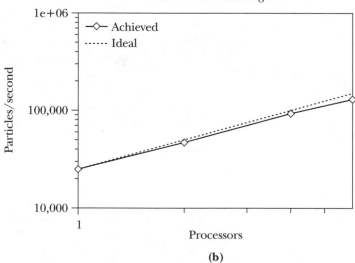

(b)

13.8
FIGURE

Scalability results for a network of multiprocessor Dell PCs (a) and the SGI Power Challenge (b).

ing results in a fourfold performance improvement, bringing the utilization up from 18 percent to 73 percent. Figure 13.7(b) shows performance on the Avalon A12, which is composed of 12 400-MHz 21164 DEC Alpha processors, each with 500 MB RAM, a 96 K secondary cache, and a 1-MB tertiary cache. Due to the small number of processors on the A12, the effect of load balancing is much smaller than on the T3D, while the A12 processors are three to four times faster than the T3D processors. Due to severe memory constraints on the T3D, it is possible to achieve only 50 percent load balance there, compared to 85 percent on the A12. These differences account for what is almost an order of magnitude difference in per-processor speed between the A12 and the T3D.

Figure 13.8(a) shows the performance results on a network of Dell PCs, each containing four 200-MHz Intel Pentium Pro processors and 1 GB RAM. For this platform, the effects of dynamic load balancing are shown, both with and without automatic granularity control. Due to the combination of multiple cabinets and multiple processors within a cabinet, it is advantageous to start simulations with one partition per cabinet, and to allow the load-balancing algorithm to split partitions in order to achieve both full utilization within a cabinet and load balance across cabinets.

Performance results on the SGI Power Challenge are shown in Figure 13.8(b). This machine uses 14 75-MHz R8000 processors and 2 GB RAM. With just one cabinet, there is no need for dynamic load balancing.

The results for each platform are combined in Figure 13.9. The highest raw performance was achieved on the Cray T3D, with 2.44 million particles per second on 256 processors. Of the machines considered in this study, the Avalon A12 demonstrated the highest per-processor performance, with 94,000 particles per second per processor. The Dell network also achieved excellent performance—the use of commodity components making it a particularly cost-effective platform.

13.5   SUMMARY

Reactor simulations of industrial interest involve asymmetric 3D flows. The use of unstructured grids, particularly with asymmetric flow patterns, leads to non-uniform load profiles. Because asymmetric solutions cannot in general be predicted a priori, they must evolve from uniform initial solutions. The result is an application that is truly irregular both in space and in time.

Simulations such as the ones presented here require approximately 200,000 grid cells, 2 million particles, and 50,000 time steps. A relatively small parallel

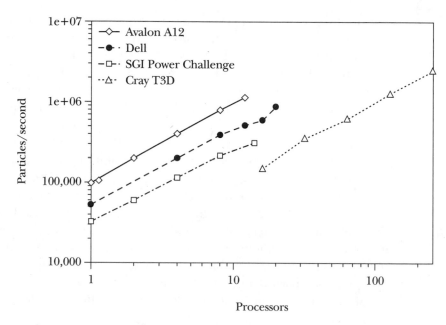

FIGURE   Performance on the Cray T3D, Avalon A12, Dell network, and SGI Power Challenge.

machine, such as a 14-processor SGI Power Challenge, can process a single time step at the rate of about 300,000 particles per second, thus completing a simulation in four days. A newer architecture, such as the 12-processor Avalon A12, can process a time step at the rate of approximately 930,000 particles per second and thus reduce simulation time to about one day.

This paper has outlined a novel concurrent DSMC method and demonstrated the method on 3D simulations of the GEC reference cell. Large-scale simulations of realistic reactor geometries are now possible within realistic engineering time scales. Simulations have been conducted on a variety of proprietary reactors that have had a direct impact on the understanding of process effects.

ACKNOWLEDGMENTS

The authors would like to gratefully acknowledge the contributions of Maura Benton, Andrew Brown, Wayne Christopher, Evan Cohn, Sergey Gimelshein, Peter Haaland, Robert Haimes, Ross Harvey, Mikhail Ivanov, Alexander

Kashkovsky, Gennady Markelov, John Maweu, Vincent McKoy, and Bradley Nelson.

Infrastructure support and computing resources for this research were provided by BMDO under contract DAAH04-96-1-0319 and by Avalon Computer Systems, Inc. The research described in this report is sponsored by Intel Corporation and the Advanced Research Projects Agency under contract number DABT63-95-C-0116. This work includes Russian participation that is supported by the U.S. Civilian Research and Development Foundation under Award No. RE1241. The information contained herein does not necessarily reflect the position or policy of the government of the United States, and no official endorsement should be inferred.

References

[13.1]   Bird, G. 1994. *Molecular Gas Dynamics and the Direct Simulation of Gas Flows*. Oxford: Clarendon Press.

[13.2]   Gimelshein, S., G. Markelov, and M. Rieffel. 1996. *Collision Models in the Hawk DSMC Implementation*. Caltech Technical Report CS-96-16.

[13.3]   Kallinderis, Y., and P. Vijayan. 1993. Adaptive Refinement-Coarsening Scheme for Three-Dimensional Unstructured Meshes. *AIAA Journal,* **31** (8), 1440–1447.

[13.4]   Koura, K., and H. Matsumoto. 1992. Variable Soft Sphere Molecular Model for Air Species. *Physics of Fluids,* **4** (5), 1083–1085.

[13.5]   Rieffel, M. 1995. *Concurrent Simulations of Plasma Reactors for VLSI Manufacturing*. Caltech Master's Thesis CS-95–012.

[13.6]   Watts, J., M. Rieffel, and S. Taylor. 1996. Practical Dynamic Load Balancing for Irregular Problems. *Parallel Algorithms for Irregularly Structured Problems: IRREGULAR '96 Proceedings, Vol. 1117*. Springer-Verlag LNCS.

[13.7]   Watts, J., M. Rieffel, and S. Taylor. 1997. A Load Balancing Technique for Multiphase Computations. *Proceedings of High Performance Computing '97,* 15–20.

[13.8]   Zhong, X., and K. Koura. 1995. Comparison of Solutions of the Burnett Equations, Navier-Stokes Equations, and DSMC for Couette Flow. *Rarefied Gas Dynamics 19,* **1,** Oxford University Press.

14 CHAPTER

Electron-Molecule Collisions for Plasma Modeling

Carl Winstead
Chuo-Han Lee
Vincent McKoy   A. A. Noyes Laboratory of Chemical Physics, California Institute of Technology

14.1 INTRODUCTION

The most sophisticated manufacturing operations taking place today may well be those carried out inside the "fabs" (fabrication plants) where, in a series of carefully controlled steps, microelectronics are created from wafers of pure silicon. A visitor would find that a high proportion of the processing equipment along the fab line employed plasma—partially ionized gas—to carry out its function, whether depositing new material in minutely specified amounts and locations, etching submicroscopic pits and trenches to tolerances defined in fractions of a micron, or any of a number of other modifications necessary to build up the intricate circuitry. Observing this amazing—and amazingly expensive—equipment in operation, the visitor might be surprised to learn that the design of plasma reactors and optimization of their operating conditions are, in fact, still largely empirical, relying not only on chemical, physical, and engineering principles but also, to a large degree, on accumulated experience and on trial and error.

The lack of a deep understanding of plasma reactor function is more than an intellectual annoyance. The apparently inexorable progress of the semiconductor industry toward the smaller, the faster, and the more complex is only sustained by continually finding ways to improve all phases of manufacturing, including plasma processing. Increasingly, the inability to model in detail the behavior of plasma reactors, and thereby to understand how the elementary physical and chemical processes within them interact to create the observed overall behavior, is becoming an obstacle to the timely and economical design and evaluation of new generations of plasma equipment.

Three factors have impeded realistic numerical modeling of plasma reactors: the lack of adequate modeling software, the high computational cost such modeling would incur, and the lack of essential input data any detailed model would require. With the development (currently under way) of 3D models incorporating fields, electron and ion transport, and reactions as well as neutral flow, the first of these impediments is gradually being surmounted. Moreover, the targeting of such models to parallel architectures (see Chapter 13 by Taylor and co-workers in this volume) addresses the second impediment, the need for greater computational power than has been available in the past. The work we will describe in this chapter addresses the third factor, the need for basic data detailing the physical and chemical processes taking place within the plasma and at the semiconductor surface.

Our research focuses on only one of the many reaction and collision processes relevant to plasma modeling—namely, the collision of electrons with molecules in the plasma—but electron-molecule collisions are an especially important process. To understand why, it is helpful to look more closely at how a processing plasma operates. Consider an etching plasma (Figure 14.1, see also color plate 14.1), in which the goal is to form features by eating away unprotected portions of the surface. The etching of silicon by fluorine, for example, proceeds through the net reaction

$$4F + Si \rightarrow SiF_4 \tag{14.1}$$

taking advantage of the fact that SiF_4 is a gas that can be pumped away. To generate free fluorine atoms (or similar highly reactive species), a molecular gas such as CF_4, or a mixture of gases, is introduced at low pressure into a chamber containing the semiconductor wafer, and an electric discharge is established. The plasma—the gas within the discharge—is partially ionized, meaning that some molecules lose an electron to become positively charged ions. The electric field between the electrodes will accelerate both the ions and the free electrons; however, by oscillating the field direction at a high frequency, the much heavier ions can be prevented from acquiring significant velocities, while still imparting high kinetic energies to the light electrons. The result is a *nonequilibrium* plasma in which the average kinetic energy (i.e., the temperature) of the heavy particles—molecules, ions, and neutral molecular fragments or radicals—remains low, thereby avoiding thermal damage to the semiconductor surface, while the average kinetic energy of the electrons is considerably higher. In such a low-temperature or "cold" plasma, collisions between energetic electrons and molecules of the feed gas are principally responsible for generating both the reactive radicals and ions that carry out useful chemistry at the surface and the additional free electrons needed to sustain the plasma.

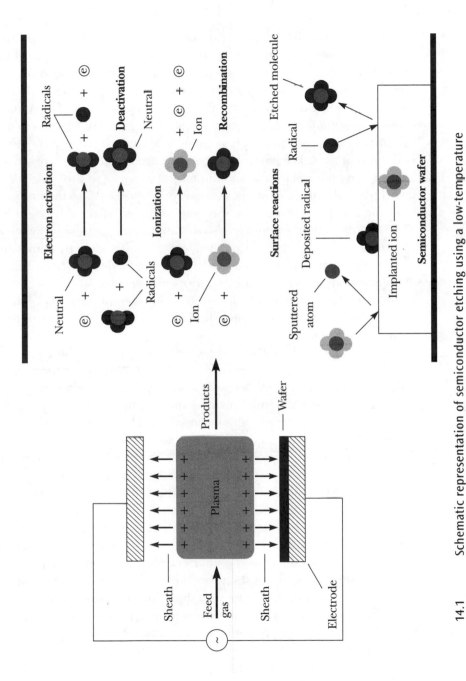

14.1
FIGURE

Schematic representation of semiconductor etching using a low-temperature plasma. (See also color plate 14.1.)

From this description, it is clear that electron-molecule collisions play a central role in low-temperature plasmas. Thus, if successful numerical models of such plasmas are to be developed, the probabilities for the various possible outcomes of an encounter between an electron and a molecule, including excitation (and possible dissociation) of the molecule, ionization of the molecule, and elastic scattering (i.e., colliding without any energy transfer) need to be known.

Interaction probabilities are conventionally expressed as *cross sections,* which have units of area. The connection between probabilities and areas may be seen by imagining the electron as an infinitely small dart and the molecule as a dartboard painted with patches whose areas are proportional to the probabilities for the various collision outcomes; the aggregate area of the dartboard is the *total scattering cross section,* or apparent size of the molecule as seen by the electron. Clearly, the cross sections so defined are at most indirectly connected to the "real" average cross-sectional area that one might deduce (e.g., from a space-filling model of the molecular structure); indeed, collision cross sections depend strongly on the energy at which the collision takes place. A set of all cross sections having significant magnitude provides the collision information needed as input to plasma models.

Electron-molecule collision cross sections can be measured in the laboratory. However, the measurements are inherently difficult, particularly for excitation and dissociation cross sections, and data are often absent or subject to large uncertainties. Moreover, many of the fragments produced within processing plasmas are experimentally inaccessible. The idea of *computing* electron-molecule collision cross sections for processing gases is thus an attractive one.

What would such a computation entail? The detailed answer is the main subject of this chapter, but by way of introduction we can sketch the principal features here. First of all, such computations must be *quantum mechanical,* for, at the size scale of molecules, quantum mechanics rules. Further, such a calculation must be of a rather high level. Although the electrons in low-temperature plasmas have energies that are high compared to the translational energies of the molecules, they are still "low-energy" electrons in the sense that their velocities are comparable to those of the valence electrons bound within the molecule. The computation must therefore treat the colliding electron on an equal footing with electrons of the target molecule, with the result that the apparently two-body electron-molecule problem is in fact a many-body problem.

Over the years, quantum chemists have advanced the study of the many-electron problem to a high art, and problems involving modest-sized molecules can be solved very accurately provided one is willing to pay the computational price. As a result, computational chemistry has developed from an academic enterprise into one with a large number of practitioners and wide application, including problems such as the computation of reaction rates that arise in plasma processing. However, virtually all of that work applies only to states in which all electrons are bound to the molecule, whereas the electron-molecule collision problem involves an electron that is free to leave. Thus, although many of the basic techniques and principles of quantum chemistry may be drawn upon, we must develop specialized methods adapted to the quantum-mechanical many-electron problem for unbound states if we are to succeed in generating accurate electron-molecule collision cross sections. Knowing that the task we have undertaken is inherently numerically intensive and will scale rapidly in difficulty with molecular size, we should aim to develop methods for the most powerful computers available if we are to tackle the polyatomic gases, such as C_3F_8 and $SiCl_4$, that are of interest in plasma processing.

14.2   COMPUTING ELECTRON-MOLECULE CROSS SECTIONS

Discussions of computational methods in chemical physics often focus either on abstract formulations or, at the other extreme, on fine algorithmic details. We prefer, especially in the present context, to set an intermediate focus: neither to presume implicitly that any method that can be formulated can be practically applied nor to get lost in technical minutiae. Rather, we will outline the formulation of our method but concentrate on its *implementation,* which we will discuss with reference to issues of *scaling* and *parallelism.* In fact, our approach is one of several alternative formulations of the low-energy electron-molecule collision problem, all having at least superficially similar abstract properties, that are in use today. Its special advantages derive, we feel, as much from its efficient implementation for MPPs as from the efficiencies inherent in its formulation. Consideration of scaling issues illuminates both the need for high-performance computations and the reasons that we expect, and achieve, high efficiencies within our parallel code.

14.2.1   Theoretical Outline

The formulation that we employ is referred to as the Schwinger Multichannel (SMC) method [14.5, 14.6]. It is a *variational* formulation, meaning that we express the approximate solution to the collision problem as the stationary point of a functional. Locating that stationary point within a function space of finite dimension determines approximate *wavefunctions* (solutions to the fundamental quantum-mechanical equation, Schrödinger's equation) and, through those wavefunctions, the collision cross sections of interest. To obtain a numerical implementation of this variational principle, we follow the common approach of reducing the problem to linear algebra through the introduction of linear-expansion representations of the trial wavefunctions. In the next several paragraphs, we outline these steps in more detail for the interested reader; others may prefer to skim the remainder of this section and Section 14.2.2, resuming with Section 14.2.3.

The fundamental equation in our work is the fixed-nuclei electronic Schrödinger equation,

$$
H\Psi(\{\vec{r}_i\};\{\vec{R}_I\}) = \left(\sum_i -\frac{1}{2}\nabla_i^2 - \sum_{i,I}\frac{Z_I}{|\vec{r}_i - \vec{R}_I|} + \sum_{i,j>i}\frac{1}{|\vec{r}_i - \vec{r}_j|}\right)\Psi(\{\vec{r}_i\};\{\vec{R}_I\})
$$
$$
= E\Psi(\{\vec{r}_i\};\{\vec{R}_I\}) \tag{14.2}
$$

where $\{\vec{r}_i\}$ is the set of electron coordinates, $\{\vec{R}_i\}$ the set of nuclear coordinates (considered as fixed parameters), ∇_i^2 is the Laplacian in $\vec{r}_i$, Z_I is the electric charge of nucleus I, E is the total electronic energy of the system, and Ψ is the wavefunction. Atomic units ($\hbar = e = m = 1$) are assumed in Equation (14.2) and in what follows. The component terms of the Hamiltonian H of Equation (14.2) have recognizable physical meanings, corresponding, respectively, to the electrons' kinetic energy, to the electron-nuclear potential energy, and to the electron-electron repulsion energy; the latter two are simple multiplicative operators whose form reflects Coulomb's law.

In the treatment of collision problems, it is often convenient to work with the integral equation associated with the Schrödinger equation, the so-called Lippmann-Schwinger equation [14.3]. We partition H into an "interaction-free" Hamiltonian H_0 describing an isolated N-electron molecule and a free electron,

$$
H_0 = \sum_{i=1}^{N+1} -\frac{1}{2}\nabla_i^2 - \sum_I \sum_{i=1}^{N}\frac{Z_I}{|\vec{r}_i - \vec{R}_I|} + \sum_{\substack{i=1 \\ j=i+1}}^{N}\frac{1}{|\vec{r}_i - \vec{r}_j|} \tag{14.3}
$$

and an electron-molecule interaction V,

$$
V = -\sum_I \frac{Z_I}{|\vec{r}_{N+1} - \vec{R}_I|} + \sum_{i=1}^{N}\frac{1}{|\vec{r}_i - \vec{r}_{N+1}|} \tag{14.4}
$$

The Lippmann-Schwinger equation is then

$$\Psi^{(\pm)}(\{\vec{r}_i\};\{\vec{R}_I\}) = \Psi_0(\{\vec{r}_i\};\{\vec{R}_I\}) + (E - H_0 \pm i\varepsilon)^{-1} V\Psi(\{\vec{r}_i\};\{\vec{R}_I\}) \quad (14.5)$$

In Equation (14.5), Ψ_0 is a solution to $H_0\Psi_0 = E\Psi_0$, the interaction-free Schrödinger equation, and the Green's function (or more accurately Green's operator) $G^{(\pm)}(E) = (E - H_0 \pm i\varepsilon)^{-1}$ is defined through a limiting process as $\varepsilon \to 0$. The $\pm$ sign appearing in the Green's function and as a label on Ψ refers to the choice of asymptotic boundary conditions: With the $+$ $(-)$ sign, Ψ behaves asymptotically as Ψ_0 plus terms containing expanding (collapsing) spherical waves. The $+$ choice, together with the choice

$$\Psi_0 = \Psi_{0,\vec{k}} = \Phi_0(\{\vec{r}_i\}_{i=1}^N;\{\vec{R}_I\})\exp(i\vec{k}\cdot\vec{r}_{N+1}) \quad (14.6)$$

where Φ_0 is the ground electronic state of the molecule, thus leads to physically appropriate scattering boundary conditions: an incident unit flux of free electrons with wave vector $\vec{k}$ and a scattered flux propagating outward in all directions. The asymptotic spherical waves are modulated by coefficients $f(\vec{k},\vec{k}')$ that describe the magnitude of the scattered flux having wave vector $\vec{k}'$. The function $f(\vec{k},\vec{k}')$, known as the *scattering amplitude,* is the quantity of interest, since the collision cross section $\sigma(\vec{k} \to \vec{k}')$ is proportional to its square modulus.

It can be shown (e.g., [14.7]) that an expression for the scattering amplitude is

$$f(\vec{k},\vec{k}') = \langle \Psi_{0,\vec{k}'} |V|\Psi_{\vec{k}}^{(+)} \rangle \quad (14.7a)$$

where the $\vec{k}$ subscript appearing on $\Psi^{(+)}$ refers to the incident electron wave vector introduced through Equations (14.5) and (14.6), and where we have adopted the "Dirac bracket" notation $\langle f|\mathcal{O}|g \rangle = \int f^*\mathcal{O}g$, with the integral taken over all electron coordinates and $*$ indicating complex conjugation. Using Equation (14.7a) together with the Lippmann-Schwinger equation, we can easily develop two alternative expressions for the scattering amplitude:

$$f(\vec{k},\vec{k}') = \langle \Psi_{\vec{k}'}^{(-)} |V|\Psi_{0,\vec{k}} \rangle \quad (14.7b)$$

and

$$f(\vec{k},\vec{k}') = \langle \Psi_{\vec{k}'}^{(-)} |V - VG^{(+)}V|\Psi_{\vec{k}}^{(+)} \rangle \quad (14.7c)$$

Schwinger [14.4] combined these three expressions to obtain a variational functional:

$$\widetilde{f}(\vec{k},\vec{k}') = \langle \Psi_{0,\vec{k}'} | V | \widetilde{\Psi}_{\vec{k}}^{(+)} \rangle + \langle \widetilde{\Psi}_{\vec{k}'}^{(-)} | V | \Psi_{0,\vec{k}} \rangle - \langle \widetilde{\Psi}_{\vec{k}'}^{(-)} | V - V G^{(+)} V | \widetilde{\Psi}_{\vec{k}}^{(+)} \rangle \qquad (14.8)$$

where $\widetilde{\Psi}_{\vec{k}}^{(+)}$ and $\widetilde{\Psi}_{\vec{k}'}^{(-)}$ are trial wavefunctions. Equation (14.8) obviously gives the correct scattering amplitude when the trial functions are equal to the exact wavefunctions; moreover, by use of the Lippmann-Schwinger equation and its adjoint, Equation (14.8) can easily be shown to be variationally stable about the correct scattering amplitude (i.e., to contain only second order errors in $\widetilde{f}$ when $\widetilde{\Psi}^{(\pm)}$ contain first order errors).

For technical reasons connected with the many-particle nature of the electron-molecule collision problem, we base our numerical method on a modified version of Schwinger's variational principle, which we refer to as the Schwinger multichannel, or SMC, variational expression. In place of Equation (14.8), we have

$$\widetilde{f}(\vec{k},\vec{k}') = \langle \Psi_{0,\vec{k}'} | V | \widetilde{\Psi}_{\vec{k}}^{(+)} \rangle + \langle \widetilde{\Psi}_{\vec{k}'}^{(-)} | V | \Psi_{0,\vec{k}} \rangle$$
$$- \langle \widetilde{\Psi}_{\vec{k}'}^{(-)} \left| \left(\frac{1}{N+1} - P \right) + VP - VPG^{(+)}V \right| \widetilde{\Psi}_{\vec{k}}^{(+)} \rangle \qquad (14.9)$$

In Equation (14.9), P is a projection operator that selects *open channels*—that is, energetically accessible final states $\Phi_n(\{\vec{r}_i\}_{i=1}^{N}) \exp(i\vec{k} \cdot \vec{r}_{N+1})$. (It is assumed in the SMC method that no electron-impact ionization channels are open, so that Φ_n is always a bound *N*-electron molecular state.)

14.2.2   Implementation

To implement the SMC expression, Equation (14.9), we introduce linear expansions for the trial functions $\widetilde{\Psi}_{\vec{k}}^{(+)}$ and $\widetilde{\Psi}_{\vec{k}'}^{(-)}$:

$$\widetilde{\Psi}_{\vec{k}}^{(+)} = \sum_m x_m(\vec{k}) \chi_m(\{\vec{r}_i\}) \qquad (14.10a)$$

and

$$\widetilde{\Psi}_{\vec{k}'}^{(-)} = \sum_\ell y_\ell(\vec{k}') \chi_\ell(\{\vec{r}_i\}) \qquad (14.10b)$$

where the χ_ℓ are known functions and the x_m and y_ℓ are coefficients to be determined. Imposing the stability conditions

$$\frac{\partial \tilde{f}(\vec{k},\vec{k}')}{\partial x_m} = \frac{\partial \tilde{f}(\vec{k},\vec{k}')}{\partial y_\ell} = 0 \quad \text{for all } \ell \text{ and } m \tag{14.11}$$

leads to the following matrix-vector equations:

$$\mathbf{Ax} = \mathbf{b}^{(0)}$$
$$\mathbf{y}^{(n)\dagger}\mathbf{A} = \mathbf{b}^{(n)} \tag{14.12}$$

where 0 and n are channel labels and $\mathbf{A}$ is a square, complex-symmetric matrix with elements

$$A_{\ell m} = \left\langle \chi_\ell \left| \left(\frac{1}{N+1} - P \right)(E - H) + VP - VPG^{(+)}V \right| \chi_m \right\rangle \tag{14.13}$$

$\mathbf{b}^{(n)}$ is a rectangular matrix with elements

$$b_{\ell,\vec{k}}^{(n)} = \langle \chi_\ell | V | \Phi_n \exp(i\vec{k} \cdot \vec{r}_{N+1}) \rangle \tag{14.14}$$

(the column label being, in practice, a quadrature set of directions $\hat{k}$ for fixed magnitude $|\vec{k}|$), and $\mathbf{x}$ and $\mathbf{y}^{(n)}$ are rectangular matrices of the unknown linear expansion coefficients x and y of Equations (14.10a) and (14.10b), the column label again being the wave vector direction; $\mathbf{y}^\dagger$ indicates the complex-conjugate transpose of $\mathbf{y}$. From the solution $\mathbf{x}$ to the first of Equation (14.12), we may express the scattering amplitude matrix $\mathbf{f}^{(n)}$ for a transition to final state n as

$$\mathbf{f}^{(n)} = \mathbf{b}^{(n)\dagger}\mathbf{x} \tag{14.15}$$

The row and column labels of this matrix refer to the directions of the incident and scattered wave vectors.

All that remains to complete the implementation of the SMC method is to choose an explicit form for the expansion functions χ_ℓ of Equations (14.10a) and (14.10b) and to work out the corresponding forms for the $\mathbf{A}$ and $\mathbf{b}$ matrix elements. In choosing a form for the $(N + 1)$-electron functions χ_ℓ, we are guided simultaneously by considerations of physical appropriateness and of ease of evaluation of the matrix elements: To keep the expansions of the trial functions compact, the χ_ℓ should approximate states of the electron-molecule system well, but it must also be possible to evaluate the various integrals that arise from Equations (14.13) and (14.14) for $A_{\ell m}$ and $b_{\ell,\vec{k}}^{(n)}$ quickly and accurately. In practice, we exploit a facet of the Schwinger variational expression that is preserved in the SMC expression—namely, the independence of the required matrix elements from the asymptotic form of the trial functions. This independence allows us to employ square-integrable basis functions, and in particular to form the χ_ℓ from *Slater determinants* of molecular orbitals, with the molecular orbitals themselves represented as combinations of Cartesian Gaussian functions. A Slater determinant has the general form

$$
\begin{vmatrix}
\phi_1(\vec{r}_1) & \phi_2(\vec{r}_1) & \cdots & \phi_{N+1}(\vec{r}_1) \\
\phi_1(\vec{r}_2) & \phi_2(\vec{r}_2) & \cdots & \phi_{N+1}(\vec{r}_2) \\
\vdots & \vdots & \ddots & \vdots \\
\phi_1(\vec{r}_{N+1}) & \phi_2(\vec{r}_{N+1}) & \cdots & \phi_{N+1}(\vec{r}_{N+1})
\end{vmatrix}
\tag{14.16}
$$

where the ϕ_p are molecular spin orbitals. In practice, we work with χ_ℓ that are eigenfunctions of the $(N+1)$-electron spin operator; these "configuration state functions," or CSFs, may consist either of a single Slater determinant or of a fixed linear combination of a few Slater determinants. The spin parts of the molecular orbitals ϕ_p can be kept track of implicitly, since the only possible values are "up" and "down," and will not be mentioned further; the spatial parts of the ϕ_p are further expanded as sums of Cartesian Gaussian functions ζ_α:

$$
\phi_p(\vec{r}') = \sum_\alpha C_{\alpha p} \zeta_\alpha(\vec{r})
\tag{14.17}
$$

The label α is shorthand for a complete set of defining parameters:

$$
\begin{aligned}
\zeta_\alpha(\vec{r}) &= \zeta(\vec{r}; \alpha, \ell, m, n, \vec{R}_I) \\
&= N_{\alpha\ell mn}(x-X)^\ell (y-Y)^m (z-Z)^n \exp(-\alpha|\vec{r}-\vec{R}|^2)
\end{aligned}
\tag{14.18}
$$

where $\vec{r} = (x,y,z)$; $\vec{R} = (X,Y,Z)$; l, m, and n, are integers; and $N_{\alpha\ell mn}$ is a normalization constant. The molecular orbitals typically represent one-electron states of motion obtained from the solution of an (approximate) independent-particle model for the molecular ground electronic state $\Phi_0(\{\vec{r}_i\}_{i=1}^N)$, together with an orthogonal complement of unoccupied orbitals, some of which may be chosen to provide good descriptions of excited electronic states or of temporarily bound states of motion of the impinging electron.

Expanding the trial functions in CSFs and the molecular orbitals within the CSFs in Cartesian Gaussians achieves a compromise between compactness in representation and efficiency of integral evaluation. Because only one- and two-electron operators occur, the determinantal structure underlying the CSFs allows the many-electron integrals to be reduced to integrals involving the coordinates of at most two electrons. Moreover, although Gaussians are not ideally suited to describe electronic charge distributions within molecules—functions of the form $r^{\ell}\exp(-\alpha|\vec{r}-\vec{R}_I|)$ would be more effective—the most numerous integrals, the two-electron integrals arising from the electron-electron Coulomb repulsion $|\vec{r}_i-\vec{r}_j|^{-1}$, are far easier to evaluate for Gaussians.

The one-electron integrals that arise in the SMC method involve either two Gaussians or a Gaussian and a plane wave; examples are the kinetic energy integrals

$$\int d^3r\,\zeta_\alpha(\vec{r})\nabla^2\zeta_\beta(\vec{r}) \tag{14.19a}$$

and the electron-nuclear interaction integrals

$$\int d^3r\,\zeta_\alpha(\vec{r})\frac{Z_I}{|\vec{r}-\vec{R}_I|}\exp(i\vec{k}\cdot\vec{r}) \tag{14.19b}$$

Two-electron integrals arise from the electron-electron Coulomb potential and involve either four Gaussians:

$$\iint d^3r_1\,d^3r_2\,\zeta_\alpha(\vec{r}_1)\zeta_\beta(\vec{r}_1)\frac{1}{|\vec{r}_1-\vec{r}_2|}\zeta_\gamma(\vec{r}_2)\zeta_\delta(\vec{r}_2) \tag{14.20a}$$

or three Gaussians and a plane wave:

$$\iint d^3r_1\,d^3r_2\,\zeta_\alpha(\vec{r}_1)\zeta_\beta(\vec{r}_1)\frac{1}{|\vec{r}_1-\vec{r}_2|}\zeta_\gamma(\vec{r}_2)\exp(i\vec{k}\cdot\vec{r}_2) \tag{14.20b}$$

Integrals involving plane waves arise both in the evaluation of the $\mathbf{b}^{(n)}$ matrix elements and in the evaluation of matrix elements involving the Green's function.

The latter have no known analytic form and are evaluated by quadrature after introducing a spectral representation of the Green's function:

$$\langle \chi_\ell | VPG^{(+)}V | \chi_m \rangle =$$

$$\lim_{\varepsilon \to 0^+} \sum_{\substack{n \in \text{open} \\ \text{channels}}} \int d^3 k_n \; \frac{\langle \chi_\ell | V | \Phi_n \, \exp(i\vec{k}_n \cdot \vec{r}_{N+1}) \rangle \langle \Phi_n \, \exp(i\vec{k}_n \cdot \vec{r}_{N+1}) | V | \chi_m \rangle}{E - (E_n + \frac{1}{2} k_n^2) + i\varepsilon} \quad (14.21)$$

the integration over $\vec{k}_n$ being performed by quadrature [14.8]; here, E_n is the energy of the molecular state Φ_n.

Let us begin to draw the steps that we have described so far together into a picture of the computational procedure that they embody. At the bottom level, we have the evaluation of integrals such as those of Equations (14.19a), (14.19b), (14.20a), and (14.20b). Through a succession of expansions, Equations (14.10) through (14.17), these elementary quantities are assembled into the matrix elements of Equations (14.13) and (14.14). Finally, Equation (14.12) is solved to yield scattering amplitudes via Equation (14.15). How much work is associated with these steps, and how is the amount of work related to the size of the molecule?

Consider first the evaluation of the integrals. The number of integrals depends strongly on the size of the molecule. Letting N_g be the number of Gaussians and $N_{\vec{k}}$ the number of plane waves, we can see from Equations (14.20a) and (14.20b) that there are approximately $N_g^4/8$ unique two-electron integrals involving four Gaussians and $N_g^3 N_{\vec{k}}/2$ unique integrals involving three Gaussians and a plane wave. On the order of half a dozen (for hydrogen) to several dozen (for heavier atoms) Cartesian Gaussians are typically centered on each atom composing the molecule; thus, for plasma etchants such as C_3F_8 or $c-C_4F_8$, several hundred Gaussians may be employed altogether. Considering that the numerical quadrature implied by Equation (14.21) typically requires on the order of 10^4 to 10^5 points in $\vec{k}_n$, we find that on the order of 10^9 four-Gaussian integrals and 10^{11} to 10^{12} three-Gaussian, one-plane-wave integrals would be required for such molecules. The number of floating-point operations required to compute any one integral, though dependent on the parameters specifying the ζ_α and the plane wave, typically ranges from dozens to hundreds. We can therefore conclude that the calculation of integrals, particularly those involving three Gaussians and a plane wave, is a substantial task for modest-sized molecules and grows rapidly more demanding as the molecular size increases.

Now consider the transformation steps required to obtain $A_{\ell m}$ and $b_{\ell,\vec{k}}^{(n)}$ matrix elements from the elementary integrals. Since the three-Gaussian, one-plane-wave integrals are most numerous, it is sufficient to consider only their transformation to obtain the scaling. Each open channel has associated with it a $\mathbf{b}^{(n)}$ matrix and a term in the Green's function quadrature, Equation (14.21); moreover, because the channels are coupled together, the number of CSFs χ_ℓ is roughly proportional to the number N_c of open channels, as well as to the size of the molecule (i.e., to N_g). From these relations for the matrix dimensions, together with the operation count for repeated application of Equation (14.17) in the transformation process, we conclude that on the order of $N_c^2 N_g^4 N_{\bar{k}}$ floating-point operations are involved in the transformation procedure. Again taking a molecule like $c\text{-}C_4F_8$ as an example and assuming that only a few channels are included (i.e., $N_c = 1$, 2, or 3), we obtain an estimate of 10^{15} to 10^{16} operations for the transformation phase of the calculation, with a rapid escalation as N_c or N_g is enlarged. (In principle, we can improve the scaling of the transformation procedure by using a version of Strassen's algorithm to carry out the matrix multiplications that arise. In practice, however, the matrices that arise, though large, are very nonsquare, and the smallest dimension—particularly after data are partitioned among processors in an MPP—is generally too small for a significant benefit to result.)

Comparing these operation counts for the principal computational steps in the SMC calculation to the speeds of current high-performance processors (on the order of 10^9 operations per second), we see clearly that such calculations would be impractical on any single-processor machine, even if we were clever enough to write code that ran at the processor's peak speed. Although efficient coding—for example, reuse of intermediate values, exploitation of molecular symmetry properties, screening out small integrals, and so on—can (and does) reduce the operation count of the actual program, it does not affect the basic scaling relations previously developed, and therefore does not affect the conclusion that *a single-processor approach will be limited to the study of small molecules*. This conclusion applies, moreover, not just to the SMC method but also to other variational methods for which the underlying scaling relations (which, in the end, reflect the problem physics) are similar.

We are thus compelled to adopt a parallel approach if we aim to tackle the polyatomic gases in use by industry today. In the next section, we will describe how the computational steps that we have outlined are divided up in space and time for execution in a parallel environment.

14.2.3 Parallel Organization

Our parallel SMC program was originally written for an early distributed-memory, multiple-instruction, multiple-data architecture, the Mark III[fp] hypercube built by JPL and Caltech [14.2]. The native message-passing system on the

Mark III^{fp}, known as CROS III [14.1], supported a fairly limited set of communication calls, at least in comparison with the parallel virtual machine (PVM) or message-passing interface (MPI) libraries, and subtly favored a single-program, multiple-data programming (SPMD) model (e.g., by providing, in addition to the usual pairwise communication calls, an explicit "shift" call to implement roll operations on distributed data structures). Although our program's design was influenced by the strengths and weaknesses of this target system, on the whole it has stood up very well through the introduction of more advanced and more flexible hardware and software. In particular, the loosely synchronous, single-program model, implemented through a limited variety of message-passing calls, has proven highly portable and easy to optimize on a succession of distributed-memory and, more recently, shared-memory architectures.

In parallelizing the SMC method, we clearly want to distribute evenly the work associated with the two main computational steps that we have identified—namely, the evaluation of two-electron integrals and the subsequent transformation of those integrals to final matrix elements. Because, moreover, the number of integrals is likely to be far larger than can be accommodated in memory, we will want to distribute the evaluation and processing of the integrals both in space (i.e., among the processors) and in time. For optimal efficiency, synchronization points should be kept to a minimum so that temporary load imbalances caused by the variable number of operations needed to evaluate different integrals may be averaged away. We are thus led to a model in which large subsets of integrals are computed in parallel, with each processor working independently on a different subset. When each processor has evaluated its subset of integrals, the transformations necessary to compute the contribution of those integrals to the $\mathbf{A}$ and $\mathbf{b}^{(n)}$ matrix elements are carried out, the integrals are discarded, and the entire procedure is repeated for a new collection of integrals. This gradual building up of the final matrix elements avoids a memory (or I/O) bottleneck, because only a tiny fraction of the complete set of integrals is needed at any time, and also provides a convenient checkpointing mechanism.

The implementation of the approach described in the preceding paragraph is schematized in Figure 14.2. A set of three-Gaussian, one-plane-wave integrals, Equation (14.20b), for fixed γ and $|\vec{k}|$ is treated as a distributed 2D array, with one dimension being a collective index to unique (α,β) pairs and the other index being the direction $\hat{k}$ of the wave vector. Assigning the (α,β) and $\hat{k}$ indices cyclically to the rows and columns of a (conceptual) 2D processor array leads to a pseudorandom distribution of integrals that helps to ensure good load balance. Because this step is perfectly parallel and rather coarse-grained—with both N_g and $N_{\hat{k}}$ (the number of $\vec{k}$ directions) typically greater than 100, there are thousands to tens of thousands of integrals per processor in a subset—load balance is essentially the only issue in achieving high parallel efficiency.

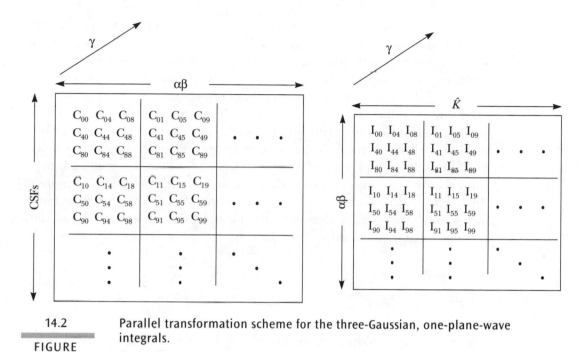

Parallel transformation scheme for the three-Gaussian, one-plane-wave integrals.

The subsequent transformation step necessarily involves interprocessor communication. In order to keep that communication simple, regular, and therefore efficient, it is encapsulated within a distributed-matrix multiplication: The integral array, considered as a distributed matrix, is multiplied with a distributed "transformation matrix" indexed in one direction by the (α,β) pair label and in the other direction by the index to CSF's χ_ℓ (again, see Figure 14.2). Both the relatively straightforward, but numerically intensive, repeated linear transformation that results from the application of Equations (14.17) through (14.20b) and the relatively complicated, but highly sparse, transformation that connects integrals over molecular orbitals to many-electron matrix elements are encoded in the transformation matrix, whose construction is itself a perfectly parallel step; only in the actual multiplication of the integral array by the transformation matrix does interprocessor communication occur. Because the arrays are large and the work-to-communication ratio scales as N^3/N^2 for large arrays, we are assured of a high parallel efficiency in this step. Moreover, because the communication is simple and well localized within the program, portability is greatly enhanced.

This above description covers the two major computational steps in the SMC method. Certainly other components are necessary to the complete program, including evaluation of one-electron integrals, numerical quadratures, and solution of linear equations. However, these are much less important to the overall performance, as far smaller operation counts are involved, and we omit discussion of them here. The remaining issue that *has* proved significant is I/O. Because, as seen in Equation (14.21), the Green's function depends on the collision energy E, we must save a considerable amount of intermediate data in order to be able to perform the quadrature over $\vec{k}_n$ for many different values of E without repeating the entire calculation. The size of this dataset scales approximately as $N_c^3 N_g^2$, where, again, N_c is the number of open channels or excitation processes considered, and N_g is the number of Gaussians. Even for small molecules, many-channel problems result in a dataset on the order of 10^{10} bytes or more in size. On some parallel machines (though not the T3D or T3E), we have found that considerable care is necessary to avoid a serious bottleneck when such data volumes are accessed in parallel [14.9].

14.3   PERFORMANCE

The performance of the SMC method depends strongly on the problem that it is asked to solve. As we have outlined above, there are two main computational tasks: constructing an enormous number of elementary quantities (three-Gaussian, one-plane-wave Coulomb integrals) and transforming those integrals into combinations that have physical meaning as matrix elements in a linear system of equations for the scattering amplitude. These two phases differ greatly in their performance characteristics and scale differently with the problem parameters. The integral computation task involves complicated logic, multiple calls to the trigonometric, square-root, and exponential functions, and the generation of substantial amounts of intermediate data for each integral. The most successful optimization approach is reuse of the intermediate data to generate batches of related integrals simultaneously; there is little scope for vector- or cache-related optimizations. In contrast, almost all of the work in the second task, transforming the integrals, can be concentrated in the multiplication of large, dense matrices, an ideal computational procedure for cache-based microprocessors (or vector supercomputers), and one whose "optimization" (apart from communication issues) is usually as simple as calling a highly tuned routine supplied in a system library. Thus, the transformation phase, in contrast to the integral evaluation phase, achieves a large fraction of peak speed, and its performance tends to improve as the problem size increases.

As discussed earlier, the number of integrals to be computed grows as the cube of the number of Gaussians, N_g, while the transformation procedure scales as N_g^4. Nonetheless, because of its inherently lower performance rate and the high operation count per integral, the integral evaluation phase consumes the majority of the total running time in single-channel calculations and in few-channel calculations on smaller molecules. However, we may recall that the amount of work in the transformation phase scales with the square of the number of channels, N_c, whereas the number of integrals to be evaluated scales much more weakly, as $a + bN_c$, with an extremely large constant term a (representing the integrals needed for the Green's function). Thus, as N_c is made larger, the relative importance of the transformation phase grows rapidly, and the transformation phase is typically dominant for N_c larger than about 4 or 5.

In light of these considerations, it should be clear that no single number can characterize the performance of the SMC program; by an appropriate choice of problem parameters, we can approach either the high-performance limit where most of the work is matrix multiplication or the lower-performance limit where most of the work is integral evaluation. To give a more realistic assessment, we instead will discuss the actual performance in each phase for a specific example calculation taken from our ongoing studies of halogenated molecules used in etching plasmas. This calculation considered electron-impact excitation of nitrogen trifluoride, NF_3, into two low-lying states, specifically $(6a_1 \rightarrow 7a_1)^{1,3}A_1$. We thus have $N_c = 3$, counting the elastic channel, while the Gaussian basis set used is characterized by $N_g = 116$. As this is a fairly small molecule and a small number of channels, we anticipate that integral evaluation will be the major computational task, and this expectation is borne out in the timings presented below.

Consider the construction of quadrature data for the Green's function—that is, the evaluation of the numerator in Equation (14.21) at quadrature points $\vec{k}_{pqr} = (k_p, \theta_q, \phi_r)$ in spherical polar coordinates, obtained through the product of one-dimensional quadratures. The program evaluates a complete set of angular quadrature points (θ_q, ϕ_r) for a fixed value of k_p, because in this way we are able to perform significant data reduction (the integration over θ_q and ϕ_r) as we go along. For larger values of the radial variable k_p, we naturally increase the number of quadrature points θ_q and ϕ_r, so that the time to evaluate a subset of quadrature data varies with k_p. For this discussion, let us examine the timings for k_p about equal to 3 atomic units, where 32 points were used in both the θ and ϕ quadratures. By exploiting symmetries of the problem, we can restrict these points to a single hemisphere and, further, can eliminate half of the ϕ points, so that the actual quadrature comprises 512 angular points distributed over one-fourth of the sphere.

From the scaling relations described earlier, we expect about $N_g^3 N_k / 2 = 4 \times 10^8$ integrals and on the order of $N_c^2 N_g^4 N_k = 8 \times 10^{11}$ operations in the transformation. The actual values are 4.03×10^8 integrals and 1.43×10^{12}

operations for the transformation phase. Using 128 of the 150-MHz processors in JPL's 256-processor Cray T3D, the elapsed time for the integral evaluation is 302 seconds, corresponding to a rate of 1.33×10^6 integrals per second overall, or 10,400 per second on a per-processor basis. Because the operation count per integral varies widely, it is difficult to convert these numbers to operations per second, but we can estimate a rough upper bound of 1 Gflop for the overall performance of the integral evaluation phase. The transformation phase (including both the actual matrix multiplications and all necessary interprocessor communication) requires 187 seconds on 128 processors, yielding an aggregate rate of 7.65 Gflops, or 59.7 Mflops per processor.

The timings just discussed provide a concrete illustration of our earlier remarks regarding the relative performance of the two phases of the calculation. They also give some idea of the benefits of parallel processing to our work: Although the throughput for this modest-sized problem is considerably below the T3D's peak speed, it is about two orders of magnitude greater than we have achieved with a sequential implementation on vector processors, where performance is severely limited by the poorly vectorizable integral evaluation task. As a result, we are able to solve, in a total running on the order of hours, a problem that we would hesitate to attempt on a sequential processor.

14.4   SUMMARY

By applying the power of MPPs such as the Cray T3D and T3E, we have been able to undertake broad studies of halogenated etchant gases used in semiconductor manufacturing. Not only are we able to address molecules like c-C_4F_8 whose sheer size might once have been an obstacle, but we are also able to pursue more detailed and comprehensive studies of individual molecules: for example, to study many different excitation processes in a single molecule and then go on to study elastic and inelastic electron collisions with all of the neutral fragments (radicals) that are formed by electron-impact dissociation of that molecule. Thorough studies of this kind are essential in building up the collision databases that will be the foundation of sophisticated plasma models.

The SMC method is one of many methods in computational science that, although designed for efficiency, nonetheless retains a faster-than-linear scaling with measures of the problem size. Certainly it is a vast improvement to replace the original combinatorial scaling of the quantum-mechanical many-body problem with scaling as a small power of some problem parameter. Without theoretical achievements of this kind, addressing any but "toy" problems would remain impossible indefinitely. With them, we can in principle simply wait for the exponential progress called for by Moore's law to make any given problem feasible on a uniprocessor. However, as the operation counts we have discussed in Section 14.2 should make clear, we are so far from being able to tackle many problems of pressing interest on uniprocessors that waiting and hoping is not a very practical strategy—especially when we could have been solving those problems on parallel machines in the meantime. As long as we remain constrained in what we can do more by computer power than by any other factor—and that appears to encompass the foreseeable future—scalable, multiprocessor implementations of the best theoretical methods will remain at the forefront of computational science.

ACKNOWLEDGMENTS

This research was supported by SEMATECH, Inc., by the National Science Foundation through the Grand Challenge project "Parallel I/O Methodologies for I/O Intensive Grand Challenge Applications," by NASA's Mission to Planet Earth through its support of the JPL/Caltech Supercomputing Project, and through the PATP program of Cray Research.

References

[14.1]   Angus, I. G., G. C. Fox, J. S. Kim, and D. W. Walker. 1990. *Solving Problems on Concurrent Processors, Vol. II: Software for Concurrent Processors*. Englewood Cliffs, NJ: Prentice Hall.

[14.2]   Burns, P., J. Crichton, D. Curkendall, B. Eng, C. Goodhart, R. Lee, R. Livingston, J. Peterson, M. Pniel, J. Tuazon, and B. Zimmermann. 1988. In G. Fox (ed.), The JPL/Caltech Mark III^{fp} Hypercube. *Proceedings of the Third Conference on Hypercube Concurrent Computers and Applications, Vol. I: Architecture, Software, Computer Systems, and General Issues* (ed.), p. 872. New York: Association for Computing Machinery.

[14.3]   Lippman, B. A., and J. Schwinger. 1950. Variational Principles for Scattering Processes. *Phys. Rev.*, **79,** 469.

[14.4]   Schwinger, J. 1947. A Variational Principle for Scattering Problems. *Phys. Rev.*, **72,** 742.

[14.5]   Takatsuka, K., and V. McKoy. 1981. Extension of the Schwinger Variational Principle beyond the Static-Exchange Approximation *Phys. Rev., A,* **24,** 2473.

[14.6]   Takatsuka, K., and V. McKoy. 1984. Theory of Electronically Inelastic Scattering of Electrons by Molecules. *Phys. Rev., A,* **30,** 1734.

[14.7]   Winstead, C., and V. McKoy. 1996. Electron Scattering by Small Molecules. *Advan. Chem. Phys.*, **96,** 103.

[14.8]   Winstead, C., and V. McKoy. 1996. Highly Parallel Computational Techniques for Electron-Molecule Collisions. *Adv. At. Mol. Opt. Phys.*, **36,** 183.

[14.9]   Winstead, C., H. P. Pritchard, and V. McKoy. 1996. In M. L. Simmons, A. H. Hayes, J. S. Brown, and D. A. Reed (eds.). Tuning I/O Performance on the Paragon: Fun with Pablo and Norma. *Debugging and Performance Tuning for Parallel Computing Systems*. Los Alamitos, CA: IEEE Computer Society.

Three-Dimensional Plasma Particle-in-Cell Calculations of Ion Thruster Backflow Contamination

Robie I. Samanta Roy   Institute for Defense Analyses

Daniel E. Hastings   Space Power and Propulsion Laboratory, Massachusetts Institute of Technology

Stephen Taylor   Scalable Concurrent Programming Laboratory, Syracuse University

15.1   INTRODUCTION

The potential problems of spacecraft contamination by the effluents of electric propulsion (EP) thrusters have been known for some time [15.2, 15.3]. However, ground-based experiments produce estimates of thruster contamination that are questionable due to vacuum chamber facility effects such as chamber wall sputtering and the presence of residual chamber gases. Only recently has massively parallel computing technology enabled large-scale fully 3D computational assessments of thruster backflow contamination over realistic spacecraft geometries. The prediction of backflow contamination is of increasing importance now that EP is earnestly being considered for a variety of applications, including station keeping on commercial geostationary communications satellites [15.9]. Among the various types of EP thrusters, ion thrusters have reached a relatively high state of maturity and thus have received much attention in regard to spacecraft contamination and integration issues.

The evaluation of the thruster-induced environmental effects that could degrade the performance of spacecraft subsystems and sensors is very important. For example, in ion thruster plumes, a low-energy plasma is created by charge-exchange (CEX) processes and can expand around a spacecraft, leading to a current drain of high-voltage surfaces. The enhanced plasma density due to a thruster plume can also lead to attenuation and refraction of electromagnetic wave transmission and reception. In addition, ion thrusters emit heavy metal-species, both charged and uncharged, due to grid and discharge chamber erosion that can easily adhere to sensitive spacecraft surfaces and decrease the operational lifetime of the satellite. It is vitally important to understand and predict the backflow transport of these species from the plume onto a spacecraft.

We have developed a model of an ion thruster plume, based on the hybrid plasma particle-in-cell (PIC) technique, to simulate the backflow contamination from the CEX plasma that is created from CEX collisions between fast beam ions and thermal neutrals that leak out of the discharge chamber. Due to the large-scale nature of the problem, which involves spatial domains of meters to encompass a realistic spacecraft, and the large numbers of computational particles that are necessary for reasonable statistics, we have developed our model to take advantage of state-of-the-art massively parallel architectures. These computers enable previously inconceivable solutions of problems. The model is applied to estimate the backflow from a 13-cm xenon ion thruster located on a model spacecraft similar to the U.S. Air Force Advanced Research and Global Observation Satellite.

In Section 15.2 of this chapter we formulate our approach to the problem and describe the physical model. Numerical methods are discussed in Section 15.3, followed by a presentation of the concurrent implementation in Section 15.4. Results of a large-scale application are presented and discussed in Section 15.5, and the concurrent performance of the model is discussed in Section 15.6. Lastly, conclusions and future work are offered in Section 15.7.

15.2   THE PHYSICAL MODEL

The ion thruster plume model used in this study accounts for four of the five major thruster effluents: (1) fast (greater than 10 km/s) propellant beam ions that provide the thrust; (2) un-ionized propellant neutrals with thermal energies that flow from both the discharge chamber and the neutralizer; (3) slow (initially thermal) propellant ions created predominantly from charge-exchange (CEX) collisions between the beam ions and neutrals; (4) nonpropellant efflux (NPE) that consists mainly of eroded grid material, typically molybdenum, of which a fraction is charged due to either CEX or electron bombardment ionization; and (5) neutralizing electrons. The NPE efflux is not considered in this chapter. In this section, brief descriptions of the other effluents are given based on the work of Samanta Roy et al. [15.12]. Some of the elements of the model are given in terms of axisymmetric coordinates for simplicity but are implemented as fully three-dimensional.

15.2.1   Beam Ions

The collimated beam ions of mass m_i that provide the thrust are accelerated electrostatically by a grid system to velocities typically on the order of 20,000–40,000 m/s. The beam ion velocity, v_{bi}, is related to the beam voltage, ϕ_b, by conservation of energy, $v_{bi} = (2e\phi/m_i)^{1/2}$. The current density of the beam ions, j_{bi}, is approximated by a parabolic axisymmetric profile given in cylindrical coordinates (r, x), where x is the axial coordinate,

$$j_{bi}(r,x) = \frac{2I_b}{\pi r_b^2}\left(1 - \frac{r^2}{r_b^2}\right) \tag{15.1}$$

which is subject to the normalization at any downstream location in the beam,

$$I_b \int_0^{2\pi}\int_0^{r_b} j_{bi}\, r\, dr\, d\Theta \tag{15.2}$$

where I_b is the ion current emitted from the thruster. The beam has a constant divergence angle, α, which is usually 15–20 degrees, and thus the beam radius is $r_b = r_T + x\tan\alpha$, where r_T is the thruster radius. The beam current is assumed to be predominantly axial, with the beam velocity remaining approximately constant over the length scale of interest of several meters, and hence the beam ion density, n_{bi}, is

$$n_{bi}(r,x) = \frac{j_{bi}(r,x)}{ev_{bi}} \tag{15.3}$$

The parabolic profile is in good agreement with experimental measurements on modern ion thrusters [15.11].

15.2.2   Neutral Efflux

Due to operating constraints, not all the propellant is ionized within the thruster. Un-ionized propellant that effuses out from the discharge chamber exits in free-molecular flow. Only the flow on the macro scale is modeled, and the effects of the multihole structure of the grids are neglected. A simple point source model gives the neutral density, n_n,

$$n_n(r,x) = \frac{n_{no}}{4} \frac{r_T^2(x + r_T)}{\left[(x + r_T)^2 + r^2\right]^{3/2}} \tag{15.4}$$

The flux of neutrals are given by the Knudsen efflux, $n_{no}\bar{C}/4$, where the mean neutral speed $\bar{C} = \sqrt{8kT_w/\pi m_i}$, is based on the temperature of the thruster walls, T_w. The neutral density at the thruster exit, n_{no}, is given as a function of the beam current, and the propellant utilization efficiency by the relation

$$n_{no} = \frac{4I_b}{e\bar{C}A_n}\left(\frac{1 - \eta_p}{\eta_p}\right) \tag{15.5}$$

where the propellant utilization efficiency, η_p, is based on the total mass flow rate (discharge + neutralizer),

$$\eta_p = \frac{I_b}{m_{total}}\left(\frac{m_i}{e}\right) \tag{15.6}$$

The neutral flow-through area, A_n, is close to the geometrical open area of the grids.

15.2.3   CEX Propellant Ions

Slow propellant ions are created inside the beam from charge-exchange reactions between the fast beam ions and the slow thermal neutrals of the following type:

$$Xe^+_{fast} + Xe^0_{slow} \rightarrow Xe^0_{fast} + Xe^+_{slow}$$

The result is a fast neutral that travels in a line-of-sight manner and a slow ion that is affected by the local radial electric fields in the beam. The volumetric production rate of these CEX ions is given by

$$N_{cex}(X) = n_n(x)n_{bi}(x)vs_{bi}\sigma_{cex}(v_{bi}) \tag{15.7}$$

	LEO (B = 0.2 G)	GEO (B = 0.001 G)
Thermal CEX ion ($T = 500°$K)	12 m	2 km
Beam ion $V > 10$ km/s	680 m	136 km

15.1

Gyroradii for xenon ions.

TABLE

where the relative collision velocity is taken to be the beam ion velocity. For a beam ion velocity of 33,200 m/s—the value used in the present simulation of the 13-cm xenon thruster—the CEX cross section, σ_{cex}, is 3.9×10^{-19}m² [15.10]. Volumetric production rates using Equation (15.7) and the simple neutral model of Equation (15.4) compare well with estimates based on measurements [15.12]. However, it must be pointed out that there is a limit to the validity of this method of CEX ion creation. If the CEX ion production rate is too high, then the beam ion density cannot be taken to be a fixed quantity. If we define a CEX ion current, $I_{cex} = 4/3\pi r_T^3 e n_{no} n_{bio} v_{bi} \sigma_{cex}(v_{bi})$, then it must be that the ratio, $I_{cex}/I_b \sim r_T n_{no} \sigma_{cex} \ll 1$. In our results, typically this ratio is less than 3 percent.

An important consideration for the transport of the slow ions is the ambient and thruster-induced magnetic fields. Table 15.1 shows the gyroradii for thermal and beam ions in various magnetic field strengths corresponding to a range of orbital altitudes. The thermal speed of the CEX ions is the minimum speed and represents ions that have not been accelerated through the potential drop of the beam. For the length scales that we are interested in currently (less than 5 m), the ions can be considered unmagnetized. In addition, thruster-induced fields outside of modern ion thrusters are weak.

15.2.4   Electrons

Ion thrusters have a device called a neutralizer that emits an electron current to balance the ion current of the beam. Essentially, the neutralizer produces a quasi-neutral plasma cloud that acts as a "bridge" for the passage of electrons to the beam. In ion thruster beam plasmas, the thermal velocity of the electrons ($T_e = 1$–5 eV $\rightarrow 4 \times 10^5$–$9 \times 10^5$ m/s) is much higher than the ion beam velocity (2–4×10^4 m/s), and thus the electrons can diffuse rapidly to provide neutralization. It is beyond the scope of this chapter to include a detailed model of the physics of an electron-emitting hollow cathode, which is still not completely understood today. Our approach is to develop and use a simple model that treats the electrons as an isothermal neutralizing fluid with a drift velocity of that of the ions. Preliminary efforts have been made recently to model the electrons kinetically [15.14].

The general momentum balance for the electrons, including electric (**E**) and magnetic fields (**B**), pressure forces, and collisional drag terms, is

$$\frac{\partial V_e}{\partial t} + v_e \cdot \nabla v_e = \frac{-e}{m_e}(\mathbf{E} + v_e \times \mathbf{B}) - \frac{\nabla P_e}{m_e n_e} + \mathbf{R}_e \tag{15.8}$$

A scaling analysis [15.11, 15.12] of the momentum equation leads to significant simplification. Since we are interested in the motion of the CEX ions, the time scales involved are much larger than electron time scales. Thus, the electron unsteady and inertia terms can be neglected.

The electron drift velocity is assumed to be on the order of the ion drift velocities. Physically, the electrons cannot overexpand the ions expanding in the plume because a large charge imbalance would result. With this estimate for the electron drift velocity, and taking typical beam potentials of 10 V or more, the ratio of the electric to magnetic forces is at least 10^2 even with magnetic field strengths of 3×10^{-5} T in low earth orbit. The collisional term consists of electron-ion and electron-neutral collisions. The electron-ion term is zero because it is proportional to the difference between the ion and electron drift velocities, and the electron-neutral term is small compared to the electric field term and the pressure term. Hence, Equation (15.8) can be simplified to a balance between the pressure, $p_e = n_e k T_e$, and electric potential, ϕ, gradient:

$$e\nabla\phi = \frac{k\nabla n_e T_e}{n_e} \tag{15.9}$$

Although experiments show that the electron temperature decreases radially and axially due to cooling as the plume expands, the variation is much less than that of the plasma density because the electron thermal conductivity is very high [15.11, 15.12]. In this chapter, we consider the case where the electron temperature is constant and Equation (15.9), upon integration, becomes

$$n_e = n_{e\infty}\exp\left(\frac{e\phi}{kT_e}\right) \tag{15.10}$$

Note that with this model, the electron density is a specified background density when the potential reaches zero, or the reference space potential far from the beam. The isothermal Boltzmann relationship, often referred to as the "barometric equation," has been studied and compared with a variable temperature model [15.11]. Comparisons show that the isothermal model yields slightly higher values of the backflowing CEX ion densities. However, comparisons of both models with experimental data show good agreement within experimental error [15.11]. The simplicity of the isothermal model outweighs the complexity of implementing the full fluid model in a multicomputer environment.

15.3   THE NUMERICAL MODEL

To model the expansion of an ion thruster plume, we employ the hybrid electrostatic plasma particle-in-cell (PIC) method [15.1]. In the electrostatic PIC technique, ions and electrons in a plasma are treated as macroparticles, where each macroparticle represents many actual particles. The charge of the simulation particles is deposited onto a computational grid, and a charge density is computed. From this density, Poisson's equation for the electrostatic potential is solved, and the particles are moved under the influence of this self-consistent electric field. A major shortcoming of explicit, fully kinetic PIC codes where electrons are treated as particles is the very small time step that is required to resolve the electron motion. Because we are interested in the ion motion, we adopt the hybrid approach, where the ions are treated as particles but the electrons are treated as a fluid. In this manner, the time step is now on the ion time scale, which, for xenon ions, is about 490 times larger than the electron time scale.

The model is fully 3D. Figure 15.1 is a schematic of the general computational domain, and Figure 15.2 shows the Cartesian grid in the x-y plane for $y > 0$. The grid is nonuniform to more efficiently handle the highly nonuniform density distribution in the plume. The grid cell size should be on the order of the Debye length, which scales with plasma density, n, as $1/n^{1/2}$, so the grids are linearly stretched in the x, y, and z directions from the thruster exit to follow the increase in Debye length due to the density decrease, which is assumed to decay as $1/R^2$ from the exit. Given that the grid cell size scales with the characteristic length scale, which is the Debye length (submillimeter inside the plume), a nonuniform grid is essential to dealing with a tractable problem. As will be seen in Section 15.5.1, the computational grid used in this study is very large (close to 10 million grid cells).

The slow CEX ions are treated as particles, with the real-to-macroparticle ratio around 10–100 million. Particles are created each time step in each grid cell based on the volumetric CEX production rate given by Equation (15.7). The velocities are those of a Maxwellian distribution with a temperature corresponding

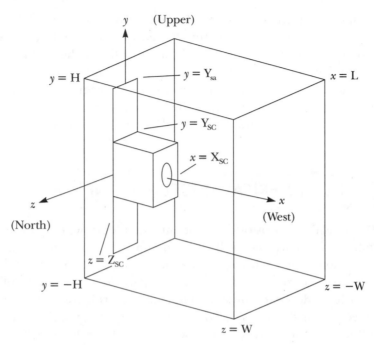

15.1 FIGURE 3D domain geometry.

to the wall of the discharge chamber (usually around 500°K). Particles that reach the simulation boundaries and spacecraft surfaces are removed, and steady-state is reached when the loss of particles at the boundaries balances the production rate in the beam. The bulk of CEX ions are produced within 2–3 beam radii downstream.

A standard linear Cartesian weighting function [15.1] is used to weight the charge of the particles to the grid. Within a cell, the charge is weighted to the eight neighboring grid points, and the volumetric charge density is computed by summing over all the particles. Once the charge density is computed, the electrostatic potential is determined by solving Poission's equation,

$$\nabla^2 \phi = \frac{e}{\varepsilon_0} \left(n_e - \sum_{species} n_i \right) \tag{15.11}$$

where n_e is given by Equation (15.10). Note that the summation over the ion species allows multiple species: the beam ions, CEX ions, and ambient ions. With

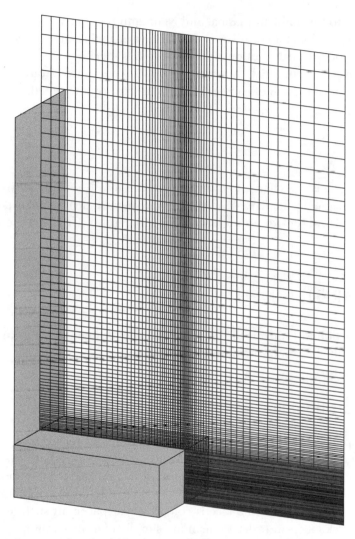

15.2

FIGURE

Computational grid in the *x-y* plane.

the Boltzmann distribution for the electron density, the Poisson equation for the electric potential becomes highly nonlinear. This equation is solved with a Newton-Raphson Successive-Over-Relaxation (SOR) scheme. For large meshes, grid relaxation techniques are the methods of choice [15.6]. Either fixed potentials are imposed on the spacecraft surfaces or the spacecraft potential can float with respect to the ambient plasma, and Neumann boundary conditions are held on all exterior domain boundaries. A solar array panel is attached to the spacecraft, and a potential distribution along its length is specified.

Given the potential, the electric field, **E,** is computed from $\mathbf{E} = -\nabla\phi$, and the equations of motion of each ion macroparticle are integrated:

$$\frac{dv_i}{dt} = \left(\frac{q}{m}\right)[\mathbf{E} + v_i \times \mathbf{B}] \cdot \frac{d\mathbf{X}_i}{dt} = v_i \qquad (15.12)$$

where q/m is the charge-to-mass ratio of the ion. The capability of including a fixed magnetic field, **B** (i.e., the geomagnetic field), is incorporated in our model. However, for these calculations, the role of the magnetic field is neglected.

15.4   PARALLEL IMPLEMENTATION

This section will address the important issue of domain decomposition, as well as the parallelization of the numerical algorithm.

15.4.1   Partitioning

The approach to parallel implementation is similar to the first general concurrent PIC algorithm developed by Liewer and Decyk [15.8]. Data decomposition is used for the partitioning of the problem. The computational domain is partitioned into blocks according to a simple rule that each block face must be of a single type; that is, a face is completely a spacecraft surface or an interior interblock face—in order to maintain simplicity in programming, it should not be a mixture. The methodology of dividing a problem into blocks actually simplifies programming structure and enables very general geometries to be handled because each block can be individually initialized with or without particles and with various boundary conditions.

Figure 15.3 shows a coarse decomposition of the domain in the x-y plane. The domain is partitioned into a minimum of two blocks in the x direction: one behind the thruster plane, and another in front. There are seven in the y direction for a full-plane simulation, and four for a half-plane simulation in order to accommodate thruster, spacecraft, solar array, and exterior boundary surfaces. Lastly, there are five in the z direction. Thus, for a half-plane simulation, there

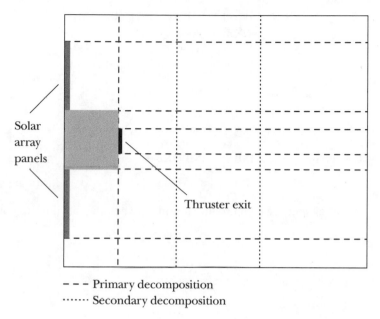

Solar
array
panels

Thruster exit

– – – Primary decomposition
······· Secondary decomposition

15.3   Example of domain decomposition in the *x-y* plane.

FIGURE

are a minimum of 40 blocks in the primary decomposition. Each block can then be decomposed into smaller blocks by a secondary decomposition, so that, depending on the total domain size, there are two to three blocks per available processor. The blocks are numbered as $N = i + jN_x + kN_xN_y$, where N_x and N_y are the number of blocks in the x and y directions, and i, j, k are the block indices, which start from $(0,0,0)$ in the lower southeast corner of the domain.

The faces of each block must be categorized for computing and communications purposes. It is important to know what types of boundary conditions to enforce for the Poisson solver and how to treat particles that cross the boundaries of each block. The face types are identified in the following manner:

✦ Hole (interior of spacecraft—no computation or communication)

✦ Interior interblock cut face

✦ Exterior boundary—Dirichlet or Neumann potential boundary condition

✦ Spacecraft surface—potential specified

✦ Thruster front—potential specified

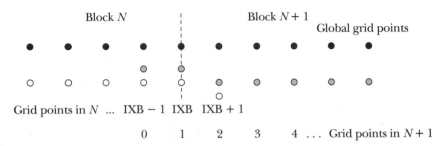

15.4

FIGURE

Detail of splitting computational grid between two neighboring blocks.

✦ Top solar array—potential specified

✦ Bottom solar array—potential specified

✦ Reflecting boundary condition on $y = 0$ plane for upper half-plane calculations (Neumann condition or potential)

The reflecting boundary condition is used for the particles; that is, a particle that hits this surface is reflected—just as on the plume centerline in an axisymmetric model. Physically, for every particle that leaves the upper half plane, there is another one that is entering from the lower half plane. On all other exterior and spacecraft boundaries, particles are absorbed. Particles are passed between processors if they share an interior interblock cut face.

The way that the global computational grid is divided at the boundary between two blocks is illustrated in Figure 15.4 (which is the same for every axis). Particles in block N whose position is greater than or equal to $x(\text{IXB})$ are passed to block $N + 1$. Similarly, particles that are less than $x(1)$ in block $N + 1$ are passed to block N.

15.4.2   Parallel PIC Algorithm

A preprocessing geometry code generates the global computational domain for a given problem and interactively decomposes the domain into N_b blocks. Generally, if M is the number of processors available, $N_b \approx (2\text{–}3)M$ to allow for overlapping of communication and computation. An input file for each block is cre-

COLOR PLATES

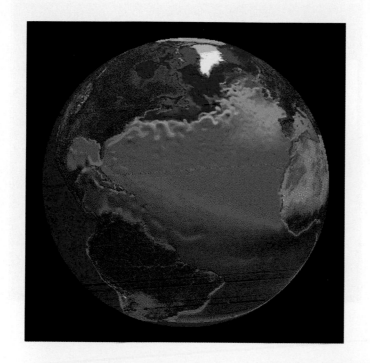

7.5
FIGURE

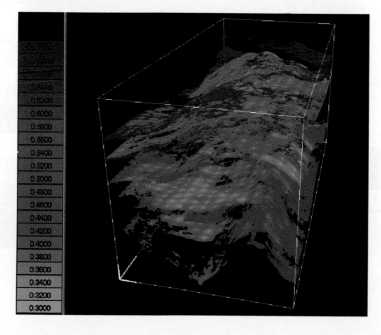

9.6
FIGURE

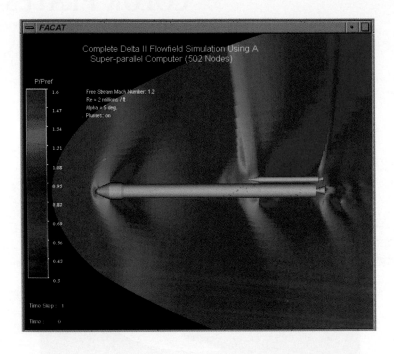

10.10 FIGURE

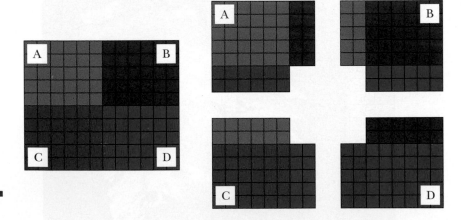

11.2 FIGURE

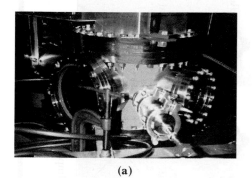

(a)

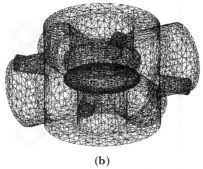

(b)

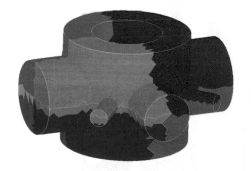

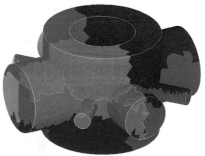

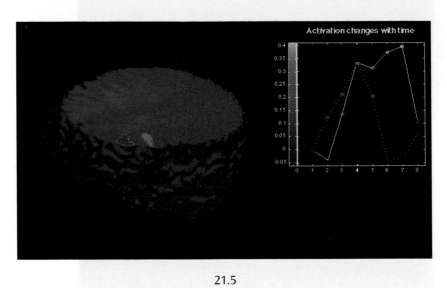

21.5
FIGURE

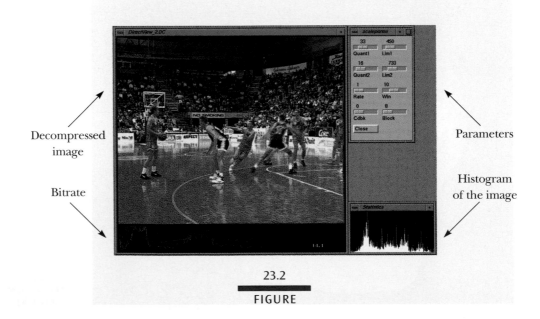

Decompressed image

Bitrate

Parameters

Histogram of the image

23.2
FIGURE

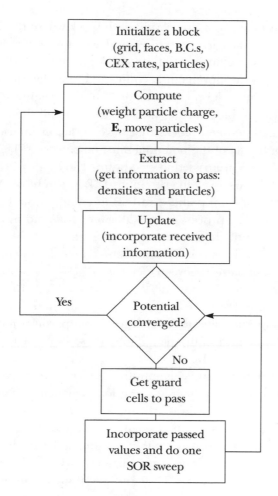

15.5   Flowchart of concurrent algorithm.

FIGURE

ated that consists of the local grid, boundary conditions, and face types. The N_b input files are mapped onto the M processors, and the same PIC code operates on each block. Each block executes the algorithm shown in Figure 15.5.

Each block in the entire domain is solved independently, and appropriate boundary conditions are used to signify what should happen at the interface between blocks. At block interfaces, there is a nonphysics boundary condition representing a "cut" in the domain. This boundary condition represents the fact that communication must occur for both particle and grid quantities. Note that the algorithm basically has two parts. Within each block where the CEX ion production rate is nonzero, particles are created and are moved. If a particle exits a block, it is communicated to an appropriate neighboring block via a face, edge, or corner. After all particle movement is conducted, the electric field is solved self-consistently in the inner loop of the algorithm. This requires only face exchanges between adjacent blocks. After an SOR sweep in all the blocks, the potentials must be passed between blocks that have common interior interblock faces. In essence, continuity of the potential must be enforced. The potential at grid points IXB in block N are passed to grid points 1 in block $N + 1$, while grid points 2 in block $N + 1$ are passed to grid points IXB + 1 in block N. Thus, each block solves the potential from points 2 to IXB, holding points 1 and IXB + 1 fixed for each iteration. The process of an SOR sweep followed by boundary cell exchange is continued until global convergence is met.

In addition to the particles being passed between blocks, the densities at the grid points on the boundaries between neighboring blocks must be superimposed to get the right values. For instance, referring to Figure 15.4, a particle in block N between $x(\text{IXB}-1)$ and $x(\text{IXB})$ is weighted to those two points. However, block $N + 1$ must know about the charge of that particle in order to have the proper density at its grid point $x(1)$. Thus, these boundary density values must be added up between blocks.

The biggest challenge to parallel computing for simulations where the computational load is dynamically changing is the load balancing of all the processors. In our simulations, the CEX ions are created within the beam and expand outwards to surround the spacecraft. Initially, all the particles are within the beam, and processors that have blocks in that region are doing all the work. Processors outside of the beam do not have any particles and are only solving the potential field in their respective blocks. Thus, initially, there is a severe load imbalance on the machine. However, as the simulation progresses, the particles travel into other processors, and the load becomes more distributed. To alleviate this problem somewhat, the blocks that are within the beam (where the particle densities are the highest) are made smaller than blocks outside so that more processors have portions of the beam. It may be noted that blocks outside are larger and hence have more grid points for the potential solver. Thus, processors outside of the beam may not have any particles but will be busy solving the field. However, the field must be solved before the particle operations, so there is no gain in this respect.

The most efficient approach is to balance the load dynamically while the simulation is in progress. There are two main approaches: one is to change dynamically the size of the blocks (and hence the number of particles within a block), and another is to move the blocks that have the most particles to processors that have the least work. Ferraro et al. [15.4] have applied the former technique to a 2D PIC simulation. By load balancing dynamically, there is always the trade-off between gains in computational efficiency and the cost associated with the repartitioning. The results of the 3D calculations in this chapter do not incorporate any form of dynamic load balancing. A static decomposition was used based on sizing the blocks so that those in the beam were about half the size of those outside. Large-scale 3D plasma simulations on massively parallel computers have been performed (without any dynamic load balancing) before on unbounded plasmas [15.15] and, recently, on spacecraft charging [15.13]. The results in this chapter are the first of their kind in 3D ion-thruster-plume contamination simulations but are quite elementary in terms of the complexity of the computer science issues. There is much room for increases in parallel efficiency, one area of future improvement beyond the work reported here.

15.5   RESULTS

This section will present the results of the 3D plume structure and compare these results to a 2D axisymmetric case.

15.5.1   3D Plume Structure

In this section, we present and discuss the 3D simulation results. The main goal of our 3D model is to investigate the CEX ion backflow structure to see whether geometrical effects of a fully 3D spacecraft are important. We will also compare the 3D results with results from an axisymmetric model [15.20]. The case considered here shows that the 2D model gives an upper bound on the CEX plasma density, and, hence, the 2D model can be used for estimates in situations that are not purely axisymmetric. This is highly desirable because the 2D model offers vast computational savings over the 3D model.

We examine the backflow from an ion thruster on a spacecraft that is similar in dimensions to the U.S. Air Force ARGOS (Advanced Research and Global Observation Satellite) spacecraft. The launch of this spacecraft, scheduled in 1998, with the Electric Propulsion Space Experiment (ESEX) payload, will be the first USAF electric propulsion flight in over 25 years and will demonstrate EP thruster operation at high power levels [15.9]. We simulate an ion thruster on this spacecraft, but, in actuality, the thruster onboard will be a 26 kW ammonia arcjet.

Following the geometry of Figure 15.1, the size of the model spacecraft in the simulation is 1.5 m long in the x direction. This is the distance from the solar array panels to the thruster exit only; the entire spacecraft was not modeled. The model spacecraft has a half height of 0.5 m in the y direction, and a width of 1 m in the z direction. A solar array panel extends 3.1 m from the top of the space-craft, 1.5 m behind the thruster exit, and is biased. The potential drop from the spacecraft to the end of the array is 28 volts, typical of most current systems, with the spacecraft grounded to the positive end. The simulation domain is a half do-main in the y direction. The ion thruster simulated is a 13-cm beam diameter xe-non thruster, and the operating conditions are a beam current of 0.404 A, a pro-pellant utilization efficiency of 0.84, and a beam ion velocity of 33,200 m/s. A constant electron temperature of 1 eV is used, and no geomagnetic field was in-cluded. To encompass the spacecraft and the solar array panel, the dimensions of the computational domain are 3.2 m $\times$ 4.5 m $\times$ 3 m in the x, y, and z direc-tions, respectively. The computational grid has 139 grid points in the x direction, 241 in the y direction, and 281 in the z direction—a total of 9,413,219 grid points.

The problem was run initially on the massively parallel Intel Touchstone Delta at Caltech and subsequently on the Cray T3D at the Jet Propulsion Labora-tory. Inaugurated in 1991, the Delta consists of 512 processors each with 16 MB of memory and a peak speed of 80 Mflops. However, the amount of user-available memory per node is closer to 12 MB, bringing the total machine capac-ity to over 6 GB. The processors are connected via a scalable 2D mesh. The Cray T3D, installed in 1994, consists of 256 nodes, each with about 55 MB of us-able memory—a total of 14 GB. The speed of each processor is about 150 Mflops peak, and they are connected via a 3D torus topology, which offers much better interprocessor communications. Message latency (time to send a message) on the Delta is about 150 μs and the bandwidth (rate of information being transmit-ted) is about 10 MB/s. In contrast, the latency is around 10 μs, and the band-width is 120 MB/s on the T3D.

Because the problem was initially targeted for the Delta, the domain was par-titioned into 1575 blocks so that there would be three or more blocks per proces-sor. The same partitioning was kept for the T3D; hence six or more blocks were allocated to each processor. We found that the simulation code performed about six times faster on the T3D due to its more powerful processors and faster com-munications network. The simulation was run until steady-state was reached, with the particle population reaching over 35 million. Due to the lack of dy-namic load balancing, at the start of the simulation only about 10 percent of the processors are utilized for particle operations. However, as the particles expand from the beam region, the number of processors utilized increases. The ratio of the time spent in interprocessor communications to computation is about 1.4 percent, and the overall speed of the code is about 30 s/time step. Due to the high demand of the machines and the availability of only 4 hour slots on week-

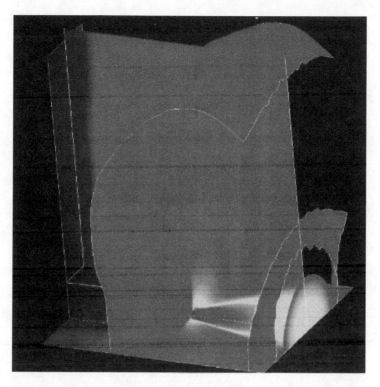

15.6

FIGURE

3D plot of potential field surrounding spacecraft. (See also color plate 15.6.)

days, the simulation took nearly 4 months to complete. The calculation required a total of approximately 128,000 node-hours.

Figure 15.6 displays a picture of the spacecraft (gray surfaces) and two planes in the x-y (vertical) and x-z (horizontal) displaying the potential in the plume. (See also color plate 15.6.) A potential iso surface is also rendered. Since the iso-thermal Boltzmann model is used for the electrons, iso-potential surfaces are also isodensity surfaces, and we can clearly see the expansion of the CEX plasma around the model spacecraft. The plume structure can be seen more clearly in Figure 15.7, which is a contour plot of the total ion density in the x-y plane cut directly through the center of the plume ($z = 0$). The plasma density de-cays from 10^{14} m^{-3} in the beam at the thruster exit to below 2×10^{10} m^{-3}. The background plasma density is fixed at 10^{10} m^{-3}, typical of the LEO environ-ment. In the region directly above the spacecraft, the CEX ions expand over the top of the spacecraft, and the density there is between 10^{10} and 2×10^{10} m^{-3}. The CEX ions propagate out of the beam and around the spacecraft due to

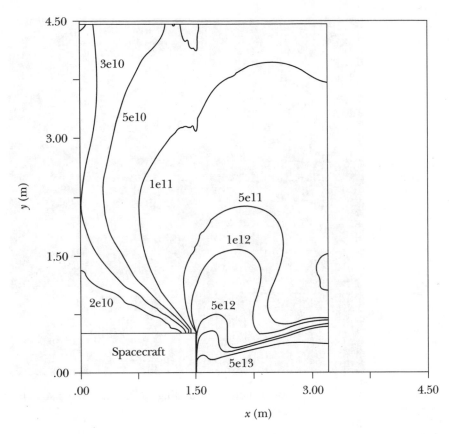

15.7

FIGURE

Total ion density in the *x-y* plane.

the electric field, which acts normal to the potential contours shown in Figure 15.8.

The geometrical effect of the rectangular spacecraft on the backflow is apparent, though, when we examine the *z-y* plane that is perpendicular to the plume axis. Figure 15.9 is a *z-y* plane that is 3 cm behind the thruster exit plane. In Figure 15.9, we can clearly see that the CEX ions flowing back around the spacecraft do not do so in a completely axisymmetrical fashion due to the rectangular geometry of the spacecraft. The CEX ions are essentially expanding around a plate that is the spacecraft face the thruster is located on, and the backflow is concentrated on the top and both sides. However, at the corners (45 degrees to the *y*-axis), the density is much less.

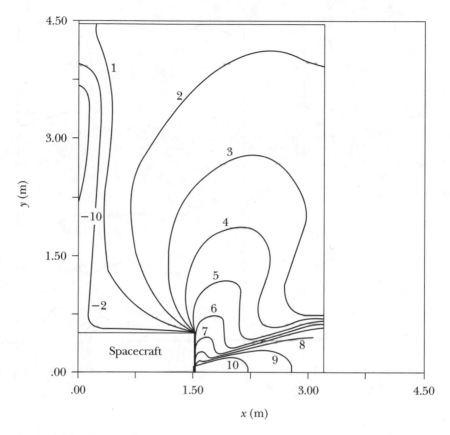

Potential in the *x-y* plane.

A clearer presentation of the asymmetry in the *z-y* plane is shown in Figure 15.10, where the total ion density along an arc 0.75 m from the center of the plume is shown for three *z-y* planes located 3, 24, and 95 cm upstream of the thruster exit plane. In the plane 3 cm upstream, the density falls by almost an order of magnitude at 45 degrees and 135 degrees—angles corresponding to the corners of the spacecraft. However, at planes further upstream, the density becomes more axisymmetric, until 95 cm upstream there is no azimuthal distinction. At distances further from the plume center, though, the structure of the CEX density still retains a distinctive asymmetric nature due to the rectangular spacecraft. Thus, this calculation demonstrates that the 3D geometry of the spacecraft influences the structure of the plume backflow.

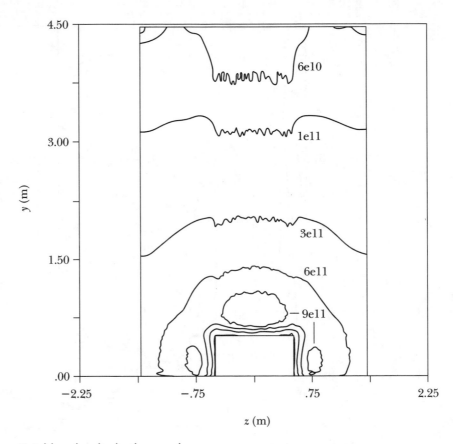

15.9   Total ion density in the z-y plane.

FIGURE

15.5.2   Comparison of 2D and 3D Results

To see how substantial the 3D effects are in comparison, an axisymmetric model [15.12] was applied to the ARGOS spacecraft in the *x-y* plane, including the solar array panel. The same number of grid points (139 × 241) and the same thruster operating conditions were used. Various numbers of particles were used, ranging from 60,000 to 300,000. The appeal of the axisymmetrical model is that low noise results could be obtained in two dimensions with less than 200,000 particles. The 2D simulation could run 24 hours a day on a workstation, and, depending on the number of particles, the overall performance was between 4 and 20 s/time step. Thus, the axisymmetric code was much more cost-effective in terms of producing results in a relatively short amount of time (less than 1 to 3

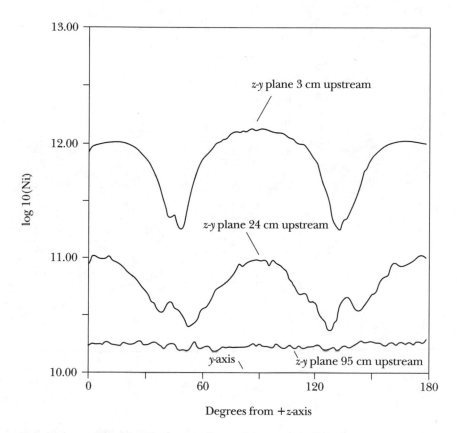

15.10

FIGURE

Comparison of density in the z-y plane along arc for distances 3, 24, and 95 cm upstream of thruster exit.

days). As a comparison between convergence of the 3D and 2D runs, the 3D runs required close to 60,000 iterations, while the axisymmetric runs were around 20,000 iterations.

Figure 15.11 compares the total ion density along a radial cut (90 degrees to plume centerline) 22 cm downstream of the thruster in the x-y plane from both the 3D and axisymmetric simulations. We can see that the comparison is very good. The plume radial expansion is axisymmetric as we expect. It is interesting to see what the decay rate in the density is due to the plume expansion. Simple backflow models [15.11] treat the CEX plasma with a constant-velocity spherical expansion and the density decays as $1/R^2$. From the density profile in Figure 15.11, we see that the density decays roughly with a rate of $1/R^{2.4}$, which is quite close. However, a difference is to be expected because the CEX ions are not ex-

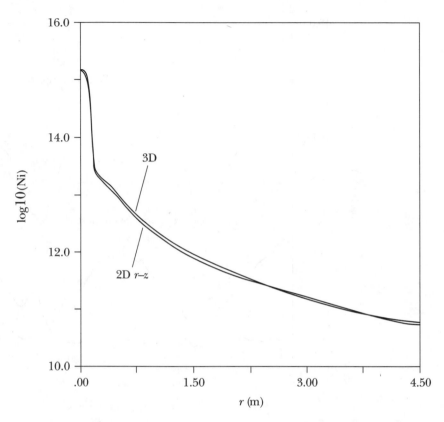

Comparison of 3D and 2D ion density along radial cut 22 cm downstream.

panding at constant velocity, but are still slowly gaining speed as they fall down
the potential hill from the plume. It must be kept in mind that with the isothermal Boltzmann electron model, the plasma density and potential follow each
other, and hence the potential is not completely flat outside of the beam.

It is important to see how the CEX plasma behaves, not only radially to the
beam but also along rays at angles greater than 90 degrees that penetrate into
the backflow region. In Figure 15.12, the total ion density along a ray 120 degrees from the plume centerline and from a point 0.75 m in front of the thruster
exit is shown. Again, we see that the agreement between the two models is very
good, with the 3D results falling slightly below the axisymmetric results at distances greater than 2 m. This may possibly be due to an insufficient number of
particles in the 3D model, but nevertheless, the axisymmetric model yields larger
densities. We note that the density decay in the backflow region along this ray is

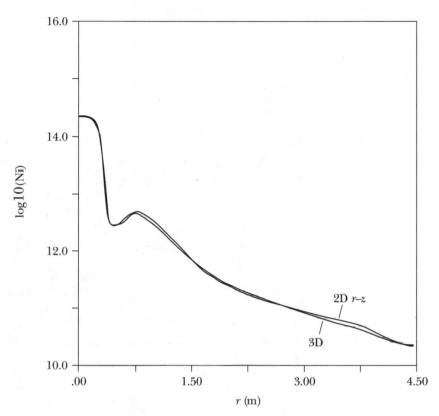

Comparison of 3D and 2D ion density along cut 120 degrees from plume axis.

also about $1/R^{2.23}$, very similar to the behavior along a ray perpendicular to the plume axis.

In addition to radial comparisons, we compare the models along an arc of constant radius. In Figure 15.13, the total ion density along an arc a distance of 1.5 m from a point 5 cm in front of the thruster is shown. In the backflow region at angles greater than 90 degrees, the axisymmetric results are again higher than the 3D results. Thus, we see that the axisymmetric model gives an upper bound on the CEX plasma density in the backflow regions.

From the comparisons of this relatively simple geometry case, we conclude (at least for asymmetric cases similar to ones explored here) that the axisymmetric model can be used to provide an upper bound on the CEX backflow in situations that are not too strongly asymmetric. However, for more complex geometries, the fully 3D model would have to be used. There are many computer

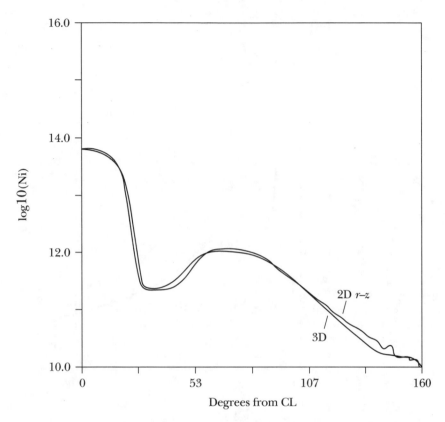

15.13

FIGURE

Comparison of 3D and 2D ion density along arc 1.5 m from point 5 cm downstream.

science issues that need to be addressed, such as dynamic load balancing, that will improve the performance of the code. Nevertheless, routine 3D calculations of this nature may have to wait for the next generation of massively parallel computers.

15.6   PARALLEL STUDY

Figure 15.14 provides a baseline performance evaluation of the simulation and is taken from an associated load balancing study [15.20]. The horizontal axis shows a timeline of the number of iterations used to generate the solution, while the

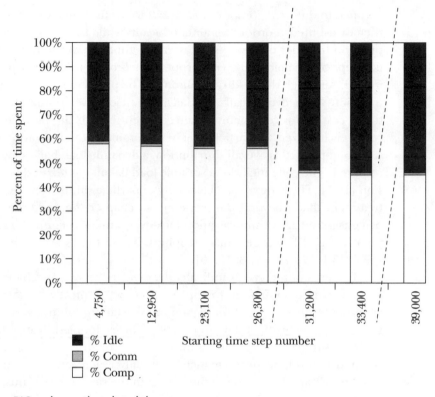

PIC code runtime breakdown.

vertical scale shows the time taken to execute 100 iterations. The time is broken down into three categories, representing computation, communication, and idle time. The communication time represents only the time to place and extract messages into and out of the network. Idle time waiting for communication has been removed by virtue of multiprocessing multiple blocks within each computer. These timing results are for the 256-node T3D using system calls. Preliminary results on the Intel Delta machine showed that the calculation was primarily communication bound. In moving to the T3D, that communication time was reduced to insignificance.

The results indicate that using a carefully hand-coded decomposition, the aggregate utilization varies during the course of the calculation between 42 and 58 percent. This hand-coded decomposition was achieved by initially mapping the grid to the processors to ensure that blocks within the thruster plume were mapped to different computers so as not to exhaust memory. These blocks were then distributed in order to maintain locality while balancing memory. The computation time per time step is in essence a function of the time to solve individual steps of the field and a cost proportional to the number of particles that are moved. Although the field calculation can be predicted a priori, the particle distribution varies dynamically. Initially, the field solver dominates the computational cost and is reasonably balanced, even though the particle distribution is relatively localized. As particles begin to dominate, the utilization drops. As a result, to improve this overall distribution, a dynamic load-balancing mechanism is required. The code includes a scalable load balancing technique based on diffusion [15.5]. The issue of load balancing in particle simulations requires extensive treatment that is beyond the scope of this chapter. Among the issues that must be considered are communication locality, granularity control, multiphase computation, and heterogeneous mappings. These topics are covered in detail in [15.7, 15.16, 15.17, 15.18, 15.19].

The area of the graph indicated by dividers represents changes to the basic constants in the simulation to improve accuracy. Typically, these represent an increase in particle production to gain more accurate solutions. Between the final two measurements the total number of particles doubled. Notice that the overall utilization remained constant, indicating that the principal blocks in the decomposition controlling performance eventually reach saturation in terms of the number of particles, as one would expect in the steady state. Thus, this study provides an accurate global picture of the overall performance of the algorithms; the utilization would not reduce further were the computations to be continued.

15.7   SUMMARY

In order to investigate geometrical effects on the backflow structure due to the 3D spacecraft, a fully 3D numerical model was developed. Due to the extremely large computational resources required for the large spatial domains encompassing a realistic spacecraft, the use of massively parallel computers was necessary and enabling. A PIC algorithm for a message-passing multicomputer environment was developed and implemented on two massively parallel computers that had sufficient memory to handle up to 3 GB memory requirements.

The propellant CEX ion backflow from a 13-cm xenon ion thruster was computed on a model spacecraft with dimensions similar to the U.S. Air Force ARGOS spacecraft. The computational domain contained over 9.4 million grid points, and the simulation employed over 35 million particles. This is the first calculation ever conducted of ion-thruster-plume backflow on such a large scale. This code employs a variety of realistic spacecraft characteristics, including floating potentials on spacecraft surfaces, potential drops across solar array panels, and self-consistent electric fields. In addition, the computational model created can be used as a test bed tool to explore many computer science issues, such as dynamic load balancing.

The plume backflow was examined for 3D effects because the spacecraft's geometry could not be captured with an axisymmetric model. The spacecraft had a box shape, so a "corner-effect," where the CEX plasma flowed over the front face of the spacecraft, was identified. This led to an asymmetry in the backflow around the spacecraft that could produce significant decreases in CEX ion density up to an order of magnitude, particularly close to the thruster exit plane.

The 3D results were compared with an axisymmetric model applied in a plane through the plume. Comparisons of CEX ion densities along radial and angular cuts throughout the backflow region away from the "corner-effect" regions did not show significant differences. That the axisymmetric model can be used to give a conservative upper bound on the backflow was shown, at least for geometries that are not highly asymmetric, as was the case.

Future work will address the use of unstructured grids for arbitrary geometries and thruster positions. Multiple thrusters will also be examined, and the effect of the CEX plasma cloud discharging charged spacecraft surfaces will be investigated.

ACKNOWLEDGMENTS

The first author was supported in part under a National Science Foundation Graduate Fellowship. Any opinions, findings, conclusions, or recommendations expressed in this publication are those of the author and do not necessarily reflect the views of the National Science Foundation. Support for the first two authors was also provided by the U.S. Air Force Office of Scientific Research under contract F49620-93-1-0317. The third author was supported by the Defense Advanced Research Projects Agency, DARPA Order 8176, monitored by the Office of Naval Research under contract N00014-91-J-1986. The authors are most grateful to Jerrell Watts, a graduate student at Caltech, for conducting the 3D production runs. The performance summary provided here was produced by Jerrell as part of his ongoing work on load-balancing methods.

References

[15.1]   Birdsall, C. K., and A. B. Langdon. 1991. *Plasma Physics via Computer Simulation.* Bristol: Adam Hilger.

[15.2]   Byers, D. C. 1979. Electron Bombardment Thruster Field and Particle Interfaces. *J. Spacecraft and Rockets,* **16,** 289.

[15.3]   Deininger, W. D. 1985. Electric Propulsion Produced Environments and Possible Interactions with the SP-100 Power System. AIAA Paper 85-2046.

[15.4]   Ferraro, R. D., P. C. Liewer, and V. K. Decyk. 1993. *J. Comput. Phys.,* **109,** 329.

[15.5]   Heirich, A., and S. Taylor. 1995. *Proceedings, International Conference on Parallel Programming.*

[15.6]   Hockney, R. W., and J. W. Eastwood. 1988. *Computer Simulation Using Particles.* Bristol: Adam Hilger.

[15.7]   Ivanov, Markelov, Taylor, and Watts. 1996. Parallel DSMC Strategies for 3D Computations. In *Proceedings of Parallel CFD '96,* 485–492.

[15.8]   Liewer, P., and V. Decyk. 1989. A General Concurrent Algorithm for Plasma Particle-in-Cell Simulation Codes. *J. Comput. Phys.,* **85,** 302.

[15.9]   Pollard, J. E., D. E. Jackson, D. C. Marvin, A. B. Jenkin, and S. W. Janson. 1993. Electric Propulsion Flight Experience and Technology Readiness. AIAA Paper 93-2221.

[15.10] Rapp, D., and W. E. Francis. 1962. Charge Exchange between Gaseous Ions and Atoms. *J. of Chemical Physics,* **37,** 2631.

[15.11] Samanta Roy, R. I. 1995. Numerical Simulation of Ion Thruster Plume Backflow for Spacecraft Contamination Assessment. Ph.D. Dissertation, MIT, Department of Aeronautics and Astronautics.

[15.12] Samanta Roy, R. I., D. E. Hastings, and N. A. Gatsonis. 1996. Modelling of Ion Thruster Plumes for Backflow Contamination. *J. Spacecraft and Rockets,* **33** (4), 525–534.

[15.13] Wang, J. 1996. AIAA Paper 96-0147.

[15.14] Wang, J., J. Brophy, P. Liewer, and G. Murphy. 1995. Modeling Ion Thruster Plumes. AIAA
         Paper 95-0596.

[15.15] Wang, J., P. Liewer, and V. Decyk. 1995. *Comput. Phys. Commun.*, **87,** 35.

[15.16] Watts, J., M. Rieffel, and S. Taylor. 1996. Practical Dynamic Load Balancing for Irregular
         Problems. In *Parallel Algorithms for Irregularly Structured Problems: IRREGULAR '96 Proceedings,*
         299–306. Vol. 1117 of LNCS. New York: Springer-Verlag.

[15.17] Watts, J., M. Rieffel, and S. Taylor. 1997. A Load Balancing Technique for Multi-phase Com-
         putations. In *Proceedings of the 1997 Simulation MultiConference; High Performance Computing '97:
         Grand Challenges in Computer Simulation,* 15–20. Society for Computer Simulation.

[15.18] Watts, J., M. Rieffel, and S. Taylor. 1998. Dynamic Management of Heterogeneous Resources.
         To appear in *High Performance Computing '98.*

[15.19] Watts, J., and S. Taylor. Communications Locality Preservation in Dynamic Load Balancing.
         To appear in *High Performance Computing '98.*

[15.20] Watts, J., and S. Taylor. A Practical Approach to Dynamic Load Balancing. *IEEE Transactions
         on Parallel and Distributed Systems.* In preparation.

16 | Advanced Atomic-Level Materials Design

Lin H. Yang   Lawrence Livermore National Laboratory

16.1   INTRODUCTION

Can novel materials with optimized properties be designed and calibrated by computer? Advances in modeling methods at the atomic level coupled with rapid increases in computer power over the last two decades have led scientists to answer this question with a resounding "yes." The ability to design new materials from quantum-mechanical principles with computers is currently one of the fastest-growing and most exciting areas of computational research. Our efforts are addressing problems in many disciplines, including physics, chemistry, materials science, and biotechnology.

The ultimate objective of a scientist involved in modeling and simulating materials at the microscopic level is to answer the following types of questions: What is matter really like at the atomic level? How can we modify the bonding between atoms to create novel materials with optimized properties? In addressing such questions, the scientist is armed with the set of laws that govern matter at the microscopic level—namely, quantum theory. Matter is made of atoms, and atoms are made of nuclei surrounded by electrons (see Figure 16.1 and color plate 16.1). The basic laws governing the behavior of nuclei and electrons were formulated in the 1920s and are collectively known as quantum theory. Quantum theory forms the basis of our microscopic understanding of the physical universe. Equipped with the laws of quantum theory and a powerful computer, why not attack the formidable task of designing novel materials by doing calculations on every atom in the material until we arrive at the properties we need? Unfortunately, such a straightforward approach is impossible. It is true that the quantum-mechanical equations governing the behavior of electrons can be written in a relatively compact form. However, practical calculations become exceedingly difficult because of the large number of degrees of freedom and interac-

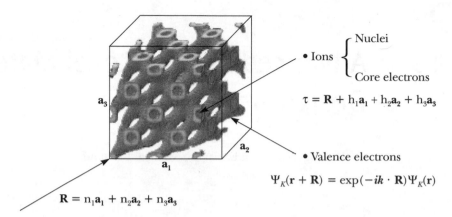

$\bullet$ Ions $\begin{cases} \text{Nuclei} \\ \\ \text{Core electrons} \end{cases}$

$$\tau = \mathbf{R} + h_1\mathbf{a}_1 + h_2\mathbf{a}_2 + h_3\mathbf{a}_3$$

$\bullet$ Valence electrons

$$\Psi_K(\mathbf{r} + \mathbf{R}) = \exp(-i\mathbf{k} \cdot \mathbf{R})\Psi_K(\mathbf{r})$$

$$\mathbf{R} = n_1\mathbf{a}_1 + n_2\mathbf{a}_2 + n_3\mathbf{a}_3$$

16.1

FIGURE

A schematic of a computational box contains ions and valence electrons. The open circles are the positions of ions that are surrounded by electronic clouds. The interactions between electrons are described by DFT. (See also color plate 16.1.)

tions between particles. An exact calculation of a system with such mind-boggling complexity is far beyond the capacity of the most powerful computers. Instead of attempting an exact—and ultimately impossible—calculation, scientists approximate physical laws to yield a feasible, yet somewhat inexact, calculation.

The key to the spectacular success of modern quantum simulations of materials is the adoption of density functional theory (DFT) in the early 1960s. The basic postulate of this important theory is that the ground-state energy (i.e., the lowest energy functional) of a system of electrons moving in a given external potential can be obtained from a knowledge of the electron charge density. This concept offers tremendous computational advantages because the electron density becomes the basic variable rather than the complicated many-body wavefunction of all the electrons. Moreover, this powerful theory reduces the problem of describing the tangled, mutually dependent motion of electrons to the one of describing the motion of a single, independent electron in an effective potential. In other words, we can describe the complex effects of all the other electrons on a single electron by an effective potential in which that electron moves. Mathematically, this approach reduces a set of complex, coupling nonlinear equations to a set of decoupling nonlinear equations without seriously upsetting the result. The framework of the DFT gives us an extremely powerful and accurate technique to calculate the properties of materials on a first-principles, or ab initio, basis—that is, from the identities of the atoms making up a material and the laws of quantum theory.

DFT, coupled with rapidly increasing computing power, led to an explosion of activity in the calculation of the properties of materials using the laws of quantum theory. By the early 1980s, it had become clear to the scientific community that the properties of simple crystals could be calculated with amazing accuracy using nothing but these laws. Soon, researchers began reproducing many material properties that previously could only be determined through experiments. Examples include the spectrum of atomic vibrations in solids; changes in crystal structure induced by applying external pressure; and the optical, electronic, and magnetic properties of materials. Researchers around the world reported similar successes for a wide variety of materials. What we learned is that computer calculations based on the microscopic laws of quantum theory really could tell how actual materials behaved.

The term *ab initio molecular dynamics,* or *quantum molecular dynamics* (QMD), is used to refer to a class of methods for studying the dynamical motion of atoms. Whereas a huge amount of computational work is spent in solving, at some level of approximation such as DFT, the entire quantum-mechanical electronic structure problem governed by the Schrödinger-like equations. When the electronic wavefunctions are reliably known, it will be possible to derive the forces on the atomic nuclei using the Hellmann-Feynman theorem. (The Hellmann-Feynman theorem of quantum mechanical forces was originally proven by P. Ehrenfest. 1927. *Z. Phys.* **45,** 455 and later discussed by Hellmann (1937) and independently rediscovered by Feynman (1939).) In the QMD simulation applied here, there are two main approximations in describing the interactions between constituent atoms of a physical system: the electrons and ions (Figure 16.1 and color plate 16.1). The first is the DFT of Hohenberg and Kohn in the local-density approximation (LDA) [16.4], which refers to the formalism for the exchange-correlation energy of the interacting electrons in the system. DFT transforms a complex many-body problem to a series of effective one-body equations. The self-consistent Schrödinger-like equations (or more precisely, the Kohn-Sham equation [16.4]) for single-electron states are solved for the solid-state or molecular system in a finite basis set of analytical functions. One widely used basis set is "plane waves," or, simply, the Fourier components of the numerical wavefunction with a truncation specified by some kinetic energy cutoff. Unlike other basis functions used for these types of equation, the plane-wave basis has the advantage of being automatic and free of bias, meaning that we can always increase the cutoff of plane-wave expansion to improve the accuracy and the convergence. However, such basis sets can only be used reliably for atomic potentials that are not too steep, and, hence, plane waves are almost always used in conjunction with pseudopotentials [16.9] that effectively represent the atomic cores as relatively smooth static effective potentials in which the valence electrons are treated. This approximation is basically a way of avoiding the need to include all the electrons in calculations. It therefore greatly reduces the number of equations for the system. The effective interaction between the valence electrons and the ion cores is described by a pseudopotential for each kind of atom. It is the introduction of the pseudopotential method that makes the QMD calculations feasible in large and complex materials systems, largely due to the reduction of degrees of freedom needed for solving the problems.

In the early days of the pseudopotential method, only a limited range of chemical elements could be handled easily, and the calculation proceeded by diagonalizing the Hamiltonian matrix, which is derived from the Schrödinger-like equations. In 1985, Car and Parrinello [16.2] introduced a unified method that put the treatment of electrons and ions on the same footing. The Car-Parrinello method is based upon the LDA and uses pseudopotentials and plane-wave basis sets but adds the concept of updating the electronic wavefunctions simultaneously with the motion of atomic nuclei (electron and nucleus dynamics are coupled). This is implemented in a standard molecular dynamics paradigm, associating dynamical degrees of freedom with each electronic Fourier component (with a small but finite mass). The efficiency of this iterative scheme has enabled not only the previously mentioned pseudopotential-based molecular dynamics studies but also analogous static calculation methods for far larger systems that had previously been inaccessible. Part of this improvement is due to the fact that some terms of the Kohn-Sham Hamiltonian can be efficiently represented in real space and other terms in Fourier space and that Fast Fourier Transforms (FFT) can be used to quickly transform from one representation to the other. The advance represented by these methods in conjunction with the increase in computer power have made it possible for ab initio plane-wave pseudopotential calculations to be routinely applied to transition metals and first-row elements, which used to be regarded as difficult to deal with. Figure 16.2 is a periodic table listing those chemical elements for which there is recent experience with our code (undoubtedly, other elements are equally accessible to our methods). Each element is coded with grayscale according to the kinetic energy cutoff that is a measure for the number of Fourier components necessary in the pseudopotential representation. In general, larger cutoff means a larger set of plane-wave expansions (number of Gs) is required for that element.

The total energy and forces supplied by first-principles calculations can be used to do many things. One of the simplest and most important is the determination of cohesive properties and equilibrium structures, such as the formation energies of imperfections and inhomogeneities of crystalline materials. Examples are point defects, grain boundaries, surfaces, and molecules at surfaces. Closely related to the treatment of equilibrium structures is the calculation of

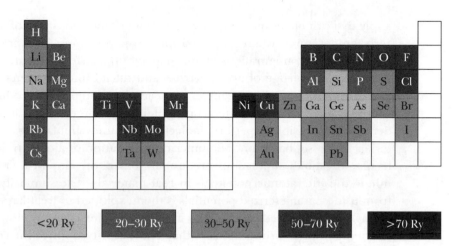

H																	
Li	Be											B	C	N	O	F	
Na	Mg											Al	Si	P	S	Cl	
K	Ca		Ti	V		Mr			Ni	Cu	Zn	Ga	Ge	As	Se	Br	
Rb				Nb	Mo					Ag		In	Sn	Sb		I	
Cs			Ta	W						Au			Pb				

<20 Ry	20–30 Ry	30–50 Ry	50–70 Ry	>70 Ry

16.2 FIGURE   A periodic table showing the chemical elements that have been applied with great success using the current PCGPP code.

vibrational properties, which is also widely practiced. However, what we get out of these calculations are those quantities at zero temperature. An extension of these first-principles methods is also being used for dynamical simulations, where the forces on the atoms are used to generate the time evolution of the atomic positions. Whereas classical molecular dynamics simulations have long been performed with semiempirical interatomic potentials, the forces can now be calculated from first principles. This means that dynamical processes involving the making and breaking of chemical bonds can be studied. Dynamical simulations allow the study of solids and liquids in thermal equilibrium through the calculation of quantities such as thermodynamic functions, radial distribution functions, diffusion coefficients, and dynamical structure factors. Even the first-principles calculation of phase diagrams and equations of states of complex materials is becoming possible. Another use of dynamical simulation is for the study of nonequilibrium processes like the dissociate chemisorption of molecules at surfaces. Conventional supercomputers can be used for first-principles calculations on systems containing a few hundreds of atoms, if the atoms are simple (silicon, for example), or a few tens of atoms if they are difficult (transition-metal oxides, for example). For large, complex or difficult systems, or for long dynamical simulations, an MPP platform is absolutely essential.

But in spite of the progress, difficulties remain with this dynamical approach. Even with the tremendous advances that emerged from density functional theory, large-scale dynamic simulations of materials and processes on a truly first-principles basis remain a formidable task. Moreover, it is not feasible to apply first-principles methods to systems containing thousands of atoms at non-zero temperatures, where the electronic properties must be averaged over the many possible configurations of ions making up a system. Fortunately, our first-principles knowledge of how electrons and nuclei interact in materials can be used as the basis to derive simple, yet accurate, models to reproduce the interactions. Once the model interaction potentials between atoms in materials are derived, it is possible to perform molecular dynamics simulations of complex materials processes based on the numerical calculation of atomic trajectories. Molecular dynamics simulations are usually based on empirical potentials that mimic the interatomic potentials in real materials. The simplicity that follows from using parameterized potentials is then exploited to treat large numbers of atoms (up to hundreds of millions) in more complex configurations. By controlling temperature (proportional to the mean velocity at which the constituent atoms move) during a molecular dynamics simulation, technologically interesting processes can be studied. These processes include melting, crystal growth and epitaxy, ion implantation, laser annealing, and defect motion, to mention just a few. Thus, molecular dynamics simulations bridge the gap between quantum theory and statistical physics. Accompanying the rapid pace of theoretical developments such as the Car-Parrinello method [16.2] is another trend that is the reason for the vitality of the field of materials physics today.

16.2   INDUSTRIAL CONSIDERATIONS

In recent years, we have seen extraordinary advances in the ways materials can be synthesized. Advanced synthesis tools now allow scientists to fabricate materials atom by atom so that they can grow thin films, build multilayers, and construct many other products such as fullerene (in which the building block is C_{60}). Indeed, it is the intimate synergy between our ability to predict accurately from quantum theory how atoms can be assembled to form new materials and our capacity to actually synthesize novel materials atom by atom that gives the field its extraordinary intellectual vitality.

Until now, materials design and processing have been, for the most part, empirical science. What this really means is that the process of coming up with an optimal material has been quite slow. For example, about one cancer drug in 40,000 has clinical significance, and perhaps one in a million would be curative. Using the old empirical methods, we could screen about 10,000 drugs a year. At that rate, it could take 100 years to obtain our first cancer-curing drug. Designing materials by computer will accelerate this process by improving our understanding of the mechanisms by which carcinogenic molecules cause cancer. Computers will also enable the design of drug molecules that either inhibit these mechanisms or remove the carcinogenic molecules from our bodies. Consequently, in designing new materials through computer simulations, our primary objective is to rapidly screen possible designs to find those few that will speed up the synthesis-processing-fabrication-manufacturing cycle. Our ultimate goal is to make this cycle more efficient by guiding appropriate experimental materials research and contributing to the goal of "materials by design" at the atomic level. Examples include screening of cancer drugs, advances in catalysis for energy production, design of new alloys and multilayers, and materials processing of semiconductors.

Industry will accelerate the achievement of these objectives by applying advanced atomic-level materials-simulation methods to specific physics or chemistry problems of importance to their research activities, such as the investigations of the atomic and electronic structure of amorphous silicon and defect energetics in semiconductor materials. However, the software that industry needs is difficult to write or upgrade from serial to parallel-style codes. New software developed in national laboratories like Lawrence Livermore National Laboratory will help the private sector make the transition to massively parallel systems, aid industry in designing better materials, and help companies insert new products into the market faster.

Material properties—whether optical, structural, or electrical—are ultimately determined by atomic structure and electronic levels. The new capability will allow the industrial sectors to routinely calculate electronic and atomic structures in much larger and complex systems with greater accuracy than was possible before. For example, research on defects and impurities in semiconductors will help scientists synthesize materials such as gallium arsenide and amorphous silicon. Gallium arsenide is a light-emitting semiconductor used in the diode laser found in laser printers. Amorphous silicon is used in imaging and scanning devices and in thin-film transistors that are part of flat-panel displays. Research on these and related materials could lead to a new generation of transistors in flat-panel displays for laptop or palmtop computers.

16.3   COMPUTATIONAL CONSIDERATIONS AND PARALLEL IMPLEMENTATIONS

In solid-state physics, the general principles of band theory start with solving the wavelike equation

$$H\psi_M(\mathbf{r}) = [-1/2\nabla^2 + V(\mathbf{r})]\psi_M(\mathbf{r}) = \varepsilon_M\psi_M(\mathbf{r}) \tag{16.1}$$

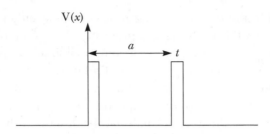

The 1D Kronig-Penney potential.

where $V(\mathbf{r})$ is a periodic function with periodicity defined by the size of the simulation box (Figure 16.1). As an idealized example, we consider a one-dimensional potential $V(x)$ of the Kronig-Penney model (Figure 16.3), which comprises square wells that are separated by barriers of height V_0 and thickness t. It has periodicity of a so that

$$V(x + na) = V(x) \tag{16.2}$$

where n is an integer. Because all the wells are equivalent, the probability of finding the electron in a given well must be the same for all wells, so that

$$\left|\psi(x + na)\right|^2 = \left|\psi(x)\right|^2 \tag{16.3}$$

For $n = 1$ this implies that

$$\psi(x + a) = e^{ika}\psi(x) \tag{16.4}$$

where k is a number (in units of $1/a$) that specifies the phase factor e^{ika} linking the wavefunction in *neighboring* wells. Repeating Equation (16.4) n times gives

$$\psi(x + na) = e^{inka}\psi(x) \tag{16.5}$$

which is the usual statement of Bloch's theorem in one dimension. Thus, the translation symmetry of the lattice leads to the eigenfunctions being characterized by the Bloch vector k. One recognizes that by replacing k in Equation (16.5) with $k + m\,(2\pi/a)$ will leave it unchanged. Therefore, it is customary to restrict the values of k in between $-\pi/a$ and π/a. In summary, the Bloch theorem enables us to solve the infinite 1D problem directly by looking for the solution in a given well (e.g., $n = 0$) and then repeating it periodically through the lattice using Equation (16.5).

In the 3D generalization, the general Bloch's theorem becomes

$$\psi_k (\mathbf{r} + \mathbf{R}) = \exp(-i \, k \cdot \mathbf{R}) \psi_k (\mathbf{r}) \tag{16.6}$$

where $\mathbf{R}$ is any direct lattice vector that may be expressed in terms of the fundamental translation vectors a_1, a_2, and a_3 as

$$\mathbf{R} = n_1 a_1 + n_2 a_2 + n_3 a_3 \tag{16.7}$$

where n_1, n_2, and n_3 are integers. The corresponding reciprocal lattice vectors are defined by

$$\mathbf{G} = m_1 b_1 + m_2 b_2 + m_3 b_3 \tag{16.8}$$

where m_1, m_2, and m_3 are integers and the fundamental basis vectors are

$$
\begin{aligned}
b_1 &= (2\pi/\Omega) \, a_2 \times a_3 \\
b_2 &= (2\pi/\Omega) \, a_3 \times a_1 \\
b_3 &= (2\pi/\Omega) \, a_1 \times a_2
\end{aligned}
\tag{16.9}
$$

with $\Omega = \left| a_1 \cdot (a_2 \times a_3) \right|$ being the volume of the simulation box defined by three vectors a_1, a_2, and a_3. The phase factor in Equation (16.6) only defines the Bloch vector k within a reciprocal lattice vector $\mathbf{G}$, since it follows from Equations (16.8) and (16.9) that $\mathbf{G} \cdot \mathbf{R}$ is an integer multiple of 2π. Just as in the one-dimensional case, it is customary to restrict the values of k to lie within a minimum volume (first Brillouin zone) defined by the three vectors b_1, b_2, and b_3. By applying the Bloch theorem, we can solve Equation (16.1) in a periodic system by simply confining the solutions within a single box (Figure 16.1), which consists of ions and electrons. The locations of ions in the box are specified by $\tau = h_1 \mathbf{a_1} + h_2 \mathbf{a_2} + h_3 \mathbf{a_3}$, with h_1, h_2, and h_3 being integer fractions. Because each box contains many electrons, the solutions of Equation (16.1) will need many eigenvectors, and eigenvalues, with each eigenvector representing the behavior of two electrons because of the Pauli exclusion principle.

A useful formulation for combining ab initio total-energy electronic structure methods with model-potential-based molecular dynamics simulations into a single framework called quantum molecular dynamics (QMD) was first proposed by Car and Parrinello [16.2]. These authors consider the general problem of minimizing an energy functional $E_{total}[\{\psi_M(\mathbf{r})\}, \{\tau_I\}, \{\alpha_v\}]$, where $\{\psi_M(\mathbf{r})\}$ represent the electronic degrees of freedom (the wave functions), $\{\tau_I\}$ represent the ionic coordinates, and $\{\alpha_v\}$ represent all the possible constraints imposed on the system (volume, strain, etc.). The minimization of the energy functional $E_{total}[\{\psi_M(\mathbf{r})\}, \{\tau_I\}, \{\alpha_v\}]$ can be performed using simulated annealing techniques if the concept of force is used to evolve not only the ionic degrees of freedom $\{\tau_I\}$, as is traditionally done in molecular dynamics, but also the electronic degrees of freedom $\{\psi_M(\mathbf{r})\}$ and the external constraints $\{\alpha_v\}$.

Since the original paper by Car and Parrinello [16.2], a number of modifications [16.6, 16.8] have been presented that improve significantly on the efficiency of the iterative solution of the Kohn-Sham (Schrödinger-like) equations. The modifications include the introduction of the conjugate gradient method [16.3, 16.6, 16.8] and a direct minimization of the total energy [16.8]. The present work is based upon the solution of the Kohn-Sham equations using the preconditioned conjugate gradient method. Our QMD code employs the serial algorithm proposed by Teter, Payne, and Allan [16.6] and has been implemented to improve the ability of treating transition metal systems. The C-language code, referred to as Preconditioned Conjugated Gradient Pseudo-potential Program (PCGPP), enables the optimizations of electronic and structural properties of complex materials at zero temperature as well as dynamical simulations at finite temperatures.

In general, there are three types of structural parameters that need to be calculated and optimized for a given material model: the electron wavefunctions $\{\psi_M(\mathbf{r})\}$, ion positions $\{\tau_I\}$, and external cell parameters $\{h_{ik}\}$. Our optimization technique is to find the best strategy to minimize the total energy by reducing the residual vectors to within some prechosen tolerances. Table 16.1 summarizes the residual vectors corresponding to these three types of parameters.

However, dealing with the electronic degrees of freedom (Schrödinger-like equation) accounts for greater than 94 percent of the total computational burden for the problems we are dealing with to date. Therefore, the implementation of the solutions to the electronic degrees of freedom will be the main focus of this section. Basically, the solutions of the Schrödinger equation involve an eigenvalue of the form given in Equation (16.1) with orthonormalization constraints between all $\psi_M(\mathbf{r})$. The solution of the electron wavefunctions involves three steps:

1. After selection of an initial state, $\psi_M(\mathbf{r}, t = 0)$, a residual vector

$$\mathfrak{R} = (H - \langle\psi_M|H|\psi_M\rangle)\psi_M(\mathbf{r}) \tag{16.10}$$

Parameters	Residual vectors
Electron wavefunctions (ψ)	$(H - <\psi_M \mid H \mid \psi_M>) \psi_M$
Ion positions (τ)	$-\partial E / \partial \tau$
Cell parameters ($h_{ik} = \Sigma_j (\delta_{ij} + \epsilon_{ij}) h^0_{jk}$)	$\partial E / 1 / \Omega \partial \epsilon_{ij}$

16.1

TABLE

The optimization parameters for structural relaxation. H is the Hamiltonian of the system, and E is the total energy function. For a given material problem, our goal is to reduce the residual vectors to values below some chosen tolerance.

is constructed, where $<\psi_M \mid H \mid \psi_M>$ is the expectation value of the Hamiltonian. During this operation, the kinetic energy term is trivially evaluated in Fourier space and the potential energy term is evaluated using the convolution theorem for Fourier transforms.

2. Once the residual vector is constructed and preconditioned, the electronic wavefunction $\psi_M(\mathbf{r}, t)$ is updated and the new wavefunctions, $\psi_M(\mathbf{r}, t + \delta t)$, at the later time $(t + \delta t)$, are made orthogonal to other wavefunctions. These operations involve basic linear algebra subroutines (BLAS) such as CAXPY operations.

3. The final step consists in Fourier transforming the wavefunctions to real space to construct the electronic charge density, $\rho(\mathbf{r}, t + \delta t) = \sum_M \left| \psi_M(\mathbf{r}, t + \delta t) \right|^2$, which enables calculation of the electron-electron and electron-ion interaction potentials, $V(\mathbf{r})$.

Before we go into detailed implementation of parallel strategies for the PCGPP code (or QMD codes in general), we need to take a close look at the data structure of eigenstates, $\psi_M(\mathbf{r})$. According to the solid-state band theory, the index M actually contains two subindexes, $\{\mathbf{k}, n\}$, where n is the index for the electron orbital and $\mathbf{k}$ is the Bloch index due to the periodicity of the physical system. Using the Fourier representation of the wave function, that is,

$$\psi_M(\mathbf{r}) = \exp(-i\, \mathbf{k} \cdot \mathbf{r}) \sum_G \mathbf{C}_G \exp(-i\, \mathbf{G} \cdot \mathbf{r}) \qquad (16.11)$$

where the $\mathbf{G}$s are reciprocal lattice vectors of the simulation box and $\mathbf{C}_G$ is the Fourier components, additional index $\mathbf{G}$ is thus introduced. A typical problem will have a few tens of $\{\mathbf{k}\}$ values, on the order of thousands of $\{n\}$ orbitals, and more than 10^5 of {$\mathbf{G}$} components. A standard serial algorithm for the solutions of $\psi_{\{n,\,k\}}$ ($\mathbf{r}$) can be summarized as follows:

```
DO k-point = 1, Number_of_k-points
DO band = 1, Number_of_bands
   DO G = 1, Number_of_G's
   Update ψ(n,k) (r) according to residual vector ℜ
     END DO
   Calculate new charge density and potentials
END DO
END DO
```

From the data structure of the wavefunction representation a number of data distribution strategies for the parallel algorithm can be considered. Our attention is on making the code more *flexible* and *portable* for different MPP platforms; therefore, the decomposition of the data structure has to be suitable for these purposes.

1. *Spatial domain decomposition.* Several groups have implemented the *ab initio* plane-wave pseudopotential MD code (in particular the Car-Parrinello algorithm) on parallel platforms. Most of them have used a spatial decomposition of the problem where each node was made responsible for calculations on a subset of the plane-wave coefficients, *G*s, used to describe each electron orbital, basically implementing a parallel 3D complex FFT. This allows efficient implementation of calculations involving several different electronic wavefunctions; most importantly, the orthonormalization of the orbital can be carried out with the same layout of the data structure. If we want the code to be flexible in running different problem sizes, this is a better way to go. However, coding this algorithm is more involving, and portability to other platforms is an issue—it concerns primarily a portable 3D complex FFT and BLAS library.

2. *Band domain decomposition.* The computations performed with respect to different electronic bands (at the same *k*-point) are largely independent and can therefore be performed simultaneously on different nodes. An attempt could be made to explore this by using a machine containing nodes equal to the number of bands in the problem. This would pose the problem of flexibility because allocating exactly the number of nodes for the problem size may not always be possible.

3. *k-point domain decomposition.* Computations performed at each of the *k*-points are relatively independent. This would be explored if a small number of

Memory (MB)	Data (GB)	3D FFT (%)	I/O (%)	BLAS (%)
104	0.5	43	9	40
1030	3.5	23	15	56

16.2

TABLE

The percentage of usage of the three routines for two different-size problems.

nodes is given with rather large memory (128 MB or more). Because traditional electronic-structure algorithms have always contained a serial loop over k-points, each iteration being in principle independent of other iterations, this is a much simpler task than the other two approaches referred to earlier. But this approach is not any better than the other approaches because it has serious stability problems, especially in that the calculations involve self-consistent loops.

A parallel implementation of the PCGPP algorithm involves three principal components: namely, a complex 3D FFT, I/O, and basic linear algebra subroutines (BLAS) such as CAXPY—all of which need to be optimized and implemented. The computational requirements of each of these three components are different. Table 16.2 shows two different problem sizes and the relative usage of these three portions of the code. As we can see, as the problem size increases, the percentage of usage of I/O and BLAS also increases. Therefore, we focus on these three items in describing our parallel stratagem.

The parallel algorithm we have described was first implemented using Cray Research Inc.'s SHMEM library, with the MPI library in the latest version. Our programming strategies contain three major elements:

1. *Automatic domain decomposition.* Based on load balance and data locality, the code automatically assigns the distributions of three indexes for a given number of nodes. In Figure 16.4, we illustrate how these assignments have been designed in the PCGPP code.

2. *Parallel I/O that can speed up the I/O linearly with the number of processors.* An example of a portion of the code is indicated in the following:

    file_Rho = fopen("rho.d", "wb+ ");
    ierror = fsetpos(file_Rho, &RhoPosMyPE);
    ierror = fwrite (&(Rho[IstartMyPE]), sizeof(double), NrhoMyPE];
    ierror = fclose(file_Rho);

   In such an arrangement, only one single file, "rho.d", is necessary for storing all the data.

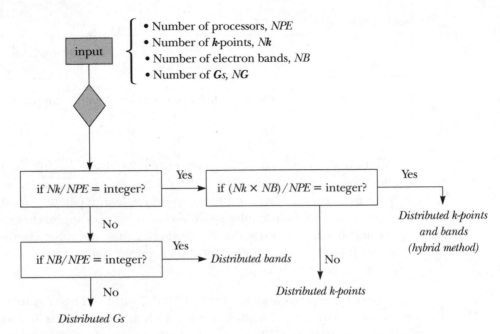

Flowchart showing the automatic domain decomposition according to the data input and number of processors to be used.

3. *Distributed 3D complex fast Fourier transform (3D CFFT) routines.* In the PCGPP code, applications of CFFTs can be summarized as follows:

1. Perform 3D CFFT on array X from **G**-space to **R**-space
2. Do calculations on array X in R-space using BLAS library
3. Perform 3D CFFT on array X from **R**-space to **G**-space

Therefore, application of the 3D FFT transforms the array X from **G**-space to **R**-space and then transforms it back to the **G**-space after some calculations have been performed in **R**-space. There is no need to keep the order of the array index in **R**-space the same as in **G**-space. As a matter of fact, in this case we can express a 3D FFT as three sets of 1D transforms corresponding to the *x*, *y*, and *z* directions. Each of the 1D transform in a set is independent of every other transform in that set and can therefore be performed in parallel. The parallel CFFT routine requires less memory than those found in the parallel library and allows the user to control the node assignments. Table 16.3 illustrates the data flow of reduced FFT operations for a transformation from **R**-space to **G**-space. We also show how step 2 is implemented in Figure

Step	x	y	z	Operations
1	NPE1	NPE2	1	1D FFT along z
2	NPE1	1	NPE2	Transpose y-z, 1D FFT along y
3	1	NPE1	NPE2	Transpose x-y, 1D FFT along x
Output	1	NPE1	NPE2	**G**-space order: y, z, x

16.3

TABLE

Three essential steps for transforming a 3D complex array from **R**-space to **G**-space. The total number of processors for this transformation is NPE = NPE1 × NPE2.

16.5. The data arrangement in **R**-space is local along the z direction but is distributed across the x-y planes, while the arrangement in **G**-space is local along x but distributed across the y-z planes. Only two transpose operations and three 1D FFT calls are needed to transform the data from **R**-space to **G**-space. The only drawback with this approach is that tedious bookkeeping is needed at the beginning of the calculations. However, compared to more than 1000 3D CFFT calls in a single calculation, the amount of bookkeeping work is small. Figure 16.6 shows an almost linear speedup of a 3D complex FFT using a SHMEM library based on the parallel scheme described earlier.

16.4   APPLICATIONS TO GRAIN BOUNDARIES IN POLYCRYSTALLINE DIAMOND

One of the areas that has become important in industrial applications is studying the electronic and atomic structure of defects in materials because these defects will affect the performance of synthesized materials. For example, the chemical vapor deposition of diamond coatings over large areas results in polycrystalline films with defects that include grain boundaries and regions of sp^2-bonded carbon. Diamond is a metastable form of carbon with sp^3-bonding and a wide electronic bandgap. It has an unusually favorable combination of characteristics, such as high mechanical strength, excellent thermal conductivity, and high resistance to radiation and temperature. Carrying out atomic-level calculations to characterize the properties of defects in diamond is, thus, important.

In this case, we have looked into different configurations of symmetrical tilt grain boundaries with all fourfold coordinated carbon atoms. The configura-

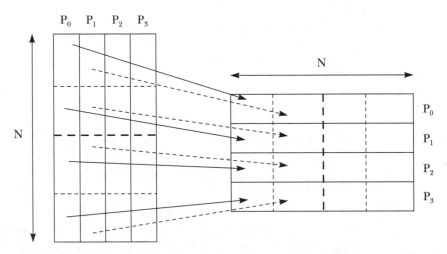

16.5

──────

FIGURE

Using four processors as an example to illustrate how step 2 in Table 16.3 is implemented. First, for each processor the local array is divided into subsections according to the number of target processors. Each subsection is then sent to the target processor for a 1D FFT operation on its local array.

tions were constructed from coincident site lattice models and were formed by rotation of two crystals around a common axis—for example, <110>—at an angle with a median plane—say, [110]. The resultant structures consist of an array of edge dislocations whose cores contain five- and seven-member rings (Figure 16.7 and color plate 16.7). The interface energies of these grain boundaries could then be calculated, and the data were used in the disinclination-structural unit model for the prediction of energies and stress fields over an entire range of misorientation [16.5]. A complete curve of grain boundary energy versus tilt angle was then obtained, which can provide a guideline for materials processing.

16.5   SUMMARY

The prospects for realistic atomic-level materials simulations and the prediction of cohesive, structural, mechanical, and electronic properties of materials have improved significantly in recent years. DFT in the LDA has yielded accurate results for a wide range of materials and has become a "standard model" for materials property calculations. Furthermore, advances in numerical algorithms and

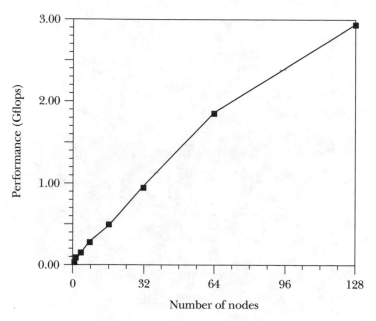

An example showing the performance efficiency in billions of floating-point operations per second (Gflops) versus the number of nodes of the 3D FFT routine implemented on the Cray T3D using the SHMEM library. The data size is a 128 × 128 × 128 complex matrix.

in computational hardware, particularly the introduction of massively parallel supercomputers, now makes feasible the *ab initio* treatment of technologically important materials, such as the semiconductors used in computer applications.

The adaptation of LDA methodology to parallel processing has been implemented within the scope of this work. We have described in detail how to design an efficient, scalable, parallel algorithm for materials simulation through the use of innovative new MPP computers in a portable manner. The data structures of eigenvectors from solution of Schrödinger-like equations have been analyzed according to their data locality. The powerful materials-modeling capability developed within the scope of this project can enable researchers to design novel materials with optimized properties solely from the identities of the constituent atoms and the law of quantum mechanics. We have given an example of applying the parallel PCGPP code to grain boundary properties in polycrystalline diamond, an important focus of materials researchers.

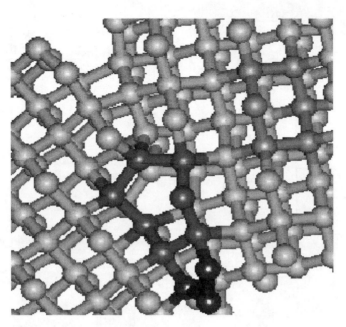

16.7

FIGURE

A ball-and-stick model of [110] projection title grain boundaries of carbon, which shows the interface core structure of five- and seven-member rings. (See also color plate 16.7.)

ACKNOWLEDGMENTS

This work was performed under the auspices of the U.S. Department of Energy under contract W-7405-ENG-48 at LLNL. The author would like to thank Dr. Roy Benedek at Argonne National Laboratory, IL, for his critical readings and comments on the manuscript. The work in diamond was in collaboration with Dr. Olga Shenderova and Professor Don Brenner at North Carolina State University.

References

[16.1]   Brommer, K. D., M. Needels, B. E. Larson, and J. D. Joannopoulos. 1992. Implementation of the Car-Parrinello Algorithm for Ab Initio Total Energy Calculations on a Massively Parallel Computer. *Comput. Phys., 7,* 350.

[16.2]   Car, R., and M. Parrinello. 1985. Unified Approach for Molecular Dynamics and Density-Functional Theory. *Phys. Rev. Lett., 55,* 2471.

[16.3]   Gillan, M. J. 1989. Calculation of the Vacancy Formation Energy in Aluminum. *J. Phys.: Condens. Matter, 1,* 689.

[16.4]   Kohn, W., and P. Vashishta. 1983. General Density Functional Theory. In S. Lundqvist and N. H. March (eds.), *Theory of the Inhomogeneous Electron Gas,* New York: Plenum Press.

[16.5]   Shenderova, O. A., D. W. Brenner, A. A. Nazarov, A. E. Romanov, and L. H. Yang. 1998. Multiscale Modeling Approach for Calculating Grain-Boundary Energies from First-Principles. *Phys. Rev., B57,* R3181.

[16.6]   Stich, I., I. Car, M. Parrinello, and S. Baroni. 1989. Conjugate Gradient Minimization of the Energy Functional: A New Method for Electronic Structure Calculation. *Phys. Rev., B39,* 4997.

[16.7]   Stich, I., M. C. Payne, R. D. King-Smith, J. S. Lin, and L. J. Clarke. 1992. Ab Initio Total-Energy Calculations for Extremely Large Systems: Application to Takayanagi Reconstruction of $S_i(111)$. *Phys. Rev. Lett., 68,* 1359.

[16.8]   Teter, M. P., M. C. Payne, and D. C. Allan. 1989. Solution of Schrodinger's Equation for Large Systems. *Phys. Rev., B40,* 12,255.

[16.9]   Troullier, N., and J. L. Martins. 1991. Efficient Pseudopotentials for Plane-Wave Calculations. *Phys. Rev., B43,* 1993.

[16.10] Wiggs, J., and H. Jonsson. 1995. A Hybrid Decomposition Parallel Implementation of the Car-Parrinello Method. *Comput. Phys. Commun., 87,* 319 and refs. therein.

17 Solving Symmetric Eigenvalue Problems

CHAPTER

David C. O'Neal
Raghurama Reddy   Pittsburgh Supercomputing Center, Carnegie Mellon University

17.1 INTRODUCTION

At the time of this work, Cray T3D software development was in its infancy. All of the available linear algebra libraries were collections of single-processor routines. This proved to be a porting obstacle for the developers of chemistry and materials science codes, whose computational models were based on eigenvalue and eigenvector analyses. Only relatively small structures would fit into local memory. Studies of larger systems would require distributed-memory diagonalization routines.

Analysis of the C70 fullerene and the DNA 6-base pair oligonucleotide generate systems of order 1000. Calculation of matrix elements describing the time evolution of molecular systems involves diagonalization of transition matrices of order 10,000 (wave packet model). In the areas of quantum dynamics and geometry optimizations, problems that result in systems of order 100,000 are on the horizon. The need for a distributed-memory eigensolver was clear, and after a review of relevant parallel algorithms, we focused on an inventive Jacobi method for symmetric systems and set out to refine it for the T3D.

Our efforts resulted in a generalization of parallel Jacobi algorithms and led to the development of PJAC, the parallel Jacobi eigensolver library. PJAC is a suite of distributed-memory routines that support the diagonalization of real symmetric and complex Hermitian matrices.

Matrix factoring methods, such as QR and QZ [17.2], are commonly used to diagonalize linear systems. These algorithms scale as $O(n^3)$. Serial Jacobi is $O(n^3$

log n), but parallel variations scale as $O(n^3 \log n/C)$, where C is the processor count. If C is of order n^2, we have the $O(n \log n)$ algorithm described by Brent and Luk [17.1] in which the global system is decomposed into a collection of 2×2 elements. But for even modest numbers of processors, the scaling of order n^3 algorithms may be matched or outdone by parallel Jacobi methods:

$$\frac{n^3}{C} \log n < n^3 \Leftrightarrow C > \log n$$

The macro-element algorithm described herein represents a generalization of the Brent-Luk work in which the grain size has been parameterized as a function of n and C. As C ranges from 1 to $(n/2)^2$, the algorithm transitions between the serial Jacobi and Brent-Luk models.

After a review of some of the basic properties of Jacobi methods in Sections 17.2 through 17.6, our macro element method is described in Section 17.7. Tests of convergence, scalability, and relative performance with respect to the fastest equivalent C90 library code we could find are reported in Section 17.8. A summary of conclusions is presented in Section 17.9.

Comments regarding the effects of load balance, network latency, and message traffic appear throughout the sections on parallel methods. Data structures and communication patterns are illustrated. Hardware and software products used for this series of experiments have been documented.

17.2   JACOBI'S METHOD

A method for reducing a symmetric matrix $A \in \mathbf{R}^{n \times n}$ to diagonal form by applying a sequence of orthogonal transformations was recorded by C. G. J. Jacobi in 1846 [17.4]. In essence, the norm of the off-diagonal coordinates of A,

$$off(A)^2 = \sum_{i=1}^{n} \sum_{\substack{j=1 \\ j \neq i}}^{n} a_{ij}^2$$

is systematically reduced by repeated application of what are now called Givens rotations. At each step, a Givens rotation matrix,

$$J(p,q,\theta) = \begin{pmatrix} 1 & \vdots & & \vdots & \\ \cdots & c & \cdots & s & \cdots \\ & \vdots & & \vdots & \\ \cdots & -s & \cdots & c & \cdots \\ & \vdots & & \vdots & 1 \end{pmatrix} \begin{matrix} \\ p \\ \\ q \\ \end{matrix}$$

is determined such that $off(B = J^T A J)$ is minimized with respect to some consistent matrix norm where $c = \cos\theta$ and $s = \sin\theta$ for some θ. The input system A is updated and the process continues until the desired level of precision has been reached. In short, this works because Givens rotations are orthogonal:

$$J^T J = I \Leftrightarrow J^T = J^{-1}$$

so A and B have the same eigenvalues:

$$Ax = \lambda x \Leftrightarrow (J^T A J)(J^T x) = \lambda(J^T x) \Leftrightarrow By = \lambda y$$

and the indicated transformation has pushed $off(B)$ a bit closer to zero. More rigorous proofs of convergence are given by Golub and Van Loan [17.2] and Schönage [17.5].

17.3   CLASSICAL JACOBI METHOD

Application of an arbitrary Givens rotation $J(p,q,\theta)$ to A yields the following relationship [17.2]:

$$off(B = J^T A J) = off(A) - 2a_{pq}^2 + 2b_{pq}^2$$

For any index pair (p,q), the value of $off(B)$ is minimized by determining J such that $b_{pq} = b_{qp} = 0$. Then $off(B)$ is just $off(A)$ reduced by the amount $2a_{pq}^2$, so it is reasonable to select rotation indices such that a_{pq} has the largest absolute value of all off-diagonal entries. The resultant procedure is called the *classical Jacobi method* (Algorithm 17.1).

Each update requires only $O(n)$ floating-point operations, but $O(n^2)$ comparisons must be made in order to locate the largest off-diagonal value. The rate

$$A^{(0)} \leftarrow A$$

$$for \; k = 0,1,\dots$$

$$\left| \begin{array}{l} choose \; (p,q) \; such \; that \left| a_{pq}^{(k)} \right| = \max_{i<j} \left| a_{i,j}^{(k)} \right| \\[2mm] compute \; c_k = \cos\theta_k \; and \; s_k = \sin\theta_k \\[2mm] J_k \leftarrow J(p,q,\theta_k) \\[2mm] A^{(k+1)} \leftarrow J_k^T A^{(k)} J_k \end{array} \right.$$

17.1   Classical Jacobi method.

ALGORITHM

of convergence of this algorithm has been shown to be quadratic for sufficiently large k [17.5].

17.4   SERIAL JACOBI METHOD

It is possible to eliminate the search time associated with the classical Jacobi method by choosing rotation pairs cyclically, for example:

$$(p,q) = (1,2),(1,3),(1,4),(1,5),\dots,(1,n),$$
$$(2,3),(2,4),(2,5),\dots,(2,n),$$
$$\vdots$$
$$(n-2,n-1),(n-2,n),$$
$$(n-1,n)$$

One complete set of $n(n-1)/2$ rotations is commonly called a *sweep*. Note that exactly one rotation is performed for each superdiagonal entry of the matrix during the course of a sweep, which implies that there are $[n(n-1)/2-1]!$ ways in which the pairings may be ordered.

Jacobi methods that employ such orderings are called *cyclic*. The row-wise pairing scheme illustrated here gives rise to the *serial Jacobi method* (Algorithm 17.2). It too has been shown to converge quadratically [17.7 and 17.8].

The serial Jacobi method requires $2n^3$ floating-point operations (flops) per sweep. If the orthogonal transformation matrix U = $J_1J_2 \dots J_N$ is accumulated, $2n^3$ additional flops per sweep are required.

$$\delta \leftarrow tolerance$$
$$while\ off(A) \geq \delta^2\ do$$
$$\quad for\ p = 1, 2, \ldots, n-1$$
$$\quad for\ q = p+1, \ldots, n$$
$$\qquad J \leftarrow J(p, q, \theta)$$
$$\qquad A \leftarrow J^t AJ$$

17.2

Serial Jacobi method.

ALGORITHM

The cyclic-by-rows (or columns) procedure for choosing rotation pairs (p, q) is not amenable to parallel processing on distributed-memory machines. Data locality is nonexistent. This leads us to review an ordering scheme that does facilitate parallel computations.

17.5 TOURNAMENT ORDERINGS

Orderings that permit rotations to be carried out simultaneously are well known to bridge and chess tournament players and are commonly called *tournament orderings*.

The communication pattern implied by a one-dimensional tournament ordering is easy to visualize. Figure 17.1 illustrates a complete sweep through all pairings for eight data points. The presence of a fixed position is apparent. Index 1 remains in the left *register* of processor P_1, while indices 2 . . . n travel through a cycle of length $n - 1$. Note that if n is odd, a zero value is introduced into the array of processors, typically into the right register of the last processor. The development of pairings associated with the two-dimensional case may be accomplished by sequential application of the one-dimensional process along each axis. The result is a diagonal communications pattern that can also be affected directly.

Reference is made to the so-called *preference factor* [17.3] for comparing convergence properties of cyclic Jacobi methods with respect to their rotation orderings. The tournament scheme asymptotically optimizes this preference factor as $n \infty$ [17.1].

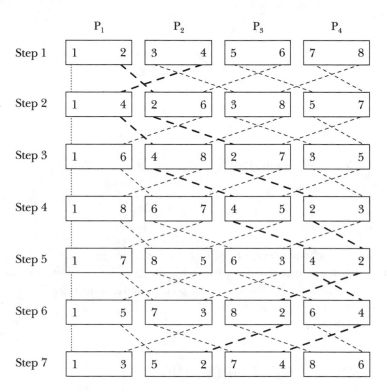

A 1D tournament ordering.

17.6 PARALLEL JACOBI METHOD

We begin by extending the ordering presented in Section 17.5 to two dimensions and applying it to a Jacobi process. The result is a matrix decomposition that promotes data locality. Input array A may be blocked into a collection of 2×2 submatrices and mapped onto a grid of processors (Figure 17.2). If n is odd, a row and column of zeros is appended.

Initially, processor P_{ij} contains the submatrix

$$\begin{pmatrix} a_{2i-1,2j-1} & a_{2i-1,2j} \\ a_{2i,2j-1} & a_{2i,2j} \end{pmatrix} \quad i,j = 1,2,\ldots,\frac{n}{2}$$

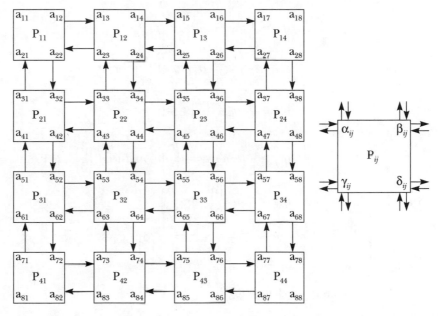

17.2   A 2D processor configuration.

FIGURE

As our view of the global system is now shifting towards that of a collection of submatrices, the introduction of a subtle change in notation would be helpful. In general, P_{ij} contains four real numbers:

$$\begin{pmatrix} \alpha_{ij} & \beta_{ij} \\ \gamma_{ij} & \delta_{ij} \end{pmatrix}$$

We refer to these submatrices as *elements* of the parallel Jacobi method.

For each step of a sweep, the processors P_{ii} ($i = 1, 2, \ldots, n/2$) lying along the main diagonal of the grid first compute the transformation values c_i and s_i associated with their data elements. Each diagonal processor must then communicate these values to the set of off-diagonal processors with which it shares a row or column index, thus allowing the formation of the global product to be completed:

$$J_i^T A J_j, \quad i, j = 1, 2, \ldots, \frac{n}{2}$$

$$if \ j = 1 \ then \ send \ \begin{pmatrix} \beta \\ \delta \end{pmatrix}_{i,1} \ to \ \mathrm{P}_{i,2}$$

$$else \ if \ j < \frac{n}{2} \ then \ send \ \begin{pmatrix} \alpha \\ \gamma \end{pmatrix}_{i,j} \ to \ \mathrm{P}_{i,j+1}$$

$$if \ j = \frac{n}{2} \ then \ \begin{pmatrix} \alpha \\ \gamma \end{pmatrix}_{tmp} \leftarrow \begin{pmatrix} \alpha \\ \gamma \end{pmatrix}_{i,\frac{n}{2}}$$

$$if \ j > 1 \ then \ receive \ \begin{pmatrix} \alpha \\ \gamma \end{pmatrix}_{i,j} \ and \ send \ \begin{pmatrix} \beta \\ \delta \end{pmatrix}_{i,j} \ to \ \mathrm{P}_{i,j\text{-}1}$$

$$if \ j = \ then \ \begin{pmatrix} \beta \\ \delta \end{pmatrix}_{i,\frac{n}{2}} \leftarrow \begin{pmatrix} \alpha \\ \gamma \end{pmatrix}_{tmp}$$

$$else \ if \ j < \frac{n}{2} \ then \ receive \ \begin{pmatrix} \beta \\ \delta \end{pmatrix}_{i,j}$$

17.1   Column interchange logic.

PROGRAM

where $J_i = J(2i - 1, 2i, \theta i)$. Exactly 2 log n messages per processor are required to accomplish this operation. All processors can then apply the transformations concurrently as indicated:

$$\begin{pmatrix} \alpha'_{ii} & \beta'_{ij} \\ \gamma'_{ji} & \delta'_{jj} \end{pmatrix} = \begin{pmatrix} c_i & -s_i \\ s_i & c_i \end{pmatrix} \begin{pmatrix} \alpha_{ii} & \beta_{ij} \\ \gamma_{ji} & \delta_{jj} \end{pmatrix} \begin{pmatrix} c_j & s_j \\ -s_j & c_j \end{pmatrix} \tag{17.1}$$

Column-wise permutation of the element data is carried out, followed by a similar row-wise reordering, thus completing the first step of the first sweep. The combined operation is completely symmetric. The logic associated with column interchanges is detailed in Program 17.1.

An equivalent diagonal communications pattern can be written. However, the number of messages that each processor must send and receive remains the same. The size of the data packets is halved (single values instead of pairs), but in either case, latency and not bandwidth is the greater concern. The implication is that there is little reason to prefer one pattern over the other.

As indicated, the element transformations associated with each step are affected simultaneously. Recall from Section 17.5 that a sweep is comprised of

$$for \; k = 1,2, \ldots, \log n$$

$$for \; L = 1,2, \ldots, 2\left(\frac{n}{2}\right) - 1$$

> *compute c_i and s_i for all P_{ii}*
> *propagate transformation values along grid rows and columns*
> *apply transformations (Equation 17.1) across all P_{ij}*
> *reorder column data (Program 17.1)*
> *reorder row data (variation of Program 17.1)*

17.3   Parallel Jacobi method (Brent-Luk).

ALGORITHM

$n - 1$ steps. Empirical data suggest that the number of sweeps, k, required to produce $off(A) < 10E-16$ is $O(\log \; n)$; hence the total time required to diagonalize A scales as $O(n \log n)$ [17.1]. An outline of the process is given by Algorithm 17.3.

Thus far, all operation counts have ignored the role of the network in the model. Communications have been assumed to scale as $O(1)$, which is unrealistic. This prompts us to itemize some of the characteristics of the fine-grained Jacobi algorithm described by Brent-Luk that presented us with problems.

First, there is little opportunity to hide the necessary network operations because the amount of work a processor performs during each step of a sweep is very small. Messages are also very small, thus amplifying the effects of latency. Traffic scales as $O(n^2)$. All of the scalable decompositions we will describe (including Brent-Luk) display load-balance problems. Processors lying along the main diagonal of the grid must perform computations and initiate broadcast operations, while off-diagonal processors sit idle or, more accurately, wait to receive data. We can also make the observation that the assumed $O(n^2)$ grid of processors runs counter to the current trend towards parallel architectures constructed of smaller numbers of more powerful processors.

Virtualization schemes can be used to overcome some of these problems and improve upon others. Two such methods were implemented. Diagrams illustrating the relevant decompositions follow.

In the first case, the global data was mapped onto an array of C processors configured as a $\sqrt{C} \times \sqrt{C}$ grid (Figure 17.3). Packet sizes and the amount of work to be performed by each processor increased while network traffic was reduced to $O(C)$. However, the load-balance problem remained. We had also restricted

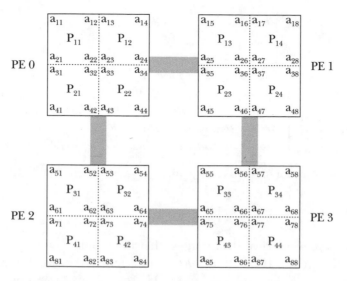

17.3

FIGURE

Scalable block virtualization.

ourselves to processor counts that were necessarily perfect squares. It was at this point that we decided to abandon the formality of a scalable method in favor of decomposition by column strips (Figure 17.4). In this case, the grid geometry moved to a simple array of C processors. Not only did this eliminate the load-balance problem, but it also cut network traffic in half (all row-shifting operations became local memory transfers).

However, as the size of the input system was scaled up, the cost of the row-shifting operations began to dominate. Use of a permutation vector to logically perform the row shifts only moved the bottleneck from the row-shifting operation to the floating-point loop, where it then became necessary to reference the row elements indirectly. Nevertheless, performance improved dramatically. Timings were now in the range of C90 library codes (libsci and IMSL), but overtaking them would not be possible.

For any given matrix, the per-processor communication costs associated with the Brent-Luk method are fixed and, unfortunately, of the same magnitude as the overall C90 timings. This led us to reexamine an idea that had been discussed during the early phases of development—one that evolved into the generalized parallel Jacobi algorithm presented in the next section.

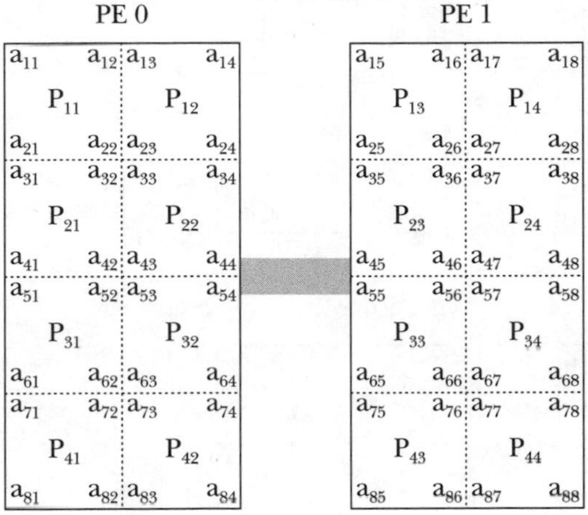

17.4

FIGURE

Column strip virtualization.

17.7   MACRO JACOBI METHOD

The macro Jacobi method represents a generalization of the Brent-Luk algorithm. It is a synthesis of the serial and parallel Jacobi methods described in Sections 17.4 and 17.6. Recalling the form of an arbitrary Jacobi element,

$$\begin{pmatrix} \alpha_{ij} & \beta_{ij} \\ \gamma_{ij} & \delta_{ij} \end{pmatrix}$$

a slight change in notation is introduced to distinguish the form of the macro Jacobi element from that of the Jacobi elements described in Section 17.6:

$$\begin{pmatrix} A_{ij} & B_{ij} \\ \Gamma_{ij} & \Delta_{ij} \end{pmatrix}$$

The coordinates of the macro elements are matrices, A_{ij}, B_{ij}, Γ_{ij}, and $\Delta_{ij} \in \mathbf{R}^{\frac{n}{\sqrt{C}} \times \frac{n}{\sqrt{C}}}$ for an arbitrary C in the range $1 \ldots \lceil n/2 \rceil^2$.

A variation of the scalable decomposition scheme (Figure 17.3) that utilized a grid geometry of $\sqrt{C} \times \sqrt{C}$ processors is presented first (Figure 17.5). This re-

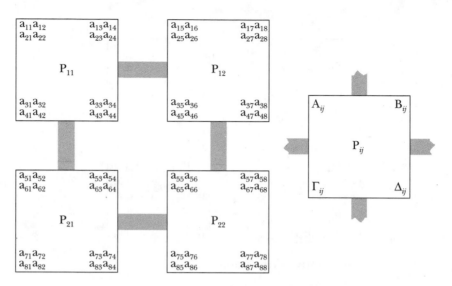

17.5

FIGURE

Scalable macro decomposition. Array of macro Jacobi elements and generic macro element P_{ij}.

places the fixed arrangement of $\lceil n/2 \rceil^2$ processors called for by the Brent-Luk model. One sweep of the column-cyclic serial Jacobi method is then applied to each of the diagonal macro elements. Rotation matrices are accumulated and propagated along the corresponding rows and columns of the grid as before. A matrix multiply routine (SGEMM) is used to complete the macro version of Equation (17.1) and the data corresponding to the next set of rotations are moved into position (following the logic of Program 17.1) in a blockwise fashion.

The resulting method is similar to Algorithm 17.3. However, while the components of a macro step are consistent with the Brent-Luk procedure, a significant difference is apparent. Scalar operations have been replaced by block operations. Algorithm 17.4 outlines these statements. Note that for macro decompositions, the number of steps per sweep becomes $2\sqrt{C} - 1$.

Algorithm 17.4 provides a description of a parameterized ordering scheme that transitions between the serial and parallel Jacobi methods in an optimal fashion. The preference factor referenced in Section 17.5 is asymptotically reduced as $\sqrt{C} \to n/2$ and $n \to \infty$. Characteristics of the scalable macro decomposition model are like those of the scalable block virtualization method presented in Section 17.6 (see Figure 17.3). Packet sizes and the amount of work each processor must perform become functions of C. The same load-balance

for k = 1, 2, ..., log n
for L = 1, 2, ..., 2√C − 1

    | *accumulate transformation matrices for all P_{ii} (cyclic Jacobi)*
    | *propagate transformation values across the element rows and*
    | *columns*
    | *apply transformations across all P_{ij}*
    | *reorder column data (blockwise variation of Program 17.1)*
    | *reorder row data (blockwise variation of Program 17.1)*

17.4   Macro element Jacobi method.

ALGORITHM

problem is apparent, and again we are limited to partition sizes that are perfect squares.

Column-wise virtualization of macro elements (Figure 17.6) resembles the column strip decomposition of Section 17.6 (see Figure 17.4). It eliminates the load-balance problem and moves the row-shifting operations on-processor. The bottleneck that had accompanied the fine-grained row-shifting pattern associated with the Brent-Luk ordering showed a distinct improvement, except as the limiting case $C = \lceil n/2 \rceil$ was approached. Performance characteristics of the virtualized macro element model are detailed in the next section. Both heterogeneous and stand-alone codes were developed. The heterogeneous version communicates with the T3D by way of a file-based transfer system. This same system may also be used to map foreign data structures into and out of macro element decompositions.

17.8   COMPUTATIONAL EXPERIMENTS

At the time of these experiments, the Cray T3D at the Pittsburgh Super-computing Center was configured with 512 PEs (processing elements) with 64 MB of memory per PE. Eight I/O gateways connected the T3D to a Cray YMP C90/16512 equipped with a 4-GB SSD. The C90 was running Unicos 8.0 with AFS. The T3D was running MAX 1.1.0.4.

The virtualized macro decomposition method described in Section 17.6 was initially implemented as a heterogeneous host-node model in Cray Fortran 77. The C90 executable was produced with the CFT77 compiler (6.0.2.3) and

Virtualized macro element decomposition.

SEGLDR (8.0f). The T3D executable was produced with the CFT77_M compiler (6.1.0.0) and MPPLDR (10.r). The MPP object codes were linked with libsci (1.1.0.0) and libsma (1.1.0.1).

17.8.1   Test Problems

Problems used for convergence and performance testing were developed by filling the upper triangular portion of an $n \times n$ array with pseudorandom numbers in the range (0,1). These values were then folded onto the corresponding lower triangular coordinates to produce a symmetric system.

Reported timings include kernel operations only. A file-based transfer scheme was implemented separately to handle local and heterogeneous mappings of the primary data structures. Initial and final distributions of the data were performed outside of the timing blocks. All timings include the accumulation of eigenvectors.

17.8.2   Convergence

Convergence characteristics were examined first. The curves shown in Figure 17.7 clearly indicate that the measured rates of convergence for various macro orderings and processor counts are quadratic.

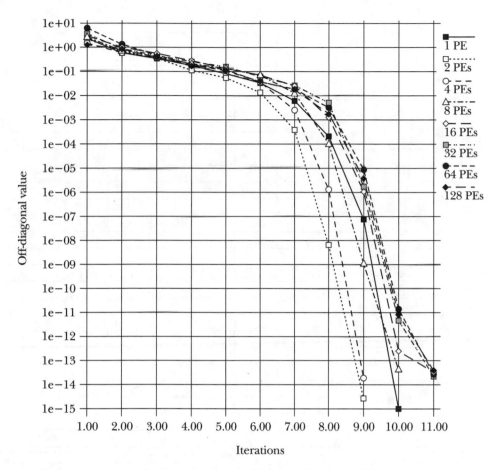

17.7

FIGURE

Convergence test showing maximum off-diagonal values with respect to iteration counts for a 512 × 512 matrix running on various partition sizes.

17.8.3   Scaling

How a method scales is of primary concern to the developers of parallel codes. Five key components of the kernel were identified and timed independently on PE0 using calls to the SECONDR utility. We expected that as more PEs were used for a given problem size, the accumulation of the transformation arrays ("Accumulate") and matrix multiply ("Apply") components would steadily decrease,

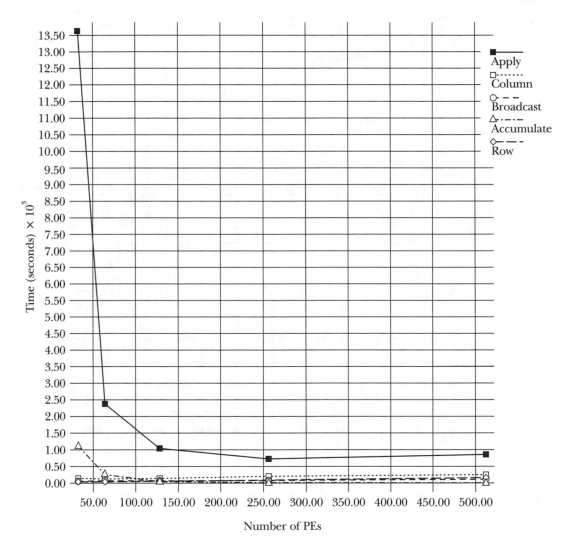

Component scaling characteristics showing kernel component timings (thousands of seconds) with respect to processor count for a 4096 × 4096 matrix.

while timings associated with communications ("Broadcast", "Row", "Column") would increase, hopefully at a slower rate.

Figure 17.8 shows that the broadcast ("Broadcast") and exchange operations ("Row", "Column") do indeed increase at a modest rate, and the accumulation routine ("Accumulate") approaches the x-axis asymptotically. However, at a point that varies with the problem size, SGEMM ("Apply") performance falls off. This can be thought of as a side effect of the virtualization scheme. For any virtualized macro decomposition (Figure 17.6), the number of macro elements per processor equals the processor count C. The order of the elements is n/C. This implies that for any n, larger values of C correspond to increasing numbers of smaller elements. Overhead associated with calls to SGEMM becomes more significant.

The performance of SGEMM also declines as the system size decreases. A curve describing the single PE performance of SGEMM appears in Figure 17.9. Note that the optimal range of system sizes for this routine is something like $16 \leq n/C \leq 64$. Cache line effects can also be seen in the regularity with which local peaks are achieved for dimensions that are multiples of 4 (the size of a cache line). The impact of SGEMM performance can also be seen in the total timing curves (Figure 17.10). For all but the largest case shown, a point is reached at which a doubling of the processor count results in an increase in runtime. This point, call it C_n, is a function of n. Each doubling of the problem size results in a similar increase in C_n. This is consistent with the fact that a doubling of the problem size implies that the order of the macro element (n/C) doubles as well. By writing out the geometries of the data structures associated with each C_n, we found that the corresponding dimension of the macro element was 16 in every case, which implies that for a problem size of $n = 8192$, $C_n = 512$. The curves of Figure 17.10 indicate that this is reasonable. By connecting the respective values of C_n for various problem sizes, the region in which the algorithm remains efficient is also determined. This allows us to predict that for $C = 1, 2, 4, 8, \ldots$, 512, the curves associated with all problem sizes $n \geq 8192$ will show decreasing timings throughout the given range of C. The simple data structures used by our current implementation will allow a problem size of $n \approx 24{,}000$ to be solved on the full machine. By exploiting symmetry, we believe that a problem size of $n \approx 40{,}000$ could be accommodated.

The timing curves of Figure 17.11 compare the performance of PJAC running on the T3D to IMSL's EVCSF routine running on the C90. Note that the clustering of timings that occurs for problem sizes between 1024 and 4096 indicates that the method is competitive for solving smaller systems on smaller partitions as well.

17.9   SUMMARY

Macro element decompositions have the effect of improving data locality for cyclic Jacobi methods implemented on distributed-memory machines, which leads to improved performance of such codes. C90 IMSL timings increase consistently by a factor of 8, which is exactly what is expected for an $O(n^3)$ algorithm as the

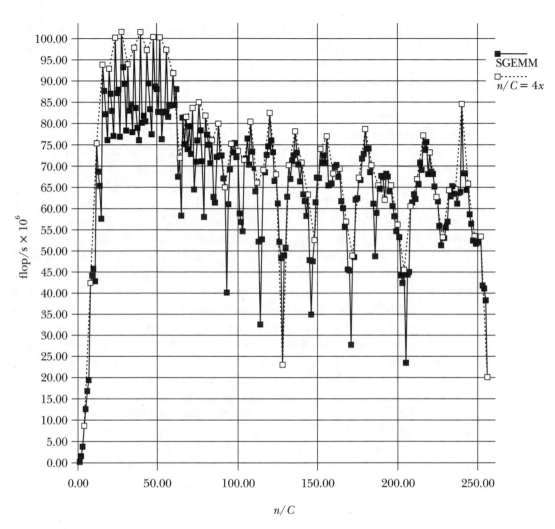

17.9 FIGURE   Single PE performance of SGEMM showing floating-point performance (Mflops) with respect to macro element size.

problem size is doubled. This predicts that given sufficient memory, IMSL would require about 17.5 and 140.4 hours to diagonalize $n = 16{,}384$ and $n = 32{,}768$ systems, respectively. T3D timing data indicate that the virtualized macro element implementation is most efficient when n/C is in the range 16 through 64. Outside of this range, the performance of SGEMM falls dramatically, but we note that for $n = 16{,}384$ and $n = 32{,}768$ problems running on the full machine ($C = 512$) the related values of n/C are 32 and 64, respectively. This leads us to predict

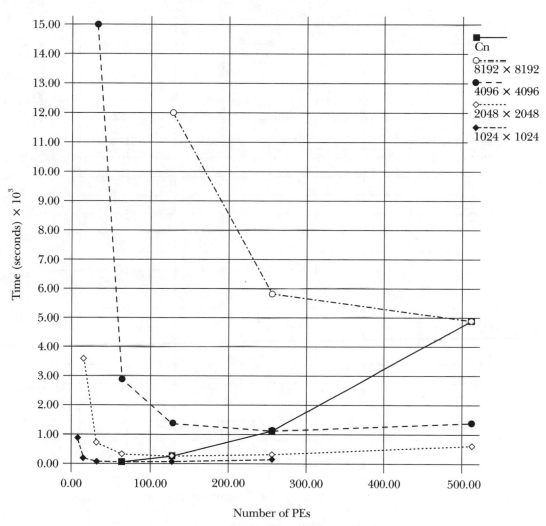

17.10

FIGURE

Overall scaling characteristics showing kernel execution time (thousands of seconds) as a function of processor count for various system sizes.

that our current implementation would require around 5.4 and 21.8 hours, respectively, to resolve these cases.

The aggregate floating-point rate of the PJAC kernel is extremely high. For the $n = 8192$ case running on the full machine, measured performance exceeded 31 Gflops/s. At the time of these tests, this was one of the highest sustained rates achieved by any T3D application, but it is also a somewhat mislead-

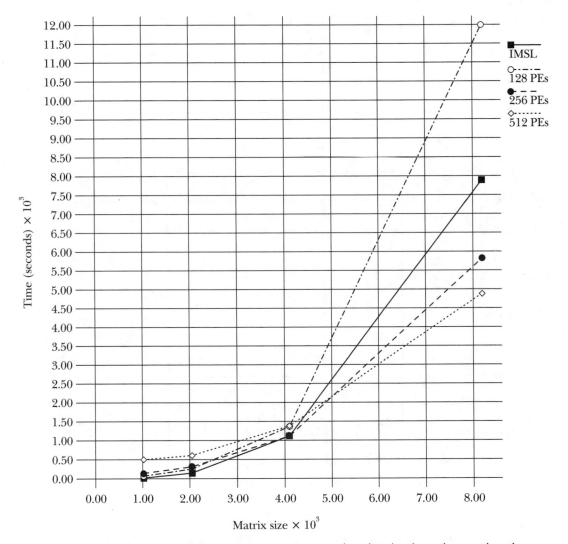

17.11

FIGURE

Performance with respect to C90 IMSL routine showing kernel execution time (thousands of seconds) with respect to system size (thousands), IMSL versus PJAC for various partition sizes.

ing result. As the global system approaches diagonal form, the macro element transformation arrays converge to the form of identity matrices; hence, an increasing number of floating-point operations involve zeros.

We remind the reader that the operation count itself is not optimal either. Recall from Section 17.1 that the cumulative floating-point count for Jacobi algorithms is in general $\log n$ greater than that for QR methods. Our macro element Jacobi method is competitive because it executes block-oriented operations that are optimal for the target architecture.

The availability of the PJAC library creates two basic possibilities. T3D codes that had been forced to perform eigenanalyses on the C90 can now "stay at home" and so eliminate the time spent transferring data between the memory spaces of the respective machines, as well as the required conversion of the dissimilar data representations. Conversely, C90 applications that perform eigenanalyses can shift this portion of the work to the T3D.

ACKNOWLEDGMENTS

We wish to thank Michael Levine and Ralph Roskies, directors of the Pittsburgh Supercomputing Center, and Robert Stock and Richard Raymond of the User Services Group for affording us the time to complete this work.

Development was partially supported by Cray Research's Parallel Applications Technology Program. Computing resources were provided by the Pittsburgh Supercomputing Center. Sketches appearing in this chapter were produced by Robert Dixon and Stephanie Dobler of PSC's Education and Training Group.

References

[17.1] Brent, R. P., and F. T. Luk. 1985. The Solution of Singular-Value and Symmetric Eigenvalue Problems on Multiprocessor Arrays. *SIAM J. Sci. Stat. Comput.,* **6** (1), 69–84.

[17.2] Golub, Gene F., and C. H. Van Loan. 1983. *Matrix Computations.* Baltimore, MD: The Johns Hopkins University Press.

[17.3] Hansen, E. R. 1963. *On Cyclic Jacobi Methods. J. Soc. Indust. Appl. Math.,* **11,** 448–459.

[17.4] Jacobi, C. G. J. 1846. Uber ein Leichtes Verfahren Die in der Theorie der Sacularstorungen Vorkommendern Gleichungen Numerich Aufzulosen. *Crelle's J.,* **30,** 51–94.

[17.5] Schönage, A. 1964. On the Quadratic Convergence of the Jacobi Process. *Numer. Math.,* **6,** 410–412.

[17.6] Stewart, G. W. 1973. *Introduction to Matrix Computations.* Orlando, FL: Academic Press.

[17.7] van Kempen, H. P. M. 1966. On Quadratic Convergence of the Special Cyclic Jacobi Method. *Numer. Math.,* **9,** 19–22.

[17.8] Wilkinson, J. H. 1962. Note on the Quadratic Convergence of the Cyclic Jacobi Process. *Numer. Math.,* **4,** 296–300.

18 | Nuclear Magnetic Resonance Simulations

CHAPTER

Alan J. Benesi
Kenneth M. Merz, Jr.
James J. Vincent   Department of Chemistry, The Pennsylvania State University

Ravi Subramanya   Pittsburgh Supercomputing Center, Carnegie Mellon University

18.1   INTRODUCTION

This chapter discusses the development and optimization of a parallel program for simulating time dependence of the powder average density matrix for Nuclear Magnetic Resonance (NMR) samples. The application is an example of an embarrassingly parallel algorithm that scales almost linearly on MPP platforms. NMR spectroscopy is the single most powerful experimental technique for characterizing the chemistry of any kind of sample. A large class of atoms characterized by quadrupolar nuclei present an interesting problem because their NMR spectra are much more complicated. A better understanding of the quantum behavior that underlies NMR experiments is essential to better interpret the NMR spectra from such atoms. Numerical simulation of the powder average density matrix provides one means of gaining this understanding. (The powder average is the term given to the average of the NMR signals from the samples that are almost always in powder form for solid-state NMR spectroscopy.) The simulated NMR signal for a powder sample is the sum of the individual signals from all the possible directions that the crystals in the sample could be oriented. Since the signal simulation from each orientation, is independent of all other orientations, we have a classic example of an embarassingly parallel application. The parallelism ensures that the application scales almost linearly on MPP platforms.

18.2   SCIENTIFIC CONSIDERATIONS

Over 65 percent of NMR-observable nuclei are quadrupoles with nuclear spin quantum numbers greater than 1/2. The majority of these are odd half-integer nuclei (I = 3/2, 5/2, 7/2, 9/2, etc.) and are usually found in solids such as metals, minerals, ceramics, and catalysts. Often, the quadrupole coupling constants of these nuclei are so large that *only* the central transition of the powder pattern is directly observable by conventional pulsed NMR techniques. In such cases, it is necessary to use second order time-independent perturbation theory to simulate powder lineshapes obtained in magic angle spinning (MAS) spectra. Odd half-integer quadrupolar nuclei can be used in Cross Polarization MAS (CPMAS) to obtain enhanced signal intensity and distance information. The problem with CPMAS is that the behavior of the magnetization (the density matrix) during the spinlock is complicated due to overlapping frequencies from first order satellite transitions. Vega [18.7, 18.8] has applied time-independent perturbation theory using both first and second order average Hamiltonians for the analysis of quadrupolar spinlocks and CPMAS involving quadrupoles. Simulations of the time dependence of the full powder average density matrix have not been made for odd half-integer quadrupolar nuclei subject to spinlock rf fields.

Our goal was to use time-dependent perturbation theory to rigorously simulate the MAS behavior of I = 3/2 quadrupolar nuclei subject to magic angle spinning, pulses, and spinlocks using both the zeroth and first order average quadrupolar Hamiltonians ($^0H_q + {}^1H_q$) over the Larmor period [18.5]. We validate the approach by comparing simulation results to experimental results. The approach is successful provided the time increment, Δt, used in the simulation is less than $\{\text{Tr}[(^0H_q + {}^1H_q)^2]\}^{-1/2}$. Simulations based on larger time increments are shown to give incorrect results for all NMR experiments on these nuclei. Furthermore, the small time increments required for successful simulations are identical to those required for propagators calculated by series expansion [18.1]. Unexpected results showing decay of powder average density matrices were obtained. The decay is attributable to destructive interference of density matrices from spins within microcrystallites with different orientations relative to the applied magnetic field.

18.3   DESCRIPTION OF THE APPLICATION

The zeroth and first order average quadrupolar Hamiltonians ($^0H_q + {}^1H_q$) in the rotating frame were calculated using the spherical tensor conventions of Mehring [18.6], the Wigner rotations tabulated by Mehring and by Brink and Satchler [18.2], and the Magnus expansion [18.4]. Although the first order average Hamiltonian over the Larmor period yields nonzero off-diagonal terms, these were eliminated to yield a secular Hamiltonian containing the sum of the zeroth and first order average quadrupolar Hamiltonian. Magic angle spinning confers time dependence onto the total quadrupolar Hamiltonian.

During periods with radio frequency (rf) irradiation, the total Hamiltonian is

$$H_{tot}(t) = H_q(t) + H_{rf} \qquad (18.1)$$

where $H_{rf} = \omega_{rf}(\cos\phi\, I_x + \operatorname{Sin}\phi\, I_y)$, ϕ is the phase of the rf relative to the x-axis of the rotating frame, and I_x and I_y are the matrix representations of the x and y components of the spin angular-momentum operators for the quadrupolar nucleus.

Neglecting relaxation, the equation of motion for the density matrix is the quantum Liouville equation:

$$\frac{d}{dt}\rho = \frac{-i}{\hbar}[H,\rho] \qquad (18.2)$$

where ρ is the "reduced" density matrix for the quadrupolar nucleus obtained using the high-temperature approximation [18.4]. At equilibrium, $\rho_{eq} = CI_z$, where C is a constant and I_z is the matrix representation of the z component of the spin angular momentum for the quadrupolar nucleus.

For time increments Δt that are sufficiently short that $H_{tot}(t) \sim$ constant, the solution to Equation (18.2) is

$$\rho(t + \Delta t) = e^{-iH\Delta t}\rho(t)e^{iH\Delta t} \qquad (18.3)$$

where the "sandwich" of complex exponentials is the propagator for the density matrix. As we will show, a more severe constraint on Δt is necessary for the time-dependent Hamiltonian of Equation (18.1)—namely, that $\Delta t < \{\operatorname{Tr}[H_{tot}^2]\}^{-1/2}$.

During periods without rf irradiation, H is diagonal and the propagators in Equation (18.3) are evaluated directly by complex exponentiation. For periods with rf irradiation, H is nonsecular, and we have evaluated the propagators in Equation (18.3) by series expansion and by the standard method (18.1). The standard method requires complex diagonalization of $H_{tot}(t)$ during periods of rf irradiation:

$$e^{\pm iH\Delta t} = S e^{\pm iS^* HS \Delta t} S*$$

(18.4)

where S is the similarity transform matrix of $H_{tot}(t)$, and $S*$ is the adjoint (inverse) of S. The series expansion method requires no diagonalization of $H_{tot}(t)$, even during periods of rf irradiation (18.1):

$$e^{\pm iH\Delta t} = \left\{ 1 + (\pm iH\Delta t) + \frac{(\pm iH\Delta t)^2}{2!} + \cdots \right\}$$

(18.5)

where $\mathbf{1}$ represents the unit matrix and all products of matrices are regular matrix products. In our simulations, we have used a sixth order expansion (i.e., to the sixth power of Δt), although we found that a fourth order expansion was adequate. As we will show, going as high as 12th order has only a small effect on the computation times, but there is no effect on accuracy.

The time-dependent powder average density matrix of the ensemble of spins is calculated by adding the properly weighted time-dependent density matrices from each "microcrystallite" in the powder. This process is *inherently parallel* as long as there is no molecular motion to change the Euler angles that relate the quadrupole principal axis system of the individual microcrystallite to the rotor reference frame for MAS (or to the laboratory reference frame for static samples). We have used two different methods to calculate the powder average, but it is important to note that any method can be used. In the first, the Euler angles ϕ, θ, and ψ (or just ϕ and θ for static samples) were divided into equal increments $\Delta\phi$, $\Delta\theta$, and $\Delta\psi$, and the latitudinal angle θ, which varies from 0 to π (or 0 to $(\pi/2)$, was weighted by $\cos| (\theta - \Delta\theta/2) - \cos (\theta + \Delta\theta/2)|$. The longitudinal angles ϕ and ψ, which vary from 0 to 2π, require no weighting. In the second method the latitudinal angle θ was divided into specified increments that yield an integral of constant value—hence the name "the method of constant integrals." These increments require no weighting.

18.4 COMPUTATIONAL CONSIDERATIONS

This section addresses algorithm design for optimal performance and choice of parallel programming model.

18.4.1 Algorithmic Considerations

Figure 18.1 describes the control-flow diagram for the program. After input of all the necessary information, the equilibrium density matrix for all spins is initialized. The dimension of the density matrix depends on both the spin quantum number and the number of coupled spins in the system. For example, the dimension of the density matrix is 2×2 for I = 1/2, 3×3 for I = 1 and 4×4 for a single spin I = 3/2. For coupled spins the dimensions increase. The matrix representation of the spin Hamiltonians has the same dimensions as the density matrix. The serial version of the code executes each of the loops sequentially and aggregates the results at the end of all the computations. Because the powder average loop is executed sequentially, the duration of a typical sequential run is a function of the number of latitudinal Euler angles that are being calculated. The small size of the Hamiltonian matrices results in small data structure sizes, making the code particularly ill conditioned for vector processing. These two factors led to substantially long turnaround times and inefficient use of available computational power.

The absence of loop dependency between successive iterations of the powder average loop led us to investigate the possibility of parallelizing the algorithm. The small sizes of the matrices make the code particularly suitable for the T3D/T3E's cache-based architecture. The base case with spin = 3/2 was particularly well suited for optimal cache utilization with a dimension of 4×4. Because the density matrices corresponding to different parts of the phase cycle loop were calculated in separate production runs, the powder average loop is the outermost loop of the code and best suited for parallelization due to load-balancing considerations. Load balancing is especially important in an MPI application on a space-sharing machine such as the Cray T3D. PEs are requested and assigned at the beginning of the job and are released at the end of the job. Optimal utiliza-

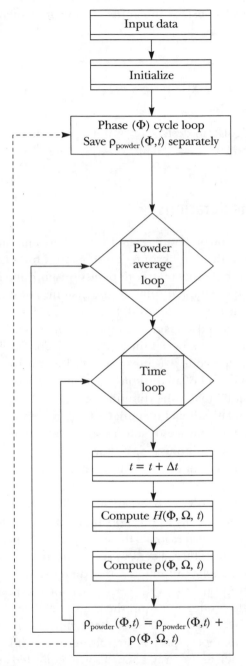

18.1
FIGURE

Control flow diagram for the NMR algorithm.

tion of available resources can be ensured by dividing the computing task equally among the available resources. The complete set of latitudinal Euler angles were divided evenly among processors. At the end of the calculations, the results from each PE are aggregated, using a global sum, to give the full powder average density matrix.

18.4.2   Programming Considerations

The SPMD paradigm was adopted as the programming model for the simulation. MPI libraries were used for doing the global reductions. Communications take up a very small fraction of the actual compute time, and any message-passing method could have been adopted. Portability considerations dictated the use of MPI. Because the code was essentially CPU bound, optimization was largely a matter of tuning the single PE performance. The small size of the powder density matrix enabled substantial cache reuse, leading to significant code speedups. Single PE optimization techniques advocated by Brooks [18.3], such as replacing divisions by reciprocals, minimizing cache conflicts by managing data structure layout, loop unrolling, and the read-ahead compile time flag, were used in the code. (See also Chapter 5.)

The code was analyzed using Apprentice. The bottlenecks identified were remedied as follows:

✦ Problem: Functional unit pipelining was poor because of a number of nested loops with relatively small iteration counts.
Solution: Addressed by unrolling the inner loops, resulting in a dramatic speedup.

✦ Problem: A loop invariant was being used to divide the values within the loops.
Solution: Computed reciprocal in the beginning and broadcast it to all the PEs. Substituted multiplication for division (inoptimal) throughout.

✦ Problem: Memory access was largely sequential.
Solution: Passed a flag to the mppldr to perform read-ahead operations, reducing page misses on data required for subsequent instructions.

✦ Problem: Cache conflicts led to cache thrashing.
Solution: Cache conflicts leading to degraded memory-access performance were minimized by managing data layout using cache alignment directives and variable declarations within commons.

✦ Complex arithmetic was performed by explicitly computing the real and imaginary parts separately. This yielded better performance than would have been achieved using the intrinsic support for complex computations.

Number of PEs	Speedup
32	1.00
64	2.00
128	3.99
256	7.83
512	15.59

18.1

TABLE

Scaling performance of the NMR code showing 512 Euler angles computed on different PE partitions.

18.5   COMPUTATIONAL RESULTS

The small amount of communication time compared to compute time enables almost linear scaling with the number of PEs, as illustrated in Table 18.1. The speedup degrades only slightly from the linear value of 16 at the largest partition size. The graph plots the ratio of the elapsed time for a run with 32 PEs to the elapsed time for a similar run performed with N PEs, where $N = \{32, 64, 128, 256, 512\}$. A linear speedup would yield speedup ratios of $\{1.0, 2.0. 4.0, 8.0, 16.0\}$. The speedup measured for the code is documented in Figure 18.2 and Table 18.2.

Performance of a 1 time-step calculation on 512 PEs of the T3D shows a record aggregate performance of 39.16 Gflops and a per PE performance of 76.48 Mflops. The original serial code ran at 80 Mflops on the C90 on a single processor. The parallel code has a per PE performance of 76.48 Mflops. The cost benefits of the parallelization are self-evident when one compares the cost of running on the C90 to the cost of running on a single PE of the T3D. Furthermore, parallelization ensures that the multiple Euler angles can be computed in the same time it takes the C90 to compute one Euler angle. This results in rapid turnaround time and accelerated research. The availability of an MPP also enables a much higher resolution study than was possible previously.

18.6   SCIENTIFIC RESULTS

Results from the NMR simulations can be broadly classified into two categories: validation of simulation and interesting scientific results. We discuss these in the following subsections.

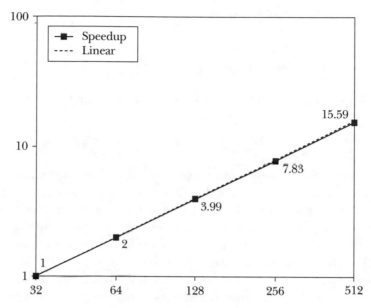

Graph of scaling performance of the NMR code.

18.6.1   Validation of Simulation

We chose to simulate various MAS and static experiments for ^{23}Na in powdered anhydrous sodium oxalate, $Na_2C_2O_4$, for which we also obtained experimental NMR data. ^{23}Na has I = 3/2, and in our sample the quadrupole coupling constant was 2.52 MHz and the asymmetry parameter, η, was 0.74. The chemical shift anisotropy of ^{23}Na and weak ^{23}Na-^{23}Na homonuclear dipolar coupling were ignored in our simulations. The Hamiltonians used in the simulations correspond to Equation (18.1). In our experiments, the magic angle spinning rate was 5240 ± 10 Hz, the on-resonance Larmor frequency was 78.6596 MHz, and the rf field strength was 35.7 kHz, as determined for a concentrated liquid solution of sodium oxalate in deuterated water. The NMR experiments were carried out at room temperature on a Chemagnetics CMX-300 operating in the quadrature mode.

The results for the single-pulse experiment and corresponding simulations are shown in Figure 18.3. Specifically, Figure 18.3 shows the comparison of the experimental MAS spectrum obtained by Fourier transformation (FT) of the FID acquired after a single 3.5-μs pulse and the FT of Tr [I$^+$ ρ] acquired after a 3.5-μs pulse for two simulations that duplicated the experimental conditions.

Total flop count	4.136e14
Total time	10561.2164 s
Total Gflops	39.161 Gflops
Single PE performance	76.48 Mflops/PE

18.2   Performance counter numbers for a 512-PE run on the T3D.

TABLE

The simulations were both carried out in an identical manner with the same Hamiltonian, except that in one case series expansion was used to propagate ρ both during and after the pulse with a time increment $\Delta t = 0.10$ μs, and in the other ρ was propagated using complex diagonalization during the pulse and by complex exponentiation after the pulse with a time increment $\Delta t = 0.954$ μs. The time increment of 0.954 μs corresponds to exactly 1.8 degrees of rotor rotation. Note that the spinning sidebands of the latter simulation are wrong both in intensity and in frequency. If a time increment of $\Delta t = 0.10$ μs is used for the simulation with complex diagonalization and complex exponentiation, the simulation exactly matches the one obtained with series expansion. This illustrates the requirement that for *both* the series expansion and the standard method, time increments must be chosen such that $\Delta t < \{Tr[(^{0}H_q + {}^{1}H_q)^2]\}^{-1/2}$. We attribute the minor differences between the experimental spectrum in Figure 18.1 and the one obtained by series expansion to at least two factors. First, we used 4 degree increments in ϕ and γ and 128 equal increments in θ for the powder average in this simulation. Second, the chemical shift anisotropy and the weak homonuclear dipolar interactions between sodium nuclei have been ignored. It should also be recognized that good precision is difficult with a matrix that contains both very large elements from $^{0}H_q$ and relatively small elements from $^{1}H_q$ and H_{rf}. The baseline dip in the experimental spectrum may be due to receiver nonlinearity.

The results for the spinlock experiment are shown in Figure 18.4. The experimental ^{23}Na MAS signal intensity as a function of spinlock time and the simulated signal intensity are compared as a function of "on-resonance" spinlock time for the experiment $(\pi/4)_x - SL_{\pm y}$ on sodium oxalate. The experimental data (thickest line) was obtained by selecting the first data point from each of a series of experiments in which the spinlock time was incremented by 20 μs. The simulation was obtained with series expansion ($\Delta t = 0.10$ μs) by adding observable traces from separate simulations for the two phases of the phase-alternated spinlock—that is, $Tr[I^+ \rho_1] + Tr[I^+ \rho_2]$, with ρ_1 corresponding to $(\pi/4)_x - SL_y$ and ρ_2 corresponding to $(\pi/4)_x - SL_{-y}$. In the simulation, the time propagation and rotor spinning were asynchronous, and the propagator was calculated anew

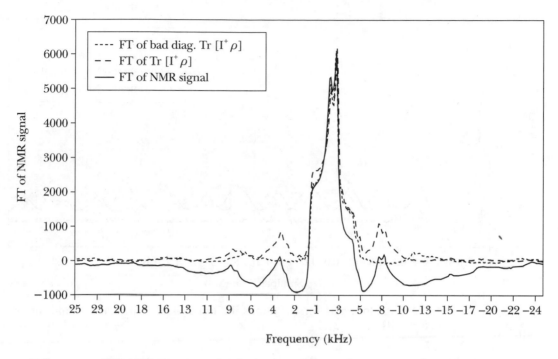

18.3

FIGURE

^{23}Na MAS spectrum of anhydrous sodium oxalate, $Na_2C_2O_4$ (I = 3/2, qcc = 2.52 MHz, η = 0.74, spinning rate = 5240 ± 10 Hz, ν_0 = 78.6596 MHz, ν_{rf} = 35.7 kHz). Experimental and simulated results obtained by FT of the NMR signal acquired after a single 3.5-μs pulse on resonance.

for each time increment. Also, the spinning rate for the asynchronous simulation was slightly off. Nevertheless, the simulation does an adequate job of duplicating the experimental data, except that the oscillations in the experimental data slowly die away, presumably due to $T_{1\rho}$ relaxation, which has been ignored in the simulations. As in the case of the single-pulse experiment, the spinlock data can also be successfully simulated with propagators calculated by complex diagonalization. Again, the results are identical to those obtained by series expansion if the time increments used in the complex diagonalization meet the criterion that $\Delta t < \{\mathrm{Tr}[H_{tot}^2]\}^{-1/2}$.

18.6.2   Interesting Scientific Results

A number of interesting results originated from this work. For the sake of brevity, we list only the most significant one. Unexpected results were obtained for $<\rho_{powder}(t)> = \mathrm{Tr}[\rho_{powder}(t)^2]$, where single-pulse $((\pi/4)_x - \mathrm{Acquire}_y)$ and

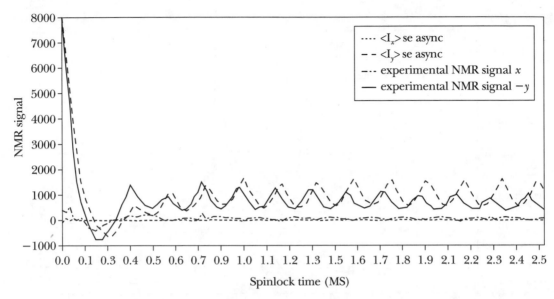

^{23}Na MAS spinlock data for anhydrous sodium oxalate. Experimental and simulated results.

spinlock $((\pi/4)_x - SL_{+y})$ simulations showed that ρ decays to a constant value over the period of a rotor cycle in the single-pulse experiment and oscillates at the rotor frequency after a sharp initial decay for the spinlock experiment. These results were initially surprising because we had naively expected to observe constant values for $<\rho_{powder}(t)>$. Serious consideration reveals that the decay in $<\rho_{powder}(t)>$ is due to destructive interference of density matrices from spins within microcrystallites with different orientations relative to the applied magnetic field. In addition, we have observed that the powder average density matrix itself can refocus as a spin echo, and we note that the phenomenon of destructive interference is the basis of the decay of the observable signal for "inhomogeneously broadened" solid-state NMR spectra. Figure 18.5 shows that the powder average expectation values $<\rho_{powder}(t)>$ and $<I_{y\text{-}powder}(t)>$ calculated for the single-pulse experiment decay sharply with time after the $(\pi/4)_x$ pulse. The loss in intensity with time for $<\rho_{powder}(t)>$ and $<I_{y\text{-}powder}(t)>$ arises from the dephasing and destructive interference of transverse components created by the pulse. For the observable signal $<I_{y\text{-}powder}(t)>$, this phenomenon is called *inhomogeneous line broadening* because of its dependence on different Euler angles and because of its effect on the spectrum obtained by Fourier transformation.

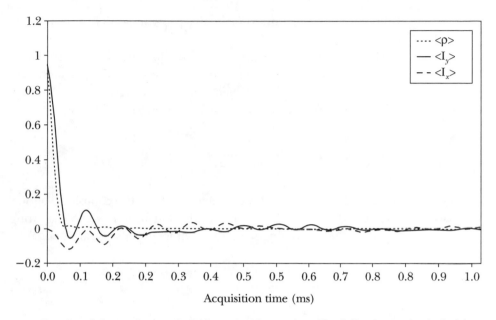

Simulated dependence of $<\rho(t)>$, $<I_{-y}(t)>$, and $<I_x(t)>$ following a single $(\pi/4)_x$ pulse to sodium oxalate undergoing MAS.

18.7 SUMMARY

Comparison between simulations with series expansion and the more standard complex diagonalization method shows that series expansion is about twice as fast at calculating the propagator for a given time increment and correspondingly faster for spectral simulations. Very small time increments are necessary for simulations when both the very large zeroth order average quadrupolar Hamiltonian (^0H_q) and the much smaller first order average quadrupolar Hamiltonian (^1H_q) are active, with $\Delta t < \{\mathrm{Tr}[(^0H_q + {}^1H_q)^2]\}^{-1/2}$. The calculation of the time dependence of the density matrix with such short time increments is a compute-intensive operation that motivated the migration to MPP platforms. The embarassingly parallel algorithm made it an ideally suited code for NUMA machines. The small size of the Hamiltonian and the powder average density matrix complemented the limited cache availability on the T3D. It therefore comes as no surprise that the resulting parallel NMR simulation program is one of the fastest scientific applications on the Cray T3D in terms of Mflops/PE. Future directions include generalization of the program to handle arbitrary Hamiltonians and pulse sequences and to make this program available to the worldwide NMR community.

The remaining challenge is to generalize the program so that it will be able to simulate solid-state powder spectra for any NMR experiment on any sample. Work is under way on this project. Once the program is validated, our plan is to make it available to solid-state NMR researchers worldwide.

ACKNOWLEDGMENTS

We thank P. D. Ellis for his valuable insight and the complex diagonalization routines. We would also like to thank the Pittsburgh Supercomputing Center for providing the computing resources that made this research possible.

References

[18.1]   Benesi, A. J. 1993. Series Expansion of Propagators. *J. Magnetic Resonance,* **103,** 230.

[18.2]   Brink, D. M., and G. R. Satchler. 1993. *Angular Momentum,* 3rd ed. Oxford: Clarendon Press.

[18.3]   Brooks, J. 1995. Single PE Optimization Techniques for the Cray T3D System. *Proc. 36th CUG,* Fall.

[18.4]   Gerstein, B. C., and C. R. Dybowski. 1985. *Transient Techniques in NMR of Solids.* New York: Academic Press.

[18.5]   Haeberlen, U. 1976. *Advances in Magnetic Resonance, Suppl. 1.* New York: Academic Press.

[18.6]   Mehring, M. 1983. *Principles of High Resolution NMR in Solids, 2nd ed.* Berlin: Springer-Verlag.

[18.7]   Vega, A. J. 1992. MAS NMR Spin Locking of Half-Integer Quadrupolar Nuclei. *J. Magnetic Resonance,* **96,** 50.

[18.8]   Vega, A. J. 1992. CP/MAS of Quadrupolar S = 3/2 Nuclei. *Solid State Nuclear Magnetic Resonance,* **1,** 17.

Molecular Dynamics Simulations Using Particle-Mesh Ewald Methods

Michael F. Crowley
David W. Deerfield II   Pittsburgh Supercomputing Center, Carnegie Mellon University

Tom A. Darden   National Institutes of Environmental Health Sciences

Thomas E. Cheatham III   DHHS/NIH/DCRT

19.1   INTRODUCTION: INDUSTRIAL CONSIDERATIONS

We report the enhancement of the molecular dynamics program AMBER by the porting of the particle-mesh Ewald method to MPP machines. The scaling with respect to number of processors has been effectively extended to more than 200 processors, a feature that makes possible multiple-nanosecond simulations of larger biomolecular systems.

19.1.1   Overview

Most biological functions can be traced back to the molecular level and the delicate interplay of the macromolecules with their environment of solvent, ions, and other molecules. An understanding of the structure of these biomolecules and of their dynamics and interactions gives insight into function or malfunction. For this reason, there is tremendous interest in developing and applying methods that elucidate the structure and dynamics of biological macromolecules, particularly under physiological conditions. X-ray crystallography gave the earliest glimpses into the structure of proteins and nucleic acids and continues to be an excellent tool for finding an average representative structure of a nucleic acid or protein, provided the molecule can be crystallized, often a major hurdle. Studies have shown that the positions of backbone atoms are not significantly affected by crystallizations, although the positions of the exposed side-chain atoms may be different than in the native conformation. This is a major problem in small molecules and small peptides but typically not a problem for proteins. Similarly, cosolvents added to aid crystallization may also interfere with the structure and lead to nonphysiological conditions. An additional limitation of X-ray crystallography is in the study of dynamics and structures that are highly flexible and tend to diffract to low resolution. NMR spectroscopy is another method that can be applied to investigate not only structure but dynamics of biological macromolecules. The difficulty of NMR is in assigning all the ^{1}H and ^{13}N resonances. Additionally, the information derived is short ranged—the only interactions detected are between atoms that are either less than 5 A apart or less than bonds away from each other. For folded proteins, this is not a terrible limitation. Even at these moderate distances, a substantial number of interactions and intramolecular contacts between residues that are distal in sequence are detected. However for double-helical nucleic acid structures, the short distances limitation makes the method less than optimal for investigating nucleic-acid bending.

An alternative method to studying the structure and dynamics is through simulation methods, such as molecular dynamics (MD). Ideally, we would like to represent all of the interactions of the protein or nucleic acid in its natural environment, which includes solvent and counter ions. Even though computer power has increased significantly over the past few years, the complexity of representing the energetics completely, such as through the application of quantum mechanics, prohibits the application to large biomolecular systems. Therefore, methods that apply a classical treatment with an empirically derived potential energy representation are often applied. Although this limits the application of the methods to systems where there is no bond forming or breaking or large polarization effects, the methods have proven extremely useful as an adjunct to experiment in providing insight into the structure and dynamics of protein and nucleic-acid systems. Thanks to advances in the empirical force field representations, the availability of significant computational resources (such as the Cray T3D and Cray T3E), and methods for performing molecular dynamics reliably, we can now simulate the dynamics of protein or nucleic acids with explicit solvent (representing on the order of 10,000 to 100,000 atoms) on a nanosecond time scale.

The focus of this discussion is on the parallelization of one of these enabling methods, the particle-mesh Ewald (PME) method. When coupled with a balanced force field and significant computational resources, it is now possible to simulate a variety of systems reliably, including highly charged systems. This chapter describes the efforts we have made to enhance the speed of AMBER and the capability to treat larger systems for longer simulation times using the large MPP machines, Cray T3D and T3E. The approach has many features that are applicable to other parallel computing arrangements.

Before the advent of the Cray MPP architecture and the PME method, simulations of highly charged systems were marked by instability and were limited to very short time scales (less than 200 ps). Specific examples include the simulation of small DNA duplexes in water and water/ethanol mixtures with the goal of representing the subtle effect of the environment on the nucleic acid and of studying the interaction of highly charged metals and ions with proteins. Thanks to the recent advances and the parallelization of the code, we look forward to future scalable node and SMP architectures to push the simulations to the next level. It is expected that the work described here will serve as a basis for this next generation.

MD is used to study many different aspects of substances and mixtures. A researcher uses MD to study the thermal motion of molecules for time periods of between 1 ps to several ns and for systems whose sizes range from tens to several hundred angstroms in each dimension. The motion is determined by the energetics of a model of the system of atoms. Differential equations for the positions and velocities of the atoms are generated from the Hamiltonian and are solved numerically to determine the time evolution of the state of the system as defined by the equations. One can determine a low energy state by removing kinetic energy from the system as the equations are solved. The interactions between molecules can be observed, and the contributions of different parts of the system can be quantified. Each time step in the simulation can be considered a state of the system and the collection of states can be used to generate ensembles of states, which, in turn, can be used to determine thermodynamic quantities. Of course, with all MD studies, care must be taken to ensure that the limitations and approximations of the method, the model, and the particular simulation are considered meticulously.

An MD step as performed in AMBER consists of three calculations: determining the energy of a system and the forces on atom centers, moving the atoms according to the forces, and adjusting temperature and pressure. Energies and forces can be approximated to many levels of precision. Ultimately, a time-dependent quantum-mechanical description of the system would yield the best models. Realistically, biomolecular simulations exceed the current computer resources even when a much simpler empirical representation of the energetics is applied. Most MD models treat atoms classically as points with mass and charge. The atomic points interact with other atomic points through pairwise interactions from chemical bonds, electrostatic interactions, and van der Waals interactions. Forces are the gradients of the energy, and particles move according to Newton's laws. With the atomic structure approximated as massive charged points, accuracy of the dynamical behavior of the model will rely heavily on the behavior of the empirical expression of the interactions, the force field. There are many excellent reviews of the methods of molecular dynamics [19.23, 19.25]; we will concentrate here on the topic of the particle-mesh Ewald method, the methods we use on MPP machines, and the issues that concern these methods.

A typical biochemical problem that MD might address has a biomolecule for solute, ions, and solvent molecules. The force on each atom is represented as the combination of the contributions from iterations with atoms that are chemically bonded to it and the nonbond iterations with the other atoms. The AMBER force field [19.5] has a simple functional form that models the energies and forces arising from the chemical bonds and angles as harmonic springs and the dihedral angles as a sum of Fourier terms. Because the functional form is simple and there are few of these bonds and angles compared to the nonbonded interactions, this part of the calculation is very fast. The nonbond energy is also broken into two contributions: van der Waals and electrostatic interactions. The simplified overall energy equation is

$$E_{\text{total}} = \sum_{\text{bonds}} K_r (r - r_{eq})^2 + \sum_{\text{angles}} K_\theta (\theta - \theta_{eq})^2 + \sum_{\text{dihedrals}} \frac{V_n}{2} [1 + \cos(n\phi - \gamma)]$$
$$+ \sum_i \sum_{j<i} \left[\frac{A_{ij}}{R_{ij}^{12}} - \frac{B_{ij}}{R_{ij}^6} \right] + \sum_i \sum_{j<i} \left[\frac{q_i q_j}{\varepsilon R_{ij}} \right]$$

(19.1)

where the first three terms are the bond terms and the latter two are the nonbond terms. Molecules are treated as permanent structures in which no covalent bond breakage or formation is allowed; the numbers of bonds, bond angles, and bond dihedrals remain constant.

19.1.2   Cutoff Problem for Long-Distance Forces

The double sum of the nonbond terms makes the number of those calculations scale with an order of N^2, where N is the number of atoms. As the size of the system increases, N^2 becomes a very large number, and, in the case of periodic boundary conditions, the nonbond sums become infinite sums.

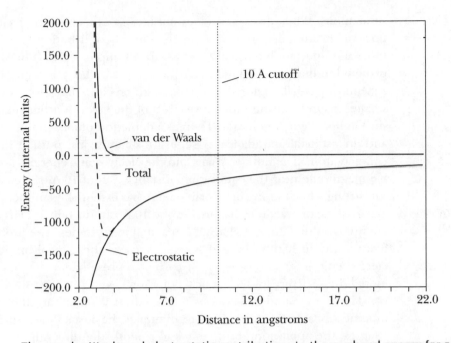

The van der Waals and electrostatic contributions to the nonbond energy for a sodium and a chloride ion in a vacuum are shown as a function of the inter atomic distance. The van der Waals contribution dominates for less than 3 A but is insignificant at 10 A or greater. The electrostatic component is dominant and significantly nonzero from 4 A out well past the 22 A limit of this figure.

The scaling problem is overcome by using a cutoff distance. Atom pairs that are separated by a distance greater than this cutoff are not included in the sums. For the van der Waals interactions, this is an acceptable solution and limits the number of nonbond interactions in the sum to $N*$(number of atoms in cutoff sphere). The value of the $(-A/r^6 + B/r^{12})$ at a cutoff of 10 A is 10^{-4} of its value at the equilibrium distance. The missing force, from atoms beyond the cutoff distance, is always attractive; the missing energy is always negative; and the magnitude of each is nearly constant and usually isotropic. The error could be estimated and corrected at each time step. On the other hand, the electrostatic sum has a very large error, 10 percent or greater, when a 10 A cutoff is introduced. The error is indeterminate in sign, and when there are charges greater than 0.5e (elementary charge), it has significant magnitude with respect to the total energy and can drastically affect the behavior of the system. Figure 19.1 illustrates the magnitude of the problem for a system with a sodium and a chloride ion. Although this is an extreme case, ions always have significant electrostatic contributions to the forces on atoms 10 A distant, and this must be accounted for in most simulations. While this system does not represent a common occurrence in nature, the magnitudes of the charges and energy contributions are comparable to those in important biological systems—for example, a Ca(II) or Mg(II) ion in a protein binding site, a bound Fe(III), or even a carboxyl group. Although many systems of partially charged molecules and ions in polar solvents show errors of smaller magnitude, the cumulative effect of the errors is artifactual and often results in nonphysical behavior. There is a depletion of ions in the 5–10 A distance and an artificial abundance of repulsive charges just outside the cutoff of a charged atom. The van der Waals and the electrostatic energies are of comparable magnitude near the equilibrium distance, but at 10 A, the electrostatics are still strong while the van der Waals energy has essentially vanished. Ignoring the electrostatic interactions that are beyond 10 A can introduce a large error in the energy, resulting in forces having artifactual magnitudes. The problem is particularly acute in highly charged systems, such as those involving ions or strong electrostatic interactions, where a correct representation is critical to reliably model the structure and dynamical behavior.

The most common solutions to the cutoff problem are the application of modifications to the force field to diminish the instabilities, such as reduced charges; the application of methods to smooth the discontinuity at the cutoff, such as switching functions at the cutoff [19.22]; particle-mesh methods [19.12]; and fast-multipole methods [19.10, 19.11]. The first method is a well-defined approximation, and the latter two are nearly exact treatments of the long-range effects. The cutoff method has been questioned and studied to determine what anomalous behavior is due to the approximations [19.17]. In this chapter, we will discuss atom-based cutoffs exclusively. Many codes use a variation of a residue- or group-based cutoff in which, for example, if one atom of a residue is within the cutoff distance, then all atoms in the residue are included in the nonbonded list. The purpose of the residue- or group-based cutoff was to help correct discontinuities at the cutoff distance. Since the PME method computes all electrostatic forces, it uses an atom-based cutoff. At present, Darden has implemented PME into AMBER [19.7], and this chapter addresses the parallel approach we have taken to use large MPP hardware for simulations using PME.

AMBER currently uses a replicated data approach to its parallel calculations [19.26]. The model provides flexibility in the methods of distributing computational work, though it suffers from communications overhead when collecting and broadcasting coordinates and forces for the entire system to all processors at each step. Each of the first three sums in Equation (19.1) is evenly divided among the processors. Non-PME AMBER divides the latter two sums using dynamic load balancing. In the PME scheme, the latter two sums are not as simple as in Equation (19.1).

19.1.3   Particle-Mesh Ewald Method

The particle-mesh Ewald method [19.7, 19.9] of determining electrostatic inter-actions was developed to enable the calculation of the long-range attractions and repulsions that are essential contributions to the structure and functioning of many macromolecules. Here, we will give an overview of the method and the equations especially as they apply to the implementation on massively parallel computers. For the complete and detailed derivation of the method, see [19.9]. In MD simulations, PME determines the energy and forces due to the collection of point charges at the atom centers. The Ewald method expands the simple sum of Coulomb's law terms, the last sum in Equation (19.1), into several sums:

$$E(\text{electrostatic}) = E(\text{direct}) + E(\text{reciprocal}) + E(\text{correction}) \qquad (19.2)$$

Except for an extra erfc factor ($\text{erf}(x) = 1 - \text{erfc}(x)$ is the error function), the direct sum, $E(\text{direct})$, is identical to the sum in the cutoff method that calculates the electrostatic potential energy:

$$E(\text{direct}) = \sum_{i,j=1}^{N} \left(\frac{q_i\, q_j\, \text{erfc}(\beta r_{ij})}{r_{ij}} \right) \qquad (19.3)$$

where r_{ij} is the distance between atom i and atom j. The erfc factor forces the val-ues of terms at a finite value of r_{ij} to be vanishingly small. The adjustable parame-ter, β, determines the cutoff radius for this sum. In practice, we choose β so that the cutoff for the direct sum is the same as that for the van der Waals sum, usually around 10 A.

The reciprocal sum is the major part of the electrostatic energy that the di-rect sum misses due to the erfc factor:

$$E(\text{reciprocal}) = \frac{1}{2\pi V} \sum_{m} \frac{\exp(-\pi^2 m^2/\beta^2)}{m^2} S(m)S(-m) \qquad (19.4)$$

where m is a reciprocal lattice vector as defined in [19.9], and the structure fac-tors, $S(m)$, are given by

$$S(m) = \sum_{j=1}^{N} q_j \exp(2\pi i m \cdot r_j) \qquad (19.5)$$

The structure factors in this sum have a form that is nearly a discrete Fourier transform. The reciprocal sum overcounts the electrostatic potential because it determines the reciprocal energy for charges with themselves and for charge interactions that are already included in other parts of the potential (such as the bond interactions). The correction sums remove this overdetermination of energy:

$$E(\text{correction}) = \frac{1}{2} \sum_{i,j \in M} \left(\frac{q_i q_j \text{erfc}(\beta r_{ij})}{r_{ij}} \right) - \frac{\beta}{\sqrt{\pi}} \sum_{i=1}^{N} q_i^2 \qquad (19.6)$$

The particle-mesh approximation, an approximation that turns the structure factors into discrete Fourier transforms, makes the reciprocal energy more computationally tractable. The structure factors as expressed in Equation (19.5) can be expanded to

$$S(m_1, m_2, m_3) = \sum_{j=1}^{N} q_j \exp[(2\pi i(m_1 s_{1j} + m_3 s_{3j})] \qquad (19.7)$$

where m_1, m_2, and m_3 are integers, and s_1, s_2, and s_3 are fractional coordinates. The structure factor has the form of a discrete Fourier transform except that the s_j's are irregularly spaced rather than being on a regular subgrid. Instead of using the atomic charges and positions, we replace them with an approximate replica of space with charges positioned on a regular 3D grid. The approximation improves when a finer grid is used. In practice, we find that a grid with 1 A between points produces a reciprocal energy to the same or better precision than the cutoff in the direct sum and the van der Waals sum. The charges can be assigned to the grid by several interpolating methods; fourth order Cardinal B-splines are used in the implementation of PME in AMBER. The approximate structure factor is now

$$S(m_1, m_2, m_3) = b_1(m_1)b_2(m_2(b_3(m_3)T(Q)(m_1, m_2, m_3) \qquad (19.8)$$

where T is the discrete Fourier transform, Q is the charge grid just described, and b_i are coefficients from the Cardinal B-spline approximation. With these approximate structure factors, a final form of $E(\text{reciprocal})$ can be generated:

$$E(\text{reciprocal}) = \frac{1}{2} \sum_{m_1} \sum_{m_2} \sum_{m_3} Q(m_1, m_2, m_3)(\Theta * Q)(m_1, m_2, m_3) \qquad (19.9)$$

where * is the convolution operator and

$$\Theta(l_1,l_2,l_3) = \Im\left[b_1(m_1)^2\, b_2(m_2)^2\, b_3(m_3)^2\, \frac{\exp\left(\frac{\pi^2 m^2}{\beta^2}\right)}{m^2}\right] \tag{19.10}$$

The Convolution theorem allows us to calculate the convolution in Equation (19.9) by

$$(\Theta*Q)(m_1,m_2,m_3) = K_1 K_2 K_3\left[T^{-1}(\Theta)T^{-1}(Q)\right](m_1,m_2,m_3) \tag{19.11}$$

The electrostatic energy, Equation (19.2), is approximated by the sum of Equations (19.3, 19.6, and 19.9). The contributions of the electrostatic interactions to the forces on the atom centers and the stress tensor are calculated analytically from the derivatives of Equations (19.3, 19.6, and 19.9).

19.2   COMPUTATIONAL CONSIDERATIONS

The quality of the scientific information produced by a MD simulation depends heavily on the length of the simulation and the severity of the approximations. Refining approximations in MD entails using longer cutoffs, larger water baths, and increased precision. There are never enough computer cycles to simulate biomolecules that are waiting to be studied. Faster algorithms and faster computers are needed before many already known biomedical problems can even begin to be solved. MPP machines were a breakthrough for some exciting research.

19.2.1   Why Use an MPP?

Unparalleled computing power was released with the Cray T3D. The structural biology community saw the possibility of starting to tackle the larger problems that were, until then, unapproachable. Methods of distributing work already existed from work on workstation clusters and older parallel architectures, but the communications bandwidth of the T3D made parallel processing a profitable method. The PME method used more CPU cycles to perform and had not yet been parallelized, and the vector version performed modestly, so a parallel version for the MPP architecture was created. The current version of the PME calculation, which includes the PME treatment of electrostatics and the normal treatment of the van der Waals interactions, scales very well and has opened the door for calculations of unprecedented size and length.

Even with the current successes of the MPP version of parallel PME, there are many improvements that can still be made to improve scaling and performance. We are pursuing these now and expect another leap in performance soon. The T3E will be the machine of choice for large and long MD computations for some time to come.

19.2.2   Parallel PME

Our goal in the work described here was to minimize wall clock time and maximize scaling with large numbers of processors; we have not yet optimized for fewer floating-point or integer operations nor included any other efficiency optimizations unless they had a significant effect on the wall clock time. Our approach to parallel computing is to distribute the work as equally as possible, keep communications to a minimum, and avoid duplicate work. Unfortunately, duplicate work is only avoided in most cases by methods that require communications; the converse is true also. We look for the combination of duplicate work and communications that will optimize the scaling of the parallel calculation; that is, the combination that takes the least time and produces the most independent parallel work. Each part of the electrostatic energy and force calculation is parallelized in a different manner and is discussed separately.

The direct energy determination, Equation (19.3), is a sum over all pairs of atoms except atoms with themselves and atom pairs whose electrostatic energy has already been included in the bonded energy determination. With β chosen so that the effective cutoff is the same as the cutoff used in the van der Waals sum—for example, 10 A—both the van der Waals and the direct electrostatic sums use the same list of pairs. In fact, both of these determinations can be done in the same loop over pairs. The pairlist, also known as the nonbond list, is the list of all atom pairs that are closer than the cutoff distance and is identical to the list used by the serial version of the PME method. The parallelization consists of no more than dividing this list equally among processors. One problem with this simple approach is that the pairlist must be known before each processor can determine and start its part of the van der Waals and direct electrostatic sum. The generation of the list is not perfectly parallel, and a brief description is appropriate.

The construction of the atom-based list is distributed by dividing the unit cell into subcells and assigning an equal number of subcells to each processor. For most simulations, a homogeneous density of atoms is a good approximation,

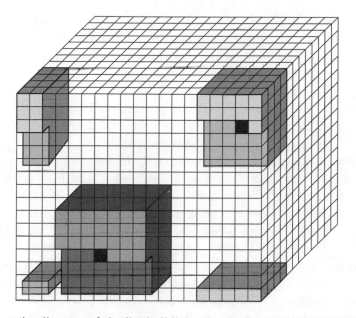

19.2

FIGURE

The diagram of the list-building subcells shows the subcells that are searched for pair atoms. For an atom in the black subcells, atoms in each of the subcells that are ahead of that subcell and within three subcells are searched for atoms that are within the cutoff distance. Atoms that are in the same subcell are also in that atom's pairlist, but not if that pair is already in another atom's pairlist. When the black subcell is near the edge of the unit cell, subcells across the periodic boundary are searched on the opposite side of the unit cell, as is evident in the hashed subcells that are searched for pairs of atoms in the black subcell on the upper right.

and the number of atoms in the assigned subcells will be nearly the same for each processor. The list of pairs for each atom in the assigned subcells is built by searching the neighboring subcells for atoms that are within the cutoff. Only subcells that are ahead in a chosen subcell numbering scheme are included in the search so that pairs are not placed in the list twice. Atom pairs that are in the bonded lists are left out because all the contributions to the energy and forces from those pair interactions are calculated in the bond sums. Figure 19.2 is a diagram of the subcells and the search scheme. Subcells are determined so that their dimension is at least one-third the cutoff distance. Only atoms in the same subcell or subcells ahead and within three subcells distance are searched for atom pairs. Although the search part of the list build scales perfectly, the setup of the subcells does not. There is no way to know which atoms are in which subcell unless all atoms are assigned to subcells first. The subcell location of each atom is determined for all atoms on all the processors. This duplicate work could be done in a distributed fashion, but the results would have to be communicated. Our present approach is to duplicate the work.

In a typical problem, the cutoff is 9 A, the unit cell edge is about 60 A, and, consequently, the subcells are cubes with edge length of approximately 3 A. There are $20 \times 20 \times 20$, or 8000, subcells numbered 1 to 8000. For 8 PEs, each PE would be assigned 1000 contiguous subcells. Assuming that the atom density in the unit cell is homogeneous, the PEs will have been assigned approximately the same number of atoms in their subcell blocks. For each atom, i, in each of the assigned subcells, all atoms that are (1) within the cutoff and (2) either in the same subcell or in a subcell numbered higher than atom i's subcell number are paired with atom i. This process generates the pairlist for each PE locally and the entire pairlist across the machine, divides the pairlist almost equally among the PEs, and divides the work of generating the pairlist fairly—all without prior knowledge of the size of the pairlist and without interprocessor communications. In the current implementation, the only duplicated work is the generation of the subcells and the lists of atoms in each subcell.

Each processor executes the direct sum on its portion of the pairlist and stores the resulting energy and forces locally. Global summing of the energy and forces across all processors is done after all other contributions—that is, bonded, reciprocal, and correction sums—are calculated. The correction sums are distributed by the simple method because all PEs have the list of atoms and the list of masked pairs, the pairs whose van der Waals and electrostatic energies are calculated in the bond sums. Each PE executes its portion of each list without communications and little duplicate work.

The calculation of the reciprocal energy and the resulting forces has several well-defined steps:

1. Determine the B-spline coefficients.

2. Fill the charge grid.

3. Calculate an inverse FFT of the grid.

4. Evaluate Equation (19.10) and overwrite Q with an inverse-transformed convolution.

5. Forward FFT on the new Q to generate the convolution.

6. Generate the forces using the convolution and Equation (4.9) of [19.9].

The entire reciprocal energy and force calculation is distributed by dividing the charge grid, Q, into equal parts for each PE. However, this division is done judiciously to optimize the FFT calculation and minimize communications between processors. The constraint we chose was to limit the breakdown of the grid to x-y planes, which limits the scaling to the number of planes. We will discuss the solution to that problem later. The parallel 3D FFT, which we discuss in Section 19.3.2, is a stand-alone routine that is tailored to this problem.

To approximate the charge density on the grid, we use a fourth order B-splines method [19.16], which spreads the charge onto a $4 \times 4 \times 4$ portion of the grid. This requires four B-spline coefficients in each of the three directions for each atom in the system. When each processor generates all of the coefficients for all of the atoms, the time taken for this duplicate work is not significant for eight or fewer processors, but becomes dominant for large numbers of processors when the other portions of the calculation are scaling well. The simplest parallelization is for each PE to determine only the coefficients for atoms that have charge density in the grid planes assigned to the processor. This improves scaling considerably, but duplicated work still remains. The B-spline coefficients for atoms that contribute to the planes of more than one PE are determined more than once. At the limit of number of PEs equal to the number of x-y planes in the grid (the z-dimension), one plane is assigned to each processor, and all the coefficients are calculated four times. In our final parallelization, each PE calculates the B-splines only for atoms in its assigned planes. Coefficients for three more planes of atoms are needed to create its portion of the grid. Neighboring PEs will have calculated those coefficients and will send them to the PEs that need them. On MPPs with fast communications, this is faster than calculating the coefficients locally and results in better scaling even with the communications. It is important to note that the communications are not global, but are only between nearby processors. There is still duplicate work because each processor must determine which atoms are in its assigned grid layers by examining the location of every atom and building a list of atoms in its assigned layers.

The charge grid is generated from the charges and the B-splines; the work is evenly distributed when the grid is evenly distributed. The list of atoms contributing to the grid points is saved from the B-spline step and is used in this step and the last step. With the charge grid filled, the inverse FFT is performed. The most efficient invocation of the FFT leaves the data distributed in *x-z* planes contiguous in the *z* direction. The orientation is irrelevant because the only work done in reciprocal space is an element-by-element multiplication (the convolution) and a sum over all elements. The convolution is produced after a forward parallel 3D FFT and is in the original *x-y* plane orientation. The final sums to produce the forces are still distributed over the *x-y* planes and add contributions to the forces on the atoms in the above list. A more detailed description of our parallel 3D FFT is in [19.6].

The nonbond energy and nonbond forces are determined in parallel. Figure 19.3 is a schematic diagram of the order of tasks performed and approximate amount of work in each task. All tasks are distributed across all processors, and a subsequent task is not performed until all processors have finished the current task. The direct calculations are parallel except for the duplication of work in setting up the list-building subcells. The reciprocal calculation is parallel to the degree that the number of PEs is a factor of the number of planes in the grid. There are no communications in this scheme except for the passing of spline coefficients between nearby processors and the communications that are used in the transpose in the 3D FFT.

19.2.3   Coarse-Grain Parallel PME

The algorithm for improving performance of AMBER/PME when the number of processors exceeds the number of planes splits the PEs into two groups, one for reciprocal energy work and the other for direct energy work (see Figure 19.4). The sums in Equations (19.3 and 19.4) are independent and can be done simultaneously by two separate groups of processors. Both the reciprocal group and the direct group of PEs accomplish their calculations using the fine-grain parallel approach we have described. With this method, a larger set of processors can be used efficiently.

The two groups should be of a size that will ensure that they finish at about the same time. All forces need to be collected and broadcast before new coordinates can be determined. The partition sizes of each group can be determined by trial and error using short test runs. The direct sum and reciprocal sum work are constant throughout the simulation, and, once the division is determined, most MD problems will not need a redistribution. A dynamic load-balancing mechanism is in place, but it unnecessarily slows the simulation; we have never seen a redistribution after the optimal distribution has been determined.

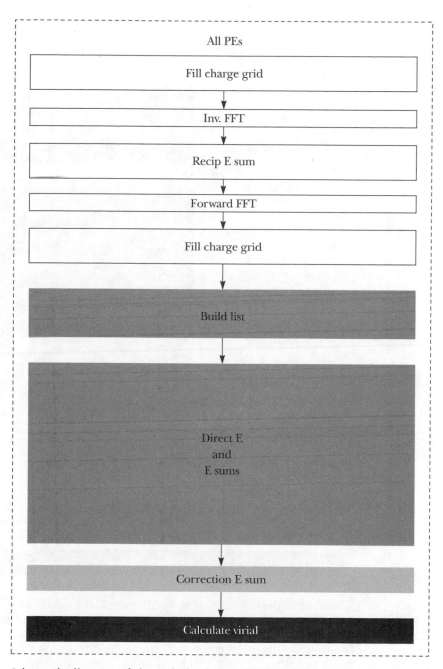

All PEs

Fill charge grid

Inv. FFT

Recip E sum

Forward FFT

Fill charge grid

Build list

Direct E
and
E sums

Correction E sum

Calculate virial

19.3

FIGURE

Schematic diagram of the tasks in the parallel PME calculation. The dashed line indicates the global group of processors over which each task is distributed. Each task in this calculation is distributed across all processors. Each task is finished by all processors before the next task is begun.

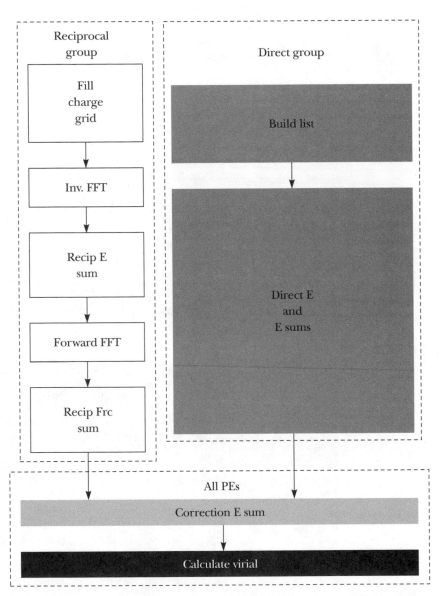

Schematic of the distribution of work for the PME calculation divided into tasks
and distributed between two different groups of processors. About one-third of
the processors are put in the reciprocal group to do the reciprocal tasks and
two-thirds in the direct group to calculate the direct sum. When both tasks are
done, all PEs rejoin the global group and complete the PME calculation with
work distributed among all PEs.

19.3 COMPUTATIONAL RESULTS

Parallel PME performs on the Cray T3D and T3E with an efficiency that makes possible the large simulations many researchers are waiting to do. There are parts of the algorithm where the duplicate work or communications hurt the performance, and to see those areas we show the performance of each part separately.

19.3.1 Performance

The whole algorithm performs at up to 70 percent efficiency on 256 processors, or at 170 times the speed of one processor doing the same work.

The parallel sums in the direct electrostatic and van der Waals sums scale perfectly; 256 processors run 256 times faster than one processor. This is no surprise because the sums are set up to be parallel with no communications or duplicate work by the list building. The only potential source of inefficiency is in the load balance, which assumes that there is a homogeneous density of atoms in the unit cell. As seen in Figure 19.5, there is no load-balancing problem with the direct sums.

Figure 19.5 also shows the performance of the list-building algorithm (diamond symbols). The scaling degrades at higher numbers of processors. The source of degradation is the duplicate work in assigning atoms to grid cells; the actual list building scales perfectly. The duplicate work can be resolved to make this part of the problem even better. The list building is performed every 10th step, in general, and does not harm the overall performance as severely as if it were determined every step.

The performance of the reciprocal space calculation is determined by its many parts. The grid-building algorithm has duplicate work, which is significant when the number of planes assigned to each processor is 2 or 1. Figure 19.6 shows as open circles the scaling performance for generating the $60 \times 60 \times 60$ grid. The scaling degrades significantly after 30 processors. The speedup plateaus from 30 to 59 processors because we have limited the grain of work division to x-y planes, and at least one PE will fill two planes while others are filling either one or two planes. The time for the grid filling will be constant and equal to the time for one PE to fill two planes. At 60 processors, the scaling is unacceptable and is due to the duplicated work and communications. Each of the 60 PEs generates one plane, searches through the entire atom list, and communicates with three neighboring PEs. For this part of the reciprocal calculation, on a $60 \times$

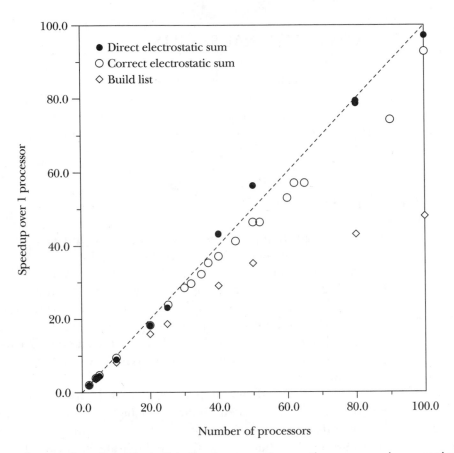

19.5 FIGURE The speedup of the list build, direct sum, and correction sum are shown against the number of processors, where Speedup for N processors = [2*(time for 2 processors)/(time for N processors)].

60×60 grid, 20 or 30 processors give the best performance. There is still a significant speedup for 60 processors over 30, but the efficiency is less than 50 percent. Above 60 processors, there will be 60 processors filling the 60 x-y planes of the grid and the rest will be idle. Figure 19.6 shows a constant time for filling the grid with 60 processors or more.

The other reciprocal work, including the FFTs, energy sum, and force sum, shows reasonable scaling in Figure 19.6 until the limit of the work distribution is reached—in this case, 60 processors. For more processors than 60, there is no speedup because the algorithm has no finer grain than the dimension of the grid.

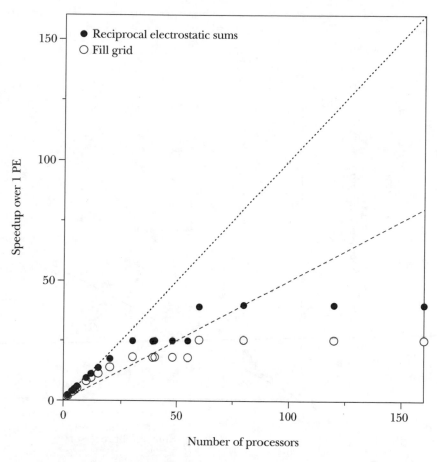

Speedup for the reciprocal calculation is shown for the 60 × 60 × 60 mesh of the sample problem. Open circles are the speedup for just the grid-building portion of the reciprocal calculation; solid circles are for the rest of the recipro-cal calculation: the FFTs, reciprocal sum in reciprocal space, and the force sum in real space.

Figure 19.7 shows the efficiency of the parallel PME force calculation on the Cray T3E. When two groups are not used, the speed of the calculation levels off because the reciprocal sum time remains constant after the number of PEs ex-ceeds the dimension of the charge grid, which, in this case, is a cubic grid of di-mension 60. When the coarse-grain parallel method is used, the speedup contin-ues past 60 PEs but will level off again when the reciprocal group size reaches the grid dimension. Adding PEs to the reciprocal group beyond this number

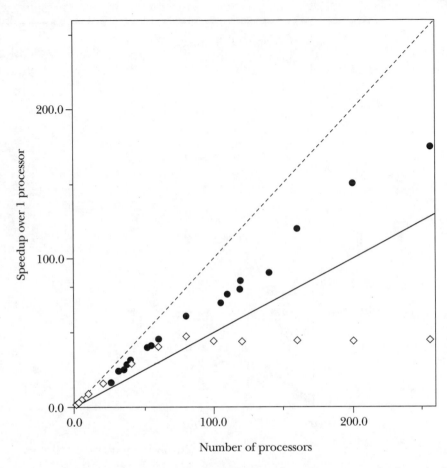

19.7

FIGURE

Speedup of the PME calculation versus the number of processors in the calculation. Diamond symbols indicate the speedup of the calculation for the single
global group operation as described in Section 19.2.2. Solid circles show
speedup of the calculation when the tasks are distributed in reciprocal and direct groups, as discussed in Section 19.3.2 and pictured in Figure 19.4. The
speedups for the fastest division between reciprocal and direct processor groups
is shown for each value of total PEs.

does not reduce the reciprocal time. The time for the direct and reciprocal
sums is a constant equal to the reciprocal time, no matter how many PEs are
added to the reciprocal or direct group. However, this limit will not be reached
until well above 200 PEs in this case, and the limit is higher the higher the FFT
dimensions are.

The coarse-grain parallel method is also advantageous for MPPs and clusters with slower communications. The transpose becomes a bottleneck in these cases. Using two groups of PEs cuts the number of reciprocal PEs by one-half to one-fourth of the global PE group. The total data that is passed may not change drastically, but the number of messages passed is considerably smaller. If the number of reciprocal group PEs, N_{rec}, is one-half of the global group with N_{tot} PEs, the ratio of data passed during the transpose with N_{rec} to the data passed with N_{tot} is

$$\frac{N_{tot} - 4}{N_{tot} - 1} \qquad (19.12)$$

For $N_{tot} = 32$, N_{rec} would be 8 and the ratio in Equation (19.12) would be 28/31; most of the data is still passed. On the brighter side, the number of messages passed would be in the ratio

$$\frac{N_{tot} - 4}{16(N_{tot} - 1)} \qquad (19.13)$$

which, for $N_{tot} = 32$, $N_{rec} = 8$, is 7/124, a small fraction of the messages sent during a transpose with 32 PEs. This is a large savings when message latency is large. In the special case of $N_{tot} = 4$ and $N_{rec} = 1$, using groups keeps the entire reciprocal energy determination on one PE. There are no communications necessary. In this way, the product of the PATP effort for producing parallel PME molecular dynamics programs for the Cray MPP machines will also benefit smaller, slower environments, though these will never approach the performance of the MPP architecture.

19.3.2 Parallel 3D FFT and Groups

The parallel 3D FFT that we developed for AMBER/PME for Cray MPP machines is distributed at the level of 2D layers. Finer-grain parallelization is possible, even at the level of the sums internal to the 1D FFTs. Knowledge of the requirements and structure of our application has helped specify the most efficient level of parallelization. The important features of the problem are that the data comes to the FFT already distributed, the array dimensions are small, and the orientation of the transformed data is not important as long as the reverse transform puts the data back in original orientation. The FFT can be done with a single transpose in this case if the data is originally distributed in complete planes.

A 3D FFT is accomplished by performing 1D FFTs in each of the three Cartesian directions. In our parallel implementation, we require that the data be already distributed in slabs of x-y planes. In the current version, we are doing complex-to-complex 3D discrete Fourier transforms, and we are implementing the real-to-complex version. First, 1D FFTs are performed locally on all PEs in the x direction and then the y direction, leaving all planes 2D transformed. The grid is then transposed across processors, leaving the data distributed in slabs of x-z planes on each processor and with the grid oriented so that the data is contiguous in the z direction. This particular transpose facilitates the z FFT. Both inverse and forward 3D FFTs can be performed in this manner. Our 1D FFTs can be any garden-variety FFT from installed libraries. Both the Cray and SGI FFTs are highly optimized and are the chosen 1D FFTs for this application, although we have found the netlib FFT to perform almost at the same speed.

The stand-alone version of the parallel 3D FFT has two options for the orientation of the final grid: It can be left in the z-x plane configuration or transposed back to the original x-y plane orientation. In the PME algorithm, it is much more efficient to leave the data in the z-x planes and eliminate the communications that the second transpose requires. The first FFT in the reciprocal energy calculation is an inverse FFT. After the inverse 3D FFT, the sum and product in reciprocal space are executed with no change in grid orientation; the grid is in the z-x planes. For the forward FFT, the grid is still in the z-x planes and facilitates a z direction 1D FFT as the first step. Data is transposed back to the original x-y planes and the y and x forward 1D FFTs are calculated. The forward 3D FFT done in this way is the exact reverse of the earlier inverse 3D FFT when the data is left in the z-x plane orientation. We have two routines for the 3D FFT: one that takes the grid distributed in x-y planes and returns the result in either the original distributed x-y planes or in the distributed z-x planes, and the other that will transform the z-x-oriented grid and returns the result in the x-y planes. The first is a general 3D FFT and can be used for both forward and inverse FFTs. The distribution of work in this 3D transform calculation is simple since all 1D FFTs are done locally: first the x and y FFTs and, after the transpose, the z FFTs are done in place and locally. The only tricky part is transposing across the processors to change the orientation of the grid in the distributed memory of the MPP and in the local memory of each PE. The transpose is the only work that will not scale in a desirable way with higher numbers of processors.

A transpose consists of moving data from PE to PE and rearranging the data on the target PE (Figure 19.8). Before our transpose, the data is in x-y planes, contiguous in the x direction. The final configuration has the data in z-x planes with the data contiguous in the z direction. The intersection of the pretranspose

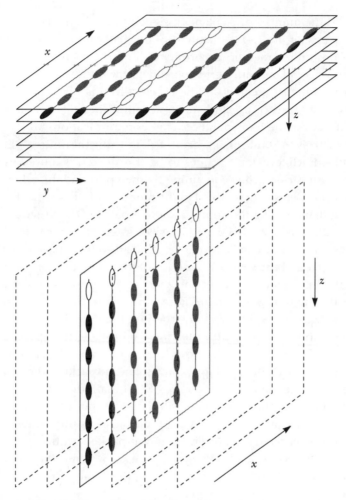

Data is distributed in slabs of *x-y* planes for the 3D FFT with the data contiguous in the *x* direction. In the transpose, an *x*-vector of complex numbers must be moved from its *x-y* plane to the n_x *z*-vectors in the appropriate *z-x* plane. The real and complex parts of the original data are in memory with stride 2, and they are stride n_x in the destination *z-x* plane so that the data will end up contiguous in the *z* direction.

x-y planes of PE_i with the *z-x* planes of PE_j contains the data that must be moved from PE_i to PE_j. The rows (*x*-vectors) that move from PE_i to PE_j are all the ones in the *x-y* planes of PE_i with *y*-index in the range of the *z* planes of PE_js *z-x* planes. This is a rectangular prism of complex numbers with dimensions $n_x * m_i^{xy} * m_j^{zx}$, where n_x is the *x* dimension of the grid, m_i^{xy} is the number of *x-y* planes of PE_i, and m_j^{zx} is the number of z-x planes assigned to PE$_j$ in the transposed grid. There are, of course, $n_x * m_i^{xy} * m_i^{zx}$ members of the grid on PE$_i$ that stay on PE$_i$ and only change position in memory according to the new orientation of data. The x-vector from r^{th} x-y plane with y grid coordinate s will transpose into the sth z-x plane and have all the rth members of the z-vectors in that plane (see Figure 19.9).

The transpose of a grid can be accomplished in several ways. The most efficient way that we have found on a fast-communications MPP machine like the T3D or T3E is to send small pieces of data from the source PE to each of the other PEs. Each x-vector of values to be transferred is moved as two vectors of length n_x and stride 2, one containing the real part and the other containing the complex part. This data is placed in the memory of PE$_j$ so that it spans the appropriate z-x plane, filling the appropriate real parts of the z-vectors—that is, with a stride of $2n_z$. The Cray SHMEM library of interprocessor communications routines has a strided put and a strided get that allow for different strides of the data on the target and the source PE and move data directly from one PE memory to the other PE memory without the send and receive protocol and processing overhead. The transpose is quite fast when we use this method of data transfer, nearly twice as fast as the second method on the Cray T3E.

The second method of transferring data for the transpose consists of packing all the data that needs to move between a pair of PEs into a single buffer array on the source PE, passing the array, and unpacking the array into the correct spots in memory on the target PE. This method is suited to clusters of workstations and other computers with large latency communications. The first method, with its large number of small messages, is unbearably slow when messages must be packed, sent, received, and unpacked, with a long latency for each message. The second method has only one pack, send, receive, unpack, and latency for each PE-to-PE transfer. Even if the bandwidth is large, the second method is preferable when latency is high.

One of the limitations of this 3D FFT is it can only divide work into at most n_z or n_y ways, whichever is smaller. If there are more PEs than x-y planes ($n_{\text{PE}} > n_z$), some PEs will not get an x-y plane and will do nothing but wait for the working PEs to finish. Further scaling (finer-grain parallelization) can be accomplished by breaking planes in half and assigning adjacent half planes to adjacent PEs. The x 1D FFTs would still be done without communications. A transpose to half y-x planes would require communications only between adjacent pairs of PEs, after which the y 1D FFT would be calculated. The transpose to z-x planes or partial z-x planes would be much the same as the x-y to z-x transpose described. This way, scaling increases to twice the PEs with a small communications price. This enhancement is a plan for the future; there are bigger barriers to scaling in other parts of parallel PME that warrant attention first.

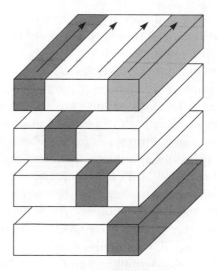

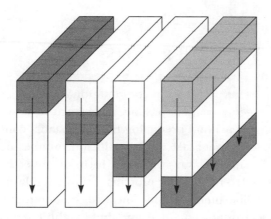

19.9
—
FIGURE

Data transfer in the transpose of the charge matrix for a four-processor system. Arrows show the direction that the data is contiguous. The wide hashed blocks of data are the data that stay on the PE but get reoriented. The corner fine-hashed block is the data that must move from PE0 to PE3. This data can be sent with fast communications a vector at a time. For slow communications, the whole block is packed in a buffer, sent to the receiving PE, unpacked on that PE, and placed in the final memory spots.

Another scaling limitation is the quantized nature of the scaling. The number of PEs used in the FFT should be a factor of the number of planes. If it is not, then there will be some PEs with $(n_{xy}/N_{PE} + 1)$, and others with (n_{xy}/N_{PE}) x-y planes to work on. This will take the same time as all PEs with $(n_{xy}/N_{PE} + 1)$ planes. For example, if n_y is 60 and N_{PE} is 29, two PEs will get 3 planes while the other 27 will get 2. The time to finish the 2D FFT will be the same as for 20 PEs doing the same problem, each PE getting 3 planes. The speed is the same for 20 to 29 processors, and only increases for 30. After that, the speed is the same until 60 PEs is reached. Although this restriction is undesirable, especially in a general-purpose distributed 3D FFT, it is not a severe restriction within the PME algorithm, particularly when we employ the coarser-grain methods that we discuss in the next section. A related problem with scaling is encountered when grid dimensions are not equal. As an extreme example, consider a grid that is $100 \times 1 \times 100$ ($n_x \times n_y \times n_z$). There is only one x-y plane in this orientation, and it will not be distributed. Reorienting the grid as $1 \times 100 \times 100$ will produce 100 x-y planes and 100 z-x planes, giving much more favorable scaling.

19.4   INDUSTRIAL STRENGTH RESULTS

Two of the most important problems in computational biology are understanding the influence of genetic mutations on the structure and function of a biomolecule (e.g., a protein) and predicting the most stable conformation of a biomolecule for a given solvent system. A significant number of biomolecules have been successfully studied using the older form of the electrostatics term, but these systems tended to be globular proteins without highly charged regions. Systems involving metalloproteins and nucleic acids tended to be problematical when using the old electrostatic potential, and these highly charged systems were not always stable for long simulations (greater than hundreds of picoseconds) without substantial changes to the assigned point charges. The development of the PME algorithm followed by the porting to MPPs has resulted in the ability to successfully simulate large biopolymers with highly charged regions. Two examples will be described in detail. The first system examines the role of single-point mutation on the structure and dynamics of a highly charged Ca(II) ion-binding domain of a coagulation protein, while the second study examines the role of the solvent system on determining the preferred conformation of a highly charged biopolymer.

The Gla domain of the coagulation proenzymes (Figure 19.10 and color plate 19.10) provides perhaps the sternest test of the electrostatic computations

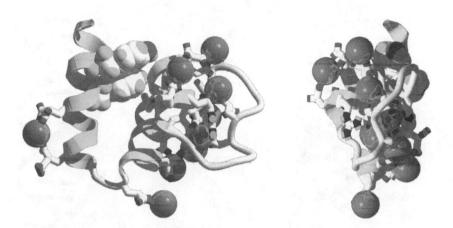

19.10

FIGURE

Molecular graphics representation of the average structure from the 500 ps simulation of the Gla domain of Factor IX complexed with Ca(II) ions [19.27]. The spline is through the C(alpha) coordinates, the sidechains of the residues that are interacting with the Ca(II) ion are shown as cylinders, and the Ca(II) ions are shown as orange spheres of the appropriate radius. (See also color plate 19.10.)

and demonstrates the value of the PME method. Gla, gamma-carboxyglutamic acid, is formed in a posttranslational vitamin K-mediated carboxylation of specific glutamyl residues resulting in a charge of 2 for Gla's sidechain in solution. The first 35 N-terminal residues of the coagulation proenzymes will contain 10 or 11 Gla residues, and this region is responsible for binding up to eight divalent metal ions (e.g., Ca(II) or Mg(II) ions). In the presence of Ca(II) ions, the Gla domain will often fold into a relatively compact domain. The PME method has been used [19.14, 19.27] to estimate the solution structure of the Gla domain of the coagulation protein, Factor IX. Mutations in this protein lead to hemophilia B, a devastating bleeding disorder. Multidimensional NMR experiments provided the initial structure with a poorly defined N-terminus and without the coordinates of the Ca(II) ions. Simulation for 500 ps of this initial geometry with Ca(II) ions placed in appropriate positions resulted in refolding of the N-terminus into a chelation complex similar to the homologous region in the X-ray crystal structure of prothrombin [19.21]. Likewise, the Ca(II) ion network generated in the simulation was similar to that seen in the prothombin structure. The observed refolding by simulation is profound; the PME method provides a new and powerful tool for highly ionic systems.

A recent success of the method is the simulation of the behavior of DNA in water and ethanol/water. Experiments show that DNA in water adopts a "B" conformation. When crystalline A-form DNA is exposed to humidity, it spontane-

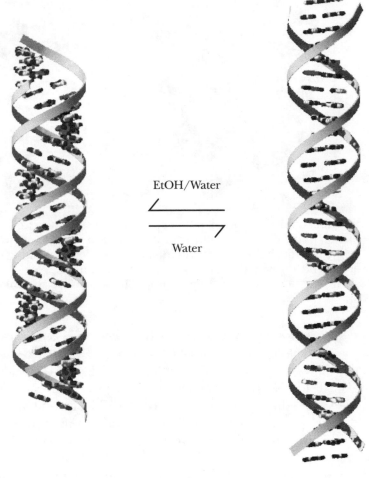

EtOH/Water

Water

A-DNA   B-DNA

19.11

FIGURE

A-form DNA and B-form DNA have significantly different geometrical features. Although the simulation described in the text was for 10 base pairs, this figure shows a 32-base-pair double-strand DNA in both the A- and the B-forms for the purpose of illustration. Note the size of the major and minor grooves (the gaps between the strands) and the tilt of the bases. A-form DNA has a much shallower pitch and is consequently shorter for the same number of pairs. In experiment and in our simulations, A-form changes geometry to B-form in water. In mixed ethanol and water solution, A-form is stable in both simulation and experiment. (See also color plate 19.11.)

ously transforms to B-form. See Figure 19.11 and color plate 19.11 for images of the A and B forms. These two forms are significantly different in their secondary structure and in their biological activity. Transitions between the two forms are important in biological regulation. Simulations with the unmodified AMBER4.1 force field [19.5] reproduce the transition, confirming not only the force field but also the importance of the long-range electrostatic interactions and the PME treatment of them. In our simulations on the T3E with parallel PME AMBER [19.4], we found that not only was B-form stable but there was a reproducible transition from A-form to B-form in water. Five simulations starting from three different starting structures—canonical A-form, canonical B-form, and the X-ray B-form—all converged to within less than 2 A RMSd (root mean square deviation) of the average structure of all five simulations. In an approximately 85 percent ethanol solution, A form DNA was stable in multi-nanosecond simulations [19.3], consistent with experiment. A transition from B-form to A-form was not observed with the unmodified force field within a few nanoseconds of simulation, but could be induced with a slight modification to one force parameter. More studies of the DNA transitions are underway on large MPP machines. We hope to discover the key parts of the mechanisms of transition and the important factors in the stabilization of the different forms of DNA.

Parallel PME has made a huge impact in the research on biological macro-molecules in two major ways. The PME method has corrected the problem of the treatment of long-range electrostatic interactions. The price of the method has been paid for by applying parallel programming to the PME algorithm and using fast MPPs like the Cray T3D and T3E. What is more important and certainly more dramatic, parallel AMBER using the PME method produces nanosecond simulations in days instead of weeks or months with results that are more accurate and reliable. Systems that are both large and highly charged can now be studied with a high degree of confidence.

19.5   THE FUTURE

In addition to the results previously described, the current state of the art in large biopolymer molecular dynamics simulations includes protein dimers complexed with duplexed DNA with a few layers of water molecules [19.8, 19.13], small lipid bilayers [19.1, 19.20], and determining the energetic landscapes for the folding of small proteins [19.2].

The future will belong to the study of larger systems, such as protein either embedded in or attached to the surface of lipid bilayers (e.g., ion channels), the study of the role of coenzymes (or organizing proteins) in defining and modulating the activity of enzymes, and, potentially, the study of the mechanism of enzymes using mixed quantum mechanics/molecular mechanics (QM/MM) techniques.

With the improved ability to properly describe the dynamics of highly charged systems, we anticipate that the role of metal ions (especially Ca(II) and Mg(II) ions) in mediating the interaction between two highly charged molecules (e.g., an acidic phospholipid surface with a highly negatively charged region of a protein) will begin to be fully understood. Over one-third of all enzymes require a metal ion for proper activity, so simulations should provide insights into the role of the metal ions in defining and maintaining the proper structure and potential activation of these metalloenzymes.

Computational studies should begin to give molecular insights into the folding of RNA sequences into local secondary structures (e.g., knots, loops, and bulges). Even though there are empirical models for predicting the local secondary structure of RNAs [19.28] and an incredible wealth of experimental thermodynamic data on short RNA sequences [19.15, 19.18, 19.19, 19.24], a significant amount of information can be gleaned from careful molecular dynamics studies of these same sequences.

19.6   SUMMARY

We have extended and substantially improved the scaling of the molecular dynamics code AMBER. The implementation and parallelization of the PME method allows for a more comprehensive treatment of the electrostatic interactions for highly charged regions. In addition, we report here a method for distributing the work that allows for greater scaling than was previously possible, permitting the effective use of larger MPPs. These improvements will allow researchers to extend their studies from relatively modest-size problems to studying protein-protein, protein-nucleic acid, and protein-lipid interactions that lay at the core of all important biological interactions.

References

[19.1]   Bassolino-Klimas, D., H. E. Alper, and T. R. Stouch. 1993. Solute Diffusion in Lipid Bilayer Membranes: An Atomic Level Study by Molecular Dynamics. *Biochemistry,* **32**(47), 12,624–12,637.

[19.2]   Boczko, E. M., and C. L. Brooks. 1995. First-Principles Calculation of the Folding Free Energy of a Three-Helix Bundle Protein. *Science,* **269**, 393–396.

[19.3]   Cheatham III, T. E., M. F. Crowley, and P. A. Kollman. 1997. A Molecular Picture of the Stabilization of A-DNA in Mixed Ethanol-Water Solutions. *Proc. Nat. Acad. Sci.,* **94**, 9626–9630.

[19.4]   Cheatham III, T. E., and P. A. Kollman. 1996. Molecular Dynamics Simulations Can Reasonably Represent the Structural Differences in DNA:DNA, RNA:DNA and DNA:RNA hybrid duplexes. *J. Mole. Biol.,* **259**, 434–444.

[19.5]   Cornell, W. D., P. Cieplak, C. I. Baylky, I. R. Gould, K. M. Merz Jr., D. M. Ferguson, D. C. Spellmeyer, T. Fox, J. W. Caldwell, and P. A. Kollman. 1995. A Second Generation Force Field for the Simulation of Proteins, Nucleic Acids and Organic Molecules. *J. Am. Chem. Soc.,* **117**, 5179–5197.

[19.6]   Crowley, M. F., T. Darden, T. Cheatham, and D. W. Deerfield III. 1997. Adventures in Improving the Scaling and Accuracy of a Parallel Molecular Dynamics Program. SC '97 **11**, 255–278.

[19.7]   Darden, T., D. York, and L. Pedersen. 1993. Particle Mesh Ewald: An N Log(N) Method for Ewald Sums in Large Systems. *J. Chem. Phys.,* **98**(12), 10,089–10,092.

[19.8]   Duan, Y., P. Wikosz, and J. M. Rosenberg. 1996. Dynamic Contributions to the DNA Binding Entropy of the Ecori and Ecorv Restriction Endonucleases. *J. Mol. Biol.,* **264**(3), 546–555.

[19.9]   Essman, U., L. Perera, M. L. Berkowitz, T. Darden, H. Lee, and L. Pedersen. 1995. A Smooth Particle Mesh Ewald Method. *J. Chem. Phys.,* **103**(19), 8577–8593.

[19.10]   Greengard, L., and V. Rokhlin. 1985. A Fast Algorithm for Particle Simulation. *J. Comp. Phys.,* **60,** 187.

[19.11]   Greengard, L., and V. Rokhlin. 1985. A Fast Algorithm for Particle Simulation. *J. Comp. Phys.,* **73,** 325.

[19.12]   Hockney, R. W., and J. W. Eastwood. 1981. *Computer Simulation Using Particles.* New York: McGraw-Hill.

[19.13]   Kumar, S., Y. Duan, P. A. Kollman, and J. M. Rosenberg. 1994. Molecular Dynamics Simulations Suggest that the eco ri Kink Is an Example of Molecular Strain. *J. Biomol. Struct. Dyn.,* **12**(3), 487–525.

[19.14]   Li, L., T. A. Darden, S. J. Freedman, B. C. Furie, B. Furie, J. D. Baleja, H. Smith, R. G. Hiskey, and L. G. Pedersen. 1997. Refinement of the NMR Solution Structure of the Gamma-Carboxyglutamic Acid Domain of Coagulation Factor IX Using Molecular Dynamics Simulation with Initial Ca(II) Positions Determined by a Genetic Algorithm. *Biochemistry,* **36,** 2132–2138.

[19.15]   McDowell, J. A., L. He, X. Chen, and D. H. Turner. 1997. Investigation of the Structural Basis for Thermodynamic Stabilities of Tandem GU Wobble Pairs: NMR Structures of (rGGAGUUCC) and (rGGAUGUCC) 2. *Biochemistry,* **36,** 8030–8038.

[19.16]   Schoenberg, I. J. 1973. *Cardinal Spline Interpolation.* Philadelphia: Society for Industrial and Applied Mathematics.

[19.17]   Schreiber, H., and O. Steinhauser. 1992. Molecular Dynamics Studies of Solvated Polypeptides: Why the Cutoff Scheme Does Not Work. *Chemical Physics,* **168,** 75–89.

[19.18]   Schroeder, S., J. Kim, and D. H. Turner. 1996. G.A and U.U Mismatches Can Stabilize RNA Internal Loops of Three Nucleotides. *Biochemistry,* **35,** 16,105–16,109.

[19.19]   Serra, M. J., and D. H. Turner. 1995. Predicting Thermodynamic Properties of RNA. *Methods Enzymol.,* **259,** 242–261.

[19.20]   Shen, L., D. Bassolino, and T. R. Stouch. 1997. Transmembrane Helix Structure, Dynamics, and Interactions: Multi-nanosecond Molecular Dynamics Simulations. *Biophys. J.,* **73**(1), 3–20.

[19.21]   Soriano-Garcia, M., K. Padmanabhan, A. M. de Vos, and A. Tulinsky. 1992. The Ca(II) Ion and Membrane Binding Structure of the Gla Domain of Ca-Prothrombin Fragment 1. *Biochemistry,* **31,** 2554–2566.

[19.22]   Steinbach, P., and B. R. Brooks. 1992. New Spherical-cutoff Methods for Long-range Forces in Macromolecular Simulation. *J. Comp. Chem.,* **15**(7), 667–683.

[19.23]   Steinbach, P., B. R. Brooks, and C. L. Brooks. 1990. *Computer Modeling of Fluids, Polymers, and Solids.* Dordrecht, the Netherlands: Kluwer Academic Publishers, 289–234.

[19.24]   Turner, D. H. 1996. Thermodynamics of Base Pairing. *Curr. Opin. Struct. Biol.,* **6,** 299–304.

[19.25]   van Gunsteren, W. F., and H. J. C. Berendsen. 1990. Computer Simulation of Molecular Dynamics: Methodology, Applications, and Perspectives in Chemistry. *Angewandte Chemie, International Edition in English,* **29**(9), 992–1023.

[19.26] Vincent, J., and K. Merz. 1995. A Highly Portable Parallel Implementation of AMBER4 Using the Message Passing Interface Standard. *J. Comp. Chem.*, **16**(11), 1420–1427.

[19.27] Wolberg, A. S., L. Leping, W.-F. Cheung, N. Hamaguchi, L. G. Pedersen, and D. W. Stafford. 1996. Characterization of gamma-Carboxyglutamic Acid Residue 21 of Human Factor IX. *Biochemistry*, **35**, 10,321–10,327.

[19.28] Zuker, M., and A. B. Jacobson. 1995. Well-determined Regions in RNA Secondary Structure Prediction: Analysis of Small Subunit Ribosomal RNA. *Nucleic Acids Res.*, **23**, 2791–2798.

20 CHAPTER · Radar Scattering and Antenna Modeling

Tom Cwik
Cinzia Zuffada
Daniel S. Katz
Jay Parker   Jet Propulsion Laboratory, California Institute of Technology

20.1   INTRODUCTION

The application of advanced computer architecture and software to a broad range of electromagnetic problems has allowed more accurate simulations of electrically larger and more complex components and systems than had been previously possible. Design and analysis in radar scattering and antenna systems can directly and repeatedly benefit from the largest and fastest computer architectures that become available. This evolution of computational methods and their use is expected to continue unfettered into the future. The work in this chapter draws from the Parallel Applications Technology Program at the Jet Propulsion Laboratory. Initially, the work in parallel computational electromagnetics at the Jet Propulsion Laboratory explored the application of early distributed-memory parallel computers to existing algorithms. This work continued with the development of methods for modeling the scattered or radiated fields from objects with penetrable or inhomogenous materials and with geometries that required modeling at the subwavelength scale size. To this end, finite element methods were developed, purposely crafted for use with high-performance, large-memory parallel computer systems. The guiding principle of this work was the development of methods that limited approximations at the theoretical formulation stage and implemented algorithms that allow generality of application when using high-performance parallel machines. The sections that follow outline the development, implementation, and results of these activities.

20.2   ELECTROMAGNETIC SCATTERING AND RADIATION

The problem of calculating electromagnetic fields scattered from a target or radiated from an antenna can be solved by various means. When the object is composed of inhomogenous penetrable materials or has geometric variations on a fraction of a wavelength, finite element methods are advantageous. A finite element method calculates fields in a volumetric region in and around the object, accounting for material parameters and shape. Far fields are then found easily by integrating equivalent sources on the computational boundary.

Although the scattering and radiation problems differ greatly in application, the fundamental formulations are very similar, differing only by the location and description of the source. After a formulation of the general problem is developed, the source term is modeled appropriately and inserted into the system of equations. For scattering problems, the source is external to the scatterer, traditionally a plane wave having a specified polarization of the electric and magnetic fields and incident on the scatterer from some direction. For antenna problems, the impressed current source exists at some specified point on the antenna. This source is appropriately modeled, typically by a known field distribution impressed on a surface or through volumetric currents.

The remainder of this section presents the formulation for a finite element solution to the scattering and radiation problem. The scattering problem is developed and the source terms for radiation are briefly outlined. The work in this section draws on [20.4, 20.5, 20.17], wherein additional material is presented and computational results for scattering and radiation geometries are found.

20.2.1   Formulation of the Problem

The scatterer and surrounding space are broken into two regions: an interior part containing the scatterers and free-space region out to a defined surface, and the exterior homogenous part (Figure 20.1). To efficiently model fields in the exterior region, the surface bounding the interior is prescribed to be a surface of revolution. The following formulation first outlines the interior finite element representation, then the exterior integral equation model, and finally the coupling of fields at the boundary separating the two regions.

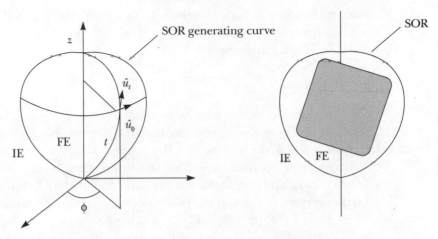

20.1

FIGURE

Geometry of computational domain showing interior and exterior regions.

The Interior Region

In the interior region, a finite element discretization of a form of the wave equation is used to model the geometry and fields. Applying a form of Green's theorem—multiplying the wave equation by a testing function $\overline{T}$, integrating over the volume, and using the divergence theorem—a weak form of the wave equation is obtained. This form includes a surface integral that provides for a boundary condition relating the field inside the selected volume to the field on the boundary, and thus provides a link to the outside field:

$$\frac{\eta_0}{jk_0} \iiint_V \left[\frac{1}{\varepsilon_r} (\nabla \times \overline{H}) \bullet (\nabla \times \overline{T}^*) - k^2 \mu_r \, \overline{H} \bullet \overline{T}^* \right] dV \\ - \iint_{\partial V} \overline{E} \times \hat{n} \bullet \overline{T}^* \, ds = 0 \tag{20.1}$$

$\overline{H}$ is the magnetic field (the $\overline{H}$-equation is used in the development; the dual $\overline{E}$-equation can be similarly developed), $\overline{T}$ is a testing function (the asterisk denotes conjugation), and $\overline{E} \times \hat{n}$ is the tangential component of $\overline{E}$ on the surface S (∂V). In general, ∂V represents all boundaries of the volume, including the surface of revolution and any perfect conductors. The surface integrals over the perfect conductors are identically zero because their integrand includes the tangential electric field $\overline{E} \times \hat{n}$. Equation (20.1) therefore represents the fields internal to and on the surface S. These fields will be modeled using a set of properly chosen finite element basis functions. In Equation (20.1), ε_r and μ_r are the relative permittivity and permeability, respectively, and k_0 and η_0 are free-space wave number and impedance, respectively.

The Exterior Region

In the formulation of the integral equation, fictitious electric ($\bar{J} = \hat{n} \times \overline{H}$) and magnetic ($\overline{M} = -\hat{n} \times \overline{E}$) currents, equivalent to the tangential magnetic and electric fields just on the exterior of the boundary surface, are defined on the boundary. These currents produce fields in the exterior region, which are the scattered fields. The sum of the scattered and the incident fields results in the total field everywhere outside the boundary surface. On the boundary itself, this sum is equal to half the total field. The scattered fields are obtained from the tangential currents via an integral over the boundary using the free-space Green's function kernel. Two equations are obtained for the electric and magnetic fields on the boundary: the electric field integral equation (EFIE) and the magnetic field integral equation (MFIE), respectively. A linear combination of the two with a constant weighting factor α results in the combined field integral equation (CFIE). The general form used in this formulation is

$$Z_m\,[\overline{M}/\eta_0] + Z_j\,[\bar{J}] = V_i \qquad (20.2)$$

where Z_m and Z_j are the integro-differential operators used in defining the CFIE, and V_i represents the incident field.

Enforcing Boundary Conditions

The two previous sections have outlined field representations for the interior and exterior regions. In the interior region, boundary conditions at any material interface, including perfect conductors, must be enforced by a proper application of the finite element basis functions. At the artificial surface of revolution separating the interior and exterior regions, boundary conditions on the continuity of tangential field components must be enforced.

Initially, four equations are written for the three unknown field quantities of interest. The first unknown is the magnetic field internal to the volume V. The other two are the electric and magnetic surface currents, $\bar{J}$ and $\overline{M}$, on the boundary.

The four equations are found from the finite element Equation (20.1), the integral equation (CFIE) relating $\bar{J}$ and $\overline{M}$ currents to the incident field (20.2), and a set of equations enforcing the continuity of $\overline{H}$ and $\overline{E}$ across the boundary. Continuity of the magnetic field across the boundary is enforced in a weak sense

$$\iint_{\partial V} (\hat{n} \times \overline{H} - \overline{J}) \cdot (\hat{n} \times \overline{U}^*) ds = 0 \qquad (20.3)$$

where $\overline{U}$ is a testing function. This is an essential boundary condition and must be explicitly enforced. Continuity of the electric field across the boundary is made implicit in the finite element equation in the surface integral term $\hat{n} \times \overline{E}$ and is termed a natural boundary condition

$$\iint_{\partial V} (\overline{E} \times \hat{n} - \overline{M}) \cdot \overline{T}^* ds = 0 \qquad (20.4)$$

This equation is combined with Equation (20.1) to produce

$$\frac{\eta_0}{jk_0} \int_V \left[\frac{1}{\varepsilon_r} (\nabla \times \overline{H}) \cdot (\nabla \times \overline{T}^*) - k^2 \mu_r \overline{H} \cdot \overline{T}^* \right] dV - \int_{\partial V} \overline{M} \cdot \overline{T}^* ds = 0 \quad (20.5)$$

Equations (20.2), (20.3), and (20.5) constitute the system of equations representing fields in all space in and about the scatterer.

20.2.2   Why This Formulation Addresses the Problem

As outlined above, the finite element method of solving for scattered fields is chosen to capture fine-scale geometry or to model inhomogenous materials in and about the scatterer or antenna. This is accomplished through the volume integral in Equation (20.5); the material parameters everywhere within the computational volume are modeled, including any perfect conducting surfaces. The magnetic fields within the volume are then calculated in the presence of the materials without approximation other than that of the numerical discretization and numerical solution. The mesh is "pulled" out from the scatterer or antenna to encompass the volume contained within a minimal surface of revolution that surrounds the scatterer or antenna. This surface, and the integral equation representation of the fields on that surface, are used to accurately model the radiation condition for fields scattered or radiated from the object. This formulation allows an accurate implementation of the radiation boundary condition that is essential for a high fidelity solution of the fields.

Additionaly, the choice of a surface of revolution as opposed to a general surface allows for a more numerically efficient integral equation. Indeed, on a surface of revolution the unknowns can be described as having a variation along the surface generator totally independent of that along the azimuthal coordinate. The azimuthal variation is expressed in terms of a Fourier series with orthogonal harmonics. As will become clear later, these features give rise to impedance matrices of a lower order than those corresponding to a surface of general shape for the same size.

20.3   FINITE ELEMENT MODELING

This theoretical formulation is discretized into a complete finite element model, ultimately creating a large system of equations to be solved. The following sections outline the internal finite element model and the surface integral equation discretizations.

20.3.1   Discretization of the Problem

Equations (20.2), (20.3), and (20.5) are discretized using appropriate sets of basis functions. In the interior region, tetrahedral, vector-edge elements (Whitney elements) are used. On the bounding surface of revolution, a set of functions with piecewise linear variation along the surface-of-revolution generator and with an azimuthal Fourier modal variation is used.

The Finite Element Model

An ensemble of elements filling the interior region, excluding any perfect conducting objects, is created using a mesh generator. The elements should accurately represent the magnetic field, the geometry of the scatterer, and the bounding surface of revolution. Since the scatterer is not a body of revolution in general, the finite element mesh will extend out from the scatterer to the surface of revolution. For an accurate model of the fields, tetrahedral, vector-edge elements are used to model $\overline{H}$ [20.11]:

$$\overline{H}(r) = \sum_i h_i \overline{W}_i(r) \tag{20.6}$$

where

$$\overline{W}_{mn}(r) = \lambda_m(r)\nabla\lambda_n(r) - \lambda_n(r)\nabla\lambda_m(r) \tag{20.6a}$$

and $\lambda(r)$ are the tetrahedral shape functions. Testing functions are also chosen to be the functions $\overline{W}(r)$.

These functions are used in the volume integral of Equation (20.5). The resultant discretized volume integral is

$$\frac{\eta_0}{jk_0}\left[\int_V \frac{1}{\varepsilon_r}(\nabla\times\overline{H})\bullet(\nabla\times\overline{W}^*) - k^2\mu_r\,\overline{H}\bullet\overline{W}^*\right]dV \Rightarrow \mathbf{KH} \qquad (20.7)$$

where $\mathbf{K}$ is the assembled sparse finite element matrix, and $\mathbf{H}$ is the vector of complex finite element basis function amplitudes.

An Efficient Exterior Integral Equation Model

To describe the surface of revolution geometry, a cylindrical coordinate system (ρ,ϕ,z) is selected for the exterior region, and orthogonal surface coordinates (t,ϕ) are used on the boundary itself; ϕ is the azimuthal angle variable and t is the contour length variable along the generating curve of the surface of revolution. In the formulation of the integral equation, the equivalent electric and magnetic surface currents ($\overline{J}$ and $\overline{M}$) are defined just on the outside of the surface through the relations

$$u\overline{E} = \overline{E}^i - L[\overline{J}] + K[\overline{M}/\eta_0] \qquad (20.8)$$

$$u\eta_0\overline{H} = \eta_0\overline{H}^i - K[\overline{J}] - L[\overline{M}/\eta_0] \qquad (20.9)$$

in which u is the Heaviside function,

$$u = \begin{cases} 1, & \text{for points outside } \partial V \\ \frac{1}{2}, & \text{for points on } \partial V \\ 0, & \text{for points inside } \partial V \end{cases} \qquad (20.9a)$$

and L and K are integro-differential operators given by

$$L[\cdots] = j\eta_0 \iint\limits_{\partial V} (k_0^2[\cdots] + \nabla\nabla'\cdot[\cdots])g(k_0|\overline{r}-\overline{r'}|)ds' \qquad (20.10)$$

$$K[\cdots] = \eta_0 \iint_{\partial V} [\cdots] \times k_0 \nabla g(k_0 |\overline{r} - \overline{r'}|) ds' \qquad (20.11)$$

In Equations (20.10) and (20.11) g is the well-known Green's function for unbounded space.

From these derivations we can write the electric field integral equation and magnetic field integral equation, respectively, to obtain the $\overline{J}$ and $\overline{M}$ surface currents. They are

$$\left(\tfrac{1}{2}\eta_0 \hat{n} \times I - K\right)[\overline{M}/\eta_0]\big|_{\text{tan}} + L[\overline{J}]\big|_{\text{tan}} = \hat{n} \times \overline{M}_i \qquad (20.12\text{a})$$

$$(\hat{n} \times L)[\overline{M}/\eta_0] + \left(\tfrac{1}{2}\eta_0 I + \hat{n} \times K\right)[\overline{J}] = \eta_0 \overline{J}_i \qquad (20.12\text{b})$$

in which, for the sake of symmetry, the source terms (tangential components of the incident field) are given as fictitious surface currents $\overline{J}_i$ and $\overline{M}_i$. They are presented in a form that is very similar both in terms of dimensions as well as vector orientations. The symbol I represents the unity operator and is introduced for notational consistency.

These two integral equations are linearly combined through a weighting factor α, and the resulting sum is cast into the compact form given by Equation (20.2), where the operators

$$\begin{aligned} Z_M &= \{(1-\alpha)\left(\tfrac{1}{2}\eta_0 \hat{n} \times I - K\right) + \alpha(\hat{n} \times L)\} \\ Z_j &= \{(1-\alpha)L + \alpha(\tfrac{1}{2}\eta_0 I + \hat{n} \times K)\} \end{aligned} \qquad (20.13)$$

and source term

$$\overline{V}_i = (1-\alpha)\hat{n} \times \overline{M}_i + \alpha\eta_0 \overline{J}_i \qquad (20.14)$$

are used. This formulation of the operators follows from the CICERO code development [20.13].

Using the method of moments, this integral equation is turned into a matrix equation. The unknown currents $\overline{M}$ and $\overline{J}$ are expanded in a finite series of basis functions $\overline{U}$ on the surface of revolution. The testing functions selected are identical to expansion functions on the surface of revolution. They are written as separable functions of t and ϕ and will have two orthogonal components along the $\hat{t}$ and $\hat{\phi}$ directions. The azimuthal function is the exponential harmonic $\exp(jn\phi)$

(Fourier harmonics). The variation along the surface-of-revolution generator is represented by a triangle function $T(t)$ divided by $\rho(t)$, the radial distance from the z-axis. Thus,

$$\overline{J}(\overline{M}) = \sum_{n,k} a^t_{n,k}\,(\eta_0 b^t_{n,k})\overline{U}^t_{n,k} - a^\phi_{n,k}\,(\eta_0 b^\phi_{n,k})\overline{U}^\phi_{n,k} \quad \text{in } \partial V \qquad (20.15)$$

$$\overline{V}_i = \sum_{n,k}(c^t_{n,k}\,\overline{U}^t_{n,k} - c^\phi_{n,k} - \overline{U}^\phi_{n,k}) \quad \text{in } \partial V \qquad (20.16)$$

and both expansion and testing functions are given as

$$\overline{U}^{t(\phi)}_{n,k} = \hat{t}(\hat{\phi})\,\frac{T_k(t)}{\rho(t)}\,e^{jn\phi} \qquad (20.17)$$

$T_k(t)$ is a triangle function spanning the kth annulus on the surface of revolution. Each annulus spans two segments along the generator, each referred to as a *strip*. Adjacent triangles overlap on one segment. These overlapping triangle functions result in approximations to $\overline{J}$ and $\overline{M}$ that are piecewise linear in t and a Fourier series in ϕ.

The original integral equation is transformed into a set of linear equations for each of the Fourier modes because the Fourier modes are orthogonal and decouple. Thus, in compact form it can be written as

$$\sum_m m_m\langle Z_{Mm}[\overline{U}_m],\overline{U}_n\rangle + \sum_m j_m\,\langle Z_{Jm}[\overline{U}_m],\overline{U}_n\rangle = \sum_m v_{im}\,\langle \overline{U}_m,\overline{U}_n\rangle \qquad (20.18)$$

where m_m and j_m are the complex unknown amplitudes for each Fourier mode. This is the second equation in the system, representing fields scattered from the object.

Coupling the Two Representations

The surface integral in Equation (20.5) and the first component of the integral in Equation (20.3) are termed the *coupling* integrals because, with a convenient choice of the unknown in the first and of the testing function in the second, they are made to couple interior and exterior field representations. The surface S in these surface integrals is chosen to be that of the surface of revolution. Because the surface of revolution is discretized when using these basis functions, the issue arises of how to represent $\overline{W}$ on S. Indeed, the outer surface of the interior volume is a union of finite element facets. These facets vary, according to the order of finite element representation chosen, from planes to curved surfaces. In general, however, this surface is not identical to the surface of revolution. Similarly, the surface of revolution is obtained by revolving a generating curve around an axis, creating a surface whose cross section is circular. However, for numerical purposes, the generator itself is not necessarily smooth, but is piecewise linear. Thus, only in the limit of fine meshing will the two surfaces coincide.

The finite element function $\overline{W}$ is evaluated approximately on the portion of the surface of revolution projected from the triangular facet of the tetrahedron onto a strip. This is accomplished by an orthogonal projection of the tetrahedral facet surface onto the surface of revolution, thus introducing an error that depends on the size of the tetrahedral facet with respect to the curvature of the surface of revolution. The coupling term is given by the integral

$$C = \iint_{\partial V} \overline{U} \cdot \overline{W}^* \, ds \tag{20.19}$$

where, for each integral equation basis and finite element testing function, the contributing surface is the union of the projections of a triangular boundary surface onto the proper number of surfaces of revolution strips (up to two in well-posed cases). Such surfaces are curved triangles, curved quadrilaterals, or curved pentagons. The evaluation of the integrals was done numerically by first inscribing these irregular surfaces into curved rectangles and then by determining the points inside the region of interest from the knowledge of the simplex coordinates of the original finite element boundary facet and their properties at points inside the facet. These coupling integrals, as well as the discretization of the second surface integral in Equation (20.3), complete the discretization of the problem.

The Complete System of Linear Equations

Having introduced the basis and testing functions for the volume as well as the surface unknowns, substitution into the complete set of equations yields

$$\begin{vmatrix} \mathbf{K} & \mathbf{C} & \mathbf{0} \\ \mathbf{C}^\dagger & \mathbf{0} & \mathbf{Z_0} \\ \mathbf{0} & \mathbf{Z_M} & \mathbf{Z_J} \end{vmatrix} \begin{vmatrix} \mathbf{H} \\ \mathbf{M} \\ \mathbf{J} \end{vmatrix} = \begin{vmatrix} \mathbf{0} \\ \mathbf{0} \\ \mathbf{V_i} \end{vmatrix} \tag{20.20}$$

where

$$\mathbf{K} = \langle K_p[\overline{W}_p] \cdot \overline{W}_q \rangle$$

$$\mathbf{C} = -\eta_0 \langle \overline{U}_m \cdot \overline{W}_q \rangle$$

$$\mathbf{Z_0} = \eta_0 \langle \overline{U}_m \cdot [\hat{n} \times \overline{U}_n] \rangle \tag{20.21}$$

$$\mathbf{Z_M} = \langle Z_{Mm} [\overline{U}_m] \cdot \overline{U}_n \rangle$$

$$\mathbf{Z_J} = \langle Z_{Jm} [\overline{U}_m] \cdot \overline{U}_n \rangle$$

The symbol † indicates the adjoint of a matrix. Note that both $\mathbf{K}$ and $\mathbf{C}$ are sparse, $\mathbf{Z_0}$ is tridiagonal, and $\mathbf{Z_M}$ and $\mathbf{Z_J}$ are banded. In particular, the system is complex, nonsymmetric, and non-Hermitian. The sparsity of the system Equation (20.20) is shown in Figure 20.2 for a case with only several hundred finite element unknowns. For larger, more representative cases, the number of finite element unknowns will grow into hundreds of thousands, while the number of columns in $\mathbf{C}$ will be several hundred to several thousand.

The parallel solution to this matrix equation system is completed in two steps. Initially, $\mathbf{H}$ in the first equation in (20.20) is written as $\mathbf{H} = -\mathbf{K}^{-1}\mathbf{CM}$ and substituted into the second equation, resulting in

$$\begin{vmatrix} \mathbf{Z_K} & \mathbf{Z_0} \\ \mathbf{Z_M} & \mathbf{Z_J} \end{vmatrix} \begin{vmatrix} \mathbf{M} \\ \mathbf{J} \end{vmatrix} = \begin{vmatrix} \mathbf{0} \\ \mathbf{V_i} \end{vmatrix} \tag{20.22}$$

where $\mathbf{Z_K} = -\mathbf{C}^\dagger\mathbf{K}^{-1}\mathbf{C}$. This relatively small system is then solved directly for $\mathbf{M}$ and $\mathbf{J}$. By solving the system in two steps, the interior solution is decoupled from the incident field, $\mathbf{V_i}$, allowing for efficient solutions when many excitation fields are present, as in monostatic radar cross-section simulations.

The relative numbers of unknowns in $\mathbf{H}$ and $\mathbf{M}$ (or $\mathbf{J}$) make the calculation of $\mathbf{K}^{-1}\mathbf{C}$ the major computational expense. This operation is the solution of a system of equations $\mathbf{KX} = \mathbf{C}$, where $\mathbf{C}$ is a rectangular matrix with a potentially large number of columns in the case of electrically large scatterers. The solution is accomplished by using a symmetric variant of the quasi-minimum residual iterative algorithm. The resulting overall matrix Equation (20.22) is treated as being dense, and the solution of this second system is accomplished via a direct dense LU decomposition because its size is relatively small.

Modeling Source Term for Antenna Modeling

The source being modeled is an unknown field distribution on an aperture represented by a mathematical surface, one of those bounding the computational

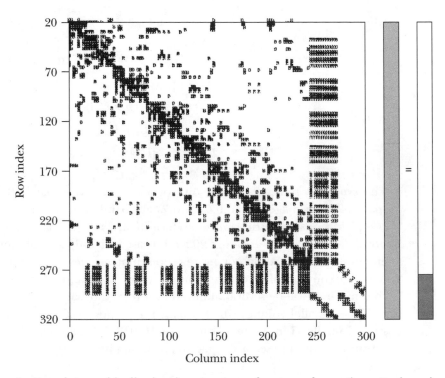

20.2

FIGURE

Scatter plot graphically showing structure of system of equations. Darkened spaces indicate nonzero matrix entries.

domain. The transverse cross section, or a portion thereof, of a waveguide or co-axial cable (or many of them, for arrays) feeding a radiating structure can be selected. This option is convenient because a representation of the transverse fields in terms of waveguide modal functions with unknown coefficients is known for certain geometries. Such a representation can then be used as a constraint on the finite element solution for the field at the surface itself, as is outlined in the following paragraphs.

Consider a waveguide directed along the ξ axis and transitioning into a radiating structure, and let S_w ($\xi = 0$) be the surface representing the aperture (for example, a complete waveguide cross section or an iris) chosen to terminate the computational domain. This means that no mesh exists beyond this point looking towards the source. For $\xi < 0$, the total tangential fields can be expressed as functions of the incident mode of unit amplitude propagating along ξ and an infinite number of modes originating at the discontinuity between the waveguide and the radiating element propagating or evanescent along the direction $-\xi$

$$\overline{E}_{t,w} = Z_0 e^{-\gamma_0 \xi^-} e_0 + \sum_{i=1}^{\infty} R_i Z_i e^{-\gamma_i \xi^-} e_i \qquad (20.23)$$

$$\overline{H}_{t,w} = e^{-\gamma_0 \xi^-} h_0 - \sum_{i=1}^{\infty} R_i e^{-\gamma_i \xi^-} h_i \qquad (20.24)$$

In Equations (20.23) and (20.24) $\bar{e}_i, \bar{h}_i$ are, respectively, the TE and TM modal functions associated with the waveguide geometry, Z_i are the modal impedances, and R_i are the unknown modal reflection coefficients. For all the definitions the reader is referred to [20.17]. From Equation (20.24), because the modes are orthogonal,

$$R_i = \int_{S_w} \overline{H}_{t,w} \cdot \bar{h}_i + \delta_{0i} \qquad (20.25)$$

is obtained, where the Kronecker delta is used.

By making use of Equations (20.23)–(20.25), the term $\overline{E} \times \hat{n}$ in the surface integral in Equation (20.1) can be expressed as

$$\overline{E} \times \hat{n} = Z_0 \bar{h}_0 + \sum_{i=0}^{\infty} Z_i R_i \bar{h}_i \qquad (20.26)$$

Therefore, with proper substitutions, the surface integral on S_w can be written as

$$\int_{S_w} 2Z_0 \overline{T}^* \cdot \bar{h}_0 ds - \sum_{i=1}^{\infty} Z_i \int_{S_w} \overline{T}^* \cdot \bar{h}_i ds \int_{S_w} \overline{H}_{t,w} \cdot \bar{h}_i ds \qquad (20.27)$$

By imposing continuity between $\overline{H}_{t,w}$ and tangential $\overline{H}$ at S_w, expressed by the finite elements, the expression finally reduces to

$$\int_{S_w} 2Z_0 \overline{T}^* \cdot \bar{h}_0 ds - \sum_{i=1}^{\infty} Z_i \int_{S_w} \overline{T}^* \cdot \bar{h}_i ds \int_{S_w} \overline{H} \cdot \bar{h}_i ds \qquad (20.28)$$

Equation (20.28) introduces additional terms to the volume integral of Equation (20.5) corresponding to the unknown coefficients of the finite element edges on S_w. In particular, Equation (20.28) shows that each unknown couples to all others on S_w through the modal function $\bar{h}_i$. After discretization of the equation, the following matrix problem is obtained:

$$
\begin{vmatrix}
\mathbf{K'} & \mathbf{C} & \mathbf{0} \\
\mathbf{C^\dagger} & \mathbf{0} & \mathbf{Z_0} \\
\mathbf{0} & \mathbf{Z_M} & \mathbf{Z_J}
\end{vmatrix}
\begin{vmatrix}
\mathbf{H} \\
\mathbf{M} \\
\mathbf{J}
\end{vmatrix}
=
\begin{vmatrix}
\mathbf{V_i} \\
\mathbf{0} \\
\mathbf{0}
\end{vmatrix}
\tag{20.29}
$$

The matrix $\mathbf{K'}$ can be viewed as mostly sparse, with the exception of a subset associated with the edges lying on S_w. Normally, the source edges represent a very small number of the overall edges, and the matrix is still treated as sparse. Furthermore, $\mathbf{V_i}$ is the impressed field of the waveguide fundamental mode.

20.3.2   Why Use a Scalable MPP?

The result of the preceding formulation and discretization is the large, sparse set of Equations (20.20). The system has a block structure, as pictured in Figure 20.2; as we have noted, the major expense involved in the solution of Equation (20.20) is an intermediate calculation that results in the system (20.23). The cost of this calculation scales directly with the electrical size of the problem being examined. By using a volumetric method, tetrahedral elements must be generated to fill the volume at a density of approximately 20 to 30 elements per wavelength; this results in 15,000 tetrahedra per cubic wavelength when there are 25 elements per linear wavelength. The number of columns in the $\mathbf{C}$ matrix has a similar scaling relationship but one that is more tied to problem geometry. It is envisioned that the number of elements needed to model problems of interest in the aerospace field (such as electrically large wing sections with coatings, or antennas mounted on or within electrically large bodies) grows to several million, and pinnacle problems envisioned today grow to several tens of millions of elements. When the coupling matrix entries are included, the need for storage growing into hundreds of GB of memory is needed and sustained floating-point rates into hundreds of Gflops per second. As outlined in the next section, these sustained rates are needed for calculations involving data structures and sparse arithmetic that do not produce performance rates (as do dense matrix algorithms) that are an appreciable fraction of the machine's peak rate. It is therefore necessary that the machine peak rate be 5 to 10 times that of the rate described to achieve useful results.

One key goal of simulation is to limit the number of physical models built and the number of experiments conducted in the iterative engineering design process. The memory size and performance rates mentioned are needed to produce turnaround times for designs that impact this engineering process. The scaling of larger and larger computer models with the increasing machine capacity envisioned for future parallel systems is the driving force behind using massive parallel processors for these calculations. Increased fidelity on more realistic models is the goal over the next few generations of hardware that will become available.

20.4   COMPUTATIONAL FORMULATION AND RESULTS

The solution of a large sparse system is the central component of the finite element simulation. (The code described in this chapter is named PHOEBUS.) Traditionally, the dependence between mesh data and the resultant sparse matrix data has been exploited in the development of mesh partitioning algorithms [20.9, 20.10, 20.14, 20.15]. These algorithms break the physical mesh or its graph into contiguous pieces that are then read into each processor of a distributed-memory machine. The mesh pieces are generated to have roughly the same number of finite elements, and, to some measure, each piece has minimal surface area. The matrix assembly routine generates nonzero matrix entries that correspond to the direct interconnection of finite elements (elements that do not physically touch do not generate a matrix entry), so the mesh partitioning algorithm attempts to create a load balance of the sparse system of equations. Processor communication in the algorithm that solves the sparse system is meant to be limited by the ability to minimize the surface area of each mesh piece.

The algorithm for mesh partitioning typically requires less computational time than the rest of the finite element simulation, but due to the complexity of algorithms needed to create good load balance and minimal processor communication, the development of parallel partitioning codes can be quite expensive. The complexity results from the irregularity of mesh data inherent in volumetric finite element modeling. The strategy followed in this application is to exploit the availability of a global address space by using compiler constructs to efficiently decompose the matrix data among processors of the Cray T3D [20.2]. Because the amount of time needed to perform the matrix decomposition is a small fraction of the overall simulation time, any minor inefficiencies in using the shared-memory compiler constructs are relatively unimportant. The matrix equation solution—the major time expense of the overall simulation—and the calculation of observables are accomplished using message-passing algorithms. This strategy allows the use of global addressing constructs to simplify the high complexity but computationally inexpensive portion of the simulation—that is, the parallel finite element matrix assembly from mesh data, and the use of message-passing algorithms on the portions of the simulation that require high performance. The direct decomposition of the matrix entries also results in regular data structures that are exploited by efficient communication patterns in the iterative solver.

20.4.1   Constructing the Matrix Problem

In the electromagnetic scattering application considered in this chapter, the system of equations under consideration is complex valued, symmetric, and nondefinite. Because the system has these properties, and because very large systems are considered (systems up to order 1 million), the quasi-minimum residual iterative algorithm is used to solve the system [20.7]. Each row (or column) of the matrix has a number of nonzero entries, typically 16 for the elements currently being used, and this number is constant and independent of the mesh size. The main expense of the solution algorithm is the sparse matrix-dense vector multiplication that is inherent in this as in most other Krylov subspace iterative algorithms. The matrix decomposition used in this implementation is based on row slabs of the sparse reordered system. The reordering algorithm is used to minimize the bandwidth of the sparse system. This decomposition and reordering is chosen to minimize communication of the overlapping vector pieces in the parallel matrix-vector multiplication, reduce storage of the resultant dense vector pieces on each processor, and allow for load balance in storage and computation.

Because the right-hand-side vectors in the parallel sparse matrix equation ($\mathbf{KX}=\mathbf{C}$) are the columns of $\mathbf{C}$, these columns are distributed as required by the row distribution of $\mathbf{K}$. When setting up the row slab decomposition, $\mathbf{K}$ is split by attempting to equalize the number of nonzeros in each processor's portion of $\mathbf{K}$ (composed of consecutive rows of $\mathbf{K}$). The rows in a given processor's portion of $\mathbf{K}$ determine the rows of $\mathbf{C}$ that processor will contain. As an example, if the total number of nonzeros in $\mathbf{K}$ is nz, a loop over the rows of $\mathbf{K}$ will be executed, counting the number of nonzeros of $\mathbf{K}$ in the rows examined. When this number becomes approximately nz/P (where P is the number of processors that will be used by the matrix equation solver), the set of rows of $\mathbf{K}$ for a given processor has been determined as has the set of rows of $\mathbf{C}$.

The reordering is chosen to minimize and equalize the bandwidth of each row over the system [20.8]. Because the amount of data communicated in the matrix-vector multiplication will depend upon the equalization of the row bandwidth, different reordering algorithms have been examined. The generalized reverse Cuthill-McKee algorithm (in both the SPARSPAK [20.8] and the Gibbs-Poole-Stockmeyer [20.12] versions) produces an ordering that minimizes system bandwidth and equalizes the bandwidth over each row of the matrix. Matrices resulting from objects that were long and thin as well as those resulting from spherical objects have been examined. The nested dissection ordering in [20.10] could produce a smaller profile of the reordered matrix, but equalization of the row bandwidth was not accomplished; row bandwidths approaching even the matrix order were found in a few rows of the matrix.

The matrix decomposition code, termed P_SLICE, consists of a number of subroutines. Initially, the potentially large mesh files are read (READ). Then the connectivity structure of the sparse matrix is generated and reordered (CONNECT), followed by the generation of the complex-valued entries of $\mathbf{K}$ (FEM), building the connectivity structure and filling the $\mathbf{C}$ matrix (COUPLING). Finally, the individual files containing the row slabs of $\mathbf{K}$ and the row slabs of $\mathbf{C}$ must be written to disk (WRITE). For each processor that will be used in the matrix equation solver, one file containing the appropriate parts of both the $\mathbf{K}$ and $\mathbf{C}$ matrices is written.

Cray Research Adaptive Fortran (CRAFT) is used for the matrix decomposition stage of the simulation. All large arrays are declared, using CDIR$ directives, to be shared in either a block manner or a cyclic manner for the leading dimension, with nonleading dimensions distributed degenerately. Using a block distribution of a matrix of size 256 on four processors leads to the first 64 elements residing on processor 0, the next 64 elements on processor 1, and so on. A cyclic distribution would lead to processor 0 having elements (1, 5, 9, . . .), processor 1 having elements (2, 6, 10, . . .), and so on. A 2D array with a degenerate distribution of the second dimension leads to all elements of the array having a given index in the first dimension on the same processor, regardless of the index in the second dimension. For example, a 2D array of size (256,10) distributed degenerately over the second dimension will have elements $((i,1), (i,2), . . . , (i,10))$ all located on the same processor. Which processor this will be is dependent on the value of i and the method of distribution over the first dimension.

Routines that could be easily parallelized by CRAFT directives were FEM and part of COUPLING. The directive CDIR$ DO SHARED was added to the parallelizable loops to automatically distribute the work over all the processors. Other routines that could be executed in parallel with a combination of CRAFT and message passing included the READ and WRITE routines. The remaining routines (CONNECT, and a second part of COUPLING) are basically sequential

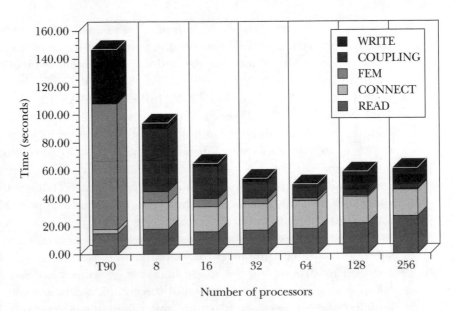

20.3

FIGURE

Computation time and scaling for a relatively small simulation (dielectric cylinder with 43,791 edges, radius = 1 cm, height = 10 cm, permittivity = 4.0 at
2.5 GHz). First column shows time for single-processor T90. Times on T90 for
CONNECT and FEM have been combined.

routines, where only one processor is doing the majority of the work while using
data spread across many (usually all) processors.

   Two files are read in the READ routine, one containing finite element data
and the other containing integral equation data. The finite element file is at least
an order of magnitude larger than the integral equation file and is read by four
processors. By using these four processors, the time of the READ routine is reduced roughly by a factor of 3 as compared to reading the file with one processor. Further reduction in this time may be possible; however, this factor of 3 is
currently sufficient. In the WRITE algorithm, data is assembled on each processing element and written to disk. On the T3D, it is faster to assemble a local array
and write out that data than to write out a distributed array directly, because as
the number of processors increases, more writes of smaller amounts of data are
being performed and disk and network contention develops. Scaling beyond this
point quickly leads to diminishing returns from each processor.

   Figures 20.3 and 20.4 show the performance of P_SLICE over varying numbers of processors for two different problems. The number of edges is the number of finite element unknowns in the problem. For the routines that have been
parallelized, doubling the number of processors reduces the amount of time by a
factor of approximately 2. For routines that are sequential, where only one pro-

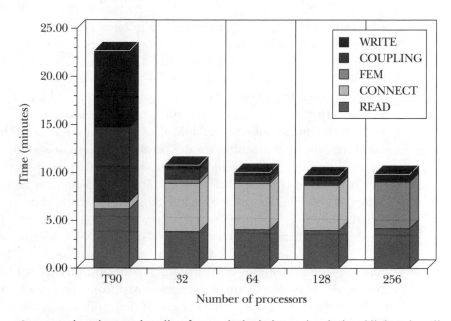

Computation time and scaling for a relatively large simulation (dielectric cylin-der with 579,993 edges, radius = 1 cm, height = 10 cm, permittivity = 4.0 at 2.5 GHz). First column shows time for single-processor T90. Times on T90 for CONNECT and FEM have been combined.

cessor is doing the work using the other processors' data, the time goes up very slightly as the number of processors for the overall code is increased. This is due strictly to communication latency. As the number of processors increases, the percentage of array elements that are not local increases, and the time to load or store these elements is longer than the time to load or store local elements. The I/O time should have roughly the same behavior, but for practical tests the I/O time is more dependent on the I/O load of the other T3D processors and the load on the front-end YMP that is between the T3D and the disks than the num-ber of T3D processors being used in P_SLICE. It is clear that the routines that benefit most from the parallel implementation on the T3D are COUPLING and WRITE.

20.4.2   Beginning the Matrix Solution

As we have outlined, the partitioned system of equations is solved in two steps, namely P_SOLVE and P_FIELD. Initially the quasi-minimum residual algorithm [20.8] is used to solve the sparse system of equations $\mathbf{KX} = \mathbf{C}$, resulting in the reduced submatrix $\mathbf{Z_K}$. The parallel quasi-minimum residual solver developed for this application operates on matrix data decomposed by row slabs in P_SLICE after reordering (Figure 20.5 shows matrix structure before and after reordering). The machine is logically considered to be a linear array of processors, with each slab of data residing in one of the processors. $\mathbf{C}$ and $\mathbf{X}$ and are also decomposed by row slabs, corresponding to the row partition of the matrix. Central components of the quasi-minimum residual algorithm that are affected by the use of a distributed-memory machine are the parallel sparse matrix–dense vector multiplication and dot products and norm calculations that need vector data distributed over the machine. The dominant component is the matrix–vector multiplication, accounting for approximately 80 percent of the time required to run P_SOLVE.

A parallel library of the needed level-one BLAS routines was developed using CRAY T3D shmem_put and shmem_get message passing. The routines required by the quasi-minimum residual algorithm are CDOTU and SCNRM2, and the parallel implementation of these was trivial, consisting of a local BLAS call to calculate each processor's contribution to the result and a call to a global sum routine to calculate the final result.

Parallel Sparse Matrix–Dense Vector Multiplication Formulation

The parallel sparse matrix–dense vector multiplication involves multiplying the $\mathbf{K}$ matrix that is distributed across the processors in row slabs, each containing a roughly equal number of nonzero elements, and a dense vector $\mathbf{x}$, which is also distributed over the processors, to form a product vector $\mathbf{y}$, distributed as is $\mathbf{x}$ (Figure 20.6). Because the $\mathbf{K}$ matrix has been reordered for minimum bandwidth, the minimum and maximum column indices of the slab are known. If the piece of the dense vector $\mathbf{x}$ local to this processor has indices within this extent of column indices, the multiplication may be done locally and the resultant vector $\mathbf{y}$ will be purely local. In general, the local row indices of the dense vector $\mathbf{x}$ do not contain the range of column indices; therefore, a communication step is required to obtain the portions of the vector $\mathbf{x}$ required by the column indices of the $\mathbf{K}$ matrix. This communication step only requires data from a few processors to the left and right. The exact number of processors communicating data is dependent on the row bandwidth of the local piece of $\mathbf{K}$ and the number of processors being used. In the simulations considered, the number of processors communicating data is typically one or two in each direction on scaled problems.

This communication could be performed using either shmem_get or shmem_put. These are one-way communication calls where the processor from whose memory the data is being gathered or to whose memory the data is being

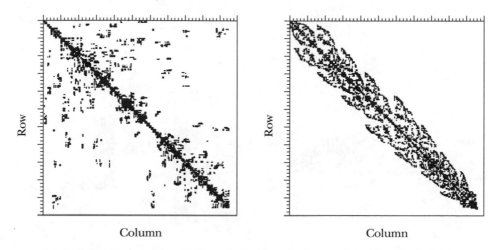

Original matrix structure (left) and after reordering (right). Filled spots indicate nonzero entries of matrix.

stored, respectively, is not interrupted by the communication. The shmem_get formulation is more intuitive and simpler to program, but the communication bandwidth of the shmem_put routine on the T3D is substantially higher than the communication bandwidth of the shmem_get routine. For this reason, the shmem_put formulation is used. This formulation requires the cache to be flushed to maintain cache coherency, but the resulting performance of the matrix–vector multiplication is still 15 percent higher than the performance obtained using the shmem_get formulation.

As described previously, the **K** matrix is stored in row slabs using row-compressed storage. As **K** is symmetric, this is equivalent to a column slab decomposition using column-compressed storage. **K** may be used in either way in the matrix–vector multiplication. In this step, a nonzero in column i requires $\mathbf{x}(i)$ to be obtained, and a nonzero in row j will produce a partial result for $\mathbf{y}(j)$. This implies that **K** stored in column slabs will require only communication of portions of **y** nonlocal to the processor after the local portion of the multiplication, and, similarly, **K** stored in row slabs will require communication only to gather **x** before the local portion of the multiplication. Because similar amounts of communication are required using either storage scheme, the scheme that minimizes the time spent in local work has been chosen for implementation. This is the row slab decomposition of **K** because the row-compressed storage scheme better reuses the T3D processor's local cache and therefore has better overall performance.

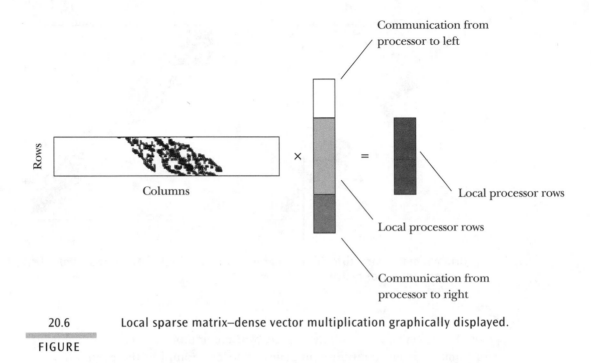

Local sparse matrix–dense vector multiplication graphically displayed.

Parallel Sparse Matrix–Dense Vector Multiplication Performance

The goal of the combination reordering-partitioning strategy discussed is to min-imize as well as equalize communication in P_SOLVE, while retaining memory load balance. The partitioning chosen clearly succeeds in evenly dividing the data among the processors; Figures 20.7 and 20.8 show the relative communica-tion time of the processors.

Figure 20.7 shows results representative of the majority of the cases that have been run. All processors, excepting those on the ends of the linear processor ar-ray, have a relatively similar amount of communication, and because the commu-nication is synchronized, all processors will require as much time as the one that uses the most time. Only the two end processors will be idle very long at the bar-rier. For this case, all processors except the first and last have to communicate with two other processors, one to the left and one to the right.

Figure 20.8 shows the other possible class of results, shared by a minority of cases that have been run. Again, the two end processors are using less time for communication than the majority of processors. However, in this example, a small subset of the processors is using more time in communication than the av-erage processor. All the processors except those in this subset have to wait a sub-

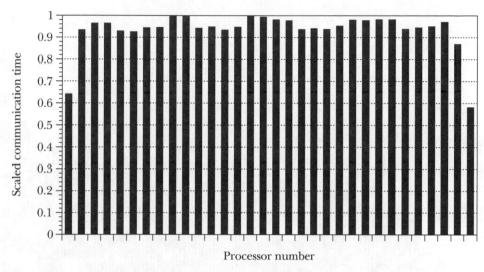

Graph of communication load balance for parallel matrix–vector multiplication of a 271,158-edge dielectric cylinder using 32 processors.

stantial amount of time at the barrier, and the speed per processor of this run is lower than that of the first example. Again in this example, all processors but the first and last have to communicate with at least two other processors, one to the left and one to the right, but here, the processors in the subset that is spending more communication time are communicating with possibly two processors in either direction. The issue in these few cases is that the decomposition of the **K** matrix was performed entirely based on storage load balance, with the assumption that the reordering would equalize the row bandwidth and create communication load balance. This assumption is generally valid, as shown in Figure 20.7, though not always, as shown in Figure 20.8.

Another factor in the performance of the parallel matrix–vector multiplication is the percentage of communication. This is mainly related to the number of processors to the left and right to which each processor must communicate and, as discussed above, the maximum number to which any processor must communicate. It is clear that running a fixed-size problem on an increasing number of processors will generate a growing amount of communication. The amount of communication is a function of how finely the **K** matrix is decomposed because its maximum row bandwidth after reordering is not a function of the number of processors used in the decomposition. If the maximum row bandwidth is m and each processor in a given decomposition has approximately m rows of **K**, then most processors will require one processor in each direction for communi-

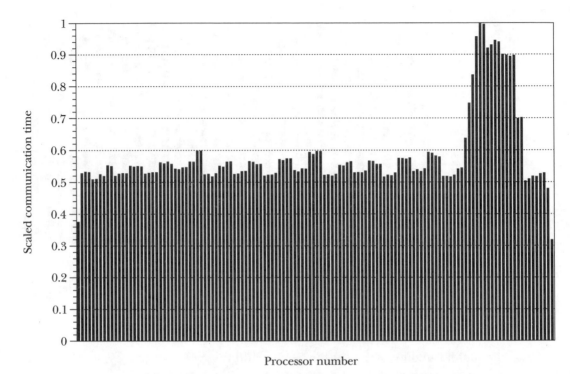

FIGURE Graph of communication load balance for parallel matrix–vector multiplication of a 579,993-edge cylinder using 128 processors.

cation. If the number of processors used for the distribution of **K** is doubled, each processor will have approximately $m/2$ rows of **K**. The row bandwidth doesn't change, so each processor will now require two processors in each direction for communication. But because the number of floating-point operations required hasn't changed, the communication percentage should roughly double. This can be seen in Figure 20.9, which shows communication percentage versus number of processors for four problem sizes.

Figure 20.10 shows the local rate of operations per second for the parallel matrix–vector multiplication. It is measured after communication has been completed. It can be seen that the performance of this operation is roughly constant and is not easily identifiable as a function of problem size or number of processors. To a limited extent, a problem that involved more data on each processor will run slightly faster than would a problem with less data on each processor, but as Figure 20.10 demonstrates, this isn't necessarily true. The storage of the data and how it fits in the T3D's cache is more important than the amount of data,

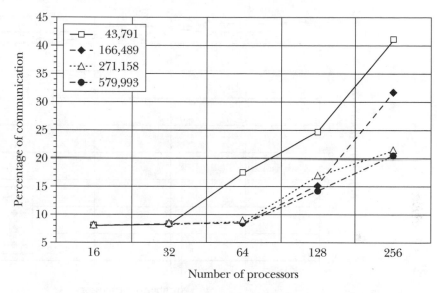

Percentage of communication versus number of processors for parallel matrix–vector multiplication for four different-size (number of edges) meshes of the dielectric cylinder.

and this forces the local performance rate not to be a simple function of problem size per processor.

Shown in Figure 20.11 are plots of time to convergence on different numbers of processors for five different problems. The number of unknowns in the finite element mesh and the number of columns of **C** are indicated on the plots. The quasi-minimum residual algorithm was stopped when the normalized residual was reduced three orders of magnitude for each column of **C**. With an initial guess being the zero vector, this results in a normalized residual of 0.1 percent, a value that is sufficient for this scattering problem. Given a fixed communication percentage and a fixed rate for local work, doubling the number of processors for a given problem would halve the total solution time. The curves in Figure 20.11 do not drop linearly at this rate because these assumptions are not met, as shown by Figures 20.9 and 20.10. The decreased amount of work per processor causes the curves to level off as the number of processors increases.

Additional Work in P_SOLVE

After each column of $\mathbf{K}^{-1}\mathbf{C}$ is computed using the quasi-minimum residual algorithm, it must be multiplied by $\mathbf{C}^{\dagger}$ to obtain the equivalent column of $\mathbf{Z_K}$. Each

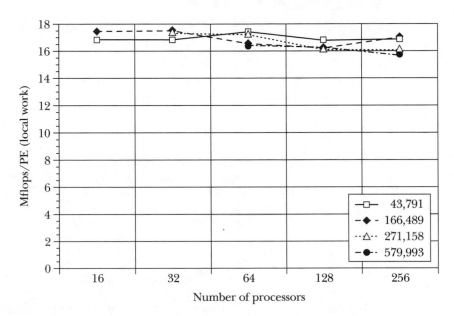

20.10

FIGURE

Local operation rate versus number of processors for parallel matrix–vector multiplication for four different-size (number of edges) meshes of the dielectric cylinder.

of these multiplies requires a global communication because **C** is distributed over the T3D by row slabs. To reduce the number of global communications, after a number of columns of $\mathbf{K}^{-1}\mathbf{C}$ are computed, these are multiplied by $\mathbf{C}^{\dagger}$, and the columns of $\mathbf{Z_K}$ obtained are written out sequentially to disk. The original quasi-minimum residual algorithm solved a single solution vector at a time. A pseudoblock (multiple right-hand-side) quasi-minimum residual variant was written, which performs each quasi-minimum residual iteration on some number of columns of **C** simultaneously. As the residual of each column of $\mathbf{K}^{-1}\mathbf{C}$ converges below the threshold, that column is no longer used in the quasi-minimum residual algorithm. This variant performs the same number of floating-point operations as the single right-hand-side quasi-minimum residual algorithm, but the **K** matrix is required to be loaded from memory much less often. This leads to a time savings of 10 to 15 percent in P_SOLVE.

20.4.3   Completing the Solution of the Matrix Problem

The final code of the simulation, P_FIELD, completes the matrix calculation shown in Equation (20.22) and computes observable quantities (radar cross sec-

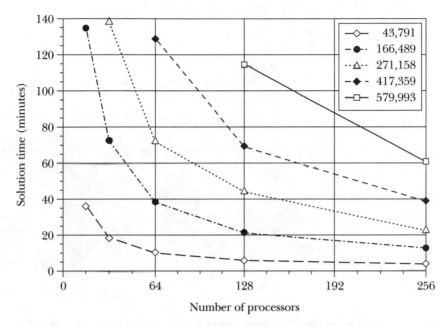

Time of convergence for five different problems. The time shown is the total execution time for the solver on different numbers of processors. The **C** matrix has
116 columns in each case.

tion, near fields, and so on). After the $\mathbf{Z_M}$, $\mathbf{Z_J}$, and $\mathbf{Z_0}$ submatrices and $\mathbf{V_i}$ vector(s)
are computed, and the submatrix $\mathbf{Z_K}$ (formed by P_SOLVE) is read in from disk,
a parallel dense matrix LU decomposition algorithm is used to solve the reduced
system [20.3]. Because this system is much smaller than the larger sparse system
solved above, the **Z** matrices may be distributed on a smaller set of processors,
chosen to optimize the solve time. The time needed to solve this system compared to the sparse system is a small fraction, typically less than 1 percent.

The radar cross section is found from the mesh surface equivalent currents
$\overline{M}$ and $\overline{J}$. This calculation—an integral over the surface—is easily parallelized on
the processors executing P_FIELD. If the radar cross section for more than one
excitation vector is needed (monostatic), a block of solution vectors is found,
and a block of radar cross sections calculated.

20.4.4 The Three Stages of the Application

Shown in Figure 20.12 is the comparison of time requirements of the three
stages of the simulation for four different problem sizes. The problem simulated
corresponds to the dielectric cylinder outlined in previous results. As is clearly

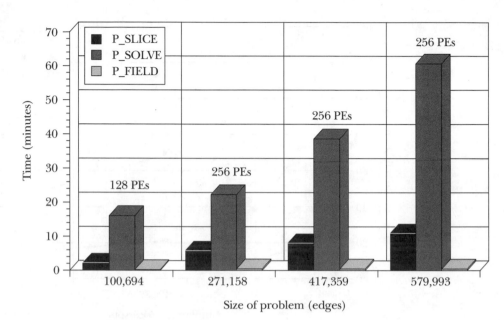

20.12

FIGURE   Comparison of time requirements for three stages of simulation for four different sizes of the cylinder problem.

shown, the dominant component of the simulation is P_SOLVE, the iterative solution of the sparse system. The matrix decomposition stage (P_SLICE) is relatively small, while the observable calculation stage (P_FIELD) is a minor fraction
of the total time. This last stage can grow if a large number of field calculations is
required, but it will typically remain a small fraction of the matrix solution time.

20.5   RESULTS FOR RADAR SCATTERING AND ANTENNA MODELING

Scattering results for various geometries can be found in [20.5]. This section
presents results for scattering from anisotropic materials and for radiation from
patch antennas.

20.5.1   Anistropic Scattering

Anisotropic materials find application in electromagnetic scattering for coatings
applied to targets or in applications where specific magnetic materials are pres-

ent. Although there is little in the software implementation that is unique to the combination of anisotropic materials and parallel computing, high-performance computing enables simulations of scattering and antenna problems that involve anisotropic materials and also have electrical sizes in the range of interesting problems. Thus it is interesting and practical to ensure that a high-performance parallel system performing electromagnetic scattering and radiation problems also handles anisotropic materials accurately.

As outlined in Section 20.1, the PHOEBUS software solves Maxwell's equations within the volume represented by the finite element mesh by the weak-form volumetric integral in Equation (20.1). This formulation enforces strict tangential continuity of the primary modeled field at material boundaries while also weakly enforcing normal continuity of the flux (in an average sense over the facets). This combination of conditions is well suited to anisotropic materials. Because we are solving frequency-domain systems, we are restricted to linear, memoryless, but general anisotropic materials. Chiral and other bianisotropic materials are not supported.

The cases of an anisotropic principal-axis dielectric material surrounded by air, a radial-oriented anisotropic sphere, and an idealized gyrotropic material considered as a cavity-mode problem have been implemented and numerically verified. This last case establishes the applicability of the finite element method used in PHOEBUS to gyrotropic materials but was performed using separate software to solve the associated eigensystem.

Several questions of suitability were considered and answered by these test cases. Does the element-by-element weak-form integral result in stable solutions to anisotropic problems without introducing vector parasite error? In particular, are the solutions continuous within materials, and do they display the correct discontinuities at the material boundaries? Do solutions within principal-axis dielectrics display the correct divergence characteristics? This was particularly in doubt because it is well known that low-order edge elements imply basis functions that are entirely divergence-free within each element volume, while fields within principal-axis dielectric volumes must be permitted to diverge; if we are primarily modeling E, then $\nabla \bullet \epsilon E = 0$ but $\nabla \bullet E \neq 0$.

For gyrotropic materials, we have tested the accuracy of the representation for finding resonant frequencies and modes in a cavity problem. This allows systematic high-order testing of the modeling physics and demonstrates in particular the behavior with respect to spurious modes. Such modes, corresponding to extrapolated behavior at the zero-frequency limit, appear to be at the root of vector parasite problems in some alternative implementations that use node-based basis functions.

Principal-axis anisotropy is incorporated in the weak-form finite element equation by direct substitution of the tensors for ϵ and/or μ. These tensors are fully specified by the three principal components—for example, ϵ_1, ϵ_2, and ϵ_3—plus a rotation matrix $\mathbf{R}$ that specifies the material principal axes as unit vectors in the global Cartesian coordinate system. Thus

$$\epsilon = \mathbf{R} \begin{bmatrix} \epsilon_1 & 0 & 0 \\ 0 & \epsilon_2 & 0 \\ 0 & 0 & \epsilon_3 \end{bmatrix} \mathbf{R}^{\mathsf{T}} \tag{20.30}$$

and

$$\mu^{-1} = \mathbf{R} \begin{bmatrix} \mu_1^{-1} & 0 & 0 \\ 0 & \mu_2^{-1} & 0 \\ 0 & 0 & \mu_3^{-1} \end{bmatrix} \mathbf{R}^{\mathsf{T}} \tag{20.31}$$

A variation is spherical anisotropy, for which every finite element volume in a sphere is assigned the same uniaxial material for which $\epsilon_2 = \epsilon_3$, $\mu_2 = \mu_3$, and $\mathbf{R}$ are constructed separately for each element so that the first principal axis is aligned with the radius vector (the vector from the sphere center to the element centroid). This forms a good approximation to a continuous spherically anisotropic material. For this case, the specification for a material is complete when ϵ_1, ϵ_2, μ_1, and μ_2 and the coordinates of the sphere center are specified.

For gyrotropic materials, we have neglected loss and dispersion. Thus we have used μ of the form

$$\mu = \begin{bmatrix} \mu_{11} & \chi_{12} & 0 \\ -\chi_{12} & \mu_{22} & 0 \\ 0 & 0 & \mu_{33} \end{bmatrix} \tag{20.32}$$

where $\mu'_{11} = \mu_{11} + \chi_{11}$ and $\mu'_{22} = \mu_{22} + \chi_{11}$, and μ denotes the unbiased permeability (usually $\mu_{11} = \mu_{22} = \mu_{33} = \mu_0$) while χ denotes the susceptibility tensor due to magnetization.

The first anisotropic test case consists of a thin dielectric slab with differing dielectic along one principal axis (Figure 20.13). The principal-axis relative dielectric constant (4.0) and propagation direction thickness ($\lambda/4$) were chosen for these test cases because of the interesting property of the corresponding infinite transverse thickness slab: polarization may be converted from linear to circular. As the linearly polarized wave from the left reaches the slab, it is concep-

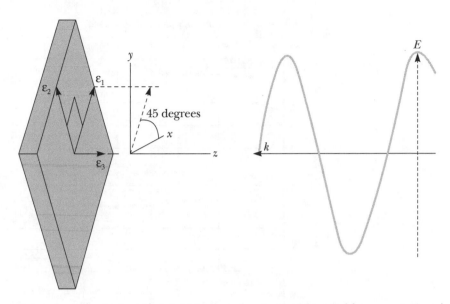

20.13

FIGURE

Geometry of anisotropic slab test cases showing incident field, computational domain, and oblique view of slab.

tually split into two components, one along each of the principal axes y' and z'. The y' component sees a quarter wavelength of free space, while the z' component sees a half wavelength of dielectric constant 4.0. Each component has perfect transmission (no reflection); but the z' wave exits 90° ahead of the y' component. Thus, incident linear polarization results in emitted circular polarization. With a 1×1 wavelength slab, this property is only partially emulated, yet clearly shows the effects of the material anisotropy. A comparison is made of the fields along the propagation axis with respect to a solution by finite difference simulation on a uniform mesh of parallelepipeds. The results for the two field polarizations show excellent agreement (Figure 20.14).

The comparisons made to date indicate that the standard mesh density rules (8–16 elements per wavelength in each medium) is adequate for anisotropic substances. Concerns for modeling the physically nonzero divergence in anisotropic objects by using edge elements have proved groundless: The elements support divergence as generalized functions at the mesh facets. That is, the total volume divergence over a cluster of finite element domains (i.e., the surface flux by Gauss's theorem) need not be zero, even though it is pointwise zero over each element interior. The paradox is resolved by recognizing that the divergence is supported at the facets between each adjoining pair of elements in a generalized function sense. Essentially, the normal component of the field is a step-function

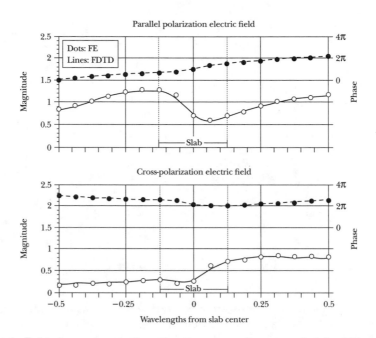

20.14

FIGURE

Electric field along propagation direction through center of slab of Figure 20.13. Magnitude and phase of total field component with polarization parallel to the incident electric field vector (top) and same with cross-polarization component of total electric field (bottom).

at the facet; hence the divergence is carried by a delta function at that point. Furthermore, the accuracy of the field treatment at dielectric interfaces is shown to be adequate and automatic. This edge-element conformability is shown to work for anisotropic-to-isotropic dielectric interfaces, as well as isotropic-to-isotropic dielectric interfaces.

The gyrotropic cavity problem consists of a height-to-radius ratio of 2 for a PEC cylinder filled with idealized gyrotropic material. The gyrotropic material constants are $\mu'_{11} = 1.0$, $\mu'_{22} = 1.0$, $\chi_{12} = 0.1i$. This problem has an analytic solution and has also been solved as a 2D body-of-revolution finite element problem [20.6]. The degrees of freedom corresponding to electric fields tangent to PEC facets are eliminated from the matrix storage data structures. The finite element matrices for the eigenvalue problem corresponding to the cavity modes are $\mathbf{R}$ (resulting from the curl-curl term) and $\mathbf{S}$ (resulting from the direct field overlap integrals), with coefficient (eigenvalue) k^2. The resulting system, $\mathbf{R} - k^2 \mathbf{S} = 0$, represents a modified eigenvalue problem, which was solved by EISPACK subroutines.

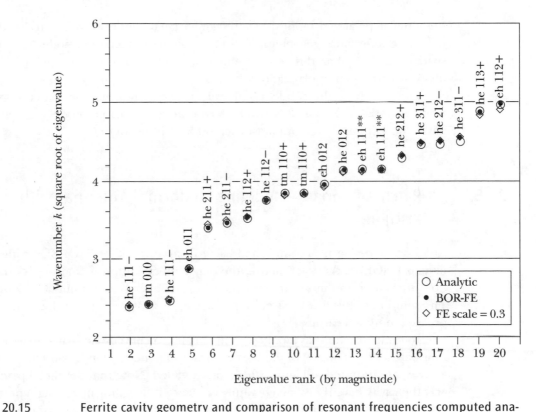

Ferrite cavity geometry and comparison of resonant frequencies computed analytically by BOR finite element code and by 3D gyrotropic prototype code

We computed eigensolutions to our 3D finite element matrices (Figure 20.15). The conducting ferrite-filled cylinder displays eigenvalues for modes in close agreement with those predicted analytically and found by the BOR technique from [20.6]. The eigensolver also finds 190 $k = 0$ modes (for the case with 190 interior finite element vertices), representing the space of functions $\mathbf{E} = \text{grad}(f)$ (for any arbitrary scalar function f) that satisfy the curl-curl equation for $k = 0$. The numerical eigenvalues imply $k < 10^{-2}$ for all of these modes, demonstrating superb separation between these mathematical modes and the physical modes that have nonzero k.

Additional validation was obtained by examining interpolated plots and animations of the interior fields on cross sections of the ferrite-filled cylinder. These were not directly compared with analytic or computational solutions, but demonstrate whether the mode structure agrees with that predicted by the analytic solution—for example, in number and type of field nodes—and the splitting of the circular polarized modes (in a ferrite, circular modes of opposite handed-ness have different eigenvalues, in contrast to the degenerate modes in empty space). The first 14 modes were examined and found to agree with the predicted mode structures and polarizations.

The quality of the results for the eigensystem indicates we may use gyro-tropic materials in PHOEBUS with high confidence. Spurious modes are well be-haved, and therefore vector parasitic errors should be absent.

20.5.2   Patch Antennas—Modeling Conformal Antennas with PHOEBE

Antenna modeling is accomplished using a variant of the PHOEBUS software named PHOEBE. As noted above, the major modification is that the source is now internal to the mesh, which results in the linear system Equation (20.29). The solution of this linear system is performed similarly to that of the scattering problem outlined earlier.

To simulate antennas mounted conformally on curved platforms, an array of four patches lying on top of the lateral surface of a metal cylinder and backed by a cavity, as illustrated in Figure 20.16, was modeled. Note that the metal patches and the cavity have the same curvature as the cylinder, thus providing a perfect match of the two structures, without protrusion. Similarly, the back of the cavity is curved so that the thickness is maintained constant at 0.25 cm. The dimension of the rectangular patches and their placement with respect to the cavity is illus-trated in Figure 20.16(c). The radius of the cylinder is 10 cm and its height is 50 cm. The cavity is placed symmetrically about the middle of the platform.

A coaxial cable feeds the right-bottom patch only, while the others act as iso-lated parasitic elements. The higher order mode (2, 0) was excited, occurring near the frequency of 4.6 GHz. A detail on how the coaxial cable attaches to the patch and the cavity is presented in cross section Figure 20.16(b) and (c). PHOEBE requires a piece of cable to be modeled with a fine element mesh, up to a truncation surface and transverse to the waveguide axis, where the mesh is terminated by imposing that the modal waveguide representation pertinent to the feed geometry be consistent with the finite element solution. In this specific case, a cable length of 1 cm protruding from the back of the cavity was included in the finite element model. The actual size of the coaxial cable is not critical; in fact, the permittivity value of the insulator can always be adjusted to achieve the desired characteristic impedance. In meshing the coaxial cable region, we find it useful to avoid very small values for the inner and outer radii and to minimize

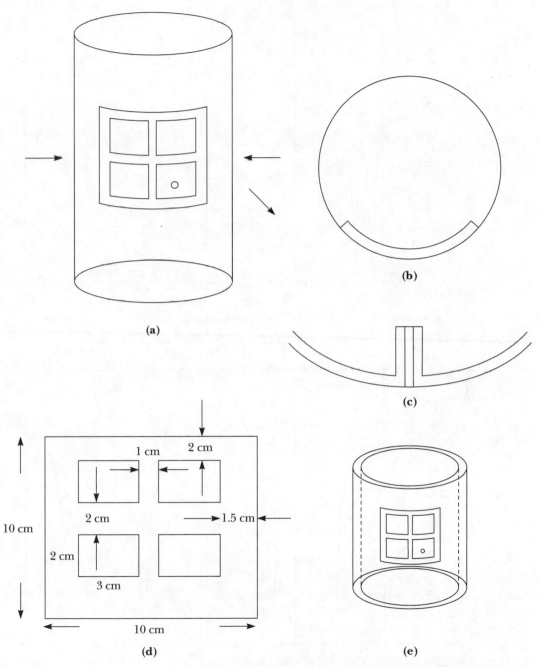

Geometry of conformal patch antenna: four-patch conformal antenna (a), cross section (b) feed detail (c), patch dimensions (d), and outer shell FE mesh (e).

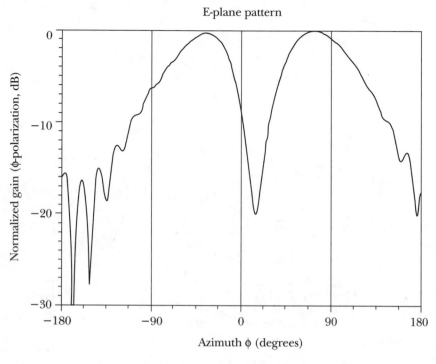

E-plane pattern

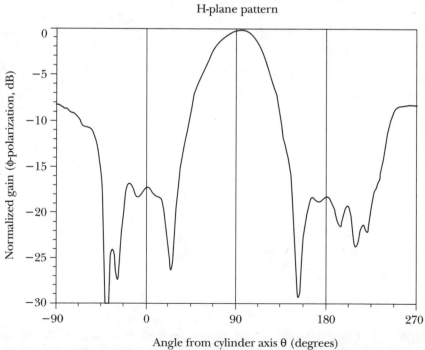

H-plane pattern

20.17 FIGURE

E (top) and H (bottom) plane radiation patterns of conformal patch antenna.

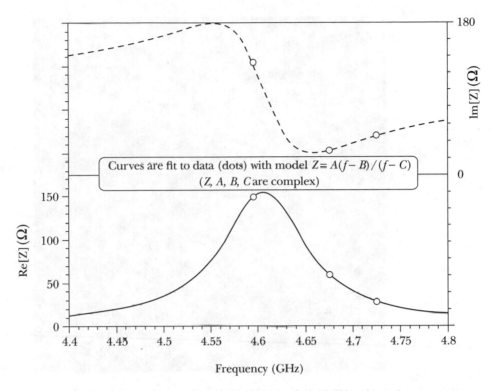

Curves are fit to data (dots) with model $Z = A(f - B)/(f - C)$
(Z, A, B, C are complex)

20.18

FIGURE

Real and imaginary parts of input impedance for conformal patch antenna.

the amount of mesh needed in this region. Because the cable transitions into a much larger structure—the volume of the patch—the mesh generator, in trying to obtain a transition between different edge lengths, tends to generate an unnecessarily large number of elements in the transition region.

The cylindrical platform is imagined to be surrounded by air, and we mesh a uniform layer of thickness 0.8 cm enclosing the structure, as illustrated in Figure 20.16(e). This choice allows for a two-element thick mesh, which is desirable for accuracy. Additionally, we mesh the cavity and the coaxial cable stub. At the frequency of interest, the electrical size of the cylinder is about 8 λ × 3.3 λ. With a nominal edge length specified to be 1/20th of the wavelength in both air (outer layer) and dielectric (cavity + feed), the number of finite elements in this mesh is 260,000, corresponding to 300,000 edges.

The radiation pattern (shown in Figure 20.17) is consistent with that of a patch antenna excited in the mode (2, 0). The slight asymmetry in the main lobes of the E-field pattern is attributed to the parasitic effect. Additionally, the

20.19

FIGURE

Phi component of magnetic field on surface of revolution boundary for conformal patch antenna. (See also color plate 20.19.)

calculated input impedance is plotted in Figure 20.18, and the tangential magnetic fields (phi component) calculated from the solution coefficients on the outer (truncating) lateral surface are shown in Figure 20.19. (See also color plate 20.19.) It is noted that the field pattern is consistent with the patch mode and that the parasitic effect is rather pronounced for the lower-left patch but is rather small for the two upper patches, which is to be expected for the chosen excitation mode.

With our choice of triangles and modes along the generator, the resulting **C** matrix has about 2500 columns. We ran this problem on 128 processors of the Cray T3D, and it took about 9.5 hours to complete. Most of this time, 8.3 hours, was taken up by the QMR solver on the 2500 right-hand sides of the **C** matrix. The solve stage was completed in multiple code runs, employing the restart feature of our QMR implementation. By comparison, filling the 5000 × 5000 dense matrix took about 40 minutes. A communication percentage time of slightly less than 5 percent was observed.

20.6   SUMMARY AND FUTURE CHALLENGES

This chapter described the motivation, formulation, and implementation of a finite element method for the calculation of electromagentic fields using massively parallel processors. Key points of this work include (a) an efficient implementation of a surface of revolution integral equation for coupling the exterior radiation boundary condition to the computational mesh, (b) the use of a matrix decomposition onto the processors that differs from mesh decomposition strategies, (c) the development of a parallel quasi-minimum residual iterative algorithm for distributed-memory massively parallel computers, and (d) the extension of the parallel scattering code to antenna modeling. From this experience, two areas stand out as future challenges: mesh generation and more efficient sparse matrix equation solvers.

The mesh generation stage involves creating the computer description of the geometry and a mesh of the region in and about the scatterer or antenna. For target sizes that require millions of elements, this is a daunting process. The mesh is generated in the region containing penetrable materials and out to the minimal surface of revolution surrounding the target or antenna. Creating elements of relatively uniform shape that conform to the target's geometry and have the necessary density is a difficult task. Additionally, it is difficult to assess the quality of a mesh after it has been generated with millions of elements. One possible approach for improving this situation is to apply adaptive-mesh refinement strategies that allow a very coarse initial mesh to be generated, with refinement being automatically performed within the finite element code [20.1].

The second challenge involves creating sparse matrix solution algorithms that are efficient for many thousands (or more) of right-hand sides. If an iterative solver is used, convergence should be relatively uniform for all right-hand sides, and on a parallel machine the solver should maintain data load balance as well as minimal communication as the problem size grows. The solver outlined in this chapter uses a matrix decomposition by row-slab partitioning following reordering that produces data structures that generally allow a balanced matrix–vector multiplication in the iterative solver. The data load balance was almost exactly uniform, while the communication overhead was moderately small and similarly uniformly balanced over the machine for the majority of problems considered. For scaled-size problems, the communication time was at most 15 percent of the total matrix–vector multiplication time. Even bringing this percentage down to zero would not lead to a major improvement in the overall performance of the code. However, major improvements are possible in two areas: the local multiplication and the number of quasi-minimum residual iterations.

First, the performance of the local portion of the sparse matrix–dense vector multiplication could be improved. This is dependent on the sparse data-storage structure of the matrix and how it is loaded into the local cache. The relative sparsity of the reordered row slab of the matrix causes the multiplication to jump around in the cache as it loads the elements of the **X** vector. If these local row slabs were reordered in such a way as to obtain a more dense matrix, the local performance could increase dramatically.

Second, an efficient parallel preconditioner, or block iterative solver, could decrease the number of iterations needed in the matrix equation solution. Naturally, the preconditioner must not increase the overhead in either setting up the problem or obtaining the final solution more than it saves by lowering the iteration count. The block solver also must not increase the time per iteration more than the amount it saves by lowering the iteration count.

ACKNOWLEDGMENTS

The authors wish to gratefully acknowledge the support of Jean Patterson, manager of the task Research in Parallel Computational Electromagnetics; Vahraz Jamnejad, a member of this task at JPL; and Mike Heroux of Cray Research, who assisted in developing an understanding of various sparse matrix–dense vector multiplication formulations. The JPL/Caltech Supercomputer used in this investigation was provided by the NASA Offices of Mission to Planet Earth, Aeronautics, and Space Science. The Cray T90 used in this investigation was provided by the Information Services Department of Cray Research. The research described was performed at the Jet Propulsion Laboratory, California Institute of Technology, under contract to the National Aeronautics and Space Administration.

References

[20.1]   Cwik, T., and J. Lou. 1997. Error Estimation and h-Adaptivity for Optimal Finite Element Analysis. *1997 Digest, USNC/URSI Radio Science Meeting, APS Digest*, Montreal, CA, July 13–18, 664–667.

[20.2]   Cwik, T., D. Katz, C. Zuffada, and V. Jamnejad. 1998. The Application of Scalable Distributed Memory Computers to the Finite Element Modeling of Electromagnetic Scattering. *Intl. Jrnl. Numer. Methods. Eng.*, **41**(4), 759–776.

[20.3]   Cwik, T., R. van de Geijn, and J. Patterson. 1994. Application of Massively Parallel Computation to Integral Equation Models of Electromagnetic Scattering (invited paper). *J. Opt. Soc. Am. A.*, **11** (4), 1538–1545.

[20.4]   Cwik, T., C. Zuffada, and V. Jamnejad. 1996. The Coupling of Finite Element and Integral Equation Representations for Efficient Three Dimensional Modeling of Electromagnetic Scattering and Radiation. In T. Itoh, G. Pelosi, P. Silvester (eds.), *Finite Element Software for Microwave Engineering*, New York: John Wiley and Sons, Inc.

[20.5]   Cwik, T., C. Zuffada, and V. Jamnejad. 1996. Modeling Three-Dimensional Scatterers Using a Coupled Finite Element–Integral Equation Representation. *IEEE Trans. Antennas Propag.*, **44** (4), 453–459.

[20.6]   Epp, Larry W., Daniel J. Hoppe, and Gilbert C Chinn. 1995. Scattering from Ferrite Bodies of Revolution Using a Hybrid Approach. *IEEE Microwave and Guided Wave Letters*, **5** (4), 111–113; and personal communications with authors.

[20.7]   Freund, R. 1992. Conjugate Gradient-Type Methods for Linear Systems with Complex Symmetric Coefficient Matrices. *SIAM J. Stat. Comput*, **13** (1), 425–448.

[20.8]   George, A., and J. Liu 1981. *Computer Solution of Large Sparse Positive Definite Systems.* Englewood Cliffs, NJ: Prentice-Hall.

[20.9]   Hendrickson, B., and R. Leland. 1995. An Improved Spectral Graph Partitioning Algorithm
          for Mapping Parallel Computations. *SIAM J. Sci. Comput.*, **16,** 452–469.

[20.10]   Karypis, G., and V. Kumar. 1995. A Fast and High Quality Multilevel Scheme for Partitioning
          Irregular Graphs. *Technical Report TR 95–035,* Department of Computer Science, University
          of Minnesota.

[20.11]   Lee, J., and R. Mittra. 1992. A Note on the Application of Edge-Elements for Modeling 3-
          Dimensional Inhomogeneously-Filled Cavities. *IEEE Transactions on Microwave Theory and Tech-
          niques,* **40** (9), 1767–1773.

[20.12]   Lewis, J. 1982. Implementation of the Gibbs-Poole-Stockmeyer and Gibbs-King Algorithms.
          ACM Trans. on Math. Software, **8,** 180–189.

[20.13]   Medgeysi-Mitschang, L., and J. Putnam. 1984. Electromagnetic Scattering from Axially
          Inhomogeneous Bodies of Revolution. *IEEE Trans. on Antennas and Propag.,* **AP-32,** 797–806.

[20.14]   Nour-Omid, B., A. Raefsky, and G. Lyzenga. 1986. Solving Finite Element Equations on Con-
          current Computers. *American Soc. Mech. Eng.,* A. Noor, ed., 291–307.

[20.15]   Pothen, A., H. Simon, and K. Liou. 1990. Partitioning Sparse Matrices with Eigenvectors of
          Graphs. *SIAM J. Matrix Anal. Appl.,* **11,** 430–452.

[20.16]   Taylor, Douglas J. 1988. Scattering and Extinction by Anisotropic Spheres. *Journal of Wave-
          Material Interaction,* **3** (4), 327–339.

[20.17]   Zuffada, C., T. Cwik, and V. Jamnejad. 1997. Modeling Radiation with an Hybrid Finite Ele-
          ment–Integral Equation–Waveguide Mode Matching Technique. *IEEE Trans. Antennas
          Propag.,* **45** (1), 34–39.

21 Functional Magnetic Resonance Imaging Dataset Analysis

Nigel H. Goddard
Greg Hood   Pittsburgh Supercomputing Center, Carnegie Mellon University

Jonathan D. Cohen
Leigh E. Nystrom   Department of Psychology, Carnegie Mellon University

William F. Eddy
Christopher R. Genovese   Department of Statistics, Carnegie Mellon University

Douglas C. Noll   Department of Radiology, University of Pittsburgh Medical Center

21.1 INTRODUCTION

Neuroscientists have long sought to understand how the brain functions. Recently, imaging techniques have become available to study the functioning of the brain in awake, behaving humans. Within the past five years, methods have been developed for the use of magnetic resonance imaging (MRI) to map functionally relevant brain activity [21.2]. An MR scanner uses controlled magnetic fields [21.14] to excite atomic nuclei in the object under study. The resulting radio signal is the Fourier transform of the density of relevant nuclei, which can be inverted to produce an image of that density. The MRI method for functional imaging that has shown the most immediate promise and on which this chapter is based is blood oxygenation level dependent (BOLD) contrast [21.1, 21.3, 21.17], which utilizes the magnetic properties of hemoglobin. These methods provide the highest spatial resolution of any method currently available for general human studies (on the order of 1 or 2 mm), and, while not as fast as

EEG and MEG recording, the temporal resolution is adequate (in the hundreds of milliseconds), with the potential for significant improvements. Furthermore, it is not associated with any known toxicity and is significantly cheaper than other, similar methods. These last two factors combine to permit large amounts of data to be collected on individual subjects, a feature that has both methodological and, ultimately, clinical significance.

In fMRI (functional magnetic resonance imaging) studies, the scanner acquires data sequentially along scan planes that pass through the brain. The data from a single plane is known as a *slice* because activity within a millimeter or so of the plane is acquired during the scan along the plane. The stack of slices form a volume. The specific volume to be scanned and the number of slices to scan within the volume are experimental factors determined by existing knowledge of brain function, the experimental task, and the particular scientific question to be addressed. A typical fMRI study consists of a number of scanning sessions with different subjects. In each session, the subject is presented with a cognitive task designed to activate the brain areas subserving the processes involved in that task. The volume is scanned repeatedly during the performance of the task. In a typical study there might be six or seven scan planes in a volume, which can be scanned in 2 seconds (although whole-brain scans are now becoming common). Because many brain areas are more or less active at all times, the simplest paradigm involves an "on" and an "off" condition. The on condition (e.g., presentation of a visual pattern) is presumed to involve the process being studied, while the off condition (e.g., presentation of a blank frame) does *not* involve it. The difference in the acquired data between these two conditions is taken to indicate which brain regions are involved in the process in question. In a typical study the on and off conditions may be alternated several times. Data is acquired by the scanner in a chunk covering several (2–4) minutes, before it is written to disk (as a single raw data file) and made available for analysis. The data rate is on the order of 150 KB/s, and quantity of data for a typical experiment might be between 500 MB and 5 GB.

21.2   INDUSTRIAL CONSIDERATIONS

Traditional post-processing of fMRI datasets can be augmented with online or realtime analyses. Here we elaborate these ideas, describe the typical analysis steps, and discuss the crucial role that parallel processing plays in achieving a realtime capability.

21.2.1   Overview

The computing costs of current methods of fMRI dataset analysis, including image reconstruction, registration, and simple statistical analysis, are extremely high. The computing time on a standard lab workstation for a single scanning session can be as much as a day. This poses a serious obstacle to the pace of research and rules out many potential clinical applications. It also has a qualitative impact on the way in which fMRI can be used in research. The need to perform analyses "offline" precludes a potentially valuable mode of functioning, in which the results of one experiment are used to guide the conduct of subsequent ones within the same scanning session. One of the strengths of fMRI is the ability to acquire meaningful data from individual subjects. This could be exploited to overcome a serious limitation in the design of neuroimaging studies. Usually, regions of interest are defined anatomically. However, there is considerable anatomic variability across subjects, and this is compounded by the likelihood that the precise anatomic location of a specific function may also vary from subject to subject, particularly within associative areas of the cortex. It would be a great advantage, therefore, to be able to identify regions of interest functionally within a given subject using probe tasks relevant to the study. This would be possible if image analysis could be performed in a reasonable amount of time (say, 5–10 minutes): An initial "scout" experiment could be conducted to precisely localize areas of interest in a given subject, and subsequent experiments could "zoom in" on those areas for closer examination [21.18]. This kind of online capability, in which analysis is completed during the experimental session in time to refine the experiment, meets the most general definition of realtime, namely, "results available when needed" [21.4]. In cognitive and many perceptual tasks, information from many images must be combined to permit meaningful interpretation of the results(e.g., [21.6]). Thus our aim is online analysis, which meets the *online criterion* [21.12] that the incremental time-cost of analyzing each new image should be no more than the time needed to acquire that image (i.e., processing keeps pace with acquisition).

21.2.2   Description of the Application

Our data processing uses FIASCO, a software suite designed to provide a highly flexible processing environment for analysis of fMRI data [21.8]. Typical analysis of an fMRI dataset can involve 5–15 separate processing steps (e.g., Figure 21.1).

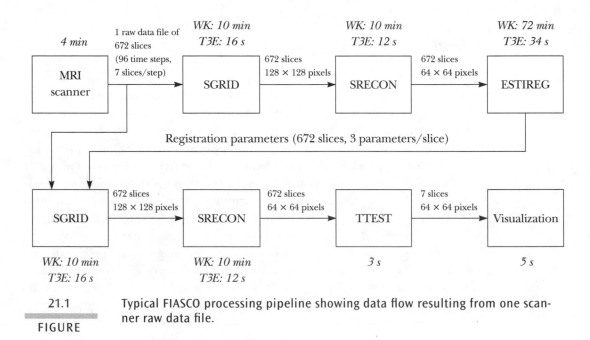

21.1 FIGURE   Typical FIASCO processing pipeline showing data flow resulting from one scanner raw data file.

FIASCO organizes these as independent programs that communicate via files and that are welded into a coherent whole by a set of customizable shell scripts. Intermediate data produced by one program to be consumed by another can be kept or discarded as specified by the user. This enables analysis of the effects of the different steps in extracting the signal from the noise. When designed, FIASCO was conceived to run in a batch environment: data being collected during a scanning session but analyzed in FIASCO much later. FIASCO contains image reconstruction tools [21.16], statistical testing modules [21.10], methods for measuring validity of a study [21.7], and other components. Figure 21.1 shows typical processing times for one data file for both a 1-processor workstation (WK) and 32-processor T3E architectures. There may be up to 12 such raw data files acquired during a single hour-long scanning session. The statistical processing and visualization steps are here assumed to be very simple but could require much longer times in some experiments. In assessing options for parallelization FIASCO is a moving target, being continually augmented with new modules as research progresses. Our initial software efforts were directed at the compute-intensive portions of the FIASCO processing stream individually rather than at a parallelization of the entire stream. In addition to addressing the immediate need for faster analysis of datasets, this approach allowed us to maintain customizability of the processing stream even while parallelizing it.

21.2.3 Parallelization and the Online Capability

The technical barriers to developing this online approach have recently become surmountable. The 1.5 Tesla MRI scanner we use generates data at a rate of about 150 KB/s, well within the capacity of current network links. In terms of computing power, we have determined that 16 Cray T3E processors provide sufficient computing and communication speed in practice to support online analysis of fMRI datasets, including motion correction. Current high-end platforms such as the SGI Onyx Reality Engine are capable of handling the visualization needs. The hardware substrate is in place, and we have integrated them into a flexible, coherent software and hardware pipeline for online analysis of fMRI datasets. We have demonstrated the capability, and in future work plan to develop it into a production tool for our scientific experiments, as well as a prototype demonstration that we hope will lead to dissemination of the technology in the clinical setting.

21.3 COMPUTATIONAL CONSIDERATIONS

In developing a parallel solution, we need to consider the potential hardware platforms, the circumstances of the software environment, and details of the algorithms employed.

21.3.1 Why Use an MPP?

The data volume (up to 500 MB) and rate (150 KB/s) together with the algorithmic complexity of the analysis, rule out a single-processor solution. The FIASCO processing pipeline described above contains one module limited by input data rate (SRECON), one limited by output data rate (SGRID), and one limited by CPU speed (ESTIREG). Even on the platforms that performed best in our benchmarks, the T3E and the Origin2000, 8–16 processors were required to meet the online criterion [21.12]. In view of the evolving MRI technology, which is increasing rapidly the data rate confronting us, this degree of parallelism must be considered a lower bound for online processing that includes motion correction. Thus, a MPP architecture was the only sensible target for this application.

21.3.2   Programming Considerations

Primary goals in our software development efforts are that code be (1) portable to many hardware platforms, (2) robust, and (3) compatible with the needs of a diverse group of researchers in the Pittsburgh community and nationally who wish to use the tools we develop. To achieve the goals of portability and robustness, we have kept the software relatively free of hardware-specific coding styles and techniques. For example, the parallel processing library described targets the PVM 21.11 software layer, an abstract parallel machine, implemented as a library, that runs on almost all machines and operating systems: workstations, symmetric multiprocessors, and massively parallel processors.

21.3.3   Algorithm Considerations

We first identified the most compute-intensive steps in the FIASCO processing stream, which can benefit most from a parallel implementation. For the spiral-acquisition Fourier-space data we were dealing with [21.16], three steps were together responsible for the bulk of this time: convolutional interpolation ("gridding"), reconstruction, and registration, which we describe below.

The raw scanner output does not consist of images where one pixel corresponds to one physical location in the brain of the subject. Rather, each slice of the raw data consists of samples acquired along spiral trajectories in Fourier space, which must then be processed to yield 2D images of the brain. Typically, the first step in processing the raw data is to convert each slice into a 2D array by resampling the data onto a uniformly spaced 2D grid, hence the term gridding. We do this using a program called SGRID. After this is done, we use a program called SRECON to apply an inverse FFT to the gridded data, thereby reconstructing the actual images.

Although the images produced by gridding and reconstruction are recognizable representations of the head and brain, they suffer from several problems that can be alleviated by further processing. One of the problems most disruptive to later statistical analysis is caused by head movement of the subject while in the scanner. This movement can result in a shift and rotation of the head and brain within the image field. With "registration" we attempt to compensate for head movement and eliminate this effect.

To accomplish registration, we consider one volume (the planes acquired during a single time step) in the dataset to be fixed and then determine what rotation and translations should be applied to all other volumes to best align them with the fixed volume. We estimate the motion correction parameters by optimizing mean squared error. We have chosen Nelder-Mead optimization [21.15] for two reasons: It does not require derivatives, which are not available here, and it is very robust. Unlike the other imaging-processing steps, this search process can take a variable amount of time, so any parallelization must cope with irregular timing patterns during this processing phase.

Estimation of motion correction parameters is performed by a program we call ESTIREG. The motion correction parameters are then applied to the original Fourier space raw data, and both the SGRID and SRECON programs are rerun to produce the final images. Because we are usually dealing with subpixel-sized corrections, it is far better to apply these in the Fourier domain than to try to directly shift the images produced in the first pass [21.9]. Estimation of motion correction parameters is currently done in only two dimensions, but there are plans to extend this to three dimensions. There are other programs for registration (such as AIR [21.21]) that already perform 3D registration that we have also parallelized, and they can be used as an alternative to ESTIREG.

Each of the image-processing operations identified as compute-intensive manipulates an image relatively independently of the other images. This allows us to employ a common embarrassingly parallel strategy that scales up to large numbers of processors. This strategy uses a master/worker model in which one processor (the master) delegates tasks to the other processors (the workers). In our case, a task is typically one of the three operations performed on a single image. In this master/worker model, the master assigns each task to free workers as they became available. The worker is responsible for fetching the appropriate input image, performing some computation on it, and then writing the resultant image to the output file. In the implementation, the task management scheme is configured as a library that can be used with any image-processing operation that treats each image independently.

Often it is the case that a worker must initialize fairly large data structures prior to commencing a task assigned to it by the master. Because this initialization is dependent on the parameters of the particular run, we have the master first send a "context" message to the worker before it sends out the first task message. In some of the programs, these contexts are established only once at the beginning of the run, while others have lighter-weight contexts that are changed more frequently. For example, during reconstruction there is a homogeneity correction array that is specific to a particular slice in all volumes. This is sent as part of the context each time a task that involves a new slice is assigned to that slave.

We added optimizations to this simple model. One such optimization was to allow a worker to execute one task while the next task assigned to the worker is in transit from the master. This overlap of computation and communication reduced the time that workers spent waiting for a new task to arrive. Separation of the parallel task management code from the core computational code allowed us to make these sorts of enhancements simultaneously to all software modules.

All program I/O is currently done to and from a shared file system to allow each process access to all of the input data and intermediate files. These intermediate files serve as a means of transferring large amounts of data from one stage in the pipeline to the next. This has both advantages and disadvantages. It allows flexibility in the pipeline because modifying the steps is as easy as changing a C-shell script. It simplifies the debugging process since each component program may be run independently. It also provides some checkpointing capability to resume processing in the event of a machine crash or preemption during runs that take hours or days. However, as we have migrated to more highly parallel machines, the disadvantages have become readily apparent. I/O is accounting for a significant fraction of the time spent in the programs. The effect of this on large eight or more workstation clusters is even more dramatic because the network and disk become bottlenecks as each machine tries to read and write from the same area. In Section 21.5.3 we describe our plans to deal with this problem.

21.4   COMPUTATIONAL RESULTS

An important component of this work was the measurement of our parallel application's performance on a variety of parallel platforms. It is also important to note the networking and scheduling technologies that were required to demonstrate the realtime solution.

21.4.1   Performance

We benchmarked the parallel code on a set of parallel platforms that covered a spectrum of currently available parallel architectures, focusing on scalability [21.12]. Here we present the T3E results in detail and compare a representative measure across the benchmarked architectures. Four speedup curves are reported: (1) the complete analysis pipeline shown in Figure 21.1, (2) the gridding module (SGRID) alone, (3) the reconstruction module (SRECON) alone, and (4) the motion estimation module (ESTIREG), which is responsible for over 50 percent of the computing needed. As described in Section 21.2.2, the FIASCO processing stream consists of independent modules that communicate intermediate data through file I/O. Thus, scalability of the entire pipeline can be severely compromised by contention for file access and/or network saturation due to disk traffic. In Section 21.5.3, we describe our future plans to produce a "compiler" for FIASCO scripts that will produce a single executable incorporating all processing steps specified by the scripts. In this case, data will be kept in memory between processing steps, obviating most of the file I/O present in the current pipeline. Speedup numbers for the motion estimation step provide a conservative estimate of what will be achieved once the FIASCO compiler is in place: There will be approximately twice as much computation in the compiled executable for the entire pipeline than there is in the motion estimation step alone, so that the proportional slowdown due to disk I/O (at the beginning and end of the pipeline) will reduce speedup numbers less than it does for the motion estimation task alone.

The Cray T3E installed at the Pittsburgh Supercomputing Center has 512 application processing elements (PEs), each consisting of an Alpha processor, 128 MB of memory, and interconnection logic. The performance reported here used up to 256 of the 450-MHz processors. There is also a high bandwidth I/O channel that is uniformly accessible from each of the PEs. Shared memory is used only indirectly when passing PVM messages. Most operations access local memory or involve disk operations executed via the I/O channel.

On the T3E we allocate one processor to the master task, leaving the remainder for the workers. The speedups we observed are displayed in Figure 21.2. In this graph we show the curves for the individual processes in addition to that for the pipeline illustrated in Figure 21.1. Note that all processes speed up linearly to 16 PEs, but with more PEs, SGRID (which does gridding) and SRECON (which does reconstruction) do not benefit substantially. The reason is that they are very I/O intensive and become I/O limited beyond this point. Although we are using high-speed fiber disks, we suspect that the disk read/write bandwidth is the limiting factor.

ESTIREG (which does the image registration) is much less I/O intensive, and here we see that it speeds up linearly to 32 processors and continues to improve up to 256 processors. Since ESTIREG accounts for the bulk of the processing time for the entire pipeline, this translates into significant speedup for the overall runtime. In production use we run with 64 or fewer processors be-

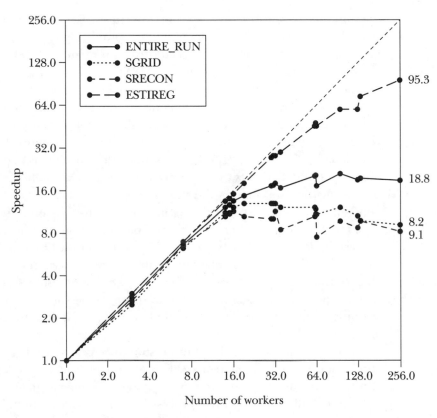

Cray T3E: speedup curves (log-log axes).

cause, while it is important to keep up with the scanner, the value of additional speedups beyond that is small in the context of our online approach.

We typically do production runs using 2^n PEs (for integral n), but in our T3E benchmarks we also did runs with $2^n - 1$ and $2^n + 1$ PEs (for $n = 4, 5, 6$) to determine if we could obtain similar speedups if we did not follow this practice. Running with $2^n - 1$ PEs yielded essentially the same speedups, while running with $2^n + 1$ PEs occasionally resulted in a slight, though not severe, dropoff in performance (see Figure 21.2). We also noticed that at high PE counts we obtained the best speedups when the number of worker PEs was a divisor of the problem size (number of images), and thus each worker received exactly the same number of tasks. This is evident in Figure 21.2 in the ESTIREG curve, where the speedup at 134 PEs (with each of the 133 workers receiving exactly 5 images) was better than with 128 PEs (in which a few workers had to process a sixth image while the other workers remained idle).

Performance Comparisons

Although we are concerned with scaling behavior, the main goal of the work described here is achieving online performance. Thus, it is also important to consider performance in absolute terms. Our measure of performance is how many image slices of a standard size (here 64×64) the system can process in a second (averaged over several hundred slices).

The top graph in Figure 21.3 shows the absolute results on a variety of platforms of our benchmarks for a pipeline consisting of gridding, reconstruction, registration, motion-corrected gridding, and motion-corrected reconstruction. In a typical scanning scenario with seven slices acquired every 2 s (and a 30 s hiatus between 192 s raw files), we have an average rate of roughly three slices/s. This critical rate is shown on the graph as a dashed horizontal line. Points at or above meet the online criterion, while those below do not. From the graph we see that, of our benchmarked machines, only the Origin2000 and T3E are able to provide this capability.

As mentioned previously, to estimate the performance of an integrated pipeline that would minimize I/O, it is useful to look at the performance curves for ESTIREG alone. These are also shown in the bottom graph in Figure 21.3. At low processor counts we see that the Origin2000 is the winner by virtue of its processor speed. However, the T3E does scale well up to a larger number of processors than we have been able to try on an Origin and has yielded the best absolute times for ESTIREG in our trials. The trend for the other three platforms suggests that they, too, may be able to meet the online criterion at larger processor counts than have been available to us. It is also noteworthy that the maximum rate (with a 256-processor T3E) is over 66 slices/s. If we assume that registration will account for half of the computation in a future pipeline, then it should be possible to have the entire pipeline operate at roughly 30 slices/s. Although this acquisition rate is not possible with our current scanner technology, it may be in the near future and, coupled with an advanced processing pipeline, would allow for online studies with high temporal resolution.

21.4.2   Subsidiary Technologies

Although the results shown above demonstrate that parallelization of the processing stream can provide speedup sufficient for online capability, implementation of this capability, and its use as a production tool by scientists and clinicians, requires integration of the parallel analysis with three other components: (1) the MRI scanner, (2) the visualization platform, and (3) the network connecting the components.

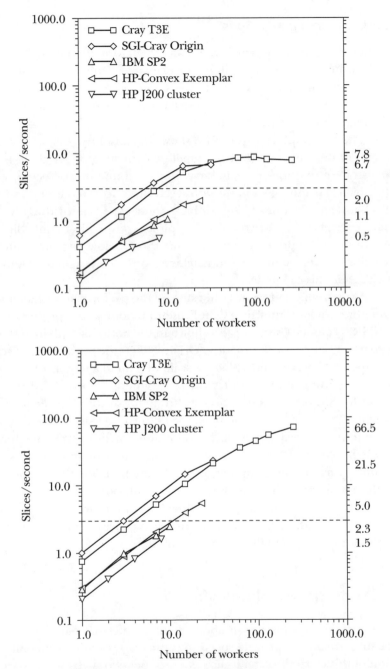

Absolute performance on the entire pipeline (top) and on the computationally intensive ESTRIG (log-log axes) step (bottom).

Network Bandwidth

Due to the multicentric nature of the hardware required for online processing, we needed to assess the network requirements for the realtime transfer of raw data from the University of Pittsburgh Medical Center Magnetic Resonance Research Center, where the scanners we use are located, to the Cray T3E at PSC.

The 1.5 T GE Signa MRI scanner (Milwaukee, WI, version 5.4.2) was retrofitted with echo-planar capabilities provided by Advanced NMR Systems (Wilmington, MA). With spiral acquisitions, the system is capable of acquiring 6–7 images/s (25 KB of raw data each) while the Echo Planar Imaging (EPI) system is capable of acquiring about 10 images/s (32 KB raw data each) over short periods of time or 4–5 images/s sustainable over a longer period. The data acquisition unit for the GE Signa is attached to Ethernet, and echo-planer retrofit is attached to an FDDI network. These data rates are well within the capacity of current network links (e.g., standard Ethernet theoretically supports four times this bandwidth). With the advent of 100base-T Ethernet and expansion of FDDI links, both operating theoretically at 100 Mb/s, bandwidth needs for online processing are even more amply met. But although the capacity is there theoretically, for online processing we require that this level of bandwidth be guaranteed for the duration of the experimental session. The ATM network protocol supports allocation of bandwidth, and new generations of IP protocol may also support this capability.

Scheduling Scanner and Processing

Our research MRI scanners are typically scheduled in hour-long units. This, however, can only provide an approximate time for the functional component of a study. The start of a scanning session may be delayed by overruns in prior studies, and training and coaching of the subjects may lead to further delays. Often, one can only predict to within one-half hour the start of the functional study.

Online capability requires that intensive computation be available during the scanning session. For the online demonstration we will describe, which used 64 300-MHz processors of the Cray T3E at Pittsburgh Supercomputing Center, we were constrained by the machine configuration to the batch mode. Typically, supercomputing sites run large machines in batch mode to maximize utilization of the resource. However, in this case the inflexibility of the batch mode, coupled with the uncertainties induced by the scanning experiment, mandated less-efficient use than a time-shared mode would have been able to achieve. In order to provide us with 64 processors when we needed them, the machine operator administered the batch queues so that all batch jobs on a 64-node partition had completed before our scanning time window began. This necessarily required some nodes to remain idle for a period preceding the scan window, a period determined by the length of the shortest job in the queues. Even worse, because of variability in the time taken to prepare the subject for the scan and to set up the scan planes, we typically did not start computing on the Cray T3E until 15–30 minutes into the scan window. Although scan termination time varied similarly, we could minimize the underutilization of the T3E by notifying the operator when our processes had finished.

This coarse scheduling of scan time results in significant underutilization of a compute platform configured in batch mode. Moreover, within a session the scanner is not acquiring data continuously, rather it is acquired in several-minute chunks interspersed with a 30-second period of inactivity, thus producing more periods of inactivity in the compute platform. These factors suggest that production use of the online processing capability we have developed motivates provision of a prioritized, time-shared mode of operation for high-end computing facilities. Under the time-shared model, our analysis processes would be accorded higher priority so that they would preempt running jobs as needed. The gang scheduler described in Chapter 6 could be utilized to enable this operating mode.

21.5   CLINICAL AND SCIENTIFIC RESULTS

The application described in this chapter is of use in scientific experiments and will be of use in a clinical setting in the near term. To illustrate this, we conducted a public demonstration of online processing at Supercomputing '96 and subsequently used the capability in the course of a scientific experiment investigating human memory.

21.5.1   Supercomputing '96 Demonstration

We developed an early demonstration of online processing for the Supercomputing '96 conference held in November 1996 in Pittsburgh. This demonstration linked the 1.5T scanner at the University of Pittsburgh Medical Center with the Cray T3E at the PSC, which delivered data to an SGI Onyx Reality Engine for visualization of brain activity on the exhibition floor at the Pittsburgh

Convention Center. There was an Internet video link provided across the same networks to allow the investigators on the exhibit floor to communicate with those controlling the MRI scanner. The conference demonstration was indeed the first of its kind: All the dry runs, as well as the first attempt during the conference, failed! These failures were due to lack of robustness in the integration of the three hardware platforms together with the network, vividly illustrating the complexities involved in embedding a computational capability, demonstrated in a batch environment, in a near-realtime application.

This demonstration illustrated how online analysis and Internet-based communication can be combined to allow new forms of experimental paradigms. In the longer term, we could see this technology developing so that researchers remote from supercomputers but with local scanners could run experiments and visualize the results online. This capability could also be used in a telemedicine setting for clinical applications, as discussed in Section 21.5.3. In the demonstration at Supercomputing '96, visualization of the results of the 8-minute experiment commenced about 6 minutes after the experiment started and was completed six minutes after the experiment ended—a constant 6-minute latency. (Recently we have used techniques similar to those outlined earlier in this chapter to achieve six-*second* latency.) Figure 21.4 shows a frame from the visualization in that demonstration. (See also color plate 21.4.)

21.5.2   Science Application

The Supercomputing '96 demonstration was intended to illustrate online processing capability, not to conduct a scientific experiment. We used a simple visual task designed to maximally activate the primary visual cortex, as this is known to be a reliable and robust effect. In subsequent work, we have begun to investigate the use of online processing in scientific studies. For example, in a study of working memory we used this capability to conduct scout experiments, which defined functional regions of interest, that were then studied more intensively in the remainder of the session (see Figure 21.5 and color plate 21.5). The yellow regions indicate the areas of left dorsolateral prefrontal cortex involved in the performance of a simple memory task, for a long interval (solid line) and a short interval (dashed line). We have implemented this procedure in an experiment that sought to determine the impulse-response function of the fMRI signal in response to manipulations of working memory load. Previous studies using visual stimuli have determined that there are linear and nonlinear regimes to this function in the primary visual cortex, depending upon the duration and intensity of

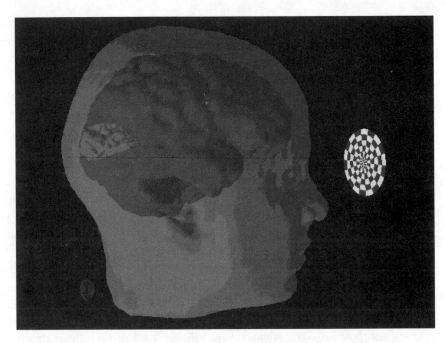

Visualization of brain regions activated by a flashing visual stimulus (from the online demonstration at Supercomputing '96). (See also color plate 21.4.)

the stimulus [21.3, 21.20]. We wished to extend this approach to study the effects of cognitive manipulations on activation within association cortex.

We designed a simple scout experiment using a robust manipulation of working memory that was known to reliably activate the regions of interest in a two-condition design [21.5]. We ran this experiment while scanning the entire frontal cortex and monitored the results using online processing until reliable activation of the regions of interest was observed. We then limited further scanning to just these regions and conducted the full impulse-response function experiment. We used this design in four subjects. On average, we were able to identify the regions of interest within 20 minutes. This left us 40 minutes in the scan session, during which we focused scanning on just those slices necessary to cover the regions of interest defined during the scout experiment (7 slices), which yielded a total of 288 scans per slice in each of the conditions of our impulse-response experiment. In the absence of the online capability, using the entire 60-minute session to scan all of the frontal cortex (12 slices), we could have achieved at most 232 scans per slice per condition. Thus, the availability of online processing, and the use of a scouting strategy, improved our acquisition rate

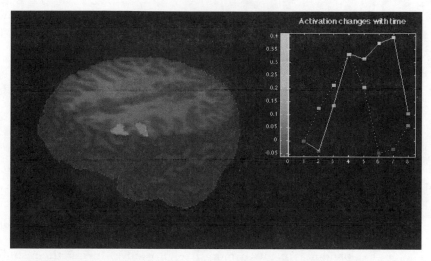

Activation changes with time

21.5

FIGURE

An example use of fMRI to investigate the mechanisms of working memory. (See also color plate 21.5.)

in the regions of interest by 24 percent, which, in turn, increased the statistical power available for the analysis.

21.5.3   What Are the Next Problems to Tackle?

Realtime Capability

A logical extension of the online capability described in this chapter is reduction of latency from several minutes to seconds. In principle this will be achievable with existing hardware. Using echo-planar fMRI [21.1, 21.13], acquired data will be immediately available for computation from the back-plane of the imaging device (see Section 21.4.2). We plan to route this data straight to the Cray T3E for reconstruction and estimation of motion correction parameters, which will then be fed back to the scanner control software so as to maintain the scan planes in their original location in the subject's brain. To the extent that this successfully stabilizes the scan planes, subsequent analysis (either offline or using the online capability described here) will be subject to reduced noise and will not require further motion correction, thus reducing processing. Development of this realtime motion-correcting feedback loop will be achieved in two stages. First, we will develop a new method that will compile a FIASCO script down into a single program that unifies the processing of all stages and allows intermediate results to be passed in memory, avoiding nearly all of the disk I/O except for reading the raw input data and writing the final results. Second, we need to link the scanner and the Cray T3E using a distributed MPI-based program in which data transfer will be handled in MPI [21.19] messages rather than via the current many-megabyte file transfers.

Clinical Applications

The requirements for clinical applications of functional MRI are very different from those of neuroscientific research applications. First, while neuroscientific research studies often involve numerous subjects over whom data are combined to increase statistical power, clinical studies involve an individual patient for whom meaningful results must be extracted. Second, our experiences indicate that patients are much more likely to move during their study than healthy young volunteers commonly used in research studies. Third, there may be a need to make therapeutic decisions in a short time frame following the clinical fMRI study. These factors combine to strongly motivate the need for online and even realtime processing of fMRI data. With online processing, the results of an fMRI study will be known before the patient leaves the scanner. Because head movement is a problem, it would be ideal if the processing included registration as well as image reconstruction and statistical processing. If the study is too corrupted by movement or other artifacts for use, then it can be repeated, much in the same way that portions of clinical MR exams are repeated when the patient moves. It would be impractical to bring many patients back for a repeat examination. Finally, many clinical applications involve therapeutic decisions based on the results of an fMRI study. For example, in neurosurgical planning it is often desirable to scan the patient the same day as surgery, further motivating the need for rapid fMRI processing.

21.6   SUMMARY

In this chapter we have described a new capability for analyzing and visualizing brain activity while a subject is performing a cognitive or perceptual task in a magnetic resonance scanner. This online capability integrated geographically distributed hardware (scanner, parallel computer, and visualization platform) via commodity networking. We described how we parallelized the existing analysis software and presented results for a diverse set of parallel platforms. Finally, we discussed some of the new possibilities this online capability presents for scientific studies and clinical intervention. The holy grail of realtime fMRI processing appears to be achievable on the Cray T3E. We have used this capability in scientific studies and anticipate it will become a routine clinical tool in the years ahead.

ACKNOWLEDGMENTS

Development of the software was supported by the National Science Foundation under grant #IBN-9418982 and grant #DMS-9505007. Benchmark runs on the Cray T3E were supported by the National Science Foundation under PSC grant #ASC960009P; runs on the SGI-Cray Origin and HP-Convex Exemplar were supported by the National Science Foundation under NCSA grant #ASC970022N. Benchmark runs on the IBM SP2 were supported by the center for the Neural Basis of Cognition, Carnegie Mellon University, and the University of Pittsburgh. We would also like to thank Jana Asher for volunteering as a subject for our experimental scans.

References

[21.1]   Bandettini, P. A., E. C. Wong, R. S. Hinks, R. S. Tikofsky, and J. S. Hyde. 1992. Time Course of EPI of Human Brain Function During Task Activation. *Magnetic Resonance in Medicine,* **25,** 390–397.

[21.2]   Belliveau, J. W., R. C. McKinstry, B. R. Buchbinder, R. M. Weisskoff, M. S. Cohen, J. M. Vevea, T. J. Brady, and B. R. Rosen. 1991. Functional Mapping of the Human Visual Cortex by Magnetic Resonance Imaging. *Science,* **254,** 716–719.

[21.3]   Boynton, G. M., S. A. Enger, G. H. Glover, and D. J. Heeger. 1996. Linear Systems Analysis of Functional Magnetic Resonance Imaging in Human V1. *J. Neuroscience,* **16,** 4207–4221.

[21.4]   Caudel, T. P., C. P. Dolan, N. Ebeid, and N. H. Goddard. 1988. Real-time Issues in Knowledge-based Decision Support Systems. In *Proceedings of the ESD/SMI Conference on Expert Systems '88—Solutions in Manufacturing,* Dearborn, MI, April.

[21.5]   Cohen, J. D., S. D. Forman, T. D. Braver, B. J. Casey, D. Servan-Schreiber, and D. C. Noll. 1994. Activation of the Prefrontal Cortex in a Nonspatial Working Memory Task with Functional MRI. *Human Brain Mapping,* **1,** 293–304.

[21.6]   Cohen, J. D., W. M. Perlstein, T. S. Braver, L. E. Nystrom, D. C. Noll, J. Jonides, and E. E. Smith. 1997. Temporal Dynamics of Brain Activation During a Working Memory Task. *Nature,* **386,** 604–608.

[21.7]   Eddy, W. F., M. Behrman, P. A. Carpenter, S. Y. Chang, J. S. Gillen, M. A. Just, T. A. Keller, A. Mockus, T. A. Tasciyan, and K. R. Thulborn. 1995. Test-Retest Reproducibility During fMRI Studies: Primary Visual and Cognitive Paradigms. In *Proceedings of the Society of Magnetic Resonanace Third Scientific Meeting and Exhibition,* **2,** 843.

[21.8]   Eddy, W. F., M. Fitzgerald, C. R. Genovese, A. Mockus, and D. C. Noll. 1996. Functional Image Analysis Software—Computational Olio. In A. Prat (editor), *Proceedings in Computational Statistics,* pp. 39–49, Heidelberg: Physica Verlag.

[21.9]   Eddy, W. F., M. Fitzgerald, and D. C. Noll. 1996. Improved Image Registration by Using Fourier Interpolation. *Magnetic Resonance in Medicine,* **36**, 923–931.

[21.10]   Forman, S. D., J. D. Cohen, M. Fitzgerald, W. F. Eddy, M. A. Mintun, and D. C. Noll. 1995. Improved Assessment of Significant Change in Functional Magnetic Resonance Imaging (fMRI): Use of a Cluster Size Threshold. *Magnetic Resonance in Medicine,* **33,** 636–647.

[21.11]   Geist, A., A. Beguelin, J. Dongarra, W. Jiang, R. Manchek, and V. Sunderam. 1994. *PVM: Parallel Virtual Machine.* Cambridge, MA: MIT Press.

[21.12]   Goddard, N. H., G. Hood, J. D. Cohen, W. F. Eddy, C. R. Genovese, D. C. Noll, and L. E. Nystrom. Online Analysis of Functional MRI Datatsets on Parallel Platforms. *Journal of Supercomputing,* **11**(3), 295–318.

[21.13]   Kwong, K. K., J. W. Belliveau, D. A. Chesler, I. E. Goldberg, R. M. Weisskoff, P. Poncelet, D. N. Kennedy, B. E. Hoppel, R. Turner, H. M. Cheng, T. J. Brady, and B. R. Rosen. 1992. Dynamic Magnetic Resonance of Human Brain Activity During Primary Sensory Stimulation. *Proceedings of the National Academy of Sciences,* **89** (June), 5675–5679.

[21.14]   Lauterbur P. C., 1973. Image Formation by Induced Local Interactions: Examples Employing Nuclear Magnetic Resonance. *Nature,* **242**, 190–191.

[21.15]   Nelder, J. A., and R. Mead. 1965. A Simplex Method for Function Minimization. *Computer Journal,* **7**, 308–313.

[21.16]   Noll, D. C., J. D. Cohen, C. H. Meyer, and W. Schneider. 1995. Spiral K-space MR Imaging of Cortical Activation. *Journal of Magnetic Resonance Imaging,* **5**, 49–56.

[21.17]   Ogawa, S., D. W. Tank, D. W. Menon, J. M. Ellermann, S. Kim, H. Merkle, and K. Ugurbil. 1992. Intrinsic Signal Changes Accompanying Sensory Stimulation: Functional Brain Mapping Using MRI. *Proceedings of the National Academy of Sciences,* **89**, 5951–5955.

[21.18]   Schneider, W., B. J. Casey, and D. C. Noll. 1994. Mapping Activation Stimulus Rate Dependence for Characters Across Multiple Visual Processing Stages with fMRI. *Human Brain Mapping,* **1**, 117–133.

[21.19]   Snir, M., S. W. Otto, S. Huss-Lederman, D. W. Walker, and J. Dongarra. 1996. *MPI: The Complete Reference.* Cambridge, MA: MIT Press.

[21.20]   Vazquez, A. L., and D. C. Noll. 1996. Non-linear Temporal Aspects of the BOLD Response in fMRI. In *International Society of Magnetic Resonance in Medicine, Proceedings, 4th Meeting,* p. 1765.

[21.21]   Woods, R. P., J. C. Mazziotta, and S. R. Cherry. 1993. Automated Image Registration. In K. Uemura et al. (eds.), *Quantification of Brain Function,* pp. 391–400. Amsterdam: Excerpta Medica.

Selective and Sensitive Comparison of Genetic Sequence Data

Alexander J. Ropelewski
Hugh B. Nicholas, Jr.
David W. Deerfield II   Pittsburgh Supercomputing Center, Carnegie Mellon University

22.1   INTRODUCTION

We have developed Msearch, a program for comparing genetic sequence data. The program implements several distinct comparison algorithms to allow researchers to perform sensitive and selective searches through genetic sequence data libraries. The comparison algorithms utilize dynamic programming, which guarantees the optimal solution and places no restriction on the underlying biological model for evolution. This program, when run on a high-performance computer such as the Cray T3E, can search through the entire National Biomedical Research Foundation's Protein Identification Resource's data library with a large protein sequence in an amount of time comparable to that required by less rigorous approaches on workstations.

22.2   INDUSTRIAL CONSIDERATIONS

A primary use of sequence data today is to identify the expression patterns of genes associated with specific diseases or involved in responses to drugs. The identification effectiveness depends on the availability of sequence data and the rapid comparison of expression pattern data with database entries.

22.2.1   Overview/Statement of the Problem

Well-characterized sequences in the genetic sequence data libraries are the result of many projects focused on diverse scientific problems. These sequence compilations are useful to researchers who are trying to categorize features contained in other sequences. These sequence compilations contain information about the biochemistry and physiology of each sequence, the species from which it was obtained, as well as cross references to scientific literature. Comparing the residues of an unknown sequence with the residues in categorized sequences will potentially allow the researcher to find fragments or homologous domains that can be used to infer structure or biochemical function.

The economic and social importance of effective sequence data library searching cannot be overestimated; comparing sequences is our most powerful tool for identifying and applying previously determined experimental knowledge to a current research problem. This knowledge greatly enhances the speed and effectiveness of new research by replacing what can be years of random search by trial-and-error experiments with carefully designed experiments that test specific, well-founded hypotheses.

The difference in medical science's progress toward a treatment or cure for cystic fibrosis and type 1 neurofibromatosis, genetic diseases that affect similar numbers of people, clearly shows the advantages of having such knowledge and in being able to apply it effectively. The genes and corresponding protein sequences that, when mutated, give rise to both diseases were discovered within a year of each other. In the case of cystic fibrosis, a successful search through categorized sequences provided insights into the biochemistry that eliminated years of costly trial-and-error experimentation at a modest cost in computer and personnel time. This, in turn, is making effective treatments available earlier than they would have been in the absence of sequence-comparison technology. Today, there are many very promising clinical trials underway for the treatment of cystic fibrosis. Research for type 1 neurofibromatosis, after almost 10 years, still focuses on discovering the basic biochemical role of the protein in cellular biology rather than on treatment or cure.

In order to search sequence data libraries effectively, the researcher needs to focus on the goal of the search. The goal of the search is to use the newly determined gene or protein sequence to accurately sort the sequence data library into two groups: a group of sequences potentially related to the newly determined sequence through evolution, and a group of sequences not related to the newly determined sequence. This requires that the researcher conduct the search using a strategy designed to find even the hard-to-find evolutionary relationships rather than, as is all too often the case, a strategy designed to minimize the computational requirements.

There are four basic factors that the researcher needs to consider in designing a search through a sequence data library. These are the algorithm used to compare the sequences; the similarity scores used in the comparisons; the scores for insertion and deletion events; and the treatment of length variation in the sequence data. Although these four factors are generally presented in terms of a computer program or data for the program, they each are fundamentally related to the biology and evolutionary processes that have given rise to both the query sequence and the sequences in the data library. Thus, each choice of these four factors is a choice of the biological and evolutionary relationships that will relate the query sequence to any sequence in the data libraries that the search will identify as related to the query.

The choice of algorithm is effectively the choice of what restriction, if any, will be placed on the pattern of substitutions, insertions, and deletions that can be detected in the common evolutionary history of the two sequences. The choice of similarity scores is the choice of how far we expect the two sequences to have diverged from each other and what substitutions we are most likely to see at that degree of divergence. The choice of scores for insertion and deletion events reflects our expectations about how rare or common insertions and deletions are relative to substitutions of one residue for another, as well as our expectations of finding either a few long insertion or deletion events or many short insertion or deletion events.

When the query sequence and all of the categorized sequences related to the query sequence are distantly related, the search will require the maximum sensitivity to discover the related sequences amidst the background of unrelated sequences. In this case, it is important to use a comparison algorithm that rigorously finds the best match between the sequences without imposing any artificial assumptions or approximations designed to save computational resources. This point seems straightforward from theoretical considerations and has been confirmed in extensive tests [22.4, 22.37, 22.38]. Unfortunately, many practicing molecular biologists are still hurrying back to their laboratories after cursory searches optimized for speed rather than sensitivity. Perhaps they have yet to realize that by taking advantage of modern supercomputers they could carry out a comprehensive and much more sensitive search in about the same time that they currently spend carrying out the cursory, less sensitive search on a workstation, departmental computer, or an e-mail/Web server.

The choice of the quantitative measure used to evaluate residue substitutions is also an important determinant of the sensitivity and effectiveness of a sequence database search. The comparison of one sequence residue with another sequence residue requires a quantitative measure of whether a residue mismatch is likely to be observed (a conservative substitution) or is unlikely to be observed compared to some statistical random model. This measure is usually based upon a log-odds substitution table that is derived from macroscopic observations for a series of sequences [22.6, 22.14]. But although these substitution matrices, based on observed mutations across several families of proteins, have been invaluable in finding related regions, it is desirable to have more specific information about the mutability of each residue at each position to reflect whether a residue must be conserved to maintain structure or function or can be mutated with little effect on biological function. This position-specific substitution matrix also provides additional information as to the likelihood of insertions and deletions in the sequence at each position.

There have been numerous approaches to defining the position-specific matrix for searching sequence data [22.3, 22.9, 22.10]. The most accurate method of creating a position-specific substitution matrix is to align, or show the residue juxtaposition of, hundreds of related sequences and examine the mutability at each position to develop a true log-odds measure [22.15]. A common approach is to create a position-specific matrix based upon a weighted average of the occurrence of each residue in a small multiple sequence alignment with a log-odds similarity matrix. Although the exact details depend upon the implementation, the approach can be summarized as (1) determining the frequency for each residue "k" in position "j" ($\text{Freq}(j,\text{Res}(k))$), and (2) computing the residue-specific score for residue "i" at position "j" ($\text{Profile}(j,\text{Res}(i))$) by summing the product of the frequency for each residue with the appropriate entry from a similarity matrix for the replacement of residue "i" by residue "k" ($\text{S}(i,k)$). Thus, the generalized form can be written as

$$\text{Profile}(j,\text{Res}(i)) = \sum_{k=1}^{20} \text{Freq}(j,\text{Res}(k)) * \text{S}(i,k) \tag{22.1}$$

The resulting term for each residue at each position represents a combination of what is observed in the multiple sequence alignment data and what has previously been seen as either conservative or nonconservative mutations in larger, more general datasets. Additional terms for gaps occurring at a particular position can also be developed. Searching a data library with a profile provides greater sensitivity and selectivity than a normal sequence-sequence comparison [22.10]. Other approaches to position-specific scoring matrices have employed explicit Baysian models of pseudocounts [22.15, 22.21].

22.3   APPROACHES USED TO COMPARE SEQUENCES

The most sensitive and selective comparison algorithms use dynamic programming to discover the optimal path (Figure 22.1) between the sequences being compared. The first sequence-comparison algorithm to use dynamic programming was for comparisons that encompass the entire length of both sequences [22.28] (global alignment). These alignments penalize gaps in the alignment equally regardless of their placement within the alignment; thus they work well when the two sequences being compared are the same size. Sellers [22.42] introduced quasi-global alignment, which penalizes gaps at the beginning and ending of the alignment differently from other gaps found in the alignment. Quasi-global alignments are ideally suited for forcing an alignment of an entire small domain within a multiple domain protein. Later, Smith and Waterman [22.44] reported a variation that produces the best matching subregions between the pair of sequences (local alignment). This algorithm has received widespread use, primarily to search sequence data libraries with unclassified sequences. Waterman and Eggert [22.47] extended the local alignment algorithm of Smith and Waterman to include identifying the "n-best" nonintersecting alignments. This derivative is extremely useful for finding repeats within a sequence (e.g., the multiple kringle domains in tissue plasminogen activator).

The computational resources (both CPU and memory) for implementing dynamic programming in sequence comparison are proportional to the product of the lengths of the sequences being compared. (There are, however, alternative implementations of these sequence-comparison algorithms that reduce the memory requirements at the cost of increased CPU usage [22.16, 22.17, 22.27].) Given the size of today's database and an average query length, the total computational requirements of a complete database search will strain workstation-class machines. Sequence databases are doubling in size every 18 months and will continue to do so for the indefinite future, while workstation performance will not increase this rapidly. Therefore, dynamic programming sequence comparisons will require high-performance computers rather than workstations if the

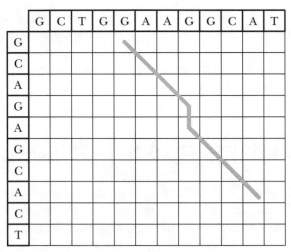

Alignment: G A A G – G C A
           G C A G A G C A

22.1

FIGURE

Path graph representing the Smith-Waterman alignment of two DNA sequences [22.40].

time necessary to receive results is to be attractively short to experimental molecular biologists.

22.3.1   Visualization of Sequence Comparison

The easiest way to visualize a sequence comparison is by the use of a *path graph*. Consider a 2D plot with one sequence along the top (from left to right) and the second sequence on the left side (from top to bottom) (Figure 22.1). A line is drawn connecting the cells that contain the best juxtaposition of residues or alignment between the two sequences. Diagonal line segments represent an extension of the alignment by either a match or mismatch, while insertions and deletions are represented by horizontal and vertical line segments (depending on which sequence has the insertion). Path graphs provide an easy and clear method for visualizing how the comparison algorithms are implemented. An advantage to using comparison algorithms utilizing dynamic programming is that all sequence juxtapositions are considered when the sequences are compared.

22.3.2   Basic Sequence-Sequence Comparison Algorithm

The local-alignment algorithm [22.44] is easily described as a recursive mathematical equation (Equation 22.2, Figure 22.2) where the value for $Cell_{i,j}$ (representing the partial alignment ending with the match of residue i from sequence A with residue j of sequence B) is the maximum of four terms. The first term ($Cell_{i-1,j-1} + S(A_i,B_j)$) corresponds to the extension of the alignment by one residue from each sequence with $S(A_i,B_j)$ being the value for substituting residue A_i for residue B_j. The next two terms are for the insertion of a gap into either Sequence A ($Cell_{i-k,j} + Gap_j$) or Sequence B ($Cell_{i,j-k} + Gap_i$). The gap penalty (Gap) is either the sum of the open gap penalty with the product of the length of the gap and the extend gap penalty (i.e., Gap = OpenGap + Length × ExtendGap) for the affine gap model or, in the case of the length-dependent gap penalty, it is the product of the length of the gap and the gap penalty (i.e., Gap = Length × GapPenalty). The last term (0), which is not used in global alignments, forces all cells to be nonnegative. That is, for local alignments, the partial scores within the table are not allowed to become negative. Thus, the best-scoring regions do not have to overcome the effects of surrounding regions of low similarity in order to achieve a high score.

$$Cell_{i,j} = \max\{Cell_{i-1,j-1} + S(A_i,B_j); Cell_{i-k,j}+Gap_j; Cell_{i,j-k}+Gap_i; 0\} \quad (22.2)$$

To recover the best alignment, or residue juxtapositions, from the table of computed similarity scores, the algorithm starts at the cell with the highest score and then determines the path that leads to this score (Figure 22.1). The backtracking ends when it reaches a cell with a value of 0. This path does not necessarily go through all local maxima, which potentially represent maxima for other suboptimal alignments. In the Waterman-Eggert [22.47] extension, the values in the cells for the best alignment are zeroed out, and the matrix is then recalculated with the restriction that the cells that were part of a previous best alignment must remain zero. The next best nonintersecting alignment is shown by the highest score in the recalculated matrix.

22.3.3   Basic Sequence-Profile Comparison Algorithm

The local-profile comparison algorithm [22.9] is also easily described as a recursive mathematical equation (Equation 22.3, Figure 22.3) where the value of

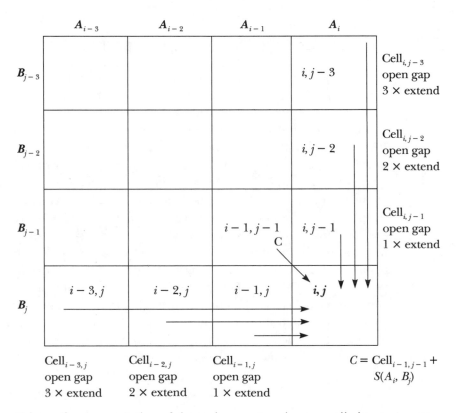

Schematic representation of dynamic programming as applied to sequence-sequence comparison [22.40].

$\text{Cell}_{i,j}$ is the maximum of four terms. The first term ($\text{Cell}_{i-1,j-1}$ + Profile(j,Res(i))) corresponds to the extension of the alignment with Profile(j,Res(i)) being the value of substituting the residue of position i of the sequence into position j of the profile. The next two terms are for the insertion of a gap into the sequence and profile, respectively. The gap penalty has the same form as was used in sequence-sequence alignment; that is, there is both an open and extend gap penalty. To provide for a position-specific term, each residue in the profile is assigned a multiplier for both the open (New Gap Multiplier, NGM) and extend gap (Extend Gap Multiplier, EGM).

The cost of inserting a gap of length k into the profile is the sum of the value of the cell where the gap is opened ($\text{Cell}_{i,j-k}$) and the open gap penalty times the New Gap Multiplier for the cell where the gap is opened (New

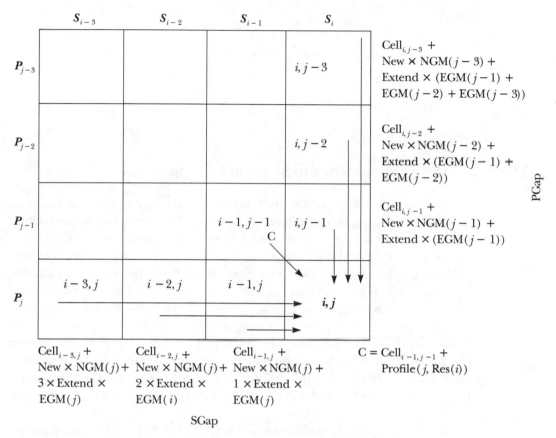

$$Cell_{i,j-3} +$$
$$New \times NGM(j-3) +$$
$$Extend \times (EGM(j-1) +$$
$$EGM(j-2) + EGM(j-3))$$

$$Cell_{i,j-2} +$$
$$New \times NGM(j-2) +$$
$$Extend \times (EGM(j-1) +$$
$$EGM(j-2))$$

$$Cell_{i,j-1} +$$
$$New \times NGM(j-1) +$$
$$Extend \times (EGM(j-1))$$

PGap

$$Cell_{i-3,j} +$$
$$New \times NGM(j) +$$
$$3 \times Extend \times$$
$$EGM(j)$$

$$Cell_{i-2,j} +$$
$$New \times NGM(j) +$$
$$2 \times Extend \times$$
$$EGM(i)$$

$$Cell_{i-1,j} +$$
$$New \times NGM(j) +$$
$$1 \times Extend \times$$
$$EGM(j)$$

$$C = Cell_{i-1,j-1} +$$
$$Profile(j, Res(i))$$

SGap

22.3

FIGURE

Schematic representation of dynamic programming as applied to Sequence-Profile comparisons.

$\times$ NGM($j \times k$)) and the extend gap penalty times the sum over the length of the gap of the extend gap multipliers (Extend* $\overset{K}{\underset{a=1}{\Sigma}}$ EGM($j - a$)). The cost of inserting a gap of length 1 into the sequence is the sum of the value of the cell where the gap was opened (Cell$_{i-1,j}$) and the open gap penalty times the appropriate new gap multiplier (New $\times$ NGM(j)) and the extend gap penalty times the length of the gap times the appropriate extend gap multiplier (1 $\times$ Extend $\times$ EGM(j)).

$$Cell_{i,j} = max\{Cell_{i-1,j-1} + Profile(j, Res(i)); SGap; PGap; 0\} \qquad (22.3)$$

where

$$SGap = \max_{1 < 1 < i} \{Cell_{i-1,j} + New * NGM(j) + 1 * Extend * EGM(j)\}$$

$$PGap = \max_{1 < k < j} \{Cell_{i,j-k} + New * NGM(j-k) + Extend * \sum_{a=1}^{k} EGM(j-a)\}$$

22.3.4   Other Approaches to Sequence Comparison

Numerous approaches [22.38] have been developed to reduce the computational resources required for database searches. This reduction is generally at the cost of reducing the sensitivity and selectivity of the database search.

One of the initial approaches used hashing to identify the regions most likely to contain the best local alignment between the two sequences [22.48]. The more successful implementations, such as FASTA [22.36], explore the identified region using dynamic programming to determine the final alignment. This procedure greatly reduces the alignment region, which accounts for the significant decrease in computational resources. However, this approach does not guarantee that the best alignment will be found because the optimal alignment may not exist within this reduced alignment region. Furthermore, if the length of an insertion is wider than the alignment region explored, the complete alignment will not be presented.

A second approach, as implemented in BLAST [22.1], is to reduce the alignment model by requiring long stretches of conservative substitutions without insertions or deletions. The alignment model, based on the idea of Maximal Segment Pairs [22.20], has well-defined properties, which allows statistical significance to be computed.

22.4   COMPUTATIONAL CONSIDERATIONS

22.4.1   Why Use an MPP?

The natural parallelism that is involved with the sequence comparison process [22.40] makes MPPs an attractive choice for sensitive searches. For simple cases, an example might be a comparison of a researcher's experimental sequence with all of the sequences in the sequence data libraries. This is likely to involve multiple searches with different choices of residue-substitution matrices. As we have discussed, the choice of residue-substitution matrix determines the level of divergence between the query sequence and the sequences identified during a database search. Thus, multiple searches with different residue-similarity matrices are necessary to probe the sequence data library with sufficient sensitivity at varying degrees of divergence.

More extensive studies have used high-performance computers to compare a large amount of sequences with themselves in order to

+ gain an understanding of the statistical distribution of alignment scores [22.23, 22.45]. These studies discovered that comparing a sequence with a sequence data library will yield an extreme value distribution.

+ understand the selection of alignment parameters and their effects. Work by Jones et al. [22.19] used a TMC CM-2 to demonstrate the existence of the phase transition with regard to gap penalties in protein sequence comparison.

+ establish the benefits of using rigorous alignment algorithms. A study by Brutlag et al. [22.4] used a MASPAR supercomputer to measure the ability of various sequence-comparison algorithms to detect the remote members of several protein superfamilies.

+ examine the differing patterns of replacement and conservation within gene families and across different gene families within a related superfamily [22.18].

None of these discoveries would have been possible at the time using conventional workstations.

22.4.2   Programming Considerations

A thorough review of implementing genetic sequence analysis codes on various supercomputers can be found in Ropelewski et al. [22.40]. A brief history of our past work related to the Msearch program is presented next.

The Msearch code traces its history to 1989, where it began life as the Pittsburgh Supercomputing Center's (PSC) MaxSegs sequence analysis code. The MaxSegs code, a fully vectorized Fortran code, is still used today on both vector supercomputers and scalar machines. In 1990, the PSC was fortunate to obtain a Thinking Machines CM-2 supercomputer. The CM-2 MPP used the SIMD architecture, and the MaxSegs code was one of the first codes ported to this machine. This port consisted of both algorithmic changes and the reworking of the CPU-intense portions of the code in the PARIS parallel subroutine library. This comparison-only code, although fast, could not retrieve the sequence alignments. This problem was solved when a heterogeneous version of the code was developed [22.3]. This heterogeneous approach, in which the initial table of scores (Figure 22.2) was computed on the CM-2 and the sequence alignments were generated on a Cray Y-MP, won third prize at the Mannheim SuParCup '91 competition.

A few years later, the PSC obtained a Thinking Machines CM-5 supercomputer. The CM-5 was one of the first SPMD machines on the market. Once again, the MaxSegs code was ported to this new platform. On the CM-5, two different implementation models were tried. The first was a data-parallel model that used CM-Fortran. This model was essentially the original CM-2 code with all of the PARIS subroutine calls replaced with Fortran90-like statements. The second model used message passing and a manager-worker arrangement. One processor on the CM-5 ran the manager code, while the remaining processors ran the worker code (Figure 22.4). The manager-worker code was essentially the original vector MaxSegs code with a few modifications to use the CMMD message-passing library. On the CM-5, the message-passing approach proved superior to the original data-parallel approach both because of reduced runtimes and the capability to generate alignments within a single machine [22.40].

In 1994, the PSC received a prototype Cray T3D. The Cray T3D required a traditional Cray vector supercomputer to act as a front end to the MPP. The front end performed many functions that were unavailable on the T3D. Because of our earlier success using message passing, we decided to port the CM-5 message-passing code to the T3D. In our original implementation, we used the Cray front end as the host processor and the T3D as nodes. We decided on this strategy because the processor speed on the Cray front end was dramatically faster than on the T3D. Heterogeneous PVM was not available at this time, so we instead converted our CM-5 CMMD code to DHSC, a high-speed communication library developed by the PSC [22.26]. This new code was one of the first to run successfully on the T3D. Unfortunately, this model was not used in production because of the relatively high latency between the T3D and the front-end Cray [22.49], and it did not improve when heterogeneous PVM became available. However, a model that used T3D processors as both the host processor and the node was successful on the T3D [22.49].

While this work was ongoing, another state-of-the-art sequence analysis code, Profile-SS, was being developed. This code, also a fully vectorized Fortran code, is still used today on both vector supercomputers and scalar machines. Because a parallel version of this code was also desired, a decision was made to merge

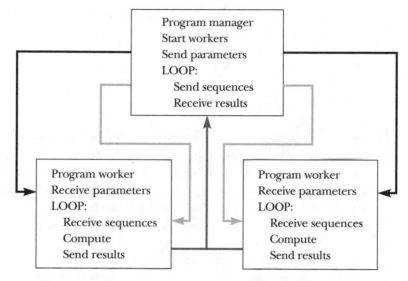

Schematic representation of the MaxSegs manager-worker code.

the MaxSegs and Profile-SS codes into a common parallel framework, called Msearch. The Msearch code is written in Fortran using the PVM [22.8] message-passing library. PVM, a public domain message-passing library developed at the Oak Ridge National Laboratory, allows the code to run essentially unchanged on a wide variety of MPPs and heterogeneous workstation clusters. Msearch incorporates four different sequence-comparison algorithms. Comparisons can be done using the MaxSegs algorithm [22.47], a quasi-global alignment algorithm similar to the Sellers [22.42] algorithm, as well as two extended profile-searching algorithms similar to Gribskov et al. [22.9]. An important feature included in the code is the capability of translating DNA sequences into implied protein sequences.

All three codes mentioned here (MaxSegs, Profile-SS, and Msearch) are in regular production use at the Pittsburgh Supercomputing Center. Over 500 users have employed the codes in their individual work and during sequence analysis workshops held by the center, and several scientific publications have resulted. The codes are available upon request from the authors and have been distributed to dozens of U.S. and several international sites. Among other outcomes, the codes have been used to disprove a published hypothesis [22.33], study the phytochrome family [22.50], and establish a potential relationship between sequence and supersecondary structure in gastrointestinal peptide hormones [22.35].

22.4.3   Algorithm Considerations

Sequence comparison is ideally suited to the manager-worker parallel programming style [22.40, 22.49]. In the general manager-worker model (Figure 22.4), one processor acts as the manager to handle all program input and output, dispatch tasks to the workers, and collect the completed results (either the comparison score or the alignments). The rest of the processors act as workers, performing the sequence-comparison task assigned by the manager and reporting the results to the manager.

There are other distinct advantages to using a manager-worker implementation. First, load balancing is easily achieved because thousands of sequences are compared on tens (or perhaps hundreds) of processors. Upon completing the current comparison, the processor is immediately assigned another pair of sequences to compare. Thus, the processors are idle only for a short period of time on startup and a short period of time upon completion. In addition to providing superior load balancing, overall communication is also reduced using this model; communication only occurs when the sequences are sent to the processors and the results are returned to the manager.

The manager-worker version of the programming model is susceptible to bottlenecks at the manager processor. For example, if a large number of processors complete tasks at the same time, all of them would then try to communicate with the manager at the same time. Using a large number of processors to compare small sequences is the primary cause of this problem, which is a side effect of the irregular communications patterns inherent in this model. In an ideal scenario, the number of processors would be balanced with the average length of the sequences.

The other disadvantage of this method is that the workers must have sufficient memory to perform the sequence comparison. This rarely causes problems when comparing protein sequences, but research programs, such as the Human Genome Project, are introducing long nucleotide sequences into the database. In the implementation described, an array is needed on each worker processor to store the table of values. The size of this table, if alignments are desired, is the product of the lengths of the sequences being compared. If only the alignment scores are desired, the size of this array can be reduced to a multiple of the largest sequence. Alternative algorithms that require more CPU time could be used to alleviate this situation [22.16], but they are not without other implementation drawbacks as well.

22.5   COMPUTATIONAL RESULTS

22.5.1   Performance

We compared two protein query sequences (Case 1: 1GPA—glycogen phosphorylase chain A—rabbit, 816 residues and Case 2: 1AAW—phosphotransferase system phosphohistidine-containing protein—Escherichia coli, 396 residues) with both the National Biomedical Research Foundation's Protein Identification Resource (PIR) database (Library 1) and the Bacterial section from the GenBank Nucleic Acid database (Library 2) using the MaxSegs algorithm [22.47]. Because we were using protein query sequences, the sequences in the GenBank database were translated into protein sequences using the three forward-reading frames. This translation process increases the number of sequences in the database by 3, while reducing the sequence lengths by one-third. The actual data used in this study came from PIR release 51 (28,888,923 residues from 91,006 sequences) and GenBank release 100, (77,151,279 bases from 33,535 reported sequences.)

Runtimes for the various test cases comparing the performance of a Cray T3D, Cray T3E, and a single processor on a Cray Y-MP/C90 are indicated in Figure 22.5. On the Cray T3D, 16 processors were needed to approximately match the performance of a single processor on the Cray C90. On the T3E, only 4 processors were needed to approximately match the performance of a single Y-MP/C90 processor. On the T3D, a bottleneck on the manager processor occurred in the two cases involving the PIR data library. The bottleneck occurred when using 128 and 64 processors, respectively, and is indicated on the graphs by the upswing in program times.

This bottleneck can also be seen by examining the resulting scaling graphs (Figure 22.6). Scaling is dependent on the lengths of the sequences being compared. A scaling factor can be used to predict how well an individual sequence and a sequence data library will scale. Simply put, the scaling factor is proportional to the length of the query sequence (816 for Case 1 or 396 for Case 2) multiplied by the average length of the sequences in the data library (317 for Library 1 or 760 for Library 2). The larger the scaling factor, the better the individual comparison problem will scale. Not surprisingly, Case 1 × Library 2 scaled the best followed by Case 2 × Library 2, Case 1 × Library 1, and Case 2 × Li-

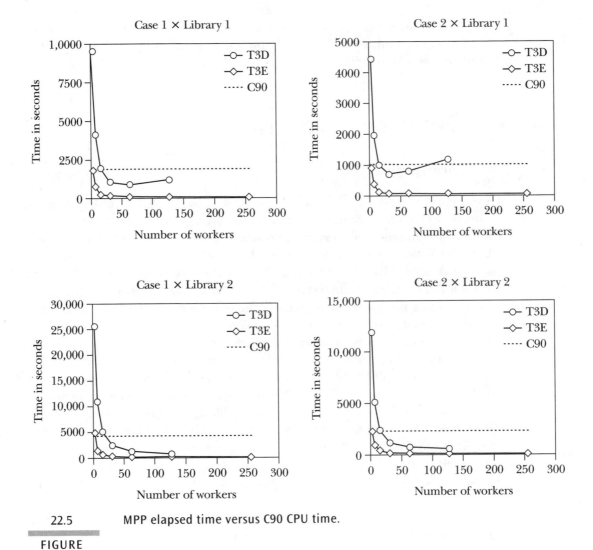

22.5

FIGURE

MPP elapsed time versus C90 CPU time.

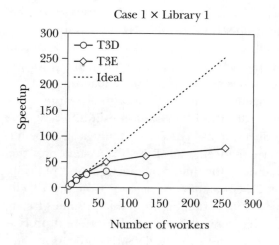

Case 1 × Library 1

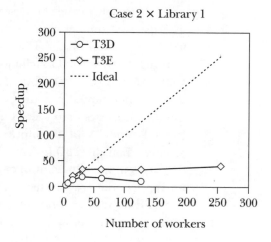

Case 2 × Library 1

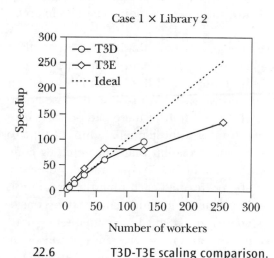

Case 1 × Library 2

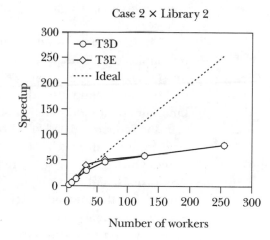

Case 2 × Library 2

22.6   T3D-T3E scaling comparison.

FIGURE

brary 1. In some cases, better-than-expected speedup was achieved because the T3E used for timings consists of both 300-MHz and 450-MHz processors.

The scalings on the T3E are superior to the scalings on the T3D for a few reasons. First, the I/O facilities on the T3D require cooperation between the C90 host and the T3D. Thus, T3D timings are affected by the load on the C90. This cooperation affects the performance in our application when large numbers of processors are used. On the T3E, the I/O system uses a different, improved model and therefore produces more consistent timings and better scalings than the T3D system. Other enhancements of the T3E system over the T3D system include equivalent bandwidth for shared-memory get and put calls and a secondary cache (see Chapter 2). For all of our test cases, from the T3D to the T3E we saw performance enhancements ranging from 5 to 10 times faster. Since the maximum performance enhancement based on the different processors alone is 4 for the 300-MHz processors and 6 for the 450-MHz processors, our application is clearly gaining performance from the additional changes in architecture.

We purposefully avoided using vendor-specific optimizations for our code in our application. Thus, we gave up some possible performance gains in exchange for portability. For example, we could have used the T3D/T3E's high-speed get and put mechanism instead of PVM for increased performance but chose not to limit our application. Another area where we could have increased performance is in the sequence data library reading. It takes a substantial amount of time to read in and parse each data library into information that can be easily compared. Our current program reads in the data libraries sequentially in their native formats, and so conversion has to be performed each time the program is run. We use this method for its ease of implementation and maintenance considerations. Sequence databases are updated frequently; all major sequence databases release new versions every 2–3 months, and most have daily or weekly incremental updates. If several database searches are to be run each day, then the benefits of reformatting the sequence data libraries become greater. A large increase in performance is possible if the sequence data libraries were to be reorganized and read in parallel.

22.6   INDUSTRIAL AND SCIENTIFIC CONSIDERATIONS

Effective sequence database searching identifies previously determined knowledge and so eliminates years of random trial-and-error experiments and makes possible experiments that test specific, well-founded hypotheses. The difference between medical science's progress toward a cure for cystic fibrosis (CF) and our progress toward a cure for type 1 neurofibromatosis (NFT1) clearly shows the advantages of having such knowledge and in being able to apply it effectively.

Both CF and NFT1 are among the most common genetic diseases in the United States. CF affects about 1 in 3300 people born in the United States, while NFT1 affects about 1 in 4000. The gene for CF and its protein product were discovered in 1989 [22.39], and researchers obtained a basic understanding of the biochemical and physiological roles of its protein product through sequence database searching that same year. The gene for NFT1 was discovered in 1990 [22.5, 22.46]; however, in contrast to CF, researchers obtained only a very limited understanding of the biochemical and physiological roles of its protein product through sequence database searches. That is, using both the gene sequence and its translated protein product as query sequences to probe sequence data libraries gave different levels of success for the CF gene and the NFT1 gene. These different levels of success have lead to very different progressions toward treatments or cures for these two inherited diseases.

Sequence searching led to the immediate identification of the protein product of the CF gene as a chloride ion channel protein, which regulates the transmembrane conductance of epithelial cells by moving chloride ions from inside the cell to outside the cell. This is an essential part of regulating the salt concentration within epithelial cells and hence their tendency to absorb water from their surroundings. Epithelial cells are the cells that form the skin as well as the surfaces of many internal organs that have contact with items brought in from outside the body. This includes the lungs and intestinal tract. The primary symptom of CF is that the epithelial cells of affected individuals secrete a very thick, nonliquified mucus rather than the normal liquid mucus. Within the year, scientists had shown that adding the normal, unmutated form of the CF protein to isolated epithelial cells afflicted with CF restored normal function to these cells.

With NFT1, only a small domain in the protein—less than 10 percent of the total protein—was identified as a regulator of the RAS protein and hence the RAS cell growth-regulating network. Experiments have confirmed that activity of the NFT1 protein but also indicate that regulation of RAS is not the major biochemical and physiological activity of the NFT1 protein. Despite strenuous efforts to identify additional biochemical and physiological functions of the NFT1 protein, these activities remain unknown. The most common techniques for experimentally identifying the unknown activities of new genes is to remove the gene completely from an experimental organism. In the case of NFT1, this is lethal early in the fetal development of organisms tested. The lack of knowledge blocks progress in treating or curing this disease because researchers cannot develop ways to test to what extent a particular therapy restores an unknown activity. Thus, finding the unknown activities of the NFT1 protein is the most urgent single task facing NFT1 researchers; it is the very knowledge that a successful data library search would have provided.

In contrast to the NFT1 case, the CF researchers succeeded in finding a well-characterized sequence similar to the CF protein in a data library. From this they learned enough about the biochemistry, the cell biology, and the physiology of the CF gene to form specific hypotheses about the disease. The single crucial experiment showing that normal CF protein added to the cell membrane would restore normal function to CF-afflicted cells put researchers in a position to begin designing specific treatments and even permanent cures for people afflicted with CF. This experiment had been successfully performed within a year of the initial identification of the gene. Additional experiments were quickly undertaken to learn about the biosynthesis and processing of the CF protein as well as the specific mechanisms by which several different common CF-causing mutations each inactivate the protein. These studies have, in turn, lead to testable hypotheses on how best to treat CF resulting from each different mutation. Work is also proceeding on several gene-therapy strategies that could provide a cure for the disease.

Researchers continue to find innovative ways to exploit comparative sequence-analysis techniques in the study of CF. One particularly innovative use of sequence comparison is a phylogenetic analysis of the CF gene and its regulatory regions to select the most effective experimental animals to use in studies. Mice and rats are the standard experimental animals in the early stages of most disease research because appropriate strains can be quickly developed and information is rarely available that another species would be a better choice. In this case, researchers took advantage of a number of known sequences along with a number of sequences that were quickly determined after the CF gene was identified to discover that the rabbit is part of a cluster of species that includes humans with very similar CF genes and regulatory regions, while the rat and mouse are in another cluster of species. CF researchers are now preparing the appropriate strains of rabbits to use in CF research with the expectation that this will make the animal research more directly applicable to humans and at the same time make it more efficient, thus reducing the total amount of animal experimentation that will be needed.

The contrast between the progress toward treatments for CF and the progress toward treatments for NFT1 should make it abundantly clear that searching sequence data libraries is an essential part of modern disease-related research programs. It has the ability to eliminate many years of costly trial-and-error experimentation at a modest cost in computer and personnel time. Where it is successful, it also makes effective treatments available earlier than they would have been in the absence of sequence database searching technology. For society as a whole, the availability of effective treatments can save great amounts of money that would have been used to maintain a patient in a reasonable degree of comfort and instead use it to allow them to live or return to a productive life. Given these potential benefits, it is important that sequence searches be carried out effectively.

22.7   THE NEXT PROBLEMS TO TACKLE

The simultaneous multiple alignment of a reasonable number of sequences requires a substantial amount of computational resources; memory is the limiting resource. Multiple sequence alignments are a powerful tool for investigating the relationship between structure and function in biological macromolecules. Such alignments represent the evolutionary history of the group of sequences [22.31] and are a record of successful mutagenesis experiments carried out by nature on a family of molecules. Thus, the alignment shows to what extent specific residues may be changed without destroying the essential structure and function of a molecule and which residues must be changed to create a new and different but related function within a similar structural framework [22.32]. As such, it is the logical starting point for directed mutagenesis laboratory experiments to study the relationship between structure and function in families of macromolecules [22.7].

Multiple sequence alignments have been essential to investigations that successfully identified the sequence residues necessary for the correct functioning of different families of transfer RNAs [22.25, 22.32] and for determining the correct secondary structure of many families of structural RNAs [22.12]. Such alignments also provide a means for testing hypotheses about gene duplication events and the origins of regulatory genes [22.33]. Multiple sequence alignments also form the basis for databases of motifs, patterns that are diagnostic for membership in particular families of molecules [22.2], or for identifying the sequence features defining the sites for posttranslational modifications [22.34, 22.41] as well as for a wide variety of investigations into macromolecular structure and function. The carefully constructed alignment of all of the aldehyde dehydrogenase sequences known at the time [22.13] is still used to guide site-directed mutagenesis studies [22.43] of important features in the recently determined crystal structure of the enzyme and in modeling paralogous members of the same superfamily [22.24].

What makes multiple sequence alignment an important supercomputing problem is that fast heuristic methods are notoriously subject to local minima problems, which leads to errors when the alignment is used to guide the analysis we have described. The most rigorous method currently available is multidimensional dynamic programming. Unfortunately, this straightforward extension of the pairwise Needleman and Wunsch sequence alignment algorithm requires CPU cycles and memory proportional to the product of the lengths of the sequences being aligned. The recent application of projective geometry techniques to this algorithm [22.11, 22.22] has made it possible to align sequences in only a small fraction of the time and memory required for the naive algorithm. At the PSC we have aligned as many as 20 real protein sequences using this technique. There are alignment problems we would like to solve by rigorous methods that involve hundreds of sequences many times longer than the 20 that we have aligned with this method.

The most fruitful current approach toward expanding the size of multiple sequence alignment problems that can be solved without systematic local minima problems is the application of the Genetic Algorithm to multiple sequence alignment. The initially successful effort has shown that a Genetic Algorithm approach can achieve the same high-quality answers that are achieved by multiple dimensional dynamic programming in a reasonable amount of computer time and with a modest amount of computer memory. This very encouraging result means that we can begin to solve large multiple sequence alignment problems with nearly the same rigor that is available for smaller problems today. Perhaps even more exciting is the prospect of overcoming some of the theoretical limitations forced on multidimensional dynamic programming by the practical constraints of CPU time. This will allow us to find alignments that have the smallest weighted sum of the changes along the branches of an evolutionary tree that relates the sequences being aligned.

Thus, a multiple sequence alignment is a valuable source of information that can be brought to bear in many ways while investigating the properties, characteristics, and functions of macromolecules. The ability to create multiple sequence alignments that more accurately reflect the evolution of the sequences in the alignment should make the alignments an even more useful and powerful guide for experimental studies.

Some families of biological macromolecules divide into distinct subfamilies that are not functionally interchangeable even though they carry out similar processes and are all descended from a common ancestral gene. High-quality multiple sequence alignments of these large families will allow us to analyze the families in terms of three categories of sequence residue:

✦ residues important to the function of the entire family

✦ residues important to the function of specific subfamilies

✦ residues that may vary freely

Understanding these subfamily relationships is essential for understanding such fundamental biological processes as communications between cells or how an organism responds to its environment. Receptors on the cell surface activate specific metabolic mechanisms through specific interactions with a complex network of mediating kinases. Both the receptors and kinases are drawn from a few large families of proteins with many subfamilies. Different malfunctions in this communications network result in many kinds of cancer as well as diseases such as high blood-fat levels and some forms of diabetes. Thus, understanding the subfamily organization of this network is important for understanding both basic human biology and many practical problems in human health. Other families of biological macromolecules are equally important to health and environmental concerns.

22.8   SUMMARY

It has been demonstrated that the use of a sensitive and selective data library search will unlock biochemical relationships that will substantially reduce the research cost and human toil. In contrast, heuristic searches, although they will reveal highly homologous relationships, are inadequate for finding distant but related sequences. High-performance computers are required in order to conduct these searches in a timely fashion, with data library searching being especially well suited for massively parallel systems.

We have implemented a full suite of alignment algorithms in an easy-to-use and well-documented program that can effectively use any high-performance computer with a high I/O throughput capability. We have shown that searching data libraries will strain even the best interprocessor networks.

ACKNOWLEDGMENTS

This work was supported by a grant to the Pittsburgh Supercomputing Center from the NIH–National Center for Research Resources (P41 RR06009) and the National Human Genome Research Institute (T15 HG00015).

References

[22.1]   Altschul, S. F., W. Gish, W. Miller, E. W. Myers, and D. J. Lipman. 1990. Basic Local Alignment Search Tool. *J. Mol. Biol.*, **215,** 403–410.

[22.2]   Bairoch, A., P. Bucher, and K. Hofmann. 1995. The PROSITE Database, Its Status in 1995. *Nucl. Acids Res.*, **24,** 189–196.

[22.3]   Bork, P., and T. Gibson. 1996. Applying Motif and Profile Searches. *Methods in Enzymology,* **266,** 162–184.

[22.4]   Brutlag, D. L., J. P., Dautricourt, R. Diaz, J. Fier, B. Moxon, and R. Stamm. 1993. Blaze. An Implementation of the Smith-Waterman Sequence Comparison Algorithm on a Massively Parallel Computer. *Computers and Chemistry,* **17,** 203–207.

[22.5]   Cawthon, R., R. Weiss, G. Xu, D. Viskochil, M. Culver, J. Stevens, M. Robertson, D. Dunn, R. Gesteland, P. O'Connell, R. White. 1990. A Major Segment of the Neurofibromatosis type 1 Gene: cDNA Sequence, Genomic Structure, and Point Mutations. *Cell,* **62,** 193–201.

[22.6]   Dayhoff, M. O., R. M. Schwartz, and B. C. Orcutt. 1978. In M. O. Dayhoff (ed.), *Atlas of Protein Sequence and Structure,* **5** (3), 345–352.

[22.7]   Eckstein, J. W., P. Beer-Romero, and I. Berdo. 1996. Identification of an Essential Acid Residue in Cdc25 Protein Phosphatase and a General Three-dimensional Model for a Core Region in Protein Phosphatases. *Prot. Sci.,* **5,** 5–12.

[22.8]   Geist, A., A. Beguelin, J. Dongarra, W. Jiang, R. Manchek, and V. Sunderam. 1994. *PVM Parallel Virtual Machine, a Users Guide and Tutorial for Networked Parallel Computing.* Cambridge MA: MIT Press.

[22.9]   Gribskov, M., R. Lüthy. and D. Eisenberg. 1990. Profile Analysis. *Methods in Enzymology,* **183,** 146–159.

[22.10]   Gribskov, M., and S. Veretnik. 1996. Identification of Sequence Patterns with Profile Analysis. *Methods in Enzymology,* **266,** 198–212.

[22.11]   Gupta, S., J. Kececioglu, and A. Schaffer. 1995. Improving the Practical Space and Time Efficiency of the Shortest-Paths Approach to Sum-of-Pairs Multiple Sequence Alignment. *J. Comput. Biol.*, **2**, 459–472.

[22.12]   Gutell, R. R., N. Larsen, and C. R. Woese. 1994. Lessons from an Evolving rRNA: 16S and 23S rRNA Structures from a Comparative Perspective. *Microbiological Review*, **58**, 10–26.

[22.13]   Hempel, J., H. Nicholas, and R. Lindahl. 1993. Aldehyde Dehydrogenases: Widespread Structural and Functional Diversity Within a Shared Framework. *Protein Science*, **2**, 1890–1900.

[22.14]   Henikoff, S., and J. Henikoff. 1992. Amino Acid Substitution Matrices Form Protein Blocks. *Proc. Natl. Acad. Sci. U.S.A.*, **89**, 10,915–10,919.

[22.15]   Henikoff, S., and J. Henikoff. 1996. Using Substitution Probabilities to Improve Position Specific Scoring Matrices. *Comput. Appl. Biosci.*, **12**, 135–143.

[22.16]   Hirschberg, D. S. 1975. A Linear Space Algorithm for Computing Maximal Common Subsequences. *Communications of the ACM*, **18**, 341–343.

[22.17]   Huang, X, R. Hardison, and W. Miller. 1990. A Space-efficient Algorithm for Local Similarities. *Comput. Appl. Biosci.*, **6**, 373–381.

[22.18]   Jones, R. 1990. *Thinking Machines Corporation Technical Report CB90-3.*

[22.19]   Jones, R., W. Taylor, X. Zhang, J. Mesirov, and E. Lander. 1990. Protein Sequence Comparison on the Connection Machine CM-2. In G. Bell, and T. Marr (eds.), *Computers and DNA.* Reading, MA: Addison-Wesley, 99–107.

[22.20]   Karlin, S., and S. F. Altschul. 1990. Methods for Assessing the Statistical Significance of Molecular Sequence Features by Using General Scoring Schemes. *Proc. Natl. Acad. Sci. U.S.A.*, **87**, 2264–2268.

[22.21]   Lawerence, C. E., S. F. Altschul, M. S. Boguski, J. S. Liu, A. F. Neuwald, and J. C. Wooton. 1993. Detecting Subtle Sequence Signals: A Gibbs Sampling Strategy for Multiple Alignment. *Science*, **262**, 208–214.

[22.22]   Lipman, D., S. Altschul, and J. Kececioglu. 1989. A Tool for Multiple Sequence Alignment. *Proc. Natl. Acad. Sci. U.S.A.*, **86**, 4412–4415.

[22.23]   Lipman, D. J., W. J. Wilbur, T. F. Smith, and M. S. Waterman. 1984. On the Statistical Significance of Nucleic Acid Similarities. *Nuc. Acids Res.*, **12**, 215–226.

[22.24]   Liu, J., Y. J. Sun, J. Rose, Y. J. Chung, C. D. Hsiao, W. R. Chang, I. Kuo, J. Perozich, R. Lindahl, J. Hempel, and B. C. Wang. 1997. Aldehyde Dehydrogenase: Crystal Structure of a Class 3 Enzyme, Novel NAD-Binding Mode and Structure-Based Mechanism. *Nature Struct. Biol.*, **4**, 317–326.

[22.25]   McClain, W. H., and H. B. Nicholas, Jr. 1987. Discrimination between Transfer RNA Molecules. *J. Mol. Biol.*, **194**, 635–642.

[22.26]   Mahdavi, J., G. Huntoon, and M. Mathis. 1992. Deployment of a HIPPI-based Distributed Supercomputing Environment at the Pittsburgh Supercomputing Center. *Proceedings of the Workshop on Heterogeneous Processing*, 93–96.

[22.27]   Myers, E., and W. Miller. 1988. Optimal Alignments in Linear Space. *Comput. Appl. Biosci.,* **4,** 11–17.

[22.28]   Needleman, S. B., and C. D. Wunsch. 1970. A General Method Applicable to the Search for Similarities in the Amino Acid Sequences of Two Proteins. *J. Mol. Biol.,* **48,** 443–453.

[22.29]   Nicholas, H. B., Jr., Y-M. Chen, and W. H. McClain. 1987. Comparisons of Transfer RNA Sequences. *Comput. Appl. Biosci.,* **3,** 53.

[22.30]   Nicholas, H. B., Jr., G. Giras, V. Hartonas-Garmhausen, M. Kopko, C. Maher, and A. Ropelewski. 1991. Distributing the Dynamic Programming Algorithm Across Heterogeneous Supercomputers. *Supercomputing 1991 Proceedings,* 139–146.

[22.31]   Nicholas, H. B., Jr., and S. B. Graves. 1983. Clustering of Transfer RNA by Cell Type and Amino Acid Specificity. *J. Mol. Biol.,* **171,** 111–118.

[22.32]   Nicholas, H. B., Jr., and W. H. McClain. 1987. An Algorithm for Discriminating Transfer RNA Sequences. *Comput. Appl. Biosci.,* **3,** 177–181.

[22.33]   Nicholas, H. B., Jr., B. Persson, H. Jornvall, and J. Hempel. 1995. Ethanol Utilization Regulatory Protein: Profile Alignments Give No Evidence of Origin Through Aldehyde and Alcohol Dehydrogenase Gene Fusion. *Prot. Sci.,* **4,** 2621–2624.

[22.34]   Nicholas, H. B., Jr., and G. L. Rosenquist. 1999. A Position Specific Scoring Matrix for Identifying Sites of Protein Tyrosine Sulfation. Manuscript in preparation.

[22.35]   Nicholas, H. B., Jr., G. L. Rosenquist, A. K. Lee, and T. Phan. 1994. Sequence Analysis for Hormone and Receptors. *Digestive Diseases and Sciences,* **39,** 1824.

[22.36]   Pearson, W. 1990. Rapid and Sensitive Sequence Comparison with FASTP and FASTA. *Methods in Enzymology,* **183,** 63–98.

[22.37]   Pearson, W. 1991. Searching Protein Sequence Libraries: Comparison of the Sensitivity and Selectivity of the Smith-Waterman and FASTA Algorithms. *Genomics,* **11,** 635–650.

[22.38]   Pearson, W. 1995. Comparison of Methods for Searching Protein Sequence Databases. *Protein Science,* **4,** 1145–1160.

[22.39]   Riordan, J., J. Rommens, B. Kerem, N. Alon, R. Rozmahel, Z. Grzelczak, J. Zielenski, S. Lok, N. Plavsic, J. Chou, M. Drumm, M. Iannuzzi, F. Collins, and L. Tsui. 1989. Identification of the Cystic Fibrosis Gene: Cloning and Characterization of Complimentary DNA. *Science,* **245,** 1055–1073.

[22.40]   Ropelewski, A. J., H. B. Nicholas, and D. W. Deerfield. 1997. Implementation of Genetic Sequence Alignment Programs on Supercomputers. *J. Supercomputing,* **11,** 237–253.

[22.41]   Rosenquist, G. L., and H. B. Nicholas, Jr. 1993. Analysis of Sequence Requirements for Protein Tyrosine Sulfation. *Protein Science,* **2,** 215–222.

[22.42]   Sellers, P. H. 1979. Pattern Recognition in Genetic Sequences. *Proc. Natl. Acad. Sci. U.S.A.,* **76,** 3041.

[22.43]   Sheikh, S., L. Ni, and H. Weiner. 1997. Mutation of the Conserved Amino Acids of Mitochondria Aldehyde Dehydrogenase. Role of the Conserved Residues in the Mechanism of Reaction. *Adv. Exp. Med. Biol.,* **414,** 195–200.

[22.44] Smith, T. F., and M. S. Waterman. 1981. Identification of Common Molecular Subsequences. *J. Mol. Biol.,* **147,** 195–197.

[22.45] Smith, T. F., M. S. Waterman, and C. Burks. 1985. The Statistical Distribution of Nucleic Acid Similarities. *Nuc. Acid Res.,* **13,** 645–656.

[22.46] Wallace, M., D. Marchuk, L. Anderson, R. Letcher, H. Odeh, A. Saulino, J. Fountain, A. Brereton, J. Nicholson, A. Mitchell, B. Brownstein, and F. Collins. 1990. Type 1 Neurofibromatosis Gene: Identification of a Large Transcript Disrupted in Three NF1 Patients. *Science,* **249,** 181–186.

[22.47] Waterman, M. S., and M. Eggert. 1987. A New Algorithm for Best Subsequence Alignments with Application to tRNA-rRNA Comparisons. *J. Mol. Biol.,* **197,** 723–728.

[22.48] Wilbur, W., and D. Lipman. 1983. Rapid Similarity Searches of Nucleic Acid and Protein Data Banks. *Proc. Natl. Acad. Sci. U.S.A.,* **80,** 726–730.

[22.49] Wimberly, F., M. Lambert, N. Nystrom, A. Ropelewski, and W. Young. 1996. Porting Third-Party Applications Packages to the Cray T3D: Programming Issues and Scalability Results. *Parallel Computing,* **22,** 1073–1089.

[22.50] Yeh, K., S. Wu, T. Murphy, and J. Lagarias. 1997. A Cyanobacterial Phytochrome Two Component Light Sensory System. *Science,* **227,** 1505–1508.

23 Interactive Optimization of Video Compression Algorithms

Henri Nicolas   Cray Research
Fred Jordan   Signal Processing Laboratory, Ecole Polytechnique Fédérale de Lausanne (EPFL), Switzerland

23.1   INTRODUCTION

One of the main difficulties for researchers when developing new digital image-processing algorithms is related to the computation time required for the scientific evaluation of the algorithms and the optimization of their parameters. This is due to the size of the manipulated data (25 or 30 images per second) and to the different thresholds or parameters that must be optimized. Furthermore, for an optimization to be correct, it must be done on several video sequences. As a consequence, in practice researchers often do not have enough time to optimize and to evaluate their algorithms correctly. This problem represents a major difficulty in the design and development of new image-processing algorithms and, consequently, leads to delay in their commercialization.

Due to the parallel nature of most low-level image-processing techniques, massively parallel computing therefore represents an attractive solution to the significant reduction of development and optimization times. In this context, some authors have already proposed efficient parallel implementations of various video compression algorithms [23.1, 23.3, 23.6, 23.7, 23.8], which demonstrates the utility of MPP technology in the video processing field. Unfortunately, even with such massively parallel implementations, the scientific evaluation of the results remains difficult due to the fact that there is no mathematical criterion to correctly evaluate the visual quality of an image. Such criteria are classically used to compare original images with their decompressed versions, but they are not sufficiently reliable. For this reason, in the ongoing development of the MPEG-4 video standard, the quality of the results is judged *only* visually [23.5].

Furthermore, image-processing algorithms often have several interdependent parameters that must be optimized simultaneously. This kind of problem remains unsolved even with existing parallel approaches.

In order to overcome these problems, we present in this chapter a new technique, an interactive system called DirectView, for realtime video processing and broadcasting system simulations [23.9, 23.10]. This system is based on efficient parallel implementation of video compression algorithms on a massively parallel computer, the Cray T3D [23.1, 23.11], with the modularity and the flexibility of a software implementation in high-level languages (C, C++) Furthermore, DirectView permits the visual evaluation of the processed image sequences as they are produced by a codec running on the parallel computer. It also allows the modification of the parameters of an algorithm in an interactive manner, thus permitting fast and efficient evaluation and optimization. This work aims to exploit, as much as possible, the parallel nature of digital image-processing algorithms to obtain almost realtime performance. This leads to a significant productivity gain when developing new video compression techniques. The possibility of performing fast and accurate optimization is of particular importance in view of the fact that the algorithms used in the MPEG-2 video standards were retained, mainly because they were fully optimized. It should be pointed out that realtime processing can also be obtained with dedicated hardware or with DSPs, but these kinds of implementations do not offer the flexibility given by our system [23.2, 23.11]. Our approach has been validated on advanced region-based video compression algorithms. The interactive facilities offered by the proposed technique permit the accurate optimization of the algorithm parameters in a few minutes rather than the several days that were previously needed. Depending on the complexity of the compression algorithms, 8–12 images are compressed, reconstructed, and visualized per second.

This chapter covers the following topics:. some industrial considerations in Section 23.2; the main characteristics of the system in Section 23.3; a description of the parallel approach used in Section 23.4; the video compression algorithm implemented in DirectView in Section 23.5; experimental results in Section 23.6; and conclusions from and perspectives on this work in Section 23.7.

23.2   INDUSTRIAL CONSIDERATIONS

Image analysis and compression of digital image sequences represent a rapidly growing market thanks to the development of such applications as digital TV, teleconferencing, medical or satellite images, and virtual or augmented reality.

As a consequence, many new video-processing techniques or algorithms must be designed in order to permit better development of these applications. As stated in the introduction, computation times and the difficulty of evaluating the results are major problems in developing new products based on new video processing algorithms. The use of the parallel approach as described here therefore represents a very promising solution for helping industries develop better products more rapidly. By using the proposed approach in an industrial context, a productivity gain can be expected.

23.3 GENERAL DESCRIPTION OF THE SYSTEM

This section presents the main technical characteristics of DirectView and its major advantages, that is, generic implementation and interactive optimization, compared to classical approaches.

23.3.1 General Principle

Two versions of the proposed system have been developed on the Cray T3D, which has been chosen to implement the DirectView concept because it is able to provide the computational power required to compress several images per second (more than 8 CIF images per second using 64 processors in the CIF format of 352×288 pixels, 8 bits/pixel, digitized at 25 frames/s). The methodology we propose does not directly depend on the characteristics of the T3D; therefore, any other parallel computer providing such computational power can be used. The proposed implementation uses the SHMEM programming model, which has been retained because it provides very low communication time due to its optimization on the T3D architecture. Nevertheless, the structure of the proposed approach does not depend on SHMEM routines. In practice, standard message-passing environments such as PVM can be used even if the communication performance decreases.

The first version of DirectView (DirectView 1.0) uses the T3D for the compression and decompression of the video data. A workstation is used only for realtime visualization of the reconstructed images. The second version (DirectView 2.0) is more ambitious, and it simulates a complete realtime video broadcasting system by exploiting the fact that for almost all video compression algorithms, the compression is significantly more complex than the decompression in terms of computational load. This property allows us to decompress one

| DirectView | Cray T3D | | | Transmission link | Workstation | |
	Compression	Bitstream generation	Decompression	Transmitted data	Decompression	Display
1.0	Yes	Yes	Yes	Decompressed images	No	Yes
2.0	Yes	Yes	No	Compressed images	Yes	Yes

23.1   **Main features of DirectView 1.0 and DirectView 2.0.**

TABLE

image on the workstation while the parallel computer compresses the following one. As a consequence, only the compressed data must be transmitted to the workstation, which is used as a decoder. Figure 23.1 and Table 23.1 give the block diagram and a synthetic comparison, respectively, of each of these versions.

With the first version of DirectView a higher transmission bandwidth is necessary (8 Mbits with a frame rate of 10 images/s and gray-level CIF images) even though the workstation is used only to visualize the decompressed images. A lower transmission bandwidth (depending on the compression ratio) is required with the second version, but higher computational load is assigned to the workstation. DirectView 2.0 works well only if the workstation is able to decompress an image as quickly as the T3D compresses an image. If it is not, the computational power of the T3D is not fully exploited (it waits for the workstation). In this case, if the transmission link capacity is sufficiently large, DirectView 1.0 is more efficient.

Apart from these differences between the two versions, DirectView works as follows: The original images are read from the hard disk of the Cray YMP by one processor of the T3D. The images are then broadcast to the other processors using optimized communication routines. Each processor compresses in parallel its own partition. The bitstream (or the decompressed images) is finally collected by a processor, which sends this data to a workstation via Ethernet or an FDDI (Fiber Distributed Data Interface) link. The reconstructed images are immediately displayed on the screen (after decompression if DirectView 2.0 is used) together with the bitrate or the compression ratio. This permits an easy evaluation of the trade-offs between the quality of the images and their transmission cost. Moreover, this system allows the interactive modification of the parameters of the algorithm running on the T3D, thus permitting their optimization.

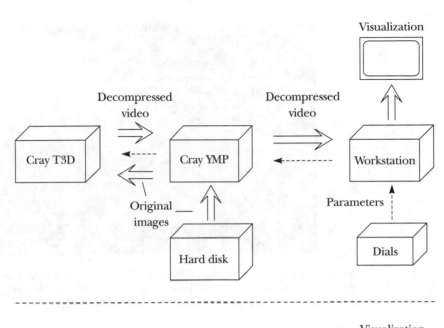

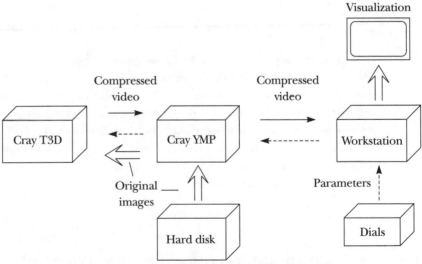

Block diagram of DirectView 1.0 (top); block diagram of DirectView 2.0 (bottom).

23.2

FIGURE

Example of data visualized on the screen: the decompressed image (top left), the current values of the dials (top right), the bitrate (bottom left), and the histogram of the image (bottom right). (See also color plate 23.2.)

This is easily done by turning a set of dials that transmit the corresponding values to the T3D.

DirectView permits not only the realtime visualization of the final result (the decompressed images) but also of other information used by the image processing algorithm, such as the segmentation of the images, various statistical information (such as the histogram), the content of the bitstream, and so on. This is of major importance for researchers because it allows fast and easy visual representation of the various data manipulated in the program. Figure 23.2 shows an example of data visualized on the screen: the decompressed image, a graph of the bitrate, the current value of the parameters, and the histogram of the displayed image. (See also color plate 23.2.)

23.3.2   Main Advantages Offered by DirectView

Generic Implementation

All the software developed for DirectView has been written using the C language, which permits flexible and modular software implementations. Consequently, the video compression algorithm can be easily changed or modified just by replacing the corresponding routines by new ones. This leads to a generic implementation that permits the testing of a wide range of video processing methods

23.3

FIGURE

Meaninglessness of the PSNR. PSNR = 25.3 dB, compression ratio = 12 (left). PSNR = 27 dB, compression ratio = 2 (right). The left image has a higher visual quality for a better compression ratio, although the PSNR is better for the right image.

or algorithms in a short time, a definite advantage for research centers in the race for the design of new multimedia systems.

Interactive Optimization

The main advantages of interactive optimization over the standard offline optimization are the following:

+ Visual evaluation: DirectView permits the visualization of the decoded images as they are being produced by the T3D. Therefore, the operator can *visually* evaluate the spatial and temporal artifacts generated by the compression algorithm. The peak signal to noise ratio (PSNR), traditionally used to compare original images with their decompressed versions, does not provide fair evaluation of the image quality, as shown in Figure 23.3. DirectView permits an evaluation of quality that is significantly better than evaluations obtained with mathematical criteria.

+ Interactive multivariable optimization: Using this system, an operator can interactively change the parameters of the compression algorithm in order to balance the trade-off between transmission cost and the quality of the decoded images. For this task, typically a multivariable optimization, for which humans are well suited, must be done. For example, a human operator will intuitively appreciate the regularity of the algorithm and will very quickly avoid local minima in which minimization algorithms are often trapped. Fur-

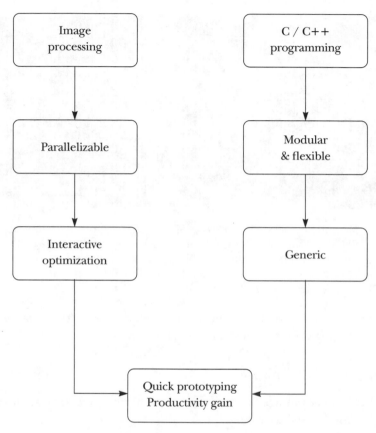

23.4   Main characteristics of DirectView.

FIGURE

thermore, DirectView avoids all the complex operations needed by classical implementations to visualize the results obtained for each value of the parameters (generation of all the results, ftp transfers between machines, format conversions for visualization, and so on). Using a classical serial implementation, the exhaustive search in the multiparameter space required to determine the optimal values is practically impossible.

✦ Debugging: Because it is possible to change the values of the algorithm parameters interactively, almost all possible values can be investigated very quickly in order to test the robustness of the algorithms. This makes possible the quick detection of special cases for which the algorithm has problems. In practice, the debugging process is significantly accelerated.

Figure 23.4 summarizes the major advantages offered by massively parallel computing in the framework of DirectView—namely, generic implementation and realtime interactive optimization. These advantages open a new perspective for researchers working in the field of video compression and analysis. The quick prototyping and productivity gain provided by DirectView permit us to improve the quality of the results and to accelerate the development of new techniques.

23.4 PARALLEL IMPLEMENTATION

Efficient visual evaluation of the images requires that they be displayed on the screen with the highest frame rate possible, which requires optimal parallelization. The iterative algorithm running on the T3D can be schematically divided into the following seven stages (see also Figure 23.6):

1. Read input images. The original images are stored on the hard disk of the YMP front-end computer and are read by one processor of the T3D. The other processors have to read this image in the local memory of PE1. In practice, PE1 reads the image at time $t + 1$ while the other PEs read the image at time t. This technique saves time by partially parallelizing the reading process.

2. Data partition. In order to optimize load balancing as much as possible among the processors while keeping a simple data partition, the images are divided into N parts of equal size, where N is the number of processors. An example with four processors is given in Figure 23.5. This data partition is independent of the compression algorithm.

3. Data compression. Each processor treats only its respective data partition. This stage represents more than 50 percent of the total computation time (for 64 PEs). Large speedups can generally be obtained for this stage because video-processing algorithms are naturally highly parallelizable.

4. Local bitstream generation. Each processor locally compresses its partition of data and generates the corresponding bitstream.

5. Generation of the entire bitstream. One processor collects the local bitstreams generated by each processor and combines them to form the complete bitstream.

6. Image reconstruction (only for DirectView 1.0). The reconstruction is performed in parallel on the T3D. The computation load is very low.

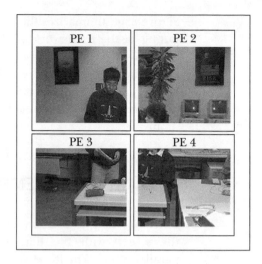

23.5   Data partition for four processors.

FIGURE

7. Communications with the workstation. The sockets of the YMP front end are used in order to accelerate the bidirectional communications between the T3D and the workstation. Two processors of the T3D are in charge of communications:

   (a) Send bitstreams: One processor is responsible for sending bitstreams to the workstation (one "send" per iteration). In order to parallelize the generation of the bitstream (stage 5) and its transmission to the workstation, the bitstream of image $t - 1$ is transmitted while the bitstream of image t is generated. This requires the transmission of the bitstream between these two processors. Nonblocking communications are used, so the communication time is negligible.

   (b) Receive new parameters: Another processor periodically tests (in every other iteration) whether new parameter values have been received from the workstation. In this case, these new values are broadcast to all other processors. In DirectView 2.0, some of these parameters are necessary for the decompression; consequently, they must be incorporated into the bitstream to be resent to the workstation. Thus we assure good synchronization between the coder and the decoder.

The left column of Figure 23.6 shows the activity of each processor of the T3D (PE1 to PEN) as a function of time together with the synchronization points

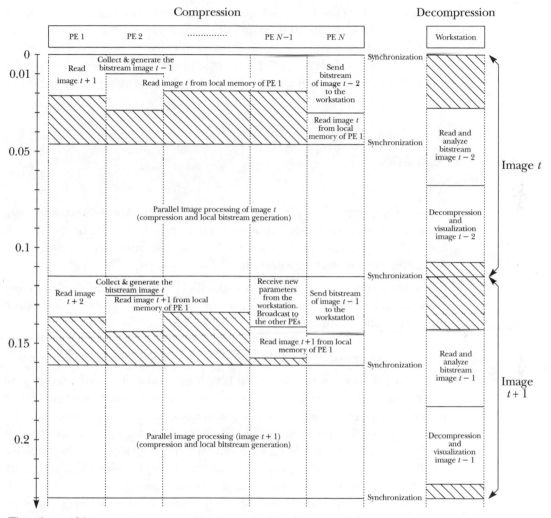

Compression

Decompression

| PE 1 | PE 2 | .... | PE N−1 | PE N | | Workstation |

Read image $t+1$

Collect & generate the bitstream image $t−1$

Read image t from local memory of PE 1

Send bitstream of image $t−2$ to the workstation

Read image t from local memory of PE 1

Parallel image processing of image t
(compression and local bitstream generation)

Synchronization

Read and analyze bitstream image $t−2$

Decompression and visualization image $t−2$

Synchronization

Read image $t+2$

Collect & generate the bitstream image t

Read image $t+1$ from local memory of PE 1

Receive new parameters from the workstation. Broadcast to the other PEs

Send bitstream of image $t−1$ to the workstation

Read image $t+1$ from local memory of PE 1

Parallel image processing (image $t+1$)
(compression and local bitstream generation)

Synchronization

Read and analyze bitstream image $t−1$

Decompression and visualization image $t−1$

Synchronization

Image t

Image $t+1$

Time (seconds)

Waiting time

23.6   Load-balancing representation (time measured for 64 processors).

FIGURE

(compression part). The right column shows the workstation activity for the reconstruction and the visualization of the images. Stages 2, 3, 4, and 6 are done in parallel by all processors. Stages 1 and 5 are performed by one processor, while two processors are used for Stage 7. Figure 23.6 illustrates the work done by each processor. We have also made a strong effort to optimize single-processor performance.

23.4.1   Remarks

+ If parallel input facilities are available, Stage 1 can be parallelized as follows: Instead of having each original image stored on only one file on the disk, N files will be used, each of them containing the data partition corresponding to a given processor. In that case, Stage 2 is cancelled.

+ In the same way, if it is possible to use parallel outputs to send the bitstream, Stage 5 can be eliminated. Each processor has to send only its portion of the bitstream. A header must be added to each local processor, however, because the workstation that will receive each of these local bitrates does not know the correspondence between them and the image that has been compressed.

+ The data partitioning just described is very general and can be used to process any kind of video sequence. The method can potentially be improved by taking into account the content of the images, for in many cases, some regions are visually more important than others or are easier to process. It would therefore be interesting to modify the data partition in order to have small data partitions for areas of interest and bigger ones elsewhere. The quality obtained after the compression-decompression process will obviously be different for these different areas. For example, the motion estimation step could be skipped in the background area in the image shown in Figure 23.5 because the background and the camera do not move. More computational power could therefore be allocated to processing the two persons.

Such an approach would seem attractive; but in practice it would be very difficult. The difficulties are from (1) defining the interesting regions, which is by nature very subjective and application dependent; (2) estimating a priori the computational load needed to process a given area with the desired quality; and (3) the change over time in the content of the video sequence, which makes impossible a definitive determination of an adaptive data partition fixed for the whole sequence. Consequentially, the use of an adaptive data partition would require the development of new, complex, and specific-image processing analysis algorithms that could also increase the computa-

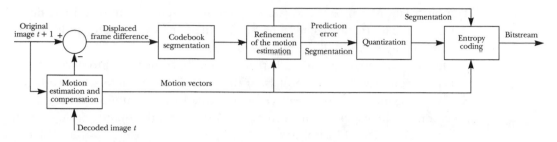

Simplified block diagram of the compression algorithm.

tional load. For these reasons, we decided to keep the data partition shown in Figure 23.5, which permits us to obtain very interesting results, as described in Section 23.6.

23.5 DESCRIPTION OF THE COMPRESSION ALGORITHM

The compression algorithm implemented in DirectView is a typical example of algorithms used or proposed for the video compression standards MPEG1 and MPEG2 and the future MPEG4, particularly in term of computational complexity. The block diagram of the proposed compression algorithm is illustrated in Figure 23.7. The temporal correlation between successive images is exploited using a classical block-based motion estimation and compensation technique. A codebook-based segmentation is then applied on each block in order to refine the segmentation, which is done by splitting the blocks when the quality obtained after motion compensation is too low. The quality evaluation is based on the PSNR. Only the blocks that have a PSNR higher than a threshold T are split [23.4]. A refinement of the motion vectors is performed in the newly created regions, using the motion displacements of the neighboring blocks in order to improve the prediction quality. Finally, the prediction error for the regions where the PSNR remains higher than T is quantized and entropy coded.

The final bitstream contains four different kinds of information:

1. Motion parameters

2. Description of the segmentation

3. Quantized prediction error

4. Flags indicating in which regions the prediction error is coded

The bitstream is sent to the decoder, where it is used for the reconstruction of the images. The reconstructed images are finally recovered after motion compensation and addition of the quantized prediction error.

In this particular algorithm, DirectView has been designed to permit the interactive modification, via the dials, of the following parameters: the codebook size, the maximal possible displacement allowed by the motion estimator, the precision of the displacement vectors, the frame rate, the quantization step, the thershold T, and the block size.

23.6   EXPERIMENTAL RESULTS

Experiments have been carried out using a Cray T3D on gray-level CIF test image sequences (352×288 gray-level pixels). The bitstream is transmitted to the workstation via a FDDI link, but Ethernet may also be used.

Figure 23.6 illustrates the load balancing of the system and the work done by each processor and by the workstation. The time spent in transmitting the bitstream (about 0.03 s) and writing a new image into the local memory of all processors (around 0.015 s per PE) explains the degradation of the speedup. Figure 23.8 shows three different speedups. The first one (curve b) corresponds to the speedup obtained for the image-processing part (Stages 2, 3, and 4). The curves c and d correspond to the whole system with and without the communications with the workstation, respectively. A speedup of around 50 is obtained with 64 PEs for the image-processing part, while the whole system achieves a speedup of around 32. Due to communication times, the speedup decreases very quickly if 128 processors or more are used. No significant degradation of the speedup is detected by taking into account the communications with the workstation.

Figure 23.9 shows the number of compressed and subsequently reconstructed images, per second, versus the number of processors. Using from 1 to 16 processors, fewer than five images are visualized per second. The operator has the impression of seeing a succession of still images and not a video sequence. With 32 processors, a frame rate of about seven per second is reached. This is the limit where we began to perceive a video sequence. With 64 processors, the frame rate is sufficiently high so as to enable a fair evaluation of the temporal characteristics and artifacts of the reconstructed video sequence, thus permitting fast and efficient evaluation and optimization. Taking into account the degradation of the speedup if more than 64 processors are used, 64 processors can be considered as the optimal number to process CIF video sequences.

We should also point out that these results depend directly on the size of the data. The proposed technique can be used for any kind of video format, such as

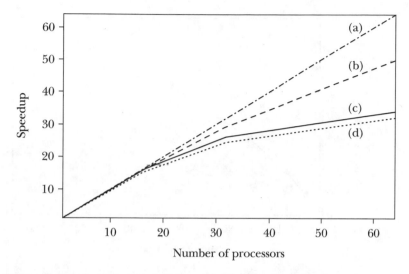

FIGURE

Speedups (DirectView 2.0): theoretical speedup (a), speedup of the compression algorithm only (b), speedup obtained for the whole system but without communication with the workstation (c), speedup for the whole system (d).

TV or HDTV (High Definition Television). In these applications, the size of the images is around 4 and 8 times bigger, respectively, than CIF images. Thus using 256 or 512 processors is necessary to reach approximately the same frame rate required for a fair evaluation and optimization of the algorithms.

After optimization of the parameters with DirectView (threshold T, quantization step, maximal displacement for the motion estimation, and so on), compression ratios of about 20 can be obtained, while retaining acceptable visual quality. Only a few minutes are necessary to optimize the algorithm. Serial implementation on a workstation and PSNR-based optimization criteria would require several days. Figure 23.3 showed two images optimized using PSNR-based criteria or visual evaluation and demonstrated that visual evaluation provides higher compression ratios with better visual qualities.

23.7 SUMMARY

The work described in this chapter demonstrates that the parallel supercomputer Cray T3D can be efficiently used for the fast development of new video-processing algorithms by exploiting their intrinsically parallel nature. In this context, the technology developed with DirectView offers realtime interactive optimization facilities, with the advantages of flexible and modular C software

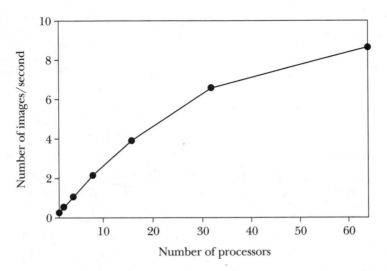

Number of processed images per second versus number of processors.

implementations. Better results are obtained in terms of both compression ratio and visual quality of the reconstructed images compared to classical approaches based on mathematical optimization criteria. Furthermore, DirectView can be used to develop and optimize a wide range of video-processing algorithms, thus permitting rapid prototyping and significant productivity gain. These characteristics provide an astounding way for universities and private companies working in this field to accelerate the development of new algorithms. The design of new multimedia applications in addition relies on the ability to test prototypes with realtime functionalities prior to hardware implementation. For this reason, the high-level implementation of DirectView compared to dedicated hardware implementation leads to a significant advantage for private companies that compete in the rapidly growing multimedia market.

ACKNOWLEDGMENTS

This work was supported by Cray Research and the Swiss Federal Institute of Technology (EPFL) in the framework of a joint project called the "Parallel Application Technology Program (PATP)". The authors are also grateful to Steve Williams of the EPFL, who helped us in the development of fast communication routines between the T3D and the workstation.

References

[23.1]   Carpentieri, B., and J. Storer. 1994. Split-Merge Video Displacement Estimation. *Proc. of IEEE*, **82** (6), 940–947.

[23.2]   Cheng, C., C. Wu, S. Pei, H. Li, and B. Jeng. 1994. High Speed Video Compression Testbed. *IEEE Transactions on Consumer Electronics*, **40** (3), 538–548.

[23.3]   Cook, G. W., and E. J. Delp. 1994. An Investigation of JPEG Image and Video Compression Using Parallel Processing. *Proc. of ICASSP*, Adelaide, Australia, April.

[23.4]   Dufaux, F., I. Moccagatta, F. Moscheni, and H. Nicolas. 1994. Vector Quantization-based Motion Field Segmentation under the Entropy Criterion. *Journal of Visual Communication and Image Representation*, **5** (4), 356–369.

[23.5]   ISO/IEC JTC1/SC29/WG11/N999. 1995. MPEG-4 Testing and Evaluation Procedures. *Document MPEG95/Tokyo*. Document Application and Operational Environments (AOE) Group.

[23.6]   Jeschke, H., K. Gaedke, and P. Pirsch. 1992. Multiprocessor Performance for Real-Time Processing of Video Coding Applications. In *Journal of VLSI Signal Processing*, **2** (2), 221–230.

[23.7]   Lee, H., J. Liu, A. Chant, and C. Chui. 1995. Parallel Vector Quantization Algorithm for SIMD Multiprocessor Systems. *Proc. of the 5th Data Compression Conference*, Snowbird, UT, 479.

[23.8]   Nicolas, H., A. Basso, E. Reusens, and M. Schutz. 1994. Parallel Implementations of Image Sequence Coding Algorithms on the CRAY T3D. *Supercomputing Review*, EPFL, **6**, 28–32.

[23.9]   Nicolas H. and F. Jordan. Interactive optimization of video compression algorithms on the CRAY T3D. In *Proceedings of CRAY User's Group Conference*, Barcelona, Spain, March 1996, 94–101.

[23.10]   Nicolas, H., and F. Jordan. 1996. Interactive Optimization and Massively Parallel Implementations of Video Compression Algorithms. In *Proceedings of ICIP Conference,* Lausanne, Switzerland, **I**, 229–232.

[23.11]   Shen, K., W. Cook, L. Jamieson, and E. Delp. 1994. An Overview of Parallel Processing Approaches to Image and Video Compression. *Proc. of Image and Video Compression, SPIE,* San Jose, CA, **1**, 197–208.

III CONCLUSIONS AND PREDICTIONS

PART

The case studies in Part II provide an in-depth look at the current state of industrial parallel computing. Part III of this book is composed of two chapters. In Chapter 24, we summarize the applications and provide general advice for parallel programming design. In Chapter 25, we use the lessons learned as a springboard into a prediction of the future.

Designing Industrial Parallel Applications

Alice E. Koniges
David C. Eder   Lawrence Livermore National Laboratory

Michael A. Heroux   SGI/Cray Research

The 17 applications presented in this book cover a wide variety of topics, but they share many salient features associated with their design, development, and optimization on parallel machines. The lessons learned are of general use to developers designing parallel applications. Here, we summarize the results in the applications chapters and follow with a section that gives advice on designing applications. The suggestions are based both on our experiences in parallel computing and on the work discussed in the applications chapters.

24.1   DESIGN LESSONS FROM THE APPLICATIONS

In general, very good performance is possible for industrial codes on MPP machines. To achieve high performance, however, advanced techniques are required. These include single-processor optimization, dealing with load-balancing issues, and developing special parallel algorithms. For some applications, the larger memory available with MPP machines permits high-resolution 3D simulations that were previously not possible. The majority of applications showed nearly linear scaling with processor number up to relatively high numbers (greater than 50) of processors. We now give more details treating the applications in groups based on the essential length scale of the physical phenomena modeled.

24.1.1   Meso- to Macroscale Environmental Modeling

Ocean and atmospheric simulations are very well suited for MPP machines, with both of our applications achieving good scaling with processor number. The domain decomposition is similar in these two applications. Each processor is given a portion of the problem in the horizontal (x, y) plane, with all the vertical (z) data for a given (x, y) being local to the processor. The ratio of computation to communication is relatively high for these simulations, making MPP machines appropriate platforms. For both applications, the requirement of very large memory is an important reason for running on a MPP machine. The larger memory allows for the higher resolution needed in the horizontal plane. In the ocean modeling simulation, a 1/6-degree resolution problem (run on a 256-processor T3D) shows significant improvements over previous lower-resolution (1/3- and 1/4-degree) runs. Still higher-resolution runs are required to determine when little qualitative improvement is obtained with increasing resolution.

Both of the applications benefited from parallel optimization. The ocean modeling code achieved a factor of 2.5 improvement (run on a 264-processor T3D) through the use of single-PE optimization. The optimized code also showed improved scaling, which contributed to the improvement. In this application, the replacement of IF and WHERE statements by masking arrays is very effective. Some optimization procedures that worked well for the T3D are not as effective on the T3E. We recommend that the Apprentice performance analysis tool (or its equivalent) be used to aid optimization every time a code is moved to a new machine. Some optimization—for example, special assembly coding—is very machine dependent. If such optimization is not done, one trades off poorer performance for increased portability. For the atmospheric code, portability is considered more important, at this time, than higher performance obtained using machine-dependent optimization. Results are presented for the atmospheric code on three MPP machines (T3D, SP2, and T3E) and a single-processor C90. Using 64 processors, the T3E is about a factor of 4 times faster (58 versus 205 hours) than the T3D, with the SP2 a bit slower (75 hours) than the T3E. The same problem took 220 hours on the C90. For both applications, the large memory possible with MPP machines is allowing high-resolution 3D calculations for the first time.

24.1.2   Applied Fluid Dynamics

The four applications in fluid dynamics require, like the two in the previous section, the large memory offered by MPP machines to solve problems at the appropriate level of resolution. In general, there is more communication required between processors for these applications than for those on larger length scales. The choices for parallel decomposition are different for each of these four applications. In the application on petroleum reservoir management, the decomposition is similar to those in Section 24.1.1, where the data in the vertical dimension (for a given subgrid in the horizontal plane) is on a given processor. In the application on flow fields around launch vehicles, a finite volume approach is used, with each processor receiving a portion of the irregular 3D grid. Three choices for parallel implementation were considered for the fluid mixing application. For high-resolution problems, the optimum choice (a combination of the other two choices) has all processors calculating trajectories on a portion of the problem with particles divided between processors. Then all processors move on to the next piece of the problem. This application shares some similarities with the plasma particle-in-cell (PIC) application in the next section. Finally, the groundwater flow application shows that parallel processing is a valid option for problems requiring iterative solution techniques. This work addresses both the scalability of an algorithm and the scalability of an algorithm's parallel implementation. For example, a multigrid algorithm is a scalable algorithm if the number of iterations required for convergence remains roughly constant, as the grid is refined.

As we saw in Part I, a good measure of performance on MPP machines is to compare results with different processors on problems that increase in size with processor number. (For a fixed problem size, the fraction of time associated with communication will generally increase with processor number. For some applications, this can give scaling results that indicate worse results than appropriate.) For example, the petroleum reservoir management code shows improved scaling with number of processors (up to 512 PEs) as the problem size is increased. As discussed in the first part of the book, scaled speedup shows the performance of an application on a problem of size $n*A$ using $n*P$ processors compared to a single processor solving a problem of size A. A good example of scaled speedup is in the application on groundwater flow, where nearly constant scaled speedup is seen up to 256 processors.

24.1.3 Applied Plasma Dynamics

The three applications in this section are solving three quite different problems but have a number of features in common. The plasma reactor application models the complex reactor geometry using an automatic grid generator that gets its input directly from the CAD/CAM description of the reactor. The initial partitioning of the grid attempts to minimize surface area and hence the amount of communication required. The code solves the Boltzmann equation by tracking individual particles. In this sense, it is similar to the application on ion thrusters, where hybrid PIC simulations are used. In these hybrid simulations, the ions are treated as particles but the electrons are treated as a fluid. As in the plasma reactor application, 3D effects are critical in solving the ion thruster problem. The application on modeling electron-molecule collisions provides data needed for plasma simulations. In this application, large subsets of integrals are given to each processor. This step does not require interprocessor communication. The second step of the transformation of these integrals into matrix elements does require communication.

The performance of a given application on different parallel computers can be quite different. This is primarily due to the differences in the machine architectures (e.g., clock speed, size and use of cache, amount of memory per node, bandwidth and latency, etc.) but is also very dependent on the given application. The performance on a range of computers is given for the plasma reactor application. Results are given for a T3D, an Avalon A12 (which uses the same chip as the T3E), a network of Dell multiprocessor workstations, and an SGI Power Challenge. In the comparisons, the number of particles used is proportional to the memory available. Load balancing is required on all machines except for the shared-memory Power Challenge. For the ion thruster application, we also compare performance on different machines. Results are given for a 512-PE Intel Delta and a 256-PE T3D. The chips in both of these machines have relatively small memories (by today's standards) of 16 and 64 MB, respectively. The small memory on the Delta chip combined with a bandwidth of only 10 MB/s (compared to 120 MB/s for the T3D) causes the application to be primarily communication-bound. In moving to the T3D, communication time is reduced to insignificance.

24.1.4   Material Design and Modeling

The parallel decomposition in these applications varies, with some applications having a decomposition that is itself problem-dependent. An example of problem-dependent decomposition is discussed for the atomic-level materials design application. This application uses an automatic domain decomposition procedure that decides among three different ways to distribute the tasks and data. In this application chapter, there is also a good general-interest discussion of using the SHMEM library to solve 3D complex fast Fourier transforms (FFTs). The solution of 3D FFTs is also given in the application chapter on the particle-mesh

Ewald method. In the application on radar scattering and antenna modeling, the use of Cray Research Adaptive Fortran (CRAFT) in the matrix decomposition stage is presented. This application provides details on many aspects of designing a parallel application.

In many cases, the algorithm used in a serial code can be adapted to a parallel machine. In other cases, new algorithms should be considered. The application on solving symmetric eigenvalue problems is an example where a significant better scaling with processor number is obtained by using a new algorithm. Another example of using different algorithms is given in the application chapter on the particle-mesh Ewald method.

The application on NMR simulations provides a nice example of the use of the Apprentice performance analysis tool. The tool is used to identify bottlenecks—for example, poor functional unit pipelining, sequential memory accessing, and cache conflicts. The remedies that are presented for these problems are of general interest. Once these problems are solved, the code achieves almost linear scaling with number of processors. The code also achieves a very high flop rate of 39.2 Gflops on 512 T3D processors for a one time-step calculation. This rate is slightly greater than 1/2 of the theoretical peak performance (r*) for the machine. In general, the performance rates for most applications in this book are 20 percent of r* or less.

24.1.5   Data Analysis

Examples of how MPP machines can be used to handle data, as compared to solving problems using data, are given in three applications. In the application on MRI datasets, the increased speed achieved by using a parallel machine is of primary importance for clinical use. The MRI data is acquired along spiral trajectories in Fourier space, and achieving an image requires three steps: (1) resampling onto a uniformly spaced 2D grid, (2) applying an inverse FFT to reconstruct an actual image, and (3) compensating for head movement using a registration procedure. Given that processing one image is relatively independent of other images, this application can be classed as "embarrassingly parallel." The major problem with scaling to a large number of processors for this application is I/O limitations. Using the current high-speed fiber link to disks, the code has linear scaling with processor number up to an order of 16 processors on a T3E. After that, there is continued speedup up to about 64 processors. Performance of this code on a number of different machines is also presented.

The application on comparison of genetic sequence data uses dynamic programming to discover the optimal path between the sequences being compared.

A history of running the code on a number of MPP machines (CM-2, CM-5, T3D, and T3E) is given along with the advantages and disadvantages of using a manager-worker programming model. The application on video compression shows that communication times can cause a degradation of speedup. The optimal number of processors to use as a function of the size of the image data is discussed.

24.2   DESIGN ISSUES

For industrial applications, the decision to use a parallel machine is based on economic factors and, generally, not on research interests. For such applications, the decision to "go parallel" is for one or both of the following reasons: (1) the need to run a larger memory problem, and (2) the need to have a problem run faster. This is to be contrasted with research in parallel computing, where achieving the maximum Gflops rate on a given machine is of interest in its own right. The relative importance of larger memory and faster time has a role in determining the appropriate machine (e.g., SMP or MPP) and the appropriate programming model. In industrial applications, product development time scales can constrain the amount of time that is allotted to parallel implementation and thus affect the approach to parallelism. In particular, time constraints can influence the decision to modify an existing code or construct a new parallel code. We discuss some code conversion issues in Section 24.2.1. The path to parallelism depends strongly on the degree of parallelism in the problem. In Section 24.2.2, we discuss various degrees of parallelism and give suggestions for appropriate machines and programming models. In Section 24.3, we give some general advice on designing industrial parallel applications.

24.2.1   Code Conversion Issues

For many industrial applications, there already exists a serial code and the developer must decide if it is better to convert this code or write a new parallel code. If the desired product is a "high-quality" parallel code, we have found that in many cases starting afresh produces such a code more quickly than converting an existing code. This was the case for a number of the applications discussed in the book. For example, in Chapter 12, the code was developed from scratch as a parallel code. In this code, the computations are organized to avoid explicit data redistribution. There can be situations in industry where a "quick fix" is needed to get a larger problem to run or when a modest speedup is all that is required. In such cases and for cases of modest parallelism (see Section 24.2.2), the best approach can be conversion of an existing code. In addition, there are applications, with even a very high degree of parallelism, where code conversion is the correct choice.

We discuss some of the code conversion issues that should be considered prior to starting a conversion as opposed to starting from scratch. The developer should determine if the I/O is confined to a single place in the code or appears in many different parts. Is a significant fraction of the code in a hard-wired serial algorithm that would be difficult to modify? On the machine for which the code is planned, the developers must determine if the libraries used by the existing code are missing or are outdated. Do parallel libraries for the same work exist? Using up-to-date libraries often gives much better performance. Does the existing code use outdated preprocessors? In some cases, the serial code can use a scripting language or precompilers that do not work on the parallel machine of interest. Should the basic language of the code—for example, Fortran 77 (or older)—be updated to a current standard—Fortran 90/95, for example? These are just a few of the questions that must be addressed in the decision to go with converting a code or to starting afresh with a new code.

24.2.2 The Degree of Parallelism in the Application

The amount of parallelism possible for a given application depends on a number of factors. Some problems have been classed as being "trivial to parallelize" because the problem naturally divides into a large number of similar-sized tasks. Sequence comparison tasks, as discussed in Chapter 22, is an example of a problem with natural parallelism. However, for some problems that appear to have natural parallelism, such as PIC codes, significant effort can be required to achieve a high level of parallelism. An example of this is discussed in Chapter 15, where a PIC code is used in 3D modeling of ion thrusters. Finally, algorithmic constraints can play an important role in determining the amount of parallelism that is possible for a given problem.

To determine the degree of parallelism, the developer of an application must decide how the problem is to be divided—that is, what work can be shared and what data is required to do this work. In an ideal situation, a given processor that is assigned some work owns all the data that is necessary to complete that work. In this case, communication speed between processors is not relevant, as no data must be shared. In real applications this is never the case, and the relative importance of communicating data is very critical in designing a parallel application and deciding the degree of parallelism that is appropriate for the application. The amount of parallelism that can be obtained in a given problem can also depend on the amount of effort that is spent by the developer. We divide the degree of parallelism into three classes: (1) modest, (2) moderate, and (3) extreme.

For the case of modest parallelism, the appropriate number of processors to consider is generally in the range of 2 to 16. None of the applications in this book have this level of parallelism. However, there are many industrial applications for which this would be an appropriate level of parallelism. For these applications, the majority of parallel speedup can often be obtained by focusing on a small number of functions. Appropriate program models for this case are OpenMP and Pthreads. OpenMP is not yet universally available but is an emerging standard that is well suited for this case. Only minimal code change is required, and a single source code for serial and parallel versions can be maintained. The code would be portable across multiple platforms. Pthreads is a good alternative in that it is more widely available than OpenMP, but it does require many more code changes. In general, MPI and HPF may not be necessary for modest parallelism because extensive code modification can be required. However, there are applications that only make use of order 16 processors, which use MPI successfully. Given the small number of processors, memory needs must be considered in deciding to use an SMP or MPP machine.

For the case of moderate parallelism, the appropriate number of processors is in the range of 16 to 64. There are only a few applications in the book that are limited to this level of parallelism. In Chapter 21, the I/O limitations to external disk drives allow linear scaling with only up to 16 processors and useful speedup up to 64 processors. In Chapter 22, bottlenecks associated with the manager-worker programming model occur when using 64 or 128 processors, depending on the dataset being studied. In both of these cases, a higher degree of parallelism is possible by increasing I/O bandwidth and changing the programming model, respectively. In general, to have this degree of parallelism the underlying algorithms must scale well with increasing processor number. Even with only modest parallelism, to date the most appropriate programming models are PVM, MPI, HPF, or similar models, where clear ownership of data and task is defined. There is a large range of machines with 16 to 64 processors, including MPPs, SMPs, NOWs, and clustered SMPs. In many cases the developmental work put into a code can be leveraged across this broad set of machines. An open question, at this time, is the use of OpenMP for this level of parallelism. One problem is the lack of portability to NOWs and clusters. In addition, OpenMP does not currently have the ability to assert placement of data on ccNUMA architectures. Finally, the operating system and not the physical processor count often limits the number of processors usable by OpenMP.

For the case of extreme parallelism, the appropriate number of processors is greater than 64, and in some cases greater than 1000. The majority of the applications in this book fall into this class of parallelism. The largest processor count used by any of the applications is 512, with the majority running on systems with 256 or 128 processors. However, for many of these applications one would expect continued good scaling with processor number up to the 1000 range. For large processor counts, issues associated with global I/O and dynamic load balancing must be addressed. No single node has the resources to handle all of the global I/O or data partitioning. (There are some applications with minimal global I/O and where data partitioning may be trivial.) MPI-2, the latest version of MPI, has some features that help treat global I/O issues, but this problem remains a research topic. The major problem with data repartitioning is that it must be done in parallel.

24.3 ADDITIONAL DESIGN ISSUES

The first step in designing a parallel application is determining the work that can be done in parallel. Next is deciding how to distribute the work and necessary data. One should be aware of data access, interprocessor communication, and overall synchronization issues. A big decision at this point is to decide on a programming model. Some programming models (e.g., message passing) generally require the developer to specify which processor does what work and the location of the data. This places work on the developer, but this knowledge can help in achieving the maximum performance from a code. In contrast, some programming models (e.g., HPF) take care of the assignment of work and data. The other big decision is to convert an existing code or to start afresh with a new code. (It is possible to do a combination of the two.) In either case, it is very important to work in steps. In modifying an existing code, pick portions to parallelize. At each step make sure one obtains the same answer when various numbers of processors (including only one processor) are used. When starting a new code, start with the core of the problem and make sure it runs from start to finish using various numbers of processors. As new features are added, make sure that each piece is bug-free in the serial mode first, and test the total code thoroughly before adding the next piece. For new and converted codes, keep unnecessary synchronization out of the code. It may hide runtime errors that will be harder to find when the code is bigger. At each stage in the building of a parallel code, it is appropriate to consider optimization issues.

25 The Future of Industrial Parallel Computing

Michael A. Heroux   SGI/Cray Research

Horst Simon   NERSC, Lawrence Berkeley National Laboratory

Alice E. Koniges   Lawrence Livermore National Laboratory

Predicting the future of industrial parallel computing is almost surely a dangerous occupation. As a case in point, consider that 10 years ago the scientific computing community predicted that MPP systems based on commodity microprocessors would be the industrial supercomputer of the future. One can claim that the first system capable of truly meeting that prediction is the Cray T3E. (This claim is supported by a recent press release from NERSC announcing that "checkpoint/restart," the ability to gracefully suspend computer operations in the middle of jobs and restart the jobs where they stopped, had been demonstrated for the first time on their T3E. This capability, which has been available for 12 years on traditional supercomputers, is essential to having a legitimate industrial supercomputer.)

Ironically, however, in 1996, the same year the T3E was introduced, a panel of leading experts strongly recommended that the National Science Foundation *deemphasize* MPP research, the rationale being that industry had proven MPP systems were too hard to use [25.5]. We believe that the panel's conclusions are not entirely correct and that there is an important role for parallel computers in industry, both now and in the future. At the same time, we believe that there are a number of trends that will have a tremendous impact on future parallel computer systems and their uses.

In the following sections we discuss our predictions for parallel computing in industry over the next 5 to 10 years. Barring any "nonlinear event," such as the successful introduction of processor-in-memory, we believe these predictions paint a credible picture of the general trends in parallel computing. It is worth noting that, if we are correct in our predictions, it will seem strange 10 years from now that we ever wrote this chapter. If parallel computing becomes as ubiquitous as we expect, there will essentially be nothing other than parallel computing. The outline of the remainder of this chapter is as follows: After a brief discussion of the role of parallel computing in industry, which we present to frame the discussion, we begin our predictions starting with microarchitecture issues. We progressively move out from there, going to macroarchitecture issues, system software issues, programming environments, applications, case studies, and finally the broad role of parallel computing in society.

25.1   THE ROLE OF PARALLEL COMPUTING IN INDUSTRY

In order to get some insight into the future of parallel computing in industry, we must understand the role it plays in the broad picture of industrial computing. To this end, we define the role of industrial computing as this:

To create valuable information via numerical simulation and deliver this information to scientists and engineers in a timely manner.

Based on this definition, we make the following observations: Parallel computing (in comparison to serial computing) can have a role in industry if parallelism either (1) provides information that is more valuable, or (2) delivers information in a timelier manner, or both. By definition, parallel computing should deliver information in a more timely manner than serial computing, assuming comparable processors are used in each case. Also, because adding processors to a computer system is relatively cheaper than the initial system cost (e.g., doubling the number of processors is much less than double the cost), parallel computing can often produce results more cheaply than serial computing. In fact, much of the focus of parallel applications efforts to date has been to deliver the same capabilities as an existing serial application, only faster and cheaper.

In some industries, doing the same thing faster and cheaper has been very valuable. However, we contend that a far more compelling motivation for the use of parallel computing in industry is in cases where parallel computing provides an affordable and unique capability not attainable with existing serial computers. In fact, we make this conjecture:

The future of parallel computing in any given industry will be largely determined by whether it can provide some unique capability for that industry at an acceptable price.

By "unique capability" we mean that the parallel application is providing information that is qualitatively better than the serial application—for example, allowing use of a 3D model instead of a 2D model. By an acceptable cost, we do not necessarily mean cheap. Each major automobile manufacturer spends more than $10 million a year for computer systems to do vehicle crash simulations. However, because of the benefit, this cost is considered acceptable.

In the following sections we discuss the future of parallel computing with this conjecture in mind. In particular, we discuss trends that we see in micro- and macroarchitecture design, system software development, programming environments, and application development. In each area, we can trace the trends to keep the cost of parallel computing acceptable and to provide unique capability.

25.2   MICROARCHITECTURE ISSUES

25.2.1   Prediction

All future parallel computers will use processors that are able to run, without modification, applications developed for the common desktop or server (deskside) computers of the day. The processor itself may be a commodity processor, or it may be an enhancement of a commodity processor with special instructions and hardware features designed for the high-performance demands of scientific and engineering applications, or a system may have some features of each. The local processor memory design will be multilevel and include increasingly large caches so that high-level application design must program for locality but lowlevel hand optimization of applications will not be necessary.

25.2.2   Discussion

One of the strongest and most visible phenomena in the computer industry is the trend toward commodity design of "core" hardware and software. This is most evident in processor design, where there is just a handful of viable generalpurpose instruction set architectures (ISAs)—for example, the Intel x86 ISA and the MIPS4 ISA—that are still under active development. Although there are many factors contributing to this phenomenon, one of the most interesting dynamics is the relationship between the ISA and the application base. The more prevalent a particular processor becomes, the more compelling it becomes for an application developer to focus primary attention on support of this platform to the detriment of other platforms. An example of this is the quality and availability of desktop applications for Windows/Intel (Wintel) systems vs. Macintosh systems. Because of the prevalence of Wintel systems, the applications set is much larger than that for Macintosh, and in cases where the application is available on both platforms, the Wintel version is typically more stable, with new features not yet available in the Macintosh version.

In addition to the ISA-application dynamic, there are many other factors that contribute to a convergence in processor ISAs. The high cost of processor design and manufacturing, systems support, and user training are a few. Thus, it seems inevitable that future parallel computers must embrace this trend. However, the performance of commodity microprocessors is currently not adequate for many strategic scientific and engineering applications, nor will they be for the near future. Thus, it is likely that future parallel computers will be compatible with commodity systems, taking advantage of the commodity system software and application base but also providing strategic enhancements to the processor design that allow it to exploit the latent performance potential of scientific and engineering applications.

25.3   MACROARCHITECTURE ISSUES

25.3.1   Prediction

As is currently the case, future parallel computers will span a spectrum whose endpoints are loosely coupled networks of workstations or PCs (NOWs) [25.1, 25.2] and tightly coupled systems (TCSs) with a single-system image OS [25.3, 25.4]. However, the distance between the endpoints, from a performance and programming perspective, will diminish dramatically. For both NOWs and TCSs, the basic building block will be a small number of processors with associated memory, network, and I/O ports, which is identical to a compatible desktop/ deskside system. Machines built in this way are often called *scalable systems*.

In the simplest cases, these building blocks will be connected by standard network technology and use enhanced system software to allow this cluster of machines to look like a single system. At the other end of the spectrum, these building blocks will be tightly coupled by a high-speed custom interconnect network (ICN) with low latency/high bandwidth communication among all processors and hardware support for barriers and synchronization. Total processor counts will range from two to four all the way to several thousand, with two- to four-processor desktop and deskside systems becoming commonplace.

NOWs will see a tremendous increase in bandwidth and decrease in latency, and it will become quite easy to connect tens or hundreds of PCs or workstations together to achieve an impressive performance capacity. From a performance standpoint, NOWs will fast approach the capabilities of a TCS, especially for applications that have a medium to high latency tolerance. However, in order to make NOWs a credible parallel computing platform, a great deal of effort will go into developing augmented system software. We will discuss this in detail in Section 25.5.

As NOWs approach the raw performance of TCSs, new TCS designs will focus not only on low latency and high bandwidth connections but will also invest in overdesigning the interconnect network. These systems will be developed using what we call *architectural overlaying*. By investing in hardware support for a global shared-address space, global cache coherence, and fast hardware barrier/synchronization mechanisms, these machines can be simultaneously viewed as

+ a single-processor machine with large memory
+ a shared-memory parallel (SMP) machine
+ a distributed-memory parallel (DMP) machine
+ or a combination of SMP within DMP

In addition to these trends in macroarchitecture, we will see that high-performance graphics and data management capabilities will be integrated into these systems so that a single computer platform can be simultaneously used for computation, graphics, and data management.

25.3.2 Discussion

NOWs

Recent advances in networking hardware and software, plus the low cost of the components, make current NOWs competitive with TCSs built 5 years ago, with a cost that is only incrementally more than that of the workstations that make up the NOW. Because many parallel distributed-memory applications were developed on older TCSs, these applications will run quite well on the new generations of NOWs, especially if fewer than 100 processors are required. However, in order for NOWs to be viable production computing platforms, a great deal of support software must be developed to handle global system activities. Mundane functions such as software upgrades across the NOW, tolerance of partial system failure, and dealing with the lack of uniformity in the NOW processors must be provided in order for industry to accept NOWs for critical application work. Up until today, these types of functions have been unavailable or have been integrated into the application codes themselves. Application developers who have been using NOWs in an industrial setting have invested heavily in fault tolerance, load-balancing techniques, and formal usage policies to schedule job execution.

TCSs and Architectural Overlaying

One of the biggest shortcomings of large-scale parallel systems up to now has been the lack of available applications. (The IBM SP series is a notable exception in that RS/6000 applications could run on a single SP processor. Therefore, the entire RS/6000 application catalog was available on SP systems.) Because large-scale parallel systems were fairly special purpose, many application developers were reluctant to do a special port of their codes to these machines. Also, even in cases where the processor was a commodity type—the DEC Alpha processor, for example, in the Cray T3E—a single-processor port of an application made little sense when a DEC Alpha workstation was available.

Architectural overlaying attempts to address this problem by overdesigning the macroarchitecture so that it can support a variety of different programming needs. One key feature required for overlaying is a directly addressable, global shared-address space. By this we mean that the ICN, which connects two or more building blocks, supports a processor from one block in directly accessing a memory location on another building block, without a severe penalty in communication latency or bandwidth. Another key required feature is fast hardware barrier and synchronization. This feature is necessary for effective use of large numbers of processors by a single application.

With desktop/deskside compatibility and these two features, it is possible to build a single macroarchitecture that can be used in a variety of ways:

✦ **Single processor with large memory:** Having a global address space, the memory resource of the entire computer system can be utilized by a single processor. This can have tremendous value and, when coupled with binary compatibility with desktop/deskside systems, provides a valuable incentive to run desktop/deskside systems codes on a parallel system. In fact, in some cases, the large memory is essential to completing the preprocessing steps (in single-processor mode) for large parallel jobs.

✦ **SMP system:** Again, because of the global address space, any subset of processors on a system can be used to run a shared-memory parallel application. In this mode, a large parallel system can be viewed as a throughput engine for multiple SMP jobs.

✦ **DMP system:** The fast hardware barrier/synchronization along with the fact that the building blocks have a natural local-memory affinity, make this type of a system an attractive DMP system.

+ **Hybrid SMP/DMP system:** There are a number of applications that can potentially benefit from using an SMP programming model within a DMP programming model, which we call *nested parallelism*. For example, given a message-passing application using MPI, it is possible to use multiple processors on each MPI subprocess to speed up execution. In addition, it is possible to correct load imbalance in some cases by assigning more processors to the MPI subprocesses that have the most work.

+ **Tightly coupled multicomputer:** With the availability of a broad set of applications (by virtue of this system being desktop/deskside compatible), it becomes possible to consider a variety of design optimization and multiphysics strategies. In this case, we can run multiple, related jobs, which, for example, have minor variations in input conditions, and then do parameter studies. It is also possible to use multiple applications—a structural dynamics and fluid dynamics application, for example—to study multiphysics problems. Furthermore, it becomes possible to tightly integrate these types of applications into an automatic design-optimization application.

The impact of architectural overlaying is dramatic. First of all, it provides users of a parallel system with a diverse, robust set of core applications. Second, and as important, it allows parallel systems to be built in a cost-effective way. In particular, hardware and system software costs are amortized across a broad set of users. Third, it allows for new advancement in applications. Nested parallelism offers an opportunity for more effective utilization of large numbers of processors, and design optimization and multiphysics strategies make numerical simulation much more valuable to the user.

Integrated Graphics and Data Management

A notable deficiency of many engineering and scientific modeling practices today is the inability to quickly and easily incorporate numerical simulation into the day-to-day business of industry. This limits our ability to bring numerical simulation to a broader group of people who simply want to use it as a means for creating and delivering information that will help their business. Integrated graphics and data management capabilities, in the same system that is performing numerical simulations, offer tremendous opportunities for numerical simulation applications to deliver information to and receive information from users, so that numerical simulation becomes an integrated component in the information system infrastructure that is critical to industry today. We mention more about this in Section 25.8.

25.4   SYSTEM SOFTWARE ISSUES

25.4.1   Prediction

System software will have an internal structure that is layered correspondingly
to the hardware building blocks. In the case of NOWs, separate operating systems (OSs) will be running independently on each NOW node with a layer of ad-
ministrative software and software libraries that allow system administrators and
users to view the NOW as a single machine. In the case of TCSs, a more highly integrated two-tiered OS will be used. The multiple lower-tier sub-OS units will
handle most system functions that are local in nature—user file-system requests,
for example. The upper tier, or meta-OS, will handle global system functions, coordinate the lower-tier sub-OS units, and have fault tolerance capabilities to
detect and isolate localized system failures without bringing the whole system
down. The sub-OS units may be Unix-based or Windows/NT-based.

25.4.2   Discussion

Following the strategy established by scalable hardware design, system software
will have a conformal layered structure. The primary component will be what we
commonly know as a single-system-image operating system (SSI OS). The SSI OS
will run on one or more hardware building blocks but will not scale to more than
a few hundred processors. In order to build a computer system that scales beyond the support of a SSI OS, a meta-OS layer will be used to coordinate multiple SSI OS units.

There are several motivations for using this layered OS approach. First of all,
it is currently very difficult to provide a SSI OS that scales well on more than 128
processors. Certainly there is a substantial effort to improve the situation, but
there are inherent synchronization issues that make a scalable SSI OS difficult to
implement. Second, there are attractive fault tolerance features that come from
a layered OS. As processor counts increase, the likelihood of a hardware or software interrupt somewhere in the computer system goes up dramatically. Users of
parallel systems are not able to tolerate the entire system going down simply because one component of the system fails. By using a layered OS, a system interrupt that occurs in one SSI OS can be isolated by the meta-OS while the remainder of the system remains up.

It is worth emphasizing that both NOWs and TCSs will have a two-tiered OS
design. In the case of NOWs, a vendor who specializes in networks for coupling
stand-alone systems will develop the meta-OS. In the case of TCSs, the meta-OS

and sub-OS will be provided by the hardware vendor and will, for all practical purposes, be a single software product.

25.5 PROGRAMMING ENVIRONMENT ISSUES

25.5.1 Prediction

SMP programming models will converge to an industry standard. The standard will cover the full range of computer systems from PCs to supercomputers. Many standard industrial applications will have SMP versions that run well on 2 to 4 processors, possibly 8 to 16. However, these parallel implementations will generally not be written in a scalable form. Instead, parallelization will be in the few areas of the application where significant runtime is used and will generally not be able to exploit large numbers of processors.

Explicit distributed-memory models (e.g., MPI), will continue to evolve, especially in an attempt to address I/O issues and different flavors of message passing (e.g., one-sided). In addition, although MPI will continue to be the standard, language standards will include extensions to support remote memory access. Proposed extensions such as Split/C, UPC, and Co-Array Fortran (see Part I) will be supported in compilers and used in a number of new applications and will extend the range of applications in which DMP implementations will be feasible.

Hybrid programming models (i.e., nested parallelism) will evolve and allow users to bring larger numbers of processors to bear on a single application than either SMP or DMP alone could effectively use.

25.5.2 Discussion

SMP Programming Models

As we have mentioned, new processor boards are being designed to have two or more processors sharing a memory resource. Future computer systems, including PCs, will typically have more than one processor by default, and the cost of the extra processors will be minimal. With this trend, there is already a strong push to standardize the SMP programming model. The proposed standard, OpenMP, discussed in Part I, is the most credible effort to date and will allow application developers to make an investment in parallel implementations that can be leveraged across all SMP platforms.

At the same time, although SMP programming will become ubiquitous, it will not satisfy all the requirements of large-scale parallel programming. There are several reasons for this. First of all, few people using an SMP programming model will make the investment in restructuring their application to eliminate those serial bottlenecks that are insignificant at lower processor counts but which throttle scalability. Second, it is often the case that the best data and work distribution for an SMP application, which is typically targeted for running on a few processors, is not the best distribution for large numbers of processors. Finally, and perhaps most importantly, the SMP programming model requires a SSI OS. As we discussed in the previous section, a SSI OS will not be able to scale to the full range of processors in large parallel systems. Thus, there is an imposed limit to SMP parallelism that has nothing to do with the scalability of the application itself.

DMP Programming Models

MPI is a de facto industry standard, and many parallel application-development efforts are based on it. However, with ambiguities in the MPI specification and the inherent overhead associated with calling library routines, there is room for improvement. In an effort to keep the implementation details of MPI away from users and give hardware vendors who support MPI as much flexibility as possible, the MPI standard allows some latitude in the exact implementation details. Because of this, an MPI-based application developed on one platform may not run on another platform because of differences in how MPI was implemented on each machine, and these differences can be very difficult to isolate. Another problem with MPI is the overhead associated with calling library routines. Data packing and unpacking, calling routine overhead, and other factors introduce higher communication latencies that can be the ultimate determining factor in how well an application implementation scales, especially for fixed problem sizes.

Because of these known deficiencies, there are several efforts that can be viewed as the next step beyond MPI. Split/C, UPC, and Co-Array Fortran each extend standard programming languages by giving the programmer an ability to express remote memory references explicitly. This allows programmers to do message passing by simply using a remote variable reference as they would any other variable reference. The actual transfer of the data is handled by the compiled code. This has three significant effects. First, the programmer is able to express complicated remote data access patterns very succinctly, making it much more feasible to implement complex algorithms. Second, the compiler now has much more information about the data access patterns and can schedule the remote memory references to hide access latency. Third, the effective latency for a remote memory reference can be minimized because the compiler will generate inline code that can utilize all communication paths of the machine in the most efficient way. All of these factors motivate us to consider language extensions as a natural step beyond MPI.

Nested Parallelism

As computer systems take on a layered appearance in both the hardware and operating systems, users will be compelled to consider a corresponding layered approach to parallelism. In particular, using an SMP model within a DMP model will be very attractive. Many domain decomposition algorithms written using a DMP model have a natural fine-grain parallelism within each subdomain that can be exploited via an SMP model.

25.6   APPLICATIONS ISSUES

25.6.1   Prediction

Usage Trends

The use of parallel computers, and all scientific/engineering computers, in industry will grow dramatically in the next 5 to 10 years. Computer simulation will be seen as an essential tool for giving unique insight into complicated problems, thereby allowing us to make much more effective decisions about our industrial design and manufacturing projects. Steady advancements will be made in modeling capabilities, both in spatial detail (size of computer model) and model complexity (accuracy of the physics). However, more dramatic will be improvements in the accessibility to the results of a computer simulation. New user interfaces will focus on providing an engineer or scientist with an environment that is more intuitive, interactive, and accessible so that the user can focus more on solving the problem at hand than on the tools—the computer system and application being used to solve the problem. These interfaces will not only be for simulation codes but will also integrate sophisticated database management capability and provide widespread accessibility via high-speed network connections.

Small-scale versus Large-scale Parallelism

Small-scale parallelism, specifically shared-memory parallel execution on four to eight processors, will become prevalent, becoming the rule instead of the exception. Because most computer systems will have more than one processor and

most applications have enough loop-level parallelism to exploit small-scale parallelism, this type of parallelism will become very cost effective. In addition, most
compilers will be able to find a good share of the parallelism without explicit
programmer intervention, making the improvement easy to obtain.

Although small-scale parallelism will grow naturally, porting and development of truly scalable parallel applications will continue to be a challenge outside of well-established application areas (e.g., CFD). Lack of robust parallel algorithms, the inability to incrementally develop scalable parallel applications,
and the difficulties associated with pre- and postprocessing of serial data files are
just a few of the major issues that must be addressed. At the same time, the tremendous computing potential of large-scale parallel systems will allow us to use
novel parallel algorithms that were previously infeasible and get a degree of accuracy that is unattainable any other way.

Ensemble and Multiphysics Applications

Many application areas will reach a state of maturity where the spatial detail and
model complexity will be good enough when run on a single high-performance
processor. This will allow us to consider new methodologies with the existing application base. For example, with inexpensive, accurate simulations, users will
conduct multiple simulations with minor variation in input parameters in order
to test the sensitivity of the analysis to key input parameters. Design of Experiment (DOE), Genetic Algorithms, and other design optimization techniques become feasible in this setting. Also, the ability to couple physical phenomena
(e.g., structures and fluid dynamics in aero-elasticity) will become commonplace. Multiple weather simulations using a range of input conditions will give
forecasters a better idea of the range of future weather conditions. In general,
this increasing ability to run many simulations will have a profound impact on
the value that scientific and engineering computing brings to society. Instead
of asking, "How good is my current design?" we will be able to ask, "What is the
best design?"

25.6.2   Discussion

Usage Trends

As we will discuss in detail in Section 25.8, numerical simulation will evolve as
an essential source of information in the Digital Information Age. As our society
comes to realize this potential, the demand for accurate, readily available simulation results will increase dramatically. This increased demand will be the result

of increasingly effective use of numerical simulation as an essential tool for industrial design and manufacturing. Some of the effectiveness will come from better application-modeling capabilities and increased computing power. However, much of it will come from our ability to integrate the information created by scientific/engineering applications into the decision-making process for each industry.

As time goes on, most popular scientific and engineering application programs evolve and mature as application developers continue to work on the programs. In general, we see the maturing process as having three distinct characteristics:

1. The degree of spatial detail the application is able to resolve: How large a model can we run and how quickly can we run it?

2. The degree of modeling complexity: How accurate is the physics modeled?

3. The degree of sophistication in the user interface: How easy is the application to use for a scientist or engineer who is not a computer expert?

Traditionally, application developers, especially those focused on parallel computers, have emphasized items 1 and 2. However, we believe that the availability of new interface environments (e.g., Web browsers) as well as the increasing integration of graphics and data management capabilities into the computing platform give us a new opportunity to develop sophisticated interfaces with minimal investments. We see this as a very significant development because the ease of use of the interface determines how many scientists and engineers can have access to the application.

Small-scale versus Large-scale Parallelism

Parallel implementations of applications can obviously have a dramatic positive impact on item 1 in the preceding section. For item 2, there can be an obvious positive impact in many cases, but there can also be a negative impact in certain cases where greater physical accuracy corresponds to handling local phenomena accurately. As an example, consider the numerical simulation of a car crash. Car-crash models can become very large, with several hundred thousand elements, and have a large degree of parallelism. However, as we add more specifics about the car structure—for example, airbag components and seat-belt connections to the frame, we necessarily add modeling requirements that hinder parallel execution and reduce the overall effectiveness of parallel processing.

Generally speaking, parallel implementations, especially distributed-memory ones, often hinder progress in item 3. Sophisticated user interfaces require intuitive representation of data—for example, graphical or icon-based representation. They also require the ability to manage data easily and in a transparent way to the user. These requirements in turn require that the computer system support graphics and data management. To date, very few parallel computer systems have been able to do this, primarily because most parallel systems were designed for fast computation and I/O. They did not have graphics capabilities or a large-enough user base to justify porting database-management tools. This situation is changing, as we see that most parallel computer systems are also general-purpose computers. As we discussed in Section 25.3, the combination of a ccNUMA macroarchitecture and the tight integration of graphics and data-management capabilities into the same system that does computing opens up tremendous opportunities for us to provide more sophisticated user interfaces than ever before. See Chapter 23 and Section 25.7.4 for examples.

Ensemble and Multiphysics Applications

Many areas of numerical modeling for scientific and engineering computing have reached a state where a numerical simulation is fairly mature. By this we mean that the numerical simulation of a particular problem is close enough to the true physical problem that differences in simulation results due to small changes in the input parameters can be interpreted, with some confidence, as being physically meaningful and, therefore, design decisions can be made based on the results. For example, modal analysis of automobile structures is accurate enough at this time for engineers to analyze the audible noise levels associated with one numerical simulation and then incrementally vary some design parameters to reduce noise levels to an acceptable range. This type of information is extremely valuable and, because numerical models can be built and tested much more rapidly than physical prototypes, it can dramatically improve the final automobile design.

25.7   PARALLEL COMPUTING IN INDUSTRY

The 17 applications chapters in this book give an in-depth look at what it takes to create an industrial strength parallel application. The following more-general remarks augment these and briefly illustrate some of the key improvements in the use of parallel computers over the past few years, and into the next few. We use the automobile industry as an example here because it currently uses each of the following areas of simulation. We note that, in general, the automobile industry is only now beginning to consider MPP computers as a valid resource for their similations, and they lag somewhat behind the applications chapters in their current level of parallel development[25.6]. Thus, this industry is a good example for the future development of parallel computing.

Area 1 illustrates that (1) as processors become cheaper, (2) parallel systems become prevalent, and (3) MPI becomes a de facto standard, then application software developers will make the investment in parallel implementations of their formerly single-processor applications. This will allow us to run the same simulation models as before, except that they will run faster and can be much larger.

Area 2 illustrates the value of our increased ability to do more accurate modeling by virtue of more powerful computers and better algorithms. It also stands as an example that cannot effectively use more than a handful of processors at once. There is nothing in principle that makes it impossible to use more processors; it is simply that the difficulty of converting these types of applications to utilize more processors is beyond the resource limits of the application developers.

Area 3 illustrates the value of having many inexpensive and powerful processors in a single computer system. Because we have so many processors, we can use them "extravagantly," at least by yesterday's standards, and run many jobs at once, where in the past we had to be much more careful with computer resource costs.

Area 4 illustrates the tremendous potential of integrated compute, data management, and graphics capabilities in a single-system frame. This development allows us to develop a new generation of applications that are useful to large new groups of engineers and scientists.

25.7.1 Area 1: Parallel Execution of a Single Analysis: Incompressible CFD Analysis

Computational fluid dynamics has historically been an area of computer simulation that is very amenable to parallel computation. Thus, it is not surprising that some of the most mature and effective industrial parallel applications come from this area. In the automotive industry, fluid flow-field reconstruction around an automobile is fundamental to the car design, but the basic concepts are applicable to many industrial areas. Chapters 9, 10, and 11 demonstrate that industrial use of fluid dynamics codes span a gamut of different industries ranging from petroleum to aerodynamics to pharmecuticals. Fluid dynamics applications are typically finite-element or finite-volume-based and often use iterative methods to solve the linear systems that are the main computational challenge in implicit solution techniques. Formulation of the discrete fluid model is straightforward to perform in parallel, as was nicely elucidated in Chapter 10. Also, most of the iterative solvers can usually be executed quite well in parallel, at least up to 100 processors. In fact the iterative solver in Chapter 12 scales nicely to 256.

In practice, this means that we can usually see significant benefit from using parallel CFD applications in an industrial setting. Speedups of 20 to 40 times on 64 processors are typical, and sometimes even superlinear speedups are possible. However, to go beyond 100 processors in most applications, it is our speculation that more work needs to be done to incorporate dynamic load balancing in the application. (Indeed 11 out of 17 of the applications chapters used some form of dynamic load balancing.) Also, we will probably need to continue the development of iterative solvers that are more scalable, such as the MGCG algorithm used in Chapter 10. However, even with these known limitations, parallel CFD applications are clearly an example of the successful use of parallel computing in industry. Analyses that routinely took days or weeks just a few years ago now complete in a few hours. This allows engineers to rely on CFD simulation even in very short, time-critical design cycles.

25.7.2   Area 2: Design Optimization: Noise, Vibration, Harshness (NVH) Analysis

One of the maturest areas of numerical simulation, in terms of model accuracy, is structural dynamics modeling. In particular, application programs that use implicit finite element methods—the various versions of NASTRAN, for example—have proven to be extremely reliable in providing accurate modeling results for many engineering purposes. In addition, recent advances in coupling optimization strategies to these codes have made the simulation results extremely valuable. This area of simulation is call Noise, Vibration, and Harshness (NVH) modeling. Using NVH analysis, automotive engineers are routinely able to modify a proposed vehicle design to reduce passenger noise levels, reduce fatigue of key components, and so on. Some of the return on investment in this area is quantitative—reduced repair costs over the life of the vehicle, for example. However, many of them are qualitative improvements related to safety and handling, which cannot have a price associated with them.

The example of NVH optimization illustrates a very significant advance in the value of simulation to industry. Prior to the use of optimization, a structural simulation result could only tell an engineer the behavior of a particular model. It gave little or no insight in how to improve the design. In other words, it did not address the question of what is a good design, which is the real goal of the design process. NVH optimization directly addresses this question, providing qualitatively better information to the design engineer.

25.7.3 Area 3: Design Studies: Crash Design Optimization

Another area of structural dynamics that is extremely important and mature is automotive crash simulation. Like parallel CFD applications, crash modeling codes have shown impressive parallel performance. Coupling the impressive single-analysis performance with a tremendous improvement in the price/performance of computing systems used to do crash analysis, crash design studies become an exciting area for tremendous advancements in crash analysis.

In this situation, the design engineer is usually looking at a few to tens of design parameters and wants to understand the impact that changing these parameters has on the crashworthiness of the automobile. However, rather than trying to specify an acceptable design a priori, the engineer would like to see a set of trade-off curves. For example, as the mass of a particular beam is reduced incrementally, how is the crashworthiness affected? Given a set of these curves, the engineer can make intelligent design choices, often taking into account other information, such as vehicle styling, that was not incorporated explicitly into the design study. In order to generate trade-off curves, dozens of independent simulations must be run, each with minor variations in input parameters. This may appear to be a trivial parallel computing exercise that could be run across a network of workstations instead of a single parallel computer. Although this is true in principle, we have found that setting up the problems, monitoring the status of job execution, and analyzing results are all much easier when done on a single system. In our experience, these ease-of-use factors are sufficient justification for calling this a legitimate parallel application, and we think it represents a significant advance in the use of parallel computers.

25.7.4 Area 4: Interactive, Intuitive, Immersive Simulation Environments: Large-Scale Particle Tracing

The final case we discuss is the emerging area of simulation environments. These environments give users an ability to do simulations and view results at or near realtime speeds. One should note that these environments are ideally suited to computer systems that have highly integrated compute, data management, and graphics capabilities. If one of these three capabilities is not present, then it becomes very difficult to provide these environments in a way that is truly useful.

In general, simulation environments have three important traits:

1. Interactive: The user does not wait long for results. Simulations are run rapidly enough to return answers within seconds of the user request, or results are precomputed and stored for rapid retrieval.

2. Intuitive: There is no manual that the user must read in order to understand how to use the environment. The interface must be natural and intuitive to a scientist or engineer who is an expert in his or her field but is not a computer expert.

3. Immersive: Although not a requirement, with this trait the user steps into a virtual world that makes use of one or more physical senses. Minimally, the user should be able to see results from the simulation in a 3D setting using stereo imaging. In addition, it is possible to use sound to enhance the experience. Smell, touch, and taste are probably not appropriate, at least at this time.

Although these traits may seem to describe the Holodeck on the Starship Enterprise more than a productive use of simulation, we have seen a few examples that indicate this is a very powerful capability for scientists and engineers. In particular, the recent development of large-scale particle tracing environments for examining flow field data has been very useful.

In full form, these environments give great insight into flow field data from any CFD simulation—for example, underhood flow analysis to test for hotspots around the automobile engine. The user provides the flow field data and the geometry of the problem, which is projected as a stereo (3D) image. Then the user can inject particles into the flow field at will by simply pointing a wand (a kind of 3D mouse) and clicking to release the particles. Once the particles are released, they follow the flow field as if they were released into the true flow. The user sees the particles moving through the 3D image of the problem domain. They can see mixing phenomena, flow blockages, dead zones, and hot spots. In many cases, the value of this kind of environment is immeasurable.

25.8   LOOKING FORWARD: THE ROLE OF PARALLEL COMPUTING IN THE DIGITAL INFORMATION AGE

Historically, the role of parallel computing has been seen as a distinctive, separate endeavor that did not touch the daily lives of most people. Activities in parallel computing and the results from its projects were limited to small numbers of highly trained specialists. The outcome of this has been that parallel computing, although having tremendous impact in some areas, has been largely unappreciated and underutilized in our society.

Today we are immersed in the Digital Information Age. The ubiquitous presence of cell phones, pagers, digital sensors, visual monitors, and so on are symbols of that. Also, the fact that most people today understand and appreciate the value of the World Wide Web shows that the impact is widespread. What is also remarkable, and why we specifically refer to this as the *Digital* Information Age, is that all of these devices can interact with each other by virtue of the underlying commonality of digital information encoding.

How does parallel computing fit into the Digital Information Age? If we recognize that it plays a critical and unique role in creating valuable data, then we can see the tremendous potential for it as an essential component of the Digital Information Age. However, parallel computing must be integrated into today's information infrastructure through the information appliances that we have come to rely upon—Web browsers, immersive environments, even pagers, cell phones, and faxes. Ultimately, this means that parallel computing must be integrated with high-performance data management and high-performance graphics in order to deliver its greatest value.

25.8.1   Increasing the Demand for Parallel Computing

Before we continue with further discussion of parallel computing in the Digital Information Age, we must make it clear that emphasizing the connection of parallel computing to today's information infrastructure does not diminish the importance of it. In fact, it is quite the opposite. By making parallel computing results readily accessible, the demand increases. Almost immediately, the ready accessibility to its results dramatically increases the demand for more accurate simulations and more rapid turnaround of simulation results.

The Role of Computer Simulation

As we mentioned at the beginning of this chapter, the role of computer simulation in science and engineering is to create valuable information about processes, product designs, and so on. We must appreciate how unique and valuable this role can be. Specifically, the data that computer simulation creates is often unattainable by any other means. For example, it is infeasible to design, build, and crash hundreds of physical automobile prototypes prior to manufacturing next year's new vehicle. However, this is possible using computer simulation. In fact, not only can you create many virtual prototypes and answer questions like "How safe is this automobile design?" but you can also begin to ask the question, "What automobile design is the safest?" This type of information is incredibly valuable and is unattainable by any other means.

Advances in computer simulation applications now allow us to model many complex physical systems with a great deal of accuracy. However, in most engineering and scientific disciplines, we have only started to approach the sophistication we need. Several issues are limiting the value of computer simulation results. In particular, the accuracy of a model and the speed at which the model generates results are two important issues.

1. **Physical accuracy:** The accuracy of a computer model, when compared to the actual physical process being modeled, provides the foundation for any scientific or engineering application. The usefulness of any application is ultimately determined by how accurate the underlying model is. For example, if we wish to use a computer model to determine if one product design is better than another, we must have confidence that our model is accurate enough to provide a reliable distinction between the two designs. Currently, in all engineering and scientific disciplines we make many simplifying assumptions in our computer models in order to be able to generate cost-effective results on today's computers. Without exception, there is an insatiable hunger for more powerful computer systems.

2. **Rapid turnaround:** In addition to providing accurate results, timeliness of generating the results is very important. Although any improvement in turnaround time is valuable, an exciting opportunity lies in the ability to run sophisticated computer models interactively.

As parallel computing results become more accessible through the digital information infrastructure, the importance of increased physical accuracy and rapid turnaround of results will increase dramatically. Thus, by increasing our focus on making parallel computing more accessible, we simultaneously increase the demand for it. How will we make parallel computing results more accessible? This is the next topic.

25.8.2   The Importance of Advanced User Interfaces

As we have mentioned, parallel computing is uniquely able to create valuable data that can in turn be used to generate information and insight into problems that impact our society today. Safer automobiles, more effective medications, and a cleaner environment are some benefits that we already see from it. However, in order to get information and insight from parallel computing data, we must have effective user interfaces.

Transforming Capability into Usability

As computer models become more complex and detailed, the role of the user interface becomes much more important. State-of-the-art simulations can generate gigabytes, terabytes, and soon petabytes of data. The latent information in this data must be extracted in a way that is meaningful to the user. The role of user interfaces is to transform capability into usability. Traditionally, parallel applications have had complicated user interfaces that require substantial training and education in order to use them effectively. This fact necessarily limits the usefulness of it to a small number of highly trained specialists. However, this is changing.

The Role of Multimedia

In the past few years we have seen tremendous progress in the use of graphics and visualization for scientific and engineering computing. In addition, the astonishing emergence of the World Wide Web as a vehicle for transmitting information has completely changed how we write user interfaces. These recent advances offer tremendous promise in making parallel computing results more accessible. The combination of realistic, 3D graphics and easy-to-write Web interfaces gives us a potent capability to provide intuitive, interactive, and immersive user environments. At the opposite end of the spectrum, it allows us to potentially feed the results of simulation directly into a spreadsheet computation, or to your pager, cell phone, or fax machine.

The Importance of High-Performance Data Management

In addition to graphics and Web tools, advanced user interfaces require sophisticated, high-performance data management. Users can and will quickly generate volumes of data that must be managed and accessed. Having both the hardware and software capabilities to handle these demands is essential to making parallel computing successful in the Digital Information Age.

25.8.3   Highly Integrated Computing

In the previous paragraphs we demonstrated that, in order for parallel computing to be successful in the Digital Information Age, parallel computer systems must have state-of-the-art graphics, networking capabilities, and data management—in addition to high-performance computing capabilities. However, graphics, data management, and computer simulation today are usually distinct functions. Because of this, we typically buy a separate computer system to handle each function and measure the value of a parallel computer system by how cost-effective it is in running a particular set of scientific/engineering applications. In fact, as the capabilities of different platforms converge, the focus turns almost solely to price/performance—that is, how cheaply a particular computer system can produce a particular, predetermined result.

Although price/performance is extremely important, we have a new opportunity to improve the value of parallel computing by increasing the benefit it provides. In particular, if we combine graphics, data management, and computing into a single high-performance system, we open up new opportunities to greatly increase the benefit of parallel computing.

25.8.4   The Future

The future of parallel computing can and will be very bright. Without a doubt, it can play an essential and unique role in curing disease, designing innovative and safer products, and protecting and enhancing our environment. However, to get the most value from parallel computing we must make the information it provides, which is truly unique, readily accessible to people who can use it. By focusing on how simulation data is managed and presented to the user, in addition to continuing to focus on more sophisticated computer models, we can bring the value of parallel computing to a broad audience. To the extent we do this, it will be seen as an essential tool that can be brought to bear on the most challenging problems facing our society today.

References

[25.1]   Beowulf Project. *cesdis.gsfc.nasa.gov/linux/beowulf/beowulf.html.*

[25.2]   Computational Plant (CPLANT) Project. *www.cs.sandia.gov/~dsgreen/cplant/main.html.*

[25.3]   Kuskin, Jeffrey, David Ofelt, Mark Heinrich, John Heinlein, Richard Simoni, Kourosh Gharachorloo, John Chapin, David Nakahira, Joel Baxter, Mark Horowitz, Anoop Gupta, Mendel Rosenblum, and John Hennessy. 1994. The Stanford FLASH Multiprocessor. In *Proceedings of the 21st International Symposium on Computer Architecture,* Chicago, IL, April, 302–313.

[25.4]   Lenoski, Daniel, James Laudon, Joe Truman, David Nakahira, Luis Stevens, Anoop Gupta, and John Hennessy. 1992. The DASH Prototype: Implementation and Performance. In *Proceedings of the 19th International Symposium on Computer Architecture,* Gold Coast, Australia, May 1992, 92–103, © 1992 by the ACM.

[25.5]   NSF Workshop on Critical Issues in Computer Architecture Research, May 21, 1996. *www.cise.nsf.gov/ccr/MSAWorkshop96/report/index.html.*

[25.6]   Stadler, Joerg. 1998. Experiences with Industrial Applications on Massively Parallel Computers. In *Proceedings of Supercomputer 1998,* 41–47. Muenchen: K. G. Sauer.

Mixed Models with Pthreads and MPI

Vijay Sonnad
Chary G. Tamirisa
Gyan Bhanot   IBM Corporation

A.1   INTRODUCTION

We present here a quick overview of POSIX threads and their use within codes that use MPI. With the advent of machines where each node consists of several processors sharing memory, this model of programming is gaining importance. Such machines represent an evolution from two opposite directions: manufacturers of shared-memory machines wishing to offer large numbers of nodes find it relatively easy to connect several machines together in a "cluster of shared-memory machines"; on the other hand, vendors of distributed-memory machines find it natural to expand the processing power of each node by using several processors sharing memory within a node. A generic illustration of this type of architecture is shown in Figure 1.4. One approach to getting the full benefits of the architecture on these hybrid machines is to use threads within a node and MPI across nodes; in this appendix, we provide a basic description and some simple examples to illustrate the concepts.

A.2   A BRIEF OVERVIEW OF POSIX THREADS

The concept of using multiple processors sharing a common memory to perform calculations in parallel has existed for several decades. In Unix-based systems, the traditional approach to making full use of such machines is to have the operating system create processes that can run in parallel on separate processors. A process defines an address space with some resources, such as user ID, open file descriptors, and current working directory, defined within it. A process embodies two features: it contains resources such as address space, and it is also the unit of execution—that is, it is schedulable. A process is a relatively heavyweight mechanism, and switching contexts between processes tends to be expensive. Separating the notion of resources from the notion of execution gives rise to the concept of a thread as the unit of execution within a process.

POSIX modified the definition of a process as a result of the separation of the execution unit and the resources within a process. A process is defined to be an address space with one or more threads. Threads can be independently scheduled on the available processors to take advantage of parallel execution on the available CPUs. Thus, threads exist within a process, and they share the resources of the process. Threads are lightweight compared to a process and hence can be scheduled more efficiently than processes.

To multithread a program, one needs to understand the programming model for threads. It is up to the application developer to identify program segments that can be executed in parallel and then create threads to execute the code. In addition, the application developer has to program so that races do not occur among the threads when they manipulate shared data. When multiple threads are created, the application writer has to decide how the threads have to be scheduled. For instance, the writer has to decide if one thread needs to have a higher priority than other threads. Another set of issues arises with respect to thread management, such as the required stack size of threads and appropriate handling of the exit status of a thread upon termination. These are just some of the issues the application programmer needs to resolve, and it is here that an understanding of the underlying threads programming model becomes necessary.

There are several programming models for threads. On Unix platforms, the predominant model is IEEE's POSIX threads (Pthreads) model; the international standard, ISO/IEC 9945–1, incorporates this standard. The Pthreads programming model is very comprehensive. It provides a set of APIs that are typically supported by a user-level library. Applications written to these APIs obtain source-level portability on all conforming platforms. POSIX defines bindings for C language; as of this writing, there is no Pthreads standard with Fortran bindings, and thus the most expedient approach to using Pthreads with Fortran is to have wrappers in C for calls to the Pthreads library. IBM provides an API for multithreaded programming in Fortran, which is not a POSIX standard but bears a strong resemblance to the Pthreads standard.

A.3   PROCESS VERSUS THREADS

Let us briefly examine the details of changes to the concept of a process. As stated earlier, a process is an address space with one or more threads of control. All threads in a process share the following features: address space, shared storage, the process ID, parent process ID, process group ID, session membership, real ID, effective ID, saved-set user ID, real group ID, effective group ID, saved-set group ID, supplementary group IDs, current working directory, root directory, file-mode creation mask, file descriptor table, signal handlers, and per-process timers. There are some thread-specific features that are unique to a thread. For instance, each thread has a unique thread ID, a scheduling policy and priority, a per-thread errno, a set of thread-specific key/value bindings, a thread stack, a set of per-thread cancellation handlers, and a per-thread signal mask.

When a process starts up, the entry point function main() of the program is invoked by the process loader. An initial thread is automatically created by the underlying system, and this initial thread is also called the *main thread* as it invokes the main() of the application. Thus, the main thread is not created by the application. Once in the main(), the application has the ability to create threads. The main or the initial thread is special. If the main thread returns, the process terminates even if there are running threads in the process. If the main thread needs to return, it has to invoke the Pthread API: pthread_exit() explicitly to avoid terminating the entire process. Another way is to wait for all threads to terminate before returning from the main() of an application.

The Pthreads programming model revolves around the creation of threads and managing their execution and the shared resources of the process. To guarantee correct results, programs have to manage asynchronous activities properly. In a multithreaded environment, if multiple threads modify the same shared data simultaneously, the contents of the shared data become unpredictable. To guard against this, the Pthreads model provides mutual exclusion through the mutex (which stands for mutual exclusion) APIs. Sometimes, it is necessary for threads to wait for some events to occur; in order to allow this, the condition variable APIs are provided. POSIX allows mutexes and condition variables to be used between threads in different processes as well. In addition to the mutex and condition variables, POSIX also defines the counting semaphore APIs that can be used to synchronize threads within the same process or across processes. With these three sets of APIs, an application developer has a very powerful set of synchronization mechanisms to use for effective synchronization within a process or between processes.

The Pthreads standard defines mechanisms for creating thread-specific memory, which is useful when one needs to provide each thread with a different dynamic memory. For instance, the error number associated with a particular function in a library needs to be specific to the thread that invoked it. POSIX also provides a thread-cancel mechanism wherein a thread can cancel another thread within the same process. This comes in handy when a thread that is no longer needed must be terminated by another thread. Because a thread that is being cancelled may be holding resources (like a mutex), provision is made in the Pthreads APIs to allow the thread to perform cleanup (that is, release the resources it holds).

The Pthreads standard extends the POSIX signals model to work in a multithreaded environment. It defines the scope of signal handlers to be processwide. It defines a per-thread signal mask so that each thread can decide whether it wants to receive or block a signal. In addition, POSIX defines a new API to allow all asynchronous signals, such as SIGALRM, to be sent to a dedicated thread waiting for the signal. When the dedicated thread receives a signal, it can do any required processing for the signal using any of the Pthread APIs. However, the Pthread APIs cannot be invoked from signal handlers; the Pthread APIs are not signal-safe. Hence, it is important to understand how to handle signals in this new fashion.

A.4   OVERVIEW OF PTHREAD APIs

The Pthreads programming model provides two data types: opaque handles to objects (not in the object-oriented sense), and attributes that define the properties of these objects. For instance, the type pthread_t defines a Pthread. Properties such as the stack size are specified through an attribute of the type pthread_attr_t. Similarly, the type pthread_mutex_t defines a mutex object; its properties are specified through an attribute of the type pthread_mutex_attr_t. The new types introduced by the Pthreads APIs are as follows:

+ Thread ID: pthread_t
+ Thread attribute: pthread_attr_t
+ Mutex: pthread_mutex_t
+ Mutex attribute: pthread_mutexattr_t
+ Condition variable: pthread_cond_t
+ Condition variable attribute: pthread_condattr_t

+ Thread-specific key: pthread_key_t

+ Once-only initialization: pthread_once_t

The counting semaphore API defined in POSIX is extended into the threads environment as stated earlier. The semaphore type is as follows:

+ Counting semaphore: sem_t

The Pthread APIs do not set the global errno; instead, they return any status (errors or success) as an integer return value of the APIs. This avoids the problem of shared global errno altogether.

Based on their functionality, the Pthreads APIs can be categorized as follows:

Thread Management Functions

These APIs deal with the issues pertaining to creating a thread, returning from a thread, joining with a thread, and detaching a thread. In addition, the once-only initialization API is provided to ensure that a specified routine is executed just once, no matter how many times it is invoked.

Thread Attribute Functions

The thread attributes that are supported are as follows: stack size, stack address, the detach state of the thread, scheduling parameters, and contention scope. There is also the notion of the default values for these attributes. The default values can be specified by providing a NULL value for the thread attribute when creating a thread.

Mutex Functions

These functions are used for locking and unlocking a critical section where shared data is modified.

Mutex Attribute Functions

These functions are used for specifying the attributes of the mutex at the time of its creation. The default mutex is obtained if the attribute is specified as NULL.

Condition Variable Functions

The condition variable functions are used for waiting for certain conditions to occur. Pthreads also provides a timeout for these waits.

Condition Variable Attribute Functions

These functions are used for specifying the attributes of the condition variable at the time of its creation. The default condition variable is obtained if the attribute is specified to be NULL.

Thread-Specific Data Functions

Thread-specific data functions are used for creating and associating dynamic memory with a thread. Such memory is unique to the thread and is not shared between threads. A thread can set and get the thread-specific memory, which is associated with a key. A thread can have several such keys.

Thread Cancel Functions

Thread cancel functions are typically used for terminating a thread from another thread. When a thread is cancelled, it needs to release any resources it holds. The application can register cleanup handlers to clean up after cancellation.

Thread Scheduling Functions

These functions are used for specifying the scheduling policy and priority of a thread. Pthreads provides realtime scheduling policies (round-robin and First-In-First-Out policies). Pthreads also allows a default policy that may not be a realtime scheduling policy.

The Pthreads standard provides APIs to contain priority inversion that can occur in a multithreaded process. Priority inversion occurs when a low-priority thread runs, starving a high-priority thread indefinitely.

Signal Handling Functions

The new API here is the sigwait() API, which allows a dedicated thread to be the sole recipient of all asynchronous signals. A thread can also send a signal to another thread using the pthread_kill() API. In addition, per-thread signal masks can be installed using the pthread_sigmask() API.

The Pthread APIs define changes to make the C runtime APIs thread-safe. Some of the C runtime functions, such as malloc() and free(), operate on shared data of the entire process, and, hence, they need to lock the data before manipulating it. This allows safety in a multithreaded environment. Similarly, some of the C string functions, such as strtok(), that use static data buffers are inherently thread-unsafe. In order to make them thread-safe, a counterpart with an "_r" suffix is defined to let the application provide the buffer that is specific to the thread that is invoking the strtok_r() API. In defining these new APIs, the Pthreads standard tries to allow applications both to obtain thread safety as well as maintain high performance.

A.5   EXAMPLES TO ILLUSTRATE THE USE OF PTHREADS WITH MPI

We begin with a simple sequential program and observe the changes that will be introduced in order to convert the code into a parallel program that will in turn utilize

1. A distributed-memory programming model with MPI

2. A shared-memory programming model using Pthreads

3. A hybrid model that will utilize both MPI and Pthreads to execute on machines that are made of clusters of SMPs

Example P.1: Dot Product Routine for a Uniprocessor

```
#include <stdio.h>
#include <malloc.h>
/*
The following structure contains the necessary information to allow
the function dotprod to access its input data and place its output
so that it can be accessed later.
*/
typedef struct
  {
    double    *a;
    double    *b;
    double    sum;
    int    veclen;
  } DOTDATA;
#define VECLEN 100
    DOTDATA dotstr;
/*
```

(*continued on page 542*)

(Example P.1 continued from page 541)

We will use a function (dotprod) to perform the scalar product. All input to this routine is obtained through a structure of type DOTDATA, and all output from this function is written into this same structure. While this is unnecessarily restrictive for a sequential program, it will turn out to be useful when we modify the program to compute in parallel.

```c
 */
void* dotprod(void)
  {
  /*Define and use local variables for convenience */
    int start, end, i;
    double mysum, *x, *y;
    start=0;
    end = dotstr.veclen;
    x = dotstr.a;
    y = dotstr.b;
  /*
```

Perform the dot product and assign result to the appropriate variable in the structure.

```c
 */
    mysum = 0;
    for (i=start; i<end ; i++)
    {
     mysum += (x[i] * y[i]);
    }
  dotstr.sum = mysum;
  return ;
  }
  /*
```

The main program initializes data and calls the dotprod() function. Finally, it prints the result.

```c
 */
  void main (int argc, char* argv[])
  {
    int i,len;
    double *a, *b;
  /*Assign storage and initialize values */
    len = VECLEN;
```

```
    a = (double*) malloc (len*sizeof(double));
    b = (double*) malloc (len*sizeof(double));
    for (i=0; i<len; i++)
     {
     a[i]=1;
     b[i]=a[i];
     }
    dotstr.veclen = len;
    dotstr.a = a;
    dotstr.b = b;
    dotstr.sum=0;
/*Perform the dotproduct */
    dotprod ();
/*Print result and release storage */
    printf ("Sum = %f \n", dotstr.sum);
    free (a);
    free (b);
  }
```

Example P.2: A Dot Product Routine for Distributed-Memory Machines Using MPI

```
   /*
This is an elementary program to illustrate the use of MPI in a pro-
gram obtained by modifying a sequential code that performs a dot
product. In this code, we have chosen to use the SPMD model and for
convenience have replicated the main data on all nodes.
   */
  #include <mpi.h>
  #include <stdio.h>
  #include <malloc.h>
   /*
The following structure contains the necessary information to allow
the function dotprod to access its input data and place its output
into the structure. Note that this structure is unchanged from the
sequential version.
   */
  typedef struct
```

(*continued on page 544*)

(*Example P.2 continued from page 543*)

```
  {
      double      *a;
      double      *b;
      double    sum;
      int     veclen;
  } DOTDATA;
 /*Define globally accessible variables */
 #define VECLEN 100
      DOTDATA dotstr;
  /*
```

The function dotprod is very similar to the sequential version except that we now have each node working on a different part of the data. As before, all access to the input is through a structure of type DOTDATA, and all output from this function is written into this same structure.

```
  */
  void* dotprod()
  {
 /*Define and use local variables for convenience */
    int i, start, end, myid, len;
    double mysum, *x, *y;
 /*Obtain rank of this node */
    MPI_Comm_rank (MPI_COMM_WORLD, &myid);
    len = dotstr.veclen;
 start = myid*len;
 end = start + len;
 x = dotstr.a;
 y = dotstr.b;
/*
```

Perform the dot product and assign result to the appropriate variable in the structure.

```
*/
 mysum = 0;
 for (i=start; i<end ; i++)
 {
 mysum += (x[i] * y[i]);
 }
```

```
  dotstr.sum += mysum;
}
/*
As before, the main program does very little computation. It does,
however, make all the calls to the MPI routines. This is not a mas-
ter-slave arrangement and all nodes participate equally in the work.
*/
void main (int argc, char* argv[])
{
  int i,len=VECLEN;
  int myid, numprocs;
  double *a, *b;
  double mysum, allsum;
/*MPI Initialization */
  MPI_Init (&argc, &argv);
  MPI_Comm_size (MPI_COMM_WORLD, &numprocs);
  MPI_Comm_rank (MPI_COMM_WORLD, &myid);
/*Assign storage and initialize values */
  a = (double*) malloc (numprocs*len*sizeof(double));
  b = (double*) malloc (numprocs*len*sizeof(double));
  for (i=0; i<len*numprocs; i++)
  {
  a[i]=1;
  b[i]=a[i];
  }
  dotstr.veclen = len;
  dotstr.a = a;
  dotstr.b = b;
  dotstr.sum=0;
/*Call the dot product routine */
  dotprod();
  mysum = dotstr.sum;
/*After the dot product, perform a summation of results on each node
*/
  MPI_Reduce (&mysum, &allsum, 1, MPI_DOUBLE, MPI_SUM, 0,
MPI_COMM_WORLD);
  if (myid == 0)
  printf ("Allsum = %f \n", allsum);
  free (a);
```

(*continued on page 546*)

(Example P.2 continued from page 545)

```
free (b);
free (dotstr);
MPI_Finalize();
```

Example P.3: A Dot Product Routine for Shared-Memory Machines Using Pthreads

```
   /*
This is an elementary program to illustrate the use of threads in a
program. This program is obtained by modifying a sequential program
that performs a dot product. The main data is made available to all
threads through a globally accessible structure. Each thread works
on a different part of the data. The main thread waits for all the
threads to complete their computations, and then it prints the re-
sulting sum.
   */
 #include <Fpthread.h>
 #include <Fstdio.h>
 #include <Fmalloc.h>
   /*
The following structure contains the necessary information to allow
the function dotprod to access its input data and place its output
into the structure. This structure is unchanged from the sequential
version.
   */
 typedef struct
  {
   double     *a;
   double     *b;
   double    sum;
   int     veclen;
  } DOTDATA;
/*Define globally accessible variables and a mutex */
#define MAXTHRDS 4
#define VECLEN 100
   DOTDATA dotstr;
```

```
      pthread_t callThd[MAXTHRDS];
      pthread_mutex_t mutexsum;
      /*
```

The function dotprod is activated when the thread is created. As before, all input to this routine is obtained from a structure of type DOTDATA, and all output from this function is written into this structure. The benefit of this approach is apparent for the multithreaded program: When a thread is created we pass a single argument to the activated function—typically, this argument is a thread number. All the other information required by the function is accessed from the globally accessible structure.

```
      */
      void* dotprod(void *arg)
      {
      /*Define and use local variables for convenience */
        int i, start, end, offset, len ;
        double mysum, *x, *y;
        offset = (int)arg;
        len = dotstr.veclen;
        start = offset*len;
        end = start + len;
        x = dotstr.a;
        y = dotstr.b;
      /*
```

Perform the dot product and assign result to the appropriate variable in the structure.

```
      */
      mysum = 0;
      for (i=start; i<end ; i++)
      {
      mysum += (x[i] * y[i]);
      }
      /*
```

Lock a mutex prior to updating the value in the shared structure, and unlock it upon updating.

```
      */
      pthread_mutex_lock (&mutexsum);
      dotstr.sum += mysum;
      pthread_mutex_unlock (&mutexsum);
      pthread_exit((void*)0);
```

(*continued on page 548*)

(*Example P.3 continued from page 547*)

```
  }
  /*
```

The main program creates threads that do all the work and then
prints out the result upon completion. Before creating the threads,
the input data is created. Because all threads update a shared
structure, we need a mutex for mutual exclusion. The main thread
needs to wait for all threads to complete, and it waits for each one
of the threads.

```
*/
  void main (int argc, char* argv[])
  {
    int i;
    double *a, *b;
    int status;
    int ret;
  /*Assign storage and initialize values */
    a = (double*) malloc (MAXTHRDS*VECLEN*sizeof(double));
    b = (double*) malloc (MAXTHRDS*VECLEN*sizeof(double));
    for (i=0; i<VECLEN*MAXTHRDS; i++)
  {
  a[i]=1;
  b[i]=a[i];
  }
  dotstr.veclen = VECLEN;
  dotstr.a = a;
  dotstr.b = b;
  dotstr.sum=0;
  pthread_mutex_init(&mutexsum, NULL);
/*Create threads to perform the dotproduct */
  for(i=0;i<MAXTHRDS;i++)
  {
      /*
  ** Each thread works on a different set of data.
  ** The offset is specified by 'i'. The size of
  ** the data for each thread is indicated by VECLEN.
  */
  ret = pthread_create( &callThd[i], NULL, dotprod, (void *)i);
          if (ret) printf ("Error in thread create \n");
```

```
    }
    /*Wait on the other threads */
    for(i=0;i<MAXTHRDS;i++)
    {
     ret = pthread_join( callThd[i], (void **)&status);
     if (ret) printf ("Error in thread join \n");
    }
/*After joining, print out the results and cleanup */
    printf ("Sum = %f \n", dotstr.sum);
    free (a);
    free (b);
    free (dotstr);
    pthread_mutex_destroy(&mutexsum);
    pthread_exit (0);
}
```

Example P.4: A Dot Product Routine for a Hybrid Machine Using Both MPI and Pthreads

```
    /*
This is a program that illustrates the simultaneous use of MPI and
Pthreads. It is essentially a simple combination of a code that im-
plements a dot product using threads and a code that uses MPI for
the same purpose. All the internode communication is done by the
main thread on each node—the other threads within that node need not
even be aware that internode communication is being performed. This
is the simplest model for mixed MPI/Pthreads programming.
    */
    #include "mpi.h"
    #include <pthread.h>
    #include <malloc.h>
    /*
This structure has been changed slightly from the previous cases to
include the number of threads per node.
    */
    typedef struct
    {
      double      *a;
```

(*continued on page 550*)

(Example P.4 continued from page 549)

```
        double    *b;
        double    sum;
        int    veclen;
        int   numthrds;
        } DOTDATA;
    /*Define globally accessible variables and a mutex */
    #define MAXTHRDS 4
    #define VECLEN 100
        DOTDATA dotstr;
        pthread_t callThd[MAXTHRDS];
        pthread_mutex_t mutexsum;
    /*
The function dotprod has only minor changes from the code that used
threads or MPI.
    */
    void* dotprod(void *arg)
    {
/*Define and use local variables for convenience */
    int i, start, end, mythrd, len, numthrds, myid;
    double mysum, *x, *y;
    /*
The number of threads and nodes defines the beginning and ending for
the dot product; each thread does work on a vector of length
VECLENGTH.
    */
    mythrd = (int)arg;
    MPI_Comm_rank (MPI_COMM_WORLD, &myid);
    numthrds = dotstr.numthrds;
    len = dotstr.veclen;
    start = myid*numthrds*len + mythrd*len;
    end = start + len;
    x = dotstr.a;
    y = dotstr.b;
/* Perform the dot product and assign the result to the appropriate
variable in the structure.
    */
    mysum = 0;
    for (i=start; i<end ; i++)
```

```
  {
  mysum += (x[i] * y[i]);
  }
  /*
Lock a mutex prior to updating the value in the structure, and un-
lock it upon updating.
*/
  pthread_mutex_lock (&mutexsum);
  dotstr.sum += mysum;
  pthread_mutex_unlock (&mutexsum);
  pthread_exit((void*)0);
  }
  /*
As before,the main program does very little computation. It creates
threads on each node and the main thread does all the MPI calls.
  */
  void main (int argc, char* argv[])
  {
    int i,len=VECLEN;
    int myid, numprocs;
    int nump1, numthrds;
    double *a, *b;
    double nodesum, allsum;
    int status;
    int ret;
  /*MPI Initialization */
  MPI_Init (&argc, &argv);
  MPI_Comm_size (MPI_COMM_WORLD, &numprocs);
  MPI_Comm_rank (MPI_COMM_WORLD, &myid);
  /*Assign storage and initialize values */
  numthrds=MAXTHRDS;
  a = (double*) malloc (numprocs*numthrds*len*sizeof(double));
  b = (double*) malloc (numprocs*numthrds*len*sizeof(double));
  for (i=0; i<len*numprocs*numthrds; i++)
  {
  a[i]=1;
  b[i]=a[i];
  }
  dotstr.veclen = len;
  dotstr.a = a;
```

(*continued on page 552*)

(Example P.4 continued from page 551)

```
    dotstr.b = b;
    dotstr.sum=0;
    dotstr.numthrds=MAXTHRDS;
    /*Create a mutex */
    pthread_mutex_init (&mutexsum, NULL);
/* Create threads within this node to perform the dotproduct */
    for(i=0;i<numthrds;i++)
    {
    ret = pthread_create( &callThd[i], NULL, dotprod, (void *)i);
    if (ret) printf ("Error in thread creation \n");
    }
/*Wait on the other threads within this node */
    for(i=0;i<numthrds;i++)
    {
        ret = pthread_join( callThd[i], (void **)&status);
        if (ret) printf ("Error in thread join \n");
    }
    nodesum = dotstr.sum;
    /*After the dot product, perform a summation of results on each
node */
    MPI_Reduce (&nodesum, &allsum, 1, MPI_DOUBLE, MPI_SUM, 0,
                MPI_COMM_WORLD);
    if (myid == 0)
    printf ("Allsum = %f \n", allsum);
    MPI_Finalize();
    free (a);
    free (b);
    free (dotstr);
    pthread_mutex_destroy(&mutexsum);
    exit (0);
}
```

Glossary

anisotropies In materials, this refers to a directional preference. For example, in fractured media, water flows preferentially in the direction of the fractures, rather than equally in all directions.

antenna systems Devices made of arrangements of components such as waveguides, dipoles, and reflecting surfaces, designed to launch electromagnetic waves with desired features such as directionality and polarization.

API Application Programming Interface.

azimuthal coordinate Angle from the x-axis to a point's projection in the x-y plane.

bandwidth (memory) The peak rate at which data can be transferred from main memory to processors.

baroclinic Departures from the vertical mean.

barotropic Vertical mean.

bianisotropic Refers to materials in which constitutive relations link both the electric flux D and magnetic flux B with both the electric and magnetic fields E and H, and these relations are functions of the field direction.

BLAS Basic Linear Algebra Subproblems.

Bloch's theorem States that the wave functions of the electrons in a crystal have a form that is modulated by a function that has the periodicity of the lattice.

Brillouin zone A Wigner-Seitz cell of a reciprocal lattice, hence the cell of smallest volume enclosed by the planes that are perpendicular bisectors of reciprocal lattice vectors.

Brownian motion The random movement of microsopic particles suspended in a fluid.

byte A unit of information that is eight bits long.

C70 fullerene A form of carbon element in which the atoms are arranged in closed shells with a very high degree of symmetry. The number of carbon atoms can vary, 60 being the most common. The C70 fullerene has 70 carbon atoms.

cache coherency A requirement that all processors use the latest data. When caches (on-chip memory) are used, multiple copies of data can exist.

Cartesian subgrids A rectangular subdivision of a larger rectangular grid.

CAXPY A complex linear algebra operation that includes the sum of a vector multiplied by a complex scalar factor and another vector. Both vectors are complex.

CGHS Conjugate Gradients Hesthenes-Steiffel. This is the original conjugate gradient algorithm invented by two mathematicians, Hesthenes and Steiffel, for solving sparse matrix equations.

checkpointing Writing the state of a computation to disk for future restarts. A checkpoint file is sometimes called a *restart* file.

chiral Refers to that type of bi-isotropic media whose constitutive relations are characterized by three scalars, the permittivity, the permeability, and the chirality admittance.

CICERO A body-of-revolution integral equation code developed by J. M. Putnam at the McDonnell Douglas Research Labs.

CMOS Chip technology based on metal oxide semiconductors.

coarse-grain parallelism Parallelism within a program may occur at many different levels. Coarse-grain indicates that the units of parallelism are of a significant length of duration relative to the whole program and usually refers to parallelism implemented at a very high level of a program.

COEF Matrix coefficient generation routine.

combined field integral equation (CFIE) Integral equation form of the frequency domain Maxwell's equations consisting of any linear combination of the magnetic field integral equation and the electric field integral equation.

compositing The last step in the parallel rendering proces, where the partial rendered images in each processor are merged to form the final image.

conformal Refers to a computational mesh constructed such that element surfaces and material surfaces coincide, especially by applying a continuous mapping from a conceptual regular mesh to the mesh that fits the material boundaries.

CPMAS Cross Polarization with Magic Angle Spinning. A useful solid state NMR technique to obtain the sensitivity enhancement of cross polarization along with the sharp lines provided by magic angle spinning.

CPU Central processing unit.

CRADA Cooperative Research and Development Agreement.

Cuthill-McKee algorithm One type of equation reordering algorithm that reduces the outer envelope of nonzeros in a sparse matrix.

Darcy's law A mathematical law describing the flow of a fluid through a porous medium.

DFT Density-functional theory.

diagonalization Diagonalization of a square matrix yields a new matrix in which only the diagonal elements are nonzero. This is an essential step in many mathematical manipulations of matrices.

dielectrics Refers to materials that support electric polarization; commonly used to describe any material that supports electromagnetic wave propagation within its volume.

discretization Representation of a continuously variable quantity such as a volumetric field by a linear combination of a countable number of basis functions times scalar coefficients, especially when each coefficient represents the value of the quantity in some local region.

DMP Distributed-Memory Parallel class of computers.

DSMC Direct Simulation Monte Carlo—alternative technique for modeling rarefied gas dynamics.

eigensolutions The eigenvalues and corresponding eigenfunctions or eigenvectors of an operator or matrix.

eigensystem A posed eigenvalue problem or the set of solutions in terms of eigenvalues and eigenvectors. The mathematical terminology corresponding to the physical problem of finding the normal modes of a system.

eigenvalues The eigenvalues of a matrix; roots of the characteristic equation for a given matrix, corresponding to frequencies of the normal modes or resonances of a physical system. Given an n-by-n matrix A, the eigenvalues of A are the n roots of its characteristic polynomial $p(z) = \det(z\mathrm{I} - \mathrm{A})$.

eigenvector Given an n-by-n matrix A with eigenvalue z, the nonzero vectors x that satisfy $\mathrm{A}x = zx$ are referred to as eigenvectors of A.

EISPACK subroutines Widely used public-domain Fortran subroutines for solving eigenvalue problems, based on Wilkinson and Reinsch's *Handbook for Automatic Computation, Vol. II, Linear Algebra* (New York: Springer-Verlag, 1971).

electric field integral equation (EFIE) Integral equation form of the frequency domain Maxwell's equations that relates the incident and total magnetic currents on a closed surface.

electromagnetics The study of time-varying electric and magnetic fields as characterized by Maxwell's equations.

elementwise A vector or matrix operation that operates on the entire vector or matrix by operating on each individual entry one at a time.

Euler angles The Euler angles are the three angles necessary to take an object (and its mathematical description) from one reference frame to another. The first angle describes the necessary rotation about the original z-axis, the second describes the necessary rotation about the new (intermediate) y-axis, and the third describes the necessary rotation about the final z-axis.

Eulerian approach A description of fluid motion employing state variables (e.g., pressure, velocity) defined as functions of the position in the fluid.

false-sharing Two distinct data items may share a cache-line. When one item is used by one processor and the other used by a different processor, the items appear to be shared to the processors. This may cause overhead on cache-coherent systems, causing the same effect as if the value was a single shared quantity.

FDDI Fiber Distributed Data Interface is a networking standard based on a dual counter-rotating ring of optical fiber.

FID NMR jargon for free induction decay, the actual NMR signal observed after a pulse or series of pulses in an NMR experiment.

fine-grain parallelism Parallelism within a program may occur at many different levels. Fine-grain indicates that the units of parallelism are of relatively short duration. It is usually used to describe loop-level parallelization or data parallelism.

fMRI Functional Magnetic Resonance Imaging, i.e., directly observing neural activity.

Fourier harmonics Expansion of a function in terms of sinusoidal series.

Galerkin operator An operator that maps a differential operator to a discrete form using a Galerkin finite element discretization method.

Gauss-Seidel (GS) smoothers The Gauss-Seidel iterative method applied to the fine-grid equations to smooth the error in a multigrid algorithm.

GEC Gaseous Electronics Conference.

GFDL Geophysical Fluid Dynamics Laboratory.

ghost cells See halo-cells.

gigabyte A measure of memory capacity that is roughly a billion bytes. A gigabyte is 2 to the 30th power, or 1,073,741,824 in decimal notation.

gigaflop A measure of a computer's speed; a billion floating-point operations per second.

GMRES The Generalized Minimial Residual Method, an iterative linear solution method for solving nonsymmetric systems of linear equations.

Godunov method A higher-order explicit algorithm for discretizing advection equations.

Green's function The response of a partial differential equation with appropriate boundary conditions to a delta-function excitation at any specified point in space.

GUI Graphic User Interface.

gyrotropic Refers to materials whose natural modes of propagation are circularly polarized waves by virtue of permittivity or permeability tensors with nonzero and antisymmetric off-diagonal imaginary components.

halo-cells In addition to the group of cells in the domain owned by a particular processor or task, a task may also carry around information for cells belonging to neighboring tasks. This is done in order to minimize remote references during computation. Sometimes called *boundary* cells or *ghost* cells.

halogenated etchant gases Gases used in the plasma etching of semiconductors whose molecules contain atoms from the highly reactive halogen group, usually fluorine or chlorine.

Hamiltonians A Hamiltonian is the mathematical descriptor for the energy of a given interaction. The total Hamiltonian describes all energies of all the interactions that affect a system.

Heaviside function The unit step function.

Hermitian matrix An n-by-n matrix A is said to be Hermitian if the conjugate transpose of A equals A. Note that any real-valued symmetric matrix is (trivially) Hermitian.

heterogeneities Refers to material properties that are spatially variable throughout a medium.

HPF High-Performance Fortran.

ILU, MILU The incomplete and modified incomplete LU factorization method, a popular preconditioning technique for solving systems of linear equations.

IMSL International Mathematical and Statistical Library. A widely used collection of mathematical subroutines used in scientific computations.

integro-differential operators Operators acting on scalar or vector fields that are composed of both differentials and integrals.

inviscid flow Flows in which the effects of viscosity, thermal conduction, and mass diffusion are ignored.

IRIX IPC library Interprocessor communications library for the Silicon Graphics IRIX operating system.

isosurface A surface defined with equal physical values.

J2CG Two-step Jacobi preconditioned conjugate gradient linear solver.

Jacobi method In this context, any of a number of methods for diagonalizing a symmetric matrix A that are based on the systematic reduction of the norm of the off-diagonal values of A.

Jacobi smoothers The Jacobi iterative method applied to the fine-grid equations to smooth the error in a multigrid algorithm.

kriging A geostatistical linear interpolation technique used to estimate rock properties in an oil reservoir.

Kronecker delta Logical function of two indices that is unity when the indices match, and otherwise zero.

Krylov subspace iterative algorithms Matrix solution techniques that rely on properties of the linear space spanned by successive powers of the matrix times an arbitrary vector, each iteration thus involving a matrix-vector multiply and gaining information about the solution in a higher-order linear space.

Lagrangian approach A description of fluid motion based on the trajectories of individual fluid particles.

Larmor frequency The resonance frequency (in the radiofrequency part of the electromagnetic spectrum) for a nucleus placed in a magnetic field. Radiofrequency pulses at this frequency generate the signals observed in NMR.

latency How long it takes to get that first bit of information to a processor (i.e., a message of size zero).

LDA Denotes the Local Density Approximation; the density within a mesh is treated as a constant value.

lossless compression A compression mechanism that allows information to be fully recovered without any loss.

lossy compression A compression mechanism in which some of the information in the original data/image will be lost during the compression process.

LU decomposition Factorization of a square matrix into the product of a lower triangular matrix with an upper triangular matrix, constituting the dominant computational step toward solving a system of equations.

magic angle spinning (MAS) spectra Solid-state NMR spectra obtained for samples spinning in cylindrical rotors, with the rotor axis held at the "magic angle" ($54.7356°$) with respect to the magnetic field axis. Spectra obtained in this way yield sharp lines for $I = 1/2$ nuclei.

magnetic field integral equation (MFIE) Integral equation form of the frequency domain Maxwell's equations that relates the incident and total electric currents on a closed surface.

Magnus expansion The Magnus expansion allows one to mathematically express a time-dependent oscillatory Hamiltonian as a sum of time-independent Hamiltonians.

matvec result The result of multiplying a matrix and a vector together.

Maxwell's equations Mathematical relations set forth in 1865 by J. C. Maxwell, describing the interaction of time-varying electric and magnetic fields, fluxes, currents, and charges, consisting of Coulomb's law, Ampere's law, Faraday's law, and the nondivergence of magnetic flux.

megabyte A measure of computer processor storage and real and virtual memory, a megabyte (MB) is 2 to the 20th power bytes, or 1,048,576 bytes in decimal notation.

megaflop A measure of a computer's speed—a million floating-point operations per second.

metastable Chemically unstable in the absence of certain conditions that would induce stability but not liable to spontaneous transformation.

MGCG Multigrid Preconditioned Conjugate Gradient method. This is an algorithm for solving a matrix equation that uses a multigrid solution as a preconditioner for a conjugate gradient method.

microcrystallites Microcrystallites are the microscopic single crystals that make up a powder.

MJCG MGCG with Jacobi smoothing.

Moore's law The prediction in 1965 by Gordon E. Moore that the complexity of integrated circuits would continue to increase at an exponential rate for many years to come. More loosely, similar expectations of exponential growth in related measures such as processor speed or memory capacity.

MPI Message-Passing Interface. A widely used message-passing standard for writing message-passing programs. Implementations are available for most platforms, e.g., MPICH, LAM, EPCC-MPI.

MPP Massively Parallel Processor.

mTorr Torr is the SI measure of pressure—1 Newton per square meter.

Navier-Stokes equations The fundamental set of equations mathematically describing the physics of viscous flows. The equations were developed, independently, by L. M. H. Navier (1785–1836) and G. G. Stokes (1819–1903).

NetCDF Network Common Data Form—a scientific data format that allows users to store array-oriented data in a self-describing and network-transparent way.

nitrogen trifluoride A gas, the perfluoro analogue of ammonia, used in plasma etching applications within the semiconductor industry.

NMR Nuclear Magnetic Resonance.

non-Hermitian Refers to complex-valued matrices that are not conjugate-symmetric.

NOW Network of Workstations.

NUMA Non-Uniform Memory Access. Refers to distributed-memory parallel computing platforms where remote memory access times differ from access times for local memory.

observables Fields, currents, or other physical properties that may, in principle, be measured.

oligonucleotides Short DNA molecules (100 bases or less) that are created chemically. If a short DNA molecule is created chemically, it is called an oligonucleotide; if it is cloned, it is called a gene.

orbitals One-electron wavefunctions in atoms or molecules usually arising as the constituents of approximate solutions to a many-particle problem. See wavefunction.

orthogonal harmonics Refers to families of functions or fields that form a convenient basis for solving partial differential equations, in that they are pairwise orthogonal with respect to some suitable integrated inner product and constitute normal modes of the equations in a coordinate system of interest.

parallelpipeds Close-packing 3D shapes that are rectilinear boxes.

PATP Parallel Applications Technology Program.

Pauli exclusion principle The principle requires that no two electrons have the same set of quantum numbers. Thus, for every one orbital only two electrons, of opposite spin, can be accommodated.

PCG method Preconditioned Conjugate Gradient method. See CGHS.

PDEs Partial differential equations.

PE Processing Element.

PE0 Processor zero. Usually corresponds to the master task.

PEC cylinder A cylinder whose surface is a perfect electrical conductor.

permittivity Proportionality scalar or tensor between the electric flux and electric field in a medium, arising from the polarizability of its atoms.

pipelined arithmetic The Alpha chip used in the Cray T3D has built-in parallel arithmetic units that allow several instructions to be executed in a pipelined fashion.

pointwise red/black GS smoothing A Gauss-Seidel smoother with the grid points ordered in a "checkerboard" pattern.

preconditioned conjugate gradient method A class of algorithms for solving sparse matrix equations.

preconditioner Matrix transformation that seeks to reduce the iterative solution time of a system of equations.

PVM The parallel virtual machine library, a standard for message passing on parallel computers.

QMD Quantum Molecular Dynamics.

QR method The QR factorization of an m-by-n matrix A is given by A = QR, where Q is an m-by-m orthogonal matrix and R is an m-by-n upper triangular matrix.

quadrature A method for approximating the integral of a function in which the values of the function at a finite set of points are multiplied by specified weights and summed.

quadrupoles Quadrupoles are atomic nuclei that possess an electric quadrupole moment. Such nuclei possess a nonuniform (positive) charge distribution. Nuclei with nuclear spin quantum numbers of 1 or greater are quadrupoles.

RISC Reduced Instruction Set Chip. A common architecture for computer chips in workstations.

Runge-Kutta scheme A multistage numerical technique used for the resolution of ordinary differential equations.

SCPLib Scalable Concurrent Programming Library—an application-independent library that provides basic programming technology to support irregular applications on scalable concurrent hardware.

SGEMM A routine from the BLAS-3 (Basic Linear Algebra Subroutine) library for doing single precision matrix multiply operations on a general matrix.

SHMEM A Cray proprietary message-passing library for Cray parallel computers.

shmem_get Cray T3D/E system call, invoked by one processor, for efficiently retrieving data from the memory of another processor.

shmem_put Cray T3D/E system call, invoked by one processor, for efficiently transferring data to the memory of another processor.

SIP Sequentially Implicit Method, a method of coupling flow and transport by first computing a flow field, then computing the advective transport.

SMC method Schwinger Multichannel method.

SMP Symmetric MultiProcessor, but occasionally refers to Shared Memory Parallel.

SOR The successive overrelaxation iterative method for solving systems of linear equations.

sparsity The proportion of zero elements in a matrix.

spinlock Spinlock refers to the locking of the nuclear spin magnetization by an applied radiofrequency field in an NMR experiment.

splatting A forward projection volume rendering algorithm that projects each voxel into the image space using a Gaussian filter.

SPMD (Single Procedure Multiple Data) paradigm Parallel programming paradigm. A single procedure is executed on multiple processors operating on different datasets. The results are aggregated at the end of the computation.

SSD Solid State Disk, a Cray Research proprietary product that is essentially an electronic memory device used to emulate a disk drive.

SSOR Symmetric Successive Overrelaxation method. A method for solving linear systems of equations.

tetrahedra A closed volumetric shape bounded by four triangle surfaces.

threads A thread is a sequence of instructions. A multithreaded process is composed of several sequences of instructions that may execute simultaneously or in an interleaved fashion, usually sharing some common areas of memory.

TVD Total-Variation-Diminishing, a mathematical property existing in the inviscid flow equations.

Variable Soft Sphere (VSS) A statistical collision model that determines the frequency of collisions and the postcollision scattering angles.

viscous flow Flows in which the effects of viscosity, thermal conduction, and mass diffusion are included.

voxel Unit of data in a three-dimensional volume dataset. Usually, it repensents a cubic area in 3D space.

wavefront A set of grid points in an ILU sweep that may all be updated independently at the same time.

wavefunction A solution to the basic equations of quantum mechanics describing a particular state of motion of a system of particles. The squared absolute value of the wavefunction evaluated at a given set of particle coordinates describes the probability of observing the system in that configuration.

waveguide Any structure designed to confine and transport wave energy from one location to another, but frequently refers to a metal tube of constant cross section.

wavelet image compression An image compression algorithm that uses a two-stage integer wavelet transform to reduce the image to lower-resolution images.

Index

Contributors

Steven F. Ashby is the Director of the Center for Applied Scientific Computing (CASC) at Lawrence Livermore National Laboratory. His research interests include numerical linear algebra, algorithm design, and scientific computing. He received a Ph.D. in Computer Science at the University of Illinois at Urbana-Champaign.

Chuck Baldwin is a Computer Scientist and Mathematician at CASC at Lawrence Livermore National Laboratory. His research interests include partial differential equations, iterative solution of linear systems, porous media fluid flow, wave propagation, and semiconductor devices. He received an M.S. in Computer Science at the University of Illinois at Urbana-Champaign.

Steven L. Baughcum is a Senior Principal Engineer in the atmospheric physics group of the Boeing Company. His research interests include combustion chemistry, atmospheric chemistry, and evaluating effects of future fleets of high-speed civil transports on the ozone layer. He received a Ph.D. in Physical Chemistry from Harvard University.

Alan J. Benesi is the Director of the NMR (Nuclear Magnetic Resonance) Facility at Pennsylvania State University. He is active in both theoretical and experimental NMR spectroscopy. He received a Ph.D. in Biophysics at the University of California, Berkeley.

Gyan Bhanot is at the IBM Thomas J. Watson Research Center. His interests are in the simulations related to statistical mechanics and particle physics on a variety of parallel computer architectures. He was an Associate Professor of Physics at Florida State University. He received a Ph.D. in Theoretical Physics from Cornell University.

William J. Bosl is a Computer Scientist at CASC at Lawrence Livermore National Laboratory and a visiting scientist at Stanford University. His research interests include the physics of coupled thermal, fluid, and elastic materials, earthquake physics, reservoir geodynamics, fault mechanics, and computational geomechanics. He received a Ph.D. in Geophysics at Stanford University.

Jeff Brooks manages the Benchmarking Group at Silicon Graphics, Inc. He received Master's degrees in Mathematics and Business Administration from the University of Minnesota.

Olivier Byrde is a Senior Application Analyst for Cray Research/Silicon Graphics at the ETH-Zurich. He has done work on the parallelization of a 3D Navier-Stokes flow solver and its application to the computation and analysis of the flow in a static chemical mixer. He received a Ph.D. in Mechanical Engineering at the Ecole Polytechnique Fédérale de Lausanne.

Margaret Cahir is a Computational Scientist with Silicon Graphics, Inc. Her areas of expertise are parallel applications and programming models. She received an M.S. in Engineering from the University of California at Berkeley.

Yi Chao is a Research Scientist in the Earth and Space Science Division of Jet Propulsion Laboratory, California Institute of Technology. His research interests are in climate ocean modeling, satellite remote sensing, air-sea interaction, and high-performance computing. He received a Ph.D. in Atmospheric and Oceanic Sciences from Princeton University.

Thomas E. Cheatham III is a Research Associate in the Laboratory of Structural Biology at the National Institutes of Health. His research has been in the application of computational chemistry techniques to problems in structural biology. He received a Ph.D. in Pharmaceutical Chemistry from the University of California at San Francisco.

Benny N. Cheng is a member of technical staff in the Earth and Space Science Division of Jet Propulsion Laboratory, California Institute of Technology. His current research interests are in statistical analysis of remote sensing data and high-performance computing. He received a Ph.D. in Mathematics from MIT and a Ph.D. in Statistics from the University of California at Santa Barbara.

Jonathan D. Cohen is an Associate Professor of Psychology at Carnegie Mellon University and the University of Pittsburgh. He does research on the neural mechanisms underlying cognitive control and brainstem systems. He received an M.D. from the University of Pennsylvania School of Medicine and a Ph.D. in Cognitive Psychology from Carnegie Mellon University.

Michael F. Crowley is on the staff at the Pittsburgh Supercomputing Center, Carnegie Mellon University. His research has centered on the mathematical description of chemical phenomena. He was a faculty member at Penn State University and a visiting faculty member at West Virginia University. He received a Ph.D. in Chemistry from the University of Montana.

Tom Cwik is the Technical Group Supervisor of the High Performance Computing Group at the Jet Propulsion Laboratory. His current activities include the application of massively parallel computer systems to electromagnetic scattering and finite element modeling methods. He received a Ph.D. degree from the University of Illinois, Urbana-Champaign.

Tom A. Darden is at the National Institutes of Environmental Health Sciences. His research is in the application of molecular modeling techniques to problems of human health. He was an instructor at the University of Wisconsin. He received his Ph.D. in Statistics from the University of California at Berkeley.

David W. Deerfield II is the Manager of the Biomedical Applications Group at the Pittsburgh Supercomputing Center. He did postdoctoral research in chemistry at the University of North Carolina. He received his Ph.D. in Chemistry from the University of Minnesota.

Michael DeLong is a Postdoctoral Fellow in the Scientific Computing Group in the Computing, Information, and Communications Division at Los Alamos. His current research includes the iterative solution of linear systems on high-performance parallel computers. He received a Ph.D. in Computer Science from the University of Virginia.

William F. Eddy is Professor of Statistics, Department of Statistics, Carnegie Mellon University. His research interests include statistical problems associated with functional magnetic resonance imaging. He received a Ph.D. in Statistics from Yale University.

David C. Eder is a member of the research staff at the Lawrence Livermore National Laboratory. His research interests are in lasers, atomic and plasma physics, and high-performance computing. He received a Ph.D. in Astrophysics from Princeton University.

Robert D. Falgout is a Mathematician at CASC at Lawrence Livermore National Laboratory. He also serves as the CASC Scalable Linear Solvers project leader. His research interests are in numerical algorithms, especially multigrid methods, and their implementation on high-performance computers. He received a Ph.D. in Applied Mathematics at the University of Virginia.

Allyson Gajraj is a Research Scientist at Amoco Production Company. His research interests include parallel oil reservoir simulation and geostatistical methods. He received a Ph.D. in petroleum engineering from the University of Tulsa.

Christopher R. Genovese is an Associate Professor of Statistics at Carnegie Mellon University. His research interests include statistical inverse problems in the physical and biological sciences, nonparametric function estimation, mixture models, game theory, and functional magnetic resonance imaging. He received a Ph.D. in Statistics from the University of California, Berkeley.

Nigel H. Goddard is a Scientific Specialist in Neural Sciences at Pittsburgh Supercomputing Center. He was at the University of Manchester, UK; University of Amsterdam, Netherlands; Phillips Telecommunications, Netherlands; and Hughes Aircraft Research Labs in Malibu, CA. He received a Ph.D. in Computer Science from the University of Rochester.

Sara Graffunder is the Director of the Computer Education Center of the Science Museum of Minnesota. She worked at Cray Research, Inc./Silicon Graphics, Inc., where she headed the Applications Department and later managed the Parallel Applications Technology Partnership with several large research groups for developing parallel applications for the CRAY T3E.

Daniel E. Hastings is a Professor of Aeronautics and Astronautics at MIT and is Chief Scientist for the U.S. Air Force. His research interests are the interaction of space environments with space systems and the development of satellite systems. He received a Ph.D. in Plasma Physics from MIT.

Michael A. Heroux is the Leader of the Scalable Applications and Capability Prototyping Groups in the Applications Division of SGI/Cray. His primary interests are in the design and implementation of new applications technologies for high-performance scientific computing. He received a Ph.D. in Numerical Methods at Colorado State University.

Greg Hood is an Applications Programmer in the Biomedical Group at the Pittsburgh Supercomputing Center. He received an M.S. in Computer Science from Carnegie Mellon University.

Morris Jette is the Leader of the Distributed Computing Group at Lawrence Livermore National Laboratory. His primary research interest is workload scheduling. This ranges in scope from the scheduling of individual processors to the management of a heterogeneous and geographically distributed computational grid.

Fred Jordan is at the Signal Processing Laboratory (Ecole Polytechnique Fédérale de Lausanne). He is working on techniques for the coding of synthetic visual information. He worked at CEA on recurrent neural networks properties using the Cray T3D. He received an engineering diploma from the Laboratoire de Chimie du Solide et Inorganique Moleculaire in Rennes.

Wayne Joubert is Team Leader of the Linear Solver team of Los Alamos National Laboratory. His research interests include parallel preconditionings, multigrid methods, parallel numerical simulations, and software development. He received a Ph.D. in Mathematics from the University of Texas at Austin.

Daniel S. Katz is a Computational Scientist at the Jet Propulsion Laboratory, California Institute of Technology. His research interests include numerical methods applied to parallel computing and computational methods in both electromagnetic wave propagation and geophysics. He received a Ph.D. in Electrical Engineering from Northwestern University.

Alice E. Koniges is Leader of the Parallel Applications Technology Program (PATP) at Lawrence Livermore National Laboratory. Her research interests include plasma physics, turbulence, parallel programming paradigms, and parallel I/O. She received a Ph.D. in Applied Mathematics and Computational Science from Princeton University.

Chuo-Han Lee is a graduate student in Physical Chemistry at the California Institute of Technology. He received a B.S. in Chemistry from the University of California, Los Angeles.

P. Peggy Li is a Computational Scientist in the Information Systems Development and Operations Division of Jet Propulsion Laboratory, California Institute of Technology. Her research interests are in parallel programming, distributed systems, and parallel visualization. She received a Ph.D. in Computer Science from the California Institute of Technology.

Olaf Lubeck is the Group Leader of the Scientific Computing Group of Los Alamos National Laboratory. His research interests include research on advanced parallel computer architectures, performance evaluation and optimization, and large-scale applications in modeling and simulation. He received a graduate degree in Numerical Meteorology from the Naval Postgraduate School.

Vincent McKoy is Professor of Theoretical Chemistry at the California Institute of Technology. His research includes theoretical and high-performance computational studies of collisions of low-energy electrons with molecules. He received a Ph.D. in Chemistry from Yale University.

Kenneth M. Merz, Jr. is a Professor of Chemistry at the Pennsylvania State University and the Senior Director of the Center for Informatics and Drug Discovery at Pharmacopeia, Inc. He is active in biological/pharmaceutical applications of computational chemistry. He received a Ph.D. in Chemistry from the University of Texas at Austin.

Robert Moench is a Software Engineer in the Vector Software Technology division of Silicon Graphics, Inc. His professional interests include parallel debugger development and object-oriented programming. He received a B.A. degree in Mathematics from St. Olaf College.

Hugh B. Nicholas, Jr. is a Senior Scientific Specialist at the Pittsburgh Supercomputing Center. He was a postdoctoral research fellow in Biology at MIT and a biophysics researcher at the University of Wisconsin. He received a Ph.D. in Chemistry from the University of Oklahoma.

Henri Nicolas is a Senior Researcher at INRIA of Rennes working on digital television. He worked at the Ecole Polytechnique Fédérale de Lausanne as the leader of the research group on digital television and at CRAY Research doing realtime implementations of digital video analysis algorithms on a T3D. He received a Ph.D. in Computer Science from the University of Rennes.

Douglas C. Noll is an Associate Professor at the University of Pittsburgh. He was a member of technical staff at AT&T Bell Laboratories in Whippany, NJ, and an Assistant Professor of Radiology and Electrical Engineering at the University of Pittsburgh. He received a Ph.D. in Electrical Engineering from Stanford University.

Leigh E. Nystrom is a Senior Research Principal in the Department of Psychiatry at the University of Pittsburgh and a Visiting Research Associate at Carnegie Mellon University. He received a Ph.D. in Cognitive Psychology from Carnegie Mellon University.

David C. O'Neal is Site Lead for Computational Structural Mechanics at the Aeronautical Systems Center and a Computational Scientist at the National Center for Supercomputing Applications. Interest areas include performance analysis, fluid and structural mechanics, and finite element methods. He received a M.A. in Applied Mathematics at the University of Pittsburgh.

Jay Parker is at the Jet Propulsion Laboratory, California Institute of Technology. His research interests include high-performance computing, electromagnetics, atmospheric remote sensing, and satellite-based geodesy. He received a Ph.D. in Electrical Engineering from the University of Illinois, Urbana-Champaign.

Raghurama Reddy is a Computational Scientist at the Pittsburgh Supercomputing Center at Carnegie Mellon University. Research interests include parallel finite elements, parallel numerical algorithms, and distributed computations. He received an M.S. in Agricultural Engineering from Colorado State University.

Marc Rieffel is a Ph.D. student at the California Institute of Technology and a staff member at the Scalable Concurrent Programming Laboratory at Syracuse University. His research interests include parallel methods for particle simulations, unstructured grid techniques, and plasma simulation. He received an M.S. in Computer Science at the California Institute of Technology.

Alexander J. Ropelewski is an Applications Programmer in the Biomedical Group at the Pittsburgh Supercomputing Center. He has implemented sequence analysis codes on a wide range of high-performance computers. He received a B.S. in Computer Science from the University of Pittsburgh.

Douglas A. Rotman is a Group Leader in the Atmospheric Sciences Division at Lawrence Livermore National Laboratory. He is interested in natural and anthropogenic effects on the atmospheric physical, chemical, and dynamical processes determining the distribution of trace chemical species. He received a Ph.D. in Mechanical Engineering from the University of California, Berkeley.

Robie I. Samanta Roy is a research staff member at the Institute for Defense Analyses. His research interests include electric propulsion for spacecraft, modeling of command and control systems, and international space policy. He received a Ph.D. in Aeronautics and Astronautics from MIT.

James Sanderson has been a staff member at Los Alamos National Laboratory. His research interests are in numerical algorithms and parallel computing. He received his Ph.D. in Numerical Analysis from the University of New Mexico.

Mark L. Sawley is a Senior Research Scientist at the Fluid Mechanics Laboratory of the Ecole Polytechnique Fédérale de Lausanne. His current research interests include the efficient parallelization of computational fluid dynamics codes. He received a Ph.D. in Physics from Flinders University of South Australia.

Sadasivan Shankar is the Group Leader of the Process Equipment Modeling Group at the Technology CAD department at Intel, Santa Clara, CA. He has worked on fluid flow simulations and heat transfer for 2D and 3D reactors and other complex systems. He received a Ph.D. in Chemical Engineering and Material Science at the University of Minnesota.

Gautam S. Shiralkar is the Technical Leader of Reservoir Simulator Development at BP Amoco's Subsurface Exploitation Division. His interests are simulator development and reservoir studies. He received a Ph.D. in Mechanical Engineering from the University of California, Berkeley.

Horst D. Simon is the Director of NERSC. He has managed SGI's university and research laboratory programs. He led a research department at NASA Ames Research Center with groups in parallel applications, scientific visualization, and numerical grid generation. He received a Ph.D. in Mathematics from the University of California, Berkeley.

Steven G. Smith is a Computer Scientist at CASC at Lawrence Livermore National Laboratory. His research interests include scientific computing on highly parallel architectures, software tools and software engineering for high-performance computing, and scientific data visualization. He received a B.S. in Computer Science at the University of Illinois at Urbana-Champaign.

Vijay Sonnad is employed by IBM on site at Lawrence Livermore National Laboratory. His interests are in parallel computational techniques in engineering with an emphasis on finite elements and iterative solution methods. He received a Ph.D. in Mechanical Engineering from MIT.

Robert E. Stephenson is a Petroleum Engineer at BP-Amoco. His research interests are in the area of developing simulators for oil and gas reservoirs and the parallelization of these codes. He received a Ph.D. in Chemical Engineering from Clemson University.

Ravi Subramanya is a Computational Science Consultant at the Pittsburgh Supercomputing Center. Research interests include code parallelization and optimization, computational fluid dynamics, software engineering, distributed systems, and data mining. He received an M.S. in Ocean Engineering from the University of Rhode Island.

Chary G. Tamirisa is a Solutions Architect at IBM. He is developing data mining solutions for the finance industry. He has worked on the DCE Multithreading library and has extensive knowledge of the POSIX model for threads. He received an M.S. in Computer Science from McGill University.

John R. Tannahill is a Computer Scientist and Group Leader of the Atmospheric Science Computer Applications Group at LLNL. He is the Lead Software Developer for the NASA GMI core model and the LLNL IMPACT model, both 3D chemical transport models. These models reside within a framework utilizing domain decomposition and message passing to achieve parallel computations.

Stephen Taylor is an Associate Professor of Computer Science at Syracuse University. He has authored three books on concurrent programming techniques and one on program design methods. He received a Ph.D. in Computer Science at the Weizmann Institute, Israel.

Andrew F. B. Tompson is a Hydrologist at Lawrence Livermore National Laboratory. His research interests include chemical transformations and transport in porous media, fluid mechanics, groundwa-